WORLD DEVELOPMENT REPORT

GOVERNANCE

and

THE LAW

A World Bank Group Flagship Report

WORLD DEVELOPMENT REPORT

2017

GOVERNANCE

and

THE LAW

WORLD BANK GROUP

ISSN, ISBN, e-ISBN, and DOI:

Softcover
ISSN: 0163-5085
ISBN: 978-1-4648-0950-7
e-ISBN: 978-1-4648-0951-4
DOI: 10.1596/978-1-4648-0950-7

Hardcover
ISSN: 0163-5085
ISBN: 978-1-4648-0952-1
DOI: 10.1596/978-1-4648-0952-1

Cover design: Kurt Niedermeier, Niedermeier Design, Seattle, Washington.

Interior design: George Kokkinidis, Design Language, Brooklyn, New York, and Kurt Niedermeier, Niedermeier Design, Seattle, Washington.

Contents

xiii   *Foreword*

xv   *Acknowledgments*

xix   *Abbreviations*

1   **Overview:** *World Development Report 2017: Governance and the Law*

2   Improving governance to meet today's development challenges

5   Drivers of effectiveness: Commitment, coordination, and cooperation

12   Levers for change: Contestability, incentives, preferences and beliefs

19   Drivers of change: Elite bargains, citizen engagement, and international influence

29   Rethinking governance for development

32   Navigating this Report

33   Notes

34   References

39   **Part I: Rethinking governance for development: A conceptual framework**

40   **Chapter 1: Governance for development: The challenges**

40   Understanding development policy: Proximate factors and underlying determinants

43   Development objectives . . . and constraints

48   Governance for the bottom half

48   Notes

48   References

51   **Chapter 2: Enhancing governance for development: Why policies fail**

52   Diverse pathways to success: Moving beyond institutional transplants

53   Drivers of effectiveness: Commitment, coordination, and cooperation

58   Policy effectiveness in the presence of power asymmetries

65   Levers for change: Incentives, preferences and beliefs, and contestability

72   A dynamic process: Drivers of change and the role of law

73   Notes

73   References

77   *Spotlight 1: Corruption*

80   *Spotlight 2: The governance challenges of managing risks*

83   **Chapter 3: The role of law**

84   Law and the policy arena

86   Ordering behavior: The command role of law

91   Ordering power: The constitutive role of law

93   Ordering contestation: The role of law in change

95   Getting to the rule of law

98   Notes

98   References

102   *Spotlight 3: How do effective and equitable legal institutions emerge?*

109   **Part II: Governance for development**

110   **Chapter 4: Governance for security**

110   Can governance solve the problem of violence in society?

111   Security, governance, and power are tightly interlinked

116   Governance can improve security in four ways

123   Conclusion

123   Notes

124   References

130   *Spotlight 4: Wartime governance*

133   *Spotlight 5: Crime*

137   **Chapter 5: Governance for growth**

137   How policy "capture" slows economic growth

138   How governance matters to growth: A microeconomic perspective

141   How policies are affected by undue influence from powerful groups

145   Policy design under risk of capture

146   How the design of public agencies mediates the influence of powerful groups

150   Finding the right approach

152   Notes

153   References

159   *Spotlight 6: The middle-income trap*

163   *Spotlight 7: Public-private partnerships*

167   **Chapter 6: Governance for equity**

170   Two key policy areas that matter for equity: Investing in public goods and expanding opportunities

171   Equity and institutional functions: The role of commitment and cooperation

173   How policies to promote equity can be affected by power asymmetries

178   Leveling the playing field and making governance more responsive to all

182   Improving policy effectiveness by taking into account asymmetries in bargaining power

183   Notes

184   References

189   *Spotlight 8: Service delivery: Education and health*

195   **Part III: Drivers of change**

196   **Chapter 7: Elite bargaining and adaptation**

196   Understanding elite bargains

203   Elite bargains and uneven state capacity

205 Broadening the policy arena to enhance elite power
207 When binding rules for accountability serve as political insurance
208 When elites adapt through rules-based mechanisms
212 Entry points for change through elite adaptation
213 Notes
213 References

217 Spotlight 9: Decentralization
220 Spotlight 10: Public service reform

225 Chapter 8: Citizens as agents of change
226 Bringing change through the ballot box
230 Bringing change through political organization: The role of political parties
234 Bringing change through social organization
239 The role of induced participation and public deliberation
241 Entry points for change: Understanding citizen agency as a collective action problem
241 Notes
242 References

247 Spotlight 11: From transparency to accountability through citizen engagement
252 Spotlight 12: The media

257 Chapter 9: Governance in an interconnected world
257 Transnationalism and the domestic policy arena
259 Transnational rules and regulations: Enhanced cooperation and focal points for change
266 Foreign aid and governance
273 Notes
274 References

278 Spotlight 13: Illicit financial flows

Boxes

O.1   3   What is governance?

O.2   4   Governance for what? Achieving the goals of security, growth, and equity

O.3   8   The idea of power and the power of ideas

O.4   10   Why some people see red when they hear "green growth"

O.5   12   The need to strengthen incentives to gather development data

O.6   14   Legal and normative pluralism

O.7   15   Transitions to the rule of law

O.8   18   The "rules game": Paying attention to where the action is

O.9   20   Elites and citizens: Who is who in the policy arena?

O.10   21   Who are elites, and what do they do? Results from a survey of elites in 12 countries

O.11   25   Direct democracy delayed women's voting rights in Switzerland

O.12   28   Domestic resource mobilization, foreign aid, and accountability

O.13   30   What does the WDR 2017 framework mean for action? The policy effectiveness cycle

O.14   31   Lessons for reformers from the "rules game": How is legitimacy ultimately built?

1.1   41   What is governance?

1.2   43   Governance for what? Achieving the goals of security, growth, and equity

1.3   46   Discontinuities of the state

2.1   53   The microfoundations of commitment, coordination, and cooperation: A perspective from game theory

2.2   55   Trust in institutions stems from delivering on commitments

2.3   59   Game theory and the roots of political power

2.4   60   Who is who in the policy arena: The case of Bolivia's social policy

2.5   62   Transaction costs, incomplete contracts, and political agreements: Why land redistribution policies often fail

2.6   63   How capacity and norms influence and are influenced by power asymmetries

2.7   64   The "rules game": Paying attention to where the action is

2.8   65   Factors that make sustaining cooperation over time more likely

2.9   66   Voluntary compliance and the building blocks of legitimacy

2.10 67   How an international commission enabled a credible commitment to fight criminals' impunity in Guatemala

2.11 69   How the introduction of electronic voting in Brazil reshaped the policy arena and led to more pro-poor policies

2.12 71   The "rules game": Lessons for reformers

3.1   84   What is law?

3.2   85   Legal and normative pluralism

3.3   87   Legal origins: Theory and practice

3.4   96   Transitions to the rule of law

3.5   97   Understanding the role of law in context

4.1   112 How modern governance was born offers lessons for today's "fragile" countries

4.2   114 The persistent links among gender-based violence, power, and norms

4.3   115 Several factors can cause conflicts, and they often combine

5.1   143 Why some people see red when they hear "green growth"

5.2   152 Participatory mechanisms in policy design: The "Bulldozer Initiative" in Bosnia and Herzegovina

6.1   168 What is equity?

6.2   169 A vicious cycle: How inequality begets inequality

6.3   174 Efforts to expand and secure access to land often lead to capture

6.4   175 Defining and measuring clientelism

6.5   181 Local elites can capture public spending despite participatory programs

6.6   183 Designing social safety nets to account for asymmetries in bargaining power

7.1   198 Expert survey to identify elites

7.2   202 When do elites have incentives to introduce rules for contestability and accountability?

7.3   204 Pockets of effectiveness in Nigeria

7.4   211 Female elites and female leaders

8.1   236 Social movements and bottom-up pressures for reform: Right to information legislation in India

8.2   237 The mobilization of women and promotion of gender-based policies in postconflict settings: The case of Sub-Saharan Africa

9.1   262 Legitimizing the second-best: Governance options for global public goods and the Paris Agreement on climate change

9.2   266 Aid as a delivery mechanism for transnational rules and ideas

9.3   270 The impact of aid on domestic resource mobilization: What does the evidence say?

9.4   271 Beyond technocratic approaches: Opening the door to considerations of politics and power in development policy

Figures

O.1   6   Long-term growth is less about how fast one grows than about not tripping along the way

O.2   9   A more even balance of power is associated with positive security outcomes

O.3   9   The value of political connections: Indonesia during President Suharto's era

O.4   11   Principals, agents, and clients: Accountability for sale

O.5   16   Recruitments of civil servants increased exponentially in Tunisia and the Arab Republic of Egypt in the aftermath of the Arab Spring uprisings of 2011

O.6   17   Formal avenues for broad-based participation in regulatory decision making are limited in low- and middle-income countries

O.7   19   WDR 2017 framework: Governance, law, and development

BO.10.1 21 Elite actors within national ruling coalitions vary greatly across countries and over time

O.8 24 Electoral democracies are spreading, but the integrity of elections is declining

O.9 26 After decades of progress, civic space is shrinking globally

O.10 27 Aid is a large share of GDP and government revenue in many developing countries

BO.13.1 30 The policy effectiveness cycle

1.1 41 Despite declining under-5 child mortality rates, inequality among and within countries is still sizable

1.2 45 Economic growth requires security

2.1 52 Despite similar rules for the management of natural resource revenue in Chile and Mongolia, Chile's expenditure patterns reveal a stronger commitment to compliance

B2.2.1 56 Welfare is higher for citizens under commitment in the lab game

B2.4.1 60 Formal and actual policy networks in Bolivia, 2010

B2.11.1 69 An electronic ballot made it much easier than a paper ballot for those with little or no education to cast their vote in Brazil

B2.11.2 70 Electronic voting reduced the number of invalid votes in Brazil

2.2 72 WDR 2017 framework: Governance, law, and development

S1.1 79 Development accounts for only about half of the variation in control of corruption

B3.3.1 87 Changes in investor protection and creditor rights have little impact on economic outcomes

3.1 91 Constitutions have become ubiquitous, but they are often replaced or amended

3.2 92 In every country, there is a gap between the laws on the books and the laws implemented, but high-income OECD countries generally do better than low- and middle-income countries

3.3 96 The rule of law is strongly correlated with high income

S3.1 103 Although high-income OECD countries generally have well-functioning legal institutions, the relationship between institutional quality and income varies in developing countries

S3.2 105 The correlation is weak between de jure and de facto measures of judicial independence

4.1 111 Violence inflicts a high cost on development

4.2 111 Violent conflict is associated with a reduction in GDP per capita

4.3 118 An even balance of power is associated with positive security outcomes

4.4 119 Constraining state power ensures security

4.5 121 Recruitment of civil servants increased exponentially in Tunisia and the Arab Republic of Egypt in the aftermath of the Arab Spring uprisings of 2011

S5.1 134 Homicide rates across Europe have declined dramatically over the last 800 years

5.1 138 Length of time needed for firms to obtain a construction permit varies widely

5.2 139 Per capita income and governance are correlated

5.3 140 Medium-term growth and governance are *not* correlated

5.4 142 In Indonesia, the stock value of politically connected firms fell when the connection was jeopardized

5.5 149 Formal checks and balances are weaker in low- and middle-income countries

5.6 150 Formal avenues for broad-based participation in regulatory decision making are limited in low- and middle-income countries

S6.1 159 Many countries have not converged toward higher incomes

S6.2 161 Checks on corruption and accountability institutions improve more in countries that escape upper-middle-income status to achieve high-income status than in countries that are "non-escapees"

S7.1 164 Private participation in infrastructure projects in developing countries remains limited

6.1 168 States can improve equity by intervening in the distribution of final outcomes through taxes and transfers and by providing access to basic services

B6.2.1 169 Capture is associated with lower levels of commitment

6.2 171 When commitment is low, countries exhibit low compliance (high shadow economy)

6.3 172 Fear of sanctions and participation in decision-making processes promote cooperation

6.4 175 A politician can become an agent of the provider in clientelist settings

6.5 176 In some countries in the Middle East and North Africa, a large proportion of citizens believe that connections are as important as or even more important than professional qualifications in obtaining a government job

6.6 177 Unofficial payments for education and health services are widespread in Europe and Central Asia

6.7 181 Empowering parents with school-based management training helps lessen capture (teacher absenteeism) in Kenya

B7.1.1 198 Elite actors within national ruling coalitions vary greatly across countries and over time

7.1 200 Preferences of economic elites predict policy adoption more than do citizen preferences in the United States

7.2 201 When the cost of losing power is high, elites are more likely to reject electoral results that support the opposition and are less likely to move toward rules-based contestability and accountability

B7.2.1 202 The interaction between political uncertainty and the cost of losing power

7.3 205 Horizontal and vertical accountability become more common as party institutionalization increases

7.4 210 Greater ideological unity among elites is associated with greater cohesion of the ruling coalition, as well as more institutionalized elite interactions

7.5 212 When economic power maps onto political power, there are fewer institutional checks on power

8.1 227 In Kenya, elections changed the incentives of the ruling elites, reducing the scope of ethnic favoritism

8.2 227 Electoral democracies are spreading, but the integrity of elections is declining

8.3 228 Although citizens value elections as an important route to economic development, less than half of respondents worldwide have confidence in the integrity of elections

8.4 228 Voter turnout worldwide from 1945 to 2015 indicates unequal citizen participation and the risk of biased representation of policy preferences

8.5 231 Although the spread of multiparty systems has increased opportunities for citizen engagement, dominant parties place de facto limits on electoral competition

8.6 231 Programmatic parties perform better than clientelist parties in improving the quality of public services, especially in competitive party systems

8.7 232 Programmatic parties tend to emerge at higher levels of development, but significant variation exists among countries at similar stages of development

8.8 233 Dominant party systems are less likely than competitive systems to introduce legal provisions for public funding, suggesting efforts to reduce contestability

8.9 234 Political parties are on average the least-trusted political institution worldwide

8.10 235 After decades of progress, civic space is shrinking globally, driven by higher government restrictions on media and CSO entry

8.11 235 Taking advantage of the digital revolution, social movements are increasingly organized across national boundaries

B8.2.1 237 The rate of political participation of women is higher in countries emerging from conflict

B8.2.2 238 In Africa, postconflict countries have been more likely to integrate women's rights in their constitutions

8.12 240 In Brazil, online voting in participatory budgeting can reinforce existing inequalities

S11.1 248 Transparency is not enough: Three conditions for the effectiveness of information initiatives

9.1 258 International actors can affect the domestic policy arena by changing the dynamics of contestation, shifting actor incentives, or shaping actor norms

9.2 260 Regulations and legal agreements have proliferated across borders

9.3 264 The "Rights Revolution" has led to a global spread of rights-related norms, facilitated and supported by global treaties and agreements

9.4 265 Human rights treaties are spreading, but de facto changes in state performance are lagging behind

9.5 265 Gender quota laws have spread worldwide since 1990

9.6   268   Aid makes up a large share of GDP and revenue in many developing countries

9.7   268   Low- and lower-middle-income countries vary greatly in the amount of aid received and improvement in GDP per capita

Maps

1.1   44   Violence is a major problem in 37 countries

B1.3.1   46   State presence in Bolivia in selected intervention domains and composite density, circa 2010

9.1   267   Aid flows amounted to over US$161 billion from donor countries to recipient countries in 2014

Tables

O.1   7   Three institutional functions— commitment, coordination, and cooperation—are essential to the effectiveness of policies

O.2   29   Three principles for rethinking governance for development

B2.1.1   53   Coordination and cooperation as modeled in game theory

B2.2.1   55   Sources of trust

B2.3.1   59   Payoffs to cooperation or noncooperation

2.1   71   Three principles for rethinking governance for development

S11.1   249   Positive and negative outcomes of citizen engagement

9.1   261   Transnational actors, instruments, and mechanisms for influencing domestic governance through incentives, preferences, and contestability

S13.1   279   Actions generating illicit financial flows

Foreword

Leaders, policy makers, and development professionals often worry that well-intentioned policies designed to improve the lives of their communities will fail to deliver results.

The global development community needs to move beyond asking "What is the right policy?" and instead ask "What makes policies work to produce life-improving outcomes?" The answer put forward in this year's *World Development Report* is better governance—that is, the ways in which governments, citizens, and communities engage to design and apply policies.

This Report is being launched at a time when global growth and productivity are continuing to slow, limiting the resources available to help the world's poorest and most vulnerable. Yet, people's demands for services, infrastructure, and fair institutions are continuing to rise. Given strained government budgets and development aid, it is vital that resources be used as effectively as possible. We can do this by harnessing the finance and skills of private businesses, working even more closely with civil society, and redoubling our efforts in the fight against corruption, one of the biggest roadblocks to effective, lasting development.

However, coordinating the efforts of this diverse set of groups requires clarity on the roles and responsibilities of each group, along with effective rules of the road to reach and sustain agreements. Without paying greater attention to stronger governance, the World Bank Group's goals of ending extreme poverty and boosting shared prosperity, as well as the transformational vision of the United Nations' broader Sustainable Development Goals, will be out of reach.

Based on extensive research and consultations conducted in many countries over the past 24 months, this Report draws attention to the importance of commitment, coordination, and cooperation as the three core functions needed to ensure that policies yield their desired outcomes. The Report also offers a helpful framework for approaching and resolving the challenges faced by our partners. Specifically, it explores how policies for security, growth, and equity can be made more effective by addressing the underlying drivers of governance.

Moving beyond the traditional concerns about implementation, such as limited state capacity, the Report then digs deeper to understand how individuals and groups with differing degrees of influence and power negotiate the choice of policies, the distribution of resources, and the ways in which to change the rules themselves.

As the Report shows, positive change is possible. Although reform efforts must be driven by local constituencies, the international community can play an active role in supporting these endeavors. In particular, we need to ensure that our future development assistance fosters the fundamental dynamics that promote better, more sustainable development.

I hope the insights presented in this Report will help countries, their communities, development institutions, and donors succeed in delivering on our shared vision to end extreme poverty and boost shared prosperity.

Jim Yong Kim
President
The World Bank Group

Acknowledgments

This Report was prepared by a team led by Luis Felipe López-Calva and Yongmei Zhou. Lead chapter authors were Edouard Al-Dahdah, David Bulman, Deborah Isser, Marco Larizza, Ezequiel Molina, Abla Safir, and Siddharth Sharma. The extended core team was composed of Kimberly Bolch, Lidia Ceriani, Samantha Lach, Bradley Larson, Annamaria Milazzo, and Evgenia Pugacheva. Brónagh Murphy and Jason Victor served as the production and logistics team for the Report. Mart Kivine led partner relations and provided strategic advice and support for resource mobilization. Stephen Commins provided consultations support and advice on the "green cover" consultation. The team received excellent research assistance from Yanina Eliana Domenella, Simona Ross, and Hari Subhash. This work was carried out under the general direction of Kaushik Basu, Shanta Devarajan, and Indermit Gill. The team is also grateful for comments and suggestions from Paul Romer.

The team received guidance from an advisory panel composed of Pranab Bardhan, Dr. Boediono, Mauricio Cárdenas, Francis Fukuyama, Avner Greif, Rebeca Grynspan, Tarja Halonen, Joel Hellman, Karuti Kanyinga, Karl Ove Moene, Benno Ndulu, James Robinson, Tharman Shanmugaratnam, and Xixin Wang.

The team would also like to acknowledge the generous support provided for preparation of the Report by Global Affairs Canada, Finland's Ministry of Foreign Affairs, Norway's Ministry of Foreign Affairs, and Sweden's Ministry of Foreign Affairs, as well as the French Development Agency, German Corporation for International Cooperation (GIZ), Knowledge for Change Program, and Nordic Trust Fund.

Consultation events were held in Argentina, Chile, China, Colombia, Estonia, Finland, France, Germany, Ghana, India, Italy, Kenya, Mexico, the Netherlands, Norway, the Philippines, Spain, Sweden, Tajikistan, Tanzania, the United Kingdom, the United States, Uruguay, and Vietnam, with participants drawn from many more countries. The team thanks those who took part in all of these events for their helpful comments and suggestions.

Bilateral and multilateral consultation events were held with the Asian Development Bank, CAF Development Bank of Latin America, European Commission, French Development Agency, German Federal Ministry of Economic Cooperation and Development, GIZ, Inter-American Development Bank, International Court of Justice, Norwegian Agency for Development Cooperation, Organisation for Economic Co-operation and Development, Swedish International Development Cooperation Agency, U.K. Department for International Development, United Nations Development Programme, and U.S. Agency for International Development.

The team also met with representatives from think tanks and civil society organizations, including the ABA Rule of Law Initiative, Afrobarometer, Berghof Foundation, Centre for Global Constitutionalism, Centro de Estudios Espinosa Yglesias, Civicus, Eurasia Foundation, Global Partnership for Social Accountability, Hague Institute for Global Justice, Innovations for Successful Societies at Princeton University, InterAction, International Food Policy Research Institute, International Institute for Democracy and Electoral Assistance,

Latin American Public Opinion Project, Mexican Competitiveness Institute, México ¿Cómo Vamos?, OpenGov Hub, Oxfam-UK, Partnership for Transparency Fund, Peace Research Institute Oslo, Stockholm International Peace Research Institute, Transparencia Mexicana, and Transparency International.

The initial findings of the Report were also discussed at several conferences and workshops, including the 2015 annual meeting of the American Political Science Association; 2015 Annual Bank Conference on Africa: Confronting Conflict and Fragility in Africa, hosted by the University of California at Berkeley; 2015 Annual Bank Conference on Development Economics; XXVIII Annual Congress of the Italian Society of Public Economics, Governance and Development: The Case of Politically Connected Businesses in Europe and Central Asia (in collaboration with the World Bank's Office of the Chief Economist, Europe and Central Asia Region); Implementing SDG 16: Good Governance Reloaded or New Opportunities for the Support of Democratic Governance? hosted by the German Development Institute; 2016 International Civil Society Week; 2016 International Conference on Inequality: Trends, Causes and the Politics of Distribution, hosted by the Friedrich-Ebert-Stiftung Foundation; 2015 International Policy Workshop on Governance and the Law, hosted by GIZ; 2016 Thinking and Working Politically Community of Practice, hosted by the Carnegie Endowment for International Peace; WDR 2017 Law Symposium, Cuentas Claras: Governance for Growth and Equity in Latin America (in collaboration with the World Bank's Office of the Chief Economist, Latin America and the Caribbean Region); 2015 World Bank Law, Justice and Development Week; and 2016 World Justice Project Scholars Conference on the Rule of Law, Non-law, and Social Order, hosted by Stanford University. Several universities sponsored events to provide feedback on the Report, including Ateneo de Manila University, Beijing University, Columbia University, Cornell University, East China University of Political Science and Law, Leiden University, Oxford University, Renmin University, Torcuato Di Tella University (Buenos Aires), University of los Andes (Bogotá), and University of the Republic (Montevideo).

A "green cover" consultation was held before submission of the draft Report to the Board of the World Bank. The team made the draft available online and explicitly contacted a set of key partners in the development community to request feedback. The team received and incorporated comments, criticism, and suggestions from members of civil society, academia, and think tanks.

Nancy Morrison was the principal editor of the Report. Sabra Ledent copyedited the Report. Bruce Ross-Larson provided editorial guidance. And Kurt Niedermeier was the principal graphic designer. Phillip Hay, Mikael Reventar, Anushka Thewarapperuma, and Roula Yazigi provided guidance on a communication and dissemination strategy. Special thanks are extended to Mary Fisk, Patricia Katayama, Stephen Pazdan, and the World Bank's Publishing Program. The team would also like to thank Vivian Hon, Surekha Mohan, Dirk Peterson, and Claudia Sepúlveda for their coordinating roles.

This Report draws on background papers, notes, and spotlight inputs prepared by Izak Atiyas, Sheheryar Banuri, Paolo Belli, Jürgen René Blum, Carles Boix, Tessa Bold, Alejandro Bonvecchi, Sarah Botton, Laurent Bouton, Juan Camilo Cárdenas Campo, Fernando Carrera, Francesco Caselli, Gonzalo Castañeda, Micael Castanheira, Simon Commander, Aline Coudouel, Manuel Eisner, Thomas Fujiwara, Scott Gates, Garance Genicot, Gaël Giraud, Alfredo González-Reyes, Helene Grandvoinnet, Ruth Guillén, Stéphane Hallegatte, Sébastien Hardy, Michael Jarvis, Patricia Justino, Daniel Kaufmann, Mushtaq H. Khan, Jenni Klugman, Sarwar Lateef, Étienne Le Roy, Andrei Levchenko, Brian Levy, Stéphanie Leyronas, Staffan Lindberg, Anna Lührmann, Ellen Lust, Nora Lustig, Yasuhiko Matsuda, Frédéric Maurel, Valeriya Mechkova, Jonathan Mellon, Alina Mungiu-Pippidi, Hamish Nixon, Ragnhild Nordas, Håvard Mokleiv Nygård, Daniel Oto-Peralias, Tiago Peixoto, Doug Porter, Franck Poupeau, Peter Reuter, Halsey Rogers, Dominique Rojat, Diego Romero, Martin Schmidt, Fredrik Sjoberg, Michael Stanley, Håvard Strand, Shawn Tan, Benno Torgler, Trang Thu Tran, John Wallis, Michael Walton, Leonard Wantchekon, and Michael Watts.

The team received expert advice during several rounds of reviews from chapter advisers Carles Boix, François Bourguignon, Francesco Caselli, Deval Desai, Avinash Dixit, Manuel Eisner, Thomas Fujiwara, Patrick Heller, Patricia Justino, Philip Keefer, Herbert Kitschelt, Andrei Levchenko, Brian Levy, María Ana Lugo, Rohini Pande, Doug Porter, Nigel Roberts, Carlos Scartascini, Brian Tamanaha, John Wallis, Leonard Wantchekon, and Michael Watts.

The team would like to acknowledge a number of people for their insightful discussions, feedback, and collaboration: Sakuntala Akmeemana, Martin Ardanaz, Omar Arias, Kathleen Beegle, Paolo Belli, Samuel Berlinski, David Bernstein, Robert Beschel, Bella Bird, Jürgen René Blum, Tessa Bold, Laurent Bouton, Miriam Bruhn, James Brumby, Hassane Cisse, Denis Cogneau, Walter Cont, Cristina Corduneanu, Aline Coudouel, Shanta Devarajan, Quy-Toan Do, Eduardo Engel, Peter Evans, Francisco Ferreira, Chloe Fevre, Deon Filmer, Varun Gauri, Tom Ginsburg, Markus Goldstein, Álvaro González, Duncan Green, Zahid Hasnain, Arturo Herrera, Joan Serra Hoffman, Robert Hunja, Ravi Kanbur, Daniel Kaufmann, Asmeen Khan, Mushtaq H. Khan, Stuti Khemani, Rachel Kleinfeld, Stephen Knack, Stefan Kossoff, Aart Kraay, Paul Lagunes, Sylvie Lambert, Ellen Lust, Nora Lustig, Syed A. Mahmood, Martha Martínez Licetti, Magdy Martínez-Solimán, Yasuhiko Matsuda, Sebastián Mazzuca, Nicolas Menzies, Samia Msadek, Gerardo Munck, Alina Mungiu-Pippidi, Kaivan Munshi, Makau Mutua, Roger Myerson, Ambar Narayan, Sara Nyman, Thiago Peixoto, Andre Portela, Gaël Raballand, Vijayendra Rao, Martin Ravallion, Nathaniel Reilly, Bob Rijkers, Daniel Rogger, Joe Saba, Audrey Sacks, Renaud Seligman, Mitchell Seligson, Harris Selod, Giancarlo Spagnolo, Jan Svejnar, Rob Taliercio, Jeff Thindwa, Florencia Torche, Benno Torgler, Dominique van de Walle, Nicolas van de Walle, Andrés Villaveces, Lorena Vinuela, Michael Walton, Deborah Wetzel, and Alan Whaites.

Many people inside and outside the World Bank Group provided helpful comments, made other contributions, and participated in consultative meetings. The team would like to thank the following: Sophie Adelman, Om Prakash Agarwal, Yayha Amir, Armando Ardila, Robert Bates, Verónica Baz, Radia Benamghar, Najy Benhassine, Luis Benveniste, Alexandra C. Bezeredi, Deepak Bhatia, Denis Biseko, Helena Bjuremalm, Eduardo Bohórquez, Francesca Bomboko, Sarah Botton, Carter Brandon, Michael Bratton, Chiara Bronchi, László Bruszt, Ruxandra Burdescu, David Calderón, Claudia Calvin, Oscar Calvo-González, Juan Camilo Cárdenas Campo, Enrique Cárdenas, Kevin Carey, Tom Carothers, Michael Chege, Donald Clarke, Roland Clarke, Pedro Conceição, Jill Cottrell, Philipp Dann, Bill Dorotinski, Alain Durand Lasserve, Ute Eckertz, Yara Esquivel, Mike Falke, Frederico Finan, Luis Foncerrada, Harald Fuhr, Bernard Funck, Yash Ghai, Frederick Golooba-Mutebi, Kristóf Gosztonyi, Donald Green, Jane Guyer, Gillian Hadfield, Jeffrey Hammer, Lucia Hanmer, Tazeen Hasan, Finn Heinrich, Hans-Joachim Heintze, Rogelio Gómez Hermosillo, Benjamin Herzberg, Ingrid-Gabriela Hoven, Alan Hudson, William Hurst, Gabriela Inchauste, Edna Jaime, Michael Jarvis, Melise Jaud, Erik Jensen, Melissa Johns, Patrick Keuleers, Anouar Ben Khelifa, Hannah Kim, Francis Kiwanga, Stephan Klasen, Anne-Lise Klausen, Verena Knippel, Matthias Kötter, David D. Laitin, George Larbi, Margaret Levi, Alberto Leyton, Doris Likwelile, Stefan Lindemann, Kathy Lindert, Mariana Llanos, Ernesto López Córdoba, Anna Lührmann, Christian Lund, Bentley MacLeod, Beatriz Magaloni, Alexander Makulilo, Ernest Mallya, Sumit Manchanda, Richard McAdams, David McKenzie, Craig Meisner, Rudolf Mellinghoff, Mauricio Merino, Edward Miguel, Omar Mohamed, Rui Monteiro, María Elena Morera, Fred Mufulukye, Ana María Muñoz, Mike Mushi, Per Norlund, Silas Olang, Virginia Oliveros, Jan Michiel Otto, Juan Pardinas, Haydee Pérez Garrido, Guillermo Perry, Lant Pritchett, Christine Qiang, Balakrishnan Rajagopal, Rita Ramalho, Juan Mauricio Ramírez, Juliana Ramirez, Viridiana Ríos, Christophe Rockmore, Carlos Rodríguez-Castelán, Lourdes Rodríguez-Chamussy, César Rodríguez Garavito, Halsey Rogers, Gérard Roland, Pallavi Roy, Eliana Rubiano, Elizabeth Ruppert Bulmer, Caroline Sage, Indhira Santos, Phillip Shelkens, Animesh Shrivastava, Dumitru Socolan, Michael Stanley, Albrecht Stockmayer, Håvard Strand, Harold Sunguisa, Hani Syed, Miguel Székely Pardo, Attilio

Tagalile, Will Taylor, Fletcher Tembo, Katy Thompson, Charles Undeland, Deus Valentine, Ingrid van Engelshoven, Roberto Vélez Grajales, Eric Verhoogen, Andrea Vigorito, Tara Vishwanath, Anya Vodopyanov, Stefan Voigt, George Mukundi Wachira, Waly Wane, Fredrick O. Wanyama, Asbjorn Wee, Barry Weingast, Jennifer Widner, George O. William, Oliver Williamson, Michael Woolcock, World Bank 1818 Society, Kaifeng Yang, Abdulqawi Ahmed Yusuf, and Davide Zucchini. We especially thank Rogier van den Brink for the very useful conversations we had in Manila and for bringing to our attention the work on fiscal management in Mongolia, including the reference to the film *Amka and the Three Golden Rules,* which we reference in chapter 2.

Despite efforts to be comprehensive, the team apologizes to any individuals or organization inadvertently omitted from this list and expresses its gratitude to all who contributed to this Report.

Abbreviations

ADR	alternative dispute resolution
ASEAN	Association of Southeast Asian Nations
CDD	community-driven development
CICIG	International Commission against Impunity in Guatemala (Comisión Internacional contra la Impunidad en Guatemala)
CPA	Comprehensive Peace Agreement (South Sudan)
CPC	Communist Party of China
CSO	civil society organization
DAC	Development Assistance Committee (of the OECD)
EU	European Union
FATF	Financial Action Task Force
FDI	foreign direct investment
FGM	female genital mutilation
FRC	Financial Reporting Centre (Kenya)
GATT	General Agreement on Tariffs and Trade
GBV	gender-based violence
GDP	gross domestic product
GNI	gross national income
ICAC	Independent Commission against Corruption (Hong Kong SAR, China)
ICTs	information and communication technologies
IFFs	illicit financial flows
IMF	International Monetary Fund
MDAs	ministries, departments, and agencies
MDGs	Millennium Development Goals
MFA	Multi Fibre Arrangement
MITI	Ministry of Trade and Industry (Japan)
NAFDAC	National Agency for Food and Drug Administration and Control (Nigeria)
NAFTA	North American Free Trade Agreement
NCPRI	National Campaign for Peoples' Right to Information (India)
NGO	nongovernmental organization
NPM	New Public Management (movement)
ODA	official development assistance
OECD	Organisation for Economic Co-operation and Development
OIRA	U.S. Office of Information and Regulatory Affairs
OSA	Official Secrets Act (India)
PPD	public-private dialogue
PPP	purchasing power parity
PPPs	public-private partnerships
PRI	Institutional Revolutionary Party (Partido Revolucionario Institucional; Mexico)
SAR	special administrative region
SBM	school-based management

SDGs	Sustainable Development Goals
SDIs	Service Delivery Indicators
SEZ	special economic zone
SOE	state-owned enterprise
SPC	Professional Career Service (Servicio Profesional de Carrera; Mexico)
StAR	Stolen Asset Recovery Initiative
TAI	transparency and accountability initiative
TFP	total factor productivity
TVEs	Township and Village Enterprises
UNFCCC	United Nations Framework Convention on Climate Change
WDR 2017	World Development Report 2017
WHO	World Health Organization
WTO	World Trade Organization

Country and economy codes

AFG	Afghanistan		COM	Comoros
AGO	Angola		CPV	Cabo Verde
ALB	Albania		CRI	Costa Rica
ARE	United Arab Emirates		CYP	Cyprus
ARG	Argentina		CZE	Czech Republic
ARM	Armenia		DEU	Germany
AUS	Australia		DJI	Djibouti
AUT	Austria		DNK	Denmark
AZE	Azerbaijan		DOM	Dominican Republic
BDI	Burundi		DZA	Algeria
BEL	Belgium		ECU	Ecuador
BEN	Benin		EGY	Egypt, Arab Rep.
BFA	Burkina Faso		ERI	Eritrea
BGD	Bangladesh		ESP	Spain
BGR	Bulgaria		EST	Estonia
BHR	Bahrain		ETH	Ethiopia
BHS	Bahamas, The		FIN	Finland
BIH	Bosnia and Herzegovina		FJI	Fiji
BLR	Belarus		FRA	France
BLZ	Belize		GAB	Gabon
BMU	Bermuda		GBR	United Kingdom
BOL	Bolivia		GEO	Georgia
BRA	Brazil		GHA	Ghana
BRB	Barbados		GIN	Guinea
BRN	Brunei Darussalam		GMB	Gambia, The
BTN	Bhutan		GNB	Guinea-Bissau
BWA	Botswana		GNQ	Equatorial Guinea
CAF	Central African Republic		GRC	Greece
CAN	Canada		GRD	Grenada
CHE	Switzerland		GTM	Guatemala
CHL	Chile		GUY	Guyana
CHN	China		HKG	Hong Kong SAR, China
CIV	Côte d'Ivoire		HND	Honduras
CMR	Cameroon		HRV	Croatia
COD	Congo, Dem. Rep.		HTI	Haiti
COG	Congo, Rep.		HUN	Hungary
COL	Colombia		IDN	Indonesia

IND	India	NZL	New Zealand
IRL	Ireland	OMN	Oman
IRN	Iran, Islamic Rep.	PAK	Pakistan
IRQ	Iraq	PAN	Panama
ISL	Iceland	PER	Peru
ISR	Israel	PHL	Philippines
ITA	Italy	PNG	Papua New Guinea
JAM	Jamaica	POL	Poland
JOR	Jordan	PRT	Portugal
JPN	Japan	PRY	Paraguay
KAZ	Kazakhstan	ROM	Romania
KEN	Kenya	RUS	Russian Federation
KGZ	Kyrgyz Republic	RWA	Rwanda
KHM	Cambodia	SAU	Saudi Arabia
KIR	Kiribati	SDN	Sudan
KNA	St. Kitts and Nevis	SEN	Senegal
KOR	Korea, Rep.	SGP	Singapore
KSV	Kosovo	SLB	Solomon Islands
KWT	Kuwait	SLE	Sierra Leone
LAO	Lao PDR	SLV	El Salvador
LBN	Lebanon	SOM	Somalia
LBR	Liberia	SRB	Serbia
LBY	Libya	SSD	South Sudan
LCA	St. Lucia	STP	São Tomé and Príncipe
LIE	Liechtenstein	SUR	Suriname
LKA	Sri Lanka	SVK	Slovak Republic
LSO	Lesotho	SVN	Slovenia
LTU	Lithuania	SWE	Sweden
LUX	Luxembourg	SWZ	Swaziland
LVA	Latvia	SYR	Syrian Arab Republic
MAC	Macau SAR, China	TCD	Chad
MAR	Morocco	TGO	Togo
MDA	Moldova	THA	Thailand
MDG	Madagascar	TJK	Tajikistan
MDV	Maldives	TKM	Turkmenistan
MEX	Mexico	TLS	Timor-Leste
MKD	Macedonia, FYR	TTO	Trinidad and Tobago
MLI	Mali	TUN	Tunisia
MLT	Malta	TUR	Turkey
MMR	Myanmar	TWN	Taiwan, China
MNG	Mongolia	TZA	Tanzania
MOZ	Mozambique	UGA	Uganda
MRT	Mauritania	UKR	Ukraine
MUS	Mauritius	URY	Uruguay
MWI	Malawi	USA	United States
MYS	Malaysia	UZB	Uzbekistan
NAM	Namibia	VEN	Venezuela, RB
NER	Niger	VNM	Vietnam
NGA	Nigeria	VUT	Vanuatu
NIC	Nicaragua	YEM	Yemen, Rep.
NLD	Netherlands	ZAF	South Africa
NOR	Norway	ZMB	Zambia
NPL	Nepal	ZWE	Zimbabwe

Overview

World Development Report 2017: Governance and the Law

The past 20 years have seen enormous progress around the world in socioeconomic indicators. The rapid diffusion of technology and greater access to capital and world markets have enabled economic growth rates that were previously unfathomable, and they have helped lift over 1 billion people out of poverty. And yet increased flows have also led to rising inequality, both within and across borders, and to greater vulnerability to global economic trends and cycles. Indeed, although the global spread of capital, technology, ideas, and people has helped many countries and people move forward, other regions and populations appear to have been left behind, and they are still facing violence, slow growth, and limited opportunities for advancement.

As ideas and resources spread at an increasingly rapid rate across countries, policy solutions to promote further progress abound. However, policies that should be effective in generating positive development outcomes are often not adopted, are poorly implemented, or end up backfiring over time. Although the development community has focused a great deal of attention on learning *what* policies and interventions are needed to generate better outcomes, it has paid much less attention to learning *why* those approaches succeed so well in some contexts but fail to generate positive results in others.

Improving governance to meet today's development challenges

Ultimately, confronting the challenges faced by today's developing countries—poor service delivery,

violence, slowing growth, corruption, and the "natural resource curse," to name a few—requires rethinking the process by which state and nonstate actors interact to design and implement policies, or what this Report calls governance (box O.1). Consider some recent cases that have attracted global attention.

State building in Somalia and Somaliland. Somalia, one of the world's most fragile countries, has been wracked by violence for more than two decades. Insurgent attacks and regional conflicts have prevented the emergence of a centralized state with a monopoly over the legitimate use of force. Warring factions, many with their own regional sources of power, have been unable to reach a credible deal that determines the makeup and responsibilities of the central state. By contrast, in Somalia's autonomous region of Somaliland, an area with similar tribal and clan tensions, 20 years of stability and economic development have followed a 1993 clan conference that brought together leaders from both the modern and traditional sectors, successfully institutionalizing these clans and elders into formal governing bodies.

Confronting corruption and the resource curse in Nigeria. In 2010, just a year after a decade-long bounty of windfall revenues from high oil prices, Nigeria was requesting budget support from its development partners. From a long-term perspective, it is unclear how much of Nigeria's oil wealth has been saved to invest in the future, although a Sovereign Wealth Fund was established in 2011 to address these concerns. According to a former governor of the central bank, the country has lost billions of dollars to corruption by the National Petroleum Company. Indeed, 2015 data from the Afrobarometer survey indicates that 78 percent of Nigerians feel that the

Ultimately, confronting the challenges faced by today's developing countries requires rethinking the process by which state and nonstate actors interact to design and implement policies, or what this Report calls governance.

Box O.1 What is governance?

For the purpose of this Report, governance is the process through which state and nonstate actors interact to design and implement policies within a given set of formal and informal rules that shape and are shaped by power.[a] This Report defines *power* as the ability of groups and individuals to make others act in the interest of those groups and individuals and to bring about specific outcomes.[b]

Depending on the context, actors may establish a government as a set of formal state institutions (a term used in the literature to denote organizations and rules) that enforce and implement policies. Also depending on the context, state actors will play a more or less important role with respect to nonstate actors such as civil society organizations or business lobbies. In addition, governance takes place at different levels, from international bodies, to national state institutions, to local government agencies, to community or business associations. These dimensions often overlap, creating a complex network of actors and interests.

Source: WDR 2017 team.

a. The general definition of *governance* used in this Report is consistent with the World Bank's corporate definition, which emphasizes formal institutions and the role of state actors.
b. Dahl (1957); Lukes (2005).

government is "doing badly in fighting corruption." Ultimately, the institutional context was unable to safeguard natural resource revenues in order to reduce fiscal volatility and promote a macroeconomic environment conducive to long-term investment. Several countries have demonstrated that this kind of "natural resource curse"—the paradox that countries with abundant natural resources face slower growth and worse development outcomes than countries without resources—can be avoided through effective economic and fiscal policies.

China's growth performance and growth challenges. For four decades, China, while increasingly integrating its economy with the global economy, grew at double-digit rates and lifted more than 700 million people out of poverty. This successful track record of economic growth is well known. Yet, according to many frequently used indicators, China's institutional environment during this period would seem not to have changed. Does this imply that institutions do not matter for growth? No. Rather, a deeper understanding of China's development shows what these indicators miss: the adaptive policy decisions and state capacity that enabled economic success were facilitated by profound changes to mechanisms of accountability and collective leadership. China's experience highlights the need to pay more attention to how institutions function and less to the specific form they take. Meanwhile, today China faces a slowdown in growth. Maintaining rapid growth requires political incentives to switch to a growth model based on firm entry, competition, and innovation. In many middle-income countries, this transformation has been blocked by the actors that benefited from early growth and have few incentives to join coalitions for further reforms. Going forward will involve addressing these governance challenges.

Slums and exclusion in India's cities. Urban development that stems from coordinated planning and investment by coalitions of developers, bureaucrats, citizens, and politicians can lead to cities that are centers of growth, innovation, and productivity. Planners can help ensure that infrastructure meets the demands of investors who seek to maximize land rents; businesses that need connectivity to consumers, employees, and other firms; and citizens who want access to services and jobs. But many cities fail to deliver on these promises. In India, massive urban slums—about 49,000 at the latest count, with tens of millions of inhabitants—represent failures to align public investments and zoning with the needs of a diverse set of urban constituents. Poorly designed cities with misallocated investments have limited connectivity among housing, affordable transportation, and utilities, driving workers into informal settlements, often in peripheral areas. Many developers and politicians have exploited the system to generate rents for themselves, but this uncoordinated urban development has prevented cities from achieving their growth potential, leading to large slums where most citizens are deprived of basic services.

Demanding better services in Brazil. In 2013 the world watched when protests erupted in Brazil's streets about the quality of public services—transport, education, and health—as the FIFA World Cup soccer tournament approached. Brazil had gone through

12 years of inclusive and sustained growth, which had lifted more than 30 million people out of poverty and strengthened the middle class. These same middle classes that contributed with their taxes to the provision of public services were now demanding better quality and coverage, including "FIFA standards" for their schools. Why did this change come about? Brazil's social contract had historically been weak and fragmented. The poor received low-quality public services, while the upper-middle classes relied on private services and were thus unwilling to contribute to the fiscal system. The creation of an expanded middle class and the reduction of poverty paradoxically heightened the perceptions of unfairness as the new middle class expected more than low-quality public services for its contributions.

"Brexit" and the growing discontent with economic integration. In June 2016, voters in the United Kingdom elected to leave the European Union (EU). The economic consequences for the country in particular and Europe in general have become a source of uncertainty in policy circles. Dissatisfaction with economic

and political integration is not, however, exclusive to this region. In countries throughout the world, populist parties have campaigned against trade and integration, some of them enjoying unprecedented electoral success. These parties often prey on citizens' increasing feelings of disenfranchisement and exclusion from decision making, as well as on a growing perception of free-riding by specific groups. Even in countries that have undoubtedly benefited from integration, the unequal distribution of such benefits and perceived ineffectiveness of "voice" have led many citizens to question the status quo, which could have consequences for social cohesion and stability.

What do these examples have in common? This Report assumes that all countries share a set of development objectives: minimizing the threat of violence (*security*), promoting prosperity (*growth*), and ensuring that prosperity is shared (*equity*), while also protecting the sustainability of the development process for future generations (box O.2). But policies do not always translate into these development outcomes in the expected ways. As the previous

Box O.2 Governance for what? Achieving the goals of security, growth, and equity

Many aspects of governance are valuable in and of themselves—that is, they have intrinsic value—in particular, the notion of freedom. In economic terms, freedom can be seen as an opportunity set, and development can be seen as "the removal of various types of unfreedoms" (exclusion from opportunities), where these unfreedoms reduce people's capacity to exercise "their reasoned agency."[a] As essential as such an intrinsic value as freedom is, its instrumental value also matters because of the "effectiveness of freedoms of particular kinds to promote freedoms of other kinds."[b] These positive relationships are what economists call complementarities. This Report acknowledges the intrinsic value of various dimensions of governance, as well as the notion of development as positive freedom, while also recognizing their instrumental value to achieving equitable development.

The analysis in this Report starts from the normative standpoint that every society cares about freeing its members from the constant threat of violence (*security*), about promoting prosperity (*growth*), and about how such prosperity is shared (*equity*). It also assumes that societies

aspire to achieving these goals in environmentally sustainable ways. This Report, then, assesses governance in terms of its capacity to deliver on these outcomes.

This approach is consistent with the transition from a dialogue based on ideology to the dialogue based on ideals that has transpired in the global development community over the past few decades. The establishment of the Millennium Development Goals (MDGs) in 2000 and the recent ratification of the Sustainable Development Goals (SDGs) by member countries of the United Nations are examples of the efforts to set common goals for social and economic advancement. SDG 16 calls for promoting "peace, justice and strong institutions," and it is explicitly related to governance. Nevertheless, as this Report will argue, beyond the intrinsic value of SDG 16, it also has important instrumental value because the attainment of the goal will aid in the attainment of all the other SDGs. Indeed, the achievement of all the development goals will require a solid understanding of governance to enable more effective policies.

Source: WDR 2017 team.

a. Sen (1999, xii).
b. Sen (1999, xii).

examples illustrate, contradictions occur in the real world. Somalia is a fragile state, whereas Somaliland seems to be doing well. Nigeria has an abundance of resources, but it is still a lower-middle-income country. China grew rapidly, even though many of its fundamental institutions did not change. India has grown, but it cannot control the propagation of slums. Brazil has experienced inclusive growth, but it is now facing widespread protests from the middle class. Great Britain had low unemployment, but it voted to leave the EU. The common thread running through these contradictions appears to be governance malfunctions: ineffective policies persist, effective policies are not chosen, and unorthodox institutional arrangements generate positive outcomes. So, what drives policy effectiveness?

Drivers of effectiveness: Commitment, coordination, and cooperation

Often, when policies and technical solutions fail to achieve intended outcomes, institutional failure takes the blame, and the solution usually proposed is to "improve" institutions. But many types of institutional arrangements and trajectories can enable development, as examples around the world demonstrate, whereas often many other "best practices" fail. In some cases, rapid progress comes about suddenly, seemingly unexpectedly. Because of this diversity of paths and perils, it becomes essential to uncover the underlying drivers of policy effectiveness. This Report identifies *commitment*, *coordination*, and *cooperation* as the three core functions of institutions that are needed to ensure that rules and resources yield the desired outcomes.[1]

Form versus function: Underlying determinants of policy effectiveness

Commitment. Commitment enables actors to rely on the credibility of policies so they can calibrate their behavior accordingly. Consistency over time in policies is not easy to achieve. Circumstances change, policy objectives may extend beyond the political cycle, and resources may fail to match, changing the incentives to implement previously chosen policies. In line with the economic theory of incomplete contracts, policies require commitment devices to ensure their credibility.

Take, for example, security—a foundation of sustained development. It is premised most basically on commitment. Are conflicting parties able to reach credible agreements to renounce violence and endow the state with a monopoly on the legitimate use of force? In Somaliland, commitment has been achieved by establishing institutional arrangements that provide sufficient incentives for all key groups to work within the rules. The commitment is credible because all parties stand to lose if any party reneges on those arrangements. In Somalia, by contrast, despite several internationally sponsored efforts at state building, polarized groups continue to believe they are better off retaining their own power or forming shifting alliances with others than conferring the monopoly of violence on a central state. Why? In large part, the nature of the agreements and the proposed institutional arrangements had failed to serve as effective commitment devices. When commitment to deals is not credible, contending sides walk away from the bargaining table and violence prevails: warring factions may renege on peace agreements, policy makers may default on promises to transfer resources to discontented groups or regions, disputants may fail to abide by court judgments, or the police may abuse citizens instead of protecting them.

A credible commitment to pro-growth policies and property rights is also essential to ensure macroeconomic stability and enable growth. According to recent evidence, most long-term growth comes not from episodes of rapid growth—as is commonly believed—but from countries not shrinking in response to an economic crisis or violent conflict (figure O.1). Growth requires an environment in which firms and individuals feel secure in investing their resources in productive activities. This commitment may arise in diverse ways. During China's take-off in the 1980s, growth success depended on a pledge to local governments, private enterprises, and rural farmers that they would be able to keep their profits—credible commitment was thus provided, even if it was still in the early stage of securing the protection of private property rights. By contrast, in Nigeria the institutional context did not provide the commitment needed to safeguard revenues from natural resource extraction in order to support long-term development. In the Nigerian context, where perceptions of corruption were negative, implementing "best-practice" fiscal rules that worked in other contexts did not constitute a credible commitment because government officials were overcome by short-term interests. State governors, for example, uncertain about whether resources would still be there in the future, had incentives to spend them straightaway.

Coordination. Credible commitment alone, however, is not sufficient; coordination is also needed.

Commitment enables actors to rely on the credibility of policies so they can calibrate their behavior accordingly.

Figure O.1 Long-term growth is less about how fast one grows than about not tripping along the way

Frequency of economies' growing and shrinking years and average rates, by GDP per capita

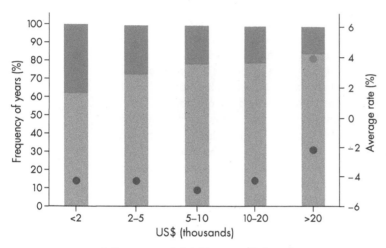

Sources: WDR 2017 team, based on Wallis 2016, with data from Penn World Table, version 8.0 (Feenstra, Inklaar, and Timmer 2015).

Note: The figure shows real GDP per capita (constant prices: chain series). Countries are first sorted into income categories based on their income in 2000, measured in 2005 U.S. dollars. Average annual growth rates are the simple arithmetic average for all the years and all the countries in the income category, without weighting. The sample underlying the figure consists of 141 countries, for which data are available from at least 1970 onward.

For investment and innovation, firms and individuals must believe that others will also invest. Institutions can help solve market failures by coordinating both investment decisions and the expectations of market participants. The insight that a failure to coordinate investment activity can lead to underdevelopment is decades old.[2] Consider the case in which large-scale factories are more efficient, but investing in them is not profitable for individual firms unless those firms invest simultaneously in a group. Perhaps the size of the market is too small to justify large-scale investments unless all the industries expand together, providing markets for one another. In such a situation, there are two possible outcomes, or equilibria. The first is one in which no firms invest in large-scale factories, and efficiency levels remain low. The second, a better outcome, is one in which firms are able to coordinate a simultaneous move to large-scale, efficient production. Such problems of coordination can occur in many contexts, ranging from finance and adoption of technology to innovation and industrial clusters to urban planning.[3] In India, the lack of coordination among urban planners, real estate developers, and

local politicians has prevented an efficient design of urban areas, hindering many cities from performing their roles in enhancing growth.

Cooperation. Finally, policy effectiveness to achieve equitable development requires cooperation, particularly citizens' willingness to contribute to public goods and not free-ride on others. The extent to which societies can ensure opportunities for all individuals depends on their ability to invest in providing high-quality services such as health, education, and connectivity, and to ensure access to economic opportunities. For such investment to take place, resources need to be collected and redistributed. Indeed, no high-income country has achieved improvements in equity without significant taxation and public spending aimed at protecting individuals against shocks (such as illness or unemployment) and reducing welfare disparities within and across generations.[4] In addition, for individuals to realize the returns of such investment, they need access to economic opportunities in adulthood, especially access to opportunities that allow them to use the human capital they have acquired. For a country to collect the taxes needed to fund investments in public goods, its citizens must be willing to comply and cooperate. Cooperation is enhanced by commitment because credible and consistent enforcement of laws is also needed to expand opportunities and level the playing field.

Sometimes, societies face a breakdown of cooperation. For example, Brazil, whose citizens organized to demand higher-quality public services, faced a problem common to many countries: the fragmentation of a social contract. In such cases, the low quality of service provision spurs the upper-middle classes to demand private services, which in turn weakens their willingness to cooperate fiscally and contribute to the provision of public goods—a perverse cycle. At other times, actors potentially affected by policies may be excluded from the design of those policies, thereby undermining their incentive to cooperate and weakening compliance. An induced perception that the EU was engaged in technocratic and exclusionary decision making and that some countries were benefiting disproportionately from the agreement, was among the reasons that led the United Kingdom to vote for "Brexit"—and led to the rise of populist parties in the world that challenge further integration.

Commitment, coordination, and *cooperation* are therefore essential institutional functions for making policies effective and thereby able to achieve development outcomes (table O.1).[5] Yet, they are effectively fulfilled under only certain conditions. This Report proposes an analytical framework to advance

Table O.1 Three institutional functions—commitment, coordination, and cooperation—are essential to the effectiveness of policies

Function	Examples of why these functions matter
Commitment	• Decision makers may want to spend windfall revenues now instead of saving them for others to spend in the future. • Politicians may resist continuing policies that have been working and prefer to pursue others that are associated with their political group. • Public service providers may push to renegotiate the terms of their contracts to their benefit when they know that the political cost of suspending service is high.
Coordination	• Investment and innovation are induced when individuals believe others will also invest. • Financial stability depends on beliefs about the credibility of policies; failures involve, for example, bank runs, where everyone believes the rest will rush to withdraw deposits. • Laws serve as a focal point for individuals to behave in certain ways, such as the convention of driving on the right side of the road.
Cooperation	• People have incentives to free-ride or to behave opportunistically—for example, by not paying taxes while enjoying the public services that other (tax-paying) individuals are funding. • Some actors potentially affected by policies may be excluded from their design, which weakens compliance and leads to fragmentation.

Source: WDR 2017 team.

understanding of how governance can help achieve these functions to promote development outcomes.

When political will is not enough: Power, bargaining, and the policy arena

This Report argues that institutions perform three key functions that enhance policy effectiveness for development: enabling credible *commitment,* inducing *coordination,* and enhancing *cooperation.* But why are policies so often ineffective in doing so? A typical response among policy practitioners is that the right policies exist, ready to be implemented, but that what is missing is political will in the national arena. This Report argues that decision makers—the elites[6]—may have the right objectives and yet may still be unable to implement the right policies because doing so would challenge the existing equilibrium—and the current balance of power. Thus the balance of power in society may condition the kinds of results that emerge from commitment, coordination, and cooperation.

Ultimately, policy effectiveness depends not only on what policies are chosen, but also on *how* they are chosen and implemented. Policy making and policy implementation both involve bargaining among different actors. The setting in which (policy) decisions are made is the *policy arena*—that is, the space in which different groups and actors interact and bargain over aspects of the public domain, and in which the resulting agreements eventually also lead to changes in the formal rules (law). It is the setting in which governance manifests itself.[7] Policy arenas can be found at the local, national, international, and supranational

levels. They can be formal (parliaments, courts, intergovernmental organizations, government agencies), traditional (council of elders), or informal (backroom deals, old boys' networks).

Who bargains in this policy arena and how successfully they bargain are determined by the relative *power* of actors, by their ability to influence others through control over resources, threat of violence, or ideational persuasion (de facto power), as well as by and through the existing rules themselves (de jure power). Power is expressed in the policy arena by the ability of groups and individuals to make others act in the interest of those groups and individuals and to bring about specific outcomes. It is a fundamental enabler of—or constraint to—policy effectiveness (box O.3).

The distribution of power is a key element of the way in which the policy arena functions. During policy bargaining processes, the unequal distribution of power—*power asymmetry*—can influence policy effectiveness. Power asymmetry is not necessarily harmful, and it can actually be a means of achieving effectiveness—for example, through delegated authority. By contrast, the negative manifestations of power asymmetries are reflected in capture, clientelism, and exclusion.

How power asymmetries matter for security, growth, and equity

Exclusion. One manifestation of power asymmetries, the *exclusion* of individuals and groups from the bargaining arena, can be particularly important for security (figure O.2). When powerful actors are excluded

Box O.3 The idea of power and the power of ideas

"The ideas of economists and political philosophers," British economist John Maynard Keynes noted in *The General Theory of Employment, Interest and Money*, "both when they are right and when they are wrong, are more powerful than is commonly understood. Indeed, the world is ruled by little else."[a] The notion of how ideas can influence historical paths in fundamental ways has long been studied by social scientists, not only from the perspective of ideology and culture but also from the viewpoint of "cultural entrepreneurship."[b] It is important, however, to distinguish two specific ways—not exhaustive but fundamental—in which ideas influence policy making and effectiveness: ideas as knowledge and ideas as a means of shaping preferences and beliefs.

From the perspective of ideas as knowledge, over the past few decades the policy discussion has been influenced by the principles of "capacity building" in the form of knowledge sharing and dissemination of "best practices." Ideas as knowledge undoubtedly play a role in strengthening the effectiveness of policies and enhancing the capacity to deliver on specific policy commitments.

But ideas also shape preferences and beliefs. Keynes ended his discussion of ideas by saying that "practical men, who believe themselves to be quite exempt from any intellectual influences, are usually slaves of some defunct economist. . . . But soon or late, it is ideas, not vested interests, which are dangerous for good or evil." In the 18th century, Hume's law established that no normative statement (such as a policy prescription) can be derived from a positive one (observation of facts) without a normative idea as an assumption. Policy prescriptions based on facts still require some normative notion—that is, an idea in the background. Acknowledging the importance of ideas, this Report discusses the relevance of shaping preferences and beliefs as a means of understanding the policy bargaining process.

It was Eric Wolf who, in 1999, called attention to the importance of understanding power and ideas as complementary to understanding social dynamics.[c] Indeed, following Michel Foucault, Wolf argues that the ability to shape other people's beliefs is a means of eliciting an action from another person—an action the other person would not otherwise take. The ability to make others act in one actor's interest or to bring about a specific outcome—the definition of power in this Report—is thus closely related to the notion of ideas as beliefs.

The dichotomy between ideas (ideology and culture) and power as a primary determinant of social dynamics is thus a false one. The idea of power cannot be understood without taking seriously the power of ideas.

Source: WDR 2017 team.

a. Keynes (1936, 383).
b. See, for example, Mokyr (2005) for a discussion of the "intellectual origins of modern economic growth."
c. Wolf (1999). See also Barrett, Stokholm, and Burke (2001).

---

from the policy arena, violence may become the preferred—and rational—way for certain individuals and groups to pursue their interests, such as in Somalia. It can lead to failed bargains between participants in the bargaining arena (such as when peace talks between rival factions break down, or when disputants fail to reach an agreement).

Exclusion, which can take the shape of lack of access to state institutions, resources, and services, often occurs along identity fault lines. The distribution of power among ethnic groups, measured by their access to central state power, is a strong predictor of violent conflict at the national level (whether in the form of repression by the state or rebellion against the state).[8] Cross-country statistical analyses using the Ethnic Power Relations data set from 1945 to 2005 indicate that states that exclude large portions of the population based on ethnic background are more likely to face armed rebellions.[9] The existence of norms that exclude certain groups, such as women and minorities, from the bargaining arena where disputes are settled tend to reinforce power asymmetries and perpetuate inequitable and insecure outcomes.[10]

Capture. A second manifestation of power asymmetries—the ability of influential groups to "capture" policies and make them serve their narrow interest—is helpful for understanding the effectiveness (or ineffectiveness) of policies in promoting long-term growth. In the 1990s, for example, some of Indonesia's largest industrial groups had strong connections to President Suharto.[11] Between 1995 and 1997, rumors about President Suharto's health circulated on several occasions. During every episode, the closer that industrial groups were to the president, the more

Figure O.2 A more even balance of power is associated with positive security outcomes

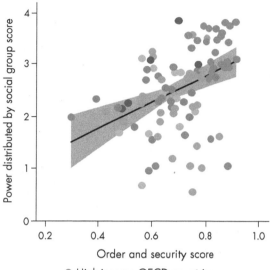

Sources: World Justice Project, Rule of Law Index 2015, Factor 5, "Order and Security" (consisting of "Crime is effectively controlled"; "Civil conflict is effectively limited"; "People do not resort to violence to redress personal grievances"); V-Dem, version 6 (consisting of "Power distributed by social group" in which a score of 0 indicates political power is monopolized by one social group, and a score of 4 indicates that social groups have equal political power).

Note: OECD = Organisation for Economic Co-operation and Development.

the value of their stock fell (figure O.3). The effects of capture can be quite costly for an economy. Politically connected firms are able to obtain preferential treatment in business regulation for themselves as well as raise regulatory barriers to entry for newcomers—such as through access to loans, ease of licensing requirements, energy subsidies, or import barriers. Such treatment can stifle competition and lead to resource misallocation, with a toll on innovation and productivity. Between 1996 and 2002, politically connected firms in Pakistan received 45 percent more government credit than other firms, even though they were less productive and had default rates that were 50 percent higher. Based on the productivity gap between firms, the annual cost of this credit misallocation could have been as high as 1.6 percent of the gross domestic product (GDP).[12]

Although it is possible for economies to grow without substantive changes in the nature of governance, it is not clear how long such growth can be sustained. Consider the case of countries apparently stuck in "development traps." Contrary to what many growth theories predict, there is no tendency for low- and middle-income countries to converge toward high-income countries. The evidence suggests that countries at all income levels are at risk of growth stagnation. What keeps some countries from transitioning to a better growth strategy when their existing growth strategy has run out of steam? With a few exceptions, policy advice for these countries has focused on the proximate causes of transition, such as the efficiency

Figure O.3 The value of political connections: Indonesia during President Suharto's era

The closer that industrial groups were to the president, the more the value of their stock fell as rumors about the president's health circulated

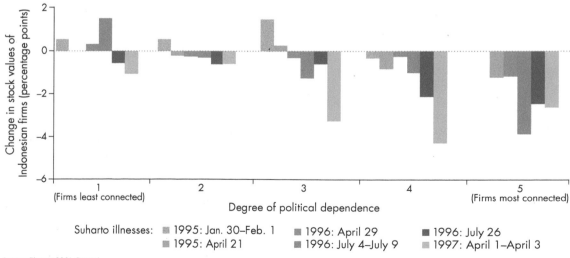

Source: Fisman 2001, figure 1.

of resource allocation or industrial upgrading. The real problem, however, may have political roots: powerful actors who gained during an earlier or current growth phase (such as the factor-intensive growth phase) may resist the switch to another growth model (such as one based on firm entry, competition, and innovation in a process of "creative destruction"). These actors may exert influence to capture policies to serve their own interests. Box O.4 presents an example of the political challenges in transitioning toward a different growth strategy—one that is related to investment in environmental sustainability.

Clientelism. A third manifestation of power asymmetries is *clientelism*—a political strategy characterized by an exchange of material goods in return for electoral support.[13] This strategy is helpful for understanding why policies that seek to promote equity are often ineffective. Although pro-equity policies can be potentially beneficial for growth in the medium and long run, they can adversely affect the interests of specific groups, particularly in the short term. Those affected by equity-oriented policies may be concerned about losing rents or about seeing their relative influence reduced, and thus they may attempt to undermine the adoption or implementation of those policies. When societies have high levels of inequality, such inequalities are reflected in the unequal capacity of groups to influence the policy-making process, making inequality more persistent. Clientelism leads to a breakdown of commitment to long-term programmatic objectives, where accountability becomes gradually up for sale.

Clientelism can shape the adoption and implementation of policies in two main ways. In the first

---

Box O.4 Why some people see red when they hear "green growth"

"Green growth is about making growth processes resource-efficient, cleaner and more resilient without necessarily slowing them."[a] For many reasons, environmental conservation is also good for long-term economic growth and development. Economic production depends on the stock of natural resources and on environmental quality ("natural capital"). Green growth strategies can increase natural capital by preventing environmental degradation. Environmental protection can also contribute indirectly to growth by correcting market failures. For example, a policy that addresses market failures leading to urban congestion can improve air quality and increase urban productivity. Greener growth can also improve well-being directly by improving air and water quality.

However, switching to greener growth strategies could impose short-term costs on some groups in society. Take the case of organic fertilizer. Smaller and more targeted doses of fertilizer (a "green" approach) are better for the environment in the long run, but conventional fertilizer is less costly and easier to use. Malawi faced this problem in 2005 when, to cope with food insecurity, it introduced a fertilizer subsidy for smallholder maize farmers. The intensive use of conventional fertilizer did lead to an immediate increase in farm output. However, because small farmers would not find it easy to adopt more organic fertilizers and

greener approaches, efforts to phase out the subsidy for conventional fertilizers could hurt maize farmers for some years.[b]

It could be that the groups who stand to lose from green growth policies in the short term have an oversized influence over the policy arena, and so they are able to block reforms and undermine commitment. Because the costs are concentrated and many of the benefits from cleaner technologies are intangible and dispersed, the potential losers from such reforms are likely better able to organize. They also can form a strong electoral constituency. For example, Malawi's fertilizer program has been popular among small farmers—an important constituency. At times, switching to greener growth strategies can entail losses for influential groups of consumers and firms. For example, South Africa announced an ambitious climate change plan in 2010 that would reduce the share of electricity generated by coal-fired plants in a country in which electricity is in short supply and coal is a relatively abundant source. The plan, despite being watered down a year later, has been opposed by consumers, labor unions, and business interests, particularly those in mining and heavy industry.[c] As these examples demonstrate, the design of green growth policies must take into account the potential resistance from those who will lose in the short term.

Sources: Hallegatte and others (2012); Resnick, Tarp, and Thurlow (2012).

a. Hallegatte and others (2012, 2).
b. Resnick, Tarp, and Thurlow (2012).
c. Resnick, Tarp, and Thurlow (2012).

type of clientelistic setting, the relationship between public officials and voters becomes distorted. Instead of a dynamic in which the official is the agent of the voter, who monitors and sanctions the agent (figure O.4, panel a), the interaction becomes a bargain in which the politician "buys" votes in exchange for (usually) short-term benefits such as transfers or subsidies (figure O.4, panel b).[14] These bargains tend to be more frequent when individuals have a higher time preference for the present with respect to the future. The poor and disadvantaged are particularly vulnerable to this sort of exchange because their pressing needs make their discount rates for the present higher than those of the better-off. In the second type of clientelistic setting, politicians become responsive to those groups that wield greater influence—for example, favoring the interests of teachers' unions over those of students (figure O.4, panel c). This happens when public officials become dependent on the support of certain groups for their political survival, including the providers of public services.

The costs of this malfunction can be high. In exchange for their political support, service providers may extract rents through the diversion of public resources, or withhold their effort in the form of absenteeism or low-quality provision, or engage in corrupt practices, hampering the delivery of services such as education, health, or infrastructure. When groups in charge of providing services capture politicians, monitoring and sanctioning these providers are no longer credible, leading to a weak commitment to service delivery. A policy experiment in Kenya illustrates this point. It compared the impact of contract teachers in interventions managed by nongovernmental organizations (NGOs) and interventions run by the government. Test scores increased only in the intervention run by NGOs, indicating that NGOs were more credible in implementing sanctions—through firing—than the government.[15] When commitment breaks down systematically, it can erode people's incentives to cooperate, and some groups may opt out by demanding private services and looking for ways to avoid contributing to the provision of public goods.[16] In clientelistic settings, states tend to have low tax revenues and provide few public goods, undermining economic activity and future taxation.

Best practice or best fit? Revisiting the notion of "first-best" through the bargaining lens

The development community has largely focused its reform attempts on designing best-practice solutions and building the capacity needed to implement them.

Figure O.4 Principals, agents, and clients: Accountability for sale

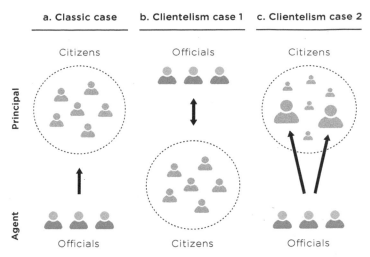

Sources: WDR 2017 team, extending World Bank 2003 and Khemani and others 2016.
Note: Arrows indicate who is responsive to whom.

Capacity, often considered a prerequisite for policy effectiveness, is certainly important, and in many cases it is even an overriding constraint. At a given point in time, it can be thought of as a stock. How and where to use such capacity, however, are also the product of a bargaining process. Even if physical and administrative capacity exists, policies may still be ineffective if groups with enough bargaining power have no incentives to pursue implementation. An example is the low investment in statistical capacity in Africa, which limits the ability to monitor policy effectiveness (box O.5). In addition, the existing power structures may be reinforced by the prevailing social norms, which are persistent shapers of behavior.[17] Such norms may reinforce or undermine policy effectiveness.

Thus investing in capacity may not be enough. Designing policies to improve security, growth, and equity requires understanding the balance of power among different actors. In the presence of powerful actors who can block or undermine policies, optimal policies from a strict economic standpoint (first-best policies) may not be the optimal implementable policies (second-best but feasible). Even when feasible, implementing what seem like first-best economic policies from a static perspective can lead to worse outcomes for society when such policies negatively affect the power equilibrium. For example, where governments are captured by firms and there is high inequality, unions may be the only way for workers to solve their collective action problem,[18] even if representation is not perfect. In such cases, passing a law to make labor contracts more flexible may undermine union membership and lead to more inequality, which in turn can perpetuate the power of the wealthy.[19]

Levers for change: Contestability, incentives, preferences and beliefs

From the perspective of power asymmetries, efforts to strengthen the ability of institutions to effectively enable commitment, coordination, and cooperation call into question many traditional practices of the development community. Anyone seeking to design more effective policies may find it helpful to recognize how the distribution of power in the policy arena could affect policy design and implementation and to consider how the policy arena can be reshaped to expand the set of policies that can be implemented.

Reshaping the policy arena occurs when changes are made in who can participate in decision-making processes (the *contestability* of the policy arena), when *incentives* to pursue certain goals are transformed, and when actors' *preferences and beliefs* shift.[20] As an illustration, consider how countries are more or less effective at redistributing income through the fiscal system. The average measure of inequality (as captured

by the Gini coefficient) based on individuals' market income is 0.47 for developed countries and 0.52 for developing countries. After the effects of taxes and transfers are taken into account, the corresponding coefficients drop to 0.31 and 0.50, respectively. If the effect of publicly provided services (in particular, education and health) is also included, inequality falls further: to 0.22 in developed countries and to 0.42 in developing countries.[21] The quantifiable redistributive capacity of these countries can be interpreted in different ways. It can be interpreted as the relative ability of different actors to influence and *contest* decisions about how resources are distributed in a given country. It can be interpreted as the *incentives* of governments to commit to the collection of taxes and allocation of spending—more checks and balances on power are associated with more redistribution.[22] Or it can be interpreted as the *preferences* for redistribution in a given country.

Contestability. Who is included and who is excluded from the policy arena are determined by the relative power of the competing actors, as well as by the barriers of entry to participation (that is, how contestable the process is). A more contestable policy arena is one in which the actors or groups who have reason to participate in the decision-making process have ways to express their interests and exert influence. Because contestability determines who is included and who is excluded from the bargain, it is closely linked to the notion of inclusion. However, it also emphasizes the barriers to participation. Although the inclusion of more actors in the decision-making process is not necessarily a guarantee of better decisions, a more contestable policy arena tends to be associated with higher levels of legitimacy and cooperation. When procedures for selecting and implementing policies are more contestable, those policies tend to be perceived as "fair" and to induce cooperation more effectively.

Incentives. The incentives that actors have to comply with agreements are fundamental to enabling commitment in the policy arena. Credible commitment requires consistency in the face of changing circumstances. Incentives for actors to commit to agreements are thus crucial for effective policy design and implementation. Stronger incentives to hold policy makers accountable can also strengthen voluntary compliance because repeatedly delivering on commitment helps build trust in institutions.

Preferences and beliefs. The preferences and beliefs of decision-making actors matter for shaping whether the outcome of the bargain will enhance welfare and whether the system is responsive to the interests of those who have less influence. Aggregating preferences, for example, can increase the latter's visibility. Because the preferences and beliefs of actors shape their policy goals, an important condition for policy effectiveness is the coordination of actors' expectations.

This Report explores in depth how changes in contestability, incentives, and preferences and beliefs can enhance policy effectiveness for security, growth, and equity. Depending on the primary functional challenge—that is, whether a policy needs to enable commitment, coordination, or cooperation—these entry points may be different. Because the functional challenges are interdependent, the entry points act as complements.

The role of law in shaping the policy arena

Law is a powerful instrument for reshaping the policy arena. Although laws generally reflect the interests of those actors with greater bargaining power, law has also proven to be an important instrument for change. By its nature, law is a device that provides a particular language, structure, and formality for ordering things, and this characteristic gives it the potential to become a force independent of the initial powers and intentions behind it. Law, often in combination with other social and political strategies, can be used as a commitment and coordination device

to promote accountability, and also to change the rules of the game to foster more equitable bargaining spaces. Effective laws are those that are able to shape bargaining spaces that increase contestability by underrepresented actors; that provide incentives by changing payoffs to lower the cost of compliance (or increase the cost of noncompliance); and that shift preferences by enhancing substantive focal points around which coordination can occur. State law, however, is but one of many rule systems that order behavior, authority, and contestation. Such legal and normative pluralism (box O.6) is neither inherently good nor bad: it can pose challenges, but it can also generate opportunities.

Law can play a role in making the policy arena more contestable. Enhancing the contestability of the arena encompasses both ex ante procedures (which relate to the means by which law is made and the extent to which it is participatory and transparent) and ex post ones (the extent to which law is applied consistently and fairly). If various actors believe the process is exclusionary or reflects only the interests of certain groups, they may not comply, or they may outright oppose it. Public hearings, stakeholder consultations, social audits, and participatory processes are some examples of instruments that can make the policy arena more contestable.[23] In this case, law serves as a tool to promote accountability, change the rules of the game, or both. This function is embodied, for example, in the advocacy to adopt right-to-information laws.

Law can play a role in shaping the incentives of actors to comply with agreements by, for example, providing a credible threat of punishment or a credible commitment to delivering the reward for compliance. Law orders behavior through rules ranging from prohibiting bribery, to establishing licensing fees and business registration, to banning child marriage, as well as through the means to enforce these rules. Following Hart's classic legal theory, laws induce particular behaviors of individuals and firms through coercive power, coordination power, and legitimating power.[24]

Law can effectively reshape preferences and coordinate expectations about how others will behave, serving as a focal point. In this way, law can act as a signpost—an expression—to guide people on how to act when they have several options, or (in economic terms) in the presence of multiple equilibria.[25] Law provides a clear reference in the midst of diverging views. People comply with the law because doing so facilitates social and economic activities.

A more contestable policy arena tends to be associated with higher levels of legitimacy and cooperation. When procedures for selecting and implementing policies are more contestable, those policies tend to be perceived as "fair" and to induce cooperation more effectively.

Box O.6 Legal and normative pluralism

The phenomenon of "legal pluralism"—the coexistence of multiple legal systems within a given community or sociopolitical space—has existed throughout history and continues today in developing and developed countries alike. Modern forms of legal pluralism have their roots in colonialism, through which Western legal systems were created for colonists, while traditional systems were maintained for the indigenous population. As is well documented, that traditional or customary law still dominates social regulation, dispute resolution, and land governance in Africa and other parts of the developing world. In some cases, customary law, including a variety of traditional and hybrid institutional forms of dispute resolution, is formally recognized and incorporated into the legal system, such as in Ghana, South Africa, South Sudan, the Republic of Yemen, and several Pacific Island states. In other cases, such forms continue to provide the primary means of social ordering and dispute resolution in the absence of access to state systems that are perceived as legitimate and effective, such as in Afghanistan, Liberia, and Somalia. Customary legal systems reflect the dominant (yet evolving, not static) values and power structures of the societies in which they are embedded, and as such are often seen to fall short of basic standards of nondiscrimination, rights, and due process. The extent to which they are considered legitimate and effective by local users is an empirical question and a relative one in light of the available alternatives.

A further source of normative pluralism is the less visible but highly influential social norms—generally accepted rules of behavior and social attitudes within a given social grouping. A vast literature documents how social norms derived from communal and identity groups, professional associations, business practices, and the like, govern the vast majority of human behavior.[a] Social norms are a fundamental way of enabling social and economic transactions by coordinating peoples' expectations about how others will act. Social sanctions, such as shame and loss of reputation, or, in some cases, socially sanctioned violence, are a powerful means of inducing cooperation to prevent what is regarded as antisocial and deviant behavior.[b]

Yet another source of normative pluralism is generated by today's globally interconnected world in which a multitude of governmental, multilateral, and private actors establish and diffuse rules about a wide range of transactions and conduct (see chapter 9). Increasingly, local experiences of law are informed by these broader interactions covering topics such as trade, labor, environment, natural resources, financial institutions, public administration, intellectual property, procurement, utility regulation, and human rights. These interactions can take the form of binding international treaties and contracts (hard law) or voluntary standards and guiding principles (soft law). These rules may reinforce, complement, or compete with state law to govern public and private spaces.[c]

Source: WDR 2017 team.

a. Ellickson (1991); Sunstein (1996); Basu (2000); Posner (2000); Dixit (2004).
b. Platteau (2000b).
c. Braithwaite and Drahos (2000); Halliday and Shaffer (2015).

Ultimately, the *rule of law*—the impersonal and systematic application of known rules to government actors and citizens alike—is needed for a country to realize its full social and economic potential. But as Gordon Brown, the former prime minister of the United Kingdom, noted, "In establishing the rule of law, the first five centuries are always the hardest." The ideal of the rule of law emerges from a home-grown (endogenous) process of contestation that shapes societies' adherence to the principles of the rule of law over time—sometimes a very long time. Box O.7 discusses the challenging process of transitioning to the rule of law. Pragmatic policy design that takes into account how these different roles of law can

bolster the effectiveness of development policies can ultimately move countries on a trajectory toward a stronger rule of law.

Enhancing policy effectiveness for security, growth, and equity: Entry points for reform

How can strengthening the role of law to change contestability, incentives, and preferences and beliefs enhance policy effectiveness for security, growth, and equity? Take the case of security. Whether formally or informally, institutions of governance can solve commitment and cooperation problems in ways that create incentives to not use violence. Four

Box O.7 Transitions to the rule of law

Compared with the extensive literature on transitions to democracy, a surprisingly small amount of systematic work has been done on transitions to a modern rule of law. History reveals three separate types of transitions which one can learn from, while other paths might be possible: (1) the shift from a customary, informal, and often highly pluralistic system of law to a unified modern one; (2) how powerful elites come to accept legal constraints on their power; and (3) how countries successfully adapt foreign legal systems to their own purposes.

The shift from a customary or pluralistic system (or both) to a codified modern one is usually motivated, at base, by actors who view a single formal system as better serving their interests, particularly their economic interests in expanded trade and investment. Scale matters: at a certain point, the personal connections that characterize customary systems become inadequate to support transactions between strangers at great remove. However, the transition costs are high, and the customary rules are often preferred by the existing stakeholders. Therefore, political power is critical in bringing about the transition.

Formal law is usually applied first to nonelites ("rule *by* law"); the shift to "rule *of* law" occurs when the elites themselves accept the law's limitations. Some have argued that constitutional constraints become self-reinforcing when power in the system is distributed evenly and elites realize that they have more to gain in the long term through constitutional rules.[a] What this theory does not explain, however, is why these same elites stick to these constraints when the power balance subsequently changes and one group is able to triumph over the others. Similarly, independent courts are always a threat to elite power; why do rulers come to tolerate them when they have the power to manipulate or eliminate them? This finding suggests that constitutionalism needs to be underpinned by a powerful normative framework that makes elites respect the law as such. Subsequent respect for law depends heavily on the degree of independence maintained by legal institutions that persist even after their normative foundations have disappeared.

Finally, as for the importation of foreign legal systems, perhaps the most important variable determining success is the degree to which indigenous elites remain in control of the process and can tailor it to their society's own traditions. Thus Japan experimented with a variety of European systems before settling on the German civil code and Bismarck constitution at the end of the 19th century. Later, in the 20th century, China, the Republic of Korea, and other Asian countries similarly adapted Western legal systems to their own purposes. In other countries and economies, such as Hong Kong SAR, China, India, and Singapore, the colonial power (Great Britain) stayed for a long time and was able to shape the local legal norms in its own image. Even so, India today practices a far higher degree of legal pluralism than does the United Kingdom itself as part of the process of local adaptation. Less successful were countries in Sub-Saharan Africa, where customary systems were undermined by colonial authorities but not replaced by well-institutionalized modern systems.

Much more research is needed on the question of legal transitions. It is clear that a fully modern legal system is *not* a precondition for rapid economic growth; legal systems themselves develop in tandem with modern economies. It may be that the necessary point of transition from a customary to a formal legal system occurs later in this process than many Western observers have thought. But relatively little is known about the historical dynamics of that transition, and thus there is too little by way of theory to guide contemporary developing countries as they seek to implement a rule of law.

Source: Francis Fukuyama for WDR 2017.

a. See North, Wallis, and Weingast (2009).

---

main governance mechanisms matter for improving security outcomes: power sharing, resource redistribution, dispute settlement, and sanctions. Power sharing and resource redistribution are highlighted in the illustrations that follow.

Power sharing and resource redistribution can reduce exclusion and the incentives to engage in violence. Just as exclusion may lead to violence, mechanisms that encourage power sharing—such as legislatures that guarantee the representation of all factions—can reduce the incentives to engage in the use of force by raising the benefits of security. Power-sharing arrangements are especially relevant for societies divided along ethnic and religious identity lines, such as in Bosnia and Herzegovina, Northern Ireland, Kenya, Lebanon, and South Africa, but also in countries in which the conflict is a legacy of opposing ideologies. Power-sharing bargains that lead to peace and security typically take place between elites. Such bargains encourage cooperative behavior by providing elite groups with the incentives to compromise with one another and to inspire inclusion among their followers, and by offering alternative avenues for contesting power.

Mechanisms to redistribute resources can also reduce violence by reordering power and changing incentives. Redistributive arrangements include budget allocation, social transfers, and victim compensation schemes. Some government interventions to reduce urban crime in Latin America follow a common pattern of increasing security by reducing poverty and inequality. Employment in the public sector could also bring about stability by ensuring the loyalty of key constituencies. An example is the dramatic increase in the numbers and salaries of public employees following the uprisings in the Arab world in 2011 (figure O.5). Although this kind of political patronage can solve the first-order problem of violence, it can also lead to corruption and can have ruinous effects on budgetary sustainability and administrative efficiency.

Implementable policies can help reduce capture, enhancing growth. Security is a precondition for prosperity, but it is not enough; economic growth must follow. When it comes to growth, if the possibility of capture looms large, policies that are first-best on the basis of economic efficiency may be less implementable

than second-best ones. Adopting an implementable second-best design could therefore be more effective than choosing the seemingly first-best policy prone to capture. Moreover, when considering alternative policy designs, the possibility of future capture can be reduced by anticipating the possible effects of a policy on the balance of decision-making ability among the actors involved.

The experience of the Russian Federation and eastern European countries in their transition to market economies is illustrative.[26] Compelled by the then-dominant economic argument that the privatization of state-owned enterprises (SOEs) was of first-order importance in enhancing economic efficiency, Russia and many eastern European countries focused on rapid, large-scale privatization of their SOEs. Although this approach may have made sense on purely economic grounds, the way in which the privatization wave was implemented created a new class of oligarchs that resisted the next generation of pro-competition reforms. As a result, many of these economies are still struggling with inefficient, oligopolistic industries. This is consistent with the view that reforms that create an initial concentration of gains may engender strong opposition to further reform from early winners.[27] By contrast, Poland chose to focus first on reforms that made it easy for new firms to enter, and to privatize the existing firms more gradually. This sequencing created a class of young firms

Figure O.5 Recruitments of civil servants increased exponentially in Tunisia and the Arab Republic of Egypt in the aftermath of the Arab Spring uprisings of 2011

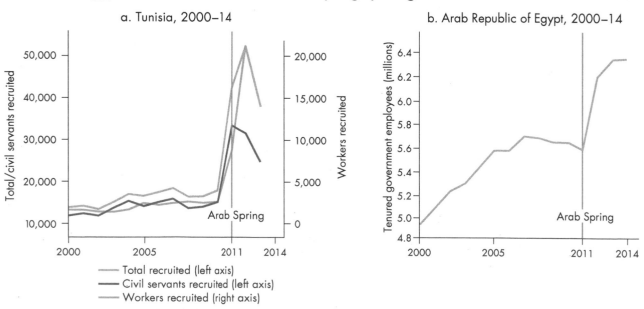

Sources: Tunisia: Brockmeyer, Khatrouch, and Raballand 2015; Arab Republic of Egypt: Bteddini 2016, based on figures from Egypt's Central Agency for Organization and Administration (CAOA).

that were collectively interested in further reforms, while preventing the sudden emergence of an influential group of large firms that could block reforms.[28]

Better design of public agencies can help expand the set of implementable policies. How public officials are selected for service, for example, and the incentive structure they face within their organizations matter, as does accounting for existing norms of behavior. Establishing and maintaining greater accountability in public agencies can also help in balancing influence in the policy arena. Mechanisms that help give less powerful, diffuse interest groups, for example, a bigger say in the policy arena could help balance the influence of more powerful, narrow interest groups. However, participatory mechanisms in regulatory institutions are still relatively uncommon in low- and middle-income countries (figure O.6).

Private interests can at times undermine policy effectiveness, but capture is not an inevitable outcome of close business-state ties. As long as influence and incentives are balanced through robust public agency design and accountability mechanisms, firms and business groups can have a positive influence on policies aimed at economic growth. Contemporary case studies suggest that business associations have helped governments improve various dimensions of the business environment—such as secure property rights, fair enforcement of rules, and the provision of public infrastructure—through lobbying efforts or better monitoring of public officials.

Controlling clientelism can help solve commitment problems related to delivering on redistributive policies.

Mechanisms that control clientelism can enhance equity by making commitment to long-term objectives credible in the political arena. At times, the incentives of elites may be aligned with taxation and public spending reforms in favor of the poor. For example, the first antipoverty programs in 19th-century Great Britain were pushed by the top 1 percent of landed elites. Against the backdrop of the French Revolution, and possible fear of revolts, these programs aimed to keep labor in the countryside and prevent it from migrating to urban areas.[29] At other times, an increase in the participation of disadvantaged groups is needed to help change the incentives of actors who bargain over policies. Increasing the direct representation of disadvantaged individuals in legislative assemblies and other political bodies can improve policy makers' commitments to reforms that improve equity. Direct participation in decision making can also improve cooperation. For example, in Ghana, when businesses are involved in the design of tax policies they are more likely to pay their taxes.[30] Greater transparency and better information can also help to change incentives by monitoring the actions of political elites and service providers. For example, an intervention designed to strengthen local accountability and community-based monitoring in the primary health care sector in Uganda was remarkably successful in improving both health services and outcomes in the participating communities.[31] However, reforms are often complex and involve frequent setbacks.

Over time, policies that effectively improve equity also reduce power asymmetries, making the policy

Figure O.6 Formal avenues for broad-based participation in regulatory decision making are limited in low- and middle-income countries

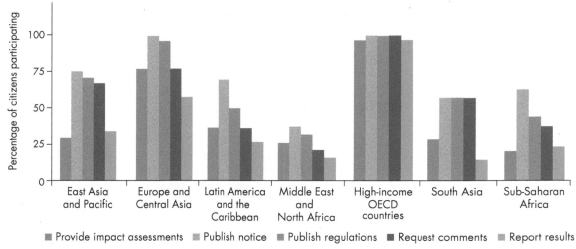

Source: WDR 2017 team, using data from the World Bank's citizen engagement in rulemaking data.

Note: OECD = Organisation for Economic Co-operation and Development.

arena more contestable. After a period of inclusive growth with greater income mobility, the growing middle class in Latin America began demanding better-quality services and demonstrating in the streets for better governance.[32] Conversely, inequitable growth and the concentration of wealth in the hands of a few led to consolidation of power and a perception of unfairness, and thus to weaker incentives for cooperation and coordination by those excluded from the benefits of development. It is thus necessary to understand how existing inequalities can be modified by reforms.

The nature of the policy arena is crucial to gauging whether actors will be able to reach and sustain agreements to enact welfare-enhancing policies. The actions that a proposed reform will trigger from other players in the arena are particularly important. The process of how reforms take place is embedded in the framework of the *World Development Report 2017* (WDR 2017) and is discussed in box O.8 from the perspective

of game theory. The discussion highlights how development reform involves playing "games" at two different levels, and actors in the quest for change often tend to neglect the game that really matters.

Figure O.7 synthesizes the conceptual framework presented in this Report. It illustrates the dynamic interaction between governance and development. At its center is the policy arena, the space where actors bargain and reach agreements about policies and rules. Given a set of rules, the right-hand side of the framework shows how commitment, coordination, and cooperation among actors lead to specific development outcomes (the *outcome game* in box O.8). But actors can also agree to change the rules, which is illustrated in the left-hand side of the framework (the *rules game* in box O.8). Both changes in development outcomes (such as the composition of growth or the concentration of wealth) and changes in rules (both formal and informal) reshape the power asymmetries manifested in the policy arena.

Box O.8 The "rules game": Paying attention to where the action is

The framework described in this Report uses game theory—the branch of social sciences that studies strategic behavior—to understand the dynamics of power, policy, and reform. Although policy makers may not consciously think in terms of game theory, they play strategy games every day, and their actions can be understood using the precision and objectivity of game theoretic models. The framework laid out in this Report aims at understanding how governance affects development over time. For that purpose, the framework involves games played at two levels. The first-level game (the *outcome game*) takes place when, given a certain set of rules and policies, actors react by making decisions about investing, consuming, working, paying taxes, allocating budgets, abiding by the rules, and so on. Those decisions lead to the realization of outcomes (security, growth, equity). The framework suggests that there is, in addition, a second-level game (the *rules game*) in which actors bargain to redefine the policies and rules that shape subsequent reactions by actors in future realizations of the games.[a]

In the abstract, the rules and policies chosen should lead to the socially desired outcomes. Economists refer to the case in which someone can pick the ideal rules for the outcome game as the "mechanism design" approach, and the rules selected are those that a "benevolent dictator" or "social planner" would pick. Although this is a useful

way to specify the ultimate *goal* of development, it is an insufficient guide to understanding the actual *process* of development. Mechanism design suggests that a reform is a once-and-done jump that takes place when someone imposes the "ideal" rules. It ignores the second-level rules game, the diversity of preferences and incentives, and the fact that different actors can have very different influences in the *rules game*. Moreover, in the process of reform and development, the *rules game is where the action is*.

Indeed, the *rules game* is where power asymmetries are manifested, whereby some actors have more direct influence (elites) and others have only indirect influence such as through voting (citizens). It has long been recognized that power is an important determinant of how a society functions and how the gains of economic activity are shared within and across nations. With game theory, one is able to formalize some of these difficult concepts and, in particular, the idea that, in the end, power depends on the circumstances, beliefs, and mores of ordinary people.

A key lesson that emerges from this approach is that rules that let players commit, coordinate, and cooperate tend to enhance efficiency in the outcome game. Ultimately, commitment devices allow actors to transform the game so that their incentives are aligned. To achieve coordination, policies need to create common knowledge that everyone will take the desirable action. Sometimes, this requires

(Box continues next page)

providing incentives for some actors to take the desirable action first so others will follow. To induce cooperation, policies need to put forth a credible mechanism of reward or penalty conditioned on players' actions to prompt other actions yielding the jointly preferred outcome.

Over time, repeated play of the rules game can lead to the establishment of a government that is better able to enforce the rules impersonally—for example, by employing legislators, judges, and police officers who can administer a formal legal order, in particular by administering a system of contract law. Contract law is a system of formal rules that

improves the efficiency of the outcome game by letting players commit to specific future actions.[b] When actors agree to a contract voluntarily, the result of a noncooperative interaction can lead to better outcomes for all. This analysis is also closely related to the concept of a "social contract" that goes back to ancient Greek thinkers. Social contracts that induce actors to abide by the rules voluntarily tend to be more efficient and sustainable. Underlying all stable societies is some form of social contract, which enables individuals to anticipate the behavior of others and react accordingly.

Source: WDR 2017 team.

a. In the WDR 2017 framework depicted in figure O.7, the right-hand side of the figure refers to the outcome game and the left-hand side to the rules game.
b. In a small social group, an informal system of rules can also encourage commitment. For example, if actor 1 does not follow through on an agreement with actor 2, actor 2 can punish actor 1 by gossiping about how actor 1 cheated.

Drivers of change: Elite bargains, citizen engagement, and international influence

Changes in contestability, incentives, and preferences and beliefs are the key levers for correcting power asymmetries in the policy arena, leading more effectively to commitment, coordination, and cooperation. But how can these changes be brought about? This Report identifies three encouraging drivers for bringing about significant changes conducive to development: elite bargains (which take the distribution of power in the policy arena as a given); citizen engagement (which tries to change the distribution of power in the policy arena); and international interventions (which indirectly affect the distribution of power in the policy arena)—see box O.9.

All countries, regardless of their level of economic and institutional development, are subject to elite bargains. Change is unlikely to occur unless powerful actors—elites—in the country agree to that change. When influential actors resist change, suboptimal policies and governance institutions that are detrimental to development tend to persist. Under certain circumstances, however, elites may voluntarily agree to limit their influence in their own self-interest. Citizens can also organize to bring about change, playing an important role in applying pressure to influence the

Figure O.7 WDR 2017 framework: Governance, law, and development

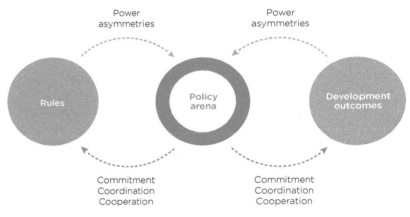

Source: WDR 2017 team.

Note: Rules refers to formal and informal rules (norms). *Development outcomes*, in the context of this Report, refers to security, growth, and equity. The actors in the *policy arena* can be grouped into elites, citizens, and international actors.

outcome of favorable bargains in the policy bargaining process. Moreover, governance does not occur solely within the boundaries of nation-states. Although international actors cannot engineer development from the outside, these transnational actors play an important role in influencing the domestic bargaining dynamics by strengthening (or weakening) local coalitions for reform.

Change occurs over time as coalitions are formed among different actors, but this is often a long and

Box O.9 Elites and citizens: Who is who in the policy arena?

Participants in the policy arena can be grouped into elites and citizens, according to their relative degree of influence in the policy-making process. What distinguishes elites from citizens is elites' ability to *directly* influence the design and implementation of a certain policy. Elites can vary from one policy to another. For example, a group that is an elite in the area of health care may not be an elite in the area of crime control. The source of elites' ability to influence policy comes not only from formal rules such as delegated authority (de jure power), but also from other means such as control over resources (de facto power). Thus even if the government changes, those who are able to influence decisions may stay the same; they keep their seat at the table. A few years ago, an entertainment magazine in a Latin American country captured this dynamic in an interview with an unlikely political observer, the chef of the presidential residence. After a tight election, the new president and his family had just moved into the residence. The interviewer asked the chef whether it was difficult for him to adjust the menu to the new presidential family's tastes. "It is really not that problematic," he reflected, "because

even though the presidents change, the guests are always the same."

Certainly, the dichotomy between elites and citizens is imperfect because it does not account for different degrees of relative power among individuals within those groups (elites or citizens), nor does it capture how their relative power differs from one policy to another. As Stephen Jay Gould notes in his classic text *Time's Arrow, Time's Cycle: Myth and Metaphor in the Discovery of Geological Time*, "Dichotomies are useful or misleading, not true or false. They are simplifying models for organizing thought, not ways of the world."[a] The reality is much more complex and nuanced.

This Report views individuals as being on a continuum with respect to their position of power in the policy arena, and thus its definition of elites and citizens is a positive (rather than a normative) one. Elites are not necessarily bad or self-interested, and citizens are not necessarily good and public-spirited. Both groups exercise their influence as people do in other spheres of life. Understanding their motivations is what matters to anticipating their conduct.

Source: WDR 2017 team.

a. Gould (1987, 8–9).

self-determining "endogenous" process. For example, success at achieving security in Somaliland arose from the collective action of a wide range of tribal and clan leaders. Sharing power among these actors helped reduce the incentives for violence by raising the benefits of security. In Nigeria, Muhammadu Buhari won the 2015 election by creating a broad coalition through a campaign platform focused on tackling corruption, potentially indicating an enhanced ability to overcome corrupt vested interests that benefit from oil rents. And in India, the Right to Information and Right to Education Acts, pushed through by grassroots coalition movements over many years, have helped poor citizens demand better services and education for their children, improving living conditions within slums.

Elites may adopt rules that constrain their own power

In December 1976, a year after the death of Gen. Francisco Franco, who had been in power since the late 1930s, a referendum was held in Spain to introduce a political reform that would allow previously banned

political parties to participate openly in Spain's political life. To the surprise of many, the Cortes Generales—Spain's parliament, which was led by members appointed by Franco—allowed this referendum, even though it would surely constrain their power and likely imply the end of the existing regime. Analysts have argued that members of the Cortes accepted the referendum because it was within the existing legal setting, which they had to protect. Gen. Pita Da Veiga, a conservative, minister of the navy, and personal friend of Franco, publicly declared, "My peace of conscience is rooted in the fact that the democratic reform is being made within the *Franquista* legality."[33] However, the Franquista legality he was praising was coming to an end precisely because of that reform, which received overwhelming public support: 97.4 percent of Spaniards voted in favor, with a turnout of 77 percent of registered voters.

Just as in the Spanish transition, elites frequently choose to constrain their own power. Changes to the "rules of the game" often reflect bargaining outcomes that result from elites acting in their own interests (box O.10). While seemingly counterintuitive, reforms

Box O.10 Who are elites, and what do they do? Results from a survey of elites in 12 countries

All social science disciplines and development practitioners recognize the importance of elite actors in determining development outcomes—from Aristotle's "oligarchy," to early 20th-century "elite theorists,"[a] to recent ambitious theories of economic and institutional coevolution.[b] The international community is increasingly looking at the consequences of different "political settlements," which can be understood as elite bargaining equilibria that emerge at critical junctures in a country's development.[c] Yet, the set of conceptual research tools available to scholars of elite bargaining and to development practitioners remains limited, as does agreement on exactly who are elites.

To help fill this gap, as part of the *World Development Report 2017*, the World Bank, in collaboration with the V-Dem Institute, has conducted expert surveys to generate cross-national indicators that enable comparison of who holds bargaining power and how they wield this influence. The surveys cover more than 100 years of data in 12 countries across six regions. The data help identify how the distribution of elites maps onto the national structure of bargaining power and the formulation and implementation of laws governing the exercise of power.

The survey reveals that the identity of the influential actors within a ruling elite coalition that decides policy at the national level differs greatly over space, time, and issue area. For example, although national chief executives are part of the elite ruling coalition in all 12 countries surveyed as of 2015, the other actors vary greatly in both number and representativeness (figure BO.10.1, panel a). With the exception of the Russian Federation, Rwanda, and Turkey, where the national chief executive monopolizes decision making, the ruling coalition in the other countries surveyed is quite varied. For example, in Bolivia the ruling coalition consists of legislators, party elites, local governments, labor unions, and civil society organizations.

Ruling elites also differ within countries over time. In the Republic of Korea, during the Park regime (1963–79), the bargaining strength of military actors, bureaucratic actors, and economic actors was relatively high (figure BO.10.1, panel b). The transition to democracy after 1987 resulted in greater strength for new actors, particularly political parties, legislators, and the judiciary, but economic and bureaucratic actors remained highly empowered. By contrast, Brazil has experienced much more volatility in empowered elites, particularly before the 1990s (figure BO.10.1, panel c).

Figure BO.10.1 Elite actors within national ruling coalitions vary greatly across countries and over time

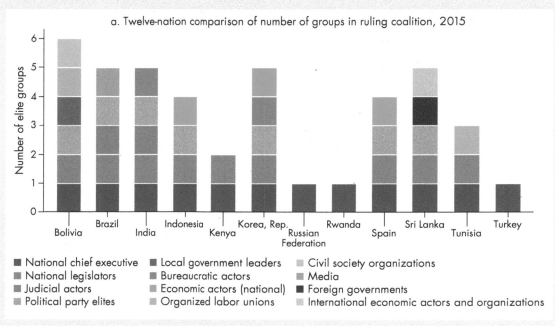

a. Twelve-nation comparison of number of groups in ruling coalition, 2015

- National chief executive
- National legislators
- Judicial actors
- Political party elites
- Local government leaders
- Bureaucratic actors
- Economic actors (national)
- Organized labor unions
- Civil society organizations
- Media
- Foreign governments
- International economic actors and organizations

(Box continues next page)

Box O.10 Who are elites, and what do they do? Results from a survey of elites in 12 countries *(continued)*

Figure BO.10.1 Elite actors within national ruling coalitions vary greatly across countries and over time *(continued)*

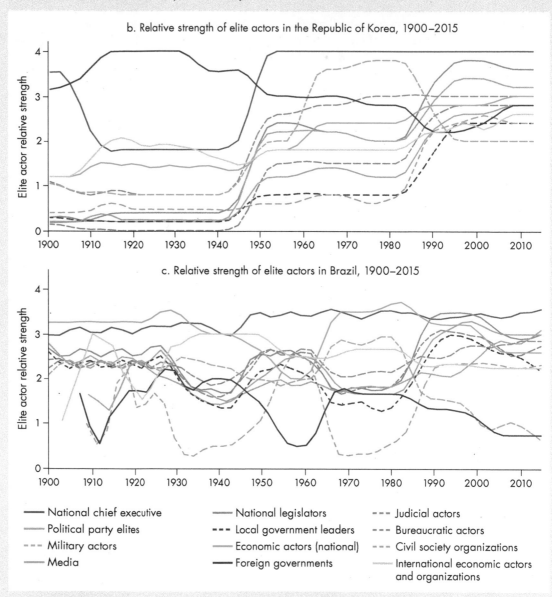

b. Relative strength of elite actors in the Republic of Korea, 1900–2015

c. Relative strength of elite actors in Brazil, 1900–2015

Legend:
- National chief executive
- Political party elites
- Military actors
- Media
- National legislators
- Local government leaders
- Economic actors (national)
- Foreign governments
- Judicial actors
- Bureaucratic actors
- Civil society organizations
- International economic actors and organizations

Source: WDR 2017 team.

Note: In this figure, relative strength is measured on a 0–4 scale, ranging from 0 (no power to influence decision making) to 4 (group has a lot of power to influence decision making on many issues). Panel a shows the number of elite groups that have relative strength greater than 3. For more information on specific variables and survey methodology, see World Bank and V-Dem (2016) and Coppedge and others (2015).

Source: WDR 2017 team.

a. See Michels ([1911] 1966); Pareto ([1927] 1971); and Mosca (1939).
b. See North, Wallis, and Weingast (2009) and Acemoglu and Robinson (2012).
c. Di John and Putzel (2009); Khan (2010); Parks and Cole (2010).

that limit the arbitrary exercise of power today may be necessary for elites to maintain or enhance their power or to provide insurance against a loss of power tomorrow. Formal institutions—moving from deals to rules—can enhance the credibility of commitments, overcome coordination challenges among elite actors, and strengthen the stability of elite bargains. In cases of long-term successful transformation, elite actors have adapted to changing circumstances by generating more capable, contestable, and accountable institutions, and these institutions themselves have helped enable further development.

To maintain their own power and influence, coalitions of decision makers may have incentives to broaden the policy arena, including adding new actors to formal decision-making bodies and increasing accountability to other elites (*horizontal accountability*). Despite a preference for keeping coalitions small, elites may choose to broaden them to improve stability when the potential for conflict rises. Bringing new actors into credible institutions for contestation may be less costly than repressing them, and expanding the formal accountability space may help provide internal commitments that facilitate agreement.

Institutionalizing accountability to citizens (*vertical accountability*)—for example, through the introduction of elections or electoral reforms—may also be a rational elite strategy to maintain privilege, particularly in the face of rising demands from the opposing elite. When splits develop among elite actors, the introduction of vertical accountability mechanisms can enhance the bargaining power of one faction. Moreover, when bottom-up citizen movements threaten elite interests, elites may choose to introduce preemptive vertical accountability mechanisms to respond to societal demands before such pressure reaches a tipping point. In Europe in the 19th century, the extension of suffrage was heralded by the threat of revolution and social upheaval in the form of revolutionary activity in neighboring countries[34] and strikes in the home country.[35]

Although elites often choose rules to maintain their position of power, sometimes—when acknowledging threats to their continued dominance—they may adopt rules to constrain their own influence as a type of political insurance. The hope is that those rules will bind not only them but also their successors. The adoption of cohesive and constraining institutions increases with the likelihood that the incumbent government will be replaced. This is an institutional variation on American philosopher John Rawls's "veil of ignorance": design institutions without knowing whether you will be subject to or master of them in the subsequent period.[36] Fiscal transparency, for example, ties not only the hands of current elites but also those of successors. This is consistent with the actions of certain states in Mexico: although access to information and transparency laws was strengthened at the federal level after the political change in 2000, and more recently in 2016, such laws were more likely to be passed at the state level when opposition parties were stronger and when there was greater executive office turnover.[37]

Leaders can also spur elite-driven change by solving coordination challenges or by transforming the preferences and beliefs of followers. *Transactional leaders* use an array of bargaining tactics and strategies to promote coordination among elite actors and reach positive-sum outcomes (win-win solutions). These leaders change the incentives of other elites by taking into consideration who wins and who loses over time. By overcoming information and coordination challenges through political strategy, they can help find areas of agreement among conflicting parties without necessarily shifting norms or preferences. In the 1960s, U.S. president Lyndon Johnson's deals, trades, threats, and ego stroking—political strategy—helped the U.S. Congress overcome a natural aversion to risk and pass civil rights legislation, a clear example of transactional leadership. *Transformational leaders* can, in addition, actually change elite preferences or gain following by shaping beliefs and preferences. They are entrepreneurial in coordinating norms and can effect large changes in society by changing the environment in which politics plays out, often by reducing the polarization of elites. In the 1990s Nelson Mandela provided a vision for South Africa based on charisma and moral persuasion, using powerful symbols to motivate and inspire his fellow citizens during the transition away from the country's apartheid policies.

Agency and collective action: Citizens influence change by voting, organizing, and deliberating

Individual citizens may not have the power to influence the policy arena to generate more equitable development on their own. However, all citizens have access to multiple mechanisms of engagement that can help them overcome collective action problems— to coordinate and cooperate—by changing contestability, incentives, and preferences and beliefs. Modes of citizen engagement can include elections, political organization, social movements, and direct participation and deliberation. Because all of these expressions of collective action are imperfect, they complement, rather than substitute for, one another.

Although elites often choose rules to maintain their position of power, sometimes—when acknowledging threats to their continued dominance—they may adopt rules to constrain their own influence as a type of political insurance.

Elections are one of the most well-established mechanisms available to citizens to strengthen accountability and responsiveness to their demands. When effective, they can help improve the level and quality of public goods and services provided by the state by selecting and sanctioning leaders based on their performance in providing these goods.[38] This effect can be particularly strong at the local level, where voters might be better able to coordinate and shape the incentives of local politicians to deliver—including by curbing corrupt behavior. For example, evidence from Kenya suggests that multiparty elections successfully constrained the ability of leaders to divert public resources for partisan goals.[39] However, elections alone are an insufficient mechanism to produce responsive and accountable governments. Although they have become the most common mechanism to elect authorities around the world, elections are increasingly perceived as unfair (figure O.8), and they are a limited instrument of control.

Political organization can serve as a complementary mechanism to represent and articulate citizens' collective interests, aggregate their preferences, and channel their demands in the policy-making process. For example, through parties, political organization can help solve citizens' coordination problems and integrate different groups into the political process, encouraging a culture of compromise. According to the evidence, *programmatic parties*—those organized around a well-defined agenda of policy priorities—are associated with a higher likelihood of adopting and successfully implementing public sector reforms.[40] However, ordinary citizens and marginalized groups sometimes find political parties unwilling to represent and articulate their demands, acting instead as "gatekeepers" to protect vested interests and existing power structures. This may help explain the disenchantment of citizens with political parties, which rank globally as the least trusted political institution.

Social organization can also help solve collective action problems by mobilizing citizens around specific issues. This mobilization can bring new demands and interests into the bargaining space, reshaping the preferences of actors and expanding the boundaries of the policy arena around previously neglected issues. Box O.11 explains how pressure from social organization by international and domestic women's groups contributed to the achievement of female suffrage in Switzerland, which led in turn to other important policy changes for gender equality. Actors in civil society and the media can play a key role in fostering policies that strengthen transparency and more widely disseminate information. Increasing the availability of reliable information—such as generating evidence on the performance of public officials—and increasing the accessibility of that information—such as strengthening the independence of media outlets or aligning the targeting and timing of information with the political process—can be fundamental first steps toward promoting greater accountability and government responsiveness.[41] However, global trends reveal that after its continual expansion over the past decades, civic space has shrunk in the past few years (figure O.9). Many governments are changing the institutional environment in which citizens engage, establishing legal barriers to restrict the functioning of media and civic society organizations and reducing their autonomy from the state.

Although social organization may succeed in giving voice to powerless groups and putting pressure on public authorities, trade-offs can be associated with the proliferation of competing interests in the policy arena. Public institutions may be quickly overloaded with multiple pressures, undermining the coherence and effectiveness of public policies. Moreover, not all social organization is necessarily motivated by a vision of a more equal and just society. In some cases, social organization can be used by narrow interest groups for exclusionary or violent purposes.

Public deliberation—spaces and processes that allow group-based discussion and weighing of alternative preferences—can also help level the playing

Figure O.8 Electoral democracies are spreading, but the integrity of elections is declining

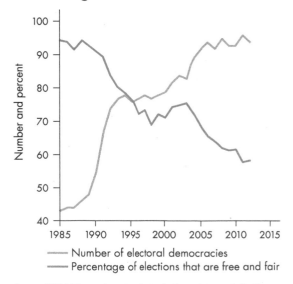

Sources: WDR 2017 team, based on Center for Systemic Peace, Polity IV (database), various years (for number of electoral democracies), and Bishop and Hoeffler 2014 (for free and fair elections).

Box O.11 Direct democracy delayed women's voting rights in Switzerland

Most European countries enfranchised women during the first decades of the 20th century. However, it was not until 1971 that Swiss women were first allowed to vote in federal elections, 65 years after the first country in Europe—Finland—did so. And yet Switzerland has had a tradition of direct democracy for centuries. What explains the late enfranchisement of Swiss women?

To change the constitution, the political system required a national referendum in which only men were allowed to vote. Several petitions and motions initiated by women's groups in the first half of the 1900s were unsuccessful in achieving women's suffrage. Who participated in the process to change the rules was thus an important determinant of which rules persisted. But so were the existing social norms and the lack of incentives for change. Reflecting those deeply held norms, Switzerland also lagged behind most Western countries in removing other legal gender inequalities, notably those preserving the legal authority of the husband.

Under heightened international pressure, Switzerland was close to a breakthrough in guaranteeing women's rights in 1957, when, for the first time, the Swiss Federal Council called for a national referendum on women's suffrage. "If Switzerland had not been a direct democracy, women's right to vote would have taken effect immediately," one

study notes.[a] The mandatory national referendum took place in 1959 when 69 percent of the entirely male electorate voted against the constitutional amendment. Still, women gained the right to vote on cantonal affairs in three Swiss cantons (Geneva, Vaud, and Neuchâtel) in 1959–60. It was not until 1971 that the majority of Swiss men voted in favor of women's suffrage. Reform coalitions among many actors played a significant role in bringing about this change, including international influence and domestic action by women's groups such as the Swiss Association for Women's Suffrage.

The change in female suffrage in Switzerland made it possible for new actors—women, in this case—to participate in the process of policy design and implementation, changing the incentives of politicians to be responsive to their preferences and interests. It also reflected a change in societies' norms with respect to women's rights. This led to further important policy changes in the 1980s. An amendment to the constitution to guarantee equal rights of all Swiss men and women was approved in a referendum in 1981. A few years later, in 1985, women were granted equal rights in marriage to men, eliminating legal requirements such as wives' need to have their husbands' permission to work outside the home, or to initiate legal proceedings, or to open a bank account.[b]

Sources: Stämpfli 1994; World Bank, Women, Business, and the Law (database), 2015.

a. Stämpfli (1994, 696).
b. World Bank (2016a).

---

field in the policy arena. Citizens' participation in local governance can be instrumental in improving the quality of deliberation and the legitimacy of decisions by clarifying the needs and demands of local constituencies. However, participatory approaches to development sometimes fail to consider the possibility of *civil society failures* in which, in weakly institutionalized environments, the poor are less likely to participate, and participatory mechanisms can be captured by local elites.[42] Such failures are not necessarily ameliorated by the availability of new technologies. As discussed in WDR 2016 on the digital divide,[43] information and communication technologies might actually reinforce socioeconomic inequalities in citizens' engagement. In Brazil, for example, the use of internet voting on municipal budget proposals revealed stark demographic differences between online and offline

voters; online voters were more likely to be male, university-educated, and wealthier.[44]

Ultimately, all expressions of citizens' collective action, including voting, political parties, social movements, civic associations, and other less conventional spaces for policy deliberation, are imperfect. Therefore, citizens, to strengthen their influence in the policy arena, need to engage through multiple mechanisms designed to solve collective action problems. This strategic combination can maximize the chances to effectively bring about changes in contestability, incentives, and preferences and beliefs.

Change with outside support: International actors enter the domestic policy arena

The dynamics of governance do not occur solely within the boundaries of nation-states. Countries

Figure O.9 After decades of progress, civic space is shrinking globally

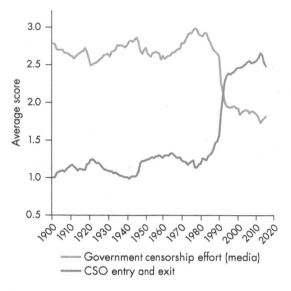

Source: WDR 2017 team, using data from V-Dem (database), 2016.

Note: The average is based on a sample of 78 countries for which there is consistent data for all years presented. The "CSO entry and exit" variable is measured on a 0–4 scale, ranging from 0 (more constrained) to 4 (less constrained). The "government censorship effort (media)" variable is reversed and measured on a 0–4 scale, ranging from 0 (less censorship) to 4 (more censorship). More information on specific variables and survey methodology can be found in World Bank and V-Dem (2016) and Coppedge and others (2015). CSO = civil society organization.

today face an interconnected, globalized world characterized by a high velocity and magnitude of flows of capital, trade, ideas, technology, and people. The world nowadays is very different from the one in which today's developed countries emerged: in those days, cross-border flows were low; the countries received no aid; and they were not subject to a proliferation of transnational treaties, norms, and regulatory mechanisms. For developing countries, the era of globalization and "global governance" presents both opportunities and challenges.

As the flows across borders expand, so too do the instruments and mechanisms that are used to manage these flows. To influence domestic policies and governance, international actors can introduce transnational rules, standards, and regulations (hereafter referred to as *transnational rules*). These rules can help induce credible commitment to domestic reform through trade and regional integration incentives. They also can help achieve international cooperation on global goods by changing incentives—such as preventing *races to the bottom* when countries compete to attract investment and gain access to markets, leading to reductions in corporate tax or environmental and

labor standards. And they can serve as focal points for domestic actors to shift preferences and improve coordination by changing ideas and diffusing norms.

International agreements on economic integration can provide credible commitments that domestic actors will follow through on economic reforms. The success of the European Union integration process demonstrates the power of these types of inducements. Prospective member countries must change domestic rules to abide by the 80,000 pages of regulations in the EU's acquis communautaire. For the countries that decided to undergo these changes, the potential economic benefits of joining the EU outweighed any loss of domestic autonomy in specific areas, and the benefits of accession were used by elites to overcome domestic resistance to the required reforms. Moreover, for member countries, accession helped change elite incentives by changing the relative power of domestic actors because some parties benefited much more than others. Meanwhile, EU membership contributed to the institutional consolidation of former dictatorships in the European periphery, such as Greece, Portugal, and Spain in the 1980s. It also played a role in the transition in central and eastern Europe after the elimination of the communist regimes in the 1990s and 2000s.

Since the end of World War II, official development assistance (ODA) or "foreign aid" has been one of the most prominent policy tools used by advanced economies to induce security, growth, and equity outcomes in developing countries.[45] Although the literature on aid effectiveness is voluminous, it tends to be inconclusive. Ultimately, the literature suggests that aid is neither inherently good nor inherently bad for development; what matters is how aid interacts with the prevailing power relations and affects governance.

In some cases, donor engagement supports the emergence of more accountable and equitable governing arrangements that become embedded in the domestic context. For example, evidence from a community-driven reconstruction program in Liberia suggests that introducing new institutions at the local level can have an effect on social cooperation that will persist beyond completion of the program.[46] In other cases, aid can undermine the relationship between the state and its citizens by making the state less responsive to their demands. For example, the more that states rely on revenues from the international community, the fewer incentives they have to build the public institutions needed to mobilize domestic revenues through taxation. And the less

Figure O.10 **Aid is a large share of GDP and government revenue in many developing countries**

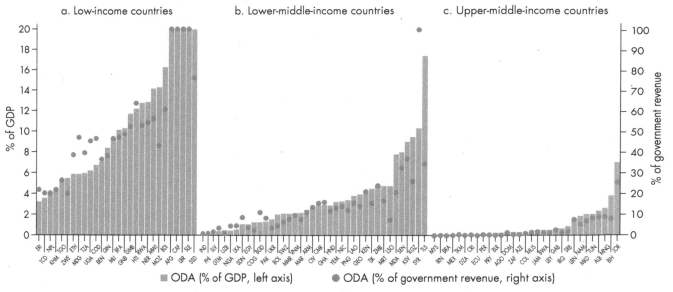

Sources: WDR 2017 team. Official development assistance (ODA) data: Organisation for Economic Co-operation and Development; government revenue data: IMF, *World Economic Outlook*, various years.

Note: The graphs show ODA from all donors to all recipients in low- and middle-income countries with a population of at least 1 million. Figures for ODA (percent of GDP) are capped at 20 percent of GDP for the sake of visualization. The underlying uncapped data are Afghanistan, 24.1 percent; Central African Republic, 35.4 percent; Liberia, 37.0 percent; and Malawi, 21.8 percent. Figures for ODA (percent of government revenue) are capped at 100 percent for the sake of visualization. The underlying uncapped data are Afghanistan, 105.2 percent; Central African Republic, 260.6 percent; Liberia, 126.0 percent; and Sierra Leone, 143.2 percent.

that states rely on their domestic tax base, the more state-citizen accountability erodes.[47]

Currently, aid represents more than 10 percent of GDP for half of all low-income countries and over 30 percent of total revenues for 26 countries (figure O.10). The empirical evidence linking aid flows to decreased taxation is mixed (box O.12). Aid has thus been likened to a natural resource curse: a windfall of unearned income that may enable inefficient government spending, unconstrained by the kind of state-citizen social contract that engages citizens in policy discussions and makes the policy arena more contestable.[48]

For a long time, the need for intervention was justified on the basis of classic market failures in which governments intervene to produce socially desirable outcomes that cannot be achieved by relying solely on markets. Later, the literature revealed the existence of government failures in which government interventions also failed because of lack of capacity, informational asymmetries, or distorted incentives.[49] One of the issues that this Report analyzes is the difficulties faced by the international community when trying to influence change in the presence of government failures. Indeed, many times well-intentioned interventions become ineffective because they reinforce

an equilibrium that sustains the outcome the intervention attempted to change. These situations can arise from interventions that do not take into account the existing power balance.

Such development assistance challenges are *not* unavoidable or intractable. Like market failures and government failures, they can be addressed. Development assistance can be more effective when donor engagement supports the emergence of more accountable and equitable governing arrangements that become embedded in the domestic context—for example, by making relevant information available to citizens to strengthen their capacity to hold political leaders accountable.[50] When and how these positive effects emerge, however, is difficult to predict in advance because of the web of intersecting and evolving factors that determine how donor initiatives engage with local political dynamics.

The development community has recently been engaging in efforts to "think politically" about aid. However, many of the operational imperatives that arise from greater attention to development assistance challenges—such as the need to increase flexibility of implementation, tolerate greater risk and ambiguity, devolve power from aid providers to aid partners, and avoid simplistic linear schemes for

Box O.12 Domestic resource mobilization, foreign aid, and accountability

There is a growing consensus that increasing domestic resource mobilization can enhance accountability, particularly if such efforts are explicitly linked to the provision of public goods. If ruling elites need to depend on broad-based taxation, they are more likely to include citizens and other elites in policy bargains. But does foreign aid undermine domestic resource mobilization—and thus accountability to citizens?

Studies testing that hypothesis initially showed a negative correlation between the two.[a] More recently, these studies have been refuted by the adoption of different data sets[b] or different econometric techniques.[c] Although the behavioral effect of aid flows undermining accountability has been tested and isolated in experimental settings,[d] in reality the relationship is more complex and seems to depend on three factors: the type of aid (for example, whether grant or debt, budget support, or project-specific); the contemporaneous effects of conditional policies associated with the aid; and, more important, the governance setting specific to each country. Moreover, even if aid were to reduce incentives to mobilize domestic resources, the removal of aid may result in societally suboptimal taxation policies to raise revenues, leaving the poor worse off.

The effects of domestic resource mobilization on accountability depend on how domestic funds are mobilized. Many available taxes may not have the capacity to enhance accountability, such as resource taxes, or may have strong distortionary effects, such as trade taxes. International corporate tax competition and trade liberalization have also diminished states' capacity for domestic resource mobilization (a race to the bottom). In settings with low savings rates or the potential for capital flight

and tax evasion, consumption taxes are the most likely to be effective, but also the most likely to be regressive. Frequently in these cases, domestic resources are mobilized in ways that may increase poverty—for example, by increasing consumption taxes—without enacting specific offsetting mechanisms of compensation for the poor. Indeed, based on household survey data for 2010, fiscal policy itself increased the US$2.50 per day poverty headcount ratio in 9 out of 25 countries analyzed.[e] In other words, more poor people were made poorer through the taxing and spending activities of governments than benefited from those activities.

Notwithstanding the importance of mobilizing domestic resources to expand responsiveness and accountability to citizens, many countries may be too poor to have the capacity to collect enough revenues to address important development goals; they may harm the poor in the process of collecting domestic resources; or they may be politically unable to pass reforms to increase revenues. In countries in which poverty rates are higher than 65 percent (mainly in Sub-Saharan Africa), for example, there is no feasible redistribution scheme that allows eradicating poverty only by transferring resources domestically from the rich to the poor.[f] Moreover, in many developing countries poor individuals are often impoverished by the fiscal system when both government taxation and spending are taken into account.[g] Finally, political power might be concentrated in the hands of a few rich individuals whose interests collide with those of the poor. In such instances, where there is need to mobilize a larger set of individuals to counterweigh the political influence in the hands of the few, domestic resource mobilization might be very difficult to achieve.[h]

Source: WDR 2017 team.

a. Most notably, Gupta and others (2004).
b. Morrissey and Torrance (2015).
c. For example, Clist and Morrissey (2011) invalidate the contemporaneous negative correlation found in Gupta and others (2004) by introducing a lagged effect of aid and taxation. They conclude that the relationship is negligible.
d. Paler (2013); Martin (2014).
e. Lustig (2016).
f. Ravallion (2010); Ceriani, Bolch, and López-Calva (2016).
g. Lustig (2016).
h. Ceriani, Bolch, and López-Calva (2016).

measuring results—run up against long-established bureaucratic structures, practices, and habits. The way forward may require a more adaptive or agile approach in which strategies are tried out locally and then adjusted based on early evidence. Moving

beyond technocratic approaches and learning how to take into account the openings and constraints presented by shifting politics are key to the ability of foreign aid to induce and sustain governance reforms that promote development.

Rethinking governance for development

More than 70 years after the Bretton Woods Conference that launched the World Bank and the International Monetary Fund, the international community continues to recognize that promoting sustained development requires taking seriously the underlying determinants related to governance. Future progress will require a new framework and new analytical tools to harness the growing evidence on what has worked and what has not.

Policies do not occur in a vacuum. Rather, they take place in complex political and social settings in which individuals and groups with unequal bargaining power interact within changing rules as they pursue conflicting interests. This Report shows that taking into account how the distribution of power in the policy arena enables or constrains institutions to effectively promote commitment, coordination, and cooperation is critical to ensuring progress toward achieving security, growth, and equity.

Past *World Development Reports* have shed light on how to solve some of the most challenging problems in key areas of development, such as jobs, gender equality, and risk management. This WDR is part of a trilogy of recent reports, alongside *Mind, Society, and Behavior* (2015) and *Digital Dividends* (2016), that examine how policy makers can make fuller use of behavioral, technological, and institutional instruments to improve state effectiveness for development. This Report starts by acknowledging that policies such as those to strengthen labor markets, overcome gender barriers, or prepare countries against shocks are often difficult to introduce and implement because certain groups in society who gain from the status quo may be powerful enough to resist the reforms needed to break the political equilibrium. Successful reforms thus are not just about "best practice." They require adopting and adjusting institutional forms in ways that solve the specific commitment and collective action problems that stand in the way of pursuing further development.

Three guiding principles

The WDR 2017 proposes three simple principles to guide those thinking about reform. First, it is important to think not only about what form institutions should have, but also about the functions that institutions must perform—that is, think not only about the form of institutions but also about their *functions*. Second, it is important to think that, although capacity building matters, how to use capacity and where to invest in capacity depend on the relative bargaining powers of actors—that is, think not only about capacity building but also about *power asymmetries*. Third, it is important to think that in order to achieve the rule of law, countries must first strengthen the different roles of law to enhance contestability, change incentives, and reshape preferences—that is, think not only about the rule of law but also about the *role of law* (table O.2).

When one is facing a specific policy challenge, what do these principles mean in practical terms? This Report identifies four key insights. Box O.13 offers a simple diagnostic road map for bringing these insights more concretely into development programming in an effort to enhance effectiveness.

The first challenge is to identify the underlying functional problem. Diagnostic approaches should home in on the specific commitment, coordination, and cooperation problems that stand in the way of achieving socially desirable outcomes, and on the ways that power asymmetries in the policy arena constrain these functions. In addition to constraints that are typically considered—such as physical and administrative capacity—policies may still be ineffective if groups with enough bargaining power have no incentives to pursue adoption or implementation. Taking into account power asymmetries means focusing on implementable (if not necessarily ideal) policies that can generate incremental progress toward inclusive growth and equitable development.

Table O.2 Three principles for rethinking governance for development

Traditional approach	Principles for rethinking governance for development
Invest in designing the right **form** of institutions.	Think not only about the form of institutions, but also about their **functions**.
Build the **capacity** of institutions to implement policies.	Think not only about capacity building, but also about **power asymmetries**.
Focus on strengthening the **rule of law** to ensure that those policies and rules are applied impersonally.	Think not only about the rule of law, but also about the **role of law**.

Source: WDR 2017 team.

Box O.13 What does the WDR 2017 framework mean for action? The policy effectiveness cycle

This Report argues that policy effectiveness cannot be understood only from a technical perspective; it is also necessary to consider the process through which actors bargain about the design and implementation of policies within a specific institutional setting. The consistency and continuity of policies over time (commitment), the alignment of beliefs and preferences (coordination), as well as the voluntary compliance and absence of free-riding (cooperation) are key institutional functions that influence how effective policies will be. But what does that mean for specific policy actions?

Figure BO.13.1 presents a way to think about specific policies in a way that includes the elements that can increase the likelihood of effectiveness. This "policy effectiveness cycle" begins by clearly defining the objective to be achieved and then following a series of well-specified steps:

Step 1. Diagnose. Identify the underlying functional problem (commitment, coordination, cooperation).

Step 2. Assess. Identify the nature of power asymmetries in the policy arena (exclusion, capture, clientelism).

Step 3. Target. Identify the relevant entry point(s) for reform (contestability, incentives, preferences and beliefs).

Step 4. Design. Identify the best mechanism for intervention (R1, R2, R3).

Step 5. Implement. Identify key stakeholders needed to build a coalition for implementation (elites, citizens, international actors).

Step 6. Evaluate and adapt.

Figure BO.13.1 The policy effectiveness cycle

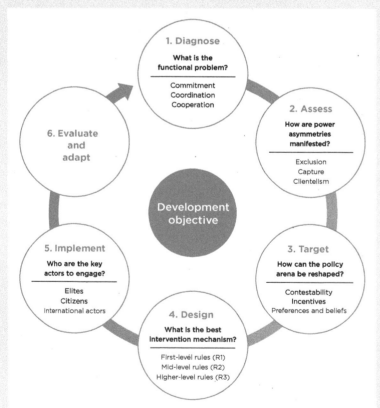

Source: WDR 2017 team.

Source: WDR 2017 team.

The second challenge is to identity the different levers of change that can help reshape the policy arena to expand the set of policies that can be implemented. Instead of taking the existing policy-making environment as a given, reformers would analyze how to lift the existing constraints to expand the space of what is politically feasible. Different levers of change can contribute to this shift. In looking at the contestability of the policy arena, reformers would take into account that incentives, as well as the preferences and beliefs of actors, are instrumental to understanding what agreements are feasible.

The third challenge is to identify the relevant interventions or changes in rules that best solve the specific functional challenges. When thinking about potential reforms of policies, actors will find it helpful to consider three "levels" of rules.[51] First-level rules, or R1, refer to specific policies (for example, the percentage of budget allocated to health care). Mid-level rules, R2, refer to organizational forms—such as the independency of the judiciary and central bank. Higher-level rules, R3, relate to "rules about changing rules"—namely, constitutional and electoral law. The "form" of policies is certainly not to be ruled out, but it is also crucial to think about their "function." For example, beyond what a fiscal rule looks like, is commitment to the rule credible? Some functional challenges may require a combination of reforms at all three rule levels. Finally, when designing and evaluating policies, anticipating opposition and considering potential unintended consequences must be part of the process (box O.14). Particularly when

---

Box O.14 Lessons for reformers from the "rules game": How is legitimacy ultimately built?

This Report encourages reformers to pay attention to the details of the *rules game* so they can avoid two basic mistakes.

First, an act of reform undertaken by one player in a rules game can backfire if the player does not consider the actions the reform will trigger in other players. For example, an outsider might advise the legislature on the benefits of contract law. In response, the legislature might pass a law that tells the courts to enforce contracts; the executive head of government might promise to promote judges who follow the executive's instructions to favor some people in court cases; wealthy elites might pay the executive to receive special treatment in the courts; the executive might use the money from the elites to finance an upcoming political campaign; and, as a result, citizens might not trust the courts to enforce contract law. Ultimately, this reform did not produce the anticipated benefits, and it may have made matters even worse. The courts, which previously offered equal protection under criminal law, may no longer be able to punish wealthy offenders who commit crimes.

Second, even if it produces better payoffs today, a reform could also backfire if it generates worse outcomes for the *rules game* that will be played in the future. This can be particularly important in terms of what political scientists call *legitimacy*, whose manifestation is voluntary acceptance of the rules and compliance with them. The citizens of a nation may be willing to delegate enough power to their government to make it a dominant player in the rules game for the nation, but only as long as they feel that the government's use of that power is legitimate.

The functional approach in this Report allows a clearer understanding of the concept of legitimacy. The legitimacy of a government can be derived from three sources. Repeated commitment builds legitimacy in terms of *outcomes*.[a] When a government repeatedly delivers on its commitments, it legitimizes itself, such as by reliably providing public services. Legitimacy can also come from a perception of fairness in the way in which policies and rules are designed and implemented—that is, *process* legitimacy. Finally, legitimacy can also be *relational*, where sharing a set of values and norms encourages individuals to recognize authority. Outcome, process, and relational legitimacy form the three types of legitimacy identified in this Report. Legitimacy matters for cooperation and coordination because it implies voluntary compliance with an act of authority. Even if a government delivers on its commitments and is able to coerce people into complying, there may be "legitimacy deficits" if the process is perceived as unfair and people may not be willing to cooperate and would rather opt out of the social contract.

Source: WDR 2017 team.

a. Outcome legitimacy is related to the notion of trust, which is defined in this Report as the probability that an actor assigns to other actors of delivering on their commitment, conditional on their past behavior.

thinking about evaluation, it must be understood that trajectories may not be linear and thus assessment requires complex methods. Anticipating the changing balance of power around the reform process and adopting an adaptive approach, such as building coalitions in anticipation of the reform, can reduce the risk of reversal. Driving sustainable change requires considering the potential opportunities presented by elite interests, the opportunities for citizen collective action, and the role of international influences.

Creating conditions for adaptability

When can meaningful changes be made in the nature of governance? The development path is bumpy: shocks (such as terms of trade shocks and natural disasters) and gradual developments (such as urbanization or a growing middle class) alter the bargaining influence and preferences of actors, often benefiting one at the expense of another. In the face of these changes, governance arrangements that cannot accommodate new actors or demands may collapse. For example, *violence traps* are unstable bargains in which elites are highly polarized and the costs of losing control are great—when the stakes are sufficiently high—leading to violent conflict. *Middle-income traps* are situations in which interest groups, currently benefiting by extracting rents, have incentives to oppose new economic conditions and thus prevent efficiency-oriented reforms from happening, leading to an unproductive equilibrium. And *inequality traps* are a vicious cycle in which a high concentration of wealth translates into a disproportionate ability of those at the top of the distribution to influence the policy process in their favor and weakens the perception of fairness of those at the bottom of the distribution, who decide to opt out and not to contest in the policy arena.[52]

Adaptability to changes in the relative bargaining power, incentives, and preferences of different actors matters. Although the conditions that determine whether countries will adapt in ways that allow for more security, growth, and equity are contingent on history and are highly specific to context, there are a few circumstances that make such adaptability more likely. In particular, when elites have reasons to find common ground, bargains can expand and adapt. When national institutions produce more effective leaders, countries are more capable of long-term development. When countries have more balanced, diversified, and organized business interests, they may be more capable of reforming institutions to adapt to changing economic conditions. Bargains that can adapt to evolving elite interests

may nevertheless struggle to adapt to growing citizen demands. Regimes may lose legitimacy when decision-making processes are insufficiently inclusive, even when other development outcomes appear successful. For example, even effective growth policies may alienate the population if public voice is lacking in the policy process. Overcoming delegitimization necessitates greater inclusion in the political process.

A focus on creating conditions, like those discussed in this Report, that prepare societies to adapt as their needs and demands change over time is critical to ensuring inclusive and sustainable development progress. Traditional development orthodoxy has so far emphasized the centrality of three assumptions in improving governance for development: the form of policies, the capacity to implement them, and the impersonal application of the rules. These assumptions have shaped the conventional solutions of the international community to the problem of policy failure in developing countries: first, invest in "good" laws and policies; second, build organizational and technical capacity to implement them; and third, strengthen the "rule of law." This Report moves beyond these approaches and emphasizes that, although it is important to look at forms that have worked in other contexts, gauge what capacity is needed, and stress the importance of the rule of law, these aspects are not enough.

Navigating this Report

Part I. Rethinking governance for development: A conceptual framework

Part I of this Report presents a conceptual framework for rethinking the role of governance and law in development. Chapter 1 motivates by unpacking critical questions facing the development community today: in particular, what are the underlying determinants of policy effectiveness? Chapter 2 proposes a new analytical approach to answering these questions, using a game theoretic approach to argue that the functional role institutions play in ensuring credible commitment, inducing coordination, and enhancing cooperation is fundamental to the effectiveness of policies to promote development. The framework presented in the chapter explores how the unequal distribution of power in society (power asymmetry) is a key factor underpinning the effectiveness of these functions. Chapter 3 approaches the conceptual framework from the perspective of law, explaining the different roles that law plays in shaping and

Adaptability to changes in the relative bargaining power, incentives, and preferences of different actors matters.

reshaping the policy arena in which actors bargain over policy design and implementation.

Part II. Governance for development

Part II of this Report applies the framework presented in part I to better understand three core development outcomes: security (chapter 4), growth (chapter 5), and equity (chapter 6). Commitment, coordination, and cooperation fundamentally underlie the effectiveness of policies to promote these outcomes, but the unequal distribution of power can constrain policy effectiveness. Moreover, characteristics of development itself—such as the composition of growth or the level of inequality—influence the relative bargaining power of certain actors. Enhancing contestability in the policy arena, effectively changing incentives, and reshaping the preferences and beliefs of different actors—for example, through leadership—can make development policies more effective in achieving their objectives.

Part III. Drivers of change

Part III of this Report explores the dynamics of how change occurs from the perspective of elite bargains (chapter 7), citizen engagement (chapter 8), and international influences (chapter 9). As discussed in part II, to improve policy effectiveness and ultimately expand the set of implementable policies, it is necessary to reshape the policy arena where actors bargain. This can be accomplished by enhancing contestability—that is, by enabling new actors to enter the bargaining space, by changing the incentives of the actors involved, or by reshaping their preferences and beliefs. Although the dynamics of governance can be very persistent and are highly endogenous, change is possible over time. In the end, change is manifested by bringing about new formal rules that reshape de jure power.

Spotlights

This Report contains 13 spotlights, which apply the conceptual framework described in the Report to key policy areas of interest, ranging from service delivery to corruption and illicit financial flows.

Notes

1. The chapters of this Report focus on the specific question of policy effectiveness for achieving these outcomes. The framework, however, can be used to address broader questions about social dynamics.
2. See Rosenstein-Rodan (1943). Murphy, Shleifer, and Vishny (1989) model a more recent version of this idea.
3. Hoff (2000) reviews models of coordination failures in a wide range of contexts, including social norms and corruption. Cooper (1999) reviews macroeconomic models of coordination failures, and Rodríguez-Clare (2005) reviews microeconomic models of coordination failures.
4. Barr (2001); Lindert (2004).
5. Including at the subnational level. Preventing crime, for example, can be explained from the functional perspective as part of what local governments provide for the public, as shown in part II of this Report.
6. What distinguishes elites from citizens in this Report is their ability to directly influence the design and implementation of a certain policy. In this way, elites are defined in a positive (as opposed to a normative) sense. See box O.9 for further detail.
7. A similar approach has been developed in a pioneering work, *The Politics of Policies*, in the context of Latin America (IDB 2005).
8. However, lack of access to state power is not the only determinant of violence; the capacity to mobilize against governments also matters (Cederman, Wimmer, and Min 2010), as does the opportunity to mobilize. On the former, see Fearon and Laitin (2000).
9. Wimmer, Cederman, and Min (2009).
10. Platteau (2000a).
11. Suharto was the second president of Indonesia. He held the office for 31 years, from the ousting of the first president, Sukarno, in 1967 until his resignation in 1998.
12. Khwaja and Mian (2005).
13. Stokes (2009).
14. Khemani and others (2016).
15. Bold and others (2012).
16. Ferreira and others (2013).
17. World Bank (2015).
18. Collective action problems include those solved through *coordination* (the coordinated actions among actors based on a shared expectation about what others will do) and *cooperation* (the cooperative behavior among actors, whereby opportunistic behavior—free-riding—is limited). Throughout this Report, the term *collective action problems* refers to these two different types of problems.
19. Acemoglu and Robinson (2012).
20. Social norms are the beliefs shared by a group or community. In this way, norms can be understood as "commonly shared beliefs."
21. See Aaberge, Langørgen, and Lindgren (2010) and Lustig (2015).
22. See Besley and Persson (2014).
23. The evidence for how some of these mechanisms lead to better outcomes, however, is mixed, as further discussed in chapter 8.
24. Hart (1961).
25. Basu (2015); McAdams (2015).
26. Roland and Verdier (1999).
27. Hellman (1998).

28. Jackson, Klich, and Poznanska (2005).
29. Lindert (2004).
30. Joshi and Ayee (2009).
31. Björkman and Svensson (2009).
32. Ferreira and others (2013).
33. Preston (2003).
34. Aidt and Jensen (2014).
35. Kim (2007).
36. Rawls (1971) proposes that citizens in an original position behind a Kantian "veil of ignorance," ignorant of their lot in life—such as class, race, social status, distribution of assets, gender—would opt for a society that maximizes the level of welfare achieved by the worst-off person in society (Maximin principle) as the accepted social contract.
37. Berliner and Erlich (2015).
38. Khemani and others (2016).
39. Burgess and others (2015).
40. Keefer (2011, 2013); Cruz and Keefer (2013).
41. Khemani and others (2016).
42. Devarajan and Kanbur (2012); Mansuri and Rao (2013).
43. World Bank (2016b).
44. WDR 2017 team, based on Spada and others (2015).
45. Foreign aid refers to official development assistance as defined by the Organisation for Economic Co-operation and Development (OECD).
46. Fearon, Humphreys, and Weinstein (2009).
47. Moore (2004).
48. The "aid curse" argument is made by Moss, Pettersson, and van de Walle (2006); Collier (2007); and Djankov, Montalvo, and Reynal-Querol (2008).
49. Devarajan and Khemani (2016).
50. Devarajan and Khemani (2016).
51. Acuña and Tommasi (1999).
52. Levy and Walton (2005).

References

Aaberge, R., A. Langørgen, and P. Lindgren. 2010. "The Impact of Basic Public Services on the Distribution of Income in European Countries." In *Income and Living Conditions in Europe*, edited by A. B. Atkinson and E. Marlier. Luxembourg: Eurostat.

Acemoglu, Daron, and James Robinson. 2012. *Why Nations Fail: The Origins of Power, Prosperity, and Poverty.* New York: Crown Business.

Acuña, C., and M. Tommasi. 1999. "Some Reflections on the Institutional Reforms Required for Latin America." In *Institutional Reforms, Growth and Human Development in Latin America.* Conference volume. New Haven, CT: Yale Center for International and Area Studies.

Aidt, Toke S., and Peter S. Jensen. 2014. "Workers of the World, Unite! Franchise Extensions and the Threat of Revolution in Europe, 1820–1938." *European Economic Review* 72 (November): 52–75.

Barr, Nicholas. 2001. *The Welfare State as Piggy Bank: Information, Risk, Uncertainty, and the Role of the State.* Oxford, U.K.: Oxford University Press.

Barrett, Stanley R., Sean Stokholm, and Jeanette Burke. 2001. "The Idea of Power and the Power of Ideas: A Review Essay." *American Anthropologist* 103 (2): 468–80.

Basu, Kaushik. 2000. *Prelude to Political Economy: A Study of the Social and Political Foundations of Economics.* Oxford, U.K.: Oxford University Press.

———. 2015. "The Republic of Beliefs: A New Approach to 'Law and Economics.'" Policy Research Working Paper 7259, World Bank, Washington, DC.

Beegle, Kathleen, Luc Christiaensen, Andrew Dabalen, and Isis Gaddis. 2016. *Poverty in a Rising Africa.* Washington, DC: World Bank.

Berliner, Daniel, and Aaron Erlich. 2015. "Competing for Transparency: Political Competition and Institutional Reform in Mexican States." *American Political Science Review* 109 (1): 110–28.

Besley, Timothy, and Torsten Persson. 2014. *Pillars of Prosperity: The Political Economics of Development Clusters.* Princeton, NJ: Princeton University Press.

Bishop, S., and A. Hoeffler. 2014. "Free and Fair Elections—A New Database." CSAE Working Paper WPS/2014-14, Centre for the Study of African Economies, Oxford, U.K.

Björkman, Martina, and Jakob Svensson. 2009. "Power to the People: Evidence from a Randomized Field Experiment on Community-Based Monitoring in Uganda." *Quarterly Journal of Economics* 124 (2): 735–69.

Bold, Tessa, Mwangi Kimenyi, Germano Mwabu, Alice Ng'ang'a, and Justin Sandefur. 2012. "Scaling-KEN-1." International Growth Centre, London School of Economics and University of Oxford.

Braithwaite, John, and Peter Drahos. 2000. *Global Business Regulation.* Cambridge, U.K.: Cambridge University Press.

Brockmeyer, Anne, Maha Khatrouch, and Gaël Raballand. 2015. "Public Sector Size and Performance Management: A Case-Study of Post-revolution Tunisia." Policy Research Working Paper 7159, World Bank, Washington, DC.

Bteddini, Lida. 2016. *Public Employment and Governance in Middle East and North Africa.* Washington, DC: World Bank.

Burgess, Robin, Remi Jedwab, Edward Miguel, Ameet Morjaria, and Gerard Padró i Miquel. 2015. "The Value of Democracy: Evidence from Road Building in Kenya." *American Economic Review* 105 (6): 1817–51.

Cederman, Lars-Erik, Andreas Wimmer, and Brian Min. 2010. "Why Do Ethnic Groups Rebel? New Data and Analysis." *World Politics* 62 (1): 87–119.

Center for Systemic Peace. Various years. Polity IV (database). Vienna, VA, http://www.systemicpeace.org/polityproject.html.

Ceriani, L., K. B. Bolch, and L. F. López-Calva. 2016. "The Arithmetics and Politics of Domestic Resource

Mobilization." Background paper, WDR 2017, World Bank, Washington, DC.

Clist, P., and O. Morrissey. 2011. "Aid and Tax Revenue: Signs of a Positive Effect since the 1980s." *Journal of International Development* 23: 165–80.

Collier, Paul. 2007. *The Bottom Billion: Why the Poorest Countries Are Failing and What Can Be Done about It.* Oxford, U.K.: Oxford University Press.

Cooper, R. 1999. *Coordination Games: Complementarities and Macroeconomics.* New York: Cambridge University Press.

Coppedge, Michael, John Gerring, Staffan I. Lindberg, Jan Teorell, David Altman, Michael Bernhard, M. Steven Fish, and others. 2015. *Varieties of Democracy: Codebook v4.* Gothenburg, Sweden: Varieties of Democracy (V-Dem) Project, V-Dem Institute University of Gothenburg; Notre Dame, Indiana: Helen Kellogg Institute for International Studies, University of Notre Dame, https://www.v-dem.net/en/.

Cruz, Cesi, and Philip Keefer. 2013. "The Organization of Political Parties and the Politics of Bureaucratic Reform." Policy Research Working Paper 6686, World Bank, Washington, DC.

Dahl, R. A. 1957. "The Concept of Power." *Behavioral Science* 2: 202–10.

Devarajan, Shantayanan. 2013. "Africa's Statistical Tragedy." *Review of Income and Wealth* 59 (October): S9–S15.

Devarajan, Shantayanan, and Ravi Kanbur. 2012. "The Evolution of Development Strategy as Balancing Market and Government Failure." Working Paper, Charles H. Dyson School of Applied Economics and Management, Cornell University, Ithaca, NY.

Devarajan, Shantayanan, and Stuti Khemani. 2016. "If Politics Is the Problem, How Can External Actors Be Part of the Solution?" Policy Research Working Paper 7761, World Bank, Washington, DC.

Di John, Jonathan, and James Putzel. 2009. "Political Settlements: Issues Paper." Governance and Social Development Resource Centre, University of Birmingham.

Dixit, Avinash. 2004. *Lawlessness and Economics.* Princeton, NJ: Princeton University Press.

Djankov, S., J. G. Montalvo, and M. Reynal-Querol. 2008. "The Curse of Aid." *Journal of Economic Growth* 13 (3): 169–94.

Economist. 2012. "For Richer—or Poorer: Re-crunching the Numbers—Whatever They Might Be." September 29. http://www.economist.com/node/21563736.

Ellickson, Robert. 1991. *Order without Law.* Cambridge, MA: Harvard University Press.

Fearon, James D., Macartan Humphreys, and Jeremy M. Weinstein. 2009. "Can Development Aid Contribute to Social Cohesion after Civil War? Evidence from a Field Experiment in Post-conflict Liberia." *American Economic Review: Papers and Proceedings* 99 (2): 287–91.

Fearon, James D., and David D. Laitin. 2000. "Violence and the Social Construction of Ethnic Identity." *International Organization* 54 (4): 845–77.

Feenstra, Robert C., Robert Inklaar, and Marcel P. Timmer. 2015. "The Next Generation of the Penn World Table." *American Economic Review* 105 (10): 3150–82. Version 8.0, http://www.rug.nl/research/ggdc/data/pwt/pwt-8.0.

Ferreira, Francisco H. G., Julian Messina, Jamele Rigolini, Luis Felipe López-Calva, María Ana Lugo, and Renos Vakis. 2013. *Economic Mobility and the Rise of the Latin American Middle Class.* Latin America and Caribbean Studies. Washington, DC: World Bank.

Fisman, Raymond. 2001. "Estimating the Value of Political Connections." *American Economic Review* 91 (4): 1095–1102.

Gould, Stephen Jay. 1987. *Time's Arrow, Time's Cycle: Myth and Metaphor in the Discovery of Geological Time.* Cambridge, MA; London: Harvard University Press.

Gupta, S., B. Clemens, A. Pivovarsky, and E. Tiongson. 2004. "Foreign Aid and Revenue Response: Does the Composition of Aid Matter?" In *Helping Countries Develop: The Role of Fiscal Policy,* edited by S. Gupta, B. Clemens, and G. Inchauste. Washington, DC: International Monetary Fund.

Hallegatte, Stéphane, Geoffrey Heal, Marianne Fay, and David Treguer. 2012. "From Growth to Green Growth—A Framework." Working Paper 17841, National Bureau of Economic Research, Cambridge, MA.

Halliday, Terence C., and Gregory Shaffer. 2015. *Transnational Legal Orders.* Cambridge, U.K.: Cambridge University Press.

Hart, H. L. A. 1961. *The Concept of Law.* London: Oxford University Press.

Hellman, Joel. 1998. "Winners Take All: The Politics of Partial Reform in Postcommunist Transitions." *World Politics* 50 (January).

Hoff, K. 2000. "Beyond Rosenstein-Rodan: The Modern Theory of Coordination Problems in Development." *Proceedings of the Annual World Bank Conference on Development Economics, 2000* (Supplement to the *World Bank Economic Review*). Washington, DC: World Bank.

IDB (Inter-American Development Bank). 2005. *The Politics of Policies: The Role of Political Process in Successful Public Policies.* Economic and Social Progress in Latin America and the Caribbean 2006 Report. Washington, DC: IDB.

IMF (International Monetary Fund). Various years. *World Economic Outlook.* Washington, DC, http://www.imf.org/external/ns/cs.aspx?id=29.

Jackson, John E., Jacek Klich, and Krystyna Poznanska. 2005. *The Political Economy of Poland's Transition: New Firms and Reform Governments.* Cambridge, U.K.: Cambridge University Press.

Joshi, A., and J. Ayee. 2009. "Autonomy or Organization? Reforms in the Ghanaian Internal Revenue Service." *Public Administration and Development* 29 (4): 289–302.

Keefer, Philip. 2011. "Collective Action, Political Parties and Pro-development Public Policy." *Asian Development Review* 28 (1): 94–118.

Keefer, Philip. 2013. "Organizing for Prosperity: Collective Action, Political Parties and the Political Economy of Development." In *Oxford Handbook of the Politics of Development*, edited by Carol Lancaster and Nicholas van de Walle. Oxford, U.K.: Oxford University Press.

Keynes, John Maynard. 1936. *The General Theory of Employment, Interest and Money*. London: Palgrave Macmillan.

Khan, Mushtaq. 2010. "Political Settlements and the Governance of Growth-Enhancing Institutions." https://www.researchgate.net/publication/265567069 _Political_Settlements_and_the_Governance_of _Growth-Enhancing_Institutions.

Khemani, Stuti, Ernesto Dal Bó, Claudio Ferraz, Frederico Finan, Corinne Stephenson, Adesinaola Odugbemi, Dikshya Thapa, and Scott Abrahams. 2016. *Making Politics Work for Development: Harnessing Transparency and Citizen Engagement*. Policy Research Report. Washington, DC: World Bank.

Khwaja, A. I., and A. Mian. 2005. "Do Lenders Favor Politically Connected Firms? Rent Provision in an Emerging Financial Market." *Quarterly Journal of Economics* 120 (4): 1371–1411.

Kim, Wonik. 2007. "Social Insurance Expansion and Political Regime Dynamics in Europe, 1880–1945." *Social Science Quarterly* 88 (2): 494–514.

Levy, S., and M. Walton. 2005. *No Growth without Equity: Inequality, Interests and Competition in Mexico*. London: Palgrave Macmillan.

Lindert, Peter H. 2004. *Growing Public: Social Spending and Economic Growth since the Eighteenth Century*. Vol. 1, *The Story*. New York: Cambridge University Press.

Lukes, Steven. 2005. *Power: A Radical Review*. 2nd ed. New York: Palgrave Macmillan.

Lustig, Nora. 2015. "The Redistributive Impact of Government Spending on Education and Health: Evidence from Thirteen Developing Countries in the Commitment to Equity Project." In *Inequality and Fiscal Policy*, edited by Benedict Clements, Ruud de Mooij, Sanjeev Gupta, and Michael Keen. Washington, DC: International Monetary Fund.

———. 2016. "Domestic Resource Mobilization and the Poor." Background paper, WDR 2017, World Bank, Washington, DC.

Mansuri, Ghazala, and Vijayendra Rao. 2013. *Localizing Development: Does Participation Work?* World Bank Policy Research Report. Washington, DC: World Bank.

Martin, Lucy. 2014. "Taxation, Loss Aversion, and Accountability: Theory and Experimental Evidence for Taxation's Effect on Citizen Behavior." Unpublished paper, Yale University, New Haven, CT.

McAdams, R. 2015. *The Expressive Powers of Law: Theories and Limits*. Cambridge, MA: Harvard University Press.

Michels, Robert. [1911] 1966. *Political Parties: A Sociological Study of the Oligarchical Tendencies of Modern Democracy*. New York: Free Press.

Mokyr, Joel. 2005. "The Intellectual Origins of Modern Economic Growth." *Journal of Economic History* 65 (2): 285–351.

Moore, Mick. 2004. "Revenues, State Formation, and the Quality of Governance in Developing Countries." *International Political Science Review* 25 (3): 297–319.

Morrissey, O., and S. Torrance. 2015. "Aid and Taxation." In *Handbook on the Economics of Foreign Aid*, edited by B. M. Arvin and B. Lew. Cheltenham, U.K.: Edward Elgar Publishing.

Mosca, Gaetano. 1939. *The Ruling Class (Elementi di Scienza Politica)*. New York: McGraw-Hill.

Moss, Todd, Gunilla Pettersson, and Nicolas van de Walle. 2006. "An Aid-Institutions Paradox? A Review Essay on Aid Dependency and State Building in Sub-Saharan Africa." Working Paper 74, Center for Global Development, Washington, DC.

Murphy, Kevin M., Andrei Shleifer, and Robert W. Vishny. 1989. "Industrialization and the Big Push." *Journal of Political Economy* 97 (5): 1003–26.

Noriega, Gustavo. 2012. *INDEC: Historia Intima de una Estafa*. New York: Penguin Random House.

North, Douglass C., John J. Wallis, and Barry R. Weingast. 2009. *Violence and Social Orders: A Conceptual Framework for Interpreting Recorded Human History*. New York: Cambridge University Press.

Paler, Laura. 2013. "Keeping the Public Purse: An Experiment in Windfalls, Taxes and the Incentives to Restrain Government." *American Political Science Review* 107 (4): 706–25.

Pareto, Vilfredo. [1927] 1971. *Manual of Political Economy*. New York: August M. Kelley.

Parks, Thomas, and William Cole. 2010. "Political Settlements: Implications for International Development Policy and Practice." Occasional Paper No. 2, Asia Foundation, San Francisco.

Platteau, Jean-Philippe. 2000a. "Allocating and Enforcing Property Rights in Land: Informal versus Formal Mechanisms in Subsaharan Africa." *Nordic Journal of Political Economy* 26: 55–81.

———. 2000b. *Institutions, Social Norms, and Economic Development*. London: Routledge.

Posner, Eric. 2000. *Law and Social Norms*. Cambridge, MA: Harvard University Press.

Preston, Paul. 2003. *Juan Carlos*. Madrid: Plaza and Janes Editories.

Ravallion, M. 2010. "Do Poorer Countries Have Less Capacity for Redistribution?" *Journal of Globalization and Development* 1 (2): 1–29.

Rawls, John. 1971. *A Theory of Justice*. Cambridge, MA: Belknap Press of Harvard University Press.

Resnick, Danielle, Finn Tarp, and James Thurlow. 2012. "The Political Economy of Green Growth: Illustrations from Southern Africa." Working Paper 2012/11, United Nations University-World Institute for Development Economics Research (UNU-WIDER), Helsinki.

Rodríguez-Clare, Andrés. 2005. "Coordination Failures, Clusters and Microeconomic Interventions." Working Paper No. 452, Inter-American Development Bank, Washington, DC.

Roitberg, G., and K. Nagasawa. 2016. "INDEC: The Machine of Lies: A Chronicle of the Destruction of Public Statistics during Argentina's Kirchner Period." *La Nacion*. http://casos.lanacion.com.ar /indec-the-lying-machine.

Roland, G., and T. Verdier. 1999. "Transition and the Output Fall." *Economics of Transition* 7 (1): 1–28.

Rosenstein-Rodan, P. N. 1943. "Problems of Industrialisation of Eastern and South Eastern Europe." *Economic Journal* 53 (210/211): 202–11.

Sen, Amartya K. 1999. *Development as Freedom*. Oxford, U.K.: Oxford University Press.

Spada, Paolo, Jonathan Mellon, Tiago Peixoto, and Fredrik Sjoberg. 2015. "Effects of the Internet on Participation: Study of a Policy Referendum in Brazil." Policy Research Working Paper 7204, World Bank, Washington, DC.

Stämpfli, Regula. 1994. "Direct Democracy and Women's Suffrage: Antagonism in Switzerland." In *Women and Politics Worldwide*, edited by Najma Chowdhury and Barbara Nelson, 690–704. New Haven, CT: Yale University Press.

Stokes, Susan. 2009. "Political Clientelism." In *The Oxford Handbook of Comparative Politics*, edited by Carles Boix and Susan Stokes. Oxford, U.K.: Oxford University Press.

Sunstein, Cass. 1996. "Social Norms and Social Roles." *Columbia Law Review* 96 (4): 903–68.

V-Dem (Varieties of Democracy). Various years. Database hosted by Gothenburg Institute (Europe) and Kellogg Institute (United States), https://www.v-dem.net/en/.

Wallis, John. 2016. "Governance and Violence." Background paper, WDR 2017, World Bank, Washington, DC.

Wimmer, Andreas, Lars-Erik Cederman, and Brian Min. 2009. "Ethnic Politics and Armed Conflict: A Configurational Analysis of a New Global Data Set." *American Sociological Review* 74 (2): 316–37.

Wolf, E. R. 1999. *Envisioning Power: Ideologies of Dominance and Crisis*. Oakland: University of California Press.

World Bank. Various years. Women, Business, and the Law (database). Washington, DC, http://wbl.world bank.org/.

———. 2003. *World Development Report 2004: Making Services Work for Poor People*. Washington, DC: World Bank.

———. 2015. *World Development Report 2015: Mind, Society, and Behavior*. Washington, DC: World Bank.

———. 2016a. *Women, Business, and the Law: Getting to Equal*. Washington, DC: World Bank.

———. 2016b. *World Development Report 2016: Digital Dividends*. Washington, DC: World Bank.

World Bank and V-Dem. 2016. "Codebook: Measuring Elite Power and Interactions." Background paper, WDR 2017, World Bank, Washington, DC.

World Justice Project. Various years. Rule of Law Index. Washington, DC, http://worldjusticeproject.org/.

PART I

Rethinking governance for development:
A conceptual framework

1.

Governance for development:
The challenges

2.

Enhancing governance for development:
Why policies fail

3.

The role of law

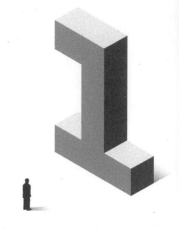

CHAPTER 1

Governance for development: The challenges

Societies worldwide have made enormous progress in improving the socioeconomic conditions for large groups of people over the last century. Just in the last 20 years, more than 1.2 billion people have been lifted out of poverty (World Bank 2015). Nobel Laureate Angus Deaton labels this achievement "the great escape": "the story of mankind's escaping from deprivation and early death, of how people have managed to make their lives better, and led the way for others to follow" (Deaton 2013, ix).

Such a positive performance hides, however, great heterogeneity within and among countries and regions in important aspects of the quality of life. Extreme poverty is still a reality for about 1 billion people, or 14 percent of the total global population. Inequalities are striking—and in many cases increasing. This persistent disparity in social and economic achievement has long concerned policy makers, academics, and development practitioners, particularly in today's world, where the links among countries are stronger and technology diffusion can be fast and cheap.

Consider, for example, the under-5 child mortality rate. This indicator is regarded as one of the most significant measures of how a society is doing in addressing the needs of its population because it reflects the quality and incidence of service provision (Buckley 2003; Andrews, Hay, and Myers 2010). Despite substantial improvements over the last 45 years, developing countries still lag many years behind the rate in developed countries for this indicator. For example, the child mortality rate in Sierra Leone matches Portugal's rate 58 years ago (figure 1.1, panel a). Moreover, within countries individuals at the bottom of the income distribution systematically lag behind those at the top. For example, the poorest 20 percent of the population of India is approximately 25 years behind the wealthiest 20 percent (figure 1.1, panel b).

Understanding development policy: Proximate factors and underlying determinants

Explanations of such vast disparities in development performance typically focus on *proximate factors*—for example, the provision of health services, connectivity infrastructure, or access to finance. "The intensive study of the problem of economic development," Hirschman (1958, 1) noted almost six decades ago, "has had one discouraging result: it has produced an ever-lengthening list of factors and conditions, of obstacles and prerequisites." This Report argues that, although proximate factors such as access to finance or the provision of health services are indeed crucial for development, the adoption and implementation of successful pro-development policies often depend on deeper *underlying determinants*. Ultimately, confronting the challenges faced by today's developing countries—to name a few, poor service delivery, violence, slowing growth, corruption, and the sustainable management of natural resources—requires a rethinking of the process by which state and nonstate actors interact to design and implement policies—that is, what this Report calls governance (box 1.1).

An understanding of governance as an underlying determinant of development is useful in examining cases of the successful and unsuccessful adoption and implementation of policies in pursuit of security, growth, and equity, and helps explain apparent

> Although proximate factors such as access to finance or the provision of health services are indeed crucial for development, the adoption and implementation of successful pro-development policies often depend on deeper *underlying determinants.*

Figure 1.1 **Despite declining under-5 child mortality rates, inequality among and within countries is still sizable**

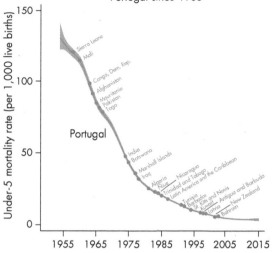

a. Child mortality rates in developing countries and regions compared with the trajectory of Portugal since 1955

Source: WDR 2017 team, using data from UN Inter-agency Group for Child Mortality Estimation (IGME).

Note: Data for all comparator countries are from the most recent year available (circa 2015).

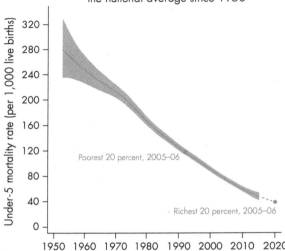

b. Child mortality rates of the poorest and the richest 20 percent in India compared with the national average since 1950

Sources: WDR 2017 team, using data from UN Inter-agency Group for Child Mortality Estimation (IGME) and on India's Demographic and Health Survey (DHS) for data by quintile.

Box 1.1 **What is governance?**

Governance is the process through which state and nonstate actors interact to design and implement policies within a given set of formal and informal rules that shape and are shaped by power.[a] This Report defines *power* as the ability of groups and individuals to make others act in the interest of those groups and individuals and to bring about specific outcomes (Dahl 1957; Lukes 2005).

Depending on the context, actors may establish a *government* as a set of formal state *institutions* (organizations and rules) that enforce and implement policies. Also depending on the context, state actors will play a more or less important role with respect to nonstate actors such as civil society organizations and business lobbies. In addition, governance takes place at different levels, from international bodies, to national state institutions, to local government agencies, to community and business associations. These dimensions often overlap, creating a complex network of actors and interests.

Source: WDR 2017 team.

a. This general definition is consistent with the World Bank's corporate definition, which emphasizes formal institutions and the role of state actors.

---

contradictions in the development trajectories of countries around the world. Some recent cases have attracted global attention.

State building in Somalia and Somaliland. Somalia, one of the world's most fragile countries, has been wracked by violence for more than two decades. Insurgent attacks and regional conflicts have prevented the emergence of a centralized state with a monopoly

over the legitimate use of force. Warring factions, many with their own regional sources of power, have been unable to reach a credible deal to determine the makeup and responsibilities of the central state. By contrast, in Somalia's autonomous region of Somaliland, an area with similar tribal and clan tensions, 20 years of stability and economic development have followed a 1993 clan conference that brought together leaders from both the modern and traditional sectors, successfully institutionalizing these clans and elders into formal governing bodies.

Confronting corruption and the resource curse in Nigeria. In 2010, just a year after experiencing a decade-long bounty of windfall revenues from high oil prices, Nigeria was requesting budget support from its development partners. From a long-term perspective, it is unclear how much of Nigeria's oil wealth has been saved to invest in the future, although a Sovereign Wealth Fund was established in 2011 to address these concerns. According to a former governor of the central bank, the country has lost billions of dollars to corruption by the National Petroleum Company. Indeed, according to 2015 data from the Afrobarometer survey, 78 percent of Nigerians feel that the government is "doing badly in fighting corruption." Ultimately, the institutional context was unable to safeguard natural resource revenues in order to reduce fiscal volatility and promote a macroeconomic environment conducive to long-term investment. Several countries have demonstrated that the "natural resource curse"— the paradox that countries with abundant natural resources face slower growth and worse development outcomes than countries without resources—can be avoided through effective economic and fiscal policies.

China's growth performance and growth challenges. For four decades, China, while increasingly integrating its economy with the global economy, grew at double-digit rates and lifted more than 700 million people out of poverty. This successful track record of economic growth is well known. Yet, according to many frequently used indicators, China's institutional environment during this period appears not to have changed. Does this imply that institutions do not matter for growth? No. Rather, a deeper understanding of China's development shows what these indicators miss: the adaptive policy decisions and state capacity that enabled economic success were facilitated by profound changes to mechanisms of accountability and collective leadership. China's experience highlights the need to pay more attention to how institutions function and less to the specific form they take. Meanwhile, today China faces a slowdown in growth. Maintaining rapid growth and avoiding a "middle-income trap" require the political will to switch to a growth model based on firm entry, competition, and innovation. In many middle-income countries, this transformation has been blocked by the actors that benefited from early growth and have mixed incentives to join coalitions for further reforms. Going forward will involve addressing these governance challenges.

Slums and exclusion in India's cities. Urban development that stems from coordinated planning and investment by coalitions of developers, bureaucrats, citizens, and politicians can lead to cities that are centers of growth, innovation, and productivity. Planners can help ensure that infrastructure meets the demands of investors who seek to maximize land rents, businesses that need connectivity to their consumers, and citizens who want access to services and jobs. But many cities fail to deliver on these promises. In India, massive urban slums—about 49,000 at the latest count, with tens of millions of inhabitants—represent failures to align public investments and zoning with the needs of a diverse set of urban constituents. Underinvestment in housing and inaccessible or unaffordable transportation options have driven workers into informal settlements, often in peripheral areas. Although many developers and politicians have exploited the system to generate rents for themselves, this uncoordinated urban development has prevented cities from achieving their growth potential, leading to large slums where most citizens are deprived of basic services.

Demanding better services in Brazil. In 2013 the world watched when protests erupted in Brazil's streets, with citizens complaining about the quality of public services—transport, education, and health—as the 2014 FIFA World Cup soccer tournament approached. Brazil had gone through 12 years of inclusive and sustained growth, which had lifted more than 30 million people out of poverty and strengthened the middle class. But these same middle classes that contributed with their taxes to the provision of public services were now demanding better quality and coverage, including "FIFA standards" for their schools. Why did this change come about? Brazil's social contract has historically been weak and fragmented. The poor received low-quality public services, while the upper-middle classes relied on private services and thus were less willing to contribute to the fiscal system. The creation of an expanded middle class and the reduction of poverty paradoxically heightened the perceptions of unfairness as the new middle class expected more than low-quality public services for its contributions.

"Brexit" and the growing discontent with economic integration. In June 2016 voters in the United Kingdom elected to leave the European Union (EU). The economic consequences for the country in particular and Europe in general have become a source of uncertainty in policy circles. Dissatisfaction with economic and political integration is not, however, exclusive to this region. In countries throughout the world,

populist parties have campaigned against trade and integration—some of them enjoying unprecedented electoral success in both developing and developed economies. These parties often prey on citizens' increasing feelings of disenfranchisement and exclusion from decision making, as well as on a growing perception of free-riding by specific groups. Even in countries that have undoubtedly benefited from integration, the unequal distribution of such benefits and perceived ineffectiveness of "voice" have led many citizens to question the status quo, which could have consequences for social cohesion and stability.

As these examples illustrate, contradictions occur in the real world. Somalia is a fragile state, while Somaliland seems to be doing well. Nigeria has an abundance of resources, but it is still a lower-middle-income country. China grew rapidly, even though many of its fundamental institutions did not change. India has grown, but it cannot control the propagation of slums. Brazil has experienced inclusive growth, but it is now facing increasing demands from the middle class. Great Britain had low unemployment, but it voted to leave the EU. The common thread running through these contradictions is governance, which helps explain why ineffective policies persist, why effective policies are often not adopted or implemented, and why unorthodox institutional arrangements may nevertheless generate positive outcomes. In other words, governance drives policy effectiveness. This is the main theme of this Report.

Governance drives policy effectiveness.

Development objectives . . . and constraints

This Report assumes that all countries share a set of development objectives: minimizing the threat of violence (security), promoting prosperity (growth), and ensuring that prosperity is shared (equity), while also protecting the sustainability of the development process for future generations (box 1.2). But policies do not always translate into these development outcomes in expected ways.

Box 1.2 Governance for what? Achieving the goals of security, growth, and equity

Many aspects of governance have intrinsic value, in particular the notion of freedom. In economic terms, freedom can be seen as an opportunity set, and development can be seen as "the removal of various types of unfreedoms" (exclusion from opportunities), where these unfreedoms reduce people's capacity to exercise "their reasoned agency" (Sen 1999, xii). As essential as such an intrinsic value as freedom is, its instrumental value also matters because of the "effectiveness of freedoms of particular kinds to promote freedoms of other kinds" (Sen 1999, xii). These positive relationships are what economists call *complementarities*. This Report acknowledges the intrinsic value of various dimensions of governance, as well as the notion of development as a positive freedom, while also recognizing their instrumental value to achieving equitable development.

As noted, the analysis in this Report starts from the normative standpoint that every society cares about freeing its members from the constant threat of violence (*security*), promoting prosperity (*growth*), and ensuring that such prosperity is shared (*equity*). It also assumes that societies aspire to achieving these goals in environmentally sustainable ways. This Report, then, assesses governance in terms of its capacity to deliver on these outcomes.

This approach is consistent with the transition from a dialogue based on ideology to the dialogue based on ideals that has transpired in the global development community over the last few decades. The establishment of the Millennium Development Goals (MDGs) in 2000 and the recent ratification of the Sustainable Development Goals (SDGs) by member countries of the United Nations are examples of the efforts to set common goals for social and economic advancement. SDG 16 calls for promoting "peace, justice, and strong institutions," and it is explicitly related to governance. Nevertheless, as this Report will argue, beyond its intrinsic value, the SDG 16 goal also has important instrumental value because its attainment will aid in the attainment of all the other SDGs. Indeed, achievement of all the development goals will require a solid understanding of governance to enable more effective policies.

Source: WDR 2017 team.

The first condition that societies want to establish in the pursuit of development is *security*—that is, people are safe from violence and the threat of violence. It is a fundamental dimension of well-being and a first-order characteristic of development (UNDP 1994; Sen 1999).

Yet, in 2014 more than 1.4 billion people lived in countries affected by violence (OECD 2015, 31). Violence is a major problem in 37 countries (map 1.1).[1] The list includes not just fragile low-income states such as Afghanistan, Somalia, and South Sudan, but also rising economic giants such as Brazil, Mexico, and South Africa. More than 740,000 people die each year as a result of armed violence. Remarkably, the majority of these deaths—about 490,000—occur in countries not affected by ongoing wars (Geneva Declaration Secretariat 2015). Homicides claimed an average of 377,000 lives between 2007 and 2012.[2] Civil wars, rebellions, and other forms of political violence caused 101,400 fatalities in 2014 alone (UCDP/PRIO

2015). At the end of 2014, 57.7 million persons worldwide were displaced (UNHCR 2015). As these figures regrettably reflect, policies to achieve security are too often ineffective; indeed, certain policies and their poor implementation can cause or exacerbate the societal problems contributing to violence.

More secure societies are also more prosperous (figure 1.2, panel a). Most of the relatively faster growth of higher-income countries between 1950 and 2011 resulted not from experiencing faster growth but rather from shrinking less—and less often—from crises or wars than lower-income countries (figure 1.2, panel b). In the even longer run, annual data on 14 European countries and the United States starting in 1820 show a sharp reduction in the frequency of the shrinking of economic growth after 1950—the period following World War II, which was the last mass-scale episode of organized violence in these countries (Wallis 2016).

Security, however, is not sufficient to achieve growth. In their quest for prosperity, countries

> More secure societies are also more prosperous.

Map 1.1 Violence is a major problem in 37 countries

Violent deaths per 100,000 residents per year, 2008-12

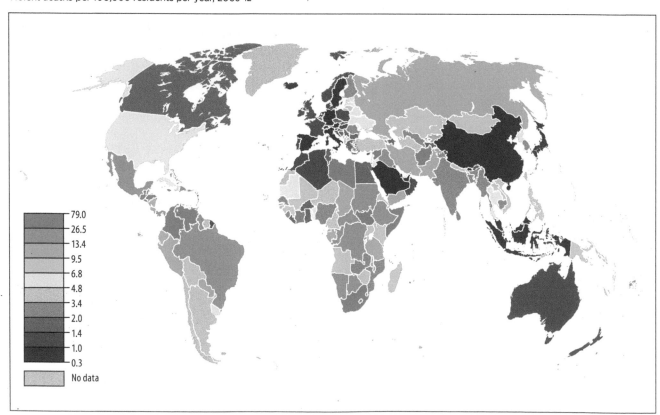

IBRD 42495 | SEPTEMBER 2016

Sources: WDR 2017 team, based on World Bank 2011; Pennsylvania State University, Correlates of War Project (COW), 2015; Geneva Declaration Secretariat 2015.

Note: Violent deaths comprise organized violence and homicide deaths.

require sustained improvements in efficiency and investment to spur economic growth. Low-income countries tend to grow as surplus labor is reallocated from agriculture to industry. Once the gains from this early industrialization process are exhausted, however, new sources of growth are needed. Economic growth arises from accumulation—such as the mobilization of savings for industrial investment—and efficiency—how well inputs are being put to use. And yet, many middle-income countries appear incapable of achieving gains in either accumulation or efficiency, becoming stuck instead in low-growth traps. Indeed, in contrast to the predictions of several growth theories, there is no evidence that low- and middle-income countries tend to converge toward high-income ones (Jones 2015).

Several countries have managed, though, to escape this middle-income trap. How? The evidence suggests that the continual reallocation of resources across sectors and firms is a substantial source of efficiency (total factor productivity, or TFP). In a dynamic setting in which new companies enter the market while uncompetitive firms exit, inputs reallocate between firms, giving way to innovation, competition, and productivity. Countries that escape the low-growth trap also tend to have a diversified export base in which coordination between domestic companies and governments contributes to shaping industrial investment. Indeed, the literature and policy forums are filled with discussions about the right sets of policies that can enable efficient resource allocation and investment upgrading. Nevertheless, as the persistent stagnation of many middle-income countries around the world reflects, very often these policies are not adopted or fail to achieve the expected results.

In addition to seeking prosperity, societies care about being equitable. In the United States, the Occupy movement's slogan, "We are the 99%," denounced the concentration of wealth among the top 1 percent. As these and other movements around the world reflect, concerns about increasing inequality are growing. The evidence indicates that these concerns are not without foundation. Even though there are signs that global income inequality is falling, inequality within countries is on the rise, and the concentration of income at the top has increased over recent years (World Bank 2015). In addition to normative concerns, a more equitable distribution of income is associated with positive outcomes, including stability and economic growth. So how do countries become more equitable?

Inequality and growth are structurally linked. Making growth more equitable involves policies that

Figure 1.2 Economic growth requires security

a. Countries with fewer episodes of violence are more prosperous

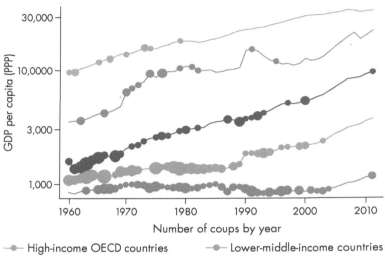

Sources: WDR 2017 team, based on data from Archigos database (Goemans, Gleditsch, and Chiozza 2009) for number of coups and Penn World Table, version 8.1 (Feenstra, Inklaar, and Timmer 2015), for level of GDP per capita.

Note: The size of the circles on each time series is relative to the number of coups per country for each income group in a given year. GDP = gross domestic product; OECD = Organisation for Economic Co-operation and Development; PPP = purchasing power parity.

b. High-income countries are better off not because they grow faster when they grow, but because they shrink less frequently and at a slower rate than low-income countries

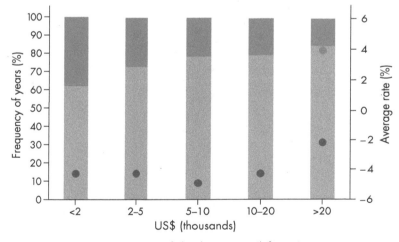

Sources: WDR 2017 team, based on Wallis 2016, with data from Penn World Table, version 8.1 (Feenstra, Inklaar, and Timmer 2015).

Note: The figure shows real GDP per capita (constant prices: chain series). Countries were first sorted into income categories based on their income in 2000, measured in 2005 U.S. dollars. Average annual growth rates are the simple arithmetic average for all the years and all the countries in the income category, without weighting. The sample underlying the figure comprises 141 countries, which have data available from at least 1970 onward. GDP = gross domestic product.

look at the bottom half of the income distribution. Consider the differences in the structure of economic activity and public services in low- compared with high-income countries. Traveling across a low-income country, one frequently observes a pattern of homogeneous economic activity—for example, large groups of people relying on agricultural activities—but rather heterogeneous public services—connectivity is uneven, and the availability and quality of services such as education and health vary dramatically from the rural to urban sectors (box 1.3). Quality and access are much lower for low-income people.

Box 1.3 Discontinuities of the state

Distribution of income is not the only factor associated with the heterogeneous coverage and quality of the provision of services and public goods. Circumstances such as gender, ethnicity, and location are also associated with the differential capacity of groups to influence the distribution of resources and the design of policies to address their needs. Location, in particular, is an important dimension because of its correlation with other circumstances. As Kanbur and Venables (2005, 3) note, "Spatial inequality is a dimension of overall inequality, but it has added significance when spatial and regional divisions align with political and ethnic tensions to undermine social and political stability."

In this sense, the state can be said to be *discontinuous* in terms of its presence and therefore its ability to respond effectively to the needs of citizens in specific territories

(O'Donnell 1993, 2003). When some regions or social groups are systematically neglected, geography becomes a prominent dimension that reflects inequities. State *discontinuity* can be approximated by a measure of the unequal *density* of the *presence* of the state in the different geographical regions of a country.

In Bolivia, a subnational analysis of the country's nine departments (*departamentos*) reveals that a few regions are systematically affected by a low state *presence*, as measured in terms of public services provided in that specific area. Map B1.3.1 shows the level of the state presence in health, education, and basic services (panels a, b, and c, respectively), for each region, and the composite *density* of the state (panel d) for these indicators—that is, the average presence across dimensions. The departments of Santa

Map B1.3.1 State presence in Bolivia in selected intervention domains and composite density, circa 2010

a. Health

b. Education

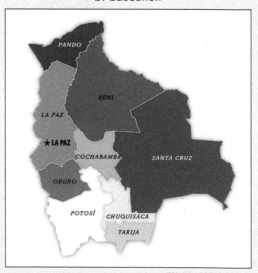

IBRD 42499 | SEPTEMBER 2016

IBRD 42500 | SEPTEMBER 2016

(Box continues next page)

Box 1.3 Discontinuities of the state *(continued)*

Map B1.3.1 State presence in Bolivia in selected intervention domains and composite density, circa 2010 *(continued)*

c. Access to water	d. Composite density

IBRD 42501 | SEPTEMBER 2016   IBRD 42502 | SEPTEMBER 2016

Sources: WDR 2017 team elaboration based on data from Bolivia's National Statistical Institute (census, 2012) for education and access to water and on data from the Demographic and Health Survey Program (2008) for health.

Note: The indicators for assessing the level of state presence are under-5 child mortality (health), share of literate adults (education), and share of households with access to piped water inside their homes (access to water). The degree of shading indicates the degree of coverage of services. The darker purple shading (panels a–c) represents a higher presence for that dimension (a better outcome or a higher coverage). State density (panel d) is the composite indicator of the different layers of state presence or coverage. The darker orange shading represents higher state density.

Cruz and Potosí are at the opposite ends of the density spectrum: Santa Cruz has the highest state density, Potosí the lowest. However, in Bolivia the overall *discontinuity* of the state has decreased over time. Using a measure of the inequality of the density across regions, the analysis finds that the presence of the state across regions in Bolivia has become more homogeneous over time.[a]

The level of state *density* in different regions is positively, although not perfectly, correlated with the level of local resources (for example, with GDP per capita). Such differences in regional development could be a result of the uneven responsiveness of the state, most likely over a long period of time, to different geographical areas and socioeconomic groups. In Bolivia, for example, the least dense region (Potosí) is also the region with the highest incidence of indigenous population, who historically have been underrepresented in state institutions and in policy making until the recent past.[b]

Source: WDR 2017 team, based on Ceriani and López-Calva (2016).

a. WDR 2017 team estimates, based on data from Bolivia's National Statistical Institute for education (census, 1992 and 2012) and access to water (census, 2001 and 2012) and on data from the National Survey on Demography and Health (1994) and Demographic and Health Survey (2008) for health.
b. According to Bolivia's latest census (2012), Castellano was not the main language spoken in Potosí by 54 percent of the population, 6 years and older, as opposed to, for example, 15 percent in Santa Cruz and 8 percent in Tarija.

Indeed, a low commitment to providing quality public services is one of the main characteristics of the most inequitable countries in the world. The opposite tends to be true in advanced countries, where one finds a more diversified economic structure and a rather homogeneous coverage and quality of public goods and services, independent of individuals' circumstances. The quest for development could thus be summarized as the transition toward more diversified economic opportunities and a more homogeneous response of public services to all individuals.

The provision of public goods and services as a way to level opportunities and to reduce poverty is undisputed. These and other social policies allow individuals to increase their stock of assets and the opportunity to use them, and they protect the most vulnerable. Fiscal policies enable the public spending behind these social transfers through taxation and help reshape the distribution of resources. Yet, policies to achieve equity are often not adopted, or they fail.

Governance for the bottom half

Why do best-practice policies to achieve security, growth, and equity so often fail to produce the desired outcomes? Why are so many potentially transformative policies not adopted? And what makes some unlikely policies succeed? As revealed in this Report, the answers to all of these questions have to do with how policies affect the interests of the actors who have the power to block them, whether actors who would benefit from policies are able to influence the decision-making process, and whether rules and norms sustain the existing equilibrium. In the following chapters, we propose a framework for thinking about these questions in pursuit of a larger objective: how policies for security, growth, and equity can be made more effective by taking governance seriously.

The analysis in this Report calls for paying particular attention to understanding the implications for those groups who tend to have less power to influence the decision-making process because of their economic or social circumstances. Groups that are typically marginalized from the policy arena—such as those at the bottom of the income distribution—should have the same access to opportunities as all others. This is an essential pillar of progress in development.

For sustained progress in development, governance needs to be responsive to all groups in society,

> For sustained progress in development, governance needs to be responsive to all groups in society, regardless of their circumstances.

regardless of their circumstances. Even though power is distributed unequally in every society—an inevitable fact—promoting *governance for the bottom half* means promoting a process through which development dividends can still be equitably distributed.

Notes

1. This is the number of countries in the first quintile of map 1.1, where the incidence of violence is measured by the number of deaths in armed conflict, in addition to the number of homicides.
2. WDR 2017 team, based on the *Global Burden of Armed Violence Report 2015: Every Body Counts* (Geneva Declaration Secretariat 2015). These figures are for intentional homicides. The number rises to 3,864,000 if unintentional homicides are included. The World Health Organization (WHO) defines homicide as "injuries inflicted by another person with intent to injure or kill, by any means."

References

Andrews, Matthew, Roger Hay, and Jerrett Myers. 2010. "Governance Indicators Can Make Sense: Under-Five Mortality Rates Are an Example." HKS Faculty Research Working Paper Series, RWP10-015, John F. Kennedy School of Government, Harvard University, Cambridge, MA.

Buckley, C. 2003. "Children at Risk: Infant and Child Health in Central Asia." William Davidson Institute Working Paper No. 523, University of Michigan, Ann Arbor.

Ceriani, L., and L. F. López-Calva. 2016. "State Discontinuity." Background Note, WDR 2017, World Bank, Washington, DC.

Dahl, R. A. 1957. "The Concept of Power." *Behavioral Science* 2: 202–10.

Deaton, A. 2013. *The Great Escape: Health, Wealth, and the Origins of Inequality.* Princeton, NJ: Princeton University Press.

Feenstra, Robert C., Robert Inklaar, and Marcel P. Timmer. 2015. "The Next Generation of the Penn World Table." *American Economic Review* 105 (10): 3150–82. Version 8.1, http://www.rug.nl/ggdc/productivity/pwt/pwt-releases/pwt8.1.

Geneva Declaration Secretariat. 2015. *Global Burden of Armed Violence 2015: Every Body Counts.* Cambridge, U.K.: Cambridge University Press.

Goemans, Henk E., Kristian Skrede Gleditsch, and Giacomo Chiozza. 2009. "Introducing Archigos: A Dataset of Political Leaders." *Journal of Peace Research* 46 (2): 269–83.

Hirschman, Albert O. 1958. *The Strategy of Economic Development.* New Haven, CT: Yale University Press.

Jones, Charles I. 2015. "The Facts of Economic Growth." NBER Working Paper 21142. National Bureau of Economic Research, Cambridge, MA. Forthcoming in John B. Taylor and Harald Uhlig, eds. *Handbook of Macroeconomics*, Vol. 2. Amsterdam: Elsevier.

Kanbur, Ravi, and Anthony J. Venables. 2005. "Spatial Inequality and Development." In *Spatial Inequality and Development*, edited by Ravi Kanbur and Anthony J. Venables, 3–11. Oxford, U.K.: Oxford University Press.

Lukes, Steven. 2005. *Power: A Radical Review*. London: Palgrave Macmillan.

O'Donnell, Guillermo. 1993. "On the State, Democratization and Some Conceptual Problems: A Latin American View with Glances at Some Postcommunist Countries." *World Development* 21 (8): 1355–69.

———. 2003. "Democracia, Desarrollo Humano y Derechos Humanos." *In Democracia, Desarrollo Humano y Ciudadanía: Reflexiones sobre la Calidad de la Democracia en América Latina*, edited by G. O'Donnell, O. Iazzetta, and J. Vargas Cullel, 25–148. Rosario, Santa Fe, Argentina: Homo Sapiens.

OECD (Organisation for Economic Co-operation and Development). 2015. *States of Fragility 2015: Meeting Post-2015 Ambitions*. Paris: OECD Publishing.

Pennsylvania State University. Various years. Correlates of War Project (COW). State College, PA, http://www.correlatesofwar.org/.

Sen, Amartya K. 1999. *Development as Freedom*. Oxford, U.K.: Oxford University Press.

UCDP/PRIO (Uppsala Conflict Data Program/Peace Research Institute Oslo). 2015. Armed Conflict Dataset Version 4-2015 (1946–2014). Uppsala University, Sweden, http://www.pcr.uu.se/research/ucdp/datasets/ucdp_prio_armed_conflict_dataset/.

UNDP (United Nations Development Programme). 1994. *Human Development Report 1994: New Dimensions of Human Security*. New York: UNDP.

UNHCR (United Nations High Commission on Refugees). 2015. *UNHCR Global Trends: Forced Displacement in 2014: World at War*. Geneva: UNHCR.

Wallis, John. 2016. "Governance and Violence." Background paper, WDR 2017, World Bank, Washington, DC.

World Bank. 2011. *World Development Report 2011: Conflict, Security, and Development*. Washington, DC: World Bank.

———. 2015. *Global Monitoring Report 2014/2015: Ending Poverty and Sharing Prosperity*. Washington, DC: World Bank.

CHAPTER 2

Enhancing governance for development: Why policies fail

Amka and the Three Golden Rules (2014) is a beautifully crafted film about a Mongolian child, Amka, whose life turns into a nightmare after he finds a golden coin and hops onto a path of overspending, abandoning family duties and taking on unmanageable levels of indebtedness. Under pressure to repay his debts, he runs away, through the astounding Mongolian landscape, to settle with an eccentric uncle who teaches him the three golden rules of life.

The Mongolian newspaper *UB Post* noted in 2014 that "the story is in many ways a symbol of how Mongolia must decide its own fate" to manage its growing levels of debt.[1] Indeed, as the movie was being released, the country was undergoing a third attempt to establish the rainy-day Future Heritage Fund to manage its windfall from mining revenues (mining is the country's largest source of revenue). The attempt to transplant the design of a "future generations fund" from international best practices had already failed twice.

Experts from around the world had visited Mongolia over the previous decade, providing advice on the best existing rules for the distribution and management of revenues from natural resources. Technical solutions were available, and political will was palpable among several state actors. Yet, since 2007, attempts to establish rules for the use of mining revenues had been thwarted by political pressures. Hard-fought parliamentary elections prompted Mongolia's political parties to promise to increase spending on programs such as cash allowances, untargeted social benefits, and investments in specific regions in order to garner support. However, such promises could be fulfilled only by depleting the resources going into the

reserve fund (Chimeddorj 2015). Thus no matter how well policy makers designed the future generations fund, unless the interests of the powerful groups in society were to change, the *commitment* to a policy of fiscal prudence would continue to fail and the country would remain in debt. The process to reach and sustain agreements among decision makers on these policies had not created the conditions for people to be willing to *cooperate* and *coordinate* actions around specific long-term goals.

The parallels between Mongolia's state of affairs and the story portrayed in the movie were not a coincidence. The metaphor in Amka's tale was a deliberate attempt, supported by opinion leaders and artists, to create awareness in Mongolian society about the importance of prudence in the management of resources (in Amka's story, the golden coin). The movie was viewed as an instrument to reinforce people's values of prudential management of wealth in an effort to coordinate support for the pursuit of the long-term goal of fiscal sustainability in Mongolia.

As this example illustrates, policy making does not take place in a vacuum. It is the result of a bargaining process among actors, who frequently have diverse and even opposing preferences and interests. More important, the bargaining power of those actors differs, derived from a variety of sources such as the existing formal rules, informal norms, their ability to represent and mobilize other groups in society, or their control over resources. The complex process in which actors bargain over the design and implementation of policies, in a very specific social, historical, and economic context, is what in this Report is called *governance*.

> Policy making does not take place in a vacuum. It is the result of a bargaining process among actors, who frequently have diverse and even opposing preferences and interests.

Diverse pathways to success: Moving beyond institutional transplants

For decades, academics as well as practitioners have acknowledged the importance of *institutions*—organizations and rules—to development. Countries that are more secure, prosperous, and equitable tend to rank higher on the existing indicators that emphasize certain institutional forms. This pattern has created a perception that certain types of institutions unambiguously determine higher levels of development, and it has led many well-intentioned policy makers and development agencies to promote institutional reforms that aim at achieving those institutional standards—often referred to as *institutional transplants*. In other words, in acknowledging that governance matters for development, one implicitly accepts the fact that the effects of governance are determined by the characteristics of formal institutions.

However, institutional forms are not enough. Consider the challenge that Mongolia faced in following its own "golden rules." The Mongolian government decided to adopt international best practices to manage fiscal revenues from natural resource extraction, but it failed to administer them with a long-term perspective. Although the countercyclical management

of fiscal policy to manage volatility has been viewed as a key role of institutions seeking to promote long-term development, the form that those institutions took in Mongolia was not enough to affect outcomes (Gill and others 2014). Political constraints, pressures from interest groups, existing social opinions about the need to accelerate progress in specific areas, and historical inertia had eroded the credibility of the commitment to prudential management of mining resources.

Contrast Mongolia with those countries viewed as examples of effective management of natural resources such as Chile and the Netherlands. Chile and Mongolia have the same institutional forms for the allocation of revenues from the extractive industry—Mongolia followed the Chilean example—but very different outcomes. Fiscal spending in Mongolia is considerably more procyclical in spite of having the same rules (see figure 2.1, panel a). Meanwhile, Chile and the Netherlands have very different institutional forms, but they are similarly effective in managing resources (for Chile, see panel b). What do the Chilean and Netherlandic cases have in common? Many factors determine effectiveness, but certainly the fact that actors are willing to accept and follow the rules, or act collectively, is one of them. In Chile, political agreements since the return to democracy in the

Figure 2.1 Despite similar rules for the management of natural resource revenue in Chile and Mongolia, Chile's expenditure patterns reveal a stronger commitment to compliance

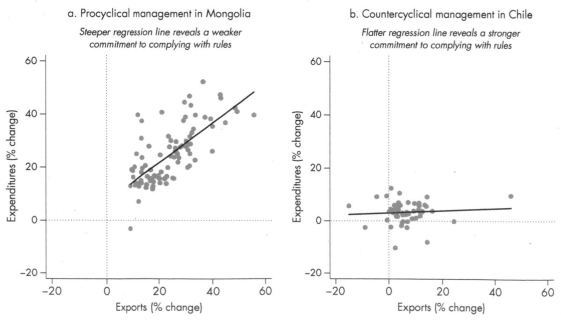

Sources: Mongolia: Mongolia Statistical Information Services, monthly data, 2005–15; Chile: World Bank, World Development Indicators (database), 1960–2014.

1990s have included a long-term perspective on economic management, a principle accepted by all actors in the political spectrum. In the Netherlands, the basic principles of fiscal management have been broadly accepted within the Netherlandic political culture for years, reinforced by the experience of living through a period of mismanagement and the so-called Dutch disease in the second half of the 20th century.[2]

Often, when policies and technical solutions fail to achieve the intended outcomes, blame falls on institutional failure, and the proposed solution is to "improve" institutions. But development can occur under a wide variety of institutional trajectories, as examples around the world and throughout history demonstrate. Thus it then becomes essential to uncover the underlying drivers of policy effectiveness. What makes some policies work while others fail? In addition to the type of institutions that matter, it is relevant to ask what those institutional forms are trying to achieve, or what *functions* they are meant to perform.

Drivers of effectiveness: Commitment, coordination, and cooperation

This Report identifies *commitment, coordination,* and *cooperation* as the three core functions of institutions that are needed to ensure that rules and resources yield the desired development outcomes. Policy effectiveness can be explained by whether and how well institutions are performing these functions. *Commitment* is about supporting consistent policies over time to ensure that promises are delivered. *Coordination* is about shaping expectations to enable complementary action. And *cooperation* is about limiting opportunistic behavior to prevent free-riding. Coordination and cooperation imply voluntary compliance—that is, the preferred social action is the one that individuals are actually willing to take. Box 2.1 discusses the ways in which commitment, coordination, and cooperation can be understood from the perspective of game

Box 2.1 The microfoundations of commitment, coordination, and cooperation: A perspective from game theory

The framework of this *World Development Report* (WDR) highlights commitment, coordination, and cooperation as the key institutional functions that shape the effectiveness of policies for development. Those terms come from game theory and are better explained using its language.[a] Table B2.1.1 presents an example.

The table can be read in the following way. The top left gray cell symbolizes the net benefits (*payoffs*) for actors when both of them decide to take action A such as mobilize, pass a law, or monitor a provider. The first number (2) is the *payoff* of actor 1 when that actor decides to take action A and actor 2 does the same. The second number (2) is actor 2's payoff when that actor decides to take

action A when actor 1 does as well. In the top right gray cell, the first number (0) is actor 1's payoff when that actor decides to take action A, but actor 2 decides against it. The second number (*x*) is actor 2's payoff when that actor decides not to take action A, but actor 1 decides to take it. The actors' payoff values can be read in the other scenarios in the same way. According to the matrix of payoffs, the value of *x* will determine whether the game is a coordination or a cooperation one. Both are *collective action problems*.

Coordination

If *x* < 2, the actors are engaged in a *coordination game*. In this game, the actors' incentives are aligned, but their

Table B2.1.1 Coordination and cooperation as modeled in game theory

		Actor 2	
		Take action A (A)	Do not take action A (NA)
Actor 1	Take action A (A)	2, 2 (A, A)	0, x (A, NA)
	Do not take action A (NA)	x, 0 (NA, A)	1, 1 (NA, NA)

(Box continues next page)

actions depend on their expectations about what the other will do. Both of them prefer to take the same action; both outcomes—(A, A) and (NA, NA)—are *equilibria* of this game. The problem is how to achieve the equilibrium that is efficient and yields the highest payoff (A, A) because each actor is unsure about what the other one will do. In game theory, this game is known as the *assurance game*, where it is in each actor's own interest to take a particular action (Y) if there is assurance that everyone else is also taking action Y. To achieve coordination, policies need to create common knowledge that everyone will take the desirable action. Sometimes, this requires providing incentives for some actors to take the desirable action first so others will follow.

Cooperation

If x > 2, the actors are engaged in a *cooperation game*. In this game, actors' incentives are not aligned. In equilibrium, both of them do not take action A—(NA, NA)—which is the worst outcome from the point of view of maximizing

the group payoff. In game theory, this is referred to as a *prisoner's dilemma game*, where the collective gain would be greater if the actors could cooperate, but each actor individually has a greater incentive to *free-ride* (take action NA). To induce cooperation, policies would have to put forth a credible mechanism of reward or penalty conditioned on players' actions in order to prompt actions yielding the jointly preferred outcome.

Commitment

Commitment refers to the ability of actors to enforce agreements. For example, if the actors were allowed to communicate with one another, they would have incentives to promise to take the action that maximizes the group's payoff. However, because there are no mechanisms to enforce those agreements (*commitment devices*), it is still in the interest of the actors to renege on their promises. Commitment devices allow actors to transform the game so that their incentives are aligned.

Source: WDR 2017 team.

a. Example adapted from Weber (2008) and reprinted in Bartolini (2013).

theory. Although policy makers may not think in terms of game theory, they play these games every day, and the models lend precision and objectivity to understanding their actions.

Commitment: Backing consistent policies over time to ensure promises are delivered

Policies are not spot transactions such as buying a book or using a taxi; they require consistency over time. However, reaching and sustaining agreements can be difficult because economic and political conditions may change, and the incentives for policy makers to deviate from established goal-oriented policies can be strong. To promote sustained development, it is particularly important to ensure that those in power can credibly deliver on promises made to citizens beyond the political cycle. Imagine that a worker would like to save for retirement by contributing funds to a pension. If that worker does not believe the government can credibly commit to not expropriating those funds and returning them in the future, he or she will likely choose not to save. In line with the economic theory of incomplete contracts,

policies must include commitment devices to ensure their credibility. Commitment devices help ensure the credibility of policies over time, even in the face of changing circumstances. In this sense, institutions can be thought of as technologies that allow society and individuals to engage in the pursuit of long-term goals, even in the face of changing circumstances.

In all countries, but mainly in low-income or fragile contexts, commitment is a fundamental condition to prevent the escalation of conflict to violence. Whether conflicting parties are able to reach credible agreements to renounce violence and endow the state with a monopoly on the legitimate use of violence is a crucial condition to prevent escalation (see chapter 4). When commitment to deals is not credible, contending sides tend to walk away from the bargaining table and violence prevails: warring factions may renege on peace agreements, policy makers may default on promises to transfer resources to discontented groups or regions, disputants may fail to abide by court judgments, or police officers may abuse citizens instead of protecting them. The influence of commitment is not exclusive to security. Economic growth requires an environment in which firms and individuals feel secure in investing their resources in productive activities. Credible commitment to pro-growth policies and property rights is, in this way, also essential to ensure macroeconomic stability and to enable growth.

People's perception of the credibility of com-mitments can also increase their willingness to cooperate—say, through tax compliance—and to coordinate, following rules in response to the belief that others will follow as well. Theoretically, deliver-ing on commitments builds trust in institutions over time and strengthens voluntary compliance (box 2.2). Empirical results from lab experiments carried out for this Report are consistent with this notion, whereby binding commitments lead to greater cooperation and more redistribution of resources among players (Banuri and others 2016)—see box 2.2.

Box 2.2 Trust in institutions stems from delivering on commitments

Trust is a central aspect of strengthening governance and delivering on development. Trust is related to positive out-comes in terms of economic growth,[a] as well as government performance (Putnam 1993; La Porta and others 1997). But what exactly is trust, where does it come from, and why does it matter? This Report defines *trust* as the probability that an actor assigns to other actors of delivering on their commitment, conditional on their past behavior. In the game theory literature, this is known as reputation. The literature distinguishes between two key kinds of trust: interpersonal trust and institutional trust.

Interpersonal trust refers to trust among individuals. It can arise from their relationships such as shared ties, or it can be present as a social norm (table B2.2.1). The notions of bonding social capital and bridging social capital are relevant to interpersonal trust (Putnam 2000). *Bonding social capital*—the horizontal ties within communities and among organizations—can bring about a sense of purpose and identity, encouraging social cohesion. *Bridging social capital* consists of the cross-cutting ties that breach social divides, such as economic class, ethnicity, and religion. If the bridging of social capital is missing, it can lead to bal-kanized societies in which strong ties within communities actually work against the collective interest, holding back development (Portes and Landolt 1996).

Institutional trust refers to society's trust in orga-nizations, rules, and the mechanisms to enforce them. Institutional trust can arise from elements based on rela-tionships, or it can be a function of repeated commitment (table B2.2.1). This Report focuses on institutional trust, built by repeatedly delivering on commitments, such as by enforcing contracts or not defaulting on pledges and obligations. This type of trust is important because it strengthens the capacity to commit (outcome legitimacy), and ultimately it enables cooperation and coordination by inducing voluntary compliance (box 2.9).

The importance of trust for enabling collective action can be illustrated in the context of game theory. In the traditional prisoner's dilemma game, even though it would be in the best interest of both prisoners to cooperate—refusing to confess—the inability to trust that the other party will indeed cooperate means that the outcome for purely rational prisoners is to defect, betraying each other (in a one-off game). Game theory predicts that cooperation comes into play in repeated games. Axelrod (1984) finds that the most successful strategies in the basic prisoner's dilemma game are related to mutual trust, engendered from paying support with support and defection with defection. This finding is supported by a lab game played for this Report (figure B2.2.1).

Table B2.2.1 Sources of trust

	Type of trust	
	Institutional trust	Interpersonal trust
Source of trust	Relationships	Relationships
	Commitment	Norms

Source: WDR 2017 team, based on Lach and López-Calva 2016.

(Box continues next page)

Figure B2.2.1 Welfare is higher for citizens under commitment in the lab game

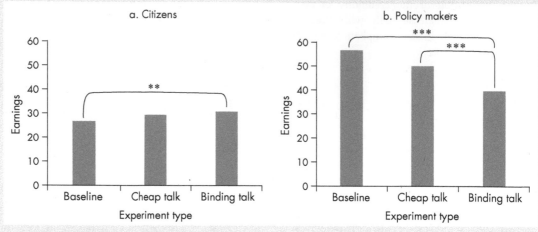

Source: Banuri and others 2016.

Note: In preparation for the *World Development Report 2017*, a series of lab experiments was carried out to explore the behavioral responses of agents in terms of cooperation and redistribution under different protocols. In the basic lab game are three citizens and one policy maker. The citizens provide resources for a group account, which the policy maker is in charge of distributing. The policy maker observes the total amount in the group account and can then distribute the resources in any manner he or she sees fit. The game is repeated over 20 periods. In the "cheap talk" treatment, the policy maker makes public the intended distribution rule prior to citizens' contributions, but the rule is not binding and can be modified after citizens make their contributions. In the "binding talk" treatment, the policy maker again makes public the distribution rule prior to citizens' contributions, but in this case the policy maker cannot amend the rule after citizens make their contributions. In this second case, there is a credible commitment because the public announcement is binding.

Significance levels: ** = significantly higher earnings of citizens in binding talk compared with baseline ($p < .05$), but not compared with cheap talk (and cheap talk is not different from the baseline). *** = significantly lower earnings of policy makers in binding talk ($p < .01$) relative to both the baseline and cheap talk ($p < .01$). Cheap talk is not significantly different from the baseline ($p = .133$).

Source: WDR 2017 team.

a. Knack and Keefer (1997); Whiteley (2000); Zak and Knack (2001).

Coordination: Shaping expectations to enable complementary action

What makes people choose to coordinate to reach socially preferred outcomes? The answer to this question is at the heart of understanding development progress. As Douglass North contends, "The disparity in the performance of economies and the persistence of disparate economies through time have not been satisfactorily explained by development economists. . . . What has been missing is an understanding of the nature of human coordination and cooperation" (North 1990a, 11). By shaping beliefs[3] and coordinating expectations, institutions can push societies on favorable paths toward better development outcomes. When actors are uncertain about what others will do, they may not make decisions that could induce socially preferred outcomes. By contrast, in the presence of strategic complementarities, coordinated actions can lead to better outcomes for all. Since the classic work on the problems of industrialization in Eastern Europe by Rosenstein-Rodan (1943) and the idea of the "big push" formalized by Murphy, Shleifer, and Vishny (1989), coordination has been viewed as a central issue in both the economic and noneconomic realms.

Particularly in middle-income countries, coordination is required to induce investment and innovation. Both depend on firms and individuals believing that others will also invest. Institutions can help solve market failures by coordinating investment decisions and the expectations of market participants. Indeed, the insight that a failure to coordinate investment activity can lead to underdevelopment is decades old.[4] Consider the case in which large-scale factories are more efficient, but investing in them is not profitable for individual firms unless carried out as a group. Perhaps the market size is too small to justify large-scale investments, unless all industries expand together, providing markets for one another. In such a situation, there are two possible outcomes, or equilibria. The first is one in which no firms invest in large-scale factories, and efficiency levels stay low. The second, better outcome is one in which firms are able to coordinate a simultaneous move to large-scale, efficient production.

Such problems of coordination can occur in many contexts, ranging from finance and adoption of technology to innovation and industrial clusters.[5] Consider a country that wants to invest in green technologies such as electric cars to improve the environmental sustainability of its growth process. Such an initiative would require the complementary investment of car manufacturers, battery producers, electricity providers, and city planners. If each actor is unsure of the willingness of the others to invest, the electric cars may never be produced. However, if institutions are able to reduce that uncertainty by creating common knowledge that other firms will also invest, or by providing incentives to first movers, they can help coordinate investment across firms and push the adoption of greener technologies (World Bank 2012). Infant industry protection and other industrial policies are ways—not always effective—in which governments have provided these types of incentives to avoid being trapped in a situation in which everyone waits for others to invest first.[6] The kinds of instruments policy makers have to coordinate expectations and lead societies to socially preferred outcomes will very much depend on the kinds of complementarities involved.

Cooperation: Limiting opportunistic behavior to prevent free-riding

Another basic type of collective action problem that institutions solve is cooperation, or reducing opportunistic behavior. By limiting free-riding, institutions can help build more cohesive societies and turn zero-sum games with no winners into positive-sum games in which all parties gain (win-wins)—see Ostrom (1990). Cooperation problems are often observed in the provision of public goods (such as collecting taxes to fund public schools or hospitals) or solving environmental concerns related to the overuse of a common resource pool (such as overexploitation of natural resources). Perhaps the most well-known example of a cooperation problem is the tragedy of the commons (Hardin 1968). In this example, all herdsmen can graze their animals in open grassland—the "commons"—without restrictions. As more and more cattle graze

in the grassland, the grass increasingly fails to grow back fast enough, ultimately depleting it until it is of no use to anyone. The notion is that rational individuals acting independently, according to their own self-interest, will deplete a shared resource, even if it is contrary to the best interest of the group. This type of problem is common in situations in which agents immediately benefit from their actions and do not experience the losses from the impacts of their actions until later. A key notion behind cooperation problems, which differentiates them from coordination problems, is that the preferable action from a social point of view is not necessarily an equilibrium. In coordination problems, multiple equilibria exist, and policy is a matter of helping make the jump to the optimal one. Solving cooperation problems, by contrast, typically requires credible rewards or penalties to prompt actions that lead to the jointly preferred outcome.

In all countries, but particularly those that have achieved higher levels of prosperity, the degree to which prosperity is shared requires cooperation, particularly citizens' willingness to contribute to public goods and not free-ride on others. The extent to which societies can ensure opportunities for all individuals relies on their ability to provide high-quality services, such as health, education, or connectivity, and to ensure access to economic opportunities, especially access to markets that allow individuals to use the assets acquired. Collecting the taxes needed to fund investments in public goods depends on individuals' willingness to cooperate. Lack of cooperation is a typical cause of segregated outcomes: for example, differential treatment of different ethnic groups. One group may not be willing to contribute to the provision of public goods if a different group will benefit. Willingness will emerge, however, if the commitment to the provision of public goods is credible—regardless of which group is in control of the resources. Such a credible commitment can be achieved by, for example, constraining the power of those to whom authority is delegated or sharing power in decision-making bodies.

Sometimes, societies face a breakdown of cooperation, and people opt out or exit, failing to comply with the rules or to contribute to the provision of public goods (Hirschman 1970). Cooperation becomes more difficult to achieve as the number of people involved increases if there is less information on and greater uncertainty about others and when the interaction is finite. Inequality may also matter for sustaining cooperation. In theory, the relationship between wealth inequality and the successful provision of a common resource pool can be ambiguous. Consider a society in which there is high wealth inequality. On the one hand, a few dominant members of that society may reap enough benefits from having a public good that they have incentives to provide and maintain it independently, even if other less wealthy individuals free-ride on it (Olson 1965). On the other hand, some individuals with better outside options (often the rich) may not want to contribute to the provision of the public good. Thus there may be higher costs for enforcing cooperation, thereby nurturing distrust that the other(s) will pay and undermining cooperative behavior.[7] For example, Brazil, where citizens organized to demand higher-quality public services, faced a problem common to many other countries: the fragmentation of the social contract. In these cases, the upper-middle class responds to the low quality of service provision by demanding private services, which in turn weakens its willingness to cooperate fiscally and contribute to the provision of public goods—a perverse cycle (Ferreira and others 2013).

Although *commitment*, *coordination*, and *cooperation* make up core institutional functions that contribute to the effectiveness of policies to achieve development outcomes, these functions are fulfilled effectively under only certain conditions.

Policy effectiveness in the presence of power asymmetries

As just described, in this Report effective policies are those that perform three key functions to improve development: enabling credible *commitment*, inducing *coordination*, and enhancing *cooperation*. But why are policies so often ineffective at doing so? The failure of policies that are good on paper to perform their intended function and the persistence of bad ones are often not the result of policy makers' lack of resources, will, or knowledge. Consider a society run by a benevolent social planner who cares about security, growth, and equity. The planner will choose policies that maximize these three objectives. However, as soon as that society deviates—as they do in real life—from the ideals of this monolithic planner, failures to commit, coordinate, and cooperate might take it far from the social optimum. Where such a society will end up will depend on the depth of these failures.

One of the key—though not the sole—contributing factors to determining policies and the resulting equilibria is the unequal distribution of power in society. This Report refers to such a distribution as a *power asymmetry*. Because policy effectiveness depends not only on *what* policies are chosen but also on *how* they are chosen and implemented, the relative degree of bargaining power of different actors may condition the kind of commitment, coordination, and cooperation that results (box 2.3).

Inside the policy arena: Policy bargaining and the distribution of power

The processes of policy making and policy implementation entail a bargaining process among different actors. The *policy arena* can be thought of as the setting in which (policy) decisions are made; different groups and actors interact and bargain over aspects of the public space; and the resulting agreements eventually lead to changes in the formal rules (law). It is the setting in which governance manifests itself.[8] Policy arenas exist at the local, national, and international levels. They can be formal (parliaments, courts, intergovernmental organizations, government agencies), traditional, or informal (backroom deals, old boys' networks). Policy arenas are issue-specific. For example, the policy arena for defense policy may not be the same as that for health or infrastructure policy.

Who bargains in this policy arena and how successfully they bargain are determined by the relative *power* of the actors. Power is expressed in the policy arena as the ability of groups and individuals to make others act in their interest and to bring about specific outcomes. It is the "production of intended effects" (Russell 1938). Actors can exercise their power by setting the agenda, by vetoing specific options, or by influencing other actors' preferences. Agenda-setting power refers to actors' abilities to influence the alternatives from which decision makers choose (Persson and Tabellini 2000). Veto power, by contrast, refers to the abilities of actors to block a change from the status quo (Tsebelis 2002). In all cases, it is about restricting the effective choices of other actors.[9]

The policy arena is shaped by both de jure and de facto power. *De jure power* refers to power that is conferred on the actors by the formal rules. For example, what the electoral rules are, whether there is a presidential or a parliamentary system, whether there is an independent judiciary, or whether the central bank is autonomous—all are formal rules that confer de jure power on different actors. *De facto power* refers to the actual power to influence other actors. It has many sources, including control over resources, control over coercive instruments, ideational persuasion, or the capacity to mobilize. Often, the formal de jure rules that confer power on actors in the policy arena do not necessarily translate into de facto power relations (box 2.4).

Who bargains in this policy arena and how successfully they bargain are determined by the relative *power* of the actors.

Box 2.3 Game theory and the roots of political power

It has long been recognized that power is an important determinant of how a society functions and how the gains of economic activity are shared within and across nations. The early writings on power were imprecise as social scientists grappled for ways to express these embryonic ideas (Dahl 1957). But such imprecision began to wane with the rise of game theory. Social scientists are now able to formalize some of these difficult concepts and, in particular, the idea that, in the end, power depends on the beliefs and mores of ordinary people. Václav Havel expressed this notion beautifully in a paper smuggled out of the prison where he was locked up for dissenting against Czechoslovakia's post-totalitarian state in the early 1980s. He argued that, in modern dictatorships, it is not always easy to separate the perpetrators from the victims. In his aptly titled essay "The Power of the Powerless" he argued that many of the oppressed are complicit in propping up the power of such regimes (Havel 1991).

This idea can be formally expressed with game theory. Consider a society with one dictator, D, and two citizens, 1 and 2. These two citizens are expected to provide some beck-and-call service and display their loyalty to D. Expressing this loyalty costs each citizen 5. The loyalty of both to D is what gives D power.

But why will people show loyalty to a dictator when it comes at a high cost? The answer lies in the nature of interaction among the citizens themselves. This can be captured by assuming that citizens can be cooperative (C) or noncooperative (N). The payoffs from such behavior are described in table B2.3.1.

This game, labeled the *assurance game* by Sen (1967), is often also called the *coordination game* (see box 2.1). Keep in mind that the assurance game has two equilibria—both players choosing C and both players choosing N.

Table B2.3.1 Payoffs to cooperation or noncooperation

	N	C
N	10, 10 (N, N)	5, 0 (N, C)
C	0, 5 (C, N)	20, 20 (C, C)

Source: Kaushik Basu.

Note: C = cooperation; N = noncooperation.

In the full game, each citizen first decides whether to display loyalty to the dictator before interacting among themselves. Suppose it is a common belief that if citizens are not loyal to the dictator, others will not cooperate with them. It is now entirely possible to become locked into a societal equilibrium in which everybody displays loyalty to the dictator and plays cooperatively among themselves. Their net return or payoff is 15—that is, 20 from the assurance game and –5 from loyalty (or obsequiousness) to the dictator, which props up the dictator's power.

All citizens would prefer not to be loyal to D, but they fear that, if they dissent, others will not cooperate with them. It is this "triadic interaction" that props up power (Basu 2000). The behavior just described is a Nash equilibrium—but it is actually more than that. It is what in game theory is called a "subgame perfect equilibrium," which is a Nash equilibrium supported by credible threats. Dictators may not know what a subgame perfect equilibrium is, but they do know how to create an atmosphere of mutual fear that props up the regime.

This example illustrates how power can be modeled without bringing any extraneous assumptions into the analysis. A pure economic analysis can lead to manifestations of power through the interplay of beliefs. But if one goes a step further and brings behavioral economics—in particular, the idea of "stigma"—into the analysis, many other phenomena can be modeled, from political mass movements to child labor (López-Calva 2003).

This analysis is closely related to the concept of the "social contract," which goes back to ancient Greek thinkers. Underlying all stable societies is some form of social contract, which enables individuals to anticipate the behavior of others. The analysis just described can yield insights into societal uprisings, such as those in the Arab world in 2010–11, which can be viewed as shifts in societal equilibria (Devarajan and Mottaghi 2015).

The analysis is a warning that, because these manifestations of power arise from the beliefs and behavior of ordinary people, all societies, even democracies, run the risk of having to confront them. The McCarthy era in the early 1950s in the United States and the Emergency in India (1975–77) are illustrations.

Source: Prepared by Kaushik Basu for WDR 2017.

Box 2.4 Who is who in the policy arena: The case of Bolivia's social policy

The divergence between the formal rules and the actual practice of formulating and implementing social policy is clearly illustrated by the process of making social policy in Bolivia. Officially, ministries are designated as the policy initiators in Bolivia because ideas and information flow from them to CONAPES (National Council for Economic and Social Policy), to the Council of Ministers, and to the president (figure B2.4.1, panel a). However, studies of the actual process of social policy making in the country, based on social network analysis, reveal a strikingly different picture (panel b). In the actual policy-making network, coordination is vertically exercised by the president, ministries interact very little, and grassroots organizations are key actors in the policy arena. Ideas and information for policy formulation flow not from the ministries to the Council of Ministers and the president, but from the grassroots organizations that constitute the electoral bases of the government party to the president, and only then to

the ministries and their deputies. In the figure, the size of each circle represents the importance of the actor in the policy-making process.

The policy-making dynamics uncovered by this social network analysis reveal two main factors that significantly shape the features of social policies. The first factor is that social policy-making units are technically weak: they are typically staffed not by specialists but by political supporters who are subject to frequent turnover and do not necessarily possess the adequate skills. For example, the average tenure of the interviewees in the Bolivian study was 14 months, and 22 percent of them had no prior experience in any social policy-making capacity. The second factor is that the actors do not have incentives to coordinate and cooperate with one another. Rather, they compete to influence policy making, often hindering the coherence and coordination of policy design as well as the quality of implementation.

Figure B2.4.1 Formal and actual policy networks in Bolivia, 2010

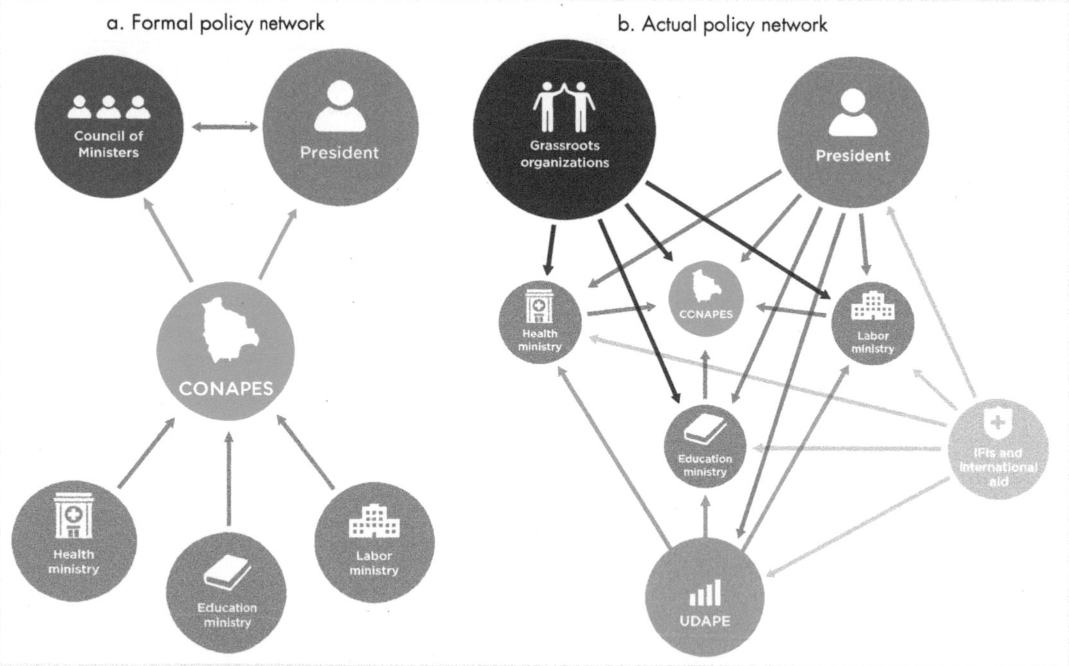

a. Formal policy network

b. Actual policy network

Source: WDR 2017 team, based on Bonvecchi 2016.

Note: CONAPES = National Council for Economic and Social Policy; UDAPE = Analytical Unit for Social and Economic Policies; "grassroots organizations" refers to Unified Central Union of Peasant Workers of Bolivia (CSUTCB), National Coordination for Change (CONALCAM), and Movement toward Socialism (MAS); "IFIs [international financial institutions] and international aid" refers to Latin American Development Bank (CAF), World Bank, Inter-American Development Bank (IDB), United Nations Children's Fund (UNICEF), and cooperation agencies from several industrialized countries.

Source: WDR 2017 team, based on Bonvecchi, Johannsen, and Scartascini (2015). See also Bonvecchi (2016).

Actors in the policy arena can be grouped into elites and citizens according to their relative degree of influence. This Report defines *elites* in a positive (as opposed to a normative) sense in that what distinguishes them from *citizens* is their ability to directly influence the design and implementation of a certain policy.[10] Thus elites are not necessarily bad or self-interested, and citizens are not necessarily good and public-spirited. Both groups act as people do in other spheres of life: understanding their motivations is important to anticipating their conduct.[11] The classification of elites and citizens is not intended to be a strict dichotomy, but rather a spectrum in which different actors have different degrees of influence.[12] The relative degree of power of actors to influence policy design or policy implementation may vary by issue. For example, although large export firms in some societies may have the power to influence trade policy and thus are an elite in this area, they may not be an elite in the areas of security or health policy.

When power gets in the way: Exclusion, capture, and clientelism

The distribution of power in the policy arena can be a fundamental enabler of—or constraint to—policy effectiveness. Unequal distributions of power in society (power asymmetries) are not necessarily harmful, and they can actually be a means of achieving effectiveness—for example, through delegated authority. However, in the presence of *transaction costs* to reach political agreements, it becomes increasingly difficult to mediate power asymmetries effectively (box 2.5).[13] If powerful actors fear that the outcome may reduce their relative power now or in the future, they may attempt to block the adoption or undermine the implementation of policies that could enhance welfare.[14] This tendency has especially significant implications for households at the bottom of the income distribution and other marginalized groups because their bargaining power tends to be more limited. Power asymmetries, in these cases, can lead to harmful consequences for society. Some common manifestations—though not the only ones—of how power asymmetries can negatively impact policy effectiveness are exclusion, capture, and clientelism.

The *exclusion* of individuals and groups from the policy arena can have particularly important implications for security outcomes (see discussion in chapter 4). When powerful actors are excluded from the policy arena, violence may become the preferred—and rational—way for certain individuals and groups to pursue their interests, thereby leading to failed bargains between participants in the policy arena. In these

instances, actors use informal mechanisms to sustain short-term transactions among themselves, but they are unable to achieve long-lasting agreements. Policies in these cases will tend not to be consistent or coherent over time, but rather to reflect which group has more power at a given moment, deeply undermining the institutional function of commitment.

Countries in which violent conflict is ongoing and groups are fighting for control over territory, such as in South Sudan, are a compelling illustration of why power gets in the way of the commitment needed to sustain mutually beneficial agreements. The outlook for the groups involved in such violent conflict is far from favorable. At best, they are looking at a costly victory, only to inherit a shattered economy. An agreement to put a stop to such violent conflict, encourage productive investment, and share its benefits in proportion to the power that each group currently holds is mutually desirable. So why are such agreements rarely reached? The reason is a commitment difficulty known as the *political hold-up problem*. Consider a situation in which the violent groups in control of different territories agree to allow those with business skills to make efficient investments in their territories in exchange for a "fee." Such an agreement could maximize the size of the benefits while redistributing them in proportion to the strength of these violent groups. But for this policy to be credible to potential investors, the violent groups would need to give up some power and establish, among other things, a system of impartial courts.[15] But the fear of not receiving a return to their "investment" makes it hard for violent groups to give up power.

A second manifestation of power asymmetries, the ability of influential groups to *capture* policies and make them serve their narrow interests, is helpful for understanding the effectiveness (or ineffectiveness) of policies in promoting long-term growth. For example, if a powerful interest group derives its power from being the most productive firm, it will advocate policies that allow it to continue to be productive and reach new markets. On the other hand, if those groups with power have the coercive capacity to cause economic and social disruption and are in the least productive sector of the economy, they will advocate policies that protect their economic power and block competition. The effects of capture can be widespread and detrimental to the well-being of society (see discussion in chapter 5).

Consider the case of regulatory capture in the building sector, which can undermine the implementation of safety standards and risk-sensitive construction. This is illustrated by the situation in Turkey after

Some common manifestations—though not the only ones—of how power asymmetries can negatively impact policy effectiveness are exclusion, capture, and clientelism.

Box 2.5 Transaction costs, incomplete contracts, and political agreements: Why land redistribution policies often fail

Land distribution schemes have been tried—and have failed—repeatedly around the world. Why? Consider the case of Surekha, a farmer who owns a large plot of land and must decide whether to lease it to smaller farmers or buy the necessary equipment and hire employees so she can farm the land herself. If the economies of scale are not significant and there are no transaction costs,[a] Surekha would be better off dividing the land and leasing it to famers, who would be willing to pay more than she would earn if she farmed it by herself because they would be more productive. This is a classic problem in economics. In the absence of transaction costs, the initial allocation of property rights should have no effect on the efficient operation of an economy (Coase 1960).

However, in the real world transaction costs abound as institutions do not always allow parties to effectively commit, coordinate, and cooperate. Because transaction costs exist—and because individuals have a limited cognitive capacity to process every possible contingency (bounded rationality)—contracts will always be incomplete. When there is room for interpretation—and renegotiation—of a contract, the nature of the relationship between the parties changes because they need to cooperate over time to enforce the contract. The process of bargaining, then, never really ends because parties to a contract will be continually adjusting their actions in response to changing circumstances (Epstein and O'Halloran 1999).

In the presence of high transaction costs, Surekha would rather hire labor and buy her own equipment to farm the

land.[b] Not only will owning the land increase Surekha's control over contingencies, but it may also give her special social status or political power to control other transactions (Bardhan 2005). For example, Surekha could threaten her employees—and if they do not accept her conditions, she will influence the village merchants not to trade with them (Basu 1986).

Suppose a local leader in Surekha's country proposes to redistribute landholdings—including compensating current landowners for the value of the land—to increase the overall productivity of the economy. Why has this type of policy failed so often and in so many places? It is because in the presence of transaction costs and incomplete contracts, the economic and political value of the land for Surekha is higher than the fair compensation. Surekha's bargaining power would be reduced if land were redistributed. As a result, she will have an incentive to block or undermine the policy.

Like economic agreements, political agreements are not independent of the distribution of power and are the result of a bargaining process among a wide set of actors. For example, state institutions emerged in history not as a voluntary contract between society members (such as producers willing to pay taxes in exchange for protection from the local bandits), but rather because some groups imposed their coercive power on others (see chapter 4). As a result, institutions and the outcomes of the bargains within those institutions reflect the power structure in a given society.[c]

Source: WDR 2017 team.

a. A world void of transaction costs is one in which there are no costs to specify, monitor, or enforce contracts between the parties (Dixit 1996). Thus the owner and the renters can foresee all possible contingencies, such as the probability of a drought or a war. It also means that a third party can observe and verify that both parties are honoring the contract and can act to enforce it in a dispute.

b. When transaction costs are high, Surekha would rather do the work herself, buying the machinery and hiring employees because ownership of the assets gives her more bargaining power over her employees when disputes arise than if she just leases the land (Hart and Moore 1990).

c. See Carneiro (1970); Tilly (1985); Boix (2015); and De la Sierra (2015). See also Boix (2016).

the 1999 Kocaeli earthquake, when the government was unable to implement a number of innovative building control regulations because of the strong influence exerted by powerful interest groups. The new regulations would have introduced higher standards for building controls, including higher qualification requirements for building designers, certified private construction supervision of building design and code compliance, and mandatory 10-year professional liability insurance for building designers. However, implementation was undermined by the strong opposition of the building and real estate industries, which believed that the new requirements could

disadvantage current professionals and translate into higher marginal costs for new construction.

A third manifestation of power asymmetries is *clientelism*, the exchange of goods and services for political support. Clientelism can shape the adoption and implementation of policies in two main ways. First, in clientelistic settings commitment to long-term objectives is hamstrung by the lack of accountability of those to whom authority is delegated (see discussion in chapter 6). Accountability is gradually put up for sale. In addition, when commitment breaks down systematically, it can erode people's incentives to cooperate, and some groups may opt out by demanding private services and avoiding contributions to the provision of public goods (Ferreira and others 2013). In clientelistic settings, states tend to have low tax revenues and provide few public goods, undermining economic activity and future taxation.

Best practice or best fit? Reconsidering the notion of "first-best" through the bargaining lens

Efforts to strengthen the ability of institutions to effectively enable commitment, coordination, and cooperation, viewed from the perspective of power asymmetries, call into question many traditional practices of the development community.

That community has largely focused its reform attempts on designing best-practice solutions and building state capacity to implement them. In this sense, capacity is often considered a prerequisite for

policy effectiveness.[16] Capacity is certainly important at a given point in time and can explain differences in performance across countries (Fukuyama 2014), but it does interact with—and can be explained by—power. At a given point in time, capacity can be thought of as a stock. Although in many cases capacity is an overriding constraint, it is also a proximate cause because it is an outcome of a bargaining process in which actors decide how and where to invest (or not) in building such capacity. Even in the presence of existing physical and administrative capacity, policies may still be ineffective if groups with enough bargaining power have no incentives to pursue implementation. An example is the low investment in statistical capacity in Africa that limits the ability to monitor policy effectiveness (box 2.6, case 1). Furthermore, prevailing norms, understood as socially accepted rules of behavior, can reinforce existing power asymmetries

---

Box 2.6 How capacity and norms influence and are influenced by power asymmetries

Case 1. The need to strengthen incentives to gather development data

For years, the development community has invested heavily—in both economic resources and technical expertise—in developing statistical capacity in Africa, but the results have been disappointing (Devarajan 2013). Many countries in the region still lack the data to monitor socioeconomic conditions such as poverty, inequality, and service delivery. As a result, demands are growing for more money and more capacity building to solve this problem. This view, however, neglects the fact that for countries to develop statistical capacity, they must muster the political incentives to do so.

In many countries, political incentives push those in power to avoid investing in capacity or to actively undermine capacity. Some elites in African countries consider high-quality data systems a tool that the opposition could use to audit their performance. Thus these elites have incentives to establish either weak statistical offices or partisan ones, staffed with political supporters rather than with technical experts (Beegle and others 2016; Hoogeveen and Nguyen 2016). But, of course, this practice is not unique to Africa. The argument for the use of existing capacity is as valid as the argument for building such capacity. In Latin America, a region well known for its capacity for data collection, there are examples where the political dynamics led to a weakening of the credibility of official statistics.[a]

Case 2. The reinforcement of existing power asymmetries through norms

Sometimes, norms reinforce existing power asymmetries—and they can constrain the effectiveness of interventions. For example, in Ghana's small-scale fisheries, men (*Fish Papas*) and women (*Fish Mamas*) have historically had different roles in fishing. Because women are not allowed to fish at sea—a norm that has been in place for over 200 years and is respected to this day—men fish while women smoke, dry, and cook the fish for sale. *Fish Mamas* traditionally buy the fish directly from the men and exercise control over the local market by setting prices and selling the day's catch (Overå 1993).

A well-intentioned project by the government of Ghana supported by the World Bank attempted to improve women's livelihoods by making the harvesting and processing of fish more sanitary and efficient. In particular, they built a facility where all fish can be processed and sold. However, by pooling the catch in one place and making it easier to process the fish, the project undermined the *Fish Mamas'* power to set the prices because it made it easier for men to do both the fishing and selling of the catch. As a result, men began selling the fish themselves, thereby reducing women's engagement in fisheries management. This project, which aimed at improving women's role in the value chain, ended up undermining their livelihood (World Bank 2015).

Source: WDR 2017 team.

a. *Economist* (2012); Noriega (2012); Roitberg and Nagasawa (2016).

and further undermine the effectiveness of capacity-building interventions (box 2.6, case 2).

In the presence of powerful actors who can block or otherwise undermine a policy, optimal policies from a strictly economic standpoint (first-best policies) may not be the optimal implementable policies (second-best but feasible policies). Consider the case of Kenya's recent education reform. Based on rigorous evidence on best practices (Duflo, Dupas, and Kremer 2015), the government introduced a new policy in 2009 to allow 18,000 contract teachers to be hired. It was thought that contract teachers, as opposed to civil servant teachers, would have greater incentives to perform well because they were on short-term contracts that, in principle, would be renewed only if their performance was satisfactory. Yet, experimental evidence from 64 government-run schools showed that learning outcomes did not improve (Bold and others 2015).

A central explanation for why the policy failed is that despite the introduction of short-term contracts, there was no credible commitment in practice to sanction underperforming teachers. Once the newly contracted teachers were in place, leaders of the teachers' union successfully mobilized to convert those new teachers into civil servants under permanent contracts, thereby undermining the reform. The children attending those schools and their families—who had little say and found it more difficult to organize and demand better service—were left with the same low-quality education. In the end, the government spent scarce budget resources on a policy that did not improve learning outcomes. Therefore, as this example illustrates, the best technical solution was not necessarily the best-fit solution to enact change in view of the distribution of power in the policy arena.

Even when feasible, implementing what seem to be first-best economic policies from a static perspective can lead to worse outcomes for society because they affect the dynamics of power. For example, when governments are captured by firms and there is high inequality, unions may be the only way for workers to solve their collective action problem, even if representation is not perfect. If so, passing a law that makes labor contracts more flexible undermines union memberships and may lead to more inequality, which in turn can perpetuate the power of the wealthy (Acemoglu and Robinson 2013).

The nature of the policy arena is crucial to gauging whether actors will be able to reach and sustain agreements to enact welfare-enhancing policies. The actions that a proposed reform will trigger in other players in the arena are particularly important. This process of how reforms take place (which is embedded in the framework) is discussed in box 2.7 from the perspective of game theory. The discussion highlights how, even though reform involves playing

---

Box 2.7 The "rules game": Paying attention to where the action is

The framework described in this Report aims at explaining how governance affects development over time. For that purpose, the framework involves games played at two levels. The first-level game (the *outcome game*) takes place when, given a certain set of rules and policies, actors react by making decisions about investing, consuming, working, paying taxes, allocating budgets, abiding by the rules, and so on. Those decisions lead to the realization of outcomes (security, growth, equity). The framework suggests that there is, in addition, a second-level game (the *rules game*) in which actors bargain to redefine the policies and rules that shape subsequent reactions by actors in future realizations of the game. The rules game is where power asymmetries are manifested, whereby some actors have more direct influence (elites) and others have only indirect influence—for example, through voting (citizens).

In the abstract, the rules and policies chosen should lead to the socially desired outcomes. Economists refer to the case in which someone can pick the ideal rules for the outcome game as the "mechanism design" approach, and the rules selected are those that a "benevolent dictator" or "social planner" would pick. Although this is a useful way to specify the ultimate *goal* of development, it is an insufficient guide to understanding the actual *process* of development. Mechanism design suggests that a reform is a once-and-done jump that takes place when someone imposes the "ideal" rules. It ignores the second-level rules game, the diversity of preferences and incentives, and the fact that different actors can have very different influences in the *rules game*. Moreover, in the process of reform and development, the *rules game is where the action is*.

Source: WDR 2017 team.

two "games" at different levels, actors in the quest for change often neglect the game that really matters.

Certain factors can make sustaining cooperation more likely. For example, it may be more difficult to reach lasting agreements in contexts in which the relative bargaining power of actors often shifts, causing a high turnover of actors entering and exiting the policy arena, or in which the short-term benefits of reneging on promises are high, compared with the benefits of maintaining a reputation for honoring agreements. Box 2.8 describes several factors that influence the likelihood that agreements will be sustained.[17]

Levers for change: Incentives, preferences and beliefs, and contestability

To more effectively enable commitment, coordination, and cooperation, it is important that one understand what agreements are feasible in the policy arena and how the policy arena can be reshaped to expand the set of policies that can be implemented. The policy arena can be reshaped when changes are made in the *incentives* that actors have to pursue certain goals, in actors' *preferences and beliefs*, and in who can participate in the decision-making processes (the *contestability* of the policy arena).

Depending on the primary functional challenge—that is, whether the institution needs to enable commitment, coordination, or cooperation—the entry point may be different. Because these functional challenges are interdependent, these entry points act as complements to one another. In all cases, for the entry points to be effective they must lead to changes that induce voluntary compliance from actors. This process of inducing voluntary compliance can be thought of as an expression of what the literature calls *legitimacy*, which is related to the voluntary acceptance of an act of authority (box 2.9).[18]

Box 2.9 Voluntary compliance and the building blocks of legitimacy

Three principal types of legitimacy matter for the effectiveness of interventions: outcome legitimacy, relational legitimacy, and process legitimacy.

Outcome legitimacy is derived from delivering on commitments, such as those to provide public services, protect property rights, or respect term limits in elections. It is related to the degree to which individuals feel that they can trust institutions (see box 2.2 for an extended discussion on the notion of trust). In this way, incentives are aligned between government and citizens. A public officer will deliver on her promises because citizens will vote for her, and citizens will vote for her because they trust that the officer will deliver on her promises. Trust is in this way a building block of outcome legitimacy (the capacity to commit). An important way to enhance outcome legitimacy is to enhance ex post accountability, so that actors will face consequences if they do not deliver the outcomes of a promised policy or action. Enhancing ex post accountability to bring about adverse consequences for not delivering on the outcomes of a promised decision is a critical entry point for strengthening outcome legitimacy: such accountability, in effect, acts as a negative reward system.

Relational legitimacy is derived from the alignment between the beliefs held by specific individuals or groups and the normative content of the rules—both formal and informal—governing the power relationship in question. It is related to the degree to which individuals share beliefs either about the qualities of the power holder or the degree to which the power arrangement serves a recognizable general interest (Nixon, Mallett, and McCullough 2016). In certain extreme cases, even if a process is not fair, a constituency could be willing to accept a government's authority because it shares its values. This arrangement is related

to how the content of the law reflects people's own social norms and views of morality. In these cases, the law can be considered irrelevant because people comply for reasons independent of its existence.

Process legitimacy is derived from a perception of fairness in the way that decisions, policies, or laws are designed and implemented. It is related to the degree to which individuals feel represented in the policy arena. When procedures for selecting and implementing policies are more contestable, those policies tend to be perceived as "fair" and to induce cooperation more effectively. Process legitimacy can exist to the extent that people feel they are represented, independent of the outcome. When individuals believe that the process has followed the rules, compliance with the law is higher, even if the outcomes are not always those that favor them (Tyler 1990; Tyler and Huo 2002). The opposite—exclusion from the process—leads to lack of legitimacy. Enhancing ex ante accountability to enable a more participatory or inclusive decision-making process can play a key role in strengthening process legitimacy.

Ultimately, legitimacy is a combined function of outcome, relational, and process legitimacy. However, although governments cannot always control outcomes directly or change beliefs quickly, they can control processes. Investing in strengthening process legitimacy may induce more voluntary compliance and enable governments to deliver on commitments more effectively. Delivering on commitments feeds in turn back into building trust in institutions and strengthening outcome legitimacy. Thus investing in process legitimacy is an important foundation of igniting positive dynamics between governance and development over time.

Source: WDR 2017 team.

Solving commitment problems: The role of incentives

The incentives that actors have to comply with agreements are fundamental to enabling commitment in the policy arena. What types of institutional arrangements can provide the right incentives to help ensure credible commitment? How can those in power bind themselves in such a way that their promises become credible, even when it is in their short-term interest to break them?

Think of Ulysses in Homer's *Odyssey*. In order to resist the short-term temptation to succumb to the

Sirens' luring song, Ulysses has his sailors bind him to the ship's mast to remove the option of jumping overboard. To understand why powerful actors would tie their own hands in this way and whether that agreement will be credible, one has to examine the context of a specific set of actors, rules, and potential incentives to break the agreement. For example, granting independence to the central bank is a mechanism that governments use to tie their hands in an attempt to gain credibility that they will not use inflation to finance public expenditures (Cukierman and Lippi 1999). Similarly, anticorruption agencies play an important role in constraining the use of public office for private gain. However, these institutions will be ineffective if they are unable to alter the existing incentive structure in a way that makes it credible to enforce the new regulations and the underlying contract of the new agency (Acemoglu and others 2008). Spotlight 1 provides a more detailed discussion on corruption from the perspective of the WDR 2017 framework.

Around the world, different institutional forms have been established to make commitment credible. In Guatemala, for example, in the aftermath of the peace agreements of the 1990s and after an increase in the political violence that raised concern among many actors, an agreement was reached to turn to international actors and create the International Commission against Impunity in Guatemala (CICIG), which has changed society's perception about its capacity to hold powerful actors accountable (box 2.10).

Often, commitment devices at a certain level may need to be complemented by devices at another level for the commitment to be taken seriously by market players. For example, international and bilateral agreements, such as multilateral trade agreements and bilateral investment agreements, can be a commitment device.[19] However, the mere presence of such agreements may not lead to a strong commitment, as demonstrated by the numerous examples of violations of the provisions of bilateral investment agreements. Thus complementary arrangements may be needed to provide a stronger signal about commitment. An example is the existence of mechanisms that systematically capture investor grievances, especially those related to violations of investment agreements,

---

Box 2.10 How an international commission enabled a credible commitment to fight criminals' impunity in Guatemala

"If you are watching this message, it is because I was assassinated by President Álvaro Colom, with help from Colom's private secretary Gustavo Alejos." The release of a YouTube video in 2009, in which Rodrigo Rosenberg makes this statement accusing the president of Guatemala of his murder, precipitated a political crisis in the country. The opposition to the president asked for his immediate resignation, and only a rapid and effective independent investigation of the situation prevented an escalation of political instability in Guatemala. The investigation revealed that the hitman who had killed Rosenberg was not hired by the president, but was in fact hired by Rosenberg himself: Rosenberg had ordered his own assassination.

The investigation was conducted by the International Commission against Impunity in Guatemala (CICIG), and it provided the credibility needed to resolve this crisis in a peaceful manner. The CICIG, backed by the United Nations, was approved in 2007 by Guatemala's Congress of the Republic. It was mandated to help Guatemala's judicial authorities in their fight against illegal criminal organizations that had infiltrated the state's security and judicial institutions. The approval came after a broad wave of homicides that infuriated citizens' organizations and the mass media. The growing perception was that the national authorities had lost any capacity to credibly prosecute large and powerful criminal networks.

Fighting impunity meant dismantling these criminal organizations and eradicating their corrupting power within state institutions, which were protecting them from being effectively prosecuted. Three of the greatest strengths of the CICIG's mandate were its independent capacity for criminal investigation; its prosecution capacity through a specific *fiscalia*[a] of the Office of the Attorney General (AG), which allowed it to investigate even in the face of internal opposition within the AG; and its independent voice in relation to the mass media. These arrangements enabled the CICIG to credibly commit to prosecuting impunity.

Since 2007, the CICIG has had a deep impact on the capacity of the Office of the Attorney General to credibly prosecute criminal networks, even leading to the peaceful resignation of the president in 2015 after the discovery of his involvement in "La Linea," a criminal network linked to customs fraud. Moreover, national security forces, judges, and members of the congress have been empowered in their public roles, and the renewed commitment to prosecution has increased pressure to reduce participation in illegal activities. The CICIG's political power today is well beyond that originally conceived for an international organization, which raises both concerns and enthusiasm in Guatemala.

Source: Carrera 2016.

a. A *fiscalia* is a district attorney or public prosecutor.

and help resolve them. The effective working of such mechanisms gives investors comfort and strengthens the commitment that governments make when they sign investment agreements. Here, the important thing is the effective working of the grievance mechanism rather than the particular form it takes.

Solving coordination problems: The role of preferences and beliefs

Preferences and beliefs play an important role in coordination. Coordination can help to understand phenomena ranging from discrimination, to corruption, to technological revolutions, to tax compliance (Tirole 1996; Mokyr 2013). For example, when Italian prime minister Silvio Berlusconi said publicly he considered the tax burden and tax enforcement for entrepreneurs to be excessive, he was sending a signal that, as long as he was in charge, tax enforcement would be weaker, actually leading to lower tax compliance by businesses (Raitano and Fantozzi 2015). By contrast, when citizens of the United Kingdom received letters informing them that most of their neighbors had already paid their taxes, tax compliance increased (BIT 2012).

Consider a society with a significant degree of political corruption. The higher the incidence of corruption, the lower is the cost of being corrupt in terms of damage to the public's perceptions of politicians. In such a situation, where corruption has become a norm, policies to deter corruption will be less effective or will require high and potentially unfeasible sanctions (Tirole 1996). However, policies to induce coordination can help countries break free from path dependence and are often needed only as a temporary intervention. For example, as Tirole (1996) points out, it may be possible for a temporary anticorruption program to move an economy from a high-corruption equilibrium (based on expectations of high corruption) to a low-corruption equilibrium (based on expectations of low corruption with respect to the behavior of others).

Solving cooperation problems: The role of contestability

Who is included and who is excluded from the policy arena are determined by the relative power of the competing actors, as well as by the barriers to participation—that is, the *contestability* of the process. A more contestable policy arena is one in which actors or groups who have reason to participate in the decision-making process have ways to express their interests and exert influence. Contestability is closely linked to the notion of inclusion, but it emphasizes the barriers to participation. Although the inclusion

of more actors in the decision-making process is not necessarily a guarantee of better decisions, a more contestable policy arena tends to be associated with higher levels of process legitimacy and cooperation.

The ability of elites and citizens to reach and sustain agreements is critical to policy effectiveness. In agreements, actors reach policy compromises that can be enforced, meaning that actors can ensure that the other actors will fulfill their part of the agreement. To reach and sustain agreements in the policy arena, citizens and elites rely on two types of mechanisms. In *deals-based mechanisms*, personal relations or mechanisms such as rent distribution are used to carry out agreements. In *rules-based mechanisms*, formal laws and legal institutions are used to enforce agreements. Deals-based mechanisms can take many forms, from gossip and stigmatization, to informal threats, to physical injury—even execution (Boix 2015). When the size of the community and its heterogeneity increase, it becomes more difficult to use relation-based mechanisms to enforce agreements and hold actors accountable. As social distance increases, societies tend to move toward rules-based mechanisms such as courts, legislatures, and political parties to enforce agreements. Although deals-based mechanisms can function well for smaller and more homogeneous groups, rules-based mechanisms become necessary to facilitate cooperation in larger and more heterogeneous groups (Li 1999; Dixit 2003, 2004).

Removing barriers to entry to the policy arena can help to enhance contestability. For example, in Brazil the replacement of paper ballots with electronic ballots effectively shifted the balance of power toward previously disengaged illiterate voters, reducing the barriers to their participation and increasing contestability (box 2.11). The electronic ballots made it much easier for those with little or no education to cast their vote, thereby de facto enfranchising more than 10 percent of the Brazilian electorate and ultimately affecting spending on public health care.

Participation and ownership in the design of rules can increase voluntary compliance. Consider the case of managing local water resources in India. In the southeastern Indian state of Tamil Nadu, cooperation to manage public irrigation systems at the community level is crucial to avoid free-riding and inefficient water use. A large survey conducted in Tamil Nadu was used to study the determinants of cooperation in these communities. The empirical analysis looked at the effects of institutional, socioeconomic, and topographic factors on cooperative behavior, measured by how well the systems are maintained, the absence of conflict, and the extent of violations of rules.

Box 2.11 How the introduction of electronic voting in Brazil reshaped the policy arena and led to more pro-poor policies

In many developed countries, the act of filling in a ballot may appear to be a trivial task. One reason is the level of education of the average citizen. The same may not be true of many illiterate or poorly educated citizens in rural and other areas of the developing world. In Brazil, illiterate citizens were not legally allowed to vote until 1985. A process that began in 1986 led to enfranchising these groups in the 1988 constitution. However, until 1996 the system involved a complex paper ballot. Because of the country's electoral rules, hundreds of candidates commonly run for state legislatures, making it impossible to list candidates in paper ballots. Voters were thus asked to write the name (or number) of the candidate on the ballot (figure B2.11.1, panel a).

At the time, roughly one-quarter of Brazilians were not functionally literate. Thus these complex paper ballots led to the de facto disenfranchisement of a large fraction

of voters—often more than one-quarter of the votes were deemed invalid and not counted. However, that situation changed in 1996 with the introduction of electronic voting devices. Their simple interface allowed voters to select the number of their candidate, and a picture of the candidate appeared on the screen before voters validated their vote (figure B2.11.1, panel b). This simplification of the voting procedures greatly reduced the number of invalid votes and effectively enfranchised more than 10 percent of the Brazilian electorate, whose votes previously had been counted.

Figure B2.11.2 shows the effect of electronic voting on valid votes. The analysis exploits the fact that in 1994 all Brazilian municipalities used paper ballots. In the 1998 election, smaller towns still used paper ballots, but municipalities with more than 40,500 voters had switched to

Figure B2.11.1 An electronic ballot made it much easier than a paper ballot for those with little or no education to cast their vote in Brazil

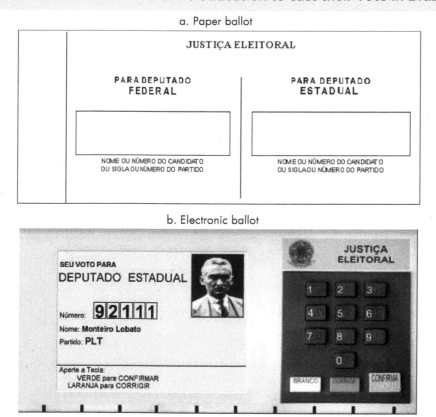

Source: Thomas Fujiwara, "Voting Technology, Political Responsiveness, and Infant Health: Evidence from Brazil," *Econometrica* 83, no. 2 (2015): 429. Printed with permission of The Econometric Society. Further permission required for reuse.

(Box continues next page)

Box 2.11 How the introduction of electronic voting in Brazil reshaped the policy arena and led to more pro-poor policies *(continued)*

Figure B2.11.2 Electronic voting reduced the number of invalid votes in Brazil

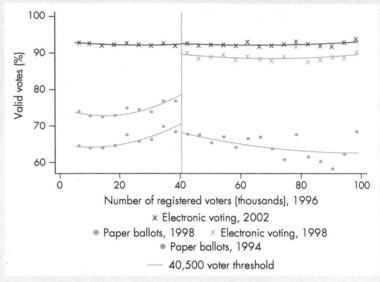

Source: Thomas Fujiwara, "Voting Technology, Political Responsiveness, and Infant Health: Evidence from Brazil," *Econometrica* 83, no. 2 (2015): 435. Adapted with permission of The Econometric Society. Further permission required for reuse.

Note: Graph shows valid votes/turnout—local averages and parametric fit. Each marker represents the average value of the variable in a 4,000-voter bin. The continuous lines are from a quadratic fit over the original ("unbinned") data.

electronic voting. By the 2002 election, electronic voting was the sole method of voting in Brazil.

The effects of the transition are illustrated by the towns of Altamira and Paracatu, which were otherwise similar. Because Altamira had 40,461 registered voters—39 less than the threshold of 40,500 for electronic voting—the municipality used paper ballots for the 1998 election, whereas Paracatu, just over the threshold with 40,917 registered voters, used electronic voting. The electronic voting led to a significant difference in valid votes: 79 percent of registered voters in Altamira versus 90 percent in Paracatu. Multiplied across many towns in Brazil, this de facto enfranchisement of millions of previously excluded

voters had substantial consequences on policy making and development outcomes.

These newly enfranchised voters chose more progressive legislators for the state assemblies, which then increased spending on public health care by 34 percent from 1998 to 2006. In Brazil, public health care is largely a pro-poor policy because the better-off citizens rely on private health services. This additional spending then increased access to prenatal health care and had an impact on health outcomes. Fujiwara (2015) estimates that electronic voting was responsible for lowering the prevalence of low birth weights (a common measure of infant health) among mothers without primary schooling by 6.8 percent.

Source: Prepared by Thomas Fujiwara for WDR 2017.

The results from the analysis highlight the importance of being involved in the crafting of the rules. The study found that when a farmer believes rules have been created jointly (along with the elite or government), the farmer is more likely to have a positive perception of both the allocation system and the compliance of other farmers with the rules. Similarly, elites violate water allocation rules less when they are the ones who crafted the rules (Bardhan 2005).

Actors marginalized from the decision-making process have fewer incentives to comply with the policy. In Tyler's classic study, individuals comply with the law primarily not out of fear of punishment (deterrence) but because they believe it to be fair (Tyler 1990). Tyler and Huo (2002) have looked at the role that being treated fairly plays in individuals' acceptance of the legal system. Based on a survey of citizens in Los Angeles and Oakland, California, who have been in contact

Table 2.1 Three principles for rethinking governance for development

Traditional approach	Principles for rethinking governance for development
Invest in designing the right **form** of institutions.	Think not only about the form of institutions, but also about their **functions**.
Build the **capacity** of institutions to implement policies.	Think not only about capacity building, but also about **power asymmetries**.
Focus on strengthening the **rule of law** to ensure that those policies and rules are applied impersonally.	Think not only about the rule of law, but also about the **role of law**.

Source: WDR 2017 team.

with judges, prosecutors, or the police, they found that members of minority groups who perceive that they have been treated unfairly are less likely to trust the subsequent decisions of law enforcement authorities and to cooperate. Being treated with respect and dignity and believing that the process has followed the rules lead to higher compliance with the law, even if the outcomes do not always favor individuals.

Three guiding principles

First, it is important to think not only about what form institutions should have, but also about the functions that institutions must perform—that is, think not only about the form of institutions, but also about their *functions*. Second, it is important to think that, although capacity building matters, how to use capacity and where to invest in capacity depend on the relative bargaining powers of actors—that is, think not only about capacity building, but also about *power asymmetries*. Third, it is important to think that in order to achieve the rule of law, countries must first strengthen the different roles of law to change

incentives, reshape preferences and beliefs, and enhance contestability—that is, think not only about the rule of law, but also about the *role of law* (table 2.1).

In practical terms, these principles mean that diagnostic approaches should zoom in on the specific commitment, coordination, and cooperation issues that limit the attainment of socially desirable outcomes and on the ways in which power asymmetries in the policy arena obstruct these functions. Identifying the different levers of change—incentives, preferences and beliefs, and contestability—can help to reshape the policy arena to expand the set of policies that can be implemented. This includes taking into account the relevant interventions or changes in rules, at different levels, to solve the specific functional challenges. Anticipating the potential opposition and taking into account the potential unintended consequences are also a central aspect of the process of designing and assessing policies (box 2.12).

Figure 2.2 synthesizes the conceptual framework presented in this Report. It illustrates the dynamic interaction between governance and development.

Box 2.12 The "rules game": Lessons for reformers

This Report encourages reformers to pay attention to the details of the *rules game* so that they can avoid two basic mistakes. First, an act of reform taken by one player in a rules game can backfire if the player does not consider the actions the reform will trigger in other players. For example, an outsider might advise the legislature on the benefits of contract law. In response, the legislature might pass a law that tells the courts to enforce contracts; the executive head of government might promise to promote judges who follow the executive's instruction to favor some people in court cases; wealthy elites might pay the executive to receive special treatment in the courts; the executive might use the money from the elites to finance an upcoming political campaign; and, as a result, citizens might not trust the

courts to enforce contract law. Ultimately, this reform did not produce the anticipated benefit, and it may even have made matters worse. The courts, which previously offered equal protection under criminal law, may no longer be able to punish wealthy offenders who commit crimes.

Second, even if it produces better payoffs today, a reform could also backfire if it generates worse outcomes for the rules game that will be played in the future. This can be particularly important in terms of legitimacy. The citizens of a nation may be willing to delegate enough power to their government to make it a dominant player in the rules game for the nation. But they may be willing to do so only as long as they feel the government's use of that power is legitimate.

Source: WDR 2017 team.

Figure 2.2 WDR 2017 framework: Governance, law, and development

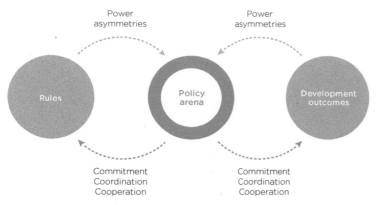

Power asymmetries

Power asymmetries

Rules

Policy arena

Development outcomes

Commitment
Coordination
Cooperation

Commitment
Coordination
Cooperation

Source: WDR 2017 team.

Note: "Rules" refers to formal and informal rules (norms). "Development outcomes" refers to security, growth, and equity. The actors in the *policy arena* can be grouped into elites, citizens, and international actors.

At its center is the policy arena, the space where actors bargain and reach agreements about policies and rules. Given a set of rules, the right-hand side of the framework shows how commitment, coordination, and cooperation among actors lead to specific development outcomes (the *outcome game* in box 2.7). But actors can also agree to change the rules, which is illustrated in the left-hand side of the framework (the *rules game* in box 2.12). Both changes in development outcomes (such as the composition of growth or the concentration of wealth) and changes in rules (both formal and informal) reshape the power asymmetries manifested in the policy arena.

A dynamic process: Drivers of change and the role of law

When can meaningful changes occur in the nature of governance? Overcoming harmful power asymmetries by adopting rules that change incentives, reshape preferences and beliefs, or enhance contestability may be difficult because those currently in power have incentives not to introduce reforms that would limit their power. Moreover, even dramatic shifts in who has power in the policy arena may not be enough if the new elites, once in power, have incentives to use the same mechanisms to extract rents from society that were used by the previous elites (Acemoglu and Robinson 2008).

However, despite the difficulties, history has shown that change can happen; many societies in

which power at a point in time was in the hands of a few have managed to develop into ones that are more open, more prosperous, and more secure (Deaton 2013; Boix 2015). Political pressure for reform can come from the top-down (elite bargains) or from the bottom-up (citizen engagement), and often it is the result of coalitions *between* elites and citizens. Elites and citizens are also influenced by international factors, which can play a role in influencing the local bargaining dynamics. Although external actors cannot engineer domestic development, they can play a role in strengthening or weakening the relative power of different actors. Part III of this Report will explore these dynamics.

Moreover, governance and development dynamics are a two-way street: the process of development is constantly reallocating resources, conferring new de facto power on actors, and shifting norms over time.[20] This process includes external (exogenous) shocks (such as a regional or worldwide financial crisis) and internal (endogenous) structural changes (such as a demographic shift) or norm-based changes (such as changes in gender roles). This feedback process alters the distribution of power and in turn affects the ability of different groups of citizens and elites to solve their collective action problems and influence the policy arena.

Law is a powerful instrument to reshape the policy arena because it is the tool through which policies are codified and implemented, as well as the tool through which power is allocated and contested. Although law generally reflects the interests of those actors with greater bargaining power, it also has proven to be an important instrument for change. By its nature, law is a device that provides a particular language, structure, and formality for ordering things, and this characteristic gives it the potential to become a force independent of the initial powers and intentions behind it. Law, often in combination with other social and political strategies, can be used as a commitment and coordination device to promote accountability, and also to change the rules of the game to foster more equitable bargaining spaces. Effective laws are those that are able to change incentives by changing payoffs to lower the cost of compliance (or increase the cost of noncompliance), change preferences by enhancing substantive focal points around which coordination can occur, and shape bargaining spaces to increase contestability by underrepresented actors. The next chapter looks at these various roles of law in greater depth.

Notes

1. "Movie Review: Amka and the Three Golden Rules | The UB Post," http://ubpost.mongolnews.mn, April 16, 2014.

2. The importance of fiscal prudence is embedded in the Netherlandic value system, as much as the importance of an open debate about policies that involve the use of public resources. Nicolaas Gerard Pierson, the Netherlands' minister of finance and one of the most respected economists in the world toward the end of the 19th century, said more than 120 years ago that taxes should be invested wisely or they would not be justified, and that opportunities for investments should be taken when "a concurrence of favorable circumstances generates a temporary budget surplus *e.g.* abundant harvests leading to extra tax revenues" (Pierson 1890).

3. Social norms are beliefs that are shared by a group or community. In this way, norms can be understood as "commonly shared beliefs."

4. See Rosenstein-Rodan (1943). Murphy, Shleifer, and Vishny (1989) model a more recent version of this idea.

5. Hoff (2000) reviews models of coordination failures in a wide range of contexts, including social norms and corruption. Cooper (1999) reviews macroeconomic models of coordination failures, while Rodríguez-Clare (2005) reviews microeconomic models of coordination failures.

6. See Hoff and Stiglitz (2001) for several other examples of coordination problems that are key to development.

7. Examples of the cohesion and inequality-conflict cycle are found in Esteban and Ray (2011) and Gintis (2000). Bardhan (2005) discusses cooperation in the context of scarcity and conflict.

8. A similar approach has been developed in a pioneering work, *The Politics of Policies: The Role of Political Process in Successful Public Policies*, in the context of Latin America (IDB 2005).

9. Lukes (1986) presents an extensive discussion of the concept of power from different perspectives, as summarized in the definition used in this Report.

10. The term *elite* is frequently used in popular writing and in academic literature, but it is often not defined. A search of the word *elite* returned 913,000 results in Google Scholar, while a search in the writings rarely reveals a clear definition.

11. In the literature of public choice tradition, this has been described as "politics without romance." See Buchanan and Tullock (1962) and Mueller (2003).

12. As Gould (1987, 9) notes, dichotomies are either "useful or misleading, not true or false" because they "are simplifying models for organizing thought, not ways of the world."

13. The problem of sustaining cooperation in transactions or agreements is known in the economics and political science literature as *transaction costs*. The term originated with Coase (1960) and Williamson (1989), and was later expanded to politics by North (1990b) and Dixit (1996).

14. This is usually called the social conflict view. It emphasizes that policies arise not because they are efficient but because of their distinct distributional consequences (Bardhan 1989; Knight 1993; Acemoglu and Robinson 2006). This section builds on the work of these as well as other scholars, including Buchanan and Tullock (1962); Weingast and Marshall (1988); Dixit (1996); Acemoglu (2003); Spiller and Tommasi (2003); IDB (2005); Stein and others (2007); North, Wallis, and Weingast (2009); Besley and Persson (2011).

15. Klein, Crawford, and Alchian (1978) note that the level of specific investments in a contractual relationship depends on the expectation of obtaining a fair rate of return on that investment. In this case, the investment refers to the fact that violent groups will need to give up power to pursue growth-enhancing policies. However, once they give up power, they fear not obtaining a fair return on their investment. Dixit (1996) extended the reasoning to political transactions.

16. This includes material (physical and financial) resources and technical ability.

17. See Ivaldi and others (2003) and Spiller and Tommasi (2003, 2007).

18. The importance of process legitimacy is captured by Levi (2003, 88): "[C]itizens are willing to go along with a policy they do not prefer as long as it is made according to a process they deem legitimate, and they are less willing to comply with a policy they like if the process was problematic."

19. See Tornell and Esquivel (1997). Also see González-Reyes (2016) for a discussion of the North American Free Trade Agreement (NAFTA) in the early 1990s.

20. Hirschman (1958); Streeten (1959); Ray (2010).

Referencesa

Acemoglu, Daron. 2003. "Why Not a Political Coase Theorem? Social Conflict, Commitment, and Politics." *Journal of Comparative Economics* 31 (4): 620–52.

Acemoglu, Daron, Simon Johnson, Pablo Querubin, and James A. Robinson. 2008. "When Does Policy Reform Work? The Case of Central Bank Independence." *Brookings Papers on Economic Activity* 2008 (1): 351–418.

---

a. References to titles of publications that include Taiwan, Hong Kong, and Macau refer to the regions currently named Taiwan, China; Hong Kong SAR, China; and Macau SAR, China, respectively.

Acemoglu, Daron, and James A. Robinson. 2006. "Economic Origins of Dictatorship and Democracy." Cambridge, U.K.: Cambridge University Press.

———. 2008. *The Role of Institutions in Growth and Development*. Washington, DC: World Bank.

———. 2013. "Economics versus Politics: Pitfalls of Policy Advice." *Journal of Economic Perspectives* 27 (2): 173–92.

Axelrod, Robert. 1984. *The Evolution of Cooperation*. New York: Basic Books.

Banuri, Sheheryar, Luis Felipe López-Calva, Ezequiel Molina, Abla Safir, and Siddharth Sharma. 2016. "The Governance Game: Lab Experiments." University of East Anglia and Centre for Behavioural and Experimental Social Science. Background paper, WDR 2017, World Bank, Washington, DC.

Bardhan, Pranab. 1989. "The New Institutional Economics and Development Theory: A Brief Critical Assessment." *World Development* 17 (9): 1389–95.

———. 2005. *Scarcity, Conflicts, and Cooperation: Essays in the Political and Institutional Economics of Development*. Cambridge, MA: MIT Press.

Bartolini, D. 2013. "The Role of Incentives in Co-operation Failures." OECD Regional Development Working Paper 2013/09, Organisation for Economic Co-operation and Development, Paris.

Basu, Kaushik. 1986. "One Kind of Power." *Oxford Economic Papers* 38 (2): 259–82.

———. 2000. *Prelude to Political Economy: A Study of the Social and Political Foundations of Economics*. Oxford, U.K.: Oxford University Press.

Beegle, Kathleen, Luc Christiaensen, Andrew Dabalen, and Isis Gaddis. 2016. *Poverty in a Rising Africa*. Washington, DC: World Bank.

Besley, Timothy, and Torsten Persson. 2011. *Pillars of Prosperity: The Political Economics of Development Clusters*. Princeton, NJ: Princeton University Press.

BIT (Behavioural Insights Team). 2012. *Applying Behavioural Insights to Reduce Fraud, Error and Debt*. London: Cabinet Office, BIT.

Boix, C. 2015. *Political Order and Inequality*. Cambridge, U.K.: Cambridge University Press.

———. 2016. "State Origins and State Consolidation." Background paper, WDR 2017, World Bank, Washington, DC.

Bold, Tessa, Mwangi Kimenyi, Germano Mwabu, Alice Ng'ang'a, and Justin Sandefur. 2015. "Interventions and Institutions: Experimental Evidence on Scaling Up Education Reforms in Kenya." Unpublished paper, Center for Global Development, Washington, DC.

Bonvecchi, Alejandro. 2016. "Bolivia Social Network Analysis of Social Policy." Background paper, WDR 2017, World Bank, Washington, DC.

Bonvecchi, Alejandro, Julia Johannsen, and Carlos Scartascini, eds. 2015. "Quiénes deciden la política social? Economía política de programas sociales en América Latina" (Who Decides Social Policy? The Political Economy of Social Programs in Latin America). Inter-American Development Bank, Washington, DC.

Buchanan, James M., and Gordon Tullock. 1962. *The Calculus of Consent: Logical Foundations of Constitutional Democracy*. Ann Arbor: University of Michigan Press.

Carneiro, Robert. 1970. "A Theory of the Origin of the State." *Science* 169 (August 21): 733–38.

Carrera, Fernando. 2016. "Guatemala's International Commission against Impunity: A Case Study on Institutions and Rule of Law." Background paper, WDR 2017, World Bank, Washington, DC.

Chimeddorj, Otgonbayar. 2015. "Managing Fiscal Revenues from Extractive Industry: The Case of Mongolia." Ministry of Finance, Mongolia, October 7. https://www.unpei.org/system/files_force/Mining%20Revenue-edited_final%20draft.pdf?download=1.

Coase, Ronald. 1960. "The Problem of Social Cost." *Journal of Law and Economics* 3 (1): 1–44.

Cooper, R. 1999. *Coordination Games*. Cambridge, U.K.: Cambridge University Press.

Cukierman, Alex, and Francesco Lippi. 1999. "Central Bank Independence, Centralization of Wage Bargaining, Inflation and Unemployment: Theory and Some Evidence." *European Economic Review* 43 (7): 1395–434.

Dahl, R. A. 1957. "The Concept of Power." *Behavioral Science* 2: 202–10.

Deaton, Angus. 2013. *The Great Escape: Health, Wealth, and the Origins of Inequality*. Princeton, NJ: Princeton University Press.

De la Sierra, Raúl Sánchez. 2015. "On the Origin of States: Stationary Bandits and Taxation in Eastern Congo." Job market paper, Department of Economics, Columbia University, New York.

Devarajan, Shantayanan. 2013. "Africa's Statistical Tragedy." *Review of Income and Wealth* 59 (S1): S9–S15.

Devarajan, Shantayanan, and Lili Mottaghi. 2015. "Towards a New Social Contract." *MENA Economic Monitor*. http://www.worldbank.org/en/region/mena/publication/mena-economic-monitor.

Dixit, Avinash. 1996. *The Making of Economic Policy: A Transaction-Cost Politics Perspective*. Cambridge, MA: MIT Press.

———. 2003. "Trade Expansion and Contract Enforcement." *Journal of Political Economy* 111 (6): 1293–1317.

———. 2004. *Lawlessness and Economics*. Princeton, NJ: Princeton University Press.

Duflo, Esther, Pascaline Dupas, and Michael Kremer. 2015. "School Governance, Teacher Incentives and Pupil-Teacher Ratios: Experimental Evidence from Kenyan Primary School." *Journal of Public Economics* 123 (March): 92–110.

Economist. 2012. "For Richer—or Poorer: Re-crunching the Numbers—Whatever They Might Be." September 29. http://www.economist.com/node/21563736.

Epstein, David, and Sharyn O'Halloran. 1999. *Delegating Powers: A Transaction Cost Politics Approach to Policy Making under Separate Powers*. Political Economy of Institutions and Decisions. Cambridge, U.K.: Cambridge University Press.

Esteban, Joan, and Debraj Ray. 2011. "Linking Conflict to Inequality and Polarization." *American Economic Review* 101 (4): 1345–74.

Fernandez, Raquel, and Dani Rodrik. 1991. "Resistance to Reform: Status Quo Bias in the Presense of Individual-Specific Uncertainty." *American Economic Review* 81 (5): 1146–55.

Ferreira, Francisco H. G., Julian Messina, Jamele Rigolini, Luis Felipe López-Calva, María Ana Lugo, and Renos Vakis. 2013. *Economic Mobility and the Rise of the Latin American Middle Class.* Latin America and Caribbean Studies. Washington, DC: World Bank.

Fujiwara, Thomas. 2015. "Voting Technology, Political Responsiveness, and Infant Health: Evidence from Brazil." *Econometrica* 83 (2): 423–64.

Fukuyama, Francis. 2014. *Political Order and Political Decay: From the Industrial Revolution to the Globalization of Democracy.* New York: Farrar, Straus and Giroux.

Gill, Indermit S., Ivailo Izvorski, Willem Van Eeghen, and Donato De Rosa. 2014. *Diversified Development: Making the Most of Natural Resources in Eurasia.* Washington, DC: World Bank.

Gintis, Herbert. 2000. "Strong Reciprocity and Human Sociality." *Journal of Theoretical Biology* 206: 169–79.

González-Reyes, Alfredo. 2016. "Searching for Growth and Development in Authoritarian Mexico: A Brief Tale of the NAFTA Commitment Device." Background paper, WDR 2017, World Bank, Washington, DC.

Gould, Stephen Jay. 1987. *Time's Arrow, Time's Cycle: Myth and Metaphor in the Discovery of Geological Time.* Cambridge, MA; London: Harvard University Press.

Green, Edward, and Robert Porter. 1984. "Noncooperative Collusion under Imperfect Price Information." *Econometrica* 52 (1): 87–100.

Hardin, Garrett. 1968. "The Tragedy of the Commons." *Science* 162 (3859): 1243–48.

Hart, Oliver, and John Moore. 1990. "Property Rights and the Nature of the Firm." *Journal of Political Economy* 98 (6): 1119–58.

Havel, Václav. 1991. "The Power of the Powerless." In *Open Letters: Selected Writings, 1965–1990,* selected and edited by Paul Wilson. New York: Knopf.

Hirschman, Albert O. 1958. *The Strategy of Economic Development.* New Haven, CT: Yale University Press.

———. 1970. *Exit, Voice, and Loyalty: Responses to Decline in Firms, Organizations, and States.* Cambridge, MA: Harvard University Press.

Hoff, K. 2000. "Beyond Rosenstein-Rodan: The Modern Theory of Coordination Problems in Development." *Proceedings of the Annual World Bank Conference on Development Economics,* edited by Boris Pleskovic and Nicholas Stern, 145–76. Washington, DC: World Bank.

Hoff, Karla, and Joseph E. Stiglitz. 2001. "Modern Economic Theory and Development." In *Frontiers of Development Economics: The Future in Perspective,* edited by Gerald Meier and Joseph E. Stiglitz, 389–459. Oxford, U.K.: Oxford University Press.

Hoogeveen, Johannes, and Nga Thi Viet Nguyen. 2016. "Statistics Reform in Africa: Aligning Incentives with Results." Background paper, *Poverty in a Rising Africa,* World Bank, Washington, DC.

IDB (Inter-American Development Bank). 2005. *The Politics of Policies: The Role of Political Process in Successful Public Policies.* Economic and Social Progress in Latin America and the Caribbean 2006 Report. Washington, DC: IDB.

Ivaldi, Marc, Bruno Jullien, Patrick Rey, Paul Seabright, and Jean Tirole. 2003. "The Economics of Tacit Collusion." Final Report for DG Competition, European Commission. http://ec.europa.eu/competition/mergers/studies_reports/the_economics_of_tacit_collusion_en.pdf.

Klein, Benjamin, Robert Crawford, and Armen Alchian. 1978. "Vertical Integration, Appropriable Rents, and the Competitive Contracting Process." *Journal of Law and Economics* 21 (2): 297–326.

Knack, S., and P. Keefer. 1997. "Does Social Capital Have an Economic Payoff? A Cross-Country Investigation." *Quarterly Journal of Economics* 112 (4): 1251–88.

Knight, J. 1993. *Institutions and Social Conflict.* Cambridge, U.K.: Cambridge University Press.

Lach, Samantha, and Luis Felipe López-Calva. 2016. "Rethinking Trust and Legitimacy: A Functionalist Approach." Background paper, WDR 2017, World Bank, Washington, DC.

La Porta, R., F. Lopez-de-Silanes, A. Shleifer, and R. W. Vishny. 1997. "Legal Determinants of External Finance." *Journal of Finance* 52 (3): 1131–50.

Levi, M. 2003. "A State of Trust." In *Trust and Governance,* edited by V. Braithwaite and M. Levi, 77–101. New York: Russell Sage Foundation.

Li, Shuhe. 1999. "The Benefits and Costs of Relation-Based Governance: An Explanation of the East Asian Miracle and Crisis." Working paper, Hong Kong City University.

López-Calva, L. F. 2003. "Social Norms, Coordination, and Policy Issues in the Fight against Child Labor." In *International Labor Standards: History, Theories, and Policy Options,* edited by K. Basu, H. Horn, L. Román, and J. Shapiro. Oxford, U.K.: Blackwell Publishing.

Lukes, S., ed. 1986. *Power (Readings in Social and Political Theory).* New York: New York University Press.

Mokyr, J. 2013. "Cultural Entrepreneurs and the Origins of Modern Economic Growth." *Scandinavian Economic History Review* 61 (1): 1–33.

Mueller, Dennis C. 2003. *Public Choice III.* Cambridge, U.K.: Cambridge University Press.

Murphy, Kevin M., Andrei Shleifer, and Robert W. Vishny. 1989. "Industrialization and the Big Push." *Journal of Political Economy* 97 (5): 1003–26.

Nixon, Hamish, Richard Mallett, and Aoife McCullough. 2016. "Are Public Services the Building Blocks of Legitimacy?" Background paper, WDR 2017, World Bank, Washington, DC.

Noriega, Gustavo. 2012. *INDEC: Historia Intima de una Estafa.* New York: Penguin Random House.

North, Douglass C. 1990a. *Institutions, Institutional Change and Economic Performance.* Cambridge, U.K.: Cambridge University Press.

———. 1990b. "A Transaction Cost Theory of Politics." Paper 144, School of Business and Political Economy, Washington University in St. Louis.

North, Douglass C., John J. Wallis, and Barry R. Weingast. 2009. *Violence and Social Orders: A Conceptual Framework for Interpreting Recorded Human History.* New York: Cambridge University Press.

Olson, M. 1965. *The Logic of Collective Action: Public Goods and the Theory of Groups.* Harvard Economic Studies 124. Cambridge, MA: Harvard University Press.

Ostrom, Elinor. 1990. *Governing the Commons: The Evolution of Institutions of Collective Action.* Cambridge, U.K.: Cambridge University Press.

Overå, R. 1993. "Wives and Traders: Women's Careers in Ghanaian Canoe Fisheries." *Maritime Anthropological Studies (MAST)* 6 (1/2).

Persson, Torsten, and Guido Tabellini. 2000. *Political Economics: Explaining Economic Policy.* Cambridge, MA: MIT Press.

Pierson, N. G. 1890. *Leerboek der staathuishoudkunde* (Textbook on Political Economy). Haarlem, The Netherlands: Erven Bohn.

Portes, A., and P. Landolt. 1996. "The Downside of Social Capital." *American Prospect* 26 (May–June): 18–21.

Putnam, Robert. 1993. *Making Democracy Work: Civic Traditions in Modern Italy.* Princeton, NJ: Princeton University Press.

———. 2000. *Bowling Alone: The Collapse and Revival of American Community.* New York: Simon and Schuster.

Raitano, Michele, and Roberto Fantozzi. 2015. "Political Cycle and Reported Labour Incomes in Italy: Quasi-experimental Evidence on Tax Evasion." *European Journal of Political Economy* 39 (C): 269–80.

Ray, Debraj. 2010. "Uneven Growth: A Framework for Research in Development Economics." *Journal of Economic Perspectives* 24 (3): 45–60.

Rodríguez-Clare, A. 2005. "Coordination Failures, Clusters, and Microeconomic Interventions" (with comments by F. Rodríguez, R. Hausmann, and J. M. Benaventa). *Economía* 6 (1): 1–42.

Roitberg, G., and K. Nagasawa. 2016. "INDEC, The Lying Machine: A Chronicle of the Destruction of Public Statistics during Argentina's Kirchner Period." *La Nacion.* http://casos.lanacion.com.ar /indec-the-lying-machine.

Rosenstein-Rodan, Paul N. 1943. "Problems of Industrialisation of Eastern and South-Eastern Europe." *Economic Journal* 53 (210/211): 202–11.

Russell, Bertrand. 1938. *Power: A New Social Analysis.* London: Allen and Unwin.

Sen, Amartya. 1967. "Isolation, Assurance and the Social Rate of Discount." *Quarterly Journal of Economics* 81 (1): 112–24.

Spiller, Pablo T., and Mariano Tommasi. 2003. "The Institutional Foundations of Public Policy: A Transactions Approach with Application to Argentina." *Journal of Law, Economics, and Organization* 19 (2): 281–306.

———. 2007. *The Institutional Foundations of Public Policy in Argentina.* Cambridge, U.K.: Cambridge University Press.

Stein, E. H., M. Tommasi, P. T. Spiller, and C. Scartascini, eds. 2007. *Policymaking in Latin America: How Politics Shapes Policies.* Inter-American Development Bank (IDB) and David Rockefeller Center for Latin American Studies, Harvard University. Washington, DC: IDB.

Stigler, George. 1964. "A Theory of Oligopoly." *Journal of Political Economy* 72 (1): 44–61.

Streeten, Paul. 1959. "Unbalanced Growth." *Oxford Economic Papers New Series* 11 (2): 167–90.

Tilly, Charles. 1985. "War Making and State Making as Organized Crime." In *Bringing the State Back,* edited by Peter Evans, Dietrich Rueschmeyer, and Theda Skocpol. Cambridge, U.K.: Cambridge University Press.

Tirole, Jean. 1996. "A Theory of Collective Reputations (with Applications to the Persistence of Corruption and to Firm Quality)." *Review of Economic Studies* 63 (1): 1–22.

Tornell, Aaron, and Gerardo Esquivel Hernández. 1997. "The Political Economy of Mexico's Entry into NAFTA." In *Regionalism versus Multilateral Trade Arrangements,* edited by Takatoshi Ito and Anne O. Krueger, 25–56. Chicago: University of Chicago Press.

Tsebelis, G. 2002. *Veto Players: How Political Institutions Work.* Princeton, NJ: Princeton University Press.

Tyler, Tom R. 1990. *Why People Obey the Law.* New Haven, CT: Yale University Press.

Tyler, Tom R., and Yuen J. Huo. 2002. *Trust in the Law: Encouraging Public Cooperation with the Police and Courts.* New York: Russell Sage Foundation.

Weber, R. A. 2008. "Organizational Coordination: A Game-Theoretic View." Department of Social and Decision Sciences, Research Showcase @ CMU, Carnegie-Mellon University, Pittsburgh.

Weingast, B. R., and W. J. Marshall. 1988. "The Industrial Organization of Congress; or, Why Legislatures, like Firms, Are Not Organized as Markets." *Journal of Political Economy* 96 (1): 132–63.

Whiteley, Paul F. 2000. "Economic Growth and Social Capital." *Political Studies* 48 (3): 443–66.

Williamson, O. E. 1989. "Transaction Cost Economics." In *Handbook of Industrial Organization,* Vol. 1, edited by Richard Schmalensee and Robert D. Willig, 135–82. Amsterdam: North-Holland.

World Bank. Various years. World Development Indicators (database). Washington, DC, http://data.world bank.org/data-catalog/world-development-indicators.

———. 2012. *Inclusive Green Growth: The Pathway to Sustainable Development.* Washington, DC: World Bank.

———. 2015. *Economic, Environmental, and Social Evaluation of Africa's Small-Scale Fisheries.* Environment and Natural Resources Global Practice Policy Note. Washington, DC: World Bank.

Zak, P. J., and S. Knack. 2001. "Trust and Growth." *Economic Journal* 111 (470): 295–321.

SPOTLIGHT 1

Corruption

Corruption is often defined as the use of public office for private gain. In the framework of this Report, corruption is a deals-based way to sustain agreements among certain individuals or groups. Although in the short term corruption may be able to "grease the wheels of the economy," in the long term it negatively affects growth by diverting resources from more productive uses and negatively affects equity by disproportionately benefiting those in power. Moreover, it undermines legitimacy because it affects public perceptions of the fairness of the decision-making process (Rose-Ackerman 2016).

The first generation of high-income member states of the Organisation for Economic Co-operation and Development (OECD) has achieved significant control of corruption through development processes and institutional forms that many other countries around the world have since tried to replicate without achieving the desired results. These anticorruption strategies often wrongly assume that aggregate levels of corruption can be reduced through a top-down combination of policies that improve enforcement of the rule of law, change the expected returns to corruption (for example, through bureaucratic pay increases, greater transparency, or harsher punishments), and simplify procedures to reduce the opportunities for corruption. These strategies have generally delivered modest reductions in corruption in contexts in which the configuration of social power does not support the enforcement of generalized rule-following behavior (Khan 2016).

WDR 2017 team, based on inputs from Alina Mungiu-Pippidi and Mushtaq H. Khan.

From the perspective of this Report, replicating these reforms may be ineffective if approaches do not also tackle the underlying reasons they are not performing their intended function, which is to ensure the credible commitment of those in power to not abuse that power for private gain. These underlying reasons are related to systemic features in the policy arena such as entrenched power structures or social norms. Consequently, corruption is less about individual transactions and more about networks of actors (Schmidt 2016). Thus changes in formal rules and anticorruption strategies are likely to be effectively enforced only when they are aligned with the interests of powerful actors in a country and are able to trigger broader changes in social expectations.

Corruption and social order: Is corruption inescapable?

The first step in rethinking corruption is to recognize that corruption is not a social "malady" or "disease" to be eradicated, but rather a built-in feature of governance interactions. Countries today are on a continuum of governance between a system in which rules are applied by virtue of personal status and one in which they are applied impersonally. Unfortunately, assuming that a particularistic system is the exception and an impersonal system is the norm is not historically accurate. In fact, the public-private separation in public affairs and the complete autonomy of state from private interests are relatively recent. All societies start from being "owned" by a few individuals who control all resources. As states develop historically, individual autonomy grows, but so too do the material resources available for spoiling (Mungiu-Pippidi 2016).

In less-developed societies, powerful groups are fewer in number and less dependent on competitiveness and market transactions for their revenues. They can feasibly interact with each other in informal or deals-based ways and generate rents through political connections. If the most powerful groups in a country do not want the enforcement of formal rules, it is unlikely that the rule of law will emerge through enforcement efforts from above. Policy makers and political parties in these countries may be able to raise significant revenues only in informal and deals-based ways because powerful groups prevent the implementation of formal rules to raise taxation. As a result, the most feasible way for policy makers and political parties to reward their supporters is to allow them to violate rules. A common manifestation is when parties buy political support in exchange for jobs in the public sector, often undermining a commitment to a merit-based performance evaluation. In general, it is difficult for political leaders to exercise the political will to enforce rules when their tenure depends on doing otherwise (Khan 2016). If the demand for control of corruption is poor because spoils are used efficiently to buy off certain strategic groups, then collective action becomes impossible to achieve and the equilibrium remains, with particularism as the norm.

Countries become more advanced when they have a more diverse set of productive organizations in different sectors and activities. As an economy becomes more productive, corruption becomes more costly because it restricts the functioning of the market. As they pay more taxes, fund political parties, and employ more people, business elites have an increasing interest in the enforcement of the formal rules required to conduct complex business and transactions (Khan 2016). Moreover, as countries develop, emergent socioeconomic classes can strengthen coalitions to demand better governance. In particular, larger middle classes have historically played an important role in pressuring governments to deliver better public services, such as education and health. These forces are illustrated by the shift of the U.S. political system in the 19th century away from patronage toward meritocracy (Fukuyama 2014). As economic development advanced, the emerging industrial urban elites began to demand more efficient government services. Moreover, the business elites found an ally against corruption in the emerging civil society, with a better-educated middle class. When newly elected president James A. Garfield was assassinated in 1881 by a would-be office seeker, this coalition of new social groups was ready to mobilize, and the Pendleton Act, which established the principle that public officials should be chosen on the basis of merit, was passed by Congress.

As the incentives of powerful actors change throughout the process of development, they can feed back into changing social norms, which reinforce the existing dynamics of corruption. In this sense, corruption can become an equilibrium because corrupt systems make it very costly for individuals to behave honestly. For example, if the majority of government bureaucrats favor their in-group or take bribes, individuals who do not do so will be criticized by their in-group and lose out on an often indispensable source of additional income. Thus entrenched corruption may lead to a higher tolerance for corrupt behavior. Because governance interventions affect development outcomes, which in turn affect governance constraints, one is confronted with a complex, coevolutionary transition process that does not follow a predictable path and requires continual adaptive interventions.

What can be done?

The development process plays an important role in reducing corruption by redistributing power and changing norms in the policy arena, but development explains only about half of the variation in control of corruption (Mungiu-Pippidi 2015). An analysis of a large sample of countries reveals how some countries overperform and others underperform in their expected levels of controlling corruption given their levels of development as measured by the Human Development Index (figure S1.1). This heterogeneity in progress suggests that reform is possible, even in countries with lower levels of development. In contexts in which levels of development and political arrangements do not yet allow the effective enforcement of formal rules, anticorruption strategies should sequentially attack corruption at critical points where anticorruption measures are both feasible and would have a high impact on development.

Anticorruption priorities will depend on the country and on the sectors and processes that are most important for accelerating development progress. A common error is to equate the impact of corruption with the magnitude of bribes. An activity with relatively small bribes can have a big impact on development if, for example, the bribes prevent the enforcement of regulations on food adulteration. Other activities characterized by significant bribes may be profit-sharing transfers to politicians with a lower impact on development if the corruption does not

Figure S1.1 Development accounts for only about half of the variation in control of corruption

Predicted control of corruption scores based on Human Development Index scores, selected countries

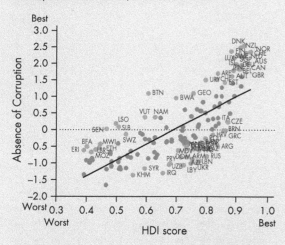

Sources: WDR 2017 team, based on data from the United Nations Development Programme (Human Development Index–HDI scores) and WDR 2017 Governance Indicators for Absence of Corruption, based on Mungiu-Pippidi 2015.

Note: Only outliers are labeled. Beige dots above (below) the line represent countries that overperform (underperform) on control of corruption given their level of development.

distort policy. A high-impact anticorruption approach therefore has to assess anticorruption priorities, but it also has to be feasible. It has to gauge whether strategies can be designed to make enforcement easier by aligning with the interests of important stakeholders or by developing new coalitions (Khan 2016).

Although this way of looking at corruption control does not allow for rigid, straightforward policy prescriptions, it is possible to identify a series of key strategies in countries that have managed in recent times to make progress in controlling corruption. To reduce corruption, reform coalitions will need to change incentives to limit the payoff of corrupt officials through increased accountability of elites

and to enhance contestability by engaging actors in civil society and the media. Increasing constraints, for example, by promoting freedom of the media and freedom of the internet, is key to strengthening an enabling environment for reform (Mungiu-Pippidi 2016). One particularly promising avenue of action is to take advantage of technology. Digitalization helps transparency and rationalization of fiscal management on the government side, and it creates empowered citizens on the society side. Internet media in general and social networks in particular are now indispensable components of citizen empowerment and collective action.

International actors, such as aid donors, also play a key role in the local fights against corruption, and they should ensure that they do not increase resources for corruption. Meaningful international anticorruption efforts should coordinate and engage with actors outside the state, including local communities, nongovernmental organizations, and multinational businesses, to support domestic anticorruption reforms through tools such as the provision of information (reform evaluations and cross-country data) or legal mechanisms (international treaties and arbitration)—see Rose-Ackerman (2016).

References

Fukuyama, Francis. 2014. *Political Order and Political Decay: From the Industrial Revolution to the Globalisation of Democracy.* New York: Farrar, Straus and Giroux.

Khan, Mushtaq H. 2016. Background note on corruption, WDR 2017, World Bank, Washington, DC.

Mungiu-Pippidi, Alina. 2015. *The Quest for Good Governance: How Societies Develop Control of Corruption.* Cambridge, U.K.: Cambridge University Press.

———. 2016. Background note on corruption, WDR 2017, World Bank, Washington, DC.

Rose-Ackerman, S. R. 2016. *Corruption and Government.* Cambridge, U.K.: Cambridge University Press.

Schmidt, M. 2016. Background note on corruption, WDR 2017, World Bank, Washington, DC.

The governance challenges of managing risks

Tackling environmental and sustainability challenges depends on the availability of commitment mechanisms to address natural hazards and to protect the environment and resources for future generations, who are not represented in the policy arena. When it comes to natural resources—and their links to risk management—cooperation is also challenging because opportunistic overexploitation of resources is the norm in many societies.

What is an acceptable level of risk?

Many natural risks are systemic—and therefore collective—by nature, and governments play a key role in the management of such risks (World Bank 2014). For example, individuals cannot protect themselves against floods independently, and thus they must rely on what is put in place at the collective level. This is particularly true in high-density population areas with geographically concentered (agglomerated) infrastructure. Despite regular claims that "disasters are unacceptable," removing all risks would be prohibitively costly to governments. Thus a certain amount of risk must be accepted. Decisions on the acceptable level of risk that individuals must bear should be made through a collective political process. What risks are mitigated through markets and what risks—and whose risks—are dealt with through public action are therefore governance-related decisions.

In *The Great Risk Shift*, Jacob Hacker (2006) describes how a larger share of economic risks were

borne by U.S. households in the 2000s than in the 1970s and 1980s, increasing their vulnerability to shocks such as illness, unemployment, and retirement. In western European countries, by contrast, there is a tendency for governments to bear some of the risks and protect households from shocks, which also has implications for the fiscal sustainability of that social contract, particularly because of the current demographic trends (World Bank 2014).

Defining an acceptable level of risk is difficult because of the complexity of the process for determining its distribution and because of the wide differences in preferences, values, and beliefs. Some individuals are more risk averse than others and may prefer a more cautionary approach. Defining a social level of acceptable risk is also difficult because of differences in sensitivity—for example, people have very different sensitivity to local air pollution. In the presence of such heterogeneity, designing homogeneous regulations is challenging and highly dependent on considerations of equity (especially when sensitivity is correlated with other social factors). The selected regulation is also unlikely to satisfy all individuals and may require compensatory action, which requires a process to decide who deserves compensation and to ensure that compensation is proportional to the losses and does not create long-term irreversible costs.

How can risk be allocated across households and over time?

When risks are borne by households, existing inequities can be manifested and reinforced. For example,

---

Stéphane Hallegatte, based on World Bank (2014) and Fay and others (2015).

when a big snowstorm in the Washington, D.C., area leaves many roads blocked and public transportation disrupted for two weeks, the option of removing the snow in order to get to work is open only to those who can afford to pay for it. Less well-off people are left not only unable to leave their homes, but also unable to generate income because of the lack of mobility, deepening the effects of the shock on their welfare.

Risk is distributed not only across households but also over time. Even more complicated are cases in which the benefits of risk management extend over the very long term. For example, for climate change the beneficiaries are not even born yet to protect their interests. Dispersed—or unrepresented—interests are a classic issue leading to government failures.

How can political will for risk management be generated in the face of dispersed benefits?

Even when they agree on an acceptable level and allocation of risk, politicians may be reluctant to devote financial and political capital to risk management efforts because the costs tend to be immediate, concentrated, and observable, whereas the benefits are longer term, distributed more broadly, and often less visible. For example, when prohibiting development in flood zones, decision makers impose a cost on landowners who will naturally tend to oppose this new regulatory constraint. On the other hand, the people protected by the regulation—for example, future buyers of apartments in the newly developed flood-prone areas—are often not aware that the regulation may eventually protect them and therefore rarely take action to support it.

To garner political support, policy packages need to be socially acceptable and thus consistent with a country's social objectives, such as protecting the poor. What does this mean in practice for designing policies that are more likely to succeed? Consider countries seeking to adopt climate change policies. Although the poor are expected to benefit in the long run from mitigation policies because they are the most vulnerable to climate change, these types of policies are not necessarily pro-poor in the short run. It is therefore critical to use the savings or new proceeds generated by climate policies to compensate poor people, promote poverty reduction, and boost safety nets. One way to do that is by recycling revenue from carbon pricing instruments through tax cuts and by increasing transfers to the population. A modeling

exercise carried out using data from developing countries shows that subtracting $100 from fossil fuel subsidies and redistributing the money equally throughout the population would on average transfer $13 to the bottom quintile of the income distribution and take away $23 from the top quintile. Redistribution has been shown to significantly increase the odds that reforms will succeed. A review of reforms in the Middle East and North Africa classifies all reforms with cash and in-kind transfers as successful, as opposed to only 17 percent of those without (Sdralevich and others 2014).

Another factor in the success of reforms is the alignment of incentives in the policy arena in such a way that the commitment to a long-term objective can be credible. Returning to the example of climate change policies, consider the role of carbon pricing. Carbon prices are critical for the efficiency of the transition toward the zero carbon emission economy that is required to stabilize climate change. However, a carbon price alone is unlikely to provide enough incentive to invest in new, radically different technologies or to change long-term investment because the long-term price signal is hardly predictable and credible. Given the expected lifetime of power plants, a credible carbon price pathway would have to be announced at least three decades in advance to spur the optimal amount of investment in low-carbon power plants. But doing so is difficult because governments have a very limited ability to commit over such long periods (Helm, Hepburn, and Mash 2003; Brunner, Flachsland, and Marschinski 2012). Thus to reduce emissions through investments with long-term consequences (such as infrastructure, research and development, and long-lived capital), additional regulations, norms, or direct investments are needed. Policy makers could, for example, kick-start the transition either by temporarily supporting investments in low-carbon technologies (Acemoglu and others 2012) or by imposing additional regulations or performance standards (Rozenberg, Vogt-Schilb, and Hallegatte 2014).

The lack of well-accepted indicators for risk makes it difficult to measure the performance of decision makers and to make them accountable for their choices in terms of risk management. However, evidence from environmental issues such as asbestos, lead paint, and tobacco use reveals that increasing transparency and providing a voice to dispersed interests help avoid capture by interest groups and improve policy decisions. Contributing factors, such as when civil society organizations are able to develop independent expertise and freely communicate their conclusions through the media, internet, and social networks, as well as when there is free access to data and some legal protection for whistle-blowers, can help to strengthen the effectiveness of risk management policies.

References

Acemoglu, D., P. Aghion, L. Bursztyn, and D. Hemous. 2012. "The Environment and Directed Technical Change." *American Economic Review* 102 (1): 131–66.

Brunner, S., C. Flachsland, and M. Marschinski. 2012. "Credible Commitment in Carbon Policy." *Climate Policy* 12 (2): 255–71.

Fay, Marianne, Stéphane Hallegatte, Adrien Vogt-Schilb, Julie Rozenberg, Ulf Narloch, and Tom Kerr. 2015. *Decarbonizing Development: Three Steps to a Zero-Carbon Future.* Climate Change and Development Series. Washington, DC: World Bank.

Hacker, Jacob. 2006. *The Great Risk Shift.* New York: Oxford University Press.

Helm, D., C. Hepburn, and R. Mash. 2003. "Credible Carbon Policy." *Oxford Review of Economic Policy* 19: 438–50.

Rozenberg, Julie, Adrien Vogt-Schilb, and Stéphane Hallegatte. 2014. "Transition to Clean Capital, Irreversible Investment, and Stranded Assets." Policy Research Working Paper 6859, World Bank, Washington, DC.

Sdralevich, Carlo, Randa Sab, Younes Zouhar, and Giorgia Albertin. 2014. *Subsidy Reform in the Middle East and North Africa: Recent Progress and Challenges Ahead.* Washington, DC: International Monetary Fund.

World Bank. 2014. *World Development Report 2014: Risk and Opportunity—Managing Risk for Development.* Washington, DC: World Bank.

CHAPTER 3

The role of law

Long before the Code of Hammurabi set the law for ancient Mesopotamia, people subjected themselves—sometimes by cooperative agreement, sometimes under threat of force—to rules that would enable social and economic activities to be ordered. As societies evolved from close-knit kinship groups to larger and more diverse communities with more complex activities, the need for more formal rules increased (Fukuyama 2010). In modern states, law serves three critical governance roles. First, it is through law and legal institutions that states seek to *order the behavior* of individuals and organizations so economic and social policies are converted into outcomes. Second, law defines the structure of government by *ordering power*—that is, establishing and distributing authority and power among government actors and between the state and citizens. And third, law also serves to *order contestation* by providing the substantive and procedural tools needed to promote accountability, resolve disputes peacefully, and change the rules.

It has long been established that the *rule of law*—which at its core requires that government officials and citizens be bound by and act consistently with the law—is the very basis of the good governance needed to realize full social and economic potential. Empirical studies have revealed the importance of law and legal institutions to improving the functioning of specific institutions, enhancing growth, promoting secure property rights, improving access to credit, and delivering justice in society.[1]

As everyday experience makes clear, however, the mere existence of formal laws by no means leads to their intended effects. In many developing countries, the laws on the books are just that; they remain unimplemented, or they are selectively implemented, or sometimes they are impossible to implement. Governments may be unable to enact "good laws"—that is, those reflecting first-best policy—or "good laws" may lead to bad outcomes. And law itself may be used as a means of perpetuating insecurity, stagnation, and inequality. For example, for decades South Africa sustained a brutal system of apartheid rooted in law. It also has become common for political leaders in illiberal regimes to legitimize nondemocratic rule through changes to the constitution, such as amendments that extend term limits. Every day, actions that exert power over others, such as displacing the poor from their land, detaining dissidents, and denying equal opportunities to women and minorities, are taken within the authority of the law. In well-documented cases, laws intended to secure property rights have served to privilege powerful actors by allowing them to seize land and register it at the expense of rural farmers, or to perpetuate class systems and power relations.[2]

Law can be a double-edged sword: although it may serve to reinforce prevailing social and economic relations, it can also be a powerful tool of those seeking to resist, challenge, and transform those relations.[3] At the local, national, and global levels, states, elites, and citizens increasingly turn to law as an important tool for bargaining, enshrining, and challenging norms, policies, and their implementation. By its nature, law is a device that provides a particular language, structure, and formality for naming and ordering things, and this characteristic gives it the potential to become a force independent of the initial powers and intentions behind it, even beyond the existence of independent and effective legal institutions. Law is thus simultaneously a product of social and power relations and

> The mere existence of formal laws by no means leads to their intended effects. In many countries, laws remain unimplemented, or they are selectively implemented, or sometimes they are impossible to implement.

a tool for challenging and reshaping those relations. Law can change *incentives* by establishing different payoffs; it can serve as a focal point for coordinating *preferences and beliefs*; and it can establish procedures and norms that increase the *contestability* of the policy arena.

Law and the policy arena

Like policy, law does not live in a vacuum. Following the discussion in chapter 2, the nature and effectiveness of laws are primarily endogenous to the dynamics of governance in the policy arena. The ability of law—"words on paper"—to achieve its aims depends on the extent to which it is backed up by a credible commitment in order to coordinate expectations about how others will behave and to induce cooperation to promote public goods. This ability in turn is shaped by the interests of elites and by the prevailing social norms.

The task of defining law has captured the minds of legal scholars, philosophers, and sociologists for centuries. H. L. A. Hart (1961, 1) observed that "few questions concerning human society have been asked with such persistence and answered by serious thinkers in so many diverse, strange and even paradoxical ways as the question 'What is law?'" Theorists have debated the essence of law for centuries, including the extent to which law refers to custom and social

ordering, requires state-backed coercion, and encompasses notions of justice (box 3.1).

This Report sidesteps these philosophical debates and uses the term *law* or *formal law* in its most conventional sense to mean positive state laws—that is, laws that are officially on the books of a given state—at the national or subnational level, whether they were passed by a legislature, enacted by fiat, or otherwise formalized. Law here means the de jure rules. The operation of law requires a *legal system* composed of *actors* and *processes* whose function it is to make, interpret, advocate, and enforce the law. This system includes legislatures, judicial and law enforcement institutions, administrative agencies, as well as the legal profession, advocates, and civil society groups.

In all societies, state law is but one of many rule systems that order behavior, authority, and contestation. These rule systems include customary and religious law, cultural and social norms, functional normative systems (rule systems developed for the common pursuit of particular aims such as sports leagues or universities), and economic transactional normative systems (Tamanaha 2008). Such legal and normative pluralism (box 3.2) is neither inherently good nor bad: it can pose challenges, but it can also generate opportunities.

Plural normative systems can complement state laws by providing order where state institutions are not accessible, by alleviating the burden on state

Box 3.1 What is law?

Countless theorists have attempted to define law. The definitions generally fall into one of three categories, which were initially set forth two millennia ago in the Platonic dialogue *Minos*: (1) law involves principles of justice and right; (2) law is an institutionalized rule system established by governments; and (3) law consists of fundamental customs and usages that order social life. Adherents of the first category are natural lawyers such as Thomas Aquinas, who assert that the defining characteristic of law is its morality, justice, and fairness. Evil legal systems or evil laws are disqualified as law in this view. The second category aligns with H. L. A. Hart and other legal positivists, who base their definition on the existence of a legal system that consists of substantive laws (primary rules) and laws governing how

those rules are made (secondary rules), without regard for the justness of the law. Under this approach, evil legal systems count as law, but customary law and international law, which lack centralized enforcement systems, are not considered fully legal. The third category is represented by anthropologists and sociologists such as Eugen Ehrlich and Bronislaw Malinowski, who focus on customary law or living law. They reject the notion that law must consist of an organized legal system and instead recognize that the central rules by which individuals abide in social interactions count as law. Three key fault lines run across these conceptions of law: the first regarding the normative value of law, the second the systematic form of law, and the third the function of law.

Source: Brian Tamanaha, Washington University in St. Louis.

Box 3.2 Legal and normative pluralism

The phenomenon of "legal pluralism"—the coexistence of multiple legal systems within a given community or sociopolitical space—has existed throughout history and continues today in developing and developed countries alike. Modern forms of legal pluralism have their roots in colonialism, through which Western legal systems were created for colonists, whereas traditional systems were maintained for the indigenous population. That traditional or customary law still dominates social regulation, dispute resolution, and land governance in Africa and other parts of the developing world is well documented. In some cases, customary law, including a variety of traditional and hybrid institutional forms of dispute resolution, are formally recognized and incorporated into the legal system, such as in Ghana, South Africa, South Sudan, the Republic of Yemen, and several Pacific Islands states. In others, such forms continue to provide the primary means of social ordering and dispute resolution in the absence of access to state systems that are perceived as legitimate and effective, such as in Afghanistan, Liberia, and Somalia. Customary legal systems reflect the dominant (yet evolving, not static) values and power structures of the societies in which they are embedded, and as such are often thought to fall short of basic standards of nondiscrimination, rights, and due process. The extent to which they are considered legitimate and effective by local users is an empirical question and a relative one in light of the available alternatives.

A further source of normative pluralism is social norms—generally accepted rules of behavior and social attitudes within a given social grouping. Although they may be less visible than codified laws, they are highly influential. A vast literature documents how social norms derived from communal and identity groups, professional associations, business practices, and the like govern the vast majority of human behavior.[a] Social norms are a fundamental way of enabling social and economic transactions by coordinating peoples' expectations about how others will act. Social sanctions, such as shame and loss of reputation, or at times socially sanctioned violence, are a powerful means of inducing cooperation to prevent what is regarded as antisocial and deviant behavior (Platteau 2000).

Yet another source of normative pluralism is generated by today's globally interconnected world, in which a multitude of governmental, multilateral, and private actors establish and diffuse rules about a wide range of transactions and conduct (see chapter 9). Increasingly, the local experiences of law are informed by these broader rules covering topics such as trade, labor, environment, natural resources, financial institutions, public administration, intellectual property, procurement, utility regulation, and human rights. These rules can take the form of binding international treaties and contracts (hard law) or voluntary standards and guiding principles (soft law). These rules may reinforce, complement, or compete with state law to govern public and private spaces (Braithwaite and Drahos 2000; Halliday and Shaffer 2015).

Source: WDR 2017 team.

a. Ellickson (1991); Sunstein (1996b); Basu (2000); Posner (2000); Dixit (2004).

---

institutions, or by enabling diversity of preferences. For example, informal mediation of land disputes by community authorities, customary or religious determination of personal and family matters, and arbitration of contract disputes by business associations complement the state legal system in many countries. However, in some cases multiple rule systems may create confusion, undermine order, and perhaps lead to perverse outcomes. These issues could arise when people can no longer rely on the expectation that others will act in accordance with a certain set of rules (Basu 2000). In West Africa, violent communal land conflict is 200–350 percent more likely where there are competing legal authorities because the lack of

certainty reduces incentives to solve disputes peacefully (Eck 2014). Where formal state laws differ sharply from the content of other prevailing social norms and rule systems, they are less likely to be obeyed and may undermine trust in the state (Isser 2011).

Finally, pluralism can help pave constructive pathways to development outcomes by enabling contestation and the shaping of preferences. Throughout history, social entrepreneurs and clever intermediaries have proven to be deft at opportunistically selecting from among legal and normative claims and authorities to advance their aims.[4] Thus legal pluralism can serve to expand the languages and sites in which contests over power are waged. In India's

Gujarat and Uttar Pradesh states, advocate groups established informal women's courts (*nari adalat*) to provide an alternative legal avenue for women subjected to domestic violence. These courts enabled women to draw on community norms, state law, and international human rights to contest unequal power relations and to shape emerging norms (Merry 2012).

The interaction of law, norms, and power is fundamental to understanding how law works to underlie persistence or change in the dynamics of the policy arena across its three core roles, to which we now turn.

Ordering behavior: The command role of law

In this role, law is an instrument of policy. It is the means by which governments codify rules about how individuals and firms are to behave in order to achieve economic and social policy outcomes, including in the criminal, civil, and regulatory domains. What makes these laws—essentially words on paper—lead to the expected outcomes, or not? How do laws interact with power, norms, and capacity to create incentives, change preferences, and generate legitimacy? Although there is agreement that the legal system affects economic performance, there is no consensus in terms of *how* it affects performance (box 3.3). This section draws on the legal, sociological, and economic scholarship to look at three interrelated ways that law serves to induce particular behavior, and why these may fail. These are the *coercive power of law*, the *coordinating power of law*, and the *legitimizing power of law*. Although they operate with distinct logic, these three mechanisms rarely work alone but rather in joint ways that interact with power, norms, and capacity to provide the commitment and collective action needed to produce results.

The coercive power of law: Incentivizing behavior change through coercion or sanctions

Perhaps the most conventional reason that people obey the law is fear of sanctions.[5] If people, acting according to their narrow self-interest, do not behave in a socially desirable way, sanctions can be used to induce cooperation by changing incentives. In other words, the coercive power of law shapes the options available to people by making some actions infeasible or just too costly. The traditional law and economics approach uses a cost-benefit analysis: people will obey the law as long as the cost of noncompliance

(factoring in the likelihood of being caught) is higher than the benefits. Thus state bureaucrats will refrain from accepting bribes if the cost and likelihood of being caught are higher than the benefit of accepting the bribe. Manufacturing companies will comply with environmental regulations if there is a high likelihood of being fined an amount greater than their profit margin gained from noncompliance. Families can be induced to send their female children to school if the consequence of noncompliance is sufficiently severe. The converse holds true as well, such as a law that generates a credible reward for compliance—for example, a law requiring people to register for an identity card to gain access to welfare benefits. This finding also extends to state entities. For example, compliance with the regulations of the European Union, World Trade Organization, or World Bank Group depends on the belief that the rewards of membership will outweigh the alternative.

The coercive power of law depends on the existence of a credible threat of being caught and punished or a credible commitment to obtaining a reward for compliance. As Basu (2015) argues, that credibility depends on the extent to which the law is able to coordinate people's beliefs and expectations about what others—fellow citizens and the officials who implement and enforce laws—will do (see also Malaith, Morris, and Postlewaite 2001). However, three conditions must be met. First, the state needs the technical, physical, and human *capacity* to carry through with consistency. Second, the law must provide strong enough incentives to overcome the gains from noncompliance, taking into account that many people may not exhibit "rational behavior" (World Bank 2015), as well as overcome adherence to any alternative conflicting *normative* order. Third, the law needs to be in line with the incentives of those with enough *power* to obstruct implementation so they will go along with it (unless truly effective restraints on such power exist). Together, these conditions will create a credible commitment that will induce rational compliance.

Take, for example, a law prohibiting bribery. First, people need to believe that the state has the capacity to detect and punish those engaged in the practice—that is, it has effective administrative and law enforcement institutions. Even if the state does not have adequate reach to detect violations everywhere, it could be aided by private enforcement to the extent the law (in combination with a broader range of related laws) incentivizes whistle-blowing by those in a position to do so. And finally, the sanction for violating the law must leave the perpetrator worse off than any benefits from engaging in bribery.

The coercive power of law depends on the existence of a credible threat of being caught and punished or a credible commitment to obtaining a reward for compliance.

Box 3.3 Legal origins: Theory and practice

One of the most influential explanations of why some countries have legal systems that support more dynamic market economies than others is the legal origins theory put forward by La Porta and others (1998) and La Porta, Lopez-de-Silanes, and Shleifer (2013). This theory posits that countries that inherited a common law rather than a civil law system from their colonial occupiers have stronger investor and creditor rights, lower legal formalism, more efficiency of contract and debt enforcement, and higher judicial independence. These strengths are attributed to the

strong role of private property as well as the adaptability of the case law system that characterize British common law.

The legal origins theory sparked a significant effort to reform laws and regulations to imitate common law rules (Besley 2015). Yet, empirical analysis shows that there is no clear relationship between changes in legal rules and changes in economic outcomes, reinforcing the idea that changes in the form of laws do not necessarily change the way the legal systems function (see figure B3.3.1). This analysis is further backed by evidence finding only

Figure B3.3.1 Changes in investor protection and creditor rights have little impact on economic outcomes

Effects of changes in legal indexes on financial indicators

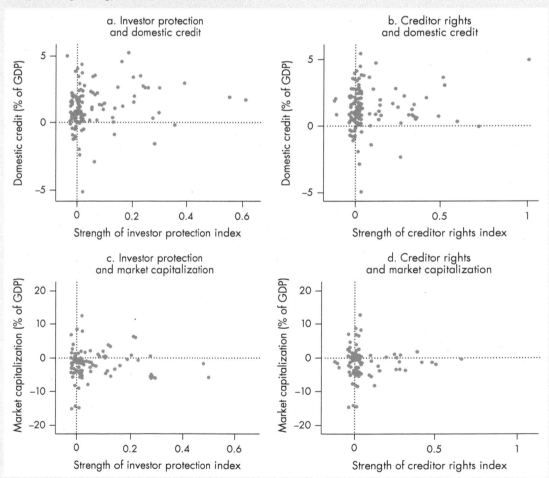

Source: WDR 2017 team, using data from Oto-Peralías and Romero-Ávila 2016.

Note: In the graphs, domestic credit extended to the private sector by banks and market capitalization of listed domestic companies are expressed in percentage of gross domestic product (GDP).

(Box continues next page)

But getting this formula right is complicated and costly. For example, too weak a sanction will be absorbed as part of the cost of doing business, while too strong a sanction for the behavior of potential whistle-blowers will reduce the number of people who will engage in private enforcement.[6]

But even with the right formula, the law must contend with powerful interests. To the extent that they benefit from bribery, enforcement will likely be blocked or not consistent or credible. Norms may also compete in ways that undermine implementation. Several studies have looked at the effect of "practical norms" or "culture" on the impact of laws. For example, laws establishing meritocratic civil service have gone unimplemented in Cameroon and Niger because of an overpowering norm that people should not be sanctioned for breaking the rules unless it is an egregious violation. The importance of social networks and neopatrimonial logic also undercuts the willingness of officials to sanction workers. As Olivier de Sardan (2015, 3) notes, "The gap between official rules and actual behavior is, per hypothesis, not a space where norms are forgotten or missing, but a space where alternative norms are in use."[7]

Competing normative orders can lead to perverse effects. For example, rigorous prosecution of domestic violence in Timor-Leste during its administration by the United Nations resulted in a significant reduction in the reporting of domestic violence because of the devastating social stigma and economic consequences for women (Chopra, Ranheim, and Nixon 2011). Similarly, stricter mandatory arrest laws for crimes related to domestic violence in the United States were found to be associated with higher murder rates of intimate partners because reporting of episodes of escalating violence to the police decreased (Iyengar 2009; Goldfarb 2011). In India, a recent law mandating the death penalty for convicted rapists could have similar effects because of the greater pressure now on women not to report a rape (Pande 2015). India has had strong laws on the books prohibiting a range of gender-based violence, including child marriage, sex-selective abortion, dowry payment, and domestic violence, but these have barely made a dent in behavior because the social sanctions associated with abandoning customary practice to follow the law are far stronger (Pistor, Haldar, and Amirapu 2010). Here the norm is likely operating at several levels. It undercuts the incentive created by the legal sanction, and it also likely undermines a credible commitment because powerful interests (and individuals in legal institutions) may also adhere to such norms.

Social norms that are not based on deep-rooted attitudes can also undercut the intended outcome of a law. As Ellickson (1991) famously documented in the study *Order without Law*, laws that conflicted with the social norms developed to regulate cattle herding in a California county confused cattlemen and led to increased conflict. A law introduced by the British in colonial India allowing agricultural lenders to enforce debts in court was intended to make credit markets more competitive to the benefit of farmers. However, in practice the law had the opposite effect because it undercut the incentives that lenders had under an informal enforcement regime to lend at favorable interest rates (Kranton and Swamy 1998).

An effective system of legal compliance based on sanctions is therefore quite difficult to achieve. It requires significant investment in capacity and infrastructure and careful analysis of the types of incentives most likely to work. However, even those measures will not suffice in the face of power and norm constraints. These considerations lead to the second and third mechanisms through which law affects behavior, which do not rely on force.

The coordinating power of law:
A focal point for change

The second way that law leads to economic and social policy outcomes is by serving as a focal point for coordinating behavior. This is also known as the expressive power of law (Cooter 1998; McAdams 2015). Here law acts as a signpost—an expression—to guide people on how to act when they have several options, or, in economic terms, when there are multiple equilibria (Basu 2015; McAdams 2015). People comply with the law because doing so facilitates economic and social activities.

The easy case is when the law establishes rules about a neutral activity to which citizens have no particular normative attachments. Thus when the law mandates driving on the right- or the left-hand side of the road, people generally comply, not because they fear punishment but because doing so facilitates road safety. The harder question is whether the law in its expressive role can coordinate behavior around more highly charged issues, where alternative norms and preferences are strong. In such cases, the law would need to shift norms and preferences away from alternative options in such a way that the law becomes the salient focal point.

Consider the astonishing success of the ban on smoking in public places in many parts of the world even in the absence of rigorous state enforcement. Here scholars have demonstrated that the ban has served to empower those persons—nonsmokers—who adhere to its substantive point to pressure smokers to refrain. In a short period of time, this empowerment has shifted societal norms so that the wrong of smoking in public places has become internalized (McAdams 2015). In other words, the ban has served to change the balance of power and norms in the policy implementation arena by legitimizing the claims of some over others. Sunstein (1996a) calls this phenomenon the *norm bandwagon* in which the lowered cost of new norms leads an increasing number of people to reject old norms until a tipping point is reached at which the old norm elicits social disapproval.

For this process to work, a critical mass of supporters of the new norm is needed, and they must be able to engage in collective action to push toward the tipping point. "When there are contestations in local norms, formal law can strengthen the stance of those whose norms are most closely aligned with the legal rule" (Shell-Duncan and others 2013, 824). The more deeply held the old norm and the weaker the supporting coalition for the new norm, the more care is needed to introduce a new norm through law so it does not backfire. Gradual or partial enforcement, coupled with education, awareness, and coaxing campaigns, allow time for norms to shift (Acemoglu and Jackson 2014).

This process of norm shifting has been analyzed and documented by legal anthropologists as a process of "translation" or "vernacularization" involving intermediaries who act as bridges between the world of formal law and the real experiences of local people (Merry 2006). For example, the introduction of an inheritance law in Ghana that was not in line with customary systems was followed by a slow evolution of custom and social change. The formal law was not enforced through coercion; rather, it served as a magnet to provide people with an alternative to custom (Aldashev and others 2012). Similarly, legal prohibition of female genital mutilation in Senegal provided an "enabling environment" for those who wished to abandon the practice. In Senegal, this legal prohibition, together with a robust education and awareness campaign, shifted more people to this category. However, among those who adhered strongly to the practice, the fear of prosecution (even though no sanctions were carried out) drove the practice underground, seriously impairing the health of some young women (Shell-Duncan and others 2013).

This is not to overstate the expressive power of law. Law does not do the work of shifting a norm by itself, but rather depends on the incentives it provides to those who already accept the new law, as well as a range of support programs that drive the process of internalizing the new norm more broadly. Although rigorous enforcement can backfire, sometimes enforcement is needed to kick-start the process of norm shifting and internalization. For example, during the first term in which a constitutional amendment mandating gender quotas in village councils in India was implemented, voters' attitudes toward women were generally negative. After two terms of repeated exposure to women candidates,

Law acts as a signpost—an expression—to guide people on how to act when they have several options.

however, men's perceptions of the ability of women to be leaders significantly improved (Beaman and others 2009). Moreover, the aspirations of parents and their adolescent daughters for education were positively affected (Beaman and others 2012), and women's entrepreneurship in the manufacturing sector increased (Ghani, Kerr, and O'Connell 2014). In the United States, a large coercive force was required to implement racial desegregation laws in the face of mass and even violent resistance, but over time these laws contributed to internalizing the norm change (Schauer 2015).

One way in which development affects governance is by changing norms. Certain norms are more responsive to a higher level of development. The introduction and effectiveness of child labor regulations have been shown to be related to income levels; as households rely less on children's incomes, the impact of formal regulations increases (Basu 1999). In India, however, child labor regulations led to a decline in child wages and a shift to greater child labor among poorer families (Bharadwaj and Lakdawala 2013). Some norms are much more persistent and less responsive to change, such as those founded on some religious or philosophical principles.

The legitimizing power of law: Creating a culture of compliance

Although sanctions can be used to control deviant behavior, and law can, under the right conditions, gradually shift certain norms, these are extremely costly and ad hoc ways of inducing changes in behavior. Ultimately, a culture of voluntary compliance with the law depends on the legitimacy of the law. Scholars point to three kinds of legitimacy: outcome, relational, and process legitimacy (as described in chapter 2). The latter two are particularly relevant to the role of law. *Relational legitimacy* (also referred to as *substantive legitimacy* in some strands of the literature) refers to a situation in which the content of the law reflects people's own social norms and views of morality. In such cases, the law is largely irrelevant because people would comply for reasons independent of the existence of the law. Even though the threat of sanctions lurks in the background, it is primarily there to handle the exceptional cases of deviance (Schauer 2015).

In heterogeneous societies, for substantive legitimacy the law must strike a balance between recognizing differences in worldviews and enabling society to function as a cohesive entity (Singer 2006). Thus debates over how states formally take into account

religious law or customary law are fraught with deeply political issues, with significant implications for legitimacy. For example, in Bolivia, Colombia, and Ecuador constitutional recognition of communal rights and indigenous law was critical in expanding state legitimacy through a sense of shared citizenship (Yashar 2005). Formal incorporation of Islamic law is at the heart of contests to define national identity in states and regions with large Muslim populations from Libya to Mindanao. And official recognition of forms of traditional or customary law remains an important issue in defining state-citizen relations in much of Sub-Saharan Africa.

Process legitimacy (also referred to as *procedural legitimacy*) refers to a situation in which laws are respected and observed to the extent that they emerge from a system deemed fair and trustworthy. Many years ago, German sociologist Max Weber (1965) argued that rational legal authority (in contrast to traditional or charismatic authority) depends on a society's belief in the legitimacy of order. In his seminal study, Tyler (2006) offers empirical support for the argument that people obey laws for reasons other than fear of punishment when they believe the laws are the product of a system they believe to be legitimate. Legitimacy here refers to procedural regularity, opportunity for citizen input, and the respectful treatment of citizens by those in authority, or what this Report refers to as *contestability*. These findings were confirmed in a study of cross-country survey data in Africa. People's compliance with the law was found to be related to their normative judgment about the legitimacy of government, based on assessments of government competence and performance, but particularly on perceptions that government is procedurally just (Levi, Tyler, and Sacks 2012).

Transplanting laws from one country to another has often failed in the absence of a process of adaptation and contestability. Based on an econometric study of 49 countries that were recipients of foreign law, Berkowitz, Pistor, and Richard (2003) found that countries that adapted the transplanted law to meet their particular socioeconomic conditions, or had a population that was already familiar with basic principles of the transplanted law, or both, had more effective legality than countries that received foreign law without any similar predispositions. Similarly, legal transplants in the context of integration into the European Union were more successful to the extent that they were accompanied by efforts to empower a variety of domestic state and nonstate actors through multiple methods of assistance and monitoring, and that they were able to merge monitoring and learning at both the national and supranational levels (Bruszt and McDermott 2014). By contrast, in parts of southeastern Europe the transplantation of judicial reform and anticorruption laws that bypassed legislative processes and other forms of adaptation did not produce the desired effects (Mendelski 2015).

Ordering power: The constitutive role of law

In this second role, law plays the more foundational constitutive role of defining the de jure governance process. It is through law—generally constitutions[8]—that states establish and confer power on state actors, defining the authority and responsibilities of different agencies and branches of government and their role in the policy-making and implementation process, as well as formal constraints on their power.[9] This task is typically carried out by drafting provisions that set out a range of checks and balances, including the horizontal allocation and separation of powers between different branches; by requiring special procedures for amendment; by establishing independent supervisory and review bodies; and, increasingly, by including a bill of rights. These formal de jure arrangements, as modified by informal and de facto arrangements, establish the nature of the policy bargaining arena. In this way, constitutions are effectively rules about making rules. This section addresses why and when the formal rules in fact determine the allocation and limits on power, or act only as "parchment barriers," as well as the other roles that constitutive laws play in shaping the dynamics of governance.

Constitutions: Rules about making rules

Constitutions are proliferating (figure 3.1). The growing number corresponds to both the increase in the number of independent states as well as the mass transition of countries in central Europe and in the former East European bloc in the post-Soviet era. It also reflects the fact that constitutions are generally short-lived. The average life span of a constitution is 19 years, and in Latin America and eastern Europe it is a mere eight years (Negretto 2008; Elkins, Ginsburg, and Melton 2009). Constitutions are thus an important object of political bargaining and ordering, with significant energy invested in designing and adopting them. This is true across all types of political regimes (Ginsburg and Simpser 2014).

And yet the effectiveness of constitutions in constraining power through rules is mixed, leading

Figure 3.1 Constitutions have become ubiquitous, but they are often replaced or amended

Number of countries with constitutions and number of constitutional events, 1789–2013

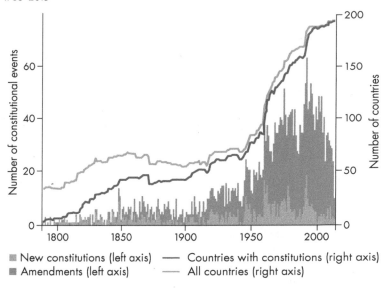

New constitutions (left axis) —— Countries with constitutions (right axis)
Amendments (left axis) —— All countries (right axis)

Source: WDR 2017 team, using data from Comparative Constitutions Project, 2015.

to two kinds of governance failures. The first—as reflected in the short life span of constitutions—is when the bargain itself fails. The second is when the words on paper persist, but the rules are ignored in the face of power and deal making. In the first failure, the result could be positive to the extent that it leads to a new, more stable, bargain. But it also could be detrimental to development outcomes if conflict ensues and if chronic failure undermines the credible commitments needed to support investment and pro-poor policies. Empirical evidence on the extent to which constitutional endurance matters is mixed. Elkins, Ginsburg, and Melton (2009) demonstrate significant associations between longer-lived constitutions and various social and political goods, including protection of rights, democracy, wealth, and stability, but establishing causality is problematic. In any event, the entrenchment of fundamental principles and its positive impact on credible commitment and coordination generally strengthen as constitutions age.

The second type of failure—widespread divergence between constitutional limitations on power and actual practice—is more directly associated with poorer development outcomes (figure 3.2). As explored in chapters 5 and 6, failure to uphold the security of property rights and basic civil, political, and economic rights has negative impacts on both growth and equity. More generally, failure to enforce rule-based limits on

Figure 3.2 In every country, there is a gap between the laws on the books and the laws implemented, but high-income OECD countries generally do better than low- and middle-income countries

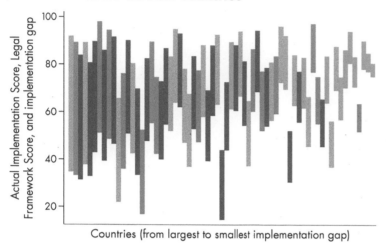

Countries (from largest to smallest implementation gap)

■ High-income OECD countries   ■ Upper-middle-income countries
■ High-income non-OECD countries   ■ Lower-middle-income countries
                    ■ Low-income countries

Sources: WDR 2017 team, based on data from World Bank, World Development Indicators (database), 2015, and Global Integrity (database), 2012.

Note: The data used are for 2009–11. Global Integrity's Legal Framework Score measures the quality of laws "on the books" in six categories: (1) nongovernmental organizations, public information, and media; (2) elections; (3) government conflicts of interest, safeguards, and checks and balances; (4) public administration and professionalism; (5) government oversight and controls; and (6) anticorruption legal framework, judicial impartiality, and law enforcement professionalism. The Actual Implementation Score measures actual practice. These scores range between 0 and 100, with 0 being the worst score and 100 being perfect. The implementation gap is the difference between the two indexes and thus the length of the bar. OECD = Organisation for Economic Co-operation and Development.

power skews the bargaining process in favor of elite interests. Nevertheless, divergence from the rules may also be an important means of holding together elite bargains. To understand what accounts for divergence between the rules and practice, it is helpful to first examine the conditions under which rules stick.

Constitutions as a commitment and coordination device

Why would rulers adhere to constitutional rules on the limits of power? Unlike regular laws that have organized institutions of enforcement, constitutions pose the ultimate question of who guards the guardians.[10] The answer is that effective constitutions need to be self-enforcing. Constitutions are essentially bargains among major interest groups about how to allocate power. As long as these groups feel they are better off with the rules than without them, the rules will stick. Thus effective constitutions establish an equilibrium by addressing problems of coordination and commitment (Weingast 2013). Constitutions

facilitate elite cohesion by coordinating which institutions play which role, thereby minimizing the costs of renegotiation and conflict. The so-called entrenchment of provisions, requiring a high standard for change in the form of amendment, provides credibility over time by guarding against shifts in preference, thereby enhancing the credibility of commitments (Ginsburg 2010; Ginsburg and Simpser 2014). Once entrenched, the rules become "sticky" as institutionalized arrangements develop around them, and it is far less easy for major interest groups to exit if they become unhappy with the allocation of power. Significantly, constitutions also serve as a coordinating device to enable collective action by citizens in the event of a transgression by those in power.

An analysis of a data set of every constitution since 1789 found that enduring constitutions generally have certain common characteristics. They need to be sufficiently inclusive to give potential spoilers an adequate payoff for staying inside the bargain (how to do so is explored further in chapter 4). They need to be flexible and adaptive so they can be resilient in the face of shocks that can change the balance of power among interest groups. And they need to be specific: the degree of specificity appears to correlate positively with endurance, perhaps because it reduces the scope for subsequent disagreement and requires more investment in negotiation, giving people a bigger stake in success (Elkins, Ginsburg, and Melton 2009).

How effective constitutions are at enabling citizen collective action for enforcement is related to the way in which constitutions act as a focal point. Even when politicians have little intention of adhering to constitutional provisions—such as when constraints on power and rights are adopted as aspirational or rhetorical appeasement—the words on paper can matter to the extent that they enable collective action. This is particularly important during times of conflict among elites, when constitutions can serve as devices of horizontal accountability. Thus, for example, in Tunisia adoption of international human rights treaties by the prior regime was largely seen as an empty gesture. Yet, during the transition to a new government, these provisions were seized upon by opposition forces and used to structure that government. Even when the legal enforceability of constitutions is limited, the language of constitutional protection has frequently been used as a basis for political mobilization by competing elite groups (Ginsburg and Simpser 2014). As will be discussed more fully, constitutions also serve as an important device of vertical accountability because the special status accorded to constitutional rights can enable citizen collective action aimed at the fulfillment of those rights.

Explaining divergence between law and practice

A number of studies have sought to demonstrate empirically how various institutional designs optimize the coordination and commitment embraced by different configurations of elite interests. In theory, different political institutions—such as presidential versus parliamentary or majority vote versus proportional representation—create different incentives that favor certain outcomes.[11] Actual outcomes, however, depend on the extent to which these de jure rules are in fact used as the main locus of political activity—that is, whether or to what extent political actors choose to invest in these institutions so that they become a self-reinforcing equilibrium (Caruso, Scartascini, and Tommasi 2015).[12]

In many developing countries—and to a certain extent, in developed ones as well—power is often exercised through a means other than those prescribed by law. Such alternative means are sometimes called "alternative political technologies" (Caruso, Scartascini, and Tommasi 2015) or "informal institutions" (Helmke and Levitsky 2004; Khan 2010). These means include a variety of ways of making bargains and deals outside the rules, including conventions for brokering power, clientelism, and purchasing favor (bribery, vote buying), as well as nonstate authority structures such as traditional or religious mechanisms. In some cases, the use of a means of exercising power not based on law is simply a matter of deviance and abuse. But often it is serving the purpose of solving commitment and collective action problems in ways more in line with elite incentives and the de facto distribution of power. In such cases, as Khan (2010, 1) explains, "informal institutions like patron-client allocative rules, and informal adaptations to the ways in which particular formal institutions work play a critical role in bringing the distribution of benefits supported by the institutional structure into line with the distribution of power." In other words, divergence between the law and practice is rarely an absence of rules but rather a matter of replacing law with rules that may be better suited—under the circumstances—to generating and meeting shared expectations in order to uphold basic stability through elite bargains (North and others 2013). The conditions under which deals-based elite bargains evolve into rule-based governance constrained by law are the subject of chapter 7.

Ordering contestation: The role of law in change

> It is true that in history the law can be seen to mediate and to legitimize existent class relations. Its forms and procedures may crystallize those relations and mask ulterior injustice. But this mediation, through the forms of law, is something quite distinct from the exercise of unmediated force. The forms and rhetoric of law acquire distinct identity which may, on occasion, inhibit power and afford some protections to the powerless.
>
> —E. P. Thompson (1975, 266)

The role of law in ordering behavior and ordering power is primarily about how elites use law to implement policies and to exercise authority. The third role of law is about how citizens—nonelites—use law to challenge and contest the exercise of power. As the quotation by the historian E. P. Thompson describes, law is both a product of social and power relations and a tool for challenging and reshaping those relations. This section examines how law, often in combination with other social and political strategies, can be used as a commitment and coordination device to promote accountability, and also to change the rules of the game to foster more equitable bargaining spaces.

In well-developed legal systems, legal institutions promote accountability by imposing horizontal checks on authorities and providing a forum for vertical claims by citizens. These legal institutions include courts and associated agencies such as prosecutors and police; special-purpose adjudicative and oversight bodies such as ombudsmen, auditors, and anticorruption or human rights commissions; and the public administrative law functions of executive agencies such as those involved in property allocation and registration, the issuance of identity documents, or the provision of health, education, and sanitation services. The extent to which these institutions are accessible and effective forums for citizens to challenge the more powerful in society varies considerably from country to country, as a function of historical circumstances as well as the political calculus of elites. Spotlight 3 on effective legal institutions discusses these conditions in depth.

Even though legal systems in many countries continue to lack effectiveness and autonomy, there has been a marked trend toward juridification of social and political contestation across the globe. As Rodrí-guez Garavito (2011, 274–75) has noted, "The planetary expansion of the law is palpable everywhere: in the

Law is both a product of social and power relations and a tool for challenging and reshaping those relations.

avalanche of constitutions in the Global South; in the growing power of judiciaries around the world; in the proliferation of 'law and order' programs and the 'culture of legality' in cities; in the judicialization of policy through anticorruption programs led by judges and prosecutors; in the explosion of private regulations, such as the voluntary standards on corporate social responsibility; and in the transmutation of social movements' struggles into human rights litigation." Law increasingly provides the common language for, and demarcates the arenas of contest among, very different contenders: citizens and states; multinational corporations and indigenous people; states, citizens, and international organizations.[13]

Law and social rights

In one example of how law is changing the contestability of policy arenas, a majority of developing countries have incorporated social and economic rights into their constitutions, and citizens are increasingly using these provisions to advance development goals (Brinks, Gauri, and Shen 2015). This trend has been most striking in Latin America, where the courts have been transformed—from weak, dependent, ineffective institutions to central players in issues at the forefront of politics and development. A key reason for this shift in role is that judicial actors have been emboldened by political fragmentation to assert the power of their institutions at the same time that citizens are demanding this role (Couso, Huneeus, and Sieder 2010; Helmke and Rios-Figueroa 2011). In India, legal institutions—at least at the level of the Supreme Court—have also proven to be an important venue for contestation, with an extensive tradition of public interest litigation and high-profile legal challenges to dominant power interests and social norms.[14] India's Supreme Court has upheld the rights of the disadvantaged and has enhanced government accountability over issues such as child and bonded labor, environmental hazards, public health, and nondiscrimination (Shankar and Mehta 2008; Deva 2009). Courts in South Africa have also made important judgments holding government accountable for the provision of housing and affordable antiretroviral drugs, among other things (Klug 2005; Berger 2008).

In social justice litigation, the legal action itself need not result in a favorable judgment to be a successful part of a contestation. Even judicial defeats can be leveraged by activists to coordinate collective action around rights consciousness (McCann 2004; Rodríguez Garavito and Rodríguez-Franco 2015). As explored further in chapter 8, the success of such efforts depends to a large degree on the ability of claimants to ground the language of rights in local social and political structures of demand—a process Brinks, Gauri, and Shen (2015) call "vernacularization." As Santos and Rodríguez Garavito (2005) argue, political mobilization at the local—and often international—level is a necessary precursor of effective rights-based strategies for the disadvantaged. Thus efforts to empower the aggrieved to use law and courts must combine legal awareness with broader strategic coalition building.

Law has also proven to be a powerful tool of accountability even outside of legal institutions by framing claims and serving as a coordinating device. For example, in China citizens are increasingly deploying official laws and policies in efforts to hold district officials accountable for illegal extraction, rigged elections, and corruption—a process dubbed "rightful resistance." Courts seldom feature in these efforts, which tend to "operate near the boundary of authorized channels, employ the rhetoric and commitments of the powerful to curb the exercise of power, hinge on locating and exploiting divisions within the state, and rely on mobilizing support from the community" (O'Brien and Li 2006, 2). The use of legal discourse, without recourse to courts, has also played a central role in tenant associations' claims to adequate housing in Kenya, indigenous groups' contests over land and natural resources in Mexico, and garment workers' efforts to gain fair labor conditions in Bangladesh (Newell and Wheeler 2006). In these cases, the law serves to "name and frame"—that is, to structure dialogue and provide a coordination device for more contentious strategies for accountability.

Legal institutions and credible commitment

Where state legal institutions have lacked the capacity for credible commitment, they have at times sought support from international actors. For example, aware of its inability to commit to fair anticorruption procedures against powerful interests, Guatemala sought support from the United Nations to establish the International Commission against Impunity in Guatemala (CICIG). The CICIG has successfully prosecuted over 150 current or former government officials, and in 2015 it charged the sitting president with corruption, leading to his resignation. Other countries, including Bosnia and Herzegovina, Cambodia, Fiji, Kosovo, and the Solomon Islands, have allowed international judges and prosecutors in their courts to enhance credible commitment around sensitive and political cases. Although these initiatives have led to the successful prosecutions of sensitive war crimes and corruption cases, they have also been criticized for lack of sustainability in that they bypass rather than engage directly in the domestic bargaining arena.

Where domestic courts are perceived as weak in the face of powerful interests, citizens have brought legal cases to other jurisdictions. This approach has been facilitated by the growing recognition of the concept of universal jurisdiction for severe crimes, as well as by the increasingly transnational character of powerful interests. For example, local communities affected by severe environmental damage caused by a mining company in Papua New Guinea sought redress in an Australian court, the home jurisdiction of the company. Although the legal case itself was settled and not wholly successful in containing the damage, it triggered a change in the local bargaining arena, mandating that community representatives be engaged in negotiating community development agreements with the company and government (Kirsch 2014).

Transnational legal pluralism and contestability

The legal arena today extends beyond the borders of nation-states in other ways as well. As discussed further in chapter 9, an era of "global governance" is under way. It is characterized by the proliferation and fragmentation of global, regional, and transnational instruments, including binding laws (so-called hard law, including treaties and conventions) and soft law (voluntary guidelines, standards, principles, and codes of conduct). The domains covered by these instruments go far beyond relations among nation-states to reach deep into the way national state and nonstate actors govern in many areas, including business, labor, crime, information, public financial management, intellectual property, procurement, utility regulation, human rights, food and safety standards, and environmental sustainability. The formation of these transnational governance regimes parallels this Report's framework: they are the product of contests among multiple actors—state, private, and civic—shaped by power, interests, and norms, which in turn are shaped and reshaped by the outcomes of these rules (Braithwaite and Drahos 2000). This web of legal pluralism creates opportunities for domestic actors seeking to contest the prevailing power and norms. Global factory workers in Mexico and Guatemala appealed to international labor standards and company codes of conduct and successfully managed to improve working conditions and to unionize in a context in which it would have been difficult otherwise to overcome entrenched resistance. Critical to their success were their links to transnational advocacy networks that exerted pressure on local governments (Rodríguez Garavito 2005). Cambodian garment workers also benefited from international labor standards that served as a commitment device for the government in order to gain favorable trade conditions (Adler and Woolcock 2009). Elsewhere, indigenous groups have been key players in the formation of international standards for extractive industries, in particular the norm of free, prior, and informed consent (Rodríguez Garavito 2011). In these examples, legal standards were converted into institutional arrangements that enhanced the contestability of the bargaining arena: collective bargaining arrangements, a tripartite labor arbitration council, and procedural requirements for consultations between extractive companies and local communities.

Getting to the rule of law

In establishing the rule of law, the first five centuries are always the hardest.

—Gordon Brown

The *rule of law* is widely recognized as necessary for the achievement of stable, equitable development. Indeed, over the last few decades no other governance ideal has been as universally endorsed.[15] There is far less agreement, however, on what it means. At a minimum, the rule of law requires that government officials and citizens be bound by and act consistent with the law (Tamanaha 2004; Fukuyama 2014). But this in turn requires that the law be clear, certain, and public and that it be applied equally to all through effective legal institutions.[16]

"Thin" versions of the rule of law have largely given way to "thicker" versions that move beyond a focus on procedure to one on substance requiring adherence to normative standards of rights, fairness, and equity.[17] The United Nations exemplifies this normative stance, defining the rule of law as "a principle of governance in which all persons, institutions and entities, public and private, including the State itself, are accountable to laws that are publicly promulgated, equally enforced and independently adjudicated, and which are consistent with international human rights norms and a principle of standards."[18]

Correlations between indicators of the rule of law and income levels are strong (figure 3.3).

The *rule of law* is widely recognized as necessary for the achievement of stable, equitable development.

Figure 3.3 The rule of law is strongly correlated with high income

Rule of Law Index versus GDP per capita, 2015

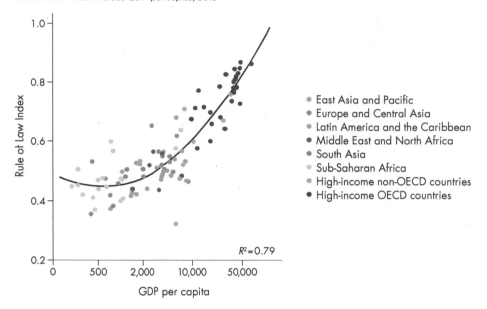

- East Asia and Pacific
- Europe and Central Asia
- Latin America and the Caribbean
- Middle East and North Africa
- South Asia
- Sub-Saharan Africa
- High-income non-OECD countries
- High-income OECD countries

$R^2 = 0.79$

Sources: WDR 2017 team, based on data from the World Justice Project, Rule of Law Index, 2015, and World Bank, World Development Indicators (database), 2015.

But the direction of causality and the mechanisms that determine this association are less well understood (box 3.4).

Meanwhile, this chapter has focused not on the rule of law but on the *role of law*—the instrumental way through which groups and individuals in society use law as a means of promoting, enforcing, and institutionalizing interests or objectives. Attention to the microfoundations of laws' effectiveness can help policy makers and citizens design laws and strategies more likely to achieve success (box 3.5). Ultimately, it is through this dynamic between power and contestation that societies shape their transitions to the rule of law.

Box 3.4 Transitions to the rule of law

Compared with the extensive literature on transitions to democracy, a surprisingly small amount of systematic work has been carried out on transitions to a modern rule of law. History reveals three separate types of transitions from which one can learn: (1) the shift from a customary, informal, and often highly pluralistic system of law to a unified modern one; (2) how powerful elites come to accept legal constraints on their power; and (3) how countries successfully adapt foreign legal systems to their own purposes.

The shift from a customary or pluralistic system to a codified modern one is usually motivated, at base, by actors who believe a single formal system will better serve their interests, particularly their economic interests in expanded trade and investment. Scale matters: at a certain point, the personal connections that characterize customary systems become inadequate to support transactions between strangers at great remove. However, the transition costs are high, and the customary rules are often preferred by the existing stakeholders. Therefore, political power is critical to bringing about the transition.

Formal law is usually applied first to nonelites ("rule *by* law"). There then is a shift to "rule *of* law" when the elites themselves accept the law's limitations. North, Wallis, and Weingast (2009) have argued that constitutional constraints become self-reinforcing when power in the system is distributed evenly and elites realize that they

(Box continues next page)

Box 3.4 Transitions to the rule of law *(continued)*

have more to gain in the long run through constitutional rules. What this theory does not explain, however, is why these same elites stick to these constraints when the power balance subsequently changes and one group is able to triumph over the others. Similarly, independent courts are always a threat to elite power, and so why do rulers come to tolerate them when they have the power to manipulate or eliminate them? These questions suggest that constitutionalism needs to be underpinned by a powerful normative framework that makes elites respect the law as such. Subsequent respect for the law will depend heavily on the degree of independence maintained by legal institutions—the judiciaries, bars, law schools, and other structures that have persisted even after their religious foundations have disappeared.

Finally, as for importing foreign legal systems, perhaps the most important variable determining success is the degree to which indigenous elites remain in control of the process and tailor it to their society's own traditions. Japan experimented with a variety of European systems before settling on the German civil code and Bismarck constitution. Later in the 20th century, China, the Republic of

Korea, and other Asian countries similarly adapted Western legal systems to their own purposes. In other cases such as Hong Kong SAR, China, Singapore, and India, the colonial power (Great Britain) stayed for a long time and was able to shape the local legal norms in its own image. Even so, today India practices a far higher degree of legal pluralism than does Great Britain itself, as part of the process of local adaptation. Less successful have been cases in Sub-Saharan Africa, where customary systems were undermined by colonial authorities but not replaced by well-institutionalized modern systems.

Much more research is needed on the question of legal transitions. It is clear that a fully modern legal system is *not* a precondition for rapid economic growth; legal systems themselves develop in tandem with modern economies. It may be that the point of transition from a customary to a formal legal system occurs later in this process than many Western observers have thought. But relatively little is known about the historical dynamics of that transition, and thus too little in the way of theory is available to guide contemporary developing countries as they seek to implement the rule of law.

Source: Prepared by Francis Fukuyama for WDR 2017.

Box 3.5 Understanding the role of law in context

As this chapter has argued, law is not an unqualified good. Depending on the context, law might functionally

- Empower change actors—*or*—reinforce existing power
- Provide order and certainty—*or*—create conflict and exacerbate confusion
- Build legitimacy—*or*— undermine legitimacy
- Structure contests—*or*—distract from real sites of contest.

To produce the effects that appear first in each line of this list, legal interventions should ensure that the forms

prescribed by law are able to demonstrate commitment and to induce collective action toward the desired end. Specifically, effective laws are able to

- Change preferences by enhancing substantive focal points around which coordination can occur
- Change incentives by changing payoffs to lower the cost of compliance or increase the cost of noncompliance
- Shape bargaining spaces that increase the contestability of underrepresented actors.

Source: WDR 2017 team.

Notes

1. Acemoglu (2003); Galiani and Schargrodsky (2010); Besley and Persson (2014).
2. See, for example, Thompson (1975); Mattei and Nader (2008); and Lund (2012).
3. Thompson (1975); Epp (1998); McCann (2004); Rodríguez Garavito (2011).
4. See, for example, Benton (2001); Belmessous (2011); and Yannakakis (2015).
5. See Schauer (2015) for an extensive argument about the importance of the role of force in law.
6. For a debate on legalizing bribe giving, see Basu (2011) and Dufwenberg and Spagnolo (2014).
7. See also Acemoglu and Jackson (2014) and d'Iribarne and Henry (2015).
8. A constitution is certainly not the only instrument that sets out rules about power, but it is the most visible one and the most systematically studied. A range of other laws that confer authority and define responsibilities and limitations on power, such as local governance laws and enabling laws for various state agencies, are also relevant.
9. Acuña and Tommasi (1999) propose a similar classification of rules applied at a more practical level (policies, organizational forms, rules about making rules).
10. Regular laws are also plagued by this same question. It is for this reason that Basu (2015) emphasizes that laws work only to the extent that they establish credible expectations about what others will do.
11. See, for example, Buchanan and Tullock (1962); Persson and Tabellini (2003); and Voigt (2011).
12. This discussion draws on Aoki (2001) and Greif (2006).
13. Comaroff and Comaroff (2001); Rajagopal (2003); Hirschl (2004); Santos and Rodríguez Garavito (2005).
14. However, the trend of public interest litigation in India has been criticized for shifting in recent years from pro-poor causes to promoting the interests of the upper classes (Gauri 2009). Indeed, if law and legal institutions can be used for pro-poor ends, they can likewise be used for other causes (Scheingold 2004).
15. Tamanaha (2004); Carothers (2006); Desai and Woolcock (2015).
16. Hadfield and Weingast (2014) model how these characteristics are necessary to achieve an equilibrium of behavior in line with the rule of law.
17. This aligns with the views of legal and moral philosophers such as Lon Fuller and John Rawls, who define law in terms of natural justice and fairness.
18. The definition continues: "It requires, as well, measures to ensure adherence to the principles of supremacy of law, equality before the law, accountability to the law, fairness in the application of the law, separation of powers, participation in decision-making, legal certainty, avoidance of arbitrariness and procedural and legal transparency" (United Nations 2004, 4).

References

Acemoglu, Daron. 2003. "Why Not a Political Coase Theorem? Social Conflict, Commitment, and Politics." *Journal of Comparative Economics* 31 (4): 620–52.

Acemoglu, Daron, and Matthew O. Jackson. 2014. "Social Norms and the Enforcement of Laws." NBER Working Paper 20369, National Bureau of Economic Research, Cambridge, MA.

Acuña, C., and M. Tommasi. 1999. "Some Reflections on the Institutional Reforms Required for Latin America." In *Institutional Reforms, Growth and Human Development in Latin America*. Conference Volume. New Haven, CT: Yale Center for International and Area Studies.

Adler, Daniel, and Michael Woolcock. 2009. "Justice without the Rule of Law? The Challenge of Rights-Based Industrial Relations in Contemporary Cambodia." Justice and Development Working Paper 2 (2), World Bank, Washington, DC.

Aldashev, Gani, Imane Chaara, Jean-Philippe Platteau, and Zaki Wahhaj. 2012. "Formal Law as a Magnet to Reform Custom." *Economic Development and Cultural Change* 60 (4): 795–828.

Aoki, Masahiko. 2001. *Toward a Comparative Institutional Analysis*. Cambridge, MA: MIT Press.

Basu, Kaushik. 1999. "Child Labor: Cause, Consequence, and Cure, with Remarks on International Labor Standards." *Journal of Economic Literature* 37 (3): 1083–1119.

———. 2000. *Prelude to Political Economy: A Study of the Social and Political Foundations of Economics*. Oxford, U.K.: Oxford University Press.

———. 2011. "Why, for a Class of Bribes, the Act of Giving a Bribe Should Be Treated as Legal." Working Paper 172011, Department of Economic Affairs, Ministry of Finance, Government of India, New Delhi.

———. 2015. "The Republic of Beliefs: A New Approach to 'Law and Economics.'" Policy Research Working Paper 7259, World Bank, Washington, DC.

Beaman, Lori, Raghebendra Chattopadhyay, Esther Duflo, Rohini Pande, and Petia Topalova. 2009. "Powerful Women: Does Exposure Reduce Bias?" *Quarterly Journal of Economics* 124 (4): 1497–1540.

Beaman, Lori, Esther Duflo, Rohini Pande, and Petia Topalova. 2012. "Female Leadership Raises Aspirations and Educational Attainment for Girls: A Policy Experiment in India." *Science* 335 (6068): 582–86.

Belmessous, Saliha, ed. 2011. *Native Claims: Indigenous Law against Empire, 1500–1920*. Oxford, U.K.: Oxford University Press.

Benton, Lauren. 2001. *Law and Colonial Cultures: Legal Regimes in World History, 1400–1900*. Cambridge, U.K.: Cambridge University Press.

Berger, Jonathan. 2008. "Litigating for Social Justice in Post-Apartheid South Africa: A Focus on Health and Education." In *Courting Social Justice: Judicial Enforcement of Social and Economic Rights in the Developing World*, edited by Varun Gauri and Daniel M. Brinks, 38–99. Cambridge, U.K.: Cambridge University Press.

Berkowitz, Daniel, Katharina Pistor, and Jean-Francois Richard. 2003. "Economic Development, Legality and the Transplant Effect." *European Economic Review* 47 (1): 165–95.

Besley, Timothy. 2015. "Law, Regulation, and the Business Climate: The Nature and Influence of the World Bank Doing Business Project." *Journal of Economic Perspectives* 29 (3): 99–120.

Besley, Timothy, and Torsten Persson. 2014. *Pillars of Prosperity: The Political Economics of Development Clusters*. Princeton, NJ: Princeton University Press.

Bharadwaj, Prashant, and Leah K. Lakdawala. 2013. "Perverse Consequences of Well-Intentioned Regulation: Evidence from India's Child Labor Ban." NBER Working Paper 19602, National Bureau of Economic Research, Cambridge, MA.

Braithwaite, John, and Peter Drahos. 2000. *Global Business Regulation*. Cambridge, U.K.: Cambridge University Press.

Brinks, Daniel M., Varun Gauri, and Kyle Shen. 2015. "Social Rights Constitutionalism: Negotiating the Tension between the Universal and the Particular." *Annual Review of Law and Social Science* 11: 289–308.

Bruszt, Laszlo, and Gerald A. McDermott. 2014. *Leveling the Playing Field: Transnational Regulatory Integration and Development*. Oxford, U.K.: Oxford University Press.

Buchanan, James, and Gordon Tullock. 1962. *The Calculus of Consent*. Ann Arbor: University of Michigan Press.

Carothers, Thomas, ed. 2006. *Promoting the Rule of Law Abroad: In Search of Knowledge*. Washington, DC: Carnegie Endowment for International Peace.

Caruso, German, Carlos Scartascini, and Mariano Tommasi. 2015. "Are We All Playing the Same Game? The Economic Effects of Constitutions Depend on the Degree of Institutionalization." *European Journal of Political Economy* 38 (C): 212–28.

Chopra, Tanja, Christian Ranheim, and Rod Nixon. 2011. "Local-Level Justice under Transitional Administration: Lessons from East Timor." In *Customary Justice and the Rule of Law in War-Torn Societies*, edited by Deborah H. Isser, 119–58. Washington, DC: United States Institute of Peace.

Comaroff, Jean, and John L. Comaroff. 2001. "Millennial Capitalism: First Thoughts on a Second Coming." In *Millennial Capitalism and the Culture of Neoliberalism*, edited by Jean Comaroff and John L. Comaroff, 1–56. Durham, NC: Duke University Press.

Comparative Constitutions Project. Various years. http://comparativeconstitutionsproject.org/#.

Cooter, Robert. 1998. "Expressive Law and Economics." *Journal of Legal Studies* 27 (S2): 585–608.

Couso, Javier A., Alexandra Huneeus, and Rachel Sieder. 2010. *Cultures of Legality: Judicialization and Political Activism in Latin America*. New York: Cambridge University Press.

Desai, Deval, and Michael Woolcock. 2015. "The Politics and Process of Rule of Law Systems in Developmental States." In *The Politics of Inclusive Development: Interrogating the Evidence*, edited by Sam Hickey, Kunal Sen, and Badru Bukenya, 174–96. Oxford, U.K.: Oxford University Press.

Deva, Surya. 2009. "Public Interest Litigation in India: A Critical Review." *Civil Justice Quarterly* 28 (1): 19–40.

d'Iribarne, Philippe, and Alain Henry. 2015. "The Cultural Roots of Effective Institutions." Background paper, WDR 2017, Agence Française de Développement, Paris.

Dixit, Avinash. 2004. *Lawlessness and Economics*. Princeton, NJ: Princeton University Press.

Dufwenberg, Martin, and Giancarlo Spagnolo. 2014. "Legalizing Bribe Giving." *Economic Inquiry* 53 (2): 836–53.

Eck, Kristine. 2014. "The Law of the Land: Communal Conflict and Legal Authority." *Journal of Peace Research* 51 (4): 441–54.

Elkins, Zachary, Tom Ginsburg, and James Melton. 2009. *The Endurance of National Constitutions*. New York: Cambridge University Press.

Ellickson, Robert. 1991. *Order without Law*. Cambridge, MA: Harvard University Press.

Epp, Charles. 1998. *The Rights Revolution*. Chicago: Chicago University Press.

Fukuyama, Francis. 2010. "Transitions to the Rule of Law." *Journal of Democracy* 21 (1): 31–44.

———. 2014. *Political Order and Political Decay*. New York: Farrar, Straus, and Giroux.

Galiani, Sebastian, and Ernesto Schargrodsky. 2010. "Property Rights for the Poor: Effects of Land Titling." *Journal of Public Economics* 94 (9–10): 700–29.

Gauri, Varun. 2009. "Public Interest Litigation in India: Overreaching or Underachieving?" Policy Research Working Paper 5109, World Bank, Washington, DC.

Ghani, Ejaz, William R. Kerr, and Stephen D. O'Connell. 2014. "Political Reservations and Women's Entrepreneurship in India." *Journal of Development Economics* 108 (2014): 138–53.

Ginsburg, Tom. 2010. "Public Choice and Constitutional Design." In *Research Handbook on Public Choice and Public Law*, edited by Daniel A. Farber and Anne Joseph O'Connell, 261–84. Research Handbooks in Law and Economics Series. Cheltenham, U.K.: Edward Edgar.

Ginsburg, Tom, and Alberto Simpser, eds. 2014. *Constitutions in Authoritarian Regimes*. Cambridge, U.K.: Cambridge University Press.

Global Integrity (database). Various years. Washington, DC, http://www.globalintegrity.org/.

Goldfarb, Sally F. 2011. "A Clash of Cultures: Women, Domestic Violence, and Law in the United States." In *Gender and Culture at the Limit of Rights*, edited by Dorothy L. Hodgson, 55–80. Pennsylvania Studies in Human Rights Series. Philadelphia: University of Pennsylvania Press.

Greif, Avner. 2006. *Institutions and the Path to the Modern Economy: Lessons from Medieval Trade.* Political Economy of Institutions and Decisions Series. Cambridge, U.K.: Cambridge University Press.

Hadfield, Gillian K., and Barry R. Weingast. 2014. "Microfoundations of the Rule of Law." *Annual Review of Political Science* 17: 21–42.

Halliday, Terence C., and Gregory Shaffer. 2015. *Transnational Legal Orders.* Cambridge Studies in Law and Society Series. New York: Cambridge University Press.

Hallward-Driemeier, Mary, and Lant Pritchett. 2011. "How Business Is Done and the 'Doing Business' Indicators: The Investment Climate When Firms Have Climate Control." Policy Research Working Paper 5563, World Bank, Washington, DC.

Hart, H. L. A. 1961. *The Concept of Law.* Clarendon Law Series. London: Oxford University Press.

Helmke, Gretchen, and Steven Levitsky. 2004. "Informal Institutions and Comparative Politics: A Research Agenda." *Perspectives on Politics* 2 (4): 725–40.

Helmke, Gretchen, and Julio Rios-Figueroa, eds. 2011. *Courts in Latin America.* Cambridge, U.K.: Cambridge University Press.

Hirschl, Ran. 2004. *Towards Juristocracy: The Origins and Consequences of the New Constitutionalism.* Cambridge, MA: Harvard University Press.

Isser, Deborah H. 2011. *Customary Justice and the Rule of Law in War-Torn Societies.* Washington, DC: United States Institute of Peace.

Iyengar, Radha. 2009. "Does the Certainty of Arrest Reduce Domestic Violence? Evidence from Mandatory and Recommended Arrest Laws." *Journal of Public Economics* 93 (1–2): 85–98.

Khan, Mushtaq H. 2010. "Political Settlements and the Governance of Growth-Enhancing Institutions." Draft research paper, SOAS, University of London, London.

Kirsch, Stuart. 2014. *Mining Capitalism: The Relationship between Corporations and Their Critics.* Oakland: University of California Press.

Klug, Heinz. 2005. "Campaigning for Life: Building a New Transnational Solidarity in the Face of HIV/AIDS and TRIPS." In *Law and Globalization from Below: Towards a Cosmopolitan Legality,* edited by Boaventura de Sousa Santos and César Rodríguez Garavito, 118–39. Cambridge Studies in Law and Society Series. Cambridge, U.K.: Cambridge University Press.

Kranton, Rachel E., and Anand V. Swamy. 1998. "The Hazards of Piecemeal Reform: British Civil Courts and the Credit Market in Colonial India." *Journal of Development Economics* 58 (1): 1–24.

La Porta, Rafael, Florencio Lopez-de-Silanes, and Andrei Shleifer. 2013. "Law and Finance after a Decade of Research." In *Corporate Finance,* Vol. 2A of *Handbook of the Economics of Finance,* edited by George M. Constantinides, Milton Harris, and Rene M. Stulz, 425–91. Amsterdam: Elsevier.

La Porta, Rafael, Florencio Lopez-de-Silanes, Andrei Shleifer, and Robert W. Vishny. 1998. "Law and Finance." *Journal of Political Economy* 106 (6): 1113–55.

Levi, Margaret, Tom R. Tyler, and Audrey Sacks. 2012. "The Reasons for Compliance with Law." In *Understanding Social Action, Promoting Human Rights,* edited by Ryan Goodman, Derek Jinks, and Andrew K. Woods, 70–99. Oxford, U.K.: Oxford University Press.

Lund, Christian. 2012. "Access to Property and Citizenship: Marginalization in a Context of Legal Pluralism." In *Legal Pluralism and Development: Scholars and Practitioners in Dialogue,* edited by Brian Z. Tamanaha, Caroline Sage, and Michael Woolcock, 197–214. Cambridge, U.K.: Cambridge University Press.

Malaith, George J., Stephen Morris, and Andrew Postlewaite. 2001. "Laws and Authority." Unpublished paper, Princeton University, Princeton, NJ.

Mattei, Ugo, and Laura Nader. 2008. *Plunder: When the Rule of Law Is Illegal.* Malden, MA: Blackwell Publishing.

McAdams, Richard. 2015. *The Expressive Power of Law.* Cambridge, MA: Harvard University Press.

McCann, Michael. 2004. "Law and Social Movements." In *The Blackwell Companion to Law and Society,* edited by Austin Sarat, 506–22. Oxford, U.K.: Blackwell Publishing.

Mendelski, Martin. 2015. "The EU's Pathological Power: The Failure of External Rule of Law Promotion in South Eastern Europe." *Southeastern Europe* 39: 318–46.

Merry, Sally Engle. 2006. *Human Rights and Gender Violence: Translating International Law into Local Justice.* Chicago: University of Chicago Press.

———. 2012. "Legal Pluralism and Legal Culture: Mapping the Terrain." In *Legal Pluralism and Development: Scholars and Practitioners in Dialogue,* edited by Brian Z. Tamanaha, Caroline Sage, and Michael Woolcock, 66–82. Cambridge, U.K.: Cambridge University Press.

Negretto, Gabriel L. 2008. "The Durability of Constitutions in Changing Environments: Explaining Constitutional Replacements in Latin America." Working Paper 350 (August), Kellogg Institute for International Studies, University of Notre Dame, South Bend, IN.

Newell, Peter, and Joanna Wheeler. 2006. *Rights, Resources, and the Politics of Accountability.* London: Zed Books.

North, Douglass C., John J. Wallis, Steven B. Webb, and Barry R. Weingast. 2013. *In the Shadow of Violence: Politics, Economics, and the Problems of Development.* New York: Cambridge University Press.

North, Douglass C., John J. Wallis, and Barry R. Weingast. 2009. *Violence and Social Orders: A Conceptual Framework for Interpreting Recorded Human History.* New York: Cambridge University Press.

O'Brien, Kevin J., and Lianjiang Li. 2006. *Rightful Resistance in Rural China.* Cambridge Studies in Contentious Politics Series. New York: Cambridge University Press.

Olivier de Sardan, Jean-Pierre. 2015. "Practical Norms: Informal Regulations within Public Bureaucracies (in Africa and Beyond)." In *Real Governance and Practical Norms in Sub-Saharan Africa: The Game of the Rules*, edited by Tom De Herdt and Jean-Pierre Olivier de Sardan, 19–62. Routledge Studies in African Politics and International Relations Series. London: Routledge.

Oto-Peralías, Daniel, and Diego Romero-Ávila. 2014. "The Distribution of Legal Traditions around the World: A Contribution to the Legal-Origins Theory." *Journal of Law and Economics* 57 (3): 561–628.

———. 2016. "Legal Reforms and Economic Performance: Revisiting the Evidence." Background paper, WDR 2017, World Bank, Washington, DC.

Pande, Rohini. 2015. "Keeping Women Safe: Addressing the Root Causes of Violence against Women in South Asia." *Harvard Magazine*, January–February. http://harvardmagazine.com/2015/01/keeping-women-safe.

Persson, Torsten, and Guido Enrico Tabellini. 2003. *The Economic Effects of Constitutions*. Cambridge, MA: MIT Press.

Pistor, Katharina, Antara Haldar, and Amrit Amirapu. 2010. "Social Norms, Rule of Law, and Gender Reality: An Essay on the Limits of the Dominant Rule of Law Paradigm." In *Global Perspectives on the Rule of Law*, edited by James J. Heckman, Robert L. Nelson, and Lee Cabatingan, 241–78. Law, Development, and Globalization Series. New York: Routledge.

Platteau, Jean-Philippe. 2000. *Institutions, Social Norms, and Economic Development*. Fundamentals of Development Economics Series. London: Routledge.

Posner, Eric. 2000. *Law and Social Norms*. Cambridge, MA: Harvard University Press.

Rajagopal, Balakrishnan. 2003. *International Law from Below: Development, Social Movements, and Third World Resistance*. Cambridge, U.K.: Cambridge University Press.

Rodríguez Garavito, César A. 2005. "Global Governance and Labor Rights: Codes of Conduct and Anti-Sweatshop Struggles in Global Apparel Factories in Mexico and Guatemala." *Politics and Society* 33 (2): 203–33.

———. 2011. "Ethnicity.gov: Global Governance, Indigenous Peoples and the Right to Prior Consultation in Social Minefields." *Indiana Journal of Global Legal Studies* 18 (1): 263–305.

Rodríguez Garavito, César, and Diana Rodríguez-Franco. 2015. *Radical Deprivation on Trial: The Impact of Judicial Activism on Socioeconomic Rights in the Global South*. Comparative Constitutional Law and Policy Series. New York: Cambridge University Press.

Santos, Boaventura de Sousa, and César Rodríguez Garavito, eds. 2005. *Law and Globalization from Below: Towards a Cosmopolitan Legality*. Cambridge Studies in Law and Society Series. Cambridge, U.K.: Cambridge University Press.

Schauer, Frederick. 2015. *The Force of Law*. Cambridge, MA: Harvard University Press.

Scheingold, Stuart A. 2004. *The Politics of Rights*. 2nd ed. Ann Arbor: University of Michigan Press.

Shankar, Shylashri, and Pratap Bhanu Mehta. 2008. "Courts and Socioeconomic Rights in India." In *Courting Social Justice: Judicial Enforcement of Social and Economic Rights in the Developing World*, edited by Varun Gauri and Daniel M. Brinks, 146–82. Cambridge, U.K.: Cambridge University Press.

Shell-Duncan, Bettina, Katherine Wander, Ylva Hernlund, and Amadou Moreau. 2013. "Legislating Change? Responses to Criminalizing Female Genital Cutting in Senegal." *Law and Society Review* 47 (4): 803–35.

Singer, Michael. 2006. "Legitimacy Criteria for Legal Systems." *King's Law Journal* 17 (2): 229–53.

Sunstein, Cass R. 1996a. "On the Expressive Function of Law." *University of Pennsylvania Law Review* 144 (5): 2021–53.

———. 1996b. "Social Norms and Social Roles." *Columbia Law Review* 96 (4): 903–68.

Tamanaha, Brian Z. 2004. *On the Rule of Law: History, Politics, and Theory*. Cambridge, U.K.: Cambridge University Press.

———. 2008. "Understanding Legal Pluralism: Past to Present, Local to Global." *Sydney Law Review* 30 (3): 375–411.

Thompson, E. P. 1975. *Whigs and Hunters: The Origin of the Black Act*. New York: Pantheon Books.

Tyler, Tom R. 2006. *Why People Obey the Law*. Princeton, NJ: Princeton University Press.

United Nations. 2004. "The Rule of Law and Transitional Justice in Conflict and Post-conflict Societies: Report of the Secretary General." Report S/2004/616, United Nations Security Council, New York.

Voigt, Stefan. 2011. "Positive Constitutional Economics II: A Survey of Recent Developments." *Public Choice* 146 (1): 205–56.

Weber, Max. 1965. *Politics as a Vocation*. Philadelphia: Fortress Press.

Weingast, Barry R. 2013. "Self-Enforcing Constitutions: With an Application to Democratic Stability in America's First Century." *Journal of Law, Economics, and Organization* 29 (2): 278–302.

World Bank. Various years. World Development Indicators (database). Washington, DC, http://data.worldbank.org/data-catalog/world-development-indicators.

———. 2015. *World Development Report 2015: Mind, Society, and Behavior*. Washington, DC: World Bank.

World Justice Project. Various years. Rule of Law Index. Washington, DC, http://worldjusticeproject.org/.

Yannakakis, Yanna. 2015. "Beyond Jurisdictions: Native Agency in the Making of Colonial Legal Cultures. A Review Essay." *Comparative Studies in Society and History* 57 (4): 1070–82.

Yashar, Deborah J. 2005. *Contesting Citizenship in Latin America*. New York: Cambridge University Press.

How do effective and equitable legal institutions emerge?

Closing the gap between law on paper and law in practice requires well-functioning legal institutions. Effective and equitable legal institutions operate as safeguards against abuses of power and as channels for the protection of rights and peaceful resolution of conflict. Well-functioning legal institutions are important to elicit voluntary compliance by signaling legitimacy. By reducing transaction costs and increasing the predictability of behavior and certainty of process, they underpin credible commitment, which is needed to modernize socioeconomic relations.

What are effective and equitable legal institutions?

Core state legal institutions include those that declare law (legislatures, government agencies), enforce law (prosecutors, regulators, police, prisons), and apply law to individual instances (courts). These institutions must operate in an integrated fashion with the cadre of private lawyers, academics, and civil society engaged in legal activity—the so-called legal complex (Karpik and Halliday 2011). They also require an appropriate enabling environment, including legal mandates, functional institutional systems and rules, and financial, human, and material resources. Meanwhile, they need to be physically and financially accessible to the population, while resonating with peoples' needs and perceptions of fairness in order to generate trust. To act as an effective check on power, courts especially need to be *independent* of political pressure, while remaining *accountable* and *effective* in

WDR 2017 team.

that they are able to compel compliance with their decisions.

Under what conditions do effective and equitable legal institutions emerge?

All high-income member countries of the Organisation for Economic Co-operation and Development (OECD) score well on de jure and de facto indicators of rule of law, including judicial independence, accountability, and effectiveness. This relationship illustrates the need for such institutions to support sophisticated and diversified economic models. But as this Report has emphasized, simply transplanting institutional forms to developing countries does not work; such forms need to emerge in a homegrown fashion from internal governance dynamics that reflect socioeconomic demands and other incentives. As shown in figure S3.1, a positive correlation between rule of law and income is observed today, but this does not explain causality or how countries move up the scale. The empirical and theoretical literature point to five sets of factors that are most likely to contribute to the development of equitable legal institutions that can act as an effective check on power: socioeconomic factors, historical factors, institutional factors, strategic factors, and ideational factors.

Socioeconomic factors. Across history and all societies, informal mechanisms for social order, dispute resolution, and checks on power have arisen in ways that meet local contexts. As Hadfield and Weingast (2013) document, predictable systems relying entirely on communal enforcement arose to bring order to the

Figure S3.1 Although high-income OECD countries generally have well-functioning legal institutions, the relationship between institutional quality and income varies in developing countries

Various rule of law indexes versus GDP per capita (log scale)

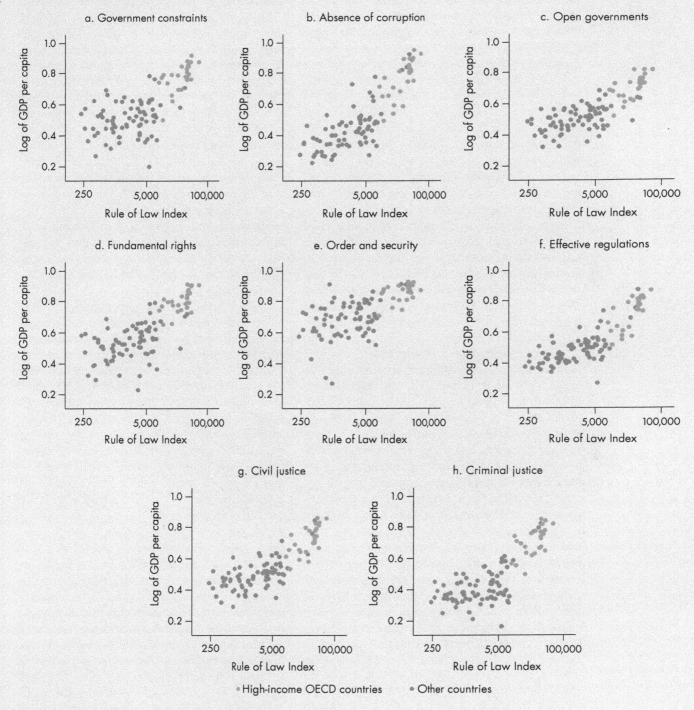

a. Government constraints

b. Absence of corruption

c. Open governments

d. Fundamental rights

e. Order and security

f. Effective regulations

g. Civil justice

h. Criminal justice

● High-income OECD countries ● Other countries

Sources: WDR 2017 team, based on data from World Justice Project, Rule of Law Index, 2014, and World Bank, World Development Indicators (database), 2016.

Note: GDP = gross domestic product; OECD = Organisation for Economic Co-operation and Development.

seemingly lawless period of the California gold rush in the mid-19th century, as well as to solve the contract enforcement dilemmas of traveling merchants in medieval Europe (see also Greif 2006). The diversification of societies and the increasing complexity of socioeconomic transactions created demands for a more formalized, arms-length mechanism for a state legal system (Dixit 2004). Even so, a wide range of alternative formal and informal mechanisms continue to exist, often proving capable of serving at least some functions of an effective legal system. Neighborhood mediation practices in urban Papua New Guinea, for example, manage disputes and maintain order in difficult urban communities in ways that formal police and courts have not (Craig, Porter, and Hukula 2016). Tribal and customary courts in Afghanistan, Liberia, and South Sudan have brought closure to vengeance killings, land disputes, and a range of social concerns, whereas the formal mechanisms used in some cases have exacerbated tensions (Isser 2011). Without discounting the important role they can play, such mechanisms are often effective precisely because they reflect the social norms and power relations in which they are embedded. Ultimately, state legal institutions are generally needed to promote equity and to serve as an effective check on power.

Historical factors. One explanation for why some judiciaries emerge as credible and effective while others do not is rooted in the historical circumstances—in particular, colonial legacies—in which the modern justice system developed. Where colonial legal systems and their national aftermaths sought to incorporate, accommodate, and adapt to the contending normative orders of society, national law and courts have emerged as relatively effective and legitimate institutions, as in India. By contrast, where colonial systems created fragmented spaces of Western law and indirect rule through which native authorities were often invented, as in Nigeria and Kenya, national law and courts faced an uphill battle in establishing credible commitments to legality. Although these dynamics tend to persist in some ways (through path dependency), they are constantly renegotiated in response to underlying patterns of social and economic change (Daniels, Trebilcock, and Carson 2011).[1]

Institutional factors. Courts are governed by an array of rules—constitutional and otherwise—that shape the independence, accountability, and effectiveness of the judiciary. These rules include judicial appointment and disciplinary procedures, the scope of judicial review, case management systems and procedures, legal standing, and access. Judicial reform efforts often focus on strengthening the formal rules, systems, and human capacity to protect judges from political pressure, incentivize efficiency, and promote access and transparency. These are important and necessary interventions, but often they are insufficient.

As figure S3.2 shows, even the most stringent constitutional guarantees of independence and best-practice forms of judicial appointment often do not correlate with de facto measures of independent judicial behavior (Feld and Voigt 2003; Ríos-Figueroa and Staton 2012). Moreover, the same formal rules can produce different incentives, depending on broader contextual factors (Helmke and Staton 2011). At the same time, empirical studies show that seemingly minor technical rule changes can have major effects on a court's role and assertiveness. For example, obscure rules on who has the right to bring a case ("standing rules") were instrumental in the rise to prominence of the courts in Costa Rica and India. In short, rules and capacity matter, but their relationship to judicial effectiveness in practice is mediated by strategic and ideational factors (Helmke and Ríos-Figueroa 2011).

Strategic factors. The first set of strategic factors relates to the calculus elites undertake to determine for what reasons they would endow courts with autonomy and effectiveness, keeping in mind that both could be used against elite interests. The literature points to five key reasons. First, elites may strengthen judiciaries to *signal a credible commitment to commercial investment* by raising the cost of political interference with economic activity, as in several fast-growing transition economies. The establishment of robust judicial institutions may also be in response to requirements for engagement in international organizations and transnational trade regimes (Moustafa and Ginsburg 2008). Second, elites may endow courts with capacity in order to use them to *enforce central policy, control agents, and maintain elite cohesion.* This was a key goal underlying Mexico's introduction of the mechanism of *amparo,* which allows citizens to challenge arbitrary action by individual bureaucrats (Magaloni 2008). Third, elites may bind their hands by establishing powerful courts during periods of political uncertainty as *political insurance* to protect their policies from being undermined in the event of a government transition (Ginsburg 2003; Staton and Moore 2011). Fourth, judicial review of legislation can serve an important *information-gathering role* for policy makers when they are unsure of how laws and policies will play out in practice (Staton and Moore 2011). Fifth, elites may empower courts in order to *channel controversial questions away from executive institutions.*

Figure S3.2 The correlation is weak between de jure and de facto measures of judicial independence

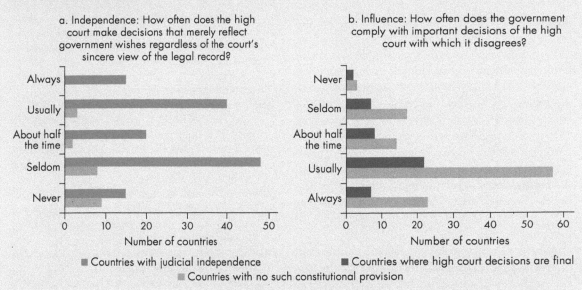

a. Independence: How often does the high court make decisions that merely reflect government wishes regardless of the court's sincere view of the legal record?

b. Influence: How often does the government comply with important decisions of the high court with which it disagrees?

■ Countries with judicial independence ■ Countries where high court decisions are final
■ Countries with no such constitutional provision

Sources: WDR 2017 team, based on data from V-Dem, 2016, and Comparative Constitutions Project, 2016.

For example, by empowering the Egyptian Supreme Constitutional Court to rule on policies related to economic liberalization, the executive was able to pass important reforms without significant political fallout (Moustafa 2007).

When used strategically by elites in these five ways, courts may be empowered with autonomy for some types of cases but not others—and that power may be taken away when it no longer serves elite interests. But even limited autonomy may create spaces for judicial actors to assert themselves and to strategically expand their role. Judges' calculus must take into account their institutional powers, but also the likelihood of compliance with their rulings. There is strong evidence that judiciaries are more likely to exercise power in cases of political uncertainty or fragmentation because this reduces the ability of others to put political pressure on the courts. This factor accounts for the emergence of autonomous judicial behavior in Brazil, Indonesia, and Mexico, among other countries (Helmke and Ríos-Figueroa 2011; Dressel and Mietzner 2012). Public expectations and demands on courts are also an important factor in this calculus, as is the broader role played by the private bar, legal academia, and other legal actors (Halliday 2013; Shapiro 2013). Judicial autonomy and effectiveness are thus an outcome of strategic interactions among the judiciary, other branches of government, and the public (McNollgast 2006).

The experience of the Supreme Court of India illustrates this process. At independence, the Court was endowed with expansive constitutional powers of judicial review and rights protection. During the period of emergency rule, the executive sought to curb these powers and pack the Court with government supporters. As India transitioned to multiparty politics and a coalition government, the Court began to reassert its independence by expanding popular access to the Court through public interest litigation. This step served to consolidate the strength of the Court through popular support and to establish precedent for a more activist role (Mate 2013).

Ideational factors. Despite their favorable institutional rules and strategic opportunities to consolidate power, some judiciaries remain constrained. The final factor is the so-called legal culture—that is, the "contested and ever-shifting repertoires of ideas and behaviors relating to law, legal justice and legal systems" (Couso, Huneeus, and Sieder 2010, 6). Simply stated, ideas, norms, beliefs, and values matter. For example, judges in Chile have been constrained by a tradition of legal formalism. By contrast, in Colombia judges' perceptions of their own role have shifted as indigenous groups have increasingly employed rights-based strategies (Domingo 2010). A social network analysis of Mexican judges depicts how professional networks can diffuse fundamental ideas about the role of judges (Ingram 2016).

Implications for judicial reform efforts

Analyzing how these factors play out in a given context can help identify what kind of reformist activities are most likely to have traction. Investments in improving the efficiency and effectiveness of commercial courts, for example, may take root where elite incentives and business demands align in favor of effective, impartial courts. Investments to strengthen citizen access and empowerment and improve judges' perceptions of their own roles are more likely to prove fruitful where strategic opportunities exist to expand the judicial role to limit abuse of power and protect rights. Conversely, the absence of such conditions may undermine efforts to build the capacity of legal institutions.

Where conditions do not favor empowerment of formal legal institutions, reformists can look to a broader set of formal and informal institutions that may be relevant in terms of meeting the key functions of commitment, coordination, and cooperation for particular issues. Commitment devices for commercial transactions include reputational considerations that might be served by industry mechanisms of alternative dispute resolution.[2] A range of customary, communal, or nonstate institutions may serve as effective cooperation mechanisms to resolve social and economic disputes peacefully. In such cases, efforts to improve the desired functions will be better served by understanding the strengths of existing institutions and seeking to enhance and complement their functional capacity by expanding accountability.

Notes

1. For a more nuanced discussion of how legal cultures were forged by a dynamic interplay between imperial policies and native agency, see Yannakakis (2015).
2. For examples of social mechanisms of commitment, see Ellickson (1991); Dixit (2004); and Greif (2006).

References

Comparative Constitutions Project. Various years. http://comparativeconstitutionsproject.org/#.

Couso, Javier A., Alexandra Huneeus, and Rachel Sieder. 2010. *Cultures of Legality: Judicialization and Political Activism in Latin America*. New York: Cambridge University Press.

Craig, D., D. Porter, and F. Hukula. 2016. "Come and See the System in Place: Mediation Capabilities in Papua New Guinea's Urban Settlements." World Bank Research Report, Justice for the Poor, Washington, DC.

Daniels, Ronald J., Michael J. Trebilcock, and Lindsey D. Carson. 2011. "The Legacy of Empire: The Common Law Inheritance and Commitments to Legality on Former British Colonies." *American Journal of Comparative Law* 59: 111–78.

Dixit, Avinash. 2004. *Lawlessness and Economics*. Princeton, NJ: Princeton University Press.

Domingo, Pilar. 2010. "Novel Appropriations of the Law in the Pursuit of Political and Social Change in Latin America." In *Cultures of Legality: Judicialization and Political Activism in Latin America*, edited by Javier A. Couso, Alexandra Huneeus, and Rachel Sieder. New York: Cambridge University Press.

Dressel, Björn, and Marcus Mietzner. 2012. "A Tale of Two Courts: The Judicialization of Electoral Politics in Asia." *Governance: An International Journal of Policy, Administration, and Institutions* 25 (3): 391–414.

Ellickson, Robert. 1991. *Order without Law*. Cambridge, MA: Harvard University Press.

Feld, Lars, and Stefan Voigt. 2003. "Economic Growth and Judicial Independence: Cross-Country Evidence Using a New Set of Indicators." Working Paper 906, Center for Economic Studies and Ifo Institute (CESifo), Munich.

Ginsburg, Tom. 2003. *Judicial Review in New Democracies: Constitutional Courts in Asian Cases*. New York: Cambridge University Press.

Greif, Avner. 2006. *Institutions and the Path to the Modern Economy: Lessons from Medieval Trade*. Cambridge, U.K.: Cambridge University Press.

Hadfield, Gillian, and Barry Weingast. 2013. "Law without the State: Legal Attributes and the Coordination of Decentralized Collective Punishment." *Journal of Law and Courts* 1 (1): 3–34.

Halliday, Terence. 2013. "Why the Legal Complex Is Integral to Theories of Consequential Courts." In *Consequential Courts: Judicial Roles in Global Perspective*, edited by Diana Kapiszewski, Gordon Silverstein, and Robert Kagan. Cambridge, U.K.: Cambridge University Press.

Helmke, Gretchen, and Julio Ríos-Figueroa. 2011. *Courts in Latin America*. Cambridge, U.K.: Cambridge University Press.

Helmke, Gretchen, and Jeffrey Staton. 2011. "The Puzzling Judicial Politics of Latin America: A Theory of Litigation, Judicial Decisions and Interbranch Conflict." In *Courts in Latin America*, edited by Gretchen Helmke and Julio Ríos-Figueroa. Cambridge, U.K.: Cambridge University Press.

Ingram, Matthew. 2016. *Crafting Courts in New Democracies: The Politics of Subnational Judicial Reform in Brazil and Mexico*. Cambridge, U.K.: Cambridge University Press.

Isser, Deborah H. 2011. *Customary Justice and the Rule of Law in War-Torn Societies*. Washington, DC: United States Institute of Peace Press.

Karpik, Lucien, and Terrence C. Halliday. 2011. "The Legal Complex." *Annual Review of Law and Social Science* 7: 217–36.

Magaloni, Beatriz. 2008. "Enforcing the Autocratic Political Order and the Role of Courts: The Case of Mexico." In *Rule by Law: The Politics of Courts in Authoritarian Regimes*, edited by Tamir Moustafa and Tom Ginsburg. New York: Cambridge University Press.

Mate, Manoj. 2013. "Public Interest Litigation and the Transformation of the Supreme Court of India." In *Consequential Courts: Judicial Roles in Global Perspective*, edited by Diana Kapiszewski, Gordon Silverstein, and Robert Kagan. Cambridge, U.K.: Cambridge University Press.

McNollgast. 2006. "Conditions for Judicial Independence." *Journal of Contemporary Legal Issues* 15 (1): 105–27.

Moustafa, Tamir. 2007. *The Struggle for Constitutional Power: Law, Politics, and Economic Development in Egypt.* New York: Cambridge University Press.

Moustafa, Tamir, and Tom Ginsburg. 2008. "Introduction: The Functions of Courts in Authoritarian Politics." In *Rule by Law: The Politics of Courts in Authoritarian Regimes*, edited by Tamir Moustafa and Tom Ginsburg. New York: Cambridge University Press.

Ríos-Figueroa, Julio, and Jeffrey Staton. 2012. "An Evaluation of Cross-National Measures of Judicial Independence." *Journal of Law, Economics, and Organization* 30 (1): 104–37.

Shapiro, Martin. 2013. "The Might Problem Continues." In *Consequential Courts: Judicial Roles in Global Perspective*, edited by Diana Kapiszewski, Gordon Silverstein, and Robert Kagan. Cambridge, U.K.: Cambridge University Press.

Staton, Jeffrey, and Will H. Moore. 2011. "Judicial Power in Domestic and International Politics." *International Organizations* 65 (3): 553–87.

V-Dem (Varieties of Democracy). Various years. Database hosted by Gothenburg Institute (Europe) and Kellogg Institute (United States), https://www.v-dem.net/en/.

World Bank. Various years. World Development Indicators (database). Washington, DC, http://data.worldbank.org/data-catalog/world-development-indicators.

World Justice Project. Various years. Rule of Law Index. Washington, DC, http://worldjusticeproject.org/.

Yannakakis, Yanna. 2015. "Beyond Jurisdictions: Native Agency in the Making of Colonial Legal Cultures. A Review Essay." *Comparative Studies in Society and History* 57 (4): 1070–82.

PART II

Governance
for development

4.

Governance
for security

5.

Governance
for growth

6.

Governance
for equity

CHAPTER 4

Governance for security

Sometime around 1775 BCE, Zimri-Lim, the king of the ancient Mesopotamian city of Mari in today's Syrian Arab Republic, wrote the world's earliest account—engraved on a clay tablet—of the use of arbitration and restitution to settle a dispute between two of his vassals. He rebuked one of them: "You have raided his country. Everything you took, gather it together and return it" (Munn-Rankin 1956, 95). On another occasion, the same king negotiated a power-sharing agreement over a contested city with his more powerful rival, King Hammurabi of Babylon. Bargaining extended over several years—"Remove [that city] from the treaty tablet and I shall commit myself!" offered Hammurabi at one point—but no agreement could be reached, a consequence of the uneven balance of power between the two kingdoms (Heimpel 2003, 379). Violence ensued, and in 1759 BCE the king of Babylon destroyed Mari, boasting that he had "turned the land into rubble heaps and ruins" and displaced its entire population (Heimpel 2003, 177).

Can governance solve the problem of violence in society?

Can dispute settlement, power sharing, restitution, and other forms of governance solve the problem of violence in society? Yes, under certain circumstances. Violence recedes when individuals, groups, and governments have *incentives* not to use it to pursue their objectives, and when not using it eventually becomes the norm. Institutions create incentives to reach agreements (cooperation) and enforce them (commitment).

When institutions of governance—the specific institutions for making and implementing policy—solve cooperation and commitment problems in ways that create *incentives* not to use violence, security prevails. When they do not, violence prevails. In the absence of cooperation, contending sides walk away from the bargaining table, and citizens do not comply with government rules. When commitment is lacking, warring factions renege on peace agreements, policy makers default on their promises to transfer resources to discontented groups or regions, disputants fail to abide by court judgments, the police abuse citizens instead of protecting them, and violence ensues.

The framework adopted by this Report emphasizes the centrality of three constitutive elements of governance for development: (1) the relative distribution of power among individuals and groups with conflicting preferences; (2) the bargaining arena where conflicting interests are mediated and policy choices are made and implemented; and (3) the barriers to entry to this arena. Accordingly, violent conflict is the result of three types of breakdowns in governance, all rooted in cooperation and commitment problems: (1) the unconstrained power of individuals, groups, and governments; (2) failed agreements between participants in the bargaining arena; or (3) the exclusion of relevant individuals and groups from this arena. Power sharing, resource redistribution, dispute settlement, and sanctions and deterrence have long been identified as potential ways governance can prevent, reduce, or end violent conflict, yet they succeed only when they constrain the power of ruling elites, achieve and sustain agreements, and do not exclude relevant individuals and groups.

> Violent conflict is the result of three types of breakdowns in governance: the unconstrained power of individuals, groups, and governments; failed agreements between participants in the bargaining arena; or the exclusion of relevant individuals and groups from this arena.

Security, governance, and power are tightly interlinked

Security—the security of people—is freedom from violence and the threat of violence (coercion).[1] Rather than representing discrete, opposed situations, security and violence are on a continuum. For that reason, this Report measures security as the reduction in the incidence of violence.[2] The threat of violence, however, is more difficult to measure. Compounding the measurement challenge is the overlapping and coexistence of violence and security.[3]

Security is a precondition for development

The cost of violence to development outcomes is staggering (figure 4.1). In 2015 violence cost the global economy US$14.3 trillion, or 13.4 percent of the global gross domestic product (GDP), and this cost has risen by more than 15 percent since 2008 (IEP 2015). Violent conflict has a negative impact on GDP per capita (figure 4.2). Civil war reduces economic growth by 2.3 percent a year (Collier 2007; Dunne and Tian 2014). Violent crime hinders economic development as well (Dell 2015). A 1.00-point decrease in homicide rates per 100,000 persons is associated with a 0.07–0.29 percentage point increase in GDP per capita growth over the next five years (World Bank 2006).

At the micro level, violence results in changes in household composition, losses in the productive capacities of household members, the destruction of productive assets and livelihoods, and displacement (Ibáñez and Vélez 2008; Justino 2009). Violence and its threat also indirectly impede trade, investment, and growth because of the uncertainty and the loss of trust and cohesion they generate (Knack and Keefer 1997; Zak and Knack 2001). For example, violent conflict directly cost Iraq 16 percent in per capita welfare from April 2011 to April 2014 and Syria 14 percent. However, when the foregone benefits of trade integration between the two countries and their neighbors are taken into account, the total cost of war almost doubles, to 28 percent for Iraq and 23 percent for Syria (Ianchovichina and Ivanic 2016).

The state's monopoly over violence is a precondition for security

In traditional societies, when security was still in the hands of private individuals and groups, the credible threat of violence through retaliation served as a deterrent against violence, and it was the main determinant of order and security.[4] The threat of revenge

Figure 4.1 Violence inflicts a high cost on development

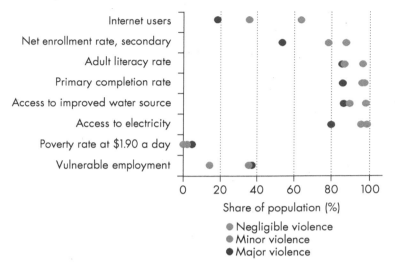

Sources: WDR 2017 team, using data from World Bank 2011; World Bank, World Development Indicators (database), 2015; Geneva Declaration Secretariat 2015; UCDP/PRIO 2015.

Note: The figure displays median values for all countries, by level of violence, for which data on development outcomes and violent deaths are available, ranging from 91 countries for poverty ratio data to 170 countries for access to electricity. Vulnerable employment is expressed as a percentage of total employment.

Figure 4.2 Violent conflict is associated with a reduction in GDP per capita

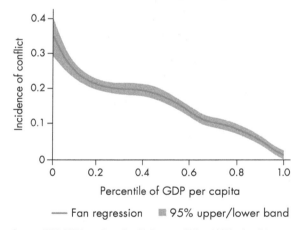

Sources: WDR 2017 team, based on Blattman and Miguel 2010 using data from World Bank, World Development Indicators (database), 2015, and UCDP/PRIO 2015.

Note: Incidence of conflict = number of violent conflicts in a country that led to at least 25 battle deaths in a year, between 1960 and 2015. GDP = gross domestic product.

largely helped reduce violence, but security was fragile, and the specter of violence always loomed (Bates 2001; North, Wallis, and Weingast 2009). Similar security arrangements based on deterrence persist in many parts of the developing world (Jacoby and Mansuri 2010).

Modern societies, by contrast, are fundamentally characterized by a concentration of security arrangements in the hands of the state, which has a monopoly over the means of violence and coercion (Weber 1965; Mann 1984). At its core, the state's monopoly over violence is the outcome of a collective agreement among powerful actors—an elite bargain, really—over who can use violence and when its use is acceptable (Wallis 2016).[5] The use of violence and coercion under this agreement is organized by the state, which typically enforces the agreement.

The monopoly over violence is an ideal that few states attain in all places at all times. It is the outcome of complex historical processes that unfold over decades, if not centuries (box 4.1). The elite bargains that give rise to this monopoly are contested, renegotiated, and reasserted every day, everywhere. The capacity—the stock of material and technological and human resources available to the state—to enforce these bargains and deter groups tempted to defect or renege on them is uneven and discontinuous over time and space.

Violence affects governance by changing power and norms

Violence and security change the distribution of power among groups and consequently affect governance—how these groups interact within a set of rules, which are themselves a function of the groups' relative power (see chapter 2 and Tilly 1978).[6] One group's use of force can strengthen or weaken—even annihilate—the power of other groups almost by definition. Assassinations, mass killings, coups, and revolutions do just that. New actors emerge and

Box 4.1 How modern governance was born offers lessons for today's "fragile" countries

Today's governance is the child of yesterday's violence. From the earliest records of human societies until the modern era, violence has been the norm (Pinker 2011). It was not until violence was constrained by the state that development began to occur on a large scale (North, Wallis, and Weingast 2009). Even the countries that enjoy the highest per capita incomes and most peaceful societies in the world, such as most of Europe, emerged from wars and violent contests for power (Tilly 1985, 1990). They were "fragile states" for most of their historical trajectory.

How these countries made this transition from violence and underdevelopment to security and prosperity reveals intriguing patterns. As commerce expanded in medieval Europe, *violence specialists*—individuals or groups that procured resources for themselves primarily through violence and coercion—traded the provision of security for financial resources to finance their wars (Braudel 1966). They allowed economic activity to flourish under their protection, founded states, and ceded some power and rights to business and other elites (Duby 1991; Bates 2001). Later, these rights were gradually expanded and eventually conceded to the majority of the population (Acemoglu and Robinson 2006). Constraints on unbridled power and other outcomes of these bargains between elites were formalized into laws. But violence did not disappear—on the contrary, more revenues were available to finance more external wars. It was now monopolized by these emerging states and channeled toward providing law and order, combating crime, and protecting property rights (Bates, Greif, and Singh 2002). Modern governance was born.[a]

Today, millions of people live under the rule of nonstate armed groups, contemporary equivalents of the medieval violence specialists who gave rise to the western European states.[b] *Wartime institutions*—the "rules of the game that result from the interaction between civilians and armed factions"—have created new, enduring realities on the ground, with profound implications for processes of state and nation building in the aftermath of violence (Justino 2016; see also spotlight 4). The relative security of places such as Somaliland provides a compelling illustration of the sustainability of the governance arrangements that arise organically—and without donor intervention—from the bargains struck among armed rebels, business communities, and civilians (Bradbury 2008). These arrangements exemplify the significance of these homegrown rules for the future governance of postwar countries—and the puzzles they pose to the international development community (Weinstein 2004).

Source: WDR 2017 team.

a. This narrative has been extended by some authors to contemporary states in eastern Africa and Southeast Asia as well. See Weinstein (2005) and Slater (2010).
b. Gambetta (1996); Weinstein (2007); Mampilly (2011); Ahmad (2015); Arjona, Kasfir, and Mampilly (2015); Sanchez de la Sierra (2015).

gain power from rebellions and wars. Historical and contemporary examples abound. Indirectly, individuals and groups can use violence and coercion to concentrate the proceeds of growth and development in their hands and increase their relative power by strengthening networks of patronage or gaining informational advantages (Levitsky and Way 2012).

Moreover, violence also affects norms of behavior and can shape new values and attitudes, including attitudes toward violence itself (box 4.2). This impact can be positive as well as negative. Exposure to violence from war has had surprisingly salutary and persistent effects on altruism (Burundi), empathy (Liberia), and political participation and social mobilization (Sierra Leone). It has also been linked to increased trust in government (Uganda), voluntary compliance with authority (Liberia), as well as higher levels of social capital, reciprocity, and interpersonal trust (Nepal).[7] Exposure to violence can also shape attitudes toward women along several fronts—including labor force participation, marriage and divorce (Germany after World War II), political participation (Peru), and bargaining among household members—and contribute positively to changes in gender roles.[8] Violence also changes identities and beliefs, including as a result of migrations and changes in the composition of households (Justino, Leavy, and Valli 2009).

The effects of violence on norms and attitudes can also be negative. The increased cooperation brought about by exposure to violence is mostly observable within groups rather than between groups, leading to forms of parochialism or identity-based insularity (Bowles and Gintis 2011). This effect could in theory generate more violence by reinforcing within-group cohesion based on distrust of others. Indeed, violence has the observed effect of hardening attitudes toward others and can also help construct identities in more rigid ways (Grossman, Manekin, and Miodownik 2015). These new norms and identities increase the support for elites who favor the continuation of violence to strengthen or extend their hold on power (Fearon and Laitin 2000; Fearon 2006). The power and resources that accrue to political elites who benefit from the use of violence then fuel more violence (Besley and Persson 2011).

So, violence affects norms, and norms affect violence. Violence affects power, and power affects violence. These two-way relationships highlight the broader point that violence can be persistent and self-sustaining. It tends to occur in interlinked episodes, with its intensity subsiding between cycles (World Bank 2011). Within-country and cross-country analysis of historical violent conflict in Africa between 1400 and 1700 reveals that it is associated with more postcolonial violent conflict, in addition to lower levels of trust and a stronger sense of ethnic identity (Besley and Reynal-Querol 2014).

Governance can prevent conflicts from becoming violent

Social choices, political change, and development itself are all inherently contentious and conflictual processes. The status quo benefits some members of society; any change is likely to benefit others, and conflict ensues (Acemoglu and Robinson 2006). This Report defines conflict as an active disagreement or dispute that arises when two or more individuals or groups believe their policy choices, interests, preferences, or concerns are incompatible. Accordingly, conflict in itself is not necessarily negative, and it can even be a constructive force for social change (Keen 1998). It is, in fact, an integral element of human interactions, and it is found in all societies at all times.

Poverty, inequality, and other manifestations of the unevenness of the development process generate tensions and distributive conflicts (Hirschman 1958; Knight 1992; Bardhan 2005). In addition to uneven development, three other broad sets of factors can also cause conflicts: identity and ideology; resources, including land, water, and extractives; and economic and other shocks. More often than not, these factors combine (box 4.3).[9]

Conflict and violence are not the same

And yet conflicts, no matter what causes them, need not erupt into organized violence. Examples are numerous. At the micro level, peaceful protests, strikes and lockouts, boycotts, and mass resignations are all examples of nonviolent manifestations of conflicts over any of these sets of drivers. At the country level, Australia, Botswana, and Norway all have oil or mineral wealth, and yet none has experienced significant violent conflict in generations. Singapore and Switzerland are ethnically, religiously, and linguistically diverse, but they enjoy some of the lowest levels of violence anywhere. Belgium recently experienced an acute crisis between parties representing its two main ethno-linguistic groups, including 541 days without a central government, but no violence erupted. Why? Because these countries have effective institutions of governance. They make all the difference in whether and when a conflict turns violent. A main message of this chapter is that institutions of governance can address conflicting interests and preferences without recourse to violence.[10]

Social choices, political change, and development itself are all inherently contentious and conflictual processes.

Box 4.2 The persistent links among gender-based violence, power, and norms

Gender-based violence (GBV) reflects power inequalities between women and men. Women and girls are more commonly the victims of GBV—a manifestation of power imbalances tilted in favor of men that characterizes many cultures around the world, most of them patriarchal. According to Watts and Zimmerman (2002, 1232), "Violence against women is not only a manifestation of sex inequality, but also serves to maintain this unequal balance of power." Collectively shared norms about women's subordinate role in society, which potentially leads to violence against them, perpetuate the power imbalance.

Female genital mutilation (FGM), sex selection, child marriage, dowry deaths, honor killings, and widowhood rituals are harmful cultural practices that are supported by various social norms and beliefs. For example, FGM is traditionally believed to preserve a girl's virginity until marriage; not conforming to the practice may lead to social exclusion, stigma, and the inability to find a husband (UNICEF 2013). Sex-selective abortions, infanticide, neglect of female children, and mistreatment of women who did not bear male children are manifestations of pervasive son preference, typically grounded in rigid patrilineal and patrilocal family systems and the special role of male children in religious rituals.[a] Dowries—a practice that strengthens son preference because it leads parents to consider daughters as liabilities—has often been linked to brutally violent acts against women—such as harassment, domestic violence, murder, and suicide—as a way to extract a higher dowry from the wife's family (UNFPA 2013). Honor killings involve murders, often committed by close relatives, in the name of "family honor." Such killings of women are a way to sanction the refusal of a female to enter an arranged marriage, an attempt by a female to marry outside her own social group, or the attack of a female by a rapist (UNFPA 2000; Pande 2015). Widows are sometimes victims of violence by in-laws and the object of humiliating rites and isolation as part of the mourning process. Such acts are intended to demonstrate a widow's grief and innocence in her husband's death (Chen 2000; Sossou 2002).

The continuation of these practices is supported by both women and men. The power imbalance can become internalized, and violence can even become acceptable for the victims, who may be afraid to challenge shared norms out of fear of backlash (they may not even be aware of alternatives to the norm). For example, more positive attitudes toward FGM are typically found in countries where its prevalence is higher. Interestingly, support for the continuation of FGM is generally similar among women and men, and among women greater support is expressed by those who themselves have undergone FGM.

Biased formal laws restricting women's economic opportunities reinforce (and are reinforced by) discriminatory gender norms, which in turn strengthen the power imbalance. Although many countries have recently carried out reforms to remove legal restrictions, about 90 percent of the 173 countries reviewed in a recent study still have at least one legal gender difference on the books, including laws requiring a woman to seek her husband's permission to work, travel, and register a business, and prohibitions on women working in certain industries or hours (World Bank 2015).

The persistence of these cultural practices depends in part on reciprocal expectations about the behavior of others.[b] As long as discriminatory norms are broadly shared by a critical mass of individuals who expect that others will conform to the practice, there will be no incentive to deviate from them. A shift requires coordination of beliefs because each individual's action depends on expectations of what the others will do. Strategic interdependence of individual beliefs will maintain the unequal distribution of power. Many state laws (such as those prohibiting FGM, domestic violence, child marriage, sex-selective abortions, and dowries, often introduced under domestic and international pressure from women's movements) have not been effective in reducing the prevalence of harmful practices because of the failure to understand the conditions needed to shift norms and the need to translate laws in the context of the local culture (see chapter 3). Other forces may lead to persistence that does not depend specifically on reciprocal social expectations, but rather on private motives that vary considerably across individuals and may require specific policy interventions (Efferson and others 2015).

Source: WDR 2017 team.

a. Das Gupta and others (2003); Milazzo (2014); Jayachandran (2015).
b. Mackie (2000), with specific reference to FGM.

Box 4.3 Several factors can cause conflicts, and they often combine

Identity is perhaps the broadest set of drivers of conflict. It encompasses ethnicity, race, language, territory, caste, gender, sexual orientation, religion, belief, and potentially all "markers" of difference between human beings. Identity carries the seeds of conflict in its womb: those who share the same identity are part of the "in-group," while those who do not are the "out-group"—the others. When people acquire a strong and exclusive sense of belonging to a single group, the stage is set for conflict (Sen 2006). Just as identities are a primary driver of conflict, conflict is the main way identities are shaped (Berman and Iannaccone 2006; Fearon 2006): "There is nothing like conflict to determine, delineate, and accentuate the sense of belonging" (Lianos 2011, 4).

Resources are another major driver of conflict, whether they are natural resources such as oil, minerals, and gemstones; common pool resources such as fisheries, forests, grazing land, and water basins; or private resources such as agricultural land and cattle. An extensive literature associates natural resources with the onset of violent conflict (Caselli, Morelli, and Rohner 2015; Ross 2015). Resources can trigger conflict whether they are scarce or abundant (Collier and Hoeffler 1998; Bardhan 2005). Conflict over the mismanagement and overuse of common pool (or open

access) resources is ubiquitous and has been the subject of landmark analyses and case studies (Ostrom 1990; Ellickson 1991). Resources also generate rents, which can be used to fuel and sustain conflict (Besley and Persson 2011).

Economic and other shocks may also drive conflict: An external (exogenous) event or condition (such as a drought, climate change, the discovery of a new trade route, or a hike in commodity prices) or an internal (endogenous) event or condition (such as technological change or demographic shifts) can disrupt a stable situation by introducing tension in the control of scarce or expanding resources.[a]

The *development process* itself—or rather its unevenness in the form of poverty, income inequality, and urban migration—can also be a powerful driver of conflict.[b]

Drivers of conflict can combine. Horizontal inequality—the confluence of ethnic identity and income inequality—is a particularly explosive combination (Esteban and Ray 2008; Esteban, Mayoral, and Ray 2012). Extreme scenarios feature all drivers. Such was the case of Darfur in Sudan, where local conflicts over land and water resources, drought, poverty and inequality, and ethnic and religious polarization all conspired, at a time when local governance broke down, to turn these drivers of conflict into one of the deadliest civil wars of the time (de Waal 2007).

Source: WDR 2017 team.

a. For drought, see Miguel, Satyanath, and Sergenti (2004); for climate change, Burke, Hsiang, and Miguel (2015); for commodity price shocks, Dube and Vargas (2013) and Bazzi and Blattman (2014); and for demographic shifts, Goldstone (2002).
b. For poverty, see Justino (2009); for income inequality, Fajnzylber, Lederman, and Loayza (2002), Montalvo and Reynal-Queyrol (2008), Stewart (2008), Enamorado and others (2016), and Ray and Esteban (2016); for urban migration, World Bank (2010).

Violent conflict is the result of a governance failure

There are converging indications that the use of organized violence to resolve a conflict is the outcome of a rational decision: leaders go to war when they believe the expected benefits of a war outweigh its expected costs (Tilly 1978; Fearon 1995), and young men join gangs and rebellions when this option is superior to the next best opportunity foregone (World Bank 2011). Institutions and norms shape behavior—including violent behavior. They create incentives for individuals and groups to use violence, or refrain from using it, to resolve conflicts by determining the expected gains from each option. These incentives differ in various institutional settings. For example, the existence of a credible threat of sanctions will discourage individuals from using violence. The absence of this deterrent will likely decrease the cost of the violent option. Violent conflict, then, is the outcome of the failure of institutions of governance to resolve a conflict, regardless of what factors or combinations of factors cause it. Three types of such governance failures can lead to violent conflicts: bargaining failures between individuals and groups; the unconstrained power of the state; and the exclusion of powerful individuals and groups from the bargaining arena where policies are made and implemented.

Bargaining failures. Violence can arise when agreements between opposing sides break down, such as when the state's monopoly over violence falls apart (Bates 2008a, 2008b). This violence becomes the preferred—and rational—way for certain individuals and

> Violent conflict is the outcome of the failure of institutions of governance to resolve a conflict, regardless of what factors or combinations of factors cause it.

groups to alter the distribution of power in their favor or to pursue their interests (Fearon 1995; Wagner 2000; Walter 2009). Such is the case in several fragile states, in the peripheral areas of many stronger states, but also in the so-called ungoverned spaces (which are often just "differently governed") (Pujol 2016) (spotlight 4). What these very different places have in common is the failure—sometimes localized only—of bargaining over who has the monopoly over violence in a territory.

Unconstrained power of the state. Although the state's monopoly over violence is a necessary condition of security, it is by no means sufficient to guarantee the long-term security of people and property. Violent conflict can, and often does, come at the hand of the state itself, particularly through its military and police. Ruling elites often resort to military force and repression against civilians to avoid having to share power (Acemoglu and Robinson 2006). Police forces may threaten and use unsanctioned violence against the population of urban slums instead of protecting them, as occurs in some U.S. and Latin American cities. Governments, or the private interests that have captured them, often violently expel local communities from their land for reasons ranging from granting concessions to mining corporations to expanding infrastructure projects (Hall, Hirsch, and Murray Li 2011; Moyo, Tsikata, and Diop 2015).

Exclusion of powerful actors. Violence can also emerge when powerful actors are excluded from the bargaining arena where policies are made and implemented—usually along identity fault lines. The distribution of power among ethnic groups, measured by their access to central state power, is a strong predictor of violent conflict, whether in the form of repression by the state or rebellion against the state. Cross-country statistical analyses using the Ethnic Power Relations data set indicate that countries in which large portions of the population are excluded from access to the state based on ethnicity are more likely to face armed rebellions and to experience violent repression by the state (Wimmer, Cederman, and Min 2009; Rørbæk and Knudsen 2015). The level of such exclusion seems to matter, too: the more excluded from state power ethnic groups are, the more likely their members are to initiate violent conflict with the government, especially if they have recently lost power (Cederman, Wimmer, and Min 2010).

Qualitative comparative and case study analyses of violent conflict in postcolonial Africa share the same finding that exclusionary elite bargains have led to trajectories of civil war, whereas countries in which elites have struck more inclusive elite bargains have succeeded in avoiding violent conflict. The extent of groups' access to state structures (in the form of jobs in the government and the military) and to state resources (such as land, commercial licenses, and other rents) determines the degree of inclusiveness or exclusiveness of these elite coalitions (Lindemann 2008, 2010).

Institutions of governance create incentives not to use violence

Ironically, some of the clearest insights into how institutions of governance shape incentives to prevent and reduce violent conflict have come from recent work on the ways violent groups maintain order and security within their own ranks (Justino 2016). Prison bands and slum gangs create informal governance rules to adjudicate disputes, divide resources, and enforce sanctions among their members (Venkatesh 2006; Skarbek 2014). Criminal associations such as the Sicilian Mafia do so as well (Gambetta 1996). Pirate organizations are a fascinating illustration of the emergence of rules of governance aimed at resolving conflicts driven by material inequalities and perceptions of unfairness and at eliciting cooperation among members of the group (Leeson 2011).

Formal and informal institutions of governance solve commitment and cooperation problems in ways that create incentives not to use violence. What these governance institutions are exactly, how they solve these functional problems, and under what conditions they work (or fail) to prevent, limit, or end violence are the subject of the rest of this chapter.

Governance can improve security in four ways

This Report identifies four categories of governance institutions that directly create incentives for individuals, groups, and governments to refrain from using violence to resolve conflicts.[11] Other types of institutions, such as markets or schools, play only indirect roles.

- *Sanction and deterrence institutions.* Governance institutions that punish and deter opportunistic behavior reduce *incentives* for violent behavior by increasing the cost of violence. Over time, they also shift *preferences* away from violence by changing norms and attitudes toward violence, leading to the internalization of new norms (see spotlight 5 on crime). Ultimately, they foster a culture of voluntary compliance based on legitimacy (chapter 2).

Examples range from speed limits and penalty fees to prison sentences.

- *Power-sharing institutions.* Governance institutions that balance, divide, and share power reduce the *incentives* to engage in violence by increasing the benefits of security. They may increase the *contestability* of policies as well. Examples include constitutions and proportional representation electoral systems.
- *Redistributive institutions.* Governance institutions that allocate and redistribute resources and resource rents are a special case of power-sharing institutions. They too reduce the *incentives* to use violence by increasing the benefits of security. Examples include budgets, social transfers, and victim compensation schemes.
- *Dispute resolution institutions.* Governance institutions that resolve and arbitrate disputes reduce incentives for using violence by stabilizing expectations. They can also shift *preferences* toward nonviolent outcomes. Examples include courts, as well as institutions of property rights such as contracts and titles.

Sanctions and deterrence can reduce violence by changing incentives and preferences

Deterrence maintains security by raising the cost of engaging in violence, whether by preventing crime (general deterrence) or by limiting recidivism (specific deterrence). Sanctions limit opportunities to use violence by way of incapacitation. Formal institutions of deterrence and sanction include the array of institutions falling under the criminal justice system such as the police, prosecutors' office, courts, prisons, penalties, and fines. Under the state's monopoly over violence, the coercion emanating from these institutions deters and constrains those tempted to use violence to pursue their objectives.

Robust empirical evidence indicates that crime responds to the *preventive* potential of incentives set by the criminal justice system, which is determined by two main parameters: a (nonabusive) police presence and number of policemen and the length of prison sentences. More police and more police presence have been shown *causally* to lead to declines in crime (Di Tella and Schargrodsky 2004; Chalfin and McCrary 2014). The length of prison sentences has as well, but to a lesser extent: for the adult population, the elasticity of crime with respect to length of sentence is small but still positive, whereas youth do not seem responsive to this incentive. Finally, because the effects of length of sentence exhibit rapidly

diminishing returns, capital punishment appears to have statistically insignificant effects on crime.[12]

On the other hand, incarceration has negative effects on recidivism, and the empirical findings are particularly troubling for youth. The experience of prison appears to create opportunities to build criminal capital and deepen criminal social networks, with the result that hardened youth frequently end up returning to crime after incarceration and at higher rates with harsher prison conditions. Incarceration can also ruin a youth's employment prospects, thereby reducing the future opportunity cost of violence (Mueller-Smith 2015).

These findings are consistent with various analytical studies suggesting that *mano dura* approaches—a set of heavy-handed government policies to combat criminal gangs in Latin America—are counterproductive (Kleiman 2011). These studies posit that heightened police engagement in crime-ridden communities may increase the risk of police abuse of innocent citizens and undermine citizen trust in government and community cohesion (Berkman 2007; World Bank 2010). Conversely, programs such as the "Youth and the Police" project in Belo Horizonte, Brazil, which organized workshops and seminars between police and youth groups, have been shown in some preliminary evaluations to improve local police-community relations (Berkman 2007).

In Rio de Janeiro, Brazil, Pacifying Police Units (UPPs) combine an increased police presence to regain control of urban territory from armed criminal groups with a new model of "proximity policing." This program seeks to build closer ties with local residents by holding community meetings and social events, providing teenagers with soccer lessons, and engaging in informal dispute settlement. In addition, it starkly reverses policemen's financial incentives by offering performance bonuses for reducing police homicides, thereby replacing an earlier policy that offered higher salaries to police officers who shot suspects in acts of legitimate defense. A recent evaluation of the impact of the introduction of the UPPs indicates that homicides by police would have been a massive 60 percent higher without UPP intervention (Magaloni, Franco, and Melo 2015).

Power sharing can reduce violence by changing incentives and increasing contestability

Power-sharing mechanisms give multiple contending elites a stake in the decision-making process and can rebalance power in the governance arena. Some form of power sharing aimed at co-opting elites and

Governance institutions that balance, divide, and share power reduce the *incentives* to engage in violence by increasing the benefits of security.

constraining majority rule has been attempted to end violence in nearly all conflicts within states over the last few decades. Power-sharing arrangements are especially relevant for societies divided along ethnic and religious identity lines such as in Bosnia and Herzegovina, Kenya, Lebanon, Northern Ireland, and South Africa, but also in countries where the conflict is a legacy of opposing ideologies.

Power-sharing institutions can take many forms. In one set of forms, particular offices or processes in national government can lower barriers to the entry of certain groups to the policy arena and increase its contestability. Examples include ensured representation of different individuals or factions in executive positions (Iraq, Kenya, Lebanon, Somalia); ensured minority voice in policy making through vetoes for minorities in coalition governments or supermajority requirements; positive action mechanisms such as legal quotas for women and marginalized groups in public office (India); and forms of legislative selection that guarantee the representation of all factions and groups such as electoral systems with proportional representation. In a second set of forms, power is distributed among groups at the subnational level. Examples include federalism (Belgium, Nigeria); administrative decentralization (Nepal, Sierra Leone); or regional autonomy (Aceh, Indonesia; Bougainville, Papua New Guinea; Catalonia, Spain; Corsica, France)—see Gates and others (2016).

Cross-country statistical analyses robustly associate institutions of power sharing with better security outcomes (Gurr 1993; Linder and Bächtiger 2005)—see figure 4.3. Executive power sharing in broad multiparty coalitions, an executive-legislative balance of power, multiparty systems, and proportional representation electoral systems are all significantly correlated with less incidence and risk of internal conflict, and less vulnerability to domestic terrorism, after controlling for economic and population characteristics. Statistical and empirical evidence in favor of decentralized and federal governance institutions is not as strong (Lijphart 2012).

Power sharing can reduce violence by giving the parties in a conflict incentives to cooperate

Mechanisms of power sharing manage conflict by encouraging cooperative behavior among rival factions. They give leadership elites incentives to collaborate, bargain, and encourage conciliation and tolerance among their followers. They also help mitigate the effects of the exclusion of minorities by majorities, reducing the likelihood of the onset of

Figure 4.3 An even balance of power is associated with positive security outcomes

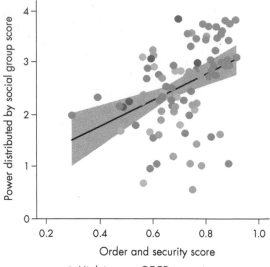

● High-income OECD countries
● High-income non-OECD countries
● Upper-middle-income countries
● Lower-middle-income countries
● Low-income countries

Sources: "Power distributed by social group" variable: V-Dem, version 6; "order and security" variable: World Justice Project, Rule of Law Index, 2015, Factor 5.

Note: The "power distributed by social group" variable is measured on a 0–4 scale, ranging from 0 (political power is monopolized by one social group) to 4 (social groups have equal political power). The "order and security" variable is measured on a 0–1 scale, ranging from 0 (low score) to 1 (high score). This composite variable consists of three dimensions measuring whether "crime is effectively controlled"; "civil conflict is effectively limited"; and "people do not resort to violence to redress personal grievances." OECD = Organisation for Economic Co-operation and Development.

identity-driven violent conflict. Where violence has already occurred, they give rebel factions incentives to lay down arms by offering them alternative avenues for contesting power in nonviolent ways, such as in Bosnia and Herzegovina, Liberia, and South Africa.[13] Over time, cooperation builds trust in the power-sharing mechanism and enhances its legitimacy—the extent to which people voluntarily comply with institutions and decisions (see chapter 2).

Cooperation is more likely when parties in a conflict can credibly commit to deals

Fighting parties are significantly more likely to cooperate and sign peace agreements to end wars if the deals contain specific assurances to share power (Walter 2002; Hartzell and Hoddie 2003). Enshrining power-sharing arrangements in peace agreements removes motives to continue fighting and has been negatively and significantly associated with renewed violent conflict (Walter 2015). Given the lack of trust among warring factions, mechanisms that ensure the credible commitment of elites, both to one another and to their followers, play a major role in ensuring that, once reached, power-sharing arrangements are implemented and violence stops (Keefer 2012).

Independent third-party mechanisms are the main mechanisms for ensuring the credibility of commitments in general (Schelling 1960; Bates 2008b). The same mechanisms can work to credibly commit parties in a conflict in the specific case of implementing power-sharing deals. For example, the deployment of international peacekeepers provided security guarantees for the agreements that ended the civil wars in Bosnia and Herzegovina, Liberia, and Sierra Leone. The commitment of regional and international powers played a similar role in reaching power-sharing accords in Lebanon, the former Yugoslav Republic of Macedonia, and Mali. However, third-party external enforcers cannot always ensure that power-sharing arrangements end the violence and restore order. Under which conditions do power-sharing arrangements promote order and security, and when do they fail?

As in the earlier example of ancient Babylon and Mari, large power asymmetries between contending factions make it easy for the stronger side to renege on its promises and hard for the weaker side to hold it to account for failing to commit (Walter 2009). Power asymmetries rooted in governments' monopoly over taxation of resources explain the likelihood of violent repression (Besley and Persson 2009). They also explain why some wars last longer than others (Fearon 2004). Conversely, power-sharing institutions can reduce violence when they constrain the power of ruling elites (figure 4.4). The more accountable a government is to a large share of the population, the easier it will be able to credibly commit to share power and the fewer incentives the sides will have to return to violence (Walter 2015; Gates and others 2016).

Redistributing resources and wealth can reduce violence by changing incentives

Redistributing wealth and sharing power affect security in similar ways. Indeed, they often go hand in hand: accessing centers of power and decision making opens the door to controlling resources and extracting rents. But elites can also redistribute wealth without having to share power by simply using fiscal policy to transfer resources to groups that threaten to use violence to pursue their interests (Bueno de Mesquita and others 2002; Acemoglu, Robinson, and

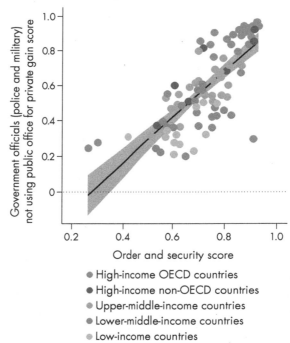

Figure 4.4 Constraining state power ensures security

Source: WDR 2017 team with data from the World Justice Project, Rule of Law Index, 2015.

Note: The "order and security" variable (Factor 5) is measured on a 0–1 scale, ranging from 0 (low score) to 1 (high score). This composite variable consists of three dimensions measuring whether "crime is effectively controlled"; "civil conflict is effectively limited"; and "people do not resort to violence to redress personal grievances." "Government officials in the police and the military do not use public office for private gain" variable (Factor 2.3) is measured on a 0–1 scale, ranging from 0 (low score) to 1 (high score). Results are presented as residuals after controlling for the natural logarithm of income per capita. OECD = Organisation for Economic Co-operation and Development.

Verdier 2004). Budgets then become the true battleground for distributive conflicts, and they reflect the bargains made among elites and between elites and citizens (Dorotinsky and Pradhan 2007).

Redistributive mechanisms address conflicts driven by poverty and inequality, usually in combination with the three other drivers. They can address conflicts rooted in grievances about the lack of access or unequal access to land and natural resources; inequalities along identity fault lines (horizontal inequality); and economic or environmental shocks. Redistribution can also address conflicts stemming from the greed of groups coveting the natural and material resources of the state and the rent extraction opportunities that access to these resources generates.[14]

Forms of redistributive governance institutions and policies include fiscal decentralization, intergovernmental transfers, taxation, social security systems and safety nets, subsidies and cash transfers, funds such as pension funds and permanent funds, and, by extension, social services such as health and education. Other institutions of governance, such as public employment, can serve both redistributive purposes and productive ones.

Redistribution can buy peace by strengthening the social contract between states and citizens

Historically, governments used social policy and other broad redistributive programs as a way to maintain order and reduce civil unrest. One example is the mainstreaming of insurance schemes in 19th-century Europe in the face of more assertive and better-organized labor movements. Much more recently, panel data from 16 Latin American countries reveal that steady increases in government expenditures on social welfare between 1980 and 2010 *caused* gradual but significant reductions in political violence in countries that witnessed reductions in inequality (Justino and Martorano 2016). Similarly, government expenditures on social services such as health, education, and welfare in 16 states of India from 1960 to 2011 were associated with a significant decrease in both the outbreak and escalation of riots across the country (Justino 2015). That such reductions occurred in the medium term further suggests that, here as well, these redistributive social policies are working through reductions in poverty and inequality. In both Afghanistan and India, more government spending on public services appears to have played a role in reducing insurgent violence (Beath, Christia, and Enikolopov 2012; Khanna and Zimmermann 2015).[15]

Government interventions to reduce urban crime in Latin America display a comparable pattern of increasing security by reducing poverty and inequality. Brazil's conditional cash transfer program, Bolsa Família, had a strong negative *causal* effect on urban crime in São Paulo as a result of increases in household incomes and changes in peer group membership (Chioda, de Mello, and Soares 2012). Colombia's Familias en Acción program in Bogotá displayed similar results (Camacho and Mejía 2013).

Redistribution can buy peace by co-opting elites

Short of committing to universalistic redistribution—usually offered in exchange for citizens abstaining from violent contestation—governing elites can credibly commit to narrower subsets of the population, whether groups with a strong capacity for mobilization or elites with veto power (Acemoglu and Robinson 2006). Bringing these smaller groups, or other elites, into the bargaining arena often happens

by way of patronage, a mode of governance in which politicians, or patrons, confer public jobs and benefits on supporters or clients (Keefer and Vlaicu 2008; Robinson and Verdier 2013). A time series cross-sectional study of 40 African countries found that expanding the size of cabinets by one additional minister reduces the risk of a coup more than the effect of a 1 percent increase in GDP—see Arriola (2009).

Governments often resort to patronage in public employment to maintain the stability of coalitions and ensure the loyalty of key constituencies whose discontent could jeopardize security (North and others 2013). During the recent uprisings in the Arab world, oil-rich governments—confronted with mounting dissent at home and concerned about the contagion from neighboring countries—decided to hike both the numbers and compensation of public employees in an effort to keep the peace and maintain the loyalty and quiescence of a key constituency (Brownlee, Masoud, and Reynolds 2013)—see figure 4.5.

Large increases in the public sector wage bill have deleterious effects on both budgetary sustainability and administrative efficiency. Attempts at curbing the trends have generally failed or have not been sustained (World Bank 1999). Despite these problems, public sector employment can solve the first-order problem of violence. Timor-Leste is a case in point. Following widespread unrest in 2006, the new government used revenues from the oil windfall to increase the budget 14-fold, from US$135 million in 2006 to US$1,850 million in 2013. Public employment spiked from 20,000 to more than 35,000 during the same period, along with social transfers to veterans (Srivastava and Blum 2016).

Redistribution can become corruption

The rent redistribution and patronage that accompany the bargains that are often necessary to maintain security and solve the first-order problem of violence frequently come at the expense of public integrity (Szeftel 1998). In few countries are these trade-offs between "buying the peace" and controlling corruption more salient than in the Republic of Yemen. Before the revolution of 2011, Republic of Yemen tribes formed a core part of the elite bargain that ensured relative security in this historically weak central state. An essential element of these armed tribes' loyalty to the central government was a vast patronage network, both formal and informal, that benefited the cooperating tribal elites. The Ministry of Tribal Affairs handed out formal monthly stipends to more than 4,500 tribal leaders across the country. In elections, the regime also favored local tribal elites, who used their position

Figure 4.5 Recruitment of civil servants increased exponentially in Tunisia and the Arab Republic of Egypt in the aftermath of the Arab Spring uprisings of 2011

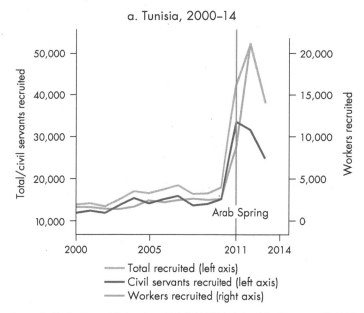

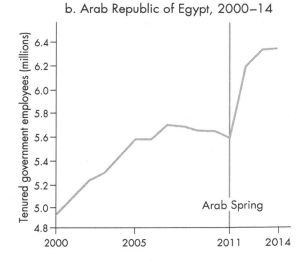

a. Tunisia, 2000–14

b. Arab Republic of Egypt, 2000–14

Total recruited (left axis)
Civil servants recruited (left axis)
Workers recruited (right axis)

Sources: Tunisia: Brockmeyer, Khatrouch, and Raballand 2015; Arab Republic of Egypt: Bteddini 2016.

as parliamentarians to secure public employment for their followers. Although some of this employment was real—particularly in the army and security forces—an informal mechanism awarded government jobs to more than 40,000 "ghost workers"—that is, clients and relatives of tribal leaders who received salaries without being expected to work. This fictitious employment consumed up to 6 percent of the national budget in the education sector alone (Egel 2013).

Redistribution can reduce violence by increasing trust in government and interpersonal trust

The exact mechanisms by which redistributive policies achieve security entail the resolution of commitment and cooperation problems between governments and groups pressing for redistribution—whether these are powerful elites or mobilized citizens (Addison, Le Billon, and Murshed 2002). Sustained and steady increases in government expenditures on social welfare, such as those in Latin America in the 1990s and 2000s, signaled governments' commitment to the social contract that ties the state to its citizens—or at least to the groups that would otherwise threaten elite control over the state (Bueno de Mesquita and others 2002, 2003). The political difficulty in rolling back these social welfare programs, which have become seen as entitlements,

makes them very credible commitment devices (Acemoglu and Robinson 2006).

Such commitment, coupled with the demonstrated and repeated capacity of governments to make good on their promises, could increase trust in government over time and reduce the chances of choosing the violent option. Conversely, the poor credibility of governments in committing to the transfer of resources can lead to violence, especially if the chances of overthrowing the government by violent means are greater than the probability of it credibly transferring the resources (Acemoglu and Robinson 2006; Murshed and Tadjoeddin 2009).

Social welfare policies can also reduce political conflict by helping to strengthen interpersonal trust between citizens. In both theory and analytical case studies, interpersonal trust has been classically linked to increased social cohesion and thus less social conflict. Empirically, it is linked to reductions in crime levels (Lederman, Loayza, and Menéndez 2002). Quantitative evidence linking social welfare to interpersonal trust is more limited, but empirical studies do show that interpersonal trust is higher among members of communities that are economically homogeneous and more equal. Conversely, participation in social activities, a close proxy of social cohesion, is lower in places where economic and social inequality are high (Alesina and La Ferrara 2002a, 2002b).

The link between fiscal decentralization and security levels is less well documented. One empirical before-and-after analysis of 98 districts in Java, Indonesia, shows that the incidence of routine violence in the form of neighborhood and village brawls and vigilante justice decreases as fiscal decentralization is implemented. This analysis suggests that the commitment to devolving resources and autonomy from distant central governments to local governments may increase the legitimacy of the local government, which in turn translates into more cooperative behavior and stronger cohesion among groups (Murshed and Tadjoeddin 2008).

Restitution and compensation also reduce incentives to engage in violence

Governance institutions that recognize and redress grievances present a special case of redistribution. They reduce incentives to engage the state through the use of violence by seeking to right past wrongs, which may help avoid repeated conflict (Walter 2015). These institutions include truth and reconciliation commissions such as in South Africa after apartheid; victim compensation schemes such as in El Salvador; and an array of material and nonmaterial measures, including symbolic ones, intended to restore people's dignity. The latter should not be underestimated. Indeed, the desire to restore a sense of dignity and self-worth as citizens and human beings appears to have been an essential element of the set of factors that triggered the Arab Spring (Brownlee, Masoud, and Reynolds 2013).

Dispute settlement can reduce violence by changing preferences

Dispute resolution institutions are critical to security and development. They help reduce violence and protect property rights. Mechanisms of dispute resolution include mediation, conciliation, and negotiation, where parties try to reach mutually satisfactory, self-enforcing agreements on their own. These mechanisms also include litigation and arbitration, where disputants rely on a third party such as a judge or a jury for resolution and the credible commitment needed to enforce the resolution. These institutions can be informal, such as elder councils in a village, or formal, such as courts, ombudsmen, and peace negotiators. Institutions of dispute resolution seek to resolve conflicts over material resources, whether scarce or abundant, such as land, water, extractives, and movable assets. They also aim to resolve conflicts over violations of norms of socially acceptable

behavior—usually codified into laws—including the use of violence and other types of offenses.

In the absence of strong formal institutions such as courts or police, individuals and communities resort to alternative dispute resolution (ADR) mechanisms—that is, a set of informal skills, practices, and norms of negotiation and mediation that aim to help parties reach self-enforcing bargains and reduce the cost and length of disputes. ADR mechanisms improve cooperation by building trust and improving communication and mutual understanding among parties and by cultivating a set of norms that encourage them to stay at the bargaining table (Blattman, Hartman, and Blair 2014). They cause a shift in preferences away from some options and in favor of others. When the third-party institutions that enforce contracts are weak or do not exist, disputants have incentives to renege on their agreements. Informal social sanctions can solve this commitment problem (Bardhan 1993). The norms promoted by ADR mechanisms, such as shaming would-be defectors, help enforce the bargains reached.

In Liberia, a large education campaign to promote ADR mechanisms for settling land disputes in 86 treated communities in 2009 resulted in a 32 percent decrease in property destruction relative to the control group (Blattman, Hartman, and Blair 2014).[16] In addition to reducing violence, the campaign in Liberia also had unintended consequences: it exposed more disputes, reflecting power struggles between village elders and youth, but these were overwhelmingly peaceful. This particular finding underscores some of the main points made in this chapter: that conflict is a normal element of the change process and is qualitatively distinct from violence, and that what matters for security is not the occurrence of conflict per se but rather its peaceful resolution by institutions.

Dispute resolution mechanisms do not always achieve security. The field experiment in Liberia remains an example of self-enforcing dispute resolution institutions helping to resolve low-intensity communal conflict, where the distribution of power between parties is relatively even. Such is not the case in the more acute conflicts over land and water resources that plague so many developing countries. These conflicts involve significant power dynamics such as land grabs by governments and closely connected local elites or extractive and agricultural concessions to multinational firms (Hall, Hirsch, and Murray Li 2011; Boone 2013). An evaluation of a donor-funded land mediation program that is also in Liberia indicates that once such power dynamics are at play,

> When the third-party institutions that enforce contracts are weak or do not exist, disputants have incentives to renege on their agreements. Informal social sanctions can solve this commitment problem.

self-enforcing dispute resolution mechanisms no longer achieve reductions in violence (Hartman, Morse, and Kitt 2014).

The uneven distribution of power among parties to a dispute stands in the way of reaching and enforcing mutually satisfactory bargains. The stronger disputants have few incentives to make concessions and relinquish power and resources, and they have many incentives to renege on agreements over time, as the rich literature on bargaining power suggests.[17] Solving disputes and enforcing contracts through the threat or use of force then become the more rational strategy for a powerful actor because the benefits of its use outweigh its costs, such as the risk of sanctions (Schelling 1960; Walter 2015). The existence of norms that exclude certain groups such as women and minorities from the bargaining arena where disputes are settled reinforces power asymmetries and perpetuates inequitable and insecure outcomes (Platteau 2000).

Conclusion

As noted in chapter 1, security is a precondition for development. However, using governance to solve the first-order problem of violence requires reaching and sustaining stable elite bargains, and it inevitably involves compromises, concessions, and trade-offs between development outcomes. The rent redistribution that accompanies the bargains necessary to maintain security can constrain development (North and others 2013; Acemoglu and others 2014). In specific cases, power-sharing arrangements between elites have helped avoid violent conflict, but they have also shackled the economy (Lindemann 2011). Similarly, elite bargains that enshrine existing inequalities can ensure security in the short term, but they are not sustainable in the long term. How governance can resolve these trade-offs among growth, equity, and security constitutes a new frontier on the development research agenda.

Notes

1. This chapter is about the security of people, as opposed to national security or the security of territories. Because of the particular threat it discusses—violence—the definition of security used here is narrower than "human security" (where threats are multiple, ranging from, in addition to violence, loss of income to food shortages, infectious diseases, and environmental threats) and yet broader than "citizen security" (where the threat is violence, but mainly that stemming from crime). This chapter does not discuss other threats, but it recognizes that they can lead to conflict and even violence. In this chapter, violence is defined as the use of physical force intended to kill, harm, or destroy.

2. Peace, a concept much broader than security, is not addressed in this chapter.

3. This chapter uses a single framework—a unifying model of violence—to address the relationships among governance, security, and development, and it applies the same framework to all types and actors of violence. The many forms of violence, which often overlap, include violence from civil war, repression, rebellion, coups, interstate conflicts, and genocide; violence from gang activity, terrorism, piracy, and organized crime; communal violence; urban violence, riots, and civil strife; and interpersonal and gender-based violence. A particular characteristic of modern violence is that the lines between forms of violence are becoming increasingly blurred (World Bank 2010, 2011; Geneva Declaration Secretariat 2015). Similarly, violence has many agents or actors. Governments, political militias, rebels, criminal gangs, communal militias, rioters, radicalized individuals and groups, and external armed forces can all be agents of violence. Sometimes, it can be difficult to tell them apart; indeed, at times different actors of violence operate side by side. Finally, violence mutates from one form to another over time, and so do the identities and affiliations of its perpetrators, making the typologies of actors and forms of violence less useful for the purposes of this Report.

4. As the British anthropologist E. E. Evans-Pritchard observed in 1940 about the Nuer, an ethnic group in today's South Sudan, "The very readiness of the Nuer to employ violence provides a reason, then, that violence so rarely takes place" (quoted in Bates 2001, 45).

5. Max Weber, in his 1965 essay *Politics as a Vocation*, originally theorized that the monopoly over violence was a single agreement among powerful groups over the use of violence. The authors are grateful to John Wallis for making this important point.

6. As Tilly (1978, 62) notes, "Great shifts in the arrangement of power have ordinarily produced—and have often depended on—exceptional moments of collective violence."

7. Bellows and Miguel (2006); Blattman (2009); Gilligan, Pasquale, and Samii (2011); Voors and others (2012); Blair (2015); Hartman and Morse (2015).

8. Calderón, Gáfaro, and Ibáñez (2011); Justino and others (2012); Buvinic and others (2013); García-Ponce (2015); Akbulut-Yuksel, Khamis, and Yuksel (2016).

9. The *World Development Report 2011: Conflict, Security, and Development* identified a very broad range of factors associated with violent conflict (World Bank 2011). It referred to them as internal and external

"stresses," whether economic, security-related, or political, adding that "they can combine and precipitate actual violence." This chapter calls a small subset of these factors "drivers" and shows instead that they cause all conflicts, but need not result in violence. It isolates governance as the precipitating element that determines whether and when conflicts caused by these drivers turn violent.

10. Engerman and Sokoloff (2002); Boix (2003); Acemoglu and Robinson (2006); North, Wallis, and Weingast (2009).

11. Some institutions of governance are intended to produce and sustain violence, such as concentration camps, slavery, or apartheid, but they are not covered in this chapter.

12. The authors are indebted to Laura Chioda for her clarification of the issues addressed in this paragraph.

13. Lijphart (2004); Norris (2008); Gates and Strøm (2013).

14. This chapter finds that the traditional distinction in the literature between conflicts motivated by greed and conflicts motivated by grievance cuts across drivers and actors of conflict. It does not find this distinction useful in concept or in practice.

15. Some caveats are necessary. In the case of Afghanistan, the reduction in violence was temporary and limited in areas with initially low levels of violence. A related study of insurgency in the Russian Federation's North Caucasus also found that in areas where insurgents were intrinsically motivated by the overthrow of the government or were receiving external support, increased government spending did not reduce violence (see Toft and Zhukov 2015).

16. Such land disputes are endemic in countries where property rights are not well defined or protected, and they often result in communal violence (Onoma 2010).

17. Wagner (2000); Fearon (2004); Powell (2004, 2006); Walter (2015).

References

Acemoglu, Daron, Suresh Naidu, Pascual Restrepo, and James A. Robinson. 2014. "Democracy Does Cause Growth." NBER Working Paper 20004, National Bureau of Economic Research, Cambridge, MA.

Acemoglu, Daron, and James A. Robinson. 2006. *Economic Origins of Dictatorship and Democracy.* Cambridge, U.K.: Cambridge University Press.

Acemoglu, Daron, James A. Robinson, and Thierry Verdier. 2004. "Kleptocracy and Divide-and-Rule: A Model of Personal Rule." *Journal of the European Economic Association* 2 (2–3): 132–92.

Addison, Tony, Philippe Le Billon, and Syed M. Murshed. 2002. "Conflict in Africa: The Cost of Peaceful Behaviour." *Journal of African Economies* 11 (3): 365–86.

Ahmad, Aisha. 2015. "The Security Bazaar: Business Interests and Islamist Power in Civil War Somalia." *International Security* 39 (3): 89–117.

Akbulut-Yuksel, Mevlude, Melanie Khamis, and Mutlu Yuksel. 2016. "For Better or for Worse: The Long-Term Effects of Postwar Reconstruction on Family Formation." *Applied Economics* 8 (29): 2771–84.

Alesina, Alberto, and Eliana La Ferrara. 2002a. "Participation in Heterogeneous Communities." *Quarterly Journal of Economics* 115 (3): 847–58.

———. 2002b. "Who Trusts Others?" *Journal of Public Economics* 85 (2): 207–34.

Arjona, Ana, Nelson Kasfir, and Zachariah Mampilly. 2015. *Rebel Governance in Civil War.* Cambridge, U.K.: Cambridge University Press.

Arriola, Leonard. 2009. "Patronage and Political Stability in Africa." *Comparative Political Studies* 42 (10): 1339–62.

Bardhan, Pranab. 1993. "Economics of Development and the Development of Economics." *Journal of Economic Perspectives* 7 (2): 129–42.

———. 2005. *Scarcity, Conflicts, and Cooperation: Essays in the Political and Institutional Economics of Development.* Cambridge, MA: MIT Press.

Bates, Robert H. 2001. *Prosperity and Violence: The Political Economy of Development.* New York: Norton.

———. 2008a. "State Failure." *Annual Review of Political Science* 11 (1): 1–12.

———. 2008b. *When Things Fall Apart: State Failure in Late-Century Africa.* Cambridge, U.K.: Cambridge University Press.

Bates, Robert H., Avner Greif, and Smita Singh. 2002. "Organizing Violence." *Journal of Conflict Resolution* 46 (5): 599–628.

Bazzi, Samuel, and Christopher Blattman. 2014. "Economic Shocks and Conflict: Evidence from Commodity Prices." *American Economic Journal: Macroeconomics* 6 (4): 1–38.

Beath, Andrew, Fotini Christia, and Ruben Enikolopov. 2012. "Winning Hearts and Minds through Development: Evidence from a Field Experiment in Afghanistan." MIT Political Science Department Research Working Paper 2011-14, Massachusetts Institute of Technology, Cambridge, MA.

Bellows, John, and Edward Miguel. 2006. "War and Institutions: New Evidence from Sierra Leone." *American Economic Review* 96 (2): 394–99.

Berkman, Heather. 2007. "Social Exclusion and Violence in Latin America and the Caribbean." Research Department Working Paper 613, Inter-American Development Bank, Washington, DC.

Berman, Eli, and Laurence R. Iannaccone. 2006. "Religious Extremism: The Good, the Bad, and the Deadly." *Public Choice* 128 (1): 109–29.

Besley, Timothy, and Torsten Persson. 2009. "Repression or Civil War?" *American Economic Review* 99 (2): 292–97.

———. 2011. *Pillars of Prosperity: The Political Economics of Development Clusters.* Princeton, NJ: Princeton University Press.

Besley, Timothy, and Marta Reynal-Querol. 2014. "The Legacy of Historical Conflict: Evidence from Africa." *American Political Science Review* 108 (2): 319–36.

Blair, Robert A. 2015. "Legitimacy after Violence: Evidence from Two Lab-in-the-Field Experiments in Liberia." Draft research paper, Brown University, Providence, RI.

Blattman, Christopher. 2009. "From Violence to Voting: War and Political Participation in Uganda." *American Political Science Review* 103 (2): 231–47.

Blattman, Christopher, Alexandra Hartman, and Robert A. Blair. 2014. "How to Promote Order and Property Rights under Weak Rule of Law? An Experiment in Changing Dispute Resolution Behavior through Community Education." *American Political Science Review* 108 (1): 100–20.

Blattman, Christopher, and Edward Miguel. 2010. "Civil War." *Journal of Economic Literature* 48 (1): 3–57.

Boix, Carles. 2003. *Democracy and Redistribution.* Cambridge, U.K.: Cambridge University Press.

Boone, Catherine. 2013. *Property and Political Order in Africa: Land Rights and the Structure of Politics.* Cambridge, U.K.: Cambridge University Press.

Bowles, Samuel, and Herbert Gintis. 2011. *A Cooperative Species: Human Reciprocity and Its Evolution.* Princeton, NJ: Princeton University Press.

Bradbury, Mark. 2008. *Becoming Somaliland: Reconstructing a Failed State.* Bloomington: Indiana University Press.

Braudel, Fernand. 1966. *La Méditerranée et le monde méditerranéen à l'époque de Philippe II.* Paris: Armand Colin.

Brockmeyer, Anne, Maha Khatrouch, and Gaël Raballand. 2015. "Public Sector Size and Performance Management: A Case-Study of Post-revolution Tunisia." Policy Research Working Paper 7159, World Bank, Washington, DC.

Brownlee, Jason, Tarek Masoud, and Andrew Reynolds. 2013. "Why the Modest Harvest?" *Journal of Democracy* 24 (4): 29–44.

Bteddini, Lida. 2016. "Middle East and North Africa: Public Employment and Governance in MENA." Report ACS18501, World Bank, Washington, DC.

Bueno de Mesquita, Bruce, James D. Morrow, Randolph M. Siverson, and Alastair Smith. 2002. "Political Institutions, Policy Choice, and the Survival of Leaders." *British Journal of Political Science* 32 (4): 559–90.

Bueno de Mesquita, Bruce, Alastair Smith, Randolph M. Siverson, and James D. Morrow. 2003. *The Logic of Political Survival.* Cambridge, MA: MIT Press.

Burke, Marshall, Solomon M. Hsiang, and Edward Miguel. 2015. "Climate and Conflict." *Annual Review of Economics* 7: 577–617.

Buvinic, Mayra, Monica Das Gupta, Ursula Casabonne, and Philip Verwimp. 2013. "Violent Conflict and Gender Inequality: An Overview." *World Bank Research Observer* 28 (1): 110–38.

Calderón, Valentina, Margarita Gáfaro, and Ana María Ibáñez. 2011. "Forced Migration, Female Labor Force Participation, and Intra-household Bargaining: Does Conflict Empower Women?" MICROCON Research Working Paper 14, Institute of Development Studies, University of Sussex, Brighton, U.K.

Camacho, Adriana, and Daniel Mejía. 2013. "Las externalidades de los programas de transferencias condicionadas sobre el crimen: El caso de Familias en Acción en Bogotá." Documento de trabajo del BID IDB-WP-406, Inter-American Development Bank, Washington, DC.

Caselli, Francesco, Massimo Morelli, and Dominic Rohner. 2015. "The Geography of Interstate Resource Wars." *Quarterly Journal of Economics* 130 (1): 267–315.

Cederman, Lars-Erik, Andreas Wimmer, and Brian Min. 2010. "Why Do Ethnic Groups Rebel? New Data and Analysis." *World Politics* 62 (1): 87–119.

Chalfin, Aaron, and Justin McCrary. 2014. "Criminal Deterrence: A Review of the Literature." Unpublished paper, University of California, Berkeley.

Chen, Martha A. 2000. *Perpetual Mourning: Widowhood in Rural India.* New Delhi: Oxford University Press.

Chioda, Laura, João M. P. de Mello, and Rodrigo R. Soares. 2012. "Spillovers from Conditional Cash Transfer Programs: Bolsa Família and Crime in Urban Brazil." IZA Discussion Paper 6371, Institute for the Study of Labor, Bonn, Germany.

Collier, Paul. 2007. *The Bottom Billion: Why the Poorest Countries Are Failing and What Can Be Done about It.* New York: Oxford University Press.

Collier, Paul, and Anke Hoeffler. 1998. "On Economic Causes of Civil War." *Oxford Economic Papers* 50 (4): 563–73.

Das Gupta, Monica, Jiang Zhenghua, Li Bohua, Xie Zhenming, Woojin Chung, and Bae Hwa-Ok. 2003. "Why Is Son Preference So Persistent in East and South Asia? A Cross-Country Study of China, India, and the Republic of Korea." *Journal of Development Studies* 40 (2): 153–87.

Dell, Melissa. 2015. "Trafficking Networks and the Mexican Drug War." *American Economic Review* 105 (6): 1738–79.

de Waal, Alex, ed. 2007. *War in Darfur and the Search for Peace.* Cambridge, MA: Harvard University Press.

Di Tella, Rafael, and Ernesto Schargrodsky. 2004. "Do Police Reduce Crime? Estimates Using the Allocation of Police Forces after a Terrorist Attack." *American Economic Review* 94 (1): 115–33.

Dorotinsky, William, and Shilpa Pradhan. 2007. "Exploring Corruption in Public Financial Management." In *The Many Faces of Corruption: Tracking Vulnerabilities at the Sector Level,* edited by Jose Edgardo Campos and Sanjay Pradhan, 267–94. Washington, DC: World Bank.

Dube, Oeindrila, and Juan Vargas. 2013. "Commodity Price Shocks and Civil Conflict: Evidence from Colombia." *Review of Economic Studies* 80 (4): 1384–1421.

Duby, Georges. 1991. *France in the Middle Ages 987–1460: From Hugh Capet to Joan of Arc.* Oxford, U.K.: Blackwell Publishers.

Dunne, J. Paul, and Nan Tian. 2014. "Conflict Spillovers and Growth in Africa." *Peace Economics, Peace Science and Public Policy* 20 (4): 539–49.

Efferson, Charles, Sonja Vogt, Amy Elhadi, Hilal El Fadil Ahmed, and Ernst Fehr. 2015. "Female Genital Cutting Is Not a Social Coordination Norm." *Science* 349 (6255): 1446–47.

Egel, Daniel. 2013. "Tribal Heterogeneity and the Allocation of Publicly Provided Goods: Evidence from Yemen." *Journal of Development Economics* 101: 228–32.

Ellickson, Robert C. 1991. *Order without Law: How Neighbors Settle Disputes.* Cambridge, MA: Harvard University Press.

Enamorado, Ted, Luis Felipe López-Calva, Carlos Rodríguez-Castelán, and Hernán Winkler. 2016. "Income Inequality and Violent Crime: Evidence from Mexico's Drug War." *Journal of Development Economics* 120 (C): 128–43.

Engerman, Stanley L., and Kenneth L. Sokoloff. 2002. "Factor Endowments, Inequality, and Paths of Development among New World Economies." NBER Working Paper 9259, National Bureau of Economic Research, Cambridge, MA.

Esteban, Joan, Laura Mayoral, and Debraj Ray. 2012. "Ethnicity and Conflict: An Empirical Study." *American Economic Review* 102 (4): 1310–42.

Esteban, Joan, and Debraj Ray. 2008. "On the Salience of Ethnic Conflict." *American Economic Review* 98 (5): 2185–2202.

Fajnzylber, Pablo, Daniel Lederman, and Norman Loayza. 2002. "Inequality and Violent Crime." *Journal of Law and Economics* 45 (1): 1–40.

Fearon, James D. 1995. "Rationalist Explanations for War." *International Organization* 49 (3): 379–414.

———. 2004. "Why Do Some Civil Wars Last So Much Longer than Others?" *Journal of Peace Research* 41 (3): 275–301.

———. 2006. "Ethnic Mobilization and Ethnic Violence." In *Oxford Handbook of Political Economy*, edited by Barry R. Weingast and Donald A. Wittman, 852–68. Oxford Handbooks of Political Science Series. New York: Oxford University Press.

Fearon, James D., and David D. Laitin. 2000. "Violence and the Social Construction of Ethnic Identity." *International Organization* 54 (4): 845–77.

Gambetta, Diego. 1996. *The Sicilian Mafia: The Business of Private Protection.* Cambridge, MA: Harvard University Press.

García-Ponce, Omar. 2015. "Women's Political Participation in the Aftermath of Civil War: Evidence from Peru." Institute of Political Economy and Governance, Barcelona.

Gates, Scott, Benjamin A. T. Graham, Yonatan Lupu, Håvard Strand, and Kaare W. Strøm. 2016. "Power-sharing, Protection, and Peace." *Journal of Politics* 78 (2): 512–26.

Gates, Scott, and Kaare Strøm, eds. 2013. "Fragile Bargains: Civil Conflict and Power-Sharing in Africa." Center for the Study of Civil War, Peace Research Institute Oslo, Oslo.

Geneva Declaration Secretariat. 2015. *Global Burden of Armed Violence 2015: Every Body Counts.* Cambridge, U.K.: Cambridge University Press.

Gilligan, Michael J., Benjamin J. Pasquale, and Cyrus D. Samii. 2011. "Civil War and Social Capital: Behavioral-Game Evidence from Nepal." Unpublished working paper, New York University, New York.

Goldstone, Jack A. 2002. "Population and Security: How Demographic Change Can Lead to Violent Conflict." *Journal of International Affairs* 56 (1): 3–22.

Grossman, Guy, Devorah Manekin, and Dan Miodownik. 2015. "The Political Legacies of Combat: Attitudes towards War and Peace among Israeli Ex-combatants." *International Organization* 69 (4): 981–1009.

Gurr, Ted R. 1993. *Minorities at Risk: A Global View of Ethnopolitical Conflicts.* Washington, DC: United States Institute of Peace.

Hall, Derek, Philip Hirsch, and Tania Murray Li. 2011. *Powers of Exclusion: Land Dilemmas in Southeast Asia.* Singapore: National University of Singapore Press.

Hartman, Alexandra C., and Benjamin S. Morse. 2015. "Wartime Violence, Empathy, and Intergroup Altruism: Theory and Evidence from the Ivoirian Refugee Crisis in Liberia." Paper presented at the Annual World Bank Conference on Africa, "Confronting Conflict and Fragility in Africa," Berkeley, CA, June 8–9.

Hartman, Alexandra C., Benjamin S. Morse, and Gregory Kitt. 2014. "The Impact of Development through Local Integration on Land Use and Conflict: An Evaluation of the '16 Villages' Policy in Liberia." Paper presented at the Annual World Bank Conference on Land and Poverty, Washington, DC, March 24–27.

Hartzell, Caroline A., and Matthew Hoddie. 2003. "Institutionalizing Peace: Power Sharing and Post-Civil War Conflict Management." *American Journal of Political Science* 47 (2): 318–32.

Heimpel, Wolfgang, ed. 2003. *Letters to the King of Mari: A New Translation, with Historical Introduction, Notes and Commentary.* Winona Lake, IN: Eisenbrauns.

Hirschman, Albert O. 1958. *The Strategy of Economic Development.* Study in Economics Series. New Haven, CT: Yale University Press.

Ianchovichina, Elena, and Maros Ivanic. 2016. "Economic Effects of the Syrian War and the Spread of the Islamic State on the Levant." *World Economy* 39 (10): 1584–1627.

Ibáñez, Ana María, and Carlos Eduardo Vélez. 2008. "Civil Conflict and Forced Migration: The Micro Determinants and Welfare Losses of Displacement in Colombia." *World Development* 36 (4): 659–76.

IEP (Institute for Economics and Peace). 2015. *Global Peace Index 2015: Measuring Peace, Its Causes, and Its Economic Value.* Sydney: IEP.

Jacoby, Hanan, and Ghazala Mansuri. 2010. "*Watta Satta:* Bride Exchange and Women's Welfare in Rural Pakistan." *American Economic Review* 100 (4): 1804–25.

Jayachandran, Seema. 2015. "The Roots of Gender Inequality in Developing Countries." *Annual Review of Economics* 7 (1): 63–88.

Justino, Patricia. 2009. "Poverty and Violent Conflict: A Micro-level Perspective on the Causes and Duration of Warfare." *Journal of Peace Research* 46 (3): 315–33.

———. 2015. "Civil Unrest and Government Transfers in India." IDS Evidence Report 108, Institute of Development Studies, University of Sussex, Brighton, U.K.

———. 2016. "Implication of War-Time Institutions for State-Building in Post-conflict Countries." Background paper, WDR 2017, World Bank, Washington, DC.

Justino, Patricia, Ivan Cardona, Rebecca Mitchell, and Catherine Müller. 2012. "Quantifying the Impact of Women's Participation in Post-conflict Economic Recovery." HiCN Working Paper 131, Households in Conflict Network, Institute of Development Studies, University of Sussex, Brighton, U.K.

Justino, Patricia, Jennifer Leavy, and Elsa Valli. 2009. "Quantitative Methods in Contexts of Everyday Violence." *IDS Bulletin* 40 (3): 41–49.

Justino, Patricia, and Bruno Martorano. 2016. "Welfare Spending and Political Conflict." Draft paper, Institute of Development Studies, University of Sussex, Brighton, U.K.

Keefer, Philip. 2012. "Why Follow the Leader? Collective Action, Credible Commitment, and Conflict." Policy Research Working Paper 6179, World Bank, Washington, DC.

Keefer, Philip, and Razvan Vlaicu. 2008. "Democracy, Credibility, and Clientelism." *Journal of Law, Economics, and Organization* 24 (2): 371–406.

Keen, David. 1998. "The Economic Functions of Violence in Civil Wars." *Adelphi Papers* 38 (320): 1–89.

Khanna, Gaurav, and Laura Zimmermann. 2015. "Guns and Butter? Fighting Violence with the Promise of Development." IZA Discussion Paper 9160, Institute for the Study of Labor, Bonn, Germany.

Kleiman, Mark. 2011. "Surgical Strikes in the Drug War: Smarter Policies for Both Sides of the Border." *Foreign Affairs* 90 (5): 89–101.

Knack, Stephen, and Philip Keefer. 1997. "Does Social Capital Have an Economic Payoff? A Cross-Country Investigation." *Quarterly Journal of Economics* 112 (4): 1251–88.

Knight, Jack. 1992. *Institutions and Social Conflict.* Cambridge, U.K.: Cambridge University Press.

Lederman, Daniel, Norman Loayza, and Ana María Menéndez. 2002. "Violent Crime: Does Social Capital Matter?" *Economic Development and Cultural Change* 50 (3): 509–39.

Leeson, Peter. 2011. *The Invisible Hook: The Hidden Economics of Pirates.* Princeton, NJ: Princeton University Press.

Levitsky, Steven, and Lucan Way. 2012. "Beyond Patronage: Violent Struggle, Ruling Party Cohesion, and Authoritarian Durability." *Perspectives on Politics* 10 (4): 869–89.

Lianos, Michalis. 2011. "Conflict as Closure." MICROCON Research Working Paper 52, Institute of Development Studies, University of Sussex, Brighton, U.K.

Lijphart, Arend. 2004. "Constitutional Design for Divided Societies." *Journal of Democracy* 15 (2): 96–109.

———. 2012. *Patterns of Democracy: Government Forms and Performance in Thirty-Six Countries.* New Haven, CT: Yale University Press.

Lindemann, Stefan. 2008. "Do Inclusive Elite Bargains Matter? A Research Framework for Understanding the Causes of Civil War in Sub-Saharan Africa." Crisis States Discussion Paper 15, Crisis States Research Center, Development Studies Institute, London School of Economics and Political Science.

———. 2010. "Exclusionary Elite Bargains and Civil War Onset: The Case of Uganda." Crisis States Discussion Paper 76, Crisis States Research Center, Development Studies Institute, London School of Economics and Political Science.

———. 2011. "Inclusive Elite Bargains and the Dilemma of Unproductive Peace." *Third World Quarterly* 32 (10): 1843–69.

Linder, Wolf, and André Bächtiger. 2005. "What Drives Democratization in Asia and Africa?" *European Journal of Political Research* 44 (6): 861–80.

Mackie, Gerry. 2000. "Female Genital Cutting: The Beginning of the End." In *Female "Circumcision" in Africa: Culture, Controversy, and Change,* edited by Bettina Shell-Duncan and Ylva Hernlund, 253–82. Directions in Applied Anthropology Series. Boulder, CO: Lynne Rienner Publishers.

Magaloni, Beatriz, Edgar Franco, and Vanessa Melo. 2015. "Killing in the Slums: An Impact Evaluation of Police Reform in Rio de Janeiro." CDDRL Working Paper 556, Center for Democracy, Development, and the Rule of Law, Freeman Spogli Institute for International Studies, Stanford University, Stanford, CA.

Mampilly, Zachariah. 2011. *Rebel Rulers: Insurgent Governance and Civilian Life during War.* Ithaca, NY: Cornell University Press.

Mann, Michael. 1984. "The Autonomous Power of the State: Its Origins, Mechanisms, and Results." *European Journal of Sociology* 25 (2): 185–213.

Miguel, Edward, Shanker Satyanath, and Ernest Sergenti. 2004. "Economic Shocks and Civil Conflict: An Instrumental Variables Approach." *Journal of Political Economy* 112 (4): 725–53.

Milazzo, Annamaria. 2014. "Why Are Adult Women Missing? Son Preference and Maternal Survival in India." Policy Research Working Paper 6802, World Bank, Washington, DC.

Montalvo, Jose G., and Marta Reynal-Querol. 2008. "Discrete Polarisation with an Application to the

Determinants of Genocides." *Economic Journal* 118 (533): 1835–65.

Moyo, Sam, Dzodzi Tsikata, and Yakham Diop, eds. 2015. *Land in the Struggles for Citizenship in Africa.* Dakar: Council for the Development of Social Science Research in Africa.

Mueller-Smith, Michael. 2015. "The Criminal and Labor Market Impacts of Incarceration." Unpublished working paper, Columbia University, New York.

Munn-Rankin, J. Margaret. 1956. "Diplomacy in Western Asia in the Early Second Millennium BC." *Iraq* 18 (1): 68–110.

Murshed, Mansoob, and Zulfan Tadjoeddin. 2008. "Is Fiscal Decentralization Conflict Abating? Routine Violence and District Level Government in Java, Indonesia." *Oxford Development Studies* 37 (4): 397–421.

———. 2009. "Revisiting the Greed and Grievance Explanations for Violent Internal Conflict." *Journal of International Development* 21 (1): 87–111.

Norris, Pippa. 2008. *Driving Democracy: Do Power-Sharing Institutions Work?* New York: Cambridge University Press.

North, Douglass C., John Joseph Wallis, Steven B. Webb, and Barry R. Weingast. 2013. *In the Shadow of Violence: Politics, Economics, and the Problems of Development.* New York: Cambridge University Press.

North, Douglass C., John Joseph Wallis, and Barry R. Weingast. 2009. *Violence and Social Orders: A Conceptual Framework for Interpreting Recorded Human History.* New York: Cambridge University Press.

Onoma, Ato Kwamena. 2010. *The Politics of Property Rights Institutions in Africa.* Cambridge, U.K.: Cambridge University Press.

Ostrom, Elinor. 1990. *Governing the Commons: The Evolution of Institutions for Collective Action.* Cambridge, U.K.: Cambridge University Press.

Pande, Rohini. 2015. "Keeping Women Safe: Addressing the Root Causes of Violence against Women in South Asia." *Harvard Magazine* (January–February). http://harvardmagazine.com/2015/01/keeping-women-safe.

Pinker, Steven. 2011. *The Better Angels of Our Nature: Why Violence Has Declined.* New York: Viking Books.

Platteau, Jean-Philippe. 2000. *Institutions, Social Norms, and Economic Development.* Amsterdam: Harwood Academic Publishers.

Powell, Robert. 2004. "The Inefficient Use of Power: Costly Conflict with Complete Information." *American Political Science Review* 98 (2): 221–41.

———. 2006. "War as a Commitment Problem." *International Organization* 60 (1): 169–203.

Pujol, Philippe. 2016. *La fabrique du monstre: 10 ans d'immersion dans les quartiers nord de Marseille, la zone la plus pauvre d'Europe.* Paris: Les Arenes.

Ray, Debraj, and Joan Esteban. 2016. "Conflict and Development." Unpublished working paper, New York University, New York.

Robinson, James A., and Thierry Verdier. 2013. "The Political Economy of Clientelism." *Scandinavian Journal of Economics* 115 (2): 260–91.

Rørbæk, Lasse Lykke, and Allan Toft Knudsen. 2015. "Maintaining Ethnic Dominance: Diversity, Power, and Violent Repression." *Conflict Management and Peace Science* (November 24).

Ross, Michael. 2015. "What Have We Learned about the Resource Curse?" *Annual Review of Political Science* 18 (1): 239–59.

Sanchez de la Sierra, Raul. 2015. "On the Origin of States: Stationary Bandits and Taxation in Eastern Congo." HiCN Working Paper 194, Households in Conflict Network, Institute of Development Studies, University of Sussex, Brighton, U.K.

Schelling, Thomas. 1960. *The Strategy of Conflict.* Cambridge, MA: Harvard University Press.

Sen, Amartya. 2006. *Identity and Violence: The Illusion of Destiny.* New York: Norton.

Skarbek, David. 2014. *The Social Order of the Underworld: How Prison Gangs Govern the American Prison System.* Oxford, U.K.: Oxford University Press.

Slater, Dan. 2010. *Ordering Power: Contentious Politics and Authoritarian Leviathans in Southeast Asia.* Cambridge, U.K.: Cambridge University Press.

Sossou, Marie-Antoinette. 2002. "Widowhood Practices in West Africa: The Silent Victims." *International Journal of Social Welfare* 11 (3): 201–09.

Srivastava, Vivek, and Jurgen Blum. 2016. "Civil Service Reform in Fragile Contexts." World Bank, Washington, DC.

Stewart, Frances. 2008. *Horizontal Inequalities and Conflict: Understanding Group Violence in Multiethnic Societies.* New York: Palgrave Macmillan.

Szeftel, Morris. 1998. "Misunderstanding African Politics: Corruption and the Governance Agenda." *Review of African Political Economy* 25 (76): 221–40.

Tilly, Charles. 1978. "Collective Violence in European Perspective." In *Violence in America,* Vol. 2 of *Protest, Rebellion, Reform,* edited by Ted Robert Gurr, 62–100. Violence, Cooperation, Peace: An International Series. Newbury Park, CA: Sage Publications.

———. 1985. "War Making and State Making as Organized Crime." In *Bringing the State Back In,* edited by Peter B. Evans, Dietrich Rueschemeyer, and Theda Skocpol, 169–91. Cambridge, U.K.: Cambridge University Press.

———. 1990. *Coercion, Capital and European States: AD 990-1990.* Oxford, U.K.: Blackwell Publishers.

Toft, Monica Duffy, and Yuri Zhukov. 2015. "Islamists and Nationalists: Rebel Motivation and Counterinsurgency in Russia's North Caucasus." *American Political Science Review* 109 (2): 222–38.

UCDP/PRIO (Uppsala Conflict Data Program/Peace Research Institute Oslo). 2015. Armed Conflict Dataset Version 4-2015 (1946–2014). Uppsala University,

Sweden, http://www.pcr.uu.se/research/ucdp/datasets/ucdp_prio_armed_conflict_dataset/.

UNFPA (United Nations Population Fund). 2000. "The State of the World Population, Lives Together, Worlds Apart: Men and Women in a Time of Change." UNFPA, New York.

———. 2013. *Laws and Son Preference in India: A Reality Check.* New Delhi: UNFPA.

UNICEF (United Nations Children's Fund). 2013. *Female Genital Mutilation/Cutting: A Statistical Overview and Exploration of the Dynamics of Change.* New York: UNICEF.

V-Dem (Varieties of Democracy). Various years. Database hosted by Gothenburg Institute (Europe) and Kellogg Institute (United States), https://www.v-dem.net/en/.

Venkatesh, Sudhir Alladi. 2006. *Off the Books: The Underground Economy of the Urban Poor.* Cambridge, MA: Harvard University Press.

Voors, Maarten J., Eleonora E. M. Nillesen, Philip Verwimp, Erwin H. Bulte, Robert Lensink, and Daan P. Van Soest. 2012. "Violent Conflict and Behavior: A Field Experiment in Burundi." *American Economic Review* 102 (2): 941–64.

Wagner, Harrison R. 2000. "Bargaining and War." *American Journal of Political Science* 44 (3): 546–76.

Wallis, John. 2016. "Governance and Violence." Background paper, WDR 2017, World Bank, Washington, DC.

Walter, Barbara F. 2002. *Committing to Peace: The Successful Settlement of Civil Wars.* Princeton, NJ: Princeton University Press.

———. 2009. "Bargaining Failures and Civil War." *Annual Review of Political Science* 12: 243–61.

———. 2015. "Why Bad Governance Leads to Repeat Civil War." *Journal of Conflict Resolution* 59 (7): 1242–72.

Watts, Charlotte, and Cathy Zimmerman. 2002. "Violence against Women: Global Scope and Magnitude." *Lancet* 359 (9313): 1232–37.

Weber, Max. 1965. *Politics as a Vocation.* Philadelphia: Fortress Press.

Weinstein, Jeremy M. 2004. "Which Path to Peace? Autonomous Recovery and International Intervention in Comparative Perspective." Paper prepared for the Centre for the Study of African Economies Conference, "The Bottom Billion," Oxford University, Oxford, U.K., June 27–29.

———. 2005. "Resources and the Information Problem in Rebel Recruitment." *Journal of Conflict Resolution* 49 (4): 598–624.

———. 2007. *Inside Rebellion: The Politics of Insurgent Violence.* Cambridge, U.K.: Cambridge University Press.

Wimmer, Andreas, Lars-Erik Cederman, and Brian Min. 2009. "Ethnic Politics and Armed Conflict: A Configurational Analysis of a New Global Data Set." *American Sociological Review* 74 (2): 316–37.

World Bank. Various years. World Development Indicators (database). Washington, DC, http://data.worldbank.org/data-catalog/world-development-indicators.

———. 1999. "Civil Service Reform: A Review of World Bank Assistance." Report 19211, World Bank, Washington, DC.

———. 2006. "Crime, Violence, and Economic Development in Brazil: Elements for Effective Public Policy." Report 36525, World Bank, Washington, DC.

———. 2010. *Violence in the City: Understanding and Supporting Community Responses to Urban Violence.* Washington, DC: World Bank.

———. 2011. *World Development Report 2011: Conflict, Security, and Development.* Washington, DC: World Bank.

———. 2015. *Women, Business, and the Law 2016: Getting to Equal.* Washington, DC: World Bank.

World Justice Project. Various years. Rule of Law Index. Washington, DC, http://worldjusticeproject.org/.

Zak, Paul, and Stephen Knack. 2001. "Trust and Growth." *Economic Journal* 111 (470): 295–321.

Wartime governance

In recent years, several concepts have emerged to describe the governance arrangements that have arisen in areas where the imprint of the state is weak or inexistent. What these concepts of "hybrid governance," "governance without government," "twilight institutions," "practical norms," and "negotiated statehood" have in common with each other and with the framework adopted in this Report is their theorization of governance as the outcome of complex bargains between different actors and groups, in this case for the purpose of filling gaps in state capacity.[1]

Underpinning these concepts is a growing literature and empirical evidence with far-reaching implications for development: "Instead of focusing on fixing 'failed states,' development practitioners and academics are asking new questions about whether more appropriate forms of order can be constructed by . . . focusing on 'function rather than form' in a context in which suboptimal hybrid arrangements are better than the total collapse of services" (Meagher, De Herdt, and Titeca 2014, 1). "Wartime governance" is a specific application of these governance arrangements to territories where the state's monopoly over the use of violence has collapsed or is being contested, and where armed groups, traditional authorities, and other informal local actors have taken over and become the de facto authority, sometimes undertaking functions normally performed by the state.

Although these territories are typically portrayed as anarchic, disordered, and ungoverned, observations from the field show that this is not the case. Different actors adopt a myriad of strategies in the areas they control, some resulting in fairly stable

forms of political control. There are abundant examples of such actors: the Revolutionary Armed Forces of Colombia (FARC), the Liberation Tigers of Tamil Eelam (LTTE) in Sri Lanka, the Taliban in Afghanistan, the National Union for the Total Independence of Angola (UNITA), Al-Shabaab in Somalia, and, more recently, the Islamic State of Iraq and the Levant (DAESH) in the Syrian Arab Republic and Iraq. These actors resort frequently to the use or threat of violence to maintain their authority through raiding, victimizing, and plundering contested territories. Yet, not all armed groups behave in solely destructive ways, nor do the more violent groups exercise violence at all times. In many of these cases, insurgent groups have taken on some (if not all) of the functions of the state in terms of providing local security and formal and informal dispute resolution mechanisms, building infrastructure, setting up systems of administration, mediating access to and in some cases providing public goods, imposing revenue-extracting systems, regulating markets—in brief, governing.[2]

To govern, armed actors establish "wartime institutions," defined as the rules of the game that result from the interaction between civilians and armed factions. Wartime institutions have three important dimensions: (1) they constrain absolute power by armed factions; (2) they establish boundaries to civilian behavior; and (3) they are negotiated, depending on shifts in power between warring factions in given localities (Stojetz and Justino 2015). These wartime institutions determine how different armed factions govern territories and populations in the absence of a unitary national government.

It is the ability and willingness to govern that distinguish "state-like" armed groups from bandits

WDR 2017 team, based on Justino (2016).

or other extractive organizations. For example, in the Democratic Republic of Congo, the Rally for Congolese Democracy-Movement for Liberation (RCD-ML) developed into an amalgam of militiamen and local businessmen who provide minimal services, levy taxes, and seek to access global markets, while still relying on coercion. The Union of Patriotic Congolese (UPC), on the other hand, remains a coercive military junta (Raeymaekers 2013). Such divergence in wartime governance across time and space is in turn shaped by several factors. Among them are the strength and nature of preexisting systems; how civilians accept and comply with different local forms of authority; the levels of competition among political actors, including the state, for a certain territory; the time horizons of different factions and how long an armed group expects to stay in a certain area; and the sources of external financing available to the group.[3]

Wartime governance arrangements may result in relative security outcomes nested within violent conflict contexts when this security benefits the strategic objectives of particular political groups. These groups need at the very least to extract revenue to fund fighting and territorial expansion. Because revenue extraction is likely to be higher in situations in which one group exercises the monopoly of violence, some armed actors may choose to levy taxes in exchange for the provision of public goods and security. This choice may in turn result in the emergence of security as postulated by Olson (1993) and Tilly (1992). The wartime systems of governance just described may also result in the emergence of security in conflict contexts when a given political actor is accepted (or tolerated) and recognized by local populations. Notably, wartime forms of governance may offer a sense of legitimacy and certainty, which may reflect civilian perceptions about the authorities who govern them and the nature of their authority (Bates 2008).

Recent research on violent conflict has found compelling evidence that local (and not just state-level) institutional structures influence political processes during and after conflicts (Kalyvas 2006; Blattman and Miguel 2010). A related body of literature has long questioned the centrality of the state in local systems of governance in areas of uneven or absent state presence—the so-called ungoverned spaces (Scott 1999; Batley 2011). This local perspective is an important supplement to national-level perspectives on state building because, as argued in a landmark study on the Democratic Republic of Congo, "The dominant international peacebuilding culture shapes the interveners' understanding of peace, violence, and intervention in

a way that overlooks the micro-foundations necessary for sustainable peace. The resulting inattention to local conflicts leads to unsustainable peacebuilding in the short term and potential war resumption in the long term" (Autesserre 2010, 39–40).

Of course, not all local political dynamics are always purely local events; they often depend on how bargains, relations, and negotiations among factions unfold in the wider political arena (Balcells and Justino 2014). Yet, a local perspective on wartime institutions and wartime governance is still important. State-building processes in conflict-affected countries are influenced by multiple actors operating at different levels of governance. This influence can be exerted through formal and informal structures and networks, and it is not always driven solely by the interests of national-level elites. Local actors are also influenced by geopolitical and external factors, ranging from foreign donor interventions to international and regional military forces, peacekeeping missions, private commercial and security organizations, private sector and foreign investment in resources and land, international and local media, and international drug and arms control systems, among others.

Understanding in more detail the role of these groups in processes of state building is important because the activities and behavior of these groups—notably, how they govern and interact with civilians—shape how institutions are formed, reinforced, and change in the postconflict period. In particular, the exclusion of elements of these groups from state-building processes in the aftermath of violent conflicts may result in further armed conflict, or may disturb political order for a long time, leading to the situations of "no peace, no war" experienced by many countries with a history of conflict (Richards 2005).

Notes

1. Migdal and Schlichte (2005); Lund (2006); Olivier de Sardan (2008); Raeymaekers, Menkhaus, and Vlassenroot (2008); Hagmann and Péclard (2010); Meagher, De Herdt, and Titeca (2014).
2. Weinstein (2007); Mampilly (2011); Arjona, Kasfir, and Mampilly (2015).
3. Snyder and Bhavnani (2005); Kalyvas (2006); Weinstein (2007); Arjona (2014); Sanchez de la Sierra (2014).

References

Arjona, Ana M. 2014. "Wartime Institutions: A Research Agenda." *Journal of Conflict Resolution* 58 (8): 1360–89.

Arjona, Ana M., Nelson Kasfir, and Zachariah Mampilly. 2015. *Rebel Governance in Civil War*. New York: Cambridge University Press.

Autesserre, Séverine. 2010. *The Trouble with the Congo: Local Violence and the Failure of International Peacebuilding*. Cambridge Studies in International Relations Series. New York: Cambridge University Press.

Balcells, Laia, and Patricia Justino. 2014. "Bridging Micro and Macro Approaches on Civil Wars and Political Violence: Issues, Challenges and the Way Forward." *Journal of Conflict Resolution* 58 (8): 1343–59.

Bates, Robert H. 2008. *When Things Fell Apart: State Failure in Late-Century Africa*. Cambridge, U.K.: Cambridge University Press.

Batley, Richard. 2011. "Structures and Strategies in Relationships between Non-government Service Providers and Government." *Public Administration and Development* 31 (4): 306–19.

Blattman, Christopher, and Edward Miguel. 2010. "Civil War." *Journal of Economic Literature* 48 (1): 3–57.

Hagmann, Tobias, and Didier Péclard. 2010. "Negotiating Statehood: Dynamics of Power and Domination in Post-colonial Africa." *Development and Change* 41 (4): 539–62.

Justino, Patricia. 2016. "Implications of Wartime Institutions for State-Building in Post-conflict Countries." Background paper, WDR 2017, World Bank, Washington, DC.

Kalyvas, Stathis N. 2006. *The Logic of Violence in Civil Wars*. New York: Cambridge University Press.

Lund, Christian. 2006. "Twilight Institutions: Public Authority and Local Politics in Africa." *Development and Change* 37 (4): 685–705.

Mampilly, Zachariah. 2011. *Rebel Rulers: Insurgent Governance and Civilian Life during War*. Ithaca, NY: Cornell University Press.

Meagher, Kate, Tom De Herdt, and Kristof Titeca. 2014. "Unravelling Public Authority: Paths of Hybrid Governance in Africa." Research Brief 10 (March), IS Academy on Human Security in Fragile States, Wageningen University, Wageningen, the Netherlands.

Migdal, Joel S., and Klaus Schlichte. 2005. "Re-thinking the State." In *The Dynamics of States: The Formation and Crises of State Domination*, edited by Klaus Schlichte, 1–40. Burlington, VT: Ashgate.

Olivier de Sardan, Jean-Pierre. 2008. "Researching the Practical Norms of Real Governance in Africa." Discussion Paper 5, Africa, Power, and Politics Programme, Overseas Development Institute, London.

Olson, Mancur. 1993. "Dictatorship, Democracy and Development." *American Political Science Review* 87 (3): 567–76.

Raeymaekers, Timothy. 2013. "Robin Hood, the Godfather, and Judge Dredd: Explaining De Facto Sovereignty in Sub-Sahara Africa." Paper presented at the "Unravelling Public Authority: Paths of Hybrid Governance in Africa" workshop, London School of Economics, December 6–7.

Raeymaekers, Timothy, Ken Menkhaus, and Koen Vlassenroot. 2008. "State and Non-state Regulation in African Protracted Crises: Governance without Government?" *Afrika Focus* 21 (2): 7–21.

Richards, Paul, ed. 2005. *No Peace, No War: An Anthropology of Contemporary Armed Conflicts*. Oxford, U.K.: James Currey.

Sanchez de la Sierra, Raul. 2014. "Defining the State: Armed Groups' Monopolies of Violence and Emergence of State-Like Behavior in Eastern Congo." Unpublished working paper, Harvard University, Cambridge, MA.

Scott, James C. 1999. *Seeing Like a State*. New Haven, CT: Yale University Press.

Snyder, Richard, and Ravi Bhavnani. 2005. "Diamonds, Blood, and Taxes: A Revenue-Centered Framework for Explaining Political Order." *Journal of Conflict Resolution* 49 (4): 563–97.

Stojetz, Wolfgang, and Patricia Justino. 2015. "Long-Run Effects of Wartime Institutions in Post-war Angola." Unpublished working paper, University of California, Berkeley.

Tilly, Charles. 1992. *Coercion, Capital, and European States: AD 990–1992*. Studies in Social Discontinuity Series. Oxford, U.K.: Blackwell.

Weinstein, Jeremy M. 2007. *Inside Rebellion: The Politics of Insurgent Violence*. Cambridge Studies in Comparative Politics Series. New York: Cambridge University Press.

Crime

How much reduction in crime is possible? A look at past trends indicates the degree to which crime can be reduced globally over the next 15 years. The broad crime drop in the United States between 1991 and 2014 amounted to an annual decline of about 2.9 percent a year, which included a range of manifestations of interpersonal violence such as homicide, child maltreatment, assault, and violence in schools. Meanwhile, Singapore has achieved its very low crime rates—including the lowest homicide, robbery, and domestic violence rates known in the world—through a sustained decline of about 5 percent a year over the last 25 years. Italy has experienced an annual decline in homicides of about 6 percent since the early 1990s. In South Africa, homicides have fallen about 4 percent a year since the mid-1990s, or just about the same yearly rate of decline as in Colombia since the early 1990s. Indeed, many countries have seen annual reductions in serious crime and violence of 2–5 percent over two decades or more. An average annual decline of 3 percent may therefore be possible at the global level, leading to a reduction of about 40 percent by the end of 2030 (Eisner and Nivette 2012).

Why do interpersonal violence and crime decline?

Why interpersonal violence and organized crime are declining is still not possible to explain with any real accuracy. However, it is currently possible to disentangle the mix of factors that influence both the cross-sectional variation in crime rates among countries and the trends of crime levels over time. First,

_____

WDR 2017 team, based on inputs from Manuel Eisner.

it appears that trends in the levels of interpersonal violence and organized crime stem only partly from factors that governments can directly influence. For example, analyses of time series going back to the 1970s suggest that factors such as changing demographics, unemployment, technological change, drug epidemics, and changes in norms and attitudes toward violence have affected trends in crime levels generally and homicides specifically (Baumer and Wolff 2014). On the other hand, changes in income inequality over the last 100 years seem to be entirely unrelated to changes in homicide rates, despite income inequality being a robust and consistent cross-sectional correlate of homicide (Brush 2007).

However, there is increasing evidence of a positive correlation between homicide and organized crime levels, on the one hand, and corruption levels, on the other (Lappi-Seppälä and Lehti 2014; Pinotti 2015). This correlation can be interpreted as empirical evidence of a role for governance in the reduction of interpersonal violence, and specifically for the theory that the failure of governments to sanction and deter organized criminal groups is one important factor contributing to high levels of homicides.

Three sets of factors explain homicide drops in the past

In addition to theories linking the decline in crime rates to demographics and access to economic opportunities (see, for example, Donohue and Levitt 2001 and de Mello and Schneider 2010), comparisons of major sustained declines in homicides by country and historical period across the globe suggest that declines in murder rates occurred when three factors came together (Eisner 2013, 2014). The first factor is changes in relative power: homicide rates declined where states gained control over private organized providers of protection and enhanced their legitimacy through effective institutions that produced benefits for broader segments of society (see chapter 4 and Rotberg 2004).

The second factor is changes in technological and human capacity: declines in homicides appear to be regularly linked to the spread of new social control technologies such as the monitoring and management of daily behaviors; increased control over disorderly conduct and substance use, especially alcohol; and systems aimed at early identification and treatment of offenders and victims (Eisner 2014). For example, the international fall in crime over the last 20 years is best seen as a result of investments in security technologies that have affected almost every aspect of daily routines (Farrell and others 2011). These technologies include electronic immobilizers to prevent car theft, burglar alarms, CCTV cameras in hot spots of disruptive behavior, a less cash-based economy, more private security personnel, and mobile telephones to call help and record crimes more easily. Many of these security and surveillance technologies are designed to reduce property crime, but they may have had an effect on violent crime as well.

The third factor is changes in norms of behavior: historical declines in homicides appear to have been catalyzed by a diminishing acceptability of violence and intentional harm to others. Historically, such change in social norms manifests itself in a growing repugnance for public executions and torture, disgust with blood revenge and duels, or increasing sensitization to child maltreatment and neglect. Political or religious leaders, philanthropists, intellectuals, and teachers are among those ushering in such changes in societal preferences (Pinker 2011).

The state's monopoly over the means of violence is the overarching factor

This report argues that the changes in capacity and in norms of behavior that affect development outcomes, including reductions in levels of violence and crime levels, are ultimately derived from changes in the relative power among actors. The sharp declines in homicide rates that occurred in more than 10 Western European countries after 1650 illustrate how shifts in the balance of power toward the state and away from private providers of security, and the resulting

Figure S5.1 Homicide rates across Europe have declined dramatically over the last 800 years

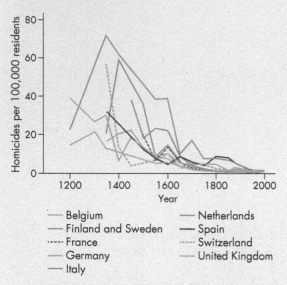

Sources: WDR 2017 team, based on Eisner 2003 with data from Eisner 2014.

expansion in state capacity, brought about changes in societal attitudes toward homicide that over time led to a drastic reduction in homicide levels (figure S5.1)—see Eisner (2003).

Before the expansion of the capacity of courts and bureaucracies that accompanied the rise of the states' monopoly over violence in 17th-century Europe, government attitudes toward homicides were lenient if the motives were passion or the defense of honor, and society perceived private retaliation as an acceptable way of restoring order. Between the 16th and 17th centuries, dispute settlement moved out of the private sphere and became the prerogative of judges and government officials, and perpetrators of homicide came to be seen as criminals. Campaigns of social awareness; societal acceptance of increased bureaucratic control of everyday life; improved trust in and the legitimacy of the state as an overarching institution; the evolution of the notion of honor, which lost its cultural significance; and the liberation of the individual from his or her obligations to the group—in short, a change in norms—eventually led to this historical decline in homicide rates (Tilly 1992; Rousseaux 1999).

References

Baumer, Eric P., and Kevin T. Wolff. 2014. "The Breadth and Causes of Contemporary Cross-National Homicide Trends." *Crime and Justice: A Review of Research* 43 (1): 231–87.

Brush, Jesse. 2007. "Does Income Inequality Lead to More Crime? A Comparison of Cross-Sectional and Time-Series Analyses of United States Counties." *Economics Letters* 96 (2): 264–68.

de Mello, J. M. P., and A. Schneider. 2010. "Assessing São Paulo's Large Drop in Homicides: The Role of Demography and Policy Interventions." In *The Economics of Crime: Lessons for and from Latin America*, edited by Rafael Di Tella, Sebastian Edwards, and Ernesto Schargrodsky, 207–35. Chicago: University of Chicago Press.

Donohue, J. J., and S. D. Levitt. 2001. "The Impact of Legalized Abortion on Crime." *Quarterly Journal of Economics* 66 (2): 379–420.

Eisner, Manuel. 2003. "Long-Term Historical Trends in Violent Crime." *Crime and Justice: A Review of Research* 30: 83–142.

———. 2013. "What Causes Large-Scale Variation in Homicide Rates?" In *Aggression in Humans and Other Primates: Biology, Psychology, Sociology*, edited by Hans-Henning Kortüm and Jürgen Heinze, 137–62. Berlin: Walter de Gruyter.

———. 2014. "From Swords to Words: Does Macro-Level Change in Self-Control Predict Long-Term Variation in Levels of Homicide?" *Crime and Justice: A Review of Research* 43 (1): 65–134.

Eisner, Manuel, and Amy Nivette. 2012. "How to Reduce the Global Homicide Rate to 2 per 100,000 by 2060." In *The Future of Criminology*, edited by Rolf Loeber and Brandon C. Welsh, 219–28. New York: Oxford University Press.

Farrell, Graham, Nick Tilley, Andromachi Tseloni, and Jen Mailley. 2011. "The Crime Drop and the Security Hypothesis." *Journal of Research in Crime and Delinquency* 48 (2): 147–75.

Lappi-Seppälä, Tapio, and Martti Lehti. 2014. "Cross-Comparative Perspectives on Global Homicide Trends." *Crime and Justice: A Review of Research* 43 (1): 135–230.

Pinker, Steven. 2011. *The Better Angels of Our Nature: Why Violence Has Declined.* New York: Penguin.

Pinotti, Paolo. 2015. "The Causes and Consequences of Organized Crime: Preliminary Evidence across Countries." *Economic Journal* 125 (586): F158–F174.

Rotberg, Robert I., ed. 2004. *When States Fail: Causes and Consequences.* Princeton, NJ: Princeton University Press.

Rousseaux, Xavier. 1999. "From Case to Crime: Homicide Regulation in Medieval and Modern Europe." In *Die Entstehung des öffentlichen Strafrechts: Bestandsaufnahme eines europäischen Forschungsproblems*, edited by Dietmar Willoweit, 143–75. Cologne: Böhlau Verlag.

Tilly, Charles. 1992. *Coercion, Capital, and European States: AD 990–1992.* Studies in Social Discontinuity Series. Oxford, U.K.: Blackwell.

CHAPTER 5

Governance for growth

If a firm in Brazil or Mexico is asked how long it has to wait to receive approval for new construction, the answer could range from as little as 1 day to more than 100 days (figure 5.1). Such remarkable variation in the wait time experienced by firms within the same country is true of almost any basic regulatory procedure in most low- and middle-income countries. Examples of such procedures are receiving a license to set up a new firm or a permit to import an item.[1]

One reason for the variance in regulatory implementation could be that some firms have more influence over the policy arena than others. For example, recent firm-level studies suggest that, to the detriment of long-term economic growth, firms with powerful political connections are unduly favored in the way certain policies are designed or implemented.[2] These firms receive preferential access to state credit, land, and import licenses. The sectors in which they operate are protected from competition from other firms through high regulatory barriers to entry. This form of policy subversion has significant negative effects on the economy.

How policy "capture" slows economic growth

This chapter explains how and when powerful groups with narrow interests can have an undue influence on policy ("capture") and slow down economic growth, even in the context of high state capacity.[3] Such dominant groups can include politically connected firms and lobbies for industry, farmers, or consumers. This chapter also analyzes cases in which shortsighted, opportunistic state actors renege on policy commitments, harming investors. In some cases, existing norms such as tolerance of corruption in public agencies can reinforce such policy failures.

That said, the influence of interest groups, while ubiquitous, does not always render growth policies ineffective; sometimes, it can even improve them. How this process plays out depends on the characteristics of the government agencies that enact the policies in question, as well as the incentives of influential groups, such as industry associations, that interact with those agencies. Understanding what drives this difference can help identify ways to improve policy effectiveness.

One lesson that emerges from such understanding is that designing second-best policies that can achieve at least the partial goals of security, growth, or equity may be more effective than designing ideal policies that are at high risk of capture (such second-best policies are considered *implementable*). A second lesson is the value of avoiding policies that look good in the short term but could end up reinforcing the power of dominant groups that could block further reforms, thereby hindering the effectiveness of policies in the future. A third lesson is that undue influence from dominant groups can be counterbalanced by the appropriate design of incentives within public agencies, checks and balances between agencies, and mechanisms that extend accountability to a broad group of firms and individuals. Such reforms can expand the set of implementable policies.

This approach assumes that the interests of high-level policy makers are aligned in the direction of reform. Whether that is the case depends on the evolution of the broader governance environment, a topic examined in part III of this Report.

> A lesson is the value of avoiding policies that look good in the short term but could end up reinforcing the power of dominant groups that could block further reforms.

Figure 5.1 Length of time needed for firms to obtain a construction permit varies widely

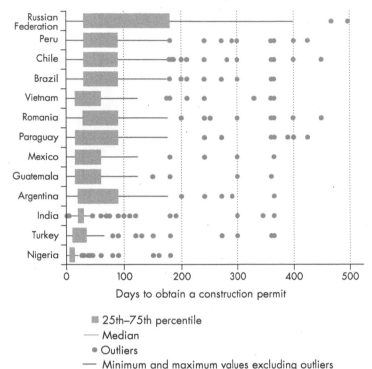

Days to obtain a construction permit

- ■ 25th–75th percentile
- — Median
- ● Outliers
- — Minimum and maximum values excluding outliers

Sources: WDR 2017 team, based on data from World Bank, Enterprise Surveys, circa 2006 to 2014.

How governance matters to growth: A microeconomic perspective

There is a clear positive correlation between aggregate measures of governance and per capita income across countries (figure 5.2). Because countries had similar levels of per capita income in the distant past, current differences in their per capita income largely reflect differences in their long-term growth rates.[4] Thus governance and long-term growth are positively associated.

This correlation should be viewed with some caveats, however. It could reflect reverse causation from growth to governance, or some third factor (such as accumulated knowledge and skills) that affects both governance and income growth. Bearing in mind these caveats, many cross-country studies suggest that the nature of governance—as reflected in broad institutional measures such as protection of property rights, rule of law, and absence of corruption—matters to long-term growth.[5]

Even within countries, historical differences in institutions that affect property rights and collective action are associated with persistent differences in levels of economic development. For example, in some regions of Peru an extensive system of forced mining labor (*mita*) was in effect from 1573 to 1812. Today, the average household consumption levels in those regions are about 25 percent lower than in adjoining regions. One explanation is that in areas without *mita*, the landowning class that emerged had an incentive to set up stable property rights institutions. Today, areas that did not have the *mita* system continue to have more secure property rights and do a better job of providing public goods (Dell 2010).

When change is viewed over the shorter time span of decades rather than centuries, the relationship between broad, aggregate measures of governance and economic growth is weaker (figure 5.3). Over the last century, growth accelerations and slowdowns that lasted as long as a decade do not seem to have been correlated with major changes in governance, nor have sustained periods of high growth lasting as long as three decades.[6] It is possible for economies to grow without big changes in the nature of governance, but it is not clear how long such growth can be sustained.

What are the mechanisms behind the aggregate relationship between governance and growth? Because different dimensions of governance are correlated across countries, it is not easy to delineate their impacts on growth using a cross-country analysis alone. A more microeconomic analysis of the mechanisms through which governance affects growth is therefore a vital complement to the macroeconomic analysis of governance and growth (Pande and Udry 2006).

Two sources of growth: Investment and efficiency

On the surface, growth in per capita income has two sources: investment and efficiency. On the one hand, investment is the process by which economies accumulate physical capital, skills, and knowledge. Efficiency, on the other hand, determines how well this labor and capital are put to use. In general, at least half of the per capita income differences across countries is attributable to differences in countries' efficiency levels (total factor productivity, or TFP). The rest is due to differences in investment (accumulation)—see Caselli (2005, 2016). Both investment and efficiency thus matter to growth.

Countries vary in the emphasis they place on various forms of investment and efficiency in their growth models. Some growth models emphasize

Figure 5.2 Per capita income and governance are correlated

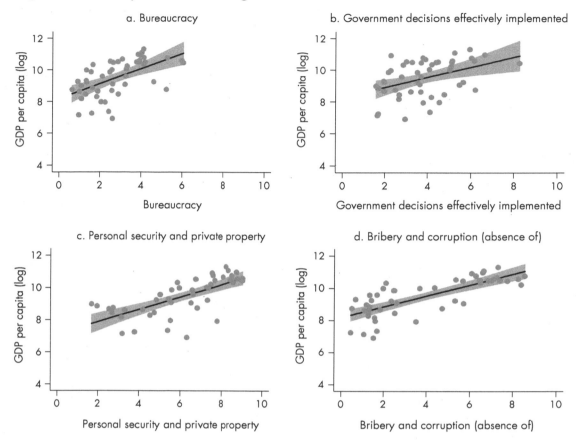

Sources: WDR 2017 team, using data from IMD World Competitiveness Online, and World Bank, World Development Indicators (database, GDP per capita). For both sources, the data are shown for 2010.

Note: "Bureaucracy" indicates to what extent bureaucracy does not hinder business activity; "government decisions effectively implemented" indicates to what extent government decisions are effectively implemented; "personal security and private property" indicates whether personal security and private property rights are adequately protected; and "bribery and corruption" indicates to what extent bribery and corruption do not exist in a country. The scale ranges from 0 (worst outcome) to 10 (best outcome). GDP = gross domestic product.

accumulation, such as the mobilization of savings for industrial investment. Other models emphasize growth in efficiency through innovation and competition among firms. Growth models based on factor accumulation may require a different governance configuration than those based on efficiency. Transitioning from one model to another has proven to be a complex policy challenge (Gill and Kharas 2015)—see spotlight 6 on the middle-income trap.

Governance can affect investment and efficiency through two types of institutional "functions." The first deals with commitment—that is, creating an environment in which firms or individuals feel secure in investing their resources in productive activities and have the incentives to use them efficiently. The second pertains to socially beneficial collective action to coordinate investment decisions and promote cooperation among investors to solve potential market failures.

The key governance functions: Enhancing commitment and collective action

In the absence of a credible commitment to the security of property rights (that is, when there is risk of expropriation), the incentives for investment or innovation will be limited. Firms and individuals that experience lower security will invest less in productive activities. Moreover, differences across firms in the level of security from expropriation will affect the efficiency of resource use. If the more productive firms in an economy experience lower security than the less productive ones, then investment by productive firms will be inefficiently low, leading to misallocating resources and thwarting growth.

Consistent with theory, household-level studies find that farmers are more likely to make long-term investments in their land when their tenure is more secure, and urban households are more likely to

Figure 5.3 Medium-term growth and governance are *not* correlated

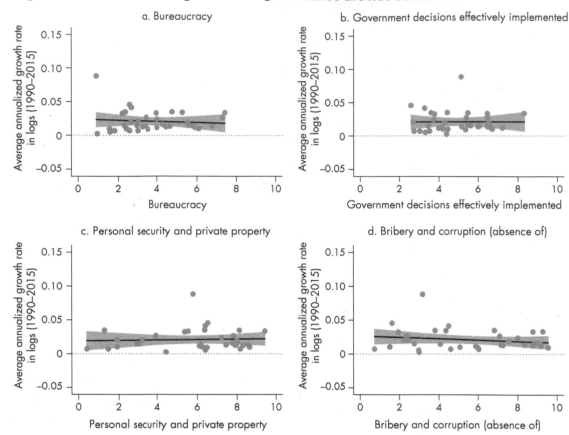

Sources: WDR 2017 team, using data from IMD World Competitiveness Online (1996 and 1998 for "government decisions effectively implemented"), and World Bank, World Development Indicators (database, average annualized growth rate in logs, 1990–2015).

Note: "Bureaucracy" indicates to what extent bureaucracy does not hinder business activity; "government decisions effectively implemented" indicates to what extent government decisions are effectively implemented; "personal security and private property" indicates whether personal security and private property rights are adequately protected; and "bribery and corruption" indicates to what extent bribery and corruption do not exist in a country. The scale ranges from 0 (worst outcome) to 10 (best outcome).

renovate homes when the risk of being dispossessed is lower.[7] Secure rights also improve labor allocation because protecting one's property is no longer a primary motivation in decisions about where to work (Field 2007). Similarly, studies find that firms that perceive themselves to be more secure from expropriation reinvest more of their profits in their business (Johnson, McMillan, and Woodruff 2002b). Theory also suggests that well-defined property rights should improve the functioning of credit and other asset markets, but empirical evidence in support of such suggestions is weak.

Enforcement of contracts governing economic transactions is also critical because problems with contract enforcement prevent specialization and an optimal division of labor (North 1990; Costinot 2009). Suppose a firm is considering whether to specialize in producing parts for a bigger firm. Once committed to this specialization, it will have no alternative but to

sell those parts at whatever price that particular buyer offers. Thus the firm will hesitate to specialize unless both parties can agree on an enforceable contract with a fair price. In small economies, reputation and relationships can be effective means of enforcement, but as growth leads to greater market size, impersonal interactions become more likely, and thus formal contract enforcement begins to matter more (Dixit 2007). Empirical studies find that a strengthened formal enforcement system (such as through the courts) can foster the creation of new business relationships, promote trade in goods, and increase the flow of credit to firms.[8]

The design and implementation of regulations that affect competition between firms are another policy dimension central to growth. For example, poorly designed licensing requirements for new firms can make it difficult for entrepreneurs to bring new investment ideas to fruition, and they can reduce the competitive pressure on existing firms to innovate and become more productive.[9] For example, a policy of industrial licensing in India required firms to obtain government permission before setting up a new factory or expanding output in an existing factory. The process of license approval was onerous and unpredictable. Loosening these requirements in some industries in the 1980s may have increased efficiency levels by as much as 22 percent (Chari 2011).

Some forms of collective action, such as coordinating investment and ensuring cooperation to prevent free-riding, can solve potential market failures that can impede growth and investment in public goods. Although discussing all possible market failures is beyond the scope of this chapter, what follows illustrates the key issues by looking at a specific type of failure.

The insight that failure to coordinate investment activity could lead to underdevelopment is decades old.[10] Suppose an industry could upgrade to a modern technology that relies on a range of specialized skills. For a worker, investing in learning those skills does not make sense if it is not clear that the modern technology will be adopted. For a firm, investing in the new technology does not make sense unless a supply of the required specialized skills will be available. Thus without some way of coordinating the decisions of workers and firms, the industry could remain trapped in a low-level equilibrium.[11] Such coordination problems can occur in many contexts, ranging from finance and adoption of technology to innovation and industrial clusters.[12]

Policies to address coordination and other collective action problems are difficult to design and implement. For example, when complementarities between firms could lead to a coordination failure, governments could use subsidies or taxes to encourage firms to invest in a coordinated manner (Rodrik 1996). But targeting such a subsidy scheme to the right set of firms requires information on precisely which firms could have spillovers on others, and on how much they are investing (Bond and Pande 2007). Because of such implementation challenges, policies to address collective action problems in growth are particularly sensitive to the quality of governance.[13]

How policies are affected by undue influence from powerful groups

A poor capacity to design or implement policies could be one reason why governments do not enact policies that are functionally optimal for aggregate growth. Yet, even when such capacity exists and a first-best policy has been identified, those in power may not have the incentive to choose that policy. Indeed, specific actors in the policy arena may be able to design or implement a policy that maximizes their private benefits rather than social welfare because they have so much bargaining power. In this Report, this arrangement is called *capture*. Capture is not easy to identify, and there is the risk of mistaking what was simply a misinformed policy choice for deliberate subversion.

Recent years have seen a burgeoning of quantitative research into this question. This research has detected specific forms of capture, and in some cases it has even measured its efficiency costs. For example, studies of trade policy suggest that even in high-income countries policy choice can unduly reflect the preferences of groups with high levels of influence in the policy arena. Although low trade barriers are generally good for long-term growth, domestic industries that compete with imports stand to lose from them in the short term. Political influence or campaign contributions from industry lobbies and labor unions have been shown to affect the setting of import tariffs. Larger and better-organized industries that compete with imports tend to win more import protection.[14]

The potential power to influence policy is distributed unevenly, not only across industries but also across firms within industries. In most countries, some firms are much better connected to the government than others. Sometimes, state actors collude with such politically connected firms to subvert a policy in the interest of those firms, possibly to the detriment of unconnected firms in the same industry.

Such capture by politically connected firms may not be easily identifiable or as large scale as, say, setting high tariffs in import-competing industries, but the evidence suggests that its economic costs are far from trivial. In the 1990s, for example, some of Indonesia's largest industrial groups had strong connections to President Suharto.[15] Between 1995 and 1997, rumors about the state of Suharto's health circulated on several occasions. Each time, the more closely industrial groups were connected to the president, the more their stock values fell (figure 5.4). In fact, the more serious the health rumor, the greater was the fall in stock values. Because this decline was not connected to other changes in market conditions or the productivity of connected firms, the drop in share prices was a proxy for the private benefits of being able to capture policy through political connections (Fisman 2001). Based on a similar method, the estimated value of political connections in the Arab

Capture by politically connected firms may not be easily identifiable, but the evidence suggests that its economic costs are far from trivial.

Figure 5.4 In Indonesia, the stock value of politically connected firms fell when the connection was jeopardized

The closer that industrial groups were to President Suharto, the more the value of their stock fell as rumors about the president's health circulated

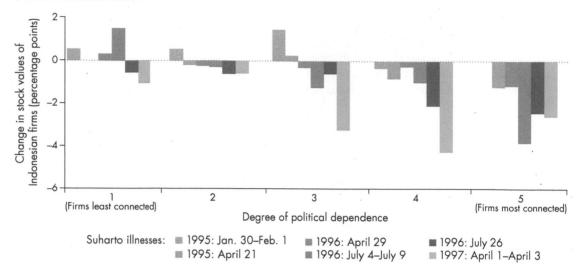

Suharto illnesses: ▪ 1995: Jan. 30–Feb. 1 ▪ 1996: April 29 ▪ 1996: July 26
▪ 1995: April 21 ▪ 1996: July 4–July 9 ▪ 1997: April 1–April 3

Source: Fisman 2001, figure 1.

Republic of Egypt during the Mubarak era was about 13–16 percent of firm value (Chekir and Diwan 2014).

How politically connected firms gain undue advantage

The benefits of policy capture to politically connected firms can be economically significant. Understanding the ways in which policy capture occurs is therefore important.

Diverting credit. One way in which state actors favor connected firms is to divert government loans to them. In Pakistan, for example, between 1996 and 2002 politically connected firms borrowed 45 percent more and had 50 percent higher loan default rates than other firms (Khwaja and Mian 2005). This preferential treatment was related entirely to loans from government banks. Moreover, it increased when the power of the connected politician increased, and it fell when there was more electoral competition within the politician's constituency. In Brazil, firms that made campaign contributions to winning candidates in the 1998 and 2002 elections had higher returns and subsequently received greater credit from banks (Claessens, Feijen, and Laeven 2008). A study of Malaysia at the time of the Asian financial crisis found that the market value of politically connected firms improved relative to that of other firms after international capital controls were imposed, suggesting that connected firms had easier access to domestic credit (Johnson and Mitton 2003).

Granting import licenses to favored firms. Another way to channel favor to connected firms is to grant import licenses only to specific (favored) firms. In Suharto-era Indonesia, being politically connected tripled the likelihood of receiving a license relative to a firm's competitors. And the licenses conferred monopolistic power on the licensee. For example, a highly connected firm in the milk industry was granted import licenses for 12 inputs necessary to produce milk, whereas some other firms in the same industry had three to four licenses at most. This situation forced competitors to rely on the connected firm or on inferior domestic supplies (Mobarak and Purbasari 2008).

Using market regulations to favor firms. Market regulations can also be used to favor connected firms. For example, regulatory barriers to the entry of new firms can be a means of protecting incumbents to the detriment of market entry and competition. In Tunisia during the regime of Zine El Abidine Ben Ali (1987–2011), firms under the control of the ruling clan accounted for a disproportionately high share (21 percent) of total private sector profits (Rijkers, Freund, and Nucifora 2014). The superior profits of these connected firms may have been due to the heavy regulation of firm entry, investment, and foreign direct investment in the sectors in which they had a heavy presence. Indeed, the gap in profits between connected firms and others was higher in the more regulated sectors, suggesting that entry regulation served to shield connected firms from competition. There is similar evidence from Mubarak-era Egypt (Diwan, Keefer, and Schiffbauer 2015).

Political cycles and populism

Potentially, any group of firms, workers, or consumers that is politically influential can influence policies. For example, the adoption of "green growth" policies that are socially beneficial and would not necessarily slow down economic growth could be blocked by influential groups of farmers or consumers who stand to lose from the policies in the short term (box 5.1). Sometimes, it is hard to predict which side will manage to tilt policies in its favor. For example, in the utilities industries, the unregulated price can be inefficiently high, and there is a valid economic argument for regulating the price. However, the regulators may set the price too high if they collude with the utility firm, whereas if the countervailing influence from consumer advocacy groups prevails, regulators may set the price too low.[16]

Tilting policies to favor politically influential groups. Sometimes, politicians direct public investment to benefit narrow groups of supporters—a practice known as *clientelism* (see chapter 6). Such a client-based allocation of public investment is likely to be highly inefficient.

More generally, public resources can be allocated in favor of politically influential groups without necessarily involving a strict patron-client relationship. For example, many countries have development programs that direct state credit to small firms, rural enterprises, and farmers. This credit can be used to favor groups that have outsized political influence. Cole (2009) found that from 1985 to 2009 in India agricultural credit from state banks increased by 5–10 percentage points in an election year. This higher lending during election years targeted places

---

Box 5.1 Why some people see red when they hear "green growth"

"Green growth is about making growth processes resource-efficient, cleaner and more resilient without necessarily slowing them" (Hallegatte and others 2012, 2). For many reasons, environmental conservation is also good for long-term economic growth and development. Economic production depends on the stock of natural resources and on environmental quality ("natural capital"). Green growth strategies can increase natural capital by preventing environmental degradation. Environmental protection can also contribute indirectly to growth by correcting market failures. For example, a policy that addresses market failures leading to urban congestion can improve air quality and increase urban productivity. Green growth can also improve well-being directly by improving air and water quality.

However, switching to green growth strategies could impose short-term costs on some groups in society. Take the case of organic fertilizer. Smaller and more targeted doses of fertilizer (a "green" approach) are better for the environment in the long run, but conventional fertilizer is less costly and easier to use. Malawi faced this problem in 2005 when, to cope with food insecurity, it introduced a fertilizer subsidy for smallholder maize farmers. The intensive use of conventional fertilizer did lead to an immediate increase in farm output. However, because small farmers would not find it easy to adopt greener approaches using smaller, targeted doses and more organic fertilizers, efforts to phase out the subsidy could hurt maize farmers for some years (Resnick, Tarp, and Thurlow 2012).

It could be that the groups who stand to lose from green growth policies in the short term have an oversized influence in the policy arena, and so they are able to block reforms and undermine commitment. Because the costs are concentrated and many of the benefits from cleaner technologies are intangible and dispersed, the potential losers from such reforms are likely better able to organize. They can also form a strong electoral constituency. For example, Malawi's fertilizer program has been popular among small farmers—an important constituency. At times, switching to green growth strategies can entail losses for influential groups of consumers and firms. For example, South Africa announced an ambitious climate change plan in 2010 that would reduce the share of electricity generated by coal-fired plants in a country in which electricity is in short supply and coal is a relatively abundant source. The plan, despite being watered down a year later, has been opposed by consumers, labor unions, and business interests, particularly those in mining and heavy industry (Resnick,Tarp, and Thurlow 2012). As these examples demonstrate, the design of green growth policies must take into account the potential resistance from short-term losers.

Sources: Hallegatte and others (2012); Resnick, Tarp, and Thurlow (2012).

---

where the electoral race was particularly close, hinting at the political motives behind the credit boom. Such political cycles in government lending during election years have been observed in many countries (Dinc 2005). In Italy, the interest rates charged in the 1990s by politically affiliated banks varied with the election cycle, which is also suggestive of political influence on lending (Sapienza 2004).

Misallocating public investment. Failed industrial development programs are another example of how political influence can undermine growth by misallocating public investment. Governments often direct public investment to specific sectors or regions, ostensibly to address coordination failures. Such programs could become a vehicle for providing hidden benefits to politically influential groups (Coate and Morris 1995). For example, landowners and workers in politically important regions might gain if an industrial zone is located in their region, raising prices and wages.

The disappointing experience of Sub-Saharan Africa with industrial coordination policies is illustrative. Defying economic logic, one program in Ghana involved the transport of cattle hides to a tannery 500 miles to the south in the country, only to send the leather back north to a footwear factory 200 miles away—all to serve a market a farther 200 miles north. Poor siting of the tannery thus rendered the program economically unviable (Robinson 2009). Some of these case studies conclude that poor location decisions were the outcomes of political influence. In Zambia, for example, the Industrial Development Corporation evidently chose economically infeasible locations for many subsidiary firms, mainly on the basis of providing employment in rural areas (Robinson 2009).

The cost of capture

The most obvious cost of policy capture is the inefficient allocation of public resources. For example, bank loans should go to the most productive firms, but that does not necessarily happen when lending is based on a firm's political connections. Corporate lending data from Pakistan for 1996–2002 reveal that connected firms received a disproportionately large share of credit, but they were more likely than other firms to default on their loans and they were less productive. Based on the gap in productivity between connected firms and other firms, the annual loss from giving disproportionate amounts of credit to connected firms could have been as high as 1.6 percent of GDP (Khwaja and Mian 2005).

Such misallocation could also have a long-term impact on growth through its detrimental effects on the basic economic process of creative destruction—that is, the entry of new firms, investment by existing firms to become more productive, and the exit of unproductive firms.[17] Entrepreneurship is likely to be discouraged in an environment in which firms with political influence earn rents (disproportionate benefits) at the expense of more efficient or more innovative firms that lack influence. By tilting the playing field against ordinary firms, such capture can also make growth less inclusive. But measuring such long-term costs is difficult.

This reckoning of the costs of undue influence on policies is relative to a benchmark in which resources are efficiently allocated. However, the removal of means of rent-seeking by influential firms could have other systemic effects on the economy. Indeed, according to one view, many low-income economies are characterized by socioeconomic relationships based not on impersonal rules but on personal connections and privilege.[18] In this political order, the elites manipulate the economy to maintain rents for powerful groups. This manipulation then serves to maintain social order and restrain violence. In such a world, "capture" is just one manifestation of deeper political economy problems, and so long as those are not addressed, simply prohibiting means of capture and rent-seeking will not lead to efficient outcomes (Acemoglu and Robinson 2013).

When interest group influence is not necessarily bad for policies

Sometimes, the self-interest of powerful businesses can coincide with policies that are good for long-term growth. The expansion of trading opportunities in the Mediterranean in the 10th to the 12th centuries, for example, led to the establishment of a broad-based merchant class in that part of the world. This merchant class was interested in market-supporting institutions that would enable trade for all its members. In Venice, it used its economic power to push for the establishment of robust contracting institutions and constraints on the executive (by ending the practice of hereditary doges and instituting a de facto parliament). Similarly, the merchant class that arose in Great Britain because of the growth of Atlantic trade in the 1600s pushed for better property rights and contracting institutions.[19]

More contemporary case studies suggest that, for their collective benefit, business associations have helped governments improve various dimensions

Sometimes, the self-interest of powerful businesses can coincide with policies that are good for long-term growth.

of the business environment (such as secure property rights, fair enforcement of rules, and provision of public infrastructure) through lobbying efforts or better monitoring of public officials (Doner and Schneider 2000). They have also helped solve coordination problems. The Republic of Korea's phase of growth through export-oriented industrialization, which lasted for three decades, exemplifies this kind of pro-growth state-business interaction.[20] Other examples include the footwear manufacturers' association in Brazil, the coffee federation in Colombia, and the textile manufacturers' association in Thailand, all of which played a coordinating role in reducing the costs of information about export markets (Doner and Schneider 2000).

Broad-based business associations are more likely to have an interest in pushing for better institutions rather than narrow rents. It is in the collective interest of firms in an industry to prevent policy capture by a few of them. Industry groups can develop collective mechanisms that prevent members from colluding with state officials and subverting policies in their narrow interest (Dixit 2015). Case studies suggest that business associations whose membership represents a large segment of the industry tend to be more influential and more "developmentally oriented" in their influence (Doner and Schneider 2000).

The extent and type of transparency also affect the nature of state-business interaction. When a state agency and the firms with which it interacts have a monopoly over critical information, there is a greater scope for them to collude and subvert policy in their mutual interest. Consider the regulation of a natural monopoly such as a public utility. Typically, the regulatory agency caps prices and compensates the utility firm based on an assessment of the firm's cost of production. In such situations, the firm could gain by colluding with the regulator to overstate its cost. The gain from such collusion is larger (and the chances it will be detected, lower) when the regulator and the firm know more than others about the cost (Laffont and Tirole 1991, 1993).

The nature of the government agencies that interact with firms also determines when state-business links will degenerate into narrow interest group capture. One example is the design of some industrial development agencies in East Asia from the 1950s to 1970s. Japan's Ministry of Trade and Industry (MITI), for example, combined bureaucratic autonomy with strong business ties. Although this step was necessary for the agency to be effective in coordinating industrialization, it also exposed the agency to

capture. MITI, however, was also highly meritocratic, with bureaucrats following long-term career paths, clear rules, and established norms. It drew staff largely from a select group of elite technocrats who had strong informal ties with one another, giving the agency an unusually high level of internal coherence. This organizational strength may have prevented MITI from being captured by narrow interests (Wade 1990; Evans 1995).

Policy design under risk of capture

How should the risk of undue influence from dominant groups be taken into account in the design of policies and by the government agencies responsible for their implementation? This section begins by discussing a pragmatic approach to policy design that duly considers the probability of capture.

Designing policies that are implementable

Sometimes, when the possibility of capture looms large, policies that are first-best on the basis of economic efficiency are less implementable than second-best ones. Why? Even a powerful interest group must expend effort and resources to gain influence. The benefits of a second-best policy may be too small to make it worth the cost for interest groups to expend such effort and resources. Building on this insight, policies are often designed to give less room for discretion at the implementation stage. For example, when a regulator mainly enforces rigid rules, there is less scope for subverting the enforcement of those rules to award undue favor. As a result, the benefit from capture is too low.[21]

Admittedly, designing policies that are less susceptible to capture involves a trade-off with efficiency. Replacing regulatory discretion with rigid rules gives the regulator less room to adapt enforcement to changing conditions. Rigid regulation thus imposes excessive costs on firms.

The risk of capture by self-interested, myopic state actors too can be addressed through pragmatic policy design—although with the same efficiency trade-offs. Think of a situation in which a government wants to attract foreign direct investment (FDI), but there is a history of FDI disputes, and investors are hesitant because they perceive a high risk of expropriation. Although strengthening checks and balances on state actors can reduce the perceived likelihood of expropriation, such institutional reforms take time. In the meantime, there are ways to design the FDI contract to make expropriation less likely. Efficiency dictates a revenue-sharing scheme in which the host country receives a fixed amount every period, leaving the investor with strong incentives to increase profitability. However, when expropriation is a possibility, a more practical revenue-sharing scheme is one in which the host country automatically receives more (less) revenue when profits are high (low)—see Engel and Fischer (2010). This scheme is more *consistent* over time, as it takes into account the government's incentives to uphold its commitment under different scenarios. Spotlight 7 addresses similar issues in the design of contracts for public-private partnerships (PPPs).

To put it in general terms, policies that are compatible with the existing balance of power may not be ideal, but they can effectively deliver growth. For example, in China the Township and Village Enterprises (TVEs) policy yielded strong investment growth until the mid-1990s (Qian 2003; Yao 2014). This policy was an unusual way of committing to property rights because TVEs were under the control of local community governments, and not, as is more common, under full private or central government control. Nevertheless, the policy was effective because of China's context at that time. From the era of central planning, China had inherited a strong ideology opposing private property, and firms lacked legal protection for their private property rights. Giving local governments control stakes in local firms and tying local fiscal outcomes and cadre incentives to TVE success were important factors in making the commitment to TVE property rights credible.

Anticipating how a policy could change the balance of power

Beyond its immediate impact on investment and production, an economic policy could have far-reaching consequences for governance—and thus growth—by altering the balance of power. Consider how a policy that promotes international trade could have such an effect. As discussed earlier, in both 11th-century Venice and 17th-century Great Britain, the growth of trade led to a rising merchant class, which in turn helped establish strong contracting and property rights institutions. But theory suggests that these effects were not inevitable, for trade does not always affect the distribution of economic power and incentives in the same way (Do and Levchenko 2009). Indeed, over time Venetian wealth from trade became concentrated in a narrower set of merchant families. No longer needing the support of smaller merchants,

they used their power to institute an oligarchy (Puga and Trefler 2014).

The sugar boom that swept over the Caribbean islands around the 1650s and lasted for more than 200 years also illustrates this point. Before the advent of large-scale sugar production, these islands were typically smallholder peasant societies. The sugar boom, however, concentrated power in the hands of large plantation owners—a development that has been associated with the rise of slavery, as well as the persistent undermining of the property rights of small farmers in the region. This institutional stunting had serious adverse consequences for long-term growth (Levchenko 2016).

Thus anyone assessing a policy that seems optimal in theory should ask if, in the given context, it could concentrate economic power in a way that would ultimately undermine institutions.[22] Consider the experience of the Russian Federation and eastern European countries in their transition toward market economies At the time, there was a consensus among economists that the privatization of state-owned enterprises (SOEs) was a priority for improving the efficiency of these economies. Russia and many eastern European countries therefore focused on rapid, large-scale privatization of SOEs. But the way in which privatization was implemented created a new class of oligarchs who were able to block other policies that could promote competition (such as easing the procedure for setting up a new business). As a result, many of these economies are still struggling with inefficient, oligopolistic industries. This is consistent with the view that reforms that create an initial concentration of gains may engender strong opposition to further reform from early winners (Hellman 1998). By contrast, Poland chose to focus first on reforms that would make it easy for new firms to enter and privatized existing firms more gradually. This sequencing created a class of young firms that were collectively interested in further reforms, while preventing the sudden emergence of a powerful group of large firms that could block reforms (Jackson, Klich, and Poznańska 2005).

How the design of public agencies mediates the influence of powerful groups

Why are some public agencies able to work with different interest groups to design and implement policies without being unduly influenced by any particular group, while others are captured by dominant groups? The answer depends on a number of features of the internal design of bureaucracies. The design features of public agencies, such as how officials are selected, how the performance of officials is assessed and rewarded, and how much discretion they have in implementing those goals, can help to mediate the influence of powerful groups. The allocation of functions across agencies and the role of oversight agencies such as auditors also matter (Tirole 1994). Finally, as discussed in the *World Development Report 2015: Mind, Society, and Behavior* (WDR 2015), bureaucratic norms can emerge that facilitate or obstruct capture.[23]

Selection methods, incentives, and intrinsic motivation

Recently, a number of studies have examined empirically how selection and incentive structures in bureaucracies affect the behavior of officials. This research can be useful for understanding how agency design could make officials less susceptible to bribery or other forms of undue influence by those seeking to capture a policy.[24]

Consider tools that provide incentives, such as pay-for-performance schemes. Randomized evaluations of these schemes in the context of the frontline provision of public services find that the performance of public officials in fulfilling their tasks improves.[25] Pay-for-performance could also weaken the incentives of officials to collude in policy capture if that would mean missing performance targets.

But there are settings in which an overreliance on financial incentives could backfire. One issue with incentive schemes is that many government agencies have multiple objectives. Making officials' pay too dependent on achieving any one objective can lead to a disproportionate focus on that objective to the exclusion of others (Tirole 1994). For example, when police agencies in the United States are allowed to keep the revenue they obtain from assets they seize in drug arrests, they make even more drug arrests, but at the cost of reducing enforcement of other petty crimes (Baicker and Jacobson 2007). Focusing on one-dimensional incentives could also encourage over-zealous or biased behavior by officials. This concern is especially salient among officials whose jobs involve exercising expert judgment, such as regulators and judges. Making their rewards dependent on taking a particular position could induce them to distort their judgments routinely in favor of that position. For example, a regulator who is rewarded according

to the number of violations detected might become too zealous in detecting "violations" or demand even higher bribes to not report violations.

In such settings, the design of selection methods for regulators may be a more effective lever. It has been shown that selection methods can influence the degree to which officials are responsive to particular interest groups. A study that compared direct election with political appointment of power utility regulators across U.S. states found that elected regulators have a more pro-consumer stance (Besley and Coate 2003). In fact, regulatory policy is just one of many policy areas for which politicians are responsible, and it is not very salient to voters. As a result, appointed regulators are more likely to respond to the interests of political elites than voters. But when regulators are elected, regulatory policy becomes more important to voters.

"Intrinsic motivation" is another lever for influencing the behavior of officials. Surveys and lab experiments suggest that public officials are intrinsically more motivated than private sector employees toward public service.[26] Such pro-social motivation is also correlated with better job performance (Perry and Hondeghem 2008).

It is possible to design the work environment in ways that enhance intrinsic motivation. For example, smaller caseloads and higher salaries have a more positive effect on the performance of judges in U.S. state supreme courts when those judges are given more discretion in selecting cases (Ash and MacLeod 2015). This is consistent with the hypothesis that judges are intrinsically motivated to work hard on important cases. Reducing caseloads and increasing salaries give them the time and financial security to focus on producing high-quality judgments, especially when they have the discretion to choose important cases.

The extent to which officials are already motivated in a pro-social direction could have an important impact on how changes in the operating environment of a public agency play out. If officials care only about monetary rewards and are susceptible to bribes, reducing the extent of discretion in decision making can restrict the scope for capture. But this approach may not be effective in an agency in which the levels of intrinsic motivation for public service are already high, because the approach could undermine that intrinsic motivation.

Designing selection methods that attract more intrinsically motivated officials is another promising approach, but evidence on it is limited. A recent field experiment randomized salaries for public sector job

The design features of public agencies, such as how officials are selected, how the performance of officials is assessed and rewarded, and how much discretion they have in implementing those goals, can help to mediate the influence of powerful groups.

offers in Mexico to test whether higher wages attract more motivated officials (Dal Bó, Finan, and Rossi 2013). Higher compensation was associated with a better-qualified applicant pool—that is, the applicants were smarter and had better personality traits, higher earnings, and a better occupation profile. Remarkably, the high-wage applicant pool was also more motivated toward public service. But some other studies suggest that offering higher wages attracts quality (as reflected in previous wages and work experience) at the expense of pro-social motivation (Finan, Olken, and Pande 2015).

Norms in public organizations

Conformity with accepted norms of behavior in one's organization could be a powerful driver of individual behavior in government organizations. Honesty can become a self-reinforcing norm in some agencies, whereas corrupt norms of behavior can take hold in others.[27] In organizations in which corruption is considered acceptable because "everyone does it," a temporary reform that shocks some officials into behaving more honestly could disrupt this bad norm, leading to a permanent, self-reinforcing improvement.

Although systematic evidence on such norm-shifting reforms is lacking, an example from the Republic of Korea's past suggests that an intervention that operates on multiple fronts to shift norms could work. In 1961 new Korean president Park Chung Hee inherited a bureaucracy known for its political decisions made on the basis of "self-enrichment." Immediately upon accepting his new office, Park took action to curb the rampant corrupt behavior in the government. Within a month, he had "dismissed the top 10 percent of bureaucrats, jailed a number of the country's leading businesspersons for corruption, and sent the rest of the bureaucracy to two-week training courses in management, efficiency, and public spiritedness" (Hoff 2001, 163). Moreover, for the bureaucrats that would remain, Park instituted strict performance monitoring practices alongside frequent office rotations. The result of these efforts was a government whose functioning was far improved.

Monitoring

Monitoring by higher agencies can deter officials from colluding in policy capture and generate useful information for third parties interested in preventing capture. Audits, for example, have been shown to reduce leakage in village-level public investment programs (Olken 2007). Informed third parties can also be recruited as monitors. Consider customs fraud

(such as the underreporting of import values), which is one way firms can subvert the implementation of trade policy through bribery or other means of influence (Fisman and Wei 2001; Sequeira and Djankov 2014). To combat this kind of fraud, foreign inspectors at the point of origin would have accurate information about the value of shipments, and they are less susceptible to the influence of domestically powerful firms. A study using data from 104 developing countries between 1980 and 2000 found that countries that hire foreign inspectors to verify the tariff classification and the value of shipments before they leave their origin country increase import duty collections by 15–30 percentage points on average (Yang 2008).

But monitoring has its limits. It can make officials overly cautious, worsening their performance.[28] And monitors themselves are not immune to capture. Such capture was revealed in a system of environmental audits of firms in an Indian state (Duflo and others 2013). In the prevailing audit system, auditors who had been hired by the firms themselves were conducting the pollution audits. But a study found that these auditors were underreporting the incidence of pollution by firms. Replacing this system with one in which auditors were randomly assigned to firms and paid fixed wages from a central pool reduced auditors' underreporting of pollution.

Accountability through horizontal checks and balances

Effective checks and balances within a government should reduce the risk of short-term, opportunistic behavior by a few state actors. Consistent with this hypothesis, there are fewer disputes about foreign direct investment in countries with stronger horizontal political constraints, as measured by the number of independent branches in government with veto power over policy change and the degree of party alignment across different branches of government (Jensen and others 2012). Even in authoritarian regimes, the existence of legislative bodies increases investment by raising the cost of expropriation (Wright 2008).

Compared with high-income countries, low- and middle-income countries have weak formal checks and balances within government on average (figure 5.5), and strengthening these institutions is a long-term project. However, the principle of accountability through horizontal checks and balances lends itself to other approaches tailored to the specifics of a context.

Allocating power among government agencies and creating independent oversight agencies can reduce the chances of "grand" capture of policy by

Honesty can become a self-reinforcing norm in some agencies, whereas corrupt norms of behavior can take hold in others.

Figure 5.5 Formal checks and balances are weaker in low- and middle-income countries

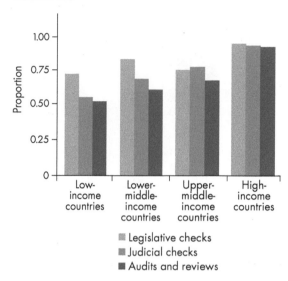

Sources: WDR 2017 team, based on data from the World Justice Project, Rule of Law Index, and World Bank, World Development Indicators (database), circa 2014.

dominant special interest groups. This principle can be illustrated by considering the design of regulatory agencies.

When regulators and the regulated firms have a monopoly over information pertinent to a regulation (such as firms' cost structure), they can collude over regulatory design. In such circumstances, the division of power across regulatory agencies can reduce the monopoly over information and thus deter collusive capture (Laffont and Martimort 1999). But such a division of power is not without its drawbacks. Acquiring the information and expertise needed for regulatory design is difficult, and it might be easier to consolidate such expertise in a single regulatory agency. Thus a multiplicity of agencies could make coordination of regulatory policy more difficult, slowing down decision making. Indeed, if regulators are motivated purely by public interest and there is little chance of collusion, splitting functions between agencies could be counterproductive.

There is evidence that review and oversight of regulatory agencies by other government branches, such as the judiciary, can help prevent or invalidate regulatory decisions that are not in the public interest. Across countries, the strength of judicial independence and constitutional review (the power of the courts to check laws passed by the legislature that contravene a rigid constitution) is associated

with stronger protection of property rights and less regulation of firm entry (La Porta and others 2004). In the United States, the delegation of decision-making authority to bureaucratic agencies and of arbitration authority to the courts has helped make regulatory policies more consistent (Spiller and Tommasi 2005). It has also helped level the playing field for less powerful actors. However, judicial review has its limits; in particular, the judiciary can step in only after being approached by an affected party with the legal standing to do so (Magill 2013).

Experience with the U.S. Office of Information and Regulatory Affairs (OIRA) suggests that the existence of an agency tasked with cross-cutting oversight of regulators, based on a cost-benefit analysis, can also help prevent capture. It has been hard for any particular narrow interest group to capture OIRA because it is a generalist institution and not focused on a single regulatory issue. Moreover, its practice of using standardized cost-benefit analysis in assessing regulations helps counteract the potential use of biased information and analysis by industry or consumer interest groups to influence regulations (Livermore and Revesz 2014).

Institutions of accountability are also politically embedded, and so they too could be subverted by powerful narrow interests. Nevertheless, even in countries with complicated and far-reaching governance environments, the state is rarely monolithic, and accountability institutions often manage to preserve autonomy. A recent case study of telecommunications in three middle-income countries—Mexico, South Africa, and Turkey—is illustrative. Although the telecom sector remains monopolistic or oligopolistic in all of these countries, recent years have seen clear improvements in access, technology, and market competition. One reason is that accountability institutions—the judiciary, competition commissions, and telecom regulators—have often acted autonomously against anticompetitive practices (Atiyas, Levy, and Walton 2016).

Mechanisms of vertical accountability and increased contestability

Economically dominant groups such as large firms have the resources to gain influence in the policy arena, whereas consumers and citizens are a diffuse interest group, facing a collective interest problem when advocating for their policy preferences.[29] Thus mechanisms of vertical accountability that facilitate contestability by citizen (or consumer) groups could help balance influence in the policy-making process.

Review and oversight of regulatory agencies by other government branches, such as the judiciary, can help prevent or invalidate regulatory decisions that are not in the public interest.

Figure 5.6 Formal avenues for broad-based participation in regulatory decision making are limited in low- and middle-income countries

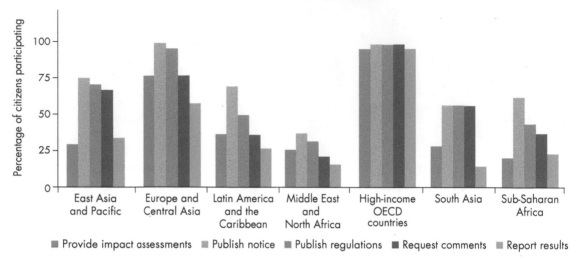

Source: WDR 2017 team, using data from World Bank, Global Indicators of Regulatory Governance, various years.

Note: OECD = Organisation for Economic Co-operation and Development.

Recent research suggests that media coverage can help reduce the influence of special-interest groups on policies by increasing the influence of ordinary voters. A study documenting the effect of "muckraking" magazines on the voting patterns of U.S. representatives and senators in the early part of the 20th century found that media coverage induces more populist legislative outcomes (Dyck, Moss, and Zingales 2013). When the benefits of preventing special-interest capture of a policy are diffuse, individual voters may lack the incentive to gather information about that policy. The media can therefore substitute for collective action in information gathering. This populist tilt is likely to be stronger when the policy issues are more newsworthy and the media are profit-maximizing because these factors increase the incentives of the media to cater to a wider consumer base, especially low-income groups.

Procedural requirements that government agencies seek diverse inputs during policy design and rollout can also balance influence. In the United States, the Administrative Procedure Act has put in place a series of procedural requirements for the participation of different interest groups in the regulatory process. Under this act, "regulatory agencies must provide notice, must inform about proposed rule makings, must make their decisions taking into account the submissions of interested parties, and cannot rush nor make decisions in the dark" (Spiller and Tommasi 2005, 535).

Mechanisms that facilitate policy input from consumer and citizen advocacy groups can also countervail the influence of dominant industry lobbies. In the United States, regulatory bodies have devised a range of mechanisms that facilitate consumer advocacy.[30] For example, in the 1970s the big oil price shocks ended a period of declining prices, and many energy utilities sought an increase in the prices they were allowed to charge. In response, many states introduced consumer advocacy groups to balance the pressure from producers. As a result, price increases were lower in these states, indicating the growing influence of consumers in regulatory price setting (Holburn and Spiller 2002).

Participatory mechanisms in regulatory institutions are still relatively uncommon in low- and middle-income countries (figure 5.6).[31] For example, most high-income countries provide advance notice of regulatory changes and make information about existing regulations publicly available. Such practices are relatively uncommon in low- and middle-income countries, however. Mechanisms to collect feedback from the public are also rare in these countries, as are mechanisms that report on the results and impact assessments of regulatory policies.

Finding the right approach

In conclusion, there are ways to alter both policy and institutional design that can reduce the harm from capture. In terms of policy design, it is important to think pragmatically about the risk of undue influence and identify implementable policies—if not first-best ones. Another lesson is to avoid policies that look good in the short term but could end up reinforcing the power of dominant groups that could block further reforms.

Better design of public agencies can help expand the set of implementable policies in two ways. First, how public officials are selected for service and the incentive structure they face within their organizations matter. This aspect of design should take into account not only economic motivations, but also the intrinsic motivation for public service and norms of behavior. In policies in which there is a significant role for discretion during implementation, credible monitoring mechanisms can further discipline implementation. Second, mechanisms of horizontal and vertical accountability in public agencies also help balance influence in the policy arena. For example, general-purpose oversight agencies can act as a check on the capture of agencies in charge of specific policy areas. Mechanisms that help less powerful, diffuse interest groups have a bigger say in the policy arena could help even out the influence of more powerful narrow interest groups.

Translating reform principles into solutions

This discussion of regulatory agency design in the United States has served to illustrate some key principles for reform. But this is not to say that low- and middle-income countries with difficult governance environments should simply copy the formal structures of horizontal and vertical accountability found to work in high-income countries.

Adapting these blueprints to specific governance environments is ultimately a matter of experimentation, but both the capacity of existing agencies and the present balance of power should factor into this process. For example, consider the design of mechanisms for strengthening regulatory advocacy by citizens and small firms. In the United States, some states have created a public agency tasked with acting as a proxy advocate for consumers, while others have opted to offer incentives and support for existing advocacy groups to participate in regulatory decision making (Magill 2013). Neither approach, though, is likely to be effective in settings in which public agencies and consumer advocacy groups have low capacity. Case studies suggest, however, that some low- and middle-income countries have successfully used participatory mechanisms such as public-private dialogues

(PPDs) as an intermediate institutional design for vertical accountability (box 5.2). PPDs do not necessarily rely on the existence of proxy advocate agencies or strong citizen and small business advocacy groups. Instead, they mobilize local communities in the context of specific reforms. Successful PPDs can go on to become institutionalized more formally.

Countries with difficult governance environments could also experiment with "ring-fencing" reforms—in other words, building "islands of effectiveness" (Fisman and Werker 2011; Levy 2014). For example, in many countries the dominance of powerful business groups or other political considerations make it difficult to liberalize firm entry or enact other business climate reforms that would increase competition between firms. In such settings, creating special economic zones (SEZs) with their own rules is a way to ring-fence competition within specific locations. China's extensive use of SEZs, beginning with coastal SEZs that were focused on export-oriented firms, is a case in point. Studies suggest that SEZs made a significant contribution to investment and productivity growth in China (Wang 2013).

Reforms at the top: The overall governance environment

Chances are that the agency-level reforms discussed so far will not be pursued seriously unless commitment is forthcoming at the highest levels of policy making. Consider the various experiences with the introduction of anticorruption agencies. In 1974 Hong Kong introduced an Independent Commission against Corruption (ICAC). The ICAC reported directly to the British governor general, recruited employees from the civilian population, and paid relatively high salaries. It has been remarkably effective: today Hong Kong SAR, China, ranks in the top 20 worldwide of Transparency International's corruption perceptions index. Nevertheless, the ICAC model has not had much success in other countries. The ICAC succeeded in part because its authorizing environment was well governed and stable, and the commitment to making the ICAC work did not depend on a fortuitous, fragile configuration of interests at the highest levels (Fisman and Werker 2011). This issue—how the broader governance environment becomes more committed to reform—is discussed in part III of this Report.

Trade-offs between growth and equity

Sometimes, a "solution" to an institutional function such as commitment can deliver growth, but with adverse consequences for equity. For example, coalitions of powerful actors can monopolize resources for investment, solving internal commitment problems but excluding less powerful actors from access to productive resources. The wave of industrialization in Latin America at the end of the 19th century and the first part of the 20th century was characterized by just such an arrangement: the state would protect politically connected, powerful business interests in exchange for a commitment to investment, rent sharing, and political support (Haber, Razo, and Maurer 2003). This arrangement delivered growth, but that growth was not shared widely. A more broad-based form of commitment to property rights would have led to a more equitable path of development. Thus issues of equity and growth cannot always be considered in isolation when thinking about governance reforms. This chapter therefore complements chapter 6, which focuses on equity and governance.

Notes

1. In recent research, Hallward-Driemeier and Pritchett (2015) use firm-level data to analyze how the implementation of simple business regulations varies across firms within the same country. They find that procedural reforms, which simplify these regulations, are not associated with a reduction in this variation.

2. See, for example, Fisman (2001); Johnson and Mitton (2003); Khwaja and Mian (2005); and Rijkers, Freund, and Nucifora (2014).

3. Traditionally, in the economics literature capture is said to occur when the design of a regulation reflects the narrow interests of specific groups of firms or consumers (Stigler 1971; Peltzman 1976). This chapter applies the term more broadly to include not only regulations but also any policy related to economic growth.

4. The gross domestic product (GDP) per capita differed only modestly across countries before 1600, so much so that the rising difference in GDP per capita across higher- and lower-income countries since then has been termed the "Great Divergence" (Jones, forthcoming).

5. See, for example, Mauro (1995); Hall and Jones (1999); and Acemoglu, Johnson, and Robinson (2001). They show that historical or culturally driven sources of difference in some dimensions of governance (such as security of property rights, corruption, and policies of economic openness) have had an impact on long-term growth in per capita GDP. Building on such approaches, Kaufmann and Kraay (2002) propose a methodology to investigate the two-way causality between governance and per capita income.

Their results also suggest a positive causal effect from governance to long-term growth, but a weak and even negative effect running from per capita income growth to better governance. See Pande and Udry (2006) for a critique of such approaches.

6. See Hausmann, Pritchett, and Rodrik (2005); Rodrik (2005); Jones and Olken (2008); Eichengreen, Park, and Shin (2012); and Levy (2014).

7. This evidence is reviewed in Galiani and Schargrodsky (2011).

8. Well-functioning courts can help firms switch to new suppliers by strengthening the level of trust between unknown parties (Johnson, McMillan, and Woodruff 2002a). Better contract enforcement is also associated with higher lending and less default (Castelar Pinheiro and Cabral 2001; Cristini, Moya, and Powell 2001; Jappelli, Pagano, and Bianco 2005). And better contract enforcement can also enhance the impact of trade liberalization on productivity (Ahsan 2013).

9. Among others, Haskel, Pereira, and Slaughter (2007) and Aghion and others (2009) present firm-level evidence on how competition (from entrants) affects productivity growth.

10. The theory of a "big push" in industrialization put forth by Rosenstein-Rodan (1943) is an early example. Murphy, Shleifer, and Vishny (1989) model a more recent version of this idea.

11. This example is from Rodríguez-Clare (2005), who reviews microeconomic models of coordination failures.

12. Hoff (2001) reviews models of coordination failures in a wider range of contexts, including social norms and corruption. Cooper (1999) reviews macroeconomic models of coordination failures.

13. Wade (1990), Evans (1995), and Kohli (2004) examine the role of governance in the industrial policy of the East Asian countries from the 1960s to the 1990s. Robinson (2009) discusses how governance issues have constrained industrial development policies in most parts of the world.

14. For evidence from developed countries, see, for example, Goldberg and Maggi (1999); Gawande and Bandyopadhyay (2000); Mitra, Thomakos, and Ulubaşoğlu (2002); and Esfahani (2005).

15. Suharto was the second president of Indonesia. After ousting the first president, Sukarno, from office in 1967, Suharto served as president for 31 years, until his resignation in 1998.

16. See, for example, Stigler (1971) and Peltzman (1976) for theory and Dal Bó (2006) for a review of the empirical evidence on capture, largely from the United States.

17. See Aghion, Akcigit, and Howitt (2014) for a summary review of this theory of growth.

18. See Pritchett and Werker (2012) for a discussion of "deals-based" systems. A similar concept of "limited

access order" is discussed in North, Wallis, and Weingast (2009).

19. See Puga and Trefler (2014) on Venice, and Acemoglu, Johnson, and Robinson (2005) on Atlantic trade. The background paper prepared for WDR 2017 by Levchenko (2016) provides a summary of recent research on the impact of trade on institutions.

20. See, for example, Evans (1995). However, the story of the Republic of Korea also suggests that productive business-state relationships can sometimes degenerate into instruments of capture. There is evidence that large businesses eventually captured some of the state support that was meant to kick-start investment (Eichengreen 2012).

21. Laffont and Tirole (1993) formalize this idea. Glaeser and Shleifer (2003) present a theory along similar lines in their study of the rise of regulation in the United States in the early decades of the 20th century.

22. See Acemoglu and Robinson (2013) for an evidence-based discussion of this argument.

23. See spotlight 1 in WDR 2015 (World Bank 2015, 60).

24. Some of the discussion in this section is based on a review paper by Finan, Olken, and Pande (2015).

25. See, for example, Banerjee, Glennerster, and Duflo (2008); Glewwe, Ilias, and Kremer (2010); Basinga and others (2011); Muralidharan and Sundararaman (2011); Duflo, Hanna, and Ryan (2012); and Gertler and Vermeersch (2012).

26. See Cowley and Smith (2014) for survey-based evidence and Banuri and Keefer (2013) for evidence from lab experiments.

27. Game theory calls this "multiple equilibria" in organizations: one in which honesty is a self-reinforcing norm; another in which corruption is the norm. See Bardhan (1997) and Hoff (2001).

28. Lichand, Lopes, and Medeiros (2015) found evidence that municipal audits to monitor the use of federal funds reduced procurement, thereby worsening health outcomes.

29. A classic exploration of this idea, in the context of regulation, is Stigler (1971).

30. Dal Bó (2006) reviews the empirical evidence on advocacy and other accountability interventions in the context of regulatory bodies. Schwarcz (2013) presents a case study of some citizen advocacy mechanisms in the context of insurance regulation across U.S. states.

31. See http://rulemaking.worldbank.org.

References

Acemoglu, Daron, Simon Johnson, and James A. Robinson. 2001. "The Colonial Origins of Comparative Development: An Empirical Investigation." *American Economic Review* 91 (5): 1369–1401.

———. 2005. "The Rise of Europe: Atlantic Trade, Institutional Change, and Economic Growth." *American Economic Review* 95 (3): 546–79.

Acemoglu, Daron, and James A. Robinson. 2013. "Economics versus Politics: Pitfalls of Policy Advice." *Journal of Economic Perspectives* 27 (2): 173–92.

Aghion, Philippe, Ufuk Akcigit, and Peter Howitt. 2014. "What Do We Learn from Schumpeterian Growth Theory?" In *Handbook of Economic Growth*, Vol. 2B, edited by Philippe Aghion and Steven N. Darlauf, 515–63. Amsterdam: Elsevier.

Aghion, Philippe, Richard Blundell, Rachel Griffith, Peter Howitt, and Susanne Prantl. 2009. "The Effects of Entry on Incumbent Innovation and Productivity." *Review of Economics and Statistics* 91 (1): 20–32.

Ahsan, Reshad N. 2013. "Input Tariffs, Speed of Contract Enforcement, and the Productivity of Firms in India." *Journal of International Economics* 90 (1): 181–92.

Ash, Elliott, and W. Bentley MacLeod. 2015. "Intrinsic Motivation in Public Service: Theory and Evidence from State Supreme Courts." *Journal of Law and Economics* 58 (4): 863–913.

Atiyas, Izak, Brian Levy, and Michael Walton. 2016. "Rent Creation and Rent Containment: The Political Economy of Telecommunications in Mexico, South Africa, and Turkey." Background paper, WDR 2017, World Bank, Washington, DC.

Baicker, Katherine, and Mireille Jacobson. 2007. "Finders Keepers: Forfeiture Laws, Policing Incentives, and Local Budgets." *Journal of Public Economics* 91 (11): 2113–36.

Banerjee, Abhijit, Rachel Glennerster, and Esther Duflo. 2008. "Putting a Band-Aid on a Corpse: Incentives for Nurses in the Indian Public Health Care System." *Journal of the European Economic Association* 6 (2–3): 487–500.

Banuri, Sheheryar, and Philip Keefer. 2013. "Intrinsic Motivation, Effort, and the Call to Public Service." Policy Research Working Paper 6729, World Bank, Washington, DC.

Bardhan, Pranab K. 1997. "Corruption and Development: A Review of Issues." *Journal of Economic Literature* 35 (3): 1320–46.

Basinga, Paulin, Paul J. Gertler, Agnes Binagwaho, Agnes L. B. Soucat, Jennifer Sturdy, and Christel M. J. Vermeersch. 2011. "Effect on Maternal and Child Health Services in Rwanda of Payment to Primary Health-Care Providers for Performance: An Impact Evaluation." *Lancet* 377 (9775): 1421–28.

Besley, Timothy J., and Stephen Coate. 2003. "Elected versus Appointed Regulators: Theory and Evidence." *Journal of the European Economic Association* 1 (5): 1176–1206.

Bond, Philip, and Rohini Pande. 2007. "Coordinating Development: Can Income-Based Incentive Schemes Eliminate Pareto Inferior Equilibria?" *Journal of Development Economics* 83 (2): 368–91.

Caselli, Francesco. 2005. "Accounting for Cross-Country Income Differences." In *Handbook of Economic Growth*, Vol. 1A, edited by Philippe Aghion and Steven N. Darlauf, 679–741. Amsterdam: Elsevier.

———. 2016. "Accounting for Cross-Country Income Differences: Ten Years Later." Background paper, WDR 2017, World Bank, Washington, DC.

Castelar Pinheiro, Armando, and Célia Cabral. 2001. "Credit Markets in Brazil: The Role of Judicial Enforcement and Other Institutions." In *Defusing Default: Incentives and Institutions*, edited by Marco Pagano, 157–88. Washington, DC: Inter-American Development Bank; Baltimore: Johns Hopkins University Press.

Chari, A. V. 2011. "Identifying the Aggregate Productivity Effects of Entry and Size Restrictions: An Empirical Analysis of License Reform in India." *American Economic Journal: Economic Policy* 3 (2): 66–96.

Chekir, Hamouda, and Ishac Diwan. 2014. "Crony Capitalism in Egypt." *Journal of Globalization and Development* 5 (2): 177–211.

Claessens, Stijn, Erik Feijen, and Luc Laeven. 2008. "Political Connections and Preferential Access to Finance: The Role of Campaign Contributions." *Journal of Financial Economics* 88 (3): 554–80.

Coate, Stephen, and Stephen Morris. 1995. "On the Form of Transfers in Special Interests." *Journal of Political Economy* 103 (6): 1210–35.

Cole, Shawn. 2009. "Fixing Market Failures or Fixing Elections? Agricultural Credit in India." *American Economic Journal: Applied Economics* 1 (1): 219–50.

Cooper, Russell W. 1999. *Coordination Games*. New York: Cambridge University Press.

Costinot, Arnaud. 2009. "On the Origins of Comparative Advantage." *Journal of International Economics* 77 (2): 255–64.

Cowley, Edd, and Sarah Louise Smith. 2014. "Motivation and Mission in the Public Sector: Evidence from the World Values Survey." *Theory and Decision* 76 (2): 241–63.

Cristini, Marcela, Ramiro A. Moya, and Andrew Powell. 2001. "The Importance of an Effective Legal System for Credit Markets: The Case of Argentina." In *Defusing Default: Incentives and Institutions*, edited by Marco Pagano, 119–56. Washington, DC: Inter-American Development Bank; Baltimore: Johns Hopkins University Press.

Dal Bó, Ernesto. 2006. "Regulatory Capture: A Review." *Oxford Review of Economic Policy* 22 (2): 203–25.

Dal Bó, Ernesto, Frederico S. Finan, and Martín A. Rossi. 2013. "Strengthening State Capabilities: The Role of Financial Incentives in the Call to Public Service." *Quarterly Journal of Economics* 128 (3): 1169–1218.

Dell, Melissa. 2010. "The Persistent Effects of Peru's Mining Mita." *Econometrica* 78 (6): 1863–1903.

Dinc, I. Serdar. 2005. "Politicians and Banks: Political Influences on Government-Owned Banks in Emerging Markets." *Journal of Financial Economics* 77 (2): 453–79.

Diwan, Ishac, Philip Keefer, and Marc Schiffbauer. 2015. "Pyramid Capitalism: Political Connections, Regulation, and Firm Productivity in Egypt." Policy Research Working Paper 7354, World Bank, Washington, DC.

Dixit, Avinash K. 2007. *Lawlessness and Economics: Alternative Modes of Governance.* Princeton, NJ: Princeton University Press.

———. 2015. "How Business Community Institutions Can Help Fight Corruption." *World Bank Economic Review* 29 (Supplement 1): S25–S47.

Do, Quy-Toan, and Andrei A. Levchenko. 2009. "Trade, Inequality, and the Political Economy of Institutions." *Journal of Economic Theory* 144 (4): 1489–1520.

Doner, Richard F., and Ben Ross Schneider. 2000. "Business Associations and Economic Development: Why Some Associations Contribute More than Others." *Business and Politics* 2 (3): 261–88.

Duflo, Esther, Michael Greenstone, Rohini Pande, and Nicholas Ryan. 2013. "Truth-Telling by Third-Party Auditors and the Response of Polluting Firms: Experimental Evidence from India." *Quarterly Journal of Economics* 128 (4): 1499–1545.

Duflo, Esther, Rema Hanna, and Stephen P. Ryan. 2012. "Incentives Work: Getting Teachers to Come to School." *American Economic Review* 102 (4): 1241–78.

Dyck, Alexander, David Moss, and Luigi Zingales. 2013. "Media versus Special Interests." *Journal of Law and Economics* 56 (3): 521–53.

Eichengreen, Barry Julian. 2012. "Government, Business, and Finance in Korean Industrial Development." *International Economic Journal* 26 (3): 357–77.

Eichengreen, Barry Julian, Donghyun Park, and Kwanho Shin. 2012. "When Fast-Growing Economies Slow Down: International Evidence and Implications for China." *Asian Economic Papers* 11 (1): 42–87.

Engel, Eduardo, and Ronald Fischer. 2010. "Optimal Resource Extraction Contracts under Threat of Expropriation." In *The Natural Resources Trap: Private Investment without Public Commitment,* edited by William Hogan and Federico Sturzenegger, 161–96. Cambridge, MA: MIT Press.

Esfahani, Hadi Salehi. 2005. "Searching for the (Dark) Forces behind Protection." *Oxford Economic Papers* 57 (2): 283–314.

Evans, Peter B. 1995. *Embedded Autonomy: States and Industrial Transformation.* Princeton, NJ: Princeton University Press.

Field, Erica. 2007. "Entitled to Work: Urban Property Rights and Labor Supply in Peru." *Quarterly Journal of Economics* 122 (4): 1561–1602.

Finan, Frederico S., Benjamin A. Olken, and Rohini Pande. 2015. "The Personnel Economics of the State." NBER Working Paper 21825, National Bureau of Economic Research, Cambridge, MA.

Fisman, Raymond. 2001. "Estimating the Value of Political Connections." *American Economic Review* 91 (4): 1095–1102.

Fisman, Raymond, and Shang-Jin Wei. 2001. "Tax Rates and Tax Evasion: Evidence from 'Missing Imports' in China." NBER Working Paper 8551, National Bureau of Economic Research, Cambridge, MA.

Fisman, Raymond, and Eric Werker. 2011. "Innovations in Governance." *Innovation Policy and the Economy,* Vol. 11, edited by Josh Lerner and Scott Stern, 79–102. Cambridge, MA: National Bureau of Economic Research; Chicago: University of Chicago Press.

Galiani, Sebastian, and Ernesto Schargrodsky. 2011. "Land Property Rights and Resource Allocation." *Journal of Law and Economics* 54 (4): S329–45.

Gawande, Kishore, and Usree Bandyopadhyay. 2000. "Is Protection for Sale? Evidence on the Grossman-Helpman Theory of Endogenous Protection." *Review of Economics and Statistics* 82 (1): 139–52.

Gertler, Paul J., and Christel Vermeersch. 2012. "Using Performance Incentives to Improve Health Outcomes." Policy Research Working Paper 6100, World Bank, Washington, DC.

Gill, Indermit S., and Homi Kharas. 2015. "The Middle-Income Trap Turns Ten." Policy Research Working Paper 7403, World Bank, Washington, DC.

Glaeser, Edward L., and Andrei Shleifer. 2003. "The Rise of the Regulatory State." *Journal of Economic Literature* 41 (2): 401–25.

Glewwe, Paul, Nauman Ilias, and Michael Kremer. 2010. "Teacher Incentives." *American Economic Journal: Applied Economics* 2 (3): 205–27.

Goldberg, Pinelopi Koujianou, and Giovanni Maggi. 1999. "Protection for Sale: An Empirical Investigation." *American Economic Review* 89 (5): 1135–55.

Haber, Stephen, Armando Razo, and Noel Maurer. 2003. *The Politics of Property Rights: Political Instability, Credible Commitments, and Economic Growth in Mexico, 1876–1929.* Political Economy of Institutions and Decisions Series. Cambridge, U.K.: Cambridge University Press.

Hall, Robert E., and Charles I. Jones. 1999. "Why Do Some Countries Produce So Much More Output per Worker than Others?" *Quarterly Journal of Economics* 114 (1): 83–116.

Hallegatte, Stéphane, Geoffrey Heal, Marianne Fay, and David Treguer. 2012. "From Growth to Green Growth: A Framework." NBER Working Paper 17841, National Bureau of Economic Research, Cambridge, MA.

Hallward-Driemeier, Mary, and Lant Pritchett. 2015. "How Business Is Done in the Developing World: Deals versus Rules." *Journal of Economic Perspectives* 29 (3): 121–40.

Haskel, Jonathan E., Sonia C. Pereira, and Matthew J. Slaughter. 2007. "Does Inward Foreign Direct Investment Boost the Productivity of Domestic Firms?" *Review of Economics and Statistics* 89 (3): 482–96.

Hausmann, Ricardo, Lant Pritchett, and Dani Rodrik. 2005. "Growth Accelerations." *Journal of Economic Growth* 10 (4): 303–29.

Hellman, Joel. 1998. "Winners Take All: The Politics of Partial Reform in Postcommunist Transitions." *World Politics* 50.

Herzberg, Benjamin. 2007. "Monitoring and Evaluation during the Bulldozer Initiative: 50 Investment Climate Reforms in 150 Days." SmartLessons 45687, International Finance Corporation, Washington, DC.

Hoff, Karla. 2001. "Beyond Rosenstein-Rodan: The Modern Theory of Coordination Problems in Development." In *Proceedings of the Annual World Bank Conference on Development Economics*, edited by Boris Pleskovic and Nicholas Stern, 145–76. Washington, DC: World Bank.

Holburn, Guy L. F., and Pablo T. Spiller. 2002. "Interest Group Representation in Administrative Institutions: The Impact of Consumer Advocates and Elected Commissioners on Regulatory Policy in the United States." Policy and Economics 002 (October), University of California Energy Institute, University of California, Berkeley.

IMD. Various years. IMD World Competitiveness Online. Lausanne, Switzerland, https://worldcompetitiveness.imd.org/.

Jackson, John E., Jacek Klich, and Krystyna Poznańska. 2005. *The Political Economy of Poland's Transition: New Firms and Reform Governments*. Political Economy of Institutions and Decisions Series. New York: Cambridge University Press.

Jappelli, Tullio, Marco Pagano, and Magda Bianco. 2005. "Courts and Banks: Effects of Judicial Enforcement on Credit Markets." *Journal of Money, Credit, and Banking* 37 (2): 223–44.

Jensen, Nathan, Glen Biglaiser, Quan Li, Edmund Malesky, Pablo M. Pinto, Santiago M. Pinto, and Joseph L. Staats. 2012. *Politics and Foreign Direct Investment*. Michigan Studies in International Political Economy Series. Ann Arbor: University of Michigan Press.

Johnson, Simon, John McMillan, and Christopher Woodruff. 2002a. "Courts and Relational Contracts." *Journal of Law, Economics, and Organization* 18 (1): 221–77.

————. 2002b. "Property Rights and Finance." *American Economic Review* 92 (5): 1335–56.

Johnson, Simon, and Todd Mitton. 2003. "Cronyism and Capital Controls: Evidence from Malaysia." *Journal of Financial Economics* 67 (2): 351–82.

Jones, Benjamin F., and Benjamin A. Olken. 2008. "The Anatomy of Start-Stop Growth." *Review of Economics and Statistics* 90 (3): 582–87.

Jones, Charles I. Forthcoming. "The Facts of Economic Growth." In *The Handbook of Macroeconomics*, Vol. 2, edited by John B. Taylor and Harald Uhlig. Amsterdam: Elsevier.

Kaufmann, Daniel, and Aart Kraay. 2002. "Growth without Governance." Policy Research Working Paper 2928, World Bank, Washington, DC.

Khwaja, Asim Ijaz, and Atif Mian. 2005. "Do Lenders Favor Politically Connected Firms? Rent Provision in an Emerging Financial Market." *Quarterly Journal of Economics* 120 (4): 1371–1411.

Kohli, Atul. 2004. *State-Directed Development: Political Power and Industrialization in the Global Periphery*. Cambridge, U.K.: Cambridge University Press.

Laffont, Jean-Jacques, and David Martimort. 1999. "Separation of Regulators against Collusive Behavior." *Rand Journal of Economics* 30 (2): 232–62.

Laffont, Jean-Jacques, and Jean Tirole. 1991. "The Politics of Government Decision-Making: A Theory of Regulatory Capture." *Quarterly Journal of Economics* 106 (4): 1089–1127.

————. 1993. *A Theory of Incentives in Procurement and Regulation*. Cambridge, MA: MIT Press.

La Porta, Rafael, Florencio Lopez-de-Silanes, Cristian Pop-Eleches, and Andrei Shleifer. 2004. "Judicial Checks and Balances." *Journal of Political Economy* 112 (2): 445–70.

Levchenko, Andrei A. 2016. "The Impact of Trade Openness on Institutions." Background paper, WDR 2017, World Bank, Washington, DC.

Levy, Brian. 2014. *Working with the Grain: Integrating Governance and Growth in Development Strategies*. New York: Oxford University Press.

Lichand, Guilherme, Marcos F. M. Lopes, and Marcelo C. Medeiros. 2015. "Is Corruption Good for Your Health?" Job Market Paper, Department of Economics, Harvard University, Cambridge, MA.

Livermore, Michael A., and Richard L. Revesz. 2014. "Can Executive Review Help Prevent Capture?" In *Preventing Regulatory Capture: Special Interest Influence in Regulation and How to Limit It*, edited by Daniel Carpenter and David A. Moss, 420–50. New York: Cambridge University Press.

Magill, M. Elizabeth. 2013. "Courts and Regulatory Capture." In *Preventing Regulatory Capture: Special Interest Influence in Regulation and How to Limit It*, edited by Daniel Carpenter and David A. Moss, 397–419. New York: Cambridge University Press.

Mauro, Paolo. 1995. "Corruption and Growth." *Quarterly Journal of Economics* 110 (3): 681–712.

Mitra, Devashish, Dimitrios D. Thomakos, and Mehmet A. Ulubaşoğlu. 2002. "'Protection for Sale' in a Developing Country: Democracy vs. Dictatorship." *Review of Economics and Statistics* 84 (3): 497–508.

Mobarak, Ahmed Mushfiq, and Denni Puspa Purbasari. 2008. "Protection for Sale to Firms: Evidence from Indonesia." Working Paper, School of Management, Yale University, New Haven, CT.

Muralidharan, Karthik, and Venkatesh Sundararaman. 2011. "Teacher Performance Pay: Experimental Evidence from India." *Journal of Political Economy* 119 (1): 39–77.

Murphy, Kevin M., Andrei Shleifer, and Robert W. Vishny. 1989. "Industrialization and the Big Push." *Journal of Political Economy* 97 (5): 1003–26.

North, Douglass C. 1990. *Institutions, Institutional Change, and Economic Performance.* Cambridge, U.K.: Cambridge University Press.

North, Douglass C., John Joseph Wallis, and Barry R. Weingast. 2009. *Violence and Social Orders: A Conceptual Framework for Interpreting Recorded Human History.* Political Economy of Institutions and Decisions Series. New York: Cambridge University Press.

Olken, Benjamin A. 2007. "Monitoring Corruption: Evidence from a Field Experiment in Indonesia." *Journal of Political Economy* 115 (2): 200–49.

Pande, Rohini, and Christopher Udry. 2006. "Institutions and Development: A View from Below." In *Advances in Economics and Econometrics: Theory and Applications, Ninth World Congress,* Vol. 2, edited by Richard Blundell, Whitney K. Newey, and Torsten Persson, 349–412. Econometric Society Monographs Series. New York: Cambridge University Press.

Peltzman, Sam. 1976. "Toward a More General Theory of Regulation." *Journal of Law and Economics* 19 (2): 245–48.

Perry, James L., and Annie Hondeghem. 2008. "Building Theory and Empirical Evidence about Public Service Motivation." *International Public Management Journal* 11 (1): 3–12.

Pritchett, Lant, and Erik Werker. 2012. "Developing the Guts of a GUT (Grand Unified Theory): Elite Commitment and Inclusive Growth." ESID Working Paper 16/12, Effective States and Inclusive Development Research Centre, School of Environment and Development, University of Manchester, Manchester, U.K.

Puga, Diego, and Daniel Trefler. 2014. "International Trade and Institutional Change: Medieval Venice's Response to Globalization." *Quarterly Journal of Economics* 129 (2): 753–821.

Qian, Yingyi. 2003. "How Reform Worked in China." In *In Search of Prosperity: Analytic Narratives on Economic Growth,* edited by Dani Rodrik, 297–333. Princeton, NJ: Princeton University Press.

Resnick, Danielle, Finn Tarp, and James Thurlow. 2012. "The Political Economy of Green Growth: Illustrations from Southern Africa." UNU-WIDER Working Paper 2012/11, United Nations University-World Institute for Development Economics Research, Helsinki.

Rijkers, Bob, Caroline L. Freund, and Antonio Nucifora. 2014. "All in the Family: State Capture in Tunisia." Policy Research Working Paper 6810, World Bank, Washington, DC.

Robinson, James A. 2009. "Industrial Policy and Development: A Political Economy Perspective." Paper presented at the World Bank "Annual Bank Conference on Development Economics Korea 2009," Seoul, June 22–24.

Rodríguez-Clare, Andrés. 2005. "Coordination Failures, Clusters, and Microeconomic Interventions." *Economía* 6 (1): 1–41.

Rodrik, Dani. 1996. "Coordination Failures and Government Policy: A Model with Applications to East Asia and Eastern Europe." *Journal of International Economics* 40 (1–2): 1–22.

———. 2005. "Growth Strategies." In *Handbook of Economic Growth,* Vol. 1A, edited by Philippe Aghion and Steven N. Darlauf, 967–1014. Amsterdam: Elsevier.

Rosenstein-Rodan, Paul N. 1943. "Problems of Industrialisation of Eastern and South-Eastern Europe." *Economic Journal* 53 (210/11): 202–11.

Sapienza, Paola. 2004. "The Effects of Government Ownership on Bank Lending." *Journal of Financial Economics* 72 (2): 357–84.

Schwarcz, Daniel. 2013. "Preventing Capture through Consumer Empowerment Programs: Some Evidence from Insurance Regulation." In *Preventing Regulatory Capture: Special Interest Influence in Regulation and How to Limit It,* edited by Daniel Carpenter and David A. Moss, 365–96. New York: Cambridge University Press.

Sequeira, Sandra, and Simeon Djankov. 2014. "Corruption and Firm Behavior: Evidence from African Ports." *Journal of International Economics* 94 (2): 277–94.

Spiller, Pablo T., and Mariano Tommasi. 2005. "The Institutions of Regulation: An Application to Public Utilities." In *Handbook of New Institutional Economics,* edited by Claude Ménard and Mary M. Shirley, 515–43. Dordrecht, the Netherlands: Springer-Verlag.

Stigler, George J. 1971. "The Theory of Economic Regulation." *Bell Journal of Economics and Management Science* 2 (1): 3–21.

Tirole, Jean. 1994. "The Internal Organization of Government." *Oxford Economic Papers* 46 (1): 1–29.

Wade, Robert. 1990. *Governing the Market: Economic Theory and the Role of Government in East Asian Industrialization.* Princeton, NJ: Princeton University Press.

Wang, Jin. 2013. "The Economic Impact of Special Economic Zones: Evidence from Chinese Municipalities." *Journal of Development Economics* 101: 133–47.

World Bank. Various years. Enterprise Surveys. Washington, DC, http://www.enterprisesurveys.org/.

———. Various years. Global Indicators of Regulatory Governance. Washington, DC, http://rulemaking.worldbank.org/.

———. Various years. World Development Indicators (database). Washington, DC, http://data.worldbank.org/data-catalog/world-development-indicators.

———. 2015. *World Development Report 2015: Mind, Society, and Behavior*. Washington, DC: World Bank.

World Justice Project. Various years. Rule of Law Index. Washington, DC, http://worldjusticeproject.org/.

Wright, Joseph. 2008. "Do Authoritarian Institutions Constrain? How Legislatures Affect Economic Growth and Investment." *American Journal of Political Science* 52 (2): 322–43.

Yang, Dean. 2008. "Integrity for Hire: An Analysis of a Widespread Customs Reform." *Journal of Law and Economics* 51 (1): 25–57.

Yao, Yang. 2014. "The Chinese Growth Miracle." In *Handbook of Economic Growth*, Vol. 2B, edited by Philippe Aghion and Steven N. Darlauf, 943–1031. Amsterdam: Elsevier.

The middle-income trap

Contrary to what many growth theories predict, there is no tendency for low- and middle-income countries to converge toward high-income countries (figure S6.1)—see Jones (2015). Recently, countries experiencing growth stagnation at middle-income levels, a condition Gill and Kharas (2007) termed the "middle-income trap," have received considerable attention. Although middle-income economies are no more likely to stagnate than economies at any other income level (Bulman, Eden, and Nguyen 2014), a compelling economic theory that can guide growth for middle-income countries is still lacking. Indeed, this lack of a "satisfactory growth theory" to inform development in middle-income countries was the original reason for referring to a middle-income trap (Gill and Kharas 2015). This spotlight uses this Report's framework to argue that the difficulty many middle-income countries have in sustaining growth can be explained by power imbalances that prevent the institutional transitions necessary for growth in productivity.

Is middle-income growth different?

Middle-income countries may face particular challenges because growth strategies that were successful while they were poor no longer suit their circumstances. For example, the reallocation of labor from agriculture to industry is a key driver of growth in low-income economies. But as this process matures, the gains from reallocating surplus labor begin to evaporate, wages begin to rise, and decreasing marginal

WDR 2017 team.

Figure S6.1 Many countries have not converged toward higher incomes

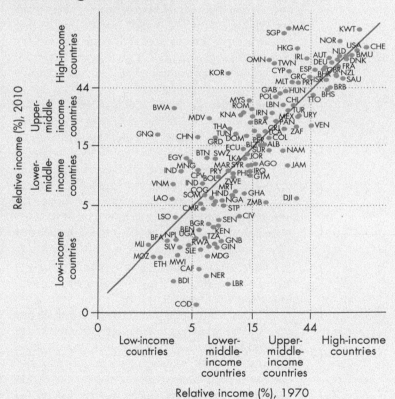

Source: WDR 2017 team, using data from Penn World Table, version 8.1 (Feenstra, Inklaar, and Timmer 2015).

returns to investment set in, implying a need for a new source of growth. Middle-income countries that become "trapped" fail to sustain total factor productivity (TFP) growth. By contrast, "escapees" find new sources of TFP growth (Daude and Fernández-Arias

2010). Indeed, 85 percent of growth slowdowns at the middle-income levels can be explained by TFP slow-downs (Eichengreen, Park, and Shin 2013).

For middle-income escapees, evidence suggests that one source of sustained TFP growth is an increasingly efficient allocation of resources. On a broad level, escaping countries experience much more rapid transitions out of agriculture and more rapid increases in manufacturing/industry (Bulman, Eden, and Nguyen 2014). Perhaps more important is the allocation of resources across subsectors and across firms within sectors. Because the productivity levels of firms in the same subsector can be markedly unequal, the entry of new firms and exit of unproductive firms (creative destruction), and the extent to which productive firms are able to gain a bigger market share by reallocating inputs between firms, are important for TFP growth (Hsieh and Klenow 2009; Bartelsman, Haltiwanger, and Scarpetta 2013; Melitz and Polanec 2015). For example, when capital and labor in Indian and Chinese manufacturing firms are hypothetically "reallocated" to match the level of efficient allocation observed in the United States, the two countries experience TFP gains of 40–60 percent and 30–50 percent, respectively (Hsieh and Klenow 2009).

Other analyses of the middle-income trap have focused on the lack of industrial upgrading (Ohno 2009; Doner and Schneider 2016). Evidence suggests that middle-income escapees have more diversified and sophisticated exports than those that remain stuck (Felipe, Abdon, and Kumar 2012). Such upgrading requires proactive government policies and coordination between domestic firms. A related view is that market failures may occur in many countries when private incentives to enter new sectors are less than social returns, necessitating a process of economic development as "self-discovery" (Hausmann and Rodrik 2003).

Efficient resource allocation and industrial upgrading require a set of institutions that differs from those that enable growth through resource accumulation. Efficient allocation requires new institutions to manage competition and creative destruction. Industrial upgrading requires the institutional capacity for greater intersector and government coordination, possibly through a strategic alliance between government and business (Doner and Schneider 2016). Product differentiation to succeed in new export markets requires "modern and more agile" property rights institutions and capital markets (Kharas and Kohli 2011).

Political economy traps

The creation of these institutions may be stymied by vested interests. Creative destruction and competition create losers—and in particular may create losers of currently powerful business and political elites. This is a more politically challenging problem than spurring productivity growth through the adoption of foreign technologies, which tends to favor economic incumbents (Acemoglu, Aghion, and Zilibotti 2006). These political challenges may be particularly great in middle-income countries because actors that gained during the transition from low to middle income may now be powerful enough to block changes that threaten their position.

In this sense, the challenges that middle-income countries face go beyond policy choice to the challenge of power imbalances. Yet, with few exceptions, discussions of the middle-income trap have generally focused on the *proximate causes* of transition difficulties and on selecting the right policies rather than the *underlying determinants* of these transitions. Understanding the policy arena in which elites bargain is essential for explaining the political economy traps faced by middle-income countries.

One such political economy trap is a persistent deals-based relationship between government and business. Deals-based, sometimes corrupt, interactions between firms and the state may not prevent growth at low income levels; indeed, such ties may actually be the "glue" necessary to ensure commitment and coordination among state and business actors (see spotlight 1 on corruption). But they become more problematic for upper-middle-income countries. For example, theory suggests that as markets expand and supply networks become more complex, deals-based relationships can no longer act as a substitute for impersonal, rules-based contract enforcement (Dixit 2004). Consistent with this hypothesis, upper-middle-income escapees lower their levels of corruption significantly before becoming high-income economies, whereas "non-escapees" do not see an improvement in corruption (figure S6.2, panel a). In non-escapees, corruption may prop up the status quo, undermining competition and the creation of new growth coalitions.

Combating entrenched corruption and creating a level playing field for firms imply a need for accountable institutions. At upper-middle-income levels, legislative, judicial, media, and civil society checks become increasingly important. Indeed, escapees tend to see much larger improvements in these institutional checks when they are at upper-middle-income levels than non-escapees, although the differences between successful and unsuccessful countries are less distinct at the low- and lower-middle-income levels (figure S6.2, panels b, c, d).

The sources of these rules-based institutions for contestation and accountability are discussed in part III of this Report, but comparing escapees and non-escapees helps identify several conditions that make institutional reforms and thus successful transitions more likely. Recently, many countries that have transitioned, including East Asian economies and Chile, have had strong, representative business groups. Well-represented business groups

helped lead to pro-growth coalitions that could push for "nonparticularistic" policies benefiting broad interests to enable broad-based growth. Other recent transitioning countries have had a source of external support/pressure for reform: nearly half of the countries that grew recently from middle to high income are in Europe, where the external commitment provided by European Union accession and membership has made institutional development credible.

Lower levels of inequality may also help prevent institutional sclerosis at middle-income levels. High levels of inequality can generate societal cleavages that prevent the emergence of the growth coalitions

Figure S6.2 Checks on corruption and accountability institutions improve more in countries that escape upper-middle-income status to achieve high-income status than in countries that are "non-escapees"

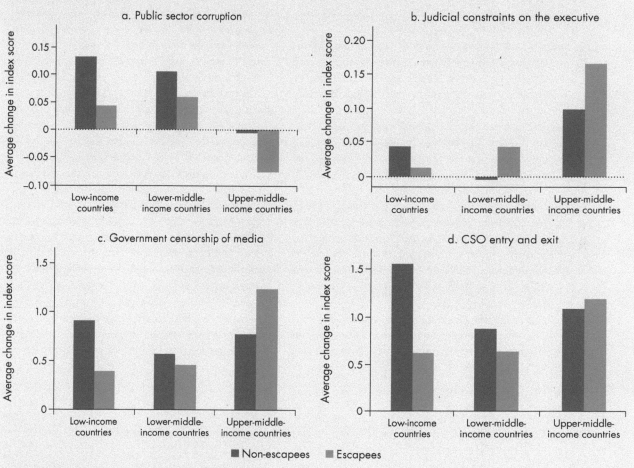

Source: WDR 2017 team, using data from V-Dem, 2015.

Note: The bars represent the average change in the relevant category for all "non-escapees" (beige) and "escapees" (blue) during the time a country is at the income level specified. Escapees are defined as those countries that reach the subsequent income levels during the sample period (1950–2011). Non-escapees are those that remain trapped at the same income level or move to a lower income level. All four panels use the same methodology. In panel a, public sector corruption (v2x_pubcorr) is an index ranging from 0 to 1, with 1 representing the most corruption. In panel b, judicial constraints on the executive (v2x_jucon) is an index ranging from 0 to 1, with 1 representing the greatest constraints. Government censorship of media (v2mecenefm) in panel c and CSO entry and exit (v2cseeorgs) in panel d are ordinal variables ranging from 0 to 4, with 4 representing the most accountability (that is, the least media censorship and the most CSO entry and exit). CSO = civil society organization.

necessary for reform (Doner and Schneider 2016). According to the data, escapees not only have lower levels of inequality when they become middle income, but also do not experience the large increases in inequality that characterize non-escapees on average (Bulman, Eden, and Nguyen 2014). Middle-income countries should therefore value equity not just as an aim in itself, but also as a precondition that increases the likelihood of escaping the middle-income growth trap.

References

Acemoglu, Daron, Philippe Aghion, and Fabrizio Zilibotti. 2006. "Distance to Frontier, Selection, and Economic Growth." *Journal of the European Economic Association* 4 (1): 37–74.

Bartelsman, Eric, John Haltiwanger, and Stefano Scarpetta. 2013. "Cross-Country Differences in Productivity: The Role of Allocation and Selection." *American Economic Review* 103 (1): 305–34.

Bulman, David, Maya Eden, and Ha Nguyen. 2014. "Transitioning from Low-Income Growth to High-Income Growth: Is There a Middle-Income Trap?" Policy Research Working Paper 7104, World Bank, Washington, DC.

Daude, Christian, and Eduardo Fernández-Arias. 2010. "On the Role of Productivity and Factor Accumulation in Economic Development in Latin America and the Caribbean." Working Paper 155, Inter-American Development Bank, Washington, DC.

Dixit, Avinash K. 2004. *Lawlessness and Economics: Alternative Modes of Governance*. Gorman Lectures in Economics Series. Princeton, NJ: Princeton University Press.

Doner, Richard F., and Ben Ross Schneider. 2016. "The Middle-Income Trap: More Politics than Economics." *World Politics* 68 (4): 608–44.

Eichengreen, Barry, Donghyung Park, and Kwanho Shin. 2013. "Growth Slowdowns Redux: New Evidence on the Middle-Income Trap." NBER Working Paper 18673, National Bureau of Economic Research, Cambridge, MA.

Feenstra, Robert C., Robert Inklaar, and Marcel P. Timmer. 2015. "The Next Generation of the Penn World Table." *American Economic Review* 105 (10): 3150–82. Version 8.1, http://www.rug.nl/ggdc /productivity/pwt/pwt-releases/pwt8.1.

Felipe, Jesus, Arnelyn Abdon, and Utsav Kumar. 2012. "Tracking the Middle-Income Trap: What Is It, Who Is in It, and Why?" Working Paper 715 (April), Levy Economics Institute of Bard College, Annandale-on-Hudson, NY.

Gill, Indermit S., and Homi Kharas. 2007. *An East Asian Renaissance: Ideas for Economic Growth*. Washington, DC: World Bank.

———. 2015. "The Middle-Income Trap Turns Ten." Policy Research Working Paper 7403, World Bank, Washington, DC.

Hausmann, Ricardo, and Dani Rodrik. 2003. "Economic Development as Self-Discovery." *Journal of Development Economics* 72 (2): 603–33.

Hsieh, Chang-Tai, and Peter J. Klenow. 2009. "Misallocation and Manufacturing TFP in China and India." *Quarterly Journal of Economics* 124 (4): 1403–48.

Jones, Charles I. 2015. "The Facts of Economic Growth." NBER Working Paper 21142, National Bureau of Economic Research, Cambridge, MA.

Kharas, Homi, and Harinder Kohli. 2011. "What Is the Middle-Income Trap, Why Do Countries Fall into It, and How Can It Be Avoided?" *Global Journal of Emerging Market Economies* 3 (3): 281–89.

Melitz, Marc, and Saso Polanec. 2015. "Dynamic Olley-Pakes Productivity Decomposition with Entry and Exit." *RAND Journal of Economics* 46 (2): 362–75.

Ohno, Kenichi. 2009. "Avoiding the Middle-Income Trap: Renovating Industrial Policy Formulation in Vietnam." *ASEAN Economic Bulletin* 26 (1): 25–43.

V-Dem (Varieties of Democracy). Various years. Database hosted by Gothenburg Institute (Europe) and Kellogg Institute (United States), https://www.v-dem.net/en/.

Public-private partnerships

In 318 BCE, the ancient Greek city of Eretria signed a contract with a wealthy citizen, Chairephanes, to drain a lake in its territory to create more usable land for agriculture. According to the contract, Chairephanes was responsible for financing and managing the drainage operation. In return, he was granted the right to use the land for 10 years and an exemption from tax duties on materials imported for the project. The contract foresaw a four-year construction schedule, renegotiable in case of war, and it bound heirs in case of the contractor's death. Anyone attempting to rescind the contract was subject to extreme sanctions. The contract was carved in marble and placed on public display (Bresson 2016, 165). Similar contracts may date as far back as the Achaemenid (First Persian) empire (6th to 4th century BCE), when, by royal decree, all individuals who dug a *quanat* (a subterranean gallery used to intercept water sources for irrigation) had the right to retain all profits for up to five generations (Goldsmith 2014, 11).

Contracts such as these are examples of what today are known as public-private partnerships (PPPs). A public entity contracts the construction and maintenance of public infrastructure to private entities, which receive the exclusive rights to profit for a fixed period of time. More specifically, PPPs are defined as "long-term contracts between a private party and a government entity, for providing a public asset or service, in which the private party bears significant risk and management responsibility, and remuneration is linked to performance" (World Bank, ADB, and IDB 2014, 14).

PPPs are considered an alternative to both public provision and private provision. Unlike public provision, where a private firm is responsible only for building the infrastructure, under PPPs the concessionaire builds, manages, maintains, and retains control of the assets for the duration of the contract, which can last more than 30 years. Unlike private provision, in PPPs the private firm has only a temporary and partial ownership of the asset. PPPs have been adopted for the provision of various services, providing mainly infrastructure in network industries such as electricity, telecommunications, water, and transport. PPPs have also been used for delivering other services traditionally connected to public provision such as health and education, garbage collection, agriculture extension services, and social housing.

PPPs were recognized as playing a key role in infrastructure financing at the recent Addis Ababa International Conference on Financing for Development (United Nations 2015, para. 48). Although the participation of the private sector in infrastructure projects has grown considerably in the last 25 years in developing countries, especially in the energy sector (figure S7.1), private financing continues to constitute a limited share of aggregate infrastructure investment. In developing countries, it is less than 25 percent (IMF 2014; World Bank 2014).

The most common argument in favor of PPPs is that they free up resources in budget-constrained governments for other projects.[1] If a country is too poor to collect enough resources domestically, or if the government cannot credibly commit to using revenues for providing public services or to repay investors in the long term, it may be difficult to collect enough funds to finance the initial investment in the form of

WDR 2017 team.

Figure S7.1 Private participation in infrastructure projects in developing countries remains limited

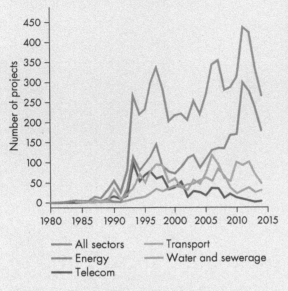

Legend:
- All sectors
- Energy
- Telecom
- Transport
- Water and sewerage

Source: WDR 2017 team, using data from World Bank, Private Participation in Infrastructure Database, 1980–2014.

either taxes or public debt. Another reason PPPs may be appealing is that they can increase efficiency in providing public services because private firms obey the rules of the financial markets. In contrast to state officials, who obey political considerations, private firms introduce competition in markets characterized by the features of natural monopolies, and they prevent investment in projects with negative social values because the profitability of the investment depends on the demand for the service.

A key challenge for PPPs in providing public services efficiently is that they must take into account the incentives of both public and private entities because PPPs allocate risks between the contracting parties over a long period of time, when circumstances often change. Actors will likely fail to reach an agreement or the PPP may be ineffective if there is no mechanism to allocate the risk in a credible way. Auction bids are based on long-term forecasts of the expected demand for a service. In reality, however, the demand may vary from the forecast. For example, forecasts may fail to accurately take into account the impact of service fees on user demand, or the service may become obsolete as technology advances. Similarly, because the government agenda may change with the political cycle and pressures for reelection,

private firms may worry that the profitability of their investment could be undermined.

For this reason, many PPPs have not resulted in the expected efficiency gains. For example, without a credible commitment to enforce the terms of the agreement, contracts are frequently renegotiated in favor of the private contractor, with considerable government spending often allocated in questionable, noncompetitive ways. Renegotiation often occurs as a consequence of an aggressive bidding strategy at the time of auction. After having been awarded the contract, the concessionaires can lobby the government to renegotiate the terms, voiding the potential efficiency gains of the auction. For example, 68 percent of the 1,700 PPP projects financed in Latin America from 1990 to 2013 (78 percent in the transport sector) were renegotiated on average one year after the contract award, according to Guasch and others (2014).

Taking into account actors' incentives and making sure that the contract's terms are consistent over time may reduce the likelihood of opportunistic behavior, such as renegotiation. However, depending on the circumstances, the form in which this commitment is credibly reached may vary. In the ancient Greek city of Eretria, it would have been very difficult to renegotiate the terms of a contract carved in marble. Publicizing the contract in a public square also helped bind the contracting parties by increasing scrutiny. Although this specific commitment device clearly may not be the best solution for PPPs today, the underlying principles remain valid.

The optimal contract may depend on whether it is possible to collect user fees, whether there is high demand, and whether the quality of the service is easily contracted. For example, the commitment device needed to effectively deliver on highway infrastructure may be very different from that needed for health services. Consider the financing of a new highway: demand is high, user fees can be collected, and quality is easily contractable. However, the returns on investment depend on future demand, which cannot be controlled by the concessionaire. If the contract is fixed-term, the risk is borne by the private contractor, who will internalize the volatility linked to traffic forecasts and ask for a higher subsidy ex ante, or renegotiate the terms of the contract once the bid is won. The higher state subsidy will in turn blunt the role of PPPs in ruling out bad investments, and renegotiation will undermine the competitive benefits of the auction. In such a context, it would be better for the planner to bear the demand risk.[2]

Notes

1. Economic theory also predicts that the present value of all the user fees that the government could have been collecting under public provision of the service equals the initial saving under PPPs. For a formal discussion, see Engel, Fischer, and Galetovic (2014).
2. For example, the tender could specify a discount rate and a user fee schedule, and the bids could be made on the present value of revenue. The contract term would then last until the winning contractor collects all the fees demanded in the bid, thereby deterring any form of renegotiation and chances for the government to subsidize the private firm with transfers (see Engel, Fischer, and Galetovic 2014).

References

Bresson, Alain. 2016. *The Making of the Ancient Greek Economy: Institutions, Markets, and Growth in the City-States.* Translated by Steven Rendall. Princeton, NJ: Princeton University Press.

Engel, Eduardo, Ronald D. Fischer, and Alexander Galetovic. 2014. *The Economics of Public-Private Partnerships: A Basic Guide.* New York: Cambridge University Press.

Goldsmith, Hugh. 2014. "The Long-Run Evolution of Infrastructure Services." CESifo Working Paper 50723, Center for Economic Studies and Ifo Institute, Munich.

Guasch, José Luis, Daniel Benitez, Irene Portabales, and Lincoln Flor. 2014. "The Renegotiation of PPP Contracts: An Overview of Its Recent Evolution in Latin America." International Transport Forum Discussion Paper 2014/18, Organisation for Economic Co-operation and Development, Paris.

IMF (International Monetary Fund). 2014. *World Economic Outlook, October 2014: Legacies, Clouds, Uncertainties.* World Economic and Financial Surveys. Washington, DC: IMF.

United Nations. 2015. "Report of the Third International Conference on Financing for Development: Addis Ababa, 13–16 July 2015." Report A/CONF.227/20 (August 3), United Nations, New York.

World Bank. Various years. Private Participation in Infrastructure Database. Washington, DC, https://ppi.worldbank.org/.

———. 2014. "Overcoming Constraints to the Financing of Infrastructure: Success Stories and Lessons Learned: Country, Sector, and Project Examples of Overcoming Constraints to the Financing of Infrastructure." World Bank, Washington, DC, January.

World Bank, ADB (Asian Development Bank), and IDB (Inter-American Development Bank). 2014. *Public-Private Partnerships: Reference Guide, Version 2.0.* Report 90384. Washington, DC: World Bank.

CHAPTER 6

Governance for equity

"We are the 99%" became the slogan of street demonstrators in the United States in August 2011 as they demanded public action against rising income inequality and the growing perception of the unfairness of the economic system after the 2008–09 global financial crisis. Observers viewed the mounting concentration of income and wealth as a threat to the sustainability of an institutional setting that responds to the needs of all citizens (Stiglitz 2011, 2012). Concerns about how to tackle the "unfair" features of the global economic system were gaining momentum throughout the world.

Indeed, as discussed in chapter 2, the perception of whether policies and rules are *fair* matters when it comes to inducing better cooperation in society.[1] Although the concept of *fairness* is complex, it certainly involves some dimensions related to outcomes and others related to process.[2] Through this lens, *equity* is associated with fairness to the extent that outcomes (income, educational attainment, or ownership of assets such as land) and the opportunities for individuals to pursue a life of their choosing are independent of their circumstances such as their ethnicity, race, gender, location, or other factors beyond their control. However, in addition to outcomes being independent of circumstances beyond their control, inequality in outcomes matters per se. Such inequality, in fact, reflects a differential ability of certain actors and groups to influence policy making and the allocation of resources in society (box 6.1).[3]

As explained in chapter 1, this Report builds on the premise that societies care about prosperity and how prosperity is shared. However, ultimately growth and inequality are jointly determined (Chenery and others 1974; Ferreira 2012). At a given moment in time, the productive assets and opportunities that individuals have determine their capacity to generate income and contribute to growth, given market conditions. In this way, economic growth reflects the aggregate productive capacity of different individuals and the accessibility and functionality of markets. In the long run, however, the potential for people to accumulate and productively use assets is influenced by policy decisions such as the allocation of public spending to public education, health, or infrastructure. Inequality and growth are thus tightly linked, and the way in which the benefits from growth translate into socioeconomic achievements across different individuals and groups is determined by how actors interact and make policy decisions about redistribution.

Many policies can enhance equity. Governments use fiscal instruments—taxes and transfers—to redistribute income ex post, and they use public spending—via the provision of public goods and services—to reshape the distribution of "opportunities" and foster mobility within and across generations (figure 6.1). The provision of quality public goods and services can help equalize opportunities, allowing individuals to increase their stock of assets—for example, in terms of human capital such as education, health, or skills; financial capital; or physical capital such as land or machinery. Promoting an environment of investment and innovation can expand access to opportunities as individuals use their capital and labor to generate income—for example, utilizing their skills to participate in the labor market or using their land for agricultural production. Social protection systems—including safety nets, subsidies, and transfers—also act as a mechanism for equity, redistributing resources to the most vulnerable.

> Perception of whether policies and rules are *fair* matters when it comes to inducing better cooperation in society.

Figure 6.1 States can improve equity by intervening in the distribution of final outcomes through taxes and transfers and by providing access to basic services

a. Gini index of market and final incomes

b. Contribution of taxes, monetary transfers, and in-kind transfers to reduce inequality varies by country

● Market income ● Final income

■ Taxes and transfers ■ In-kind transfers

Source: WDR 2017 team, based on Inchauste and Lustig, forthcoming, table 1.1.

Note: In panel a, *market income* refers to income before taxes and transfers. *Final income* is defined as income after direct and indirect taxes and transfers, also taking into account transfers in kind (access to basic services). The graph presents lower-bound estimates of redistributive impact.

Pro-equity policies can boost overall growth in the medium and long term, but they also can adversely affect specific groups, particularly in the short term. The groups likely to lose out from these policies—in terms of income, rents, or influence—may attempt to undermine their adoption or implementation. For example, influential actors may block land reform policies or shape the allocation of public spending for their personal benefit. Civil servants may undermine the access and quality of public services. When societies have high levels of inequality, such inequalities are reflected in the unequal capacity of groups to influence the policy-making process, which makes inequality even more persistent (box 6.2).

Box 6.2 A vicious cycle: How inequality begets inequality

In societies in which inequality is high, the effectiveness of governance to deliver on equity outcomes can be weakened structurally because those at the top of the income ladder not only have control over a disproportionate amount of wealth and resources, but also have a disproportionate ability to influence the policy process. This type of power asymmetry may lead even a benevolent planner, who is fair and freely elected and is seeking efficiency (and even more so, a corrupted official) to end up systematically favoring the interests of those at the top over those at the bottom. The result is a more inefficient allocation of resources and further entrenchment of existing inequalities over time (Esteban and Ray 2006).

This undue influence can be illustrated by looking at countries in which lobbying is integrated in the political system. Igan and Mishra (2014) find compelling results using data on the politically targeted activities of the financial industry (including lobbying, campaign contributions, and political connections) from 1999 to 2006 in the United States. They find that lobbying expenditures and network connections are associated with a greater probability that legislators will switch their position from advocating tighter financial market regulations to voting in favor of deregulation. More broadly, levels of commitment are lower in countries with higher shares of billionaires whose wealth comes from sectors prone to capture and rent-seeking, including those who are heavily dependent on government concessions such as in the financial, real estate, and natural resources sectors (figure B6.2.1).[a]

Theory suggests that, in most cases, the overall gains from equity-enhancing redistribution policies are greater than gains from inequality-neutral growth policies for the top 1 percent or 5 percent (Milanović 2016). Nevertheless, for those at the top, policies that increase inequality can be preferable to those that would enable a more efficient allocation of public resources and lead to higher overall economic growth. For example, Stiglitz (2012) finds that as market income became more unequal in the United

Figure B6.2.1 Capture is associated with lower levels of commitment

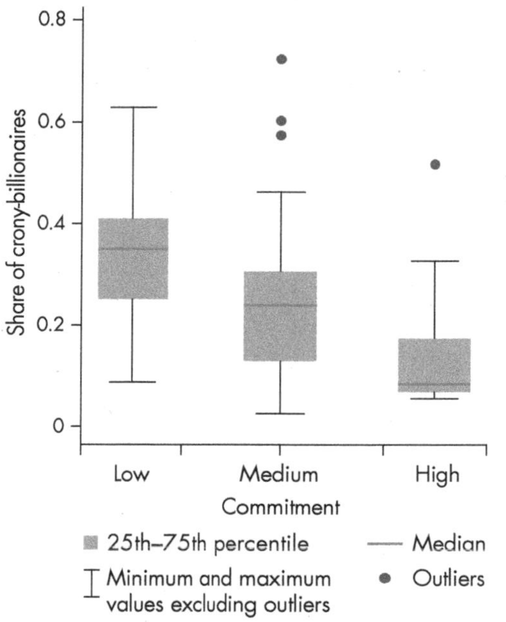

Sources: WDR 2017 team estimates, based on Forbes, "The World's Billionaires," http://www.forbes.com/billionaires/, and WDR 2017 Governance Indicators.

Note: Commitment is measured as protection of property rights, contract enforcement, and lack of arbitrary expropriation without proper compensation. The classification of commitment levels is as follows: low = < 0; medium = 0–2; high = > 2. The categories comprise 11, 29, and 9 countries, respectively. Crony-billionaires are defined as the subset of billionaires whose fortunes belong to the following sectors: agriculture, communication, construction, oil, gas, chemicals and other energy, financial and insurance activities, mining and quarrying, real estate activities, and conglomerates.

States, the government also approved more generous tax cuts on capital gains. Unsurprisingly, these tax cuts mainly favored those who were already at the top of the income

(Box continues next page)

Box 6.2 A vicious cycle: How inequality begets inequality *(continued)*

distribution (including the members of Congress who were voting for those policy reforms).

Inequality affects governance not only by means of capture, but also by weakening how individuals perceive the fairness of the society they live in. When a country fails to deliver on its commitment to improve and equalize opportunities for all citizens, and it responds only to the interests of those at the top of the distribution, citizens may decide to *opt out* of or *exit* the existing political processes instead of contesting the outcomes in the policy arena. This decision leads to a weakening of cooperation. Even in countries in which the benefits of economic growth reach all members of society, the discontent arising from a perception of an increase in relative deprivation (when those at the top of

the distribution are moving ahead more quickly than those at the bottom) may be larger than the contentment from an absolute improvement in living standards—as documented, for example, for Europe and central Asia by Dávalos and others (2016).

The concern about the vicious cycle of inequality and governance, in which initial conditions of inequality promote a policy arena that further entrenches that inequality, is exacerbated by the surge in the concentration at the top of the income and wealth distributions in many countries (Atkinson, Piketty, and Saez 2011; World Bank 2016). Understanding the entry points to break this persistent loop is crucial to restoring a social contract that can promote greater and more equal access to opportunities for everyone.

Source: WDR 2017 team.

a. During the 2015–16 election cycle in the United States, the largest disbursement (27 percent of all outlays) came from the financial sectors, which include insurance companies, securities and investment firms, real estate interests, and commercial banks (Center for Responsive Politics). These are the sectors with the largest number of billionaires (WDR 2017 team, based on *Forbes*, "The World's Billionaires," http://www.forbes.com/billionaires/).

To increase the success of reforms opposed by powerful interests, it may be necessary to modify the bargaining process by changing the *incentives* or *preferences* of the actors who bargain or allowing new actors to *contest* policies. At times, members of the elite may have incentives to become aligned with actors pushing for reforms in taxation and public spending that favor the poor. For example, the first antipoverty programs in 19th-century England and Wales were pushed by the top 1 percent of the landed gentry. Against the backdrop of the French Revolution, this group sought to keep cheap labor in rural areas and prevent it from migrating to urban areas, at a time when the French Revolution spurred fear of revolts (Lindert 2004; Ravallion 2015). Increasing the participation of disadvantaged groups can also help change the incentives of actors who bargain over policies. Direct participation and contestation in decision making can improve cooperation as well. For example, in Ghana, when businesses were involved in tax collection they became more likely to pay their taxes (Joshi and Ayee 2009). By building common interest, political organization can aggregate citizens' preferences and demand in policy-making processes. However, such reforms can be complex and frequently involve setbacks.

This chapter explores how power asymmetries matter for equity. It begins by looking at how they can lead to breakdowns in institutional functions,

constraining the effectiveness of policies. The second part of the chapter then looks at the levers of change and how constraints can be alleviated to level the playing field and make policies more responsive to all.

Two key policy areas that matter for equity: Investing in public goods and expanding opportunities

Although income inequality *between* countries has declined over the last 20 years as low- and middle-income countries have grown faster than those at the top of the world income distribution, the level of income inequality *within* countries has increased.[4] This trend can be explained in part by governance environments that prevent the successful adoption and implementation of policies to enhance equity.

This chapter considers two key policy areas that matter for equity: investment that helps equalize opportunities through the accumulation of assets, and policies that increase access to economic opportunities to utilize those assets. As emphasized in the *World Development Report 2006: Equity and Development* (World Bank 2005), the opportunities of individuals arise to a considerable extent from investments in public goods and services, particularly in terms of health and education. But such investments depend on collecting and redistributing resources. Indeed, no high-income country has improved equity without significant taxation and public spending to protect individuals against shocks (such as illness, unemployment, and old age) and to reduce welfare disparities within and across generations (Barr 2001; Lindert 2004). In addition, for individuals to realize the returns on such investments, they need access to economic opportunities in adulthood, especially those opportunities that allow them to use the human capital they have acquired.

Although the focus of this chapter is not on labor markets, it does touch on important determinants of labor income inequality. Consider Latin America, the most unequal region in the world, which has experienced an important decline in income inequality over the last two decades (Rodríguez-Castelán and others 2016). This decline is largely explained by the decline in labor income inequality—associated with an expansion of education—as well as the decline in nonlabor income inequality, largely explained by more progressive government transfers (Lustig, López-Calva, and Ortiz-Juárez 2015). Indeed, the provision of quality public goods and services as a means of leveling the playing field and reducing poverty has been unambiguous (World Bank 2005).

Equity and institutional functions: The role of commitment and cooperation

As argued in this Report, the effectiveness of policies to achieve equitable development is related to how well institutions perform certain key functions. Policies that require long-term objectives, for example, are often truncated (a *commitment* failure). Effective policies tend to have long-term objectives (extending beyond the political cycle), matching resources, and well-aligned incentives for the actors involved. Actors must trust that promises will be kept, even in the face of changing circumstances. Often, however, the incentives of public officials become misaligned with those of the constituencies they are meant to serve. In clientelistic settings, the interaction between public officials and citizens is distorted: public officials "buy" the votes of citizens in exchange for short-term benefits (see box 6.4 later in this chapter for a definition of *clientelism*). Or public officials may become accountable only to certain influential groups, or "clients," promoting their interests in exchange for their political support.

A low commitment to providing quality public services is one of the main characteristics of the poorest countries in the world, as well as the most unequal ones. Pro-equity policies require state capacity, including a bureaucracy able to collect taxes and teachers well trained to educate children. A professional bureaucracy has been identified as a significant feature of any state seeking to achieve development (Rauch and Evans 2000). "Weak states," particularly in Sub-Saharan Africa, are characterized by a limited state presence beyond the capital and coastal areas and by a limited ability to tax (Migdal 1988; Herbst 2000). In middle-income countries with high inequality, such as in Latin America, "truncated" welfare states exclude a large share of the population from public spending (De Ferranti and others 2004; Ferreira and others 2013).

When the commitment to deliver on policies, such as the provision of quality services, breaks down, individuals tend to opt out and demonstrate less cooperation in, for example, their willingness to pay taxes. Figure 6.2 shows how lower levels of

Figure 6.2 When commitment is low, countries exhibit low compliance (high shadow economy)

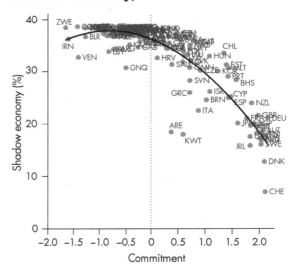

Sources: Commitment: WDR 2017 Governance Indicators; shadow economy: Schneider, Buehn, and Montenegro 2011.

Note: "Shadow economy" is defined as the share of the market-based legal production of goods and services that is deliberately concealed from public authorities for any of the following reasons: (1) to avoid payment of income, value added, or other taxes; (2) to avoid payment of social security contributions; (3) to avoid having to meet certain legal labor market standards such as minimum wage, maximum working hours, and safety standards; and (4) to avoid complying with certain administrative procedures such as completing statistical questionnaires or other administrative forms (Schneider, Buehn, and Montenegro 2011). The variable "shadow economy" is the predicted value of the measure, controlling for the gross domestic product (GDP) per capita. "Commitment" is measured as protection of property rights, contract enforcement, and lack of arbitrary expropriation without proper compensation.

commitment are associated with larger "shadow economies," in which individuals opt out by not complying with the existing rules. Collecting the taxes needed to fund investments in public goods crucially requires the willingness of taxpayers—individuals and firms—to cooperate and comply with the rules. Perceptions of free-riding by others or low-quality services can lead to breakdowns in cooperation. In middle-income countries with high inequality, such as in Latin America, citizens may exit—for example, by opting out of basic public education—because they obtain little from the state (Hirschman 1970; Perry and others 2007). The low quality of service provision prompts the upper-middle class to demand private services, which in turn weakens their willingness to fiscally cooperate and contribute to the provision of public goods—a perverse cycle. At other times, actors potentially affected by policies may be excluded from their design, undermining their incentive to cooperate and weakening compliance.

What makes people cooperate so they do not free-ride on others and do comply with the rules? Cooperative behavior results in part from the credibility of sanctions against those who do not comply. For example, ethnic networks may be able to induce cooperation in the form of school funding among their members because they have more credible sanctions against free-riders (Miguel and Gugerty 2005). This view was tested in a lab game with players from a multiethnic neighborhood in Kampala, Uganda. Players in charge of allocating resources shared much higher amounts with others when their actions were taken in full view of others than when they were not. In both cases, other players were from their same ethnic group. These results indicate that for individuals who are not willing to share, the risk of a social sanction shapes their behavior rather than altruism toward coethnics (figure 6.3, panel a).

Cooperation is enhanced by commitment. The credibility of policy makers is essential for the enforcement of sanctions and the payment of compensation when redistribution reforms are carried out. Consider the difficulties in reforming energy subsidies. Such subsidies are often inequitable because they benefit relatively richer households, which devote a larger share of their total consumption to energy-related goods. They are inefficient because their high fiscal cost precludes other public spending (Coady and others 2015). Therefore, eliminating these subsidies while setting up compensatory measures for the poor could improve both efficiency and equity. Yet, virtually all countries that have attempted energy subsidy reforms have faced social and political unrest. This is

Figure 6.3 Fear of sanctions and participation in decision-making processes promote cooperation

a. Cooperation in a lab experiment in Uganda

Average offers in a "dictator game" paid by egoist players to coethnics

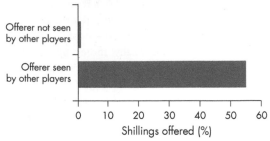

Source: WDR 2017 team, based on Habyarimana and others 2007.

Note: The figure shows the average offer paid by egoist players (those who always employ the most selfish strategy available in all rounds of the game) in a "dictator game"—that is, a game in which a player (the dictator) determines how to split an endowment with other players. Subjects were given 1,000 Ugandan shillings—10 coins of 100 shillings each—and asked to distribute them among themselves and the two other players in any way they pleased. The figure shows the "benchmark coethnic" measure: any pair of players who identified themselves as belonging to the same ethnic category in their pre-experiment questionnaire was coded as coethnics.

b. Cooperation in rural Indonesia

Increase in the probability that individuals state they will contribute to project construction when plebiscites are held compared with representative-based meetings

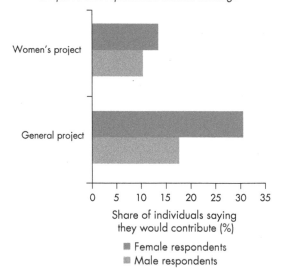

Source: WDR 2017 team, based on Olken 2010.

Note: In an experiment conducted in rural Indonesia, villages were randomly assigned to choose development projects either through meetings at which representatives would make the selection (the majority of attendees were government officials, neighborhood heads, and those selected to represent village groups) or through direct election plebiscites (in which all adults eligible to vote in the last national parliamentary election could vote). The villages had to select a general project and a women's project. After conclusion of the project selection process, respondents were asked about their plans to make voluntary contributions to the project (labor, money, food).

often because policy makers are not credible in their commitment to redistribute the savings from efficiency gains.

Perceptions of fairness also matter for cooperation. Experimental evidence indicates that individuals adjust their behavior and are willing to incur a cost in order to sanction behaviors that they perceive to be unfair. More specifically, the fairness of the processes through which decisions are made matters. Participation in the decision-making process has an intrinsic value in allowing more legitimate choices (Habermas 1996; Rawls 1997). But participation may also have an instrumental value by increasing cooperation—for example, in the form of contribution to the funding of projects or in the form of compliance with decisions made. Experimental evidence supports this view (Dal Bó, Foster, and Putterman 2010; Goeree and Yariv 2011). A study from Indonesia indicates greater cooperation when participatory processes are in place: individuals are more willing to contribute to projects when the whole village can cast a vote directly in plebiscites than when the usual decision-making meetings, run by representatives, are held (figure 6.3, panel b).

Fairness and "process legitimacy" also matter for economic opportunities. The credible and consistent enforcement of laws and regulations, including property rights, can help expand opportunities and level the playing field. For example, if property rights are secure only for some, then those who are not protected as much as others will respond by underinvesting (Goldstein and Udry 2008). Furthermore, if individuals think their effort will not be rewarded because of discrimination, they may exert less effort (Hoff and Pandey 2006).

How policies to promote equity can be affected by power asymmetries

In the Indian state of Maharashtra, villages dominated politically by the Maratha caste are 10 percent less likely to implement nationally funded antipoverty programs than other villages, even though their population—who votes in free elections—consists largely of poor or landless laborers.[5] Why? A credible explanation is that the local landed class from the Maratha caste uses its political power—leading village councils—to block antipoverty programs, "buying" votes instead through the provision of informal insurance to voters in times of financial crisis. The Marathas are particularly successful in clientelist strategies thanks to the other "services" they can provide, such as their trading networks. Prevailing social norms in the villages—the caste system—help the Marathas maintain their political influence because they are the traditionally dominant caste in Maharashtra and are better able to enforce sanctions (Anderson, Francois, and Kotwal 2015).

On paper, allowing village councils to select the beneficiaries of antipoverty programs in a setting in which the councils are freely elected should enhance equity outcomes: local governments can be held accountable, and beneficiaries can better observe and control their effort because of their proximity. Village councils, in theory, would also be better at targeting beneficiaries and selecting public works projects that are most useful for the community. In reality, however, as the example in Maharashtra shows, local influential actors may take advantage of their role in the allocation of resources to block redistribution, exchanging political support for short-term benefits.

More generally, asymmetries in bargaining power shape how commitment and cooperation are sustained, ultimately affecting whether equity-enhancing policies are adopted and implemented. Although a policy to improve equity may look good on paper, such as strengthening access to land, it may also be prone to clientelism and capture (box 6.3). Groups that directly influence policies—called *elites* in this Report—may have more bargaining power than others because of the existing inequalities in income or wealth, or the difficulties that other actors face in organizing and lobbying effectively. Indeed, in the presence of weakly organized constituencies, political elites may have fewer incentives to invest in public goods and improve equity. They may instead engage in narrow patron-client relationships that maintain their ability to influence decision making.

Clientelism and capture: Weakening the commitment to service delivery

This Report, like the *World Development Report 2004: Making Services Work for Poor People* (World Bank 2003), views service provision as a series of relationships between principals and agents. In the classic case, the official is the agent of the voter (who monitors and sanctions the agent). However, this dynamic of monitoring by citizens is often undermined by political incentives. Committing to a broad provision of public goods can be politically disadvantageous because the benefits of public goods become diluted among nonsupporters and are more difficult to monitor—and reverse. By contrast, political candidates may commit to targeted benefits for narrow

Although a policy to improve equity may look good on paper, it may also be prone to clientelism and capture.

Box 6.3 Efforts to expand and secure access to land often lead to capture

Expanding and securing access to land are important policy areas in efforts to increase economic opportunities. Indeed, in 2008 an estimated 75 percent of the world's poor lived in rural areas and their incomes depended, directly or indirectly, on agriculture (Ravallion 2015). Thus, improving and securing their access to land are important to increase investments and productivity. More equitable access to land has also been associated with higher equity and efficiency, both directly and indirectly, through better institutions and increased citizen participation—an important element of collective action.[a]

Land tenure reforms, however, can be used for patronage. The security of land tenure varies considerably across and within countries, depending greatly on systems of inheritance, existing social hierarchies, and gender norms—all of which can hamper the ability of disadvantaged groups to improve their livelihoods. In Vietnam, for example, individuals with connections to politicians and bureaucrats have much more tenure security than others (Markussen and Tarp 2014). In Ghana, property rights are particularly insecure for women, who are less likely than men to play local political or social roles.

Interventions to change land tenure, including in cities, have often been captured and used for patronage. In many African cities, a range of land interventions, such as land regularization and resettlement operations, have been captured by local elites and used for political patronage, including through corruption of civil servants (such as staff of the land registry). Bribes may be used to facilitate access to land, obtain formal tenure, or obtain plots for friends and political clients (Durand-Lasserve, Durand-Lasserve, and Selod 2015).

When inequality is too entrenched to expect sales and rental markets to reallocate land, land redistribution reforms become necessary. However, because of the difficulty in reaching agreement on such reforms, they often take place at times of significant political change, such as the end of colonial rule, or with strong pressure from outside, as in the Republic of Korea. When no such major political changes have occurred, land redistribution has been spurred by collective action by citizens, including peasant movements that increased pressure for reform, such as in Brazil (Binswanger-Mkhize, Bourguignon, and van den Brink 2009).

Source: WDR 2017 team.

a. For microeconomic evidence in India, see Banerjee and Iyer (2005). For a comparison of North and South America, see Engerman and Sokoloff (2002).

---

groups of "clients"—such as their ethnic group or their caste—because they can more credibly deliver, and control, these benefits. For example, politicians can target input subsidies for farming to supporters, while maintaining a threat to remove the subsidies. Such arrangements ensure that supporters credibly commit to backing politicians, while politicians also have a credible tool to "punish" supporters if they defect (Bates 1981).

In such clientelist settings (see box 6.4), the traditional principal-agent relationship between citizens and officials breaks down, and accountability becomes up for sale (figure 6.4). Clientelism can affect the adoption and implementation of policies in two main ways. In the first, citizens' expectations of politicians become skewed (some receive targeted benefits, whereas many may go without). In the second, service providers extract rents because they play a role in politicians' reelection (Bold and others 2016). Both cases lead to breakdowns in commitments to long-term objectives.

In the first form of clientelism (clientelism case 1 in figure 6.4), the interaction between public officials and citizens is distorted: rather than officials acting as the agents of citizens and voters monitoring and sanctioning officials, the dynamic becomes a bargain in which the politician "buys" the citizen's vote for what usually are short-term gains (Khemani and others 2016). These bargains tend to be more frequent where individuals have a higher time preference for the present with respect to the future. The poor and disadvantaged are particularly vulnerable to exchanging their votes for short-term benefits in the form of transfers because their pressing needs make their discount rates for the present higher than those of the better-off. Where commitments to broad-based policies do not appear to be credible—for example, in situations with limited state capacity—such voting behavior is rational, not merely short-sighted. This clientelist bargain tends to lead to a breakdown in commitment to programmatic objectives. Evidence suggests that clientelism in the form of vote buying

Clientelism is a political strategy characterized by giving material goods in return for electoral support (Stokes 2009). Clientelism can be viewed as a two-party encounter between a politician and a voter (Hicken 2011). It is, however, often organized in networks, which can be based on districts or regions. As a result, a central part of clientelism's organizational structure is an intermediary or a broker, whose role is to mobilize a network of local voters in exchange for financial payment or patronage jobs. The behavior and strategy of a broker and the contractual arrangement with the national politician are thus an important element of clientelism.[a]

A number of studies mentioned in this chapter emphasize the negative impact of clientelism on the provision of public goods. Indeed, it can entail significant welfare costs for societies (Bardhan 2002). When it is prevalent, voters

act to pursue short-term benefits rather than focus on broad policy considerations such as equitable and sustainable reforms.

Measuring clientelism is a challenge. Distinguishing empirically between public goods and private goods can be complex. For example, infrastructure projects, typically considered a public good, can be locally targeted to a specific geographic area.[b] By contrast, redistribution promised by politicians to win votes can be beneficial to broad groups. For example, in the cases of the Peruvian Social Fund (Schady 2000) and the investment in infrastructure in Spain from 1964 to 2004 (Solé-Ollé 2013), even though welfare-enhancing transfers were targeted to secure votes, the policies benefited large swaths of the population, beyond those targeted to win elections.

Source: WDR 2017 team, based on Wantchekon (2016).

a. See Stokes (2005); Cruz (2013); Holland and Palmer-Rubin (2015); and Schneider (2015).
b. See review in Bouton, Castanheira, and Genicot (2016).

is associated with a lower provision of public services (Khemani 2015).

In a second form of clientelism (clientelism case 2 in figure 6.4), specific groups capture policy-making processes, reducing the incentives of public officials to adopt and implement policies for their constituency as a whole. This capture takes place when public officials grant benefits in exchange for the political support of a single-issue or homogeneous group. In this equilibrium, public officials become accountable to such groups, including—but not limited to—service providers, whose support becomes indispensable for officials' political survival. Public sector providers, such as teachers' unions, may extract rents through the diversion of public resources or through lower effort in the form of absenteeism or low-quality service provision, which can hamper the delivery of services such as education, health, or infrastructure (see spotlight 8 for a broader discussion of the governance challenges in service delivery).

When groups in charge of providing services capture politicians, monitoring and sanctioning of these providers are no longer credible, leading to a weak commitment to service delivery. A policy experiment in Kenya illustrates this point. It compared the impact of contract teachers in interventions managed by nongovernmental organizations (NGOs) and interventions run by the government. Test scores

Figure 6.4 A politician can become an agent of the provider in clientelist settings

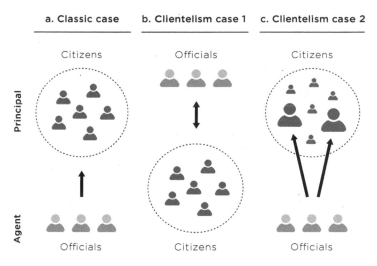

Sources: WDR 2017 team, extending World Bank 2003 and Khemani and others 2016.

Note: Arrows indicate who is responsive to whom.

increased only in the intervention run by NGOs, indicating that the NGOs were more credible in implementing sanctions—through firing—than the government (Bold and others 2013).

Policy makers' lack of credibility in sanctioning public sector workers results in part from the role that the latter play in politics. In clientelist contexts, public sector jobs may be awarded in exchange for political support. For example, in surveys conducted by the Program on Governance and Local Development (GLD) in countries in the Middle East and North Africa, between 40 and 70 percent of respondents stated that political connections are as important as or more important than qualifications to obtain a government job (figure 6.5)—see GLD (2016). In theory, a job is an attractive way for politicians to reward supporters. Politicians can exercise control over the careers of public sector workers, such as their location and promotions, and thus have a credible threat to maintain the workers' support. And it is in the interest of public sector workers to support politicians, thereby obtaining help for their careers.[6]

When sanctioning of service providers is not credible, the most blatant consequence is the diversion of financial resources. For example, in most countries in Europe and central Asia, more than one-third of

individuals report that informal payments (such as bribes and under-the-table payments) are made to access health services; this proportion rises to 9 out of 10 persons in Azerbaijan (figure 6.6). In education, corruption also affects learning outcomes. In Brazil, students' test scores in mathematics and Portuguese are higher when corruption is lower in the municipalities where the schools are located (Ferraz, Finan, and Moreira 2012).

Capture that undermines the role of officials in sanctioning service providers goes beyond the diversion of financial resources; it also helps to explain absenteeism and lack of work effort. Averaging across Bangladesh, Ecuador, India, Indonesia, Peru, and Uganda, a survey conducted by unannounced enumerators found that about 19 percent of teachers were absent from primary schools (Chaudhury and others 2006). Absentee rates for health workers in the same countries were even higher: 35 percent on average. Recent data measuring teacher absenteeism in the classroom in seven countries in Sub-Saharan Africa reveal very high rates: as much as 56 percent in Mozambique. Even when teachers are in the classroom, they often are not teaching or not teaching well. Similarly, health workers often exert little effort: in Senegal, clinicians spend an average of only 39 minutes a day counseling patients (Bold and others 2011).

Clientelism and capture further hamper a government's ability to raise resources and commit to service delivery in the future. Providing few public goods can undermine economic activity and future taxation. In theory, this is one way politicians can maintain power over "clients"; they can reduce the alternatives in the private sector (Robinson and Verdier 2013). For example, in Sierra Leone President Siaka Stevens dismantled the railway leading to a region with a high concentration of supporters from the opposition party. Although interpretations of the underlying reason for this differ, some argue that the "presence" of the state in certain parts of the country was deliberately maintained at a low level (Abraham and Sesay 1993, 120; Acemoglu and Robinson 2012).

Figure 6.5 In some countries in the Middle East and North Africa, a large proportion of citizens believe that connections are as important as or even more important than professional qualifications in obtaining a government job

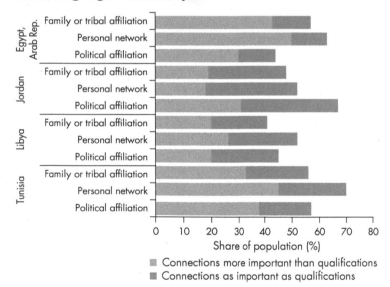

Share of population (%)

■ Connections more important than qualifications
■ Connections as important as qualifications

Sources: University of Gothenburg 2016, using data from GLD 2016.

Note: The question: "What is the importance of a person's professional qualifications in obtaining a government job relative to other factors? Please indicate whether each is more important, equally important, or less important as a person's experience and professional qualifications? 1. A person's political affiliations. 2. A person's personal network, relation to influential people. 3. A person's family or tribal affiliation." The graph shows the percentage stating that each factor is more important (or as important) than (as) experience and qualifications in obtaining a government job in each country. Data are for the following years: Egypt, 2012; Jordan, 2014; Libya, 2013; Tunisia, 2015. Surveys are administered among a nationally representative sample of citizens in each country (using probability proportion to size sampling).

Breakdowns in cooperation: Contributing (or not) to public goods

Actors potentially affected by reforms, such as on fiscal policy, may prevent the adoption of such reforms, especially when the actors are part of a cohesive group. Consider the contrasting examples of a failed land tax reform and a successful personal income tax reform in Uruguay. In 2006 Uruguay introduced a reform aimed at increasing the efficiency and the progressivity of its fiscal system. Its central feature was the introduction of a progressive personal income tax intended to improve redistribution, reduce the tax burden on the poorest taxpayers, and increase revenue collection.[7] The government was able to limit opposition to the reform by offering transparent information on the impact of the reform and publicizing the government's commitment to fight and punish evasion. Moreover, opponents did not object with a united voice. By contrast, a few years later, in 2012, when the government proposed a progressive tax on land assets, medium and large landholders, together with cattle-raisers and managers of large rural estates, rallied together against it. The reform then failed to pass and was ruled unconstitutional by the Supreme Court. A plausible explanation for this result was the organized legal action of the two main associations representing the interests of the landed elites (Rius 2015).

However, even when economic elites form a cohesive group, changes in their incentives can affect whether taxation and public spending reforms in favor of the poor are adopted. Faced with changing economic conditions or fear of citizen-led regime change, even cohesive elites can push for increased taxation and social spending. As noted earlier, the first antipoverty programs in 19th-century England and Wales were pushed by the landed aristocracy to keep cheap labor in the countryside and prevent it from migrating to urban areas at a time when the French Revolution spurred fear of revolts. In South Africa during apartheid, white elites financed the eradication of white poverty through direct taxation, seeking to stabilize segregation and prevent interracial solidarity among the poor white minority and the black majority (Lieberman 2003).

Social norms: At times hindering the effectiveness of de jure reforms aimed at increasing cooperation

Social norms and individuals' beliefs about how other people—both fellow citizens and public officials—will behave also matter for equity. Policies may fail to expand opportunities when deeply rooted social norms, such as those related to gender or racial discrimination, are not addressed. For example, evidence suggests that entrenched norms and beliefs about the ability of women to be effective political leaders are associated with lower representation of women in national parliaments, which has negative effects on the introduction of inclusive policies (see chapter 7).

Figure 6.6 Unofficial payments for education and health services are widespread in Europe and Central Asia

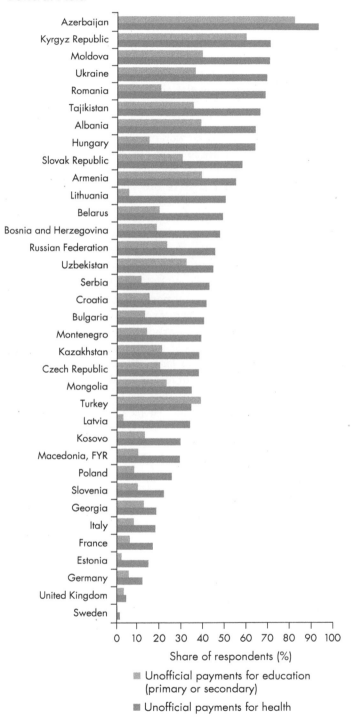

Source: WDR 2017 team, using data from the European Bank for Reconstruction and Development, Life in Transition Survey, 2010.

Note: The graph shows the percentage of each country's respondents who answered "Always," "Usually," or "Sometimes" to the question "In your opinion, how often do people like you have to make unofficial payments or gifts in these situations? Receive public education (primary or secondary)/Receive medical treatment in the public health system?" Other possible answers are "Seldom" and "Never."

At times, even when a specific reform passes and is not captured, entrenched power or norms may make it ineffective. Indeed, de jure reforms are often not enough to improve economic opportunities sustainably. A good example is what happened to the African-American population in the U.S. South following the end of the Civil War in 1865, despite radical changes on paper. Although slavery had been abolished, little else changed for African Americans in the South. The white elites adopted measures to maintain low wages and restricted mobility for African-American workers (Ransom and Sutch 2001). And a measure to grant each freed slave 40 acres of land failed to pass (Wiener 1978). Another hundred years would pass before more profound changes occurred.

De jure reforms are particularly at risk of not being implemented when they clash with prevailing social norms, including customary law (see chapter 3). Efforts to expand opportunities—such as legal reforms to improve women's rights and opportunities—can remain ineffective if norms that consolidate existing asymmetries in bargaining power are not changed (Milazzo 2016). For example, norms can hinder the effectiveness of land titling programs in improving women's access to land. Women may be afraid to claim their titles for fear of social sanctions and backlash from their husbands and families, as occurred in Bolivia and the Lao People's Democratic Republic (Giovarelli and others 2005; World Bank/FAO/IFAD 2009).

On the other hand, the introduction of formal rules may, in some circumstances, undermine pro-equity social norms and voluntary compliance—for example, in terms of philanthropic giving or tax compliance. Consider progressive tax reform in ancient Greece (Christ 1990). Before the reform, the wealthy were responsible for financing public goods and services, especially festivals and military campaigns, through a practice called *liturgies*. As a reward for their cooperation in fiscal affairs, the wealthy liturgists enjoyed the prestige of being appointed to public office and could claim leniency if tried in court. In this sense, tax compliance was seen as a civic honor. Under a tax reform, however, *liturgies* moved from voluntary to compulsory. This shift resulted in diminished social recognition of the taxpayers, who could no longer claim privileges before the judges on the basis of their cooperation. As a result, the wealthy liturgists became increasingly reluctant to pay taxes and tried to conceal their wealth or transfer the role of paying taxes to even wealthier individuals.

> **Efforts to expand opportunities—such as legal reforms to improve women's rights and opportunities—can remain ineffective if norms that consolidate existing asymmetries in bargaining power are not changed.**

Leveling the playing field and making governance more responsive to all

Expanding opportunities for disadvantaged individuals is potentially beneficial for growth in the medium and long term, but it may threaten the interests of certain groups. When such groups have a direct influence on policy design or implementation, including because of existing patterns of inequality in income or wealth, they may be able to block or undermine reforms. Effective policy design should therefore take into account the bargaining power of the different actors involved. Threats to policy adoption and implementation need to be fully considered, incorporating ways to increase the cost of blocking reforms. Designing policies that are based on the existing bargaining power among actors may be more likely to make them successful in the short run. Ultimately, however, it may be necessary to modify the policy arena in order to enlarge the set of policies that can be successfully adopted and implemented.

Expanding the set of equity-oriented policies that can be effectively implemented will depend on modifying the policy bargaining process by changing the incentives and preferences of actors who bargain or by reducing the entry barriers for actors who are more likely to adopt redistributive policies—including those from disadvantaged groups. Efforts to adopt policies that imply losses for certain powerful actors may benefit from providing those actors with *incentives* to support the reform (such as bundling the policy with others that benefit them). Another entry point, shaping *preferences*, can enhance collective action—for example, by building common interest around certain policies. Moreover, enhancing *contestability* is a key entry point to help solve power asymmetries. For example, increasing the direct representation of disadvantaged individuals in legislative assemblies can promote policy makers' commitment to reforms that improve equity.

Changing actors' incentives in the policy arena through voting and information

Understanding the incentives needed to convince influential actors to adopt and implement policies that will benefit the poor and disadvantaged is key to improving equity. In the example from Kenya discussed earlier, even though involving parents in school monitoring after new contract teachers were hired helped improve outcomes, this success was not scaled up because the government lacked incentives to credibly implement sanctions (Bold and others 2013; Duflo, Dupas, and Kremer 2015). This example illustrates the need to change the incentives of elected leaders. Faced with new incentives in the context of changing economic conditions or rising citizen pressure, elites may increase taxation and social spending, as illustrated in the previously discussed example of the adoption of antipoverty programs in 19th-century England and Wales (Lindert 2004).

In some contexts, when political elites face stiff competition as well as high demand for public goods, they may be under more than the usual pressure to deliver services because they may need to broaden their support base. In the United States, there is evidence that greater political competition has led to more new infrastructure (Besley, Persson, and Sturm 2010). In Brazil, there is also evidence of less corruption among mayors who face reelection (Ferraz and Finan 2011). When politicians face increased competition, they may delegate implementation decisions to better-trained bureaucrats to whom they also give more autonomy (Rasul and Rogger 2015). However, in clientelist settings more competition may not always result in more public goods. The effects of competition depend on whether the constituencies whose support politicians require are easier to win over with public goods or targeted policies. For example, competing for the votes of the middle class—which demands public goods—can make politicians opt out of clientelism (Weitz-Shapiro 2012).

The engagement of disadvantaged groups through voting can change the incentives of political leaders. In the United States, laws that extended women's suffrage were followed by increases in public health spending and door-to-door hygiene campaigns (Miller 2008). In Brazil, the effective enfranchisement of poorer and less educated voters, thanks to improvements in voting technology using electronic ballots, contributed to an increase in the number of prenatal visits by health professionals, and possibly to a decrease in the prevalence of low birth weights among less educated voters (Fujiwara 2015).

New experimental evidence indicates that communication and deliberation can help overcome clientelism. More avenues for communication can allow politicians and voters to uncover common interests. They can also allow voters to learn about one another's preferences and expectations and to update beliefs about candidate quality. For example, experimental evidence from Benin suggests that town hall meetings reduce the prevalence of clientelism

(Fujiwara and Wantchekon 2013). The effects may be ambiguous, however, because increased communication may also help to better identify targeted short-term benefits.

The provision of information can help transform incentives and overcome collective action problems, but information alone is not enough. In the case of tax reforms, people may misinterpret the effects of a redistributive reform, prompting them to oppose it even though it would benefit them (Cruces, Perez-Truglia, and Tetaz 2013). For example, Bolivia tried to introduce a progressive personal income tax with a flat rate of 12.5 percent and a no-tax threshold of twice the minimum wage. The announcement of the reform led to massive public protests, including by certain professionals who believed they would bear the largest cost of the reform, even though their salaries fell in the no-tax area. The government's inadequate effort to explain that the tax would have affected only a small group of high earners and mistakes in communicating the reform, such as addressing the group of potential losers as the "middle class," contributed to the demise of the tax (Fairfield 2013). By contrast, in Uruguay, during the successful personal income tax reform in 2006, the government effectively communicated that only wealthier individuals would be affected (Rius 2015).

Information is, in theory, a critical tool to monitor elites, including service providers. For example, an experiment in primary health care in Uganda that mimicked traditional community-driven development approaches found that the quality of care or health outcomes improved only in the subgroup in which communities were also provided with information on the relative performance of the facilities. Such information helps identify what is within the control of policy makers or service providers (Bjorkman, De Walque, and Svensson 2014). In Pakistan, a randomized experiment that gave parents information on the performance of private and public schools increased test scores, decreased private school fees, and increased primary enrollment (Andrabi, Das, and Khwaja 2015).

However, the provision of information on its own often fails to improve delivery because many implicit assumptions link the provision of information to improving services. In particular, information on local interventions may improve outcomes only when the constraints related to asymmetries in bargaining power are alleviated. For example, in an experiment in Kenya, providing information on children's performance in schools and how parents could

> The provision of information can help transform incentives and overcome collective action problems, but information alone is not enough.

take action to help their children did not increase parents' participation in monitoring. The study suggests that experiments providing information make many implicit assumptions; two important ones in this case that seem to be wrong are that parents think that monitoring services is their responsibility and that they can do anything about it (Lieberman, Posner, and Tsai 2014).

Other mechanisms, such as earmarking resources, can also change incentives for adopting policies. Bundling reforms that improve equity with other reforms that matter to opposing elites may increase their buy-in. For example, in tax reforms earmarking can help garner support. Although earmarking has been criticized for generating rigidities in the fiscal system, it has been used often to improve commitment and convince elites to accept reforms (Fairfield 2013). Colombia, for example, managed to pass a wealth tax levied on the richest 1 percent of the population because the tax revenues were explicitly devoted to security and crime reduction.

Shaping preferences to increase cooperation

Collective action—particularly cooperation—can be enhanced by building common interest. It is argued that external conflicts have played a role in development by helping build common interest against a common enemy (Besley and Persson 2010). However, stressing the identity of certain groups and improving their participation in policies may improve the outcomes for these groups, but it could come at the expense of other groups, or at the expense of longer-term benefits. For example, in India the political reservations (electoral quotas) for scheduled tribes increased social welfare spending in their favor, but they decreased spending on education (Pande 2003). Scheduled tribes may perceive that they will receive low returns on their education and thus may decide to invest less in it. Although higher social welfare spending is beneficial to them, it comes at the expense of redistribution that could benefit other groups and that may be more beneficial in the long term.

Rigorous work on how to build common interest in times of peace is lacking, but there is evidence that education can play a role. A study of border regions in Kenya and Tanzania that were "artificially" divided by colonial powers and thus share many common characteristics found that ethnic fractionalization does not lead to the underprovision of public goods on the Tanzanian side of the border as much as it does on the Kenyan side of the border. Miguel (2004) attributes this finding to the fact that schools in Tanzania more actively foster a national identity than do schools in Kenya, thereby improving cooperation in the provision of public goods.

Enhancing contestability

Increasing the direct representation of disadvantaged or minority individuals in legislative assemblies and other political bodies can help sustain commitment to pro-equity reforms. For example, the significant increase in the proportion of women in national legislative assemblies over the last 20 years (even though, at below 30 percent, it remains low) has helped to bring about policies that are more aligned with women's preferences. Evidence from India demonstrates that women taking part in village councils vote for public goods that are more aligned with their preferences and that improve health, such as investments in safe drinking water (Chattopadhyay and Duflo 2004). Other studies find that political reservations (electoral quotas) for scheduled tribes and castes lead to higher spending on social welfare for scheduled tribes and more jobs for scheduled castes (Pande 2003). Ultimately, the political representation of disadvantaged groups seems to be effective in reducing poverty (Chin and Prakash 2011).

Involving excluded groups in the design and implementation of specific policies, such as taxation, can help increase cooperation. One promising example is explicitly taxing the informal sector in developing countries.[8] In Ghana, as of 1981 informal public transport workers were successfully incorporated into formal tax policy, thanks to the delegation of tax collection to informal sector associations. This arrangement is believed to have increased tax revenues (Joshi and Ayee 2009), and it was extended to 32 other informal sector associations (Joshi, Prichard, and Heady 2014). An important element of the success of this policy is that it improved taxpayer services, providing incentives for cooperation. Importantly, it introduced a culture of tax compliance in a sector previously neglected by the tax authorities. Ultimately, the associational form of taxation moved in 2003 to a more cost-efficient presumptive tax regime in which drivers are asked every quarter to buy a sticker and display it on their vehicle's windshield (Prichard 2009).

In service delivery, "empowering" users by involving them in management can help improve services and reduce capture. For example, when parents' councils at schools are well trained and have credible sanctions, they can improve educational outcomes (Bruns,

Involving excluded groups in the design and implementation of specific policies, such as taxation, can help increase cooperation.

Filmer, and Patrinos 2011). In a reform experiment in Kenya to hire contract teachers, capture by civil service teachers was lower by a third in the subgroup of schools in which school committees received training in school-based management. In this subgroup, the school committee was better able to monitor the hiring of contract teachers and reduce absenteeism and the hiring of relatives (figure 6.7).

Reducing power asymmetries through contestability mechanisms is not without challenges, however. Capture can occur even in participatory programs, such as community-driven development, that specifically seek to include disadvantaged individuals in policy-making processes. These individuals may participate less in these processes because of the higher opportunity costs of their leisure time, or because entrenched social norms make it hard to oppose those who traditionally hold more power (box 6.5). This is an example of how good institutional forms sometimes fail to perform their functions.

Measures to empower users may work best if they are linked to political authorities in order to change the power dynamics with providers. In Indonesia, for example, a field experiment compared various mechanisms to strengthen school committees. The results suggested that linking school committees,

Figure 6.7 Empowering parents with school-based management training helps lessen capture (teacher absenteeism) in Kenya

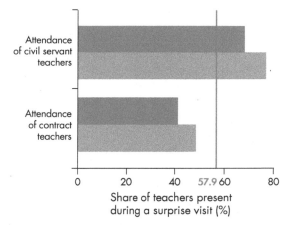

Share of teachers present during a surprise visit (%)

■ Schools that hired additional contract teachers

■ Schools that hired additional contract teachers and had school-based management training

— Teacher attendance in schools that did not hire additional contract teachers (control group)

Source: WDR 2017 team, based on Duflo, Dupas, and Kremer 2015.

Note: Attendance was measured by the percentage of teachers present in school during a surprise visit.

Box 6.5 Local elites can capture public spending despite participatory programs

Reforms to increase public spending in favor of disadvantaged individuals may be captured by local elites, who can disproportionately sway expenditure decisions (Galasso and Ravallion 2005). Capture occurs even in participatory programs such as community-driven development (CDD), despite program objectives to include disadvantaged individuals in spending decisions. CDDs are a form of decentralization of spending that seeks to allow decisions to be better aligned with the preferences of local communities and, through participation, foster collective action. A review of participatory programs, however, has found evidence that the poor benefit less from these programs than the better-off (Mansuri and Rao 2013).

Existing patterns of inequality and poverty shape how collective action takes place in villages. One reason CDDs may not benefit poor people is that even when, on paper, the poor are supposed to take part in decisions, in practice

they do so less often and to a lesser extent than more advantaged individuals—that is, in the framework of this Report, CDDs often fail to improve contestability because they do not lower the entry barriers for the poor in decision making. As a review of participatory programs found, participants in "civic activities tend to be wealthier, more educated, of higher social status (by caste and ethnicity), male, and more politically connected than nonparticipants" (Mansuri and Rao 2013, 5). The opportunity cost to participate is higher for the poor because they have less leisure time and need to work longer hours to generate income. In addition, when they participate, it is more difficult for them to influence outcomes because they are less educated or may find it difficult to debate with and contradict individuals who traditionally hold influence and authority (Abraham and Platteau 2004).

Source: WDR 2017 team.

which are considered relatively powerless, to elected village councils through joint meetings and action plans was the most cost-effective method to increase test scores. Linking school committees to village councils alleviated some of the power constraints that committees faced on their own (Pradhan and others 2014).

If the credibility of sanctions by parents and communities is limited, empowering parents may not be effective. In the absence of formal sanctions to hire and fire (such as in well-trained school councils), school-based management may exercise influence by exerting social pressure on providers. However, when teachers or health workers are wealthier or more influential than the users of their services, the latter may not be able to exert social pressure. For example, interventions to empower communities to monitor health clinics in Uganda are less successful in areas with higher inequality (Bjorkman and Svensson 2010). In Mexico, grade failure and dropout rates were not reduced in poorer communities after a school-based management program was rolled out (Gertler, Patrinos, and Rubio-Codina 2012).

Given the limits of local actors, what matters for more significant reforms is the balance of power between providers and politicians and how they bargain. Some reforms that have managed to include unions and balance their power have succeeded. For example, in Chile ambitious education reforms were passed because of the inclusion of unions in a setting in which the executive had high credibility. Workers approved the increase in spending in exchange for performance pay reforms (Mizala and Schneider 2014).

Improving policy effectiveness by taking into account asymmetries in bargaining power

Policies can be blocked, captured, or rendered ineffective when their design does not account for asymmetries in bargaining power. Assuming that some actors want to implement reforms that improve equity, how can these reforms be designed, passed, and implemented effectively?

Asymmetries in bargaining power need not result in failed policies. Reforms can be successful in improving equity if their design takes into account how the bargaining power of different actors will affect policy implementation, including at the national and local

levels, across income groups, and between service providers and users.

To design more effective policies, those in the policy arena must understand the existing patterns of inequality. For example, anyone considering at which level reforms should be implemented should take into account how national and local elites shape policies. Although decentralization or participatory development may seem promising on paper, elites may be more entrenched at the local level than at the national level (Bardhan 2002). Indeed, one of the founding documents of the United States, *The Federalist Papers*, argued for the need for federal intervention because of the risk that vested interests would capture local governments, leaving minorities less protected (Hamilton, Madison, and Jay 1788).[9] Decentralization can also create spaces where de jure power and de facto power conflict, potentially undermining policies. In some Sub-Saharan African countries, opportunities for bribes stem in part from incomplete decentralization; central authorities may, for example, try to retain power over land allocation in practice despite de jure decentralization (Durand-Lasserve, Durand-Lasserve, and Selod 2015). Policy design needs to be comprehensive and reduce room for local elites to intervene adversely. For example, increasing resources that aim to fund pro-poor policies may increase the incentives of local elites to be involved in policy making in order to capture these new resources (Mansuri and Rao 2013).

Beyond national and local elites, it is important to weigh how different groups in society will shape the effective implementation of policies. In the case of social safety nets, failing to take into account the different bargaining power of the actors involved, at every stage of the design, may lead to the failure of reforms. For example, although social safety nets that target the poor may be cost-effective for reducing poverty, such policies may face opposition from groups that do not benefit from them (box 6.6). Project design can partly improve the performance of community projects and decrease the adverse impacts of local inequality. For example, in 99 rural communities in northern Pakistan, projects that required more labor inputs (to which villagers could contribute directly and thus monitor) and less capital (which is more difficult to monitor) were better maintained, even in communities where land inequality was high (Khwaja 2009).

This chapter has described various mechanisms for adopting and effectively implementing equity-oriented policies, but these mechanisms come into

Box 6.6 Designing social safety nets to account for asymmetries in bargaining power

Asymmetries in bargaining power matter at every stage of the design of social safety nets. Policy makers and development practitioners need to decide whether to target a particular group, how to target it, how to operationalize the program, and how to choose the nature of the benefits.

Whether to target a particular group. Gauging the influence and bargaining power of actors matters at the earliest design stages when deciding whether to target a particular group at all. Because of financial constraints, targeting the poor may be the most cost-efficient policy to reduce poverty. The "first-best" approach may be to reform consumer subsidies to protect the poor from price increases. However, passing the reform may require compensating other groups that may be more connected to political elites or better able to organize to demonstrate. For example, when the Dominican Republic adopted gasoline subsidy reforms, the transport industry was influential enough to obtain compensation for the reforms. Such compensation may not be cost-efficient, but failing to compensate the industry could have stopped the reform from passing altogether. Similarly, the compensatory cash transfers for removing the electricity subsidy also covered part of the middle class to preempt opposition (Gallina and others, forthcoming).

Targeting methodology. The choice of targeting methodology also needs to take into account the existing bargaining power among actors. Indeed, when it is not easy to target the poorest, putting communities in charge of allocating benefits may appear to be the best technical solution. However, in practice it may allow members of the elites to block or capture programs or use them for political gain.

Operationalization. For a given reform design, its operationalization must also take into account asymmetries in bargaining power: who registers applicants, who validates applications, and who is present during the process. Politicians may want to be involved at every step for political gain. However, when they are, the benefits of the reform may shift toward political supporters, although there is no clear evidence about the extent of the bias (Weitz-Shapiro 2012).

Amount and nature of benefits. In choosing the amount and nature of benefits, the approach that is the technical first-best may not be the preferred tool of policy makers. Giving cash to households is usually the technically first-best approach because it allows them to better allocate their total expenditure. Incumbent authorities, however, may prefer to distribute food because it is easier to publicize and exploit for political gain. This loss of efficiency may be further aggravated if the authorities prefer food for more lucrative reasons—because it may benefit influential food-importing and transporting groups (Graham 1994).

All the initial choices in program design can have longer-term or spillover negative consequences by further entrenching power relations. These choices could, however, help pass reforms in the short term. Reforms, by improving the livelihoods of the poor and their investment in human capital, can ultimately help rebalance power in their favor. Some cash transfer programs in Latin America are credited with contributing to the empowerment of the poorest citizens. However, these trade-offs may also reinforce vested interests, such as food importers when benefits are in kind, or local elites when the only way to implement reforms is to involve the elites in the allocation of benefits. Such trade-offs need to be carefully considered when designing reforms.

Sources: Aline Coudouel, World Bank Social Protection, Labor, and Jobs Global Practice, and WDR 2017 team.

---

play only if processes for change have already begun. Part III of this Report delves into these processes. Chapter 7 examines when and how elites permit new actors to bargain over policies, including through changes in incentives or preferences. When elite bargains are not conducive to more accountability to citizens, disadvantaged groups may organize in order to have more voice in society. This possibility is discussed in chapter 8. Chapter 9 concludes this Report by examining the role of international actors and processes in influencing the domestic policy arena.

Notes

1. Philosopher John Rawls (1971) starts his classic *A Theory of Justice* by saying that "justice is the first virtue of social institutions, as truth is of systems of thought." Rawls associated the notion of justice precisely with *fairness*.
2. Along the same lines, Sen (2002) discusses the notion of opportunity freedom and process freedom.
3. In 1974 sociologist James Coleman wrote a critique of Rawls's *A Theory of Justice* in the *American Journal of Sociology* (Coleman 1974). In that critique, he mentions

that Rawls dismissed a whole line of work in sociology that discusses the notions of "ascription versus achievement." Ascription refers to status. Every child born—even though he or she does not have any achievement yet (related to effort)—has a position in the distribution of power in society, as determined by the status of his or her parent or parents.

4. Atkinson (2015); Bourguignon (2015); Milanović (2016).
5. This estimate includes village-level controls (among others, distance to natural water sources, distance to railways and national roads, soil quality measures, rainfall levels, total village population, proportion of village population belonging to the Maratha caste, whether the seat in the *gram panchayat* is reserved) and regional fixed effects (Anderson, Francois, and Kotwal 2015).
6. Gordin (2002); Calvo and Murillo (2004); Robinson and Verdier (2013).
7. Barreix and Roca (2008); Martorano (2014); OECD/ECLAC (2014).
8. The informal sector may already be indirectly affected by taxation on intermediate goods or trade taxes (Stiglitz 2010).
9. See especially *Federalist* No. 10, "The Same Subject Continued: The Union as a Safeguard Against Domestic Faction and Insurrection," written by James Madison and originally published anonymously in the *New York Daily Advertiser*, November 22, 1787.

References

Abraham, Anita, and Jean-Philippe Platteau. 2004. "Participatory Development: When Culture Creeps." In *Culture and Public Action*, edited by Vijayendra Rao and Michael Walton, 210-33. Stanford Social Sciences Series. Stanford, CA: Stanford University Press.

Abraham, Arthur, and Habib Sesay. 1993. "Regional Politics and Social Service Provision since Independence." In *The State and the Provision of Social Services in Sierra Leone since Independence, 1961–1991*, edited by C. Magbaily Fyle. Oxford, U.K.: Codesaria.

Acemoglu, Daron, and James A. Robinson. 2012. *Why Nations Fail: The Origins of Power, Prosperity, and Poverty*. New York: Crown Business.

Anderson, Siwan, Patrick Francois, and Ashok Kotwal. 2015. "Clientelism in Indian Villages." *American Economic Review* 105 (6): 1780–1816.

Andrabi, Tahir, Jishnu Das, and Asim I. Khwaja. 2015. "Report Cards: The Impact of Providing School and Child Test Scores on Educational Markets." Policy Research Working Paper 7226, World Bank, Washington, DC.

Atkinson, Anthony B. 2015. *Inequality: What Can Be Done?* London: Harvard University Press.

Atkinson, Anthony B., Thomas Piketty, and Emmanuel Saez. 2011. "Top Incomes in the Long Run of History." *Journal of Economic Literature* 49 (1): 3–71.

Banerjee, Abhijit, and Lakshmi Iyer. 2005. "History, Institutions, and Economic Performance: The Legacy of Colonial Land Tenure Systems in India." *American Economic Review* 95 (4): 1190–1213.

Bardhan, Pranab. 2002. "Decentralization of Governance and Development." *Journal of Economic Perspectives* 16 (4): 185–205.

Barr, Nicholas. 2001. *The Welfare State as Piggy Bank: Information, Risk, Uncertainty, and the Role of the State*. New York: Oxford University Press.

Barreix, A., and J. Roca. 2008. "Uruguay." In *Tax Systems and Tax Reforms in Latin America*, edited by L. Bernardi, A. Barreix, A. Marenzi, and P. Profeta. London: Routledge.

Bates, Robert H. 1981. *Markets and States in Tropical Africa: The Political Basis of Agricultural Policy*. California Series on Social Choice and Political Economy. Berkeley: University of California Press.

Besley, Timothy, and Torsten Persson. 2010. "State Capacity, Conflict, and Development." *Econometrica* 78 (1): 1–34.

Besley, Timothy, Torsten Persson, and Daniel M. Sturm. 2010. "Political Competition, Policy and Growth: Theory and Evidence from the US." *Review of Economic Studies* 77 (4): 1329–52.

Binswanger-Mkhize, Hans, Camille Bourguignon, and Rogier van den Brink. 2009. *Agricultural Land Redistribution: Toward Greater Consensus*. Washington, DC: World Bank.

Bjorkman, Martina, Damien De Walque, and Jakob Svensson. 2014. "Information Is Power: Experimental Evidence on the Long-Run Impact of Community-Based Monitoring." Policy Research Working Paper 7015, World Bank, Washington, DC.

Bjorkman, Martina, and Jakob Svensson. 2010. "When Is Community-Based Monitoring Effective? Evidence from a Randomized Experiment in Primary Health in Uganda." *Journal of the European Economic Association* 8 (2–3): 571–81.

Bold, Tessa, Yanina Domenella, Ezequiel Molina, and Abla Safir. 2016. "Clientelism in the Public Sector: Why Public Service Reforms May Not Succeed and What to Do about It." Background paper, WDR 2017, World Bank, Washington, DC.

Bold, Tessa, Bernard Gauthier, Jakob Svensson, and Waly Wane. 2011. *Service Delivery Indicators: Pilot in Education and Health Care in Africa*. Washington, DC: World Bank.

Bold, Tessa, Mwangi Kimenyi, Germano Mwabu, Alice Ng'ang'a, and Justin Sandefur. 2013. "Scaling-Up What Works: Experimental Evidence on External Validity in Kenyan Education," CSAE Working Paper Series 2013-04, Centre for the Study of African Economies, University of Oxford.

Bold, Tessa, Mwangi Kimenyi, Germano Mwabu, Alice Ng'ang'a, and Justin Sandefur. 2015. "Interventions and Institutions: Experimental Evidence on Scaling Up Education Reforms in Kenya." Unpublished paper, Center for Global Development, Washington, DC.

Bourguignon, François. 2015. *The Globalization of Inequality*. Translated by Thomas Scott-Railton. Princeton, NJ: Princeton University Press.

Bouton, Laurent, Micael Castanheira, and Garance Genicot. 2016. "Inequalities in Government Interventions: Literature Review." Background paper, WDR 2017, World Bank, Washington, DC.

Bruns, Barbara, Deon Filmer, and Harry Anthony Patrinos. 2011. *Making Schools Work: New Evidence on Accountability Reforms*. Human Development Perspectives Series. Washington, DC: World Bank.

Calvo, Ernesto, and Maria Victoria Murillo. 2004. "Who Delivers? Partisan Clients in the Argentine Electoral Market." *American Journal of Political Science* 48 (4): 742–57.

Chattopadhyay, Raghabendra, and Esther Duflo. 2004. "Women as Policy Makers: Evidence from a Randomized Policy Experiment in India." *Econometrica* 72 (5): 1409–43.

Chaudhury, Nazmul, Jeffrey Hammer, Michael Kremer, Karthik Muralidharan, and F. Halsey Rogers. 2006. "Missing in Action: Teacher and Health Worker Absence in Developing Countries." *Journal of Economic Perspectives* 20 (1): 91–116.

Chenery, Hollis B., Montek S. Ahluwalia, C. L. G. Bell, John H. Daly, and Richard Jolly. 1974. *Redistribution with Growth: Policies to Improve Income Distribution in Developing Countries in the Context of Economic Growth*. London: Oxford University Press.

Chin, Aimee, and Nishith Prakash. 2011. "The Redistributive Effects of Political Reservation for Minorities: Evidence from India." *Journal of Development Economics* 96 (2): 265–77.

Christ, Matthew R. 1990. "Liturgy Avoidance and Antidosis in Classical Athens." *Transactions of the American Philological Association* 120: 147–69.

Coady, David, Ian W. H. Parry, Louis Sears, and Baoping Shang. 2015. "How Large Are Global Energy Subsidies?" IMF Working Paper 15/105, International Monetary Fund, Washington, DC.

Coleman, J. 1974. "Inequality, Sociology, and Moral Philosophy." *American Journal of Sociology* 80 (3).

Cruces, Guillermo, Ricardo Perez-Truglia, and Martin Tetaz. 2013. "Biased Perceptions of Income Distribution and Preferences for Redistribution: Evidence from a Survey Experiment." *Journal of Public Economics* 98 (February): 100–12.

Cruz, Cesi. 2013. "Social Networks and the Targeting of Vote Buying." Paper presented at the American Political Science Association's Annual Meeting, APSA 2013, Chicago, August 29–September 1.

Dal Bó, Pedro, Andrew Foster, and Louis Putterman. 2010. "Institutions and Behavior: Experimental Evidence on the Effects of Democracy." *American Economic Review* 100 (5): 2205–29.

Dávalos, María Eugenia, Giorgia DeMarchi, Indhira V. Santos, Barbara Kits, and Isil Oral. 2016. "Voices of Europe and Central Asia: New Insights on Shared Prosperity and Jobs." World Bank, Washington, DC.

De Ferranti, David, Guillermo E. Perry, Francisco H. G. Ferreira, and Michael Walton. 2004. *Inequality in Latin America: Breaking with History?* World Bank Latin American and Caribbean Studies Series. Washington, DC: World Bank.

Duflo, Esther, Pascaline Dupas, and Michael Kremer. 2015. "School Governance, Teacher Incentives, and Pupil-Teacher Ratios: Experimental Evidence from Kenyan Primary School." *Journal of Public Economics* 123 (March): 92–110.

Durand-Lasserve, Alain, Maÿlis Durand-Lasserve, and Harris Selod. 2015. *Land Delivery Systems in West African Cities: The Example of Bamako, Mali*. Africa Development Forum Series. Washington, DC: World Bank.

Engerman, Stanley L., and Kenneth L. Sokoloff. 2002. "Factor Endowments, Inequality, and Paths of Development among New World Economies." NBER Working Paper 9259, National Bureau of Economic Research, Cambridge, MA.

Esteban, Joan, and Debraj Ray. 2006. "Inequality, Lobbying, and Resource Allocation." *American Economic Review* 96 (1): 257–79.

European Bank for Reconstruction and Development. 2010. Life in Transition Survey. http://www.ebrd.com/what-we-do/economic-research-and-data/data/lits.html.

Fairfield, Tasha. 2013. "Going Where the Money Is: Strategies for Taxing Economic Elites in Unequal Democracies." *World Development* 47 (7): 42–57.

Ferraz, Claudio, and Frederico Finan. 2011. "Electoral Accountability and Corruption: Evidence from the Audits of Local Governments." *American Economic Review* 101 (4): 1274–1311.

Ferraz, Claudio, Frederico Finan, and Diana B. Moreira. 2012. "Corrupting Learning: Evidence from Missing Federal Education Funds in Brazil." *Journal of Public Economics* 96 (9–10): 712–26.

Ferreira, Francisco H. G. 2012. "Distributions in Motion: Economic Growth, Inequality, and Poverty Dynamics." *The Oxford Handbook of the Economics of Poverty*, edited by Philip N. Jefferson, 427–62. New York: Oxford University Press.

Ferreira, Francisco H. G., Julián Messina, Jamele Rigolini, Luis Felipe López-Calva, María Ana Lugo, and Renos Vakis. 2013. *Economic Mobility and the Rise of the Latin American Middle Class*. Washington, DC: World Bank.

Ferreira, Francisco H. G., and Vito Peragine. 2015. "Equality of Opportunity: Theory and Evidence." Policy Research Working Paper 7217, World Bank, Washington, DC.

Fujiwara, Thomas. 2015. "Voting Technology, Political Responsiveness, and Infant Health: Evidence from Brazil." *Econometrica* 83 (2): 423–64.

Fujiwara, Thomas, and Leonard Wantchekon. 2013. "Can Informed Public Deliberation Overcome Clientelism?

Experimental Evidence from Benin." *American Economic Journal: Applied Economics* 5 (4): 241–55.

Galasso, Emanuela, and Martin Ravallion. 2005. "Decentralized Targeting of an Antipoverty Program." *Journal of Public Economics* 89 (4): 705–27.

Gallina, Andrea, Gabriela Inchauste, Pavel Isa, Catherine Lee, and Miguel Sanchez. Forthcoming. "Dominican Republic." In *The Political Economy of Energy Subsidy Reform*, edited by Gabriela Inchauste and David Victor. Washington, DC: World Bank.

Gertler, Paul, Harry Patrinos, and Marta Rubio-Codina. 2012. "Empowering Parents to Improve Education: Evidence from Rural Mexico." *Journal of Development Economics* 99 (1): 68–79.

Giovarelli, Renee, Elizabeth Katz, Susan Lastarria-Cornhiel, and Sue Nichols. 2005. "Gender Issues and Best Practices in Land Administration Projects: A Synthesis Report." Report 32571-GLB, World Bank, Washington, DC.

GLD (Program on Governance and Local Development). 2016. Governance and Local Development Surveys. University of Gothenburg, Gothenburg, Sweden, http://gld.gu.se/.

Goeree, Jacob, and Leeal Yariv. 2011. "An Experimental Study of Collective Deliberation." *Econometrica* 79 (3): 893–921.

Goldstein, Markus, and Christopher Udry. 2008. "The Profits of Power: Land Rights and Agricultural Investment in Ghana." *Journal of Political Economy* 116 (6): 981–1022.

Gordin, Jorge P. 2002. "The Political and Partisan Determinants of Patronage in Latin America, 1960–1994: A Comparative Perspective." *European Journal of Political Research* 41 (4): 513–49.

Graham, Carol L. 1994. *Safety Nets, Politics, and the Poor: Transitions to Market Economies.* Washington, DC: Brookings Institution Press.

Habermas, Jurgen. 1996. *Between Facts and Norms: Contributions to a Discourse Theory of Law and Democracy.* Cambridge, MA: MIT Press.

Habyarimana, James, Macartan Humphreys, Daniel N. Posner, and Jeremy M. Weinstein. 2007. "Why Does Ethnic Diversity Undermine Public Goods Provision?" *American Political Science Review* 101 (4): 709–25.

Hamilton, Alexander, James Madison, and John Jay. 1788. *The Federalist: A Collection of Essays, Written in Favour of the New Constitution, as Agreed upon by the Federal Convention, September 17, 1787.* 2 vols. New York: J. and A. M'Lean.

Herbst, Jeffrey I. 2000. *States and Power in Africa: Comparative Lessons in Authority and Control.* Princeton, NJ: Princeton University Press.

Hicken, Allen. 2011. "Clientelism." *Annual Review of Political Science* 14 (1): 289–310.

Hirschman, Albert O. 1970. *Exit, Voice, and Loyalty: Responses to Decline in Firms, Organizations, and States.* Cambridge, MA: Harvard University Press.

Hoff, Karla, and Priyanka Pandey. 2006. "Discrimination, Social Identity, and Durable Inequalities." *American Economic Review* 96 (2): 206–11.

Holland, Alisha, and Brian Palmer-Rubin. 2015. "Beyond the Machine: Clientelist Brokers and Interest Organizations in Latin America." *Comparative Political Studies* 48 (9): 1186–1223.

Igan, Deniz, and Prachi Mishra. 2014. "Wall Street, Capitol Hill, and K Street: Political Influence and Financial Regulation." *Journal of Law and Economics* 57 (4): 1063–84.

Inchauste, Gabriela, and Nora Lustig. Forthcoming. "Fiscal Policy and Redistribution." In *Distributional Impact of Taxes and Transfers: Evidence from Eight Developing Countries*, edited by Gabriela Inchauste and Nora Lustig. Washington, DC: World Bank.

Joshi, Anuradha, and Joseph Ayee. 2009. "Autonomy or Organization? Reforms in the Ghanaian Internal Revenue Service." *Public Administration and Development* 29 (4): 289–302.

Joshi, Anuradha, Wilson Prichard, and Christopher J. Heady. 2014. "Taxing the Informal Economy: The Current State of Knowledge and Agendas for Future Research." *Journal of Development Studies* 50 (10): 1325–47.

Khemani, Stuti. 2015. "Buying Votes versus Supplying Public Services: Political Incentives to Under-Invest in Pro-poor Policies." *Journal of Development Economics* 177 (C): 84–93.

Khemani, Stuti, Ernesto Dal Bó, Claudio Ferraz, Frederico Finan, Corinne Stephenson, Adesinaola Odugbemi, Dikshya Thapa, and Scott Abrahams. 2016. *Making Politics Work for Development: Harnessing Transparency and Citizen Engagement.* Policy Research Report. Washington, DC: World Bank.

Khwaja, Asim. 2009. "Can Good Projects Succeed in Bad Communities?" *Journal of Public Economics* 93 (7): 899–916.

Lieberman, Evan. 2003. "Race and Regionalism in the Politics of Taxation in Brazil and South Africa." Cambridge, U.K.: Cambridge University Press.

Lieberman, Evan S., Daniel N. Posner, and Lily L. Tsai. 2014. "Does Information Lead to More Active Citizenship? Evidence from an Education Intervention in Rural Kenya." *World Development* 60 (C): 69–83.

Lindert, Peter H. 2004. *Growing Public: Social Spending and Economic Growth since the Eighteenth Century,* Vol. 1 of *The Story.* New York: Cambridge University Press.

Lustig, Nora, Luis F. López-Calva, and Eduardo Ortiz-Juárez. 2015. "Deconstructing the Decline in Inequality in Latin America." In *Proceedings of IEA Roundtable on Shared Prosperity and Growth,* edited by Kaushik Basu and Joseph Stiglitz. New York: Palgrave Macmillan.

Mansuri, Ghazala, and Vijayendra Rao. 2013. *Localizing Development: Does Participation Work?* Policy Research Report. Washington, DC: World Bank.

Markussen, Thomas, and Finn Tarp. 2014. "Political Connections and Land-Related Investment in Rural Vietnam." *Journal of Development Economics* 110 (C): 291–302.

Martorano, Bruno. 2014. "The Impact of Uruguay's 2007 Tax Reform on Equity and Efficiency." *Development Policy Review* 32 (6): 701–14.

Migdal, Joel S. 1988. *Strong Societies and Weak States: State-Society Relations and State Capabilities in the Third World*. Princeton, NJ: Princeton University Press.

Miguel, Edward. 2004. "Tribe or Nation? Nation-Building and Public Goods in Kenya versus Tanzania." *World Politics* 56 (3): 327–62.

Miguel, Edward, and Mary Kay Gugerty. 2005. "Ethnic Diversity, Social Sanctions, and Public Goods in Kenya." *Journal of Public Economics* 89 (11–12): 2325–68.

Milanović, Branko. 2016. "Why Might the Rich Be Indifferent to Income Growth of Their Own Countries?" *Economics Letters* 147 (October): 108–11.

Milazzo, Annamaria. 2016. "Governance and Women's Economic and Political Participation: Formal Constraints, Norms and Power." Background paper, WDR 2017, World Bank, Washington, DC.

Miller, Grant. 2008. "Women's Suffrage, Political Responsiveness, and Child Survival in American History." *Quarterly Journal of Economics* 123 (3): 1287–1327.

Mizala, Alejandra, and Ben Ross Schneider. 2014. "Negotiating Education Reform: Teacher Evaluations and Incentives in Chile (1990–2010)." *Governance* 27 (1): 87–109.

OECD/ECLAC (Organisation for Economic Co-operation and Development/Economic Commission for Latin America and the Caribbean). 2014. *Multi-dimensional Review of Uruguay*, Vol. 1 of *Initial Assessment, OECD Development Pathways*. Paris: OECD Publishing.

Olken, Benjamin A. 2010. "Direct Democracy and Local Public Goods: Evidence from a Field Experiment in Indonesia." *American Political Science Review* 104 (2): 243–67.

Pande, Rohini. 2003. "Can Mandated Political Representation Increase Policy Influence for Disadvantaged Minorities?" *American Economic Review* 93 (4): 1132–51.

Perry, Guillermo E., William F. Maloney, Omar S. Arias, Pablo Fajnzylber, Andrew D. Mason, and Jaime Saavedra-Chanduvi. 2007. *Informality: Exit and Exclusion*. World Bank Latin American and Caribbean Studies Series. Washington, DC: World Bank.

Pradhan, Menno, Daniel Suryadarma, Amanda Beatty, Maisy Wong, Armida Alisjahbana, Arya Gaduh, and Rima Prama Artha. 2014. "Improving Educational Quality through Enhancing Community Participation: Results from a Randomized Field Experiment in Indonesia." *American Economic Journal: Applied Economics* 6 (2): 105–26.

Prichard, Wilson. 2009. "The Politics of Taxation and Implications for Accountability in Ghana, 1981–2008." Working Paper 330, Institute of Development Studies, University of Sussex, Brighton, U.K.

Ransom, Roger L., and Richard Sutch. 2001. *One Kind of Freedom: The Economic Consequence of Emancipation*. New York: Cambridge University Press.

Rasul, IImran, and Daniel Rogger. 2015. "Management of Bureaucrats and Public Service Delivery: Evidence from the Nigerian Civil Service." LSE Research Online Documents on Economics 58161, London School of Economics and Political Science.

Rauch, James E., and Peter B. Evans. 2000. "Bureaucratic Structure and Bureaucratic Performance in Less Developed Countries." *Journal of Public Economics* 75 (1): 49–71.

Ravallion, Martin. 2015. *The Economics of Poverty: History, Measurement, and Policy*. New York: Oxford University Press.

Rawls, John. 1971. *A Theory of Justice*. Cambridge, MA: Harvard University Press.

———. 1997. "The Idea of Public Reason Revisited." *University of Chicago Law Review* 64 (3): 765–807.

Rius, Andrés. 2015. "The Uruguayan Tax Reform of 2006: Why Didn't It Fail?" In *Progressive Tax Reforms and Equality in Latin America*, edited by James E. Mahon Jr., Marcelo Bergman, and Cynthia J. Arnson, 64–100. Washington, DC: Woodrow Wilson International Center for Scholars.

Robinson, James A., and Thierry Verdier. 2013. "The Political Economy of Clientelism." *Scandinavian Journal of Economics* 115 (2): 260–91.

Rodríguez-Castelán, Carlos, Luis F. López-Calva, Nora Lustig, and Daniel Valderrama. 2016. "Understanding the Dynamics of Labor Income Inequality in Latin America." Working Paper 1608, Department of Economics, Tulane University, New Orleans.

Schady, Norbert R. 2000. "Seeking Votes: The Political Economy of Expenditures by the Peruvian Social Fund (FONCODES), 1991–95." *American Political Science Review* 94 (2): 289–304.

Schneider, Friedrich, Andreas Buehn, and Claudio E. Montenegro. 2011. "Shadow Economies All over the World: New Estimates for 162 Countries from 1999 to 2007." In *Handbook on the Shadow Economy*, edited by Friedrich Schneider, 9–77. Cheltenham, U.K.: Edward Elgar.

Schneider, Mark. 2015. "Does Clientelism Work? A Test of Guessability in India." Working Paper 2015–13, Center on the Politics of Development, University of California, Berkeley.

Sen, Amartya. 2002. *Rationality and Freedom*. Cambridge, MA: Harvard University Press.

Solé-Ollé, Albert. 2013. "Inter-regional Redistribution through Infrastructure Investment: Tactical or Programmatic?" *Public Choice* 156 (1–2): 229–52.

Stiglitz, Joseph E. 2010. "Development-Oriented Tax Policy." In *Taxation in Developing Countries, Six Case Studies and Policy Implications*, edited by Roger H. Gordon, 11–36. New York: Columbia University Press.

———. 2011. "Of the 1%, by the 1%, for the 1%." *Vanity Fair*, March 31. http://www.vanityfair.com/news/2011/05/top-one-percent-201105.

Stiglitz, Joseph E. 2012. *The Price of Inequality: How Today's Divided Society Endangers Our Future.* New York: Norton.

Stokes, Susan C. 2005. "Perverse Accountability: A Formal Model of Machine Politics with Evidence from Argentina." *American Political Science Review* 99 (3): 315–25.

———. 2009. "Political Clientelism," In *The Oxford Handbook of Comparative Politics*, edited by Carles Boix and Susan C. Stokes, 604–27. Oxford Handbooks of Political Science Series. New York: Oxford University Press.

University of Gothenburg. 2016. "Governance and Service Delivery in the Middle East and North Africa." Background paper, WDR 2017, World Bank, Washington, DC.

Wantchekon, Leonard. 2016. "Clientelism, Programmatic Politics, and Governance." Background paper, WDR 2017, World Bank, Washington, DC.

Weitz-Shapiro, Rebecca. 2012. "What Wins Votes: Why Some Politicians Opt Out of Clientelism." *American Journal of Political Science* 56 (3): 568–83.

Wiener, Jonathan M. 1978. *Social Origins of the New South: Alabama, 1860–1885.* Baton Rouge: Louisiana State University Press.

World Bank. 2003. *World Development Report 2004: Making Services Work for Poor People.* Washington, DC: World Bank; New York: Oxford University Press.

———. 2005. *World Development Report 2006: Equity and Development.* Washington, DC: World Bank; New York: Oxford University Press.

———. 2016. *Poverty and Shared Prosperity 2016: Taking On Inequality.* Washington, DC: World Bank.

World Bank, FAO (Food and Agriculture Organization of the United Nations), and IFAD (International Fund for Agricultural Development). 2009. "Module 4: Gender Issues in Land Policy and Administration." In *Gender in Agriculture Sourcebook*, 125–72. Agriculture and Rural Development Series. Washington, DC: World Bank.

Service delivery: Education and health

Improving access to health services and ensuring that students learn are essential to expanding opportunities for all citizens. Various market failures explain the need for collective action to deliver these services. However, power asymmetries often prevent the successful implementation of policies that improve health and education.

Public interventions: Needed for investments in human capital

Various market failures may make individuals underinvest in health and education. First, certain aspects of health and education are public goods, and many individuals can benefit from investments in them without paying. For example, spraying against mosquitoes in a neighborhood benefits all residents; those who do not pay for spraying cannot be excluded. As a result, some residents may free-ride and not pay for the spraying because they will benefit from it anyway. If all residents adopted this logic, spraying would ultimately not be funded.

Second, investments in human capital present externalities: the benefits to society from educating or promoting the health of individuals can be larger than their private benefits. Some may argue, for example, that education matters not only because of the economic gains it produces, but also because of its contribution to shaping civic behavior (Andrabi, Das, and Khwaja 2015). In addition, some levels of

education may be optimal only if all actors move together. Individuals may not invest in skills if they think that firms are not investing in complementary technologies, and firms may not invest in new technologies if they think they will not be able to find skilled workers (Acemoglu 1998). In some instances, such as the fight against communicable diseases, an individual has no incentive to invest in his or her own welfare if others do not invest as well.

Third, failures in other markets affect investments in human capital: individuals may not be able to borrow to make investments, or they may be misinformed about the gains from them. This is especially true for poorer or disadvantaged individuals. For example, because of credit constraints only those who have enough wealth may be able to invest in education. And because of lack of information, poorer children may be more likely to underestimate how wages increase with education, as a study in the Dominican Republic found (Jensen 2010).

Education: The challenges of delivering learning for all

The problems outlined in chapter 6 hamper education systems from achieving their goals. Bureaucratic forms do not necessarily serve their intended functions, often because power relationships prevent systems from promoting student learning equitably and efficiently. Moreover, norms consolidate power further and prevent laws and policies from being implemented as written.

In 2014 in Mozambique, 45 percent of primary school teachers and 44 percent of directors were absent from school during an unannounced visit by

WDR 2017 team, based on inputs from Paolo Belli and Halsey Rogers.

survey enumerators of the Service Delivery Indicators (SDI) initiative. However, even if schools managed to reduce teacher absenteeism to zero, pupils would not be able to learn what their teachers do not know. The survey found that in Mozambique only 65 percent of mathematics teachers could calculate 86 minus 55, and just 19 percent of teachers were able to develop a sound lesson plan.

Power dynamics undermine education reforms

In many cases, although policies seem to be in place to improve educational outcomes—for example, governments train teachers or carry out national assessments of student learning—such policies are nevertheless ineffective in improving outcomes.

Reforms have failed because they were thwarted by power dynamics. Indeed, reforms for hiring contract teachers have failed frequently. The idea behind hiring contract teachers is to reduce class size and employ teachers who are easier to sanction (thanks to the threat of firing or at least contract nonrenewal). Thus these teachers face stronger incentives.

However, teachers and their unions are a potent political force. When contract teachers ally with civil service teachers, they also become a potent political force that can lobby to be absorbed into the civil service. Over the last decade or two, large numbers of contract teachers have been "regularized" (given civil service status) in Kenya, Peru (Webb and Valencia 2006), Indonesia, and other countries. As discussed in chapter 6, this power dynamic demonstrates that, although policy makers should monitor teachers to ensure they deliver better learning, policy makers may in fact be dependent on teachers for political support. This dependence diminishes the willingness of policy makers to monitor and enforce performance.

This example reveals that if policy design ignores the power dynamics, a reform can leave the system worse off than before the reform. Teachers hired on contract are often less qualified than civil servant teachers, at least in terms of formal qualifications. Yet, schools, communities, and governments are willing to hire these contract teachers because they are willing to trade qualifications for effort. In the end, though, they have received the worst of both worlds from a service delivery perspective: once the less qualified contract teachers have been incorporated into the civil service, the country ends up with the same low effort, lower skills, and a higher budgetary cost.

Difficult education reforms can be effectively adopted and implemented

How can reforms change the power dynamics to improve the outcomes of education systems? Despite the gloomy picture overall, change can happen, most likely when reforms are successful in changing the incentives of teachers and policy makers, involving new actors in the policy bargaining arena, and changing norms.

Changing the incentives of policy makers and teachers through public awareness. Information is often viewed as a way in which policy makers can better monitor providers. However, information as a purely technical tool may not be enough. Rather, information is useful when it can be easily understood and targets those with incentives to act.

Improving public awareness of the unacceptably low levels of learning in many areas of a country has proven to be a successful policy for changing the incentives of teachers and policy makers and improving the quality of education. This idea underlies citizen-led assessments of student learning, such as the ASER Centre program in India and the Uwezo program in East Africa, both of which aim to improve data on and public awareness of the levels of learning. The same theory inspired efforts such as the SDI initiative in Sub-Saharan Africa. The SDI gathers data on both inputs and outcomes in representative samples of schools in many countries, and its data are useful for diagnosing problems and targeting support. But ultimately, the SDI effort is not just about fine-tuning an education system by turning technocratic dials, but also about shifting the equilibrium by marshaling public awareness to support reform.

Combining information and sequencing to build support for reforms. Many important education reforms have taken place over the last two decades, including in settings in which teacher unions play important roles. Policy makers who want to implement reforms can reach out to build support from other actors by first using information on student performance and directly communicating with the public. In some cases, such as in Ecuador, Mexico, and Peru, the resistance to efforts to reform education has been strong. But in Chile, where policy makers had high credibility with the unions because they were traditional allies, a process of continual negotiation paved the way for the passage of important reforms, such as bonus pay, including by bundling them with higher spending on education (Bruns and Luque 2015).

Bringing new actors into education policy: The role of parents. Directly involving parents in school policies is another way to change the power dynamics. However, it can work only when parents can credibly enforce sanctions. For example, why did giving more power to parents through school-based management (SBM) reforms work in Honduras but fail in Guatemala? Ganimian (2016) argues that in Honduras teachers' unions focused on higher-order problems such as wages, and the investment from the national government was small, especially in the beginning. As a result, SBM was able to endure through different administrations. In Guatemala, by contrast, the high cost of maintaining the program made it more vulnerable to special-interest groups, who managed to organize and successfully advocate to revert the reform.

Changing norms. Changing education systems also means promoting norms that support better behavior and promoting teachers who share these norms. Many teachers throughout the developing world make heroic efforts to educate children in extraordinarily difficult circumstances, contending with a lack of learning materials, student absenteeism, and threats to their safety. They do this at times out of altruistic concern for children, but they also may subscribe to a norm of teacher professionalism and a sense of duty. Ensuring that more such teachers are selected into public service and rewarded appropriately can help shift the composition of the teacher body and change the power dynamics.

Health: The challenges of improving access

Investments in health early in life are key to health later in life, as well as for education and learning outcomes (Almond, Chay, and Lee 2005; Black, Devereux, and Salvanes 2007). However, in many developing countries, and especially in low-income countries, the quality of health care is poor. As discussed in chapter 6, doctors are absent, and when they are present, they exert little effort or make mistakes in diagnosing and treating patients.

The state of Madhya Pradesh in India illustrates the challenge of poor availability and quality of care (Chaudhury and others 2006; Das and Hammer 2007). In a representative sample of rural areas of Madhya Pradesh, 40 percent of doctors in public health facilities were absent at any given time. Doctors in public facilities spent on average 2.4 minutes with a patient and completed only 16 percent of a checklist of examination items and questions on medical history. The same doctors performed better when they were in the private sector, indicating the importance of incentives. Nevertheless, virtually no doctors conducted all the examinations indicated when a child had diarrhea. Meanwhile, patients were much more likely to receive an unnecessary treatment than a correct one. Only 3 percent of doctors gave a correct treatment (Das and others 2015).

In addition, household out-of-pocket expenditures dominate health financing in low-income countries and in many middle-income countries (World Bank 2007). Ukraine illustrates the problem of out-of-pocket expenditures—including a gap between formal rules and actual practice. As in several other countries of the former Soviet Union, all Ukrainians have a constitutional right to access free health services. Nevertheless, direct payments by patients account for more than 40 percent of total health expenditures and are a heavy burden for the majority of Ukrainians.[1] De facto, patients pay an informal fee for almost every service offered by public health providers. These informal payments seem to be partly pocketed as informal income and split among the care providers (physicians and nurses), other health care personnel (chief doctors, hospital administrators), and political authorities at various levels. They are also used to finance the recurrent expenses of health facilities such as various supplies, refurbishment, and reconstruction (Belli, Dzhygyr, and Maynzyuk 2015).

Poor quality of care and high out-of-pocket payments are in part a result of the political equilibrium between the different actors involved in the process of adopting and implementing health policy. The following policy principles, however, can help to guide more effective health care reform.

Change the actors involved in health policy adoption and implementation

Involve more actors in hiring practices to break patronage. In Ukraine and other countries, patronage plays a decisive role in the recruitment and placement of doctors, especially for attractive positions—that is, those in which it is possible to extract more and larger informal payments. This scheme consolidates networks of personal connections and erects high entry barriers. Several Ukrainian health workers reported that they had to pay to secure a job or to retain their positions, and also that they had to maintain their discipline and loyalty to their line managers (Belli, Dzhygyr, and Maynzyuk 2015).

The patronage system, especially among doctors, should be reformed. In Ukraine, for example, broadening the set of actors involved in the process of hiring doctors holds promise. Some cities have introduced the requirement that the municipal health care department approve any appointment and dismissal of medical staff to stem the power of chief doctors.

Involve users, including through good use of information and monitoring. Involving communities can work to strengthen the quality of care and decrease absenteeism, provided that they have clear mandates and tools to monitor providers. An intervention designed to strengthen local accountability and community-based monitoring in the primary health care sector in Uganda was remarkably successful in improving both health services and outcomes in the participating communities (Björkman and Svensson 2009). The intervention consisted of a series of community meetings facilitated by a nongovernmental organization, using report cards on the quality of services and resulting in action plans. Utilization of outpatient services increased by 20 percent, and there were significant improvements in treatment practices, waiting time, examination procedures, and absenteeism. Most important, the weight of infants increased significantly, and the under-5 mortality rate fell by one-third in the treatment villages.

Change the incentives of politicians and providers

There are limits, however, to how much local control can achieve, in part because important components of the quality of service delivery are not determined locally. It may be necessary to change the incentives at a higher level or through top-down approaches to improve the delivery of health services.

Better incentives for policy makers can work if effectively implemented. The example of decentralization is often seen as an attempt to increase accountability because users/voters can better observe the efforts of policy makers. In Brazil, the public health system, which is funded primarily by transfers from the federal government and administered by the states and municipalities, is the main source of health care for the poor. Because of the competition for the votes of the uninsured (poor) who want public health care and the insured (richer) who do not, spending on health care is higher in municipalities where the proportion of poor is higher and where voter turnout is higher (Mobarak, Rajkumar, and Cropper 2011).

Decentralization can, however, be ineffective, simply adding a bureaucratic layer. And that is what happened in Ukraine. In the 1990s, following the disintegration of the centralized Soviet Union and the collapse of central revenues, most public services financing and administration, including health, were decentralized to the regional, district, and municipal levels. But only the municipal level was governed by elected officials; all other levels were governed by officials appointed from the center, thereby limiting the representativeness of local authorities. In addition, there was no clear assignment of new accountabilities. The process thus increased fragmentation because several levels of government financed, owned, and ran health facilities. Decentralization, then, ended up "crystalizing" the status quo—for example, making it impossible to streamline the excess infrastructure because health services became a source of patronage and informal revenue for local elites and senior doctors (Belli, Dzhygyr, and Maynzyuk 2015).

Better incentives for providers can work if effectively implemented. The introduction of performance-based budgeting schemes may improve the level and distribution of key health outcomes and change the incentives of health providers by making them more accountable. More research is needed to assess the effectiveness of these schemes, and their impact may depend on existing conditions. For example, in Ukraine the introduction of program-based budgeting collided with the existing detailed spending requirements and simply added a layer of bureaucracy. On the other hand, in Argentina the introduction of performance incentives to finance a provincial insurance scheme for maternal and child health care (Plan Nacer) improved not only the number of prenatal care visits, but also the quality of prenatal care and delivery. The incidence of low birth weight and neonatal mortality fell (Gertler, Giovagnoli, and Martinez 2014).

Note

1. In 2010, for example, about 60 percent of Ukrainians had at least partially forgone health care services because they could not afford them (Tambor and others 2014).

References

Acemoglu, Daron. 1998. "Why Do New Technologies Complement Skills? Directed Technical Change and Wage Inequality." *Quarterly Journal of Economics* 113 (4): 1055–89.

Almond, Douglas, Kenneth Y. Chay, and David S. Lee. 2005. "The Costs of Low Birth Weight." *Quarterly Journal of Economics* 120 (3): 1031–83.

Andrabi, Tahir, Jishnu Das, and Asim I. Khwaja. 2015. "Report Cards: The Impact of Providing School and Child Test Scores on Educational Markets." Policy Research Working Paper 7226, World Bank, Washington, DC.

Belli, Paolo, Yuriy Dzhygyr, and Kateryna Maynzyuk. 2015. *How Is It Working? A New Approach to Measure Governance in the Health System in Ukraine.* Washington, DC: World Bank.

Björkman, Martina, and Jakob Svensson. 2009. "Power to the People: Evidence from a Randomized Field Experiment on Community-Based Monitoring in Uganda." *Quarterly Journal of Economics* 124 (2): 735–69.

Black, Sandra E., Paul J. Devereux, and Kjell G. Salvanes. 2007. "From the Cradle to the Labor Market? The Effect of Birth Weight on Adult Outcomes." *Quarterly Journal of Economics* 122 (1): 409–39.

Bruns, Barbara, and Javier Luque. 2015. *Great Teachers: How to Raise Student Learning in Latin America and the Caribbean.* Latin American Development Forum Series. Washington, DC: World Bank.

Chaudhury, Nazmul, Jeffrey S. Hammer, Michael Kremer, Karthik Muralidharan, and F. Halsey Rogers. 2006. "Missing in Action: Teacher and Health Worker Absence in Developing Countries." *Journal of Economic Perspectives* 20 (1): 91–116.

Das, Jishnu, and Jeffrey S. Hammer. 2007. "Money for Nothing: The Dire Straits of Medical Practice in Delhi, India." *Journal of Development Economics* 83 (1): 1–36.

Das, Jishnu, Alaka Holla, Aakash Mohpal, and Karthik Muralidharan. 2015. "Quality and Accountability in Healthcare Delivery: Audit Evidence from Primary Care Providers in India." Policy Research Working Paper 7334, World Bank, Washington, DC.

Ganimian, Alejandro J. 2016. "Why Do Some School-Based Management Reforms Survive While Others Are Reversed? The Cases of Honduras and Guatemala." *International Journal of Educational Development* 47: 33–46.

Gertler, Paul, Paula Giovagnoli, and Sebastian Martinez. 2014. "Rewarding Provider Performance to Enable a Healthy Start to Life: Evidence from Argentina's Plan Nacer." Policy Research Working Paper 6884, World Bank, Washington, DC.

Jensen, Robert. 2010. "The (Perceived) Returns to Education and the Demand for Schooling." *Quarterly Journal of Economics* 125 (2): 515–48.

Mobarak, Ahmed Mushfiq, Andrew Sunil Rajkumar, and Maureen Cropper. 2011. "The Political Economy of Health Services Provision in Brazil." *Economic Development and Cultural Change* 59 (4): 723–51.

Tambor, Marzena, Milena Pavlova, Bernd Rechel, Stanislawa Golinowska, Christoph Sowada, and Wim Groot. 2014. "The Inability to Pay for Health Services in Central and Eastern Europe: Evidence from Six Countries." *European Journal of Public Health* 24 (3): 378–85.

Webb, Richard, and Sofía Valencia. 2006. "Human Resources in Public Health and Education in Peru." In *A New Social Contract for Peru: An Agenda for Improving Education, Health Care, and the Social Safety Net,* edited by Daniel Cotlear, 191–244. World Bank Country Study Series. Washington, DC: World Bank.

World Bank. Various years. Service Delivery Indicators (database). Washington, DC, http://datatopics.world bank.org/sdi/.

———. 2007. *Healthy Development: The World Bank Strategy for Health, Nutrition, and Population Results.* Washington, DC: World Bank.

PART III

Drivers of change

7.

**Elite bargaining
and adaptation**

8.

**Citizens as
agents of change**

9.

**Governance in an
interconnected world**

CHAPTER 7

Elite bargaining and adaptation

For the past four decades, China has been the world's fastest-growing country. Meanwhile, it has lifted over 700 million people out of poverty. According to many commonly used indicators, China's institutional environment during this period appears to have not changed. And yet these indicators fail to identify the deep changes to China's policy arena that facilitated adaptive policy decisions and enhanced state capacity and thus enabled China's economic and social transformation.

In China, the Communist Party of China (CPC) has been the sole governing party since 1949, consulting on a limited basis with eight minor parties. Nevertheless, China has significantly increased contestability by gradually changing processes for leadership selection and collective decision making at both central and local levels. In the years following Deng Xiaoping's 1980 assertion that "over-concentration of power is liable to give rise to arbitrary rule by individuals at the expense of collective leadership," the CPC broadened horizontal accountability and institutionalized collective leadership through norms on leadership transitions, rules on selection and retirement, consultative decision making, greater party institutionalization, bureaucratic professionalization, and the introduction of village elections. The growth of state and party bureaucracies, as well as organized business and societal interests, combined with decentralized economic power, led to a proliferation of organizational bases with bargaining power (Lampton 1987). All these reforms reflected the incentives and preferences of those in power: broader accountability and a more rules-based space for contestability helped solve commitment and collective action challenges within the ruling elite and thus

enhanced the stability of the ruling party during a period of tremendous change.

When powerful interests resist change, governance institutions that stunt inclusive development can persist. Yet history is rife with examples of countries that improved rules, institutions, and processes that constrained powerful interests and facilitated development progress. All of today's high-income countries were once poor and had unaccountable governments. These countries sustained economic growth over long periods, while improving social welfare and preventing violence. Sustained inclusive growth was facilitated by evolving institutions and rules of the game that constrained arbitrary behavior by decision makers, enhancing contestation in policy making, and increasing the accountability of decision makers. Such changes have been accomplished using different institutional forms. Some countries have broadened accountability within dominant political parties or opened the space for contestation only in specific domains or at the local administrative levels; others have introduced free and fair competitive elections and broad corporatist consultative arrangements.

Understanding elite bargains

The institutions and rules these countries established facilitated nonviolent and equitable development. But *why* did these durable institutions develop? Changes to the rules of the game that determine policy formulation and implementation result from a bargaining process among elite actors acting in their own interests. Reforms that limit the arbitrary exercise of power today may be necessary for maintaining or enhancing power or providing insurance against a loss of power

Changes to the rules of the game that determine policy formulation and implementation result from a bargaining process among elite actors acting in their own interests.

in the future. Formal institutions—moving from deals to rules—can enhance the credibility of commitments, overcoming coordination challenges and strengthening the stability of bargains among elites. In cases of long-term successful transformation, elite actors have adapted to changing circumstances by generating more capable, contestable, and accountable institutions. These institutions themselves helped enable further development.

The processes through which elite actors and the organizations that support them coordinate and commit to one another to determine outcomes can be thought of as *elite bargains*. Elite bargains are dynamic, constantly adapting to changes in the relative power, incentives, and preferences of elite actors. The development path is bumpy: shocks (such as terms of trade shocks and natural disasters) and gradual developments (such as urbanization or a growing middle class) alter elite power and preferences, often benefiting one group of elites at the expense of another. In the face of these changes, many deals-based bargains that cannot accommodate new actors or demands collapse. At other times, elite bargains successfully adapt to changes in the relative power, incentives, and preferences of societal interests by accommodating new demands through credible rules for elite-elite and elite-citizen interactions (see chapter 2).

Long-term development progress is predicated on this ability to adapt to changing circumstances. The institutional forms selected to solve commitment and collective action challenges at particular junctures in a country's development may produce trade-offs: growth with higher inequality; more redistribution or less violence accompanied by lower long-term growth; successful growth episodes but with higher environmental costs; or growing levels of injustice or exclusion despite good growth outcomes. The introduction of contestability and accountability mechanisms can help countries adapt when tensions related to these trade-offs arise. When adaptation takes place through rules-based mechanisms, virtuous cycles of continued adaptation and development progress are more likely. However, the conditions under which such rules-based adaptation occurs are limited: in most of the world and most of human history unstable deals-based bargains have dominated.

Who bargains?

Actors in the policy arena bargain over the design and implementation of policies and the definition of rules. *Elites* are those actors with the ability to directly influence outcomes within a given sector or issue. But identifying these elites can be difficult (box 7.1).

This chapter focuses on *national elites*—those elites who have direct influence over the formulation and implementation of national policy, as well as the rules of the game by which national power is allocated, exercised, and constrained.[1] Even at the national level, elites differ by sector: those with agenda-setting or veto control over health policy may not have control over constitutional reforms. At the national level, political (state) elites are of particular importance. However, formal political elites wield variable amounts of de facto power. In highly institutionalized countries, political power may flow from official positions, but in most countries—developed and developing alike—nonstate elites also directly influence bargaining outcomes. In the United States, a high-income institutionalized democracy, policies are much more likely to match the preferences of economic elites than the preferences of average citizens, despite a de jure commitment to equal representation (figure 7.1)—see Gilens and Page (2014). Elsewhere, relational or ideological informal power may trump economic or military might: in history, the de facto "power behind the throne" has often been a trusted adviser or counselor who lacked formal de jure powers.

Organizations empower elites, help them overcome coordination problems, and enable them to credibly commit to one another. Elites differ in their capacity to organize: can they credibly commit to those they seek to influence and thus coordinate their behavior? Certain wealthy oligarchic elites may not depend on internal organization directly, but money is fungible, and it can buy collective action when necessary. For example, during periods of political unrest in Thailand economic elites paid "protestors" to occupy public spaces and demand a change in government (Winters 2011). Similarly, intellectual or charismatic leaders may become powerful elites because of their ability to generate large mass followings by shifting preferences. In this sense, elites are elite by virtue of their capacity to organize collective action and thus exercise influence (Mosca 1939; Mills 1956).

The use of an elite bargaining framework helps move beyond the black box view of the state. A state is not monolithic, but rather a reflection of bargaining outcomes among groups of empowered economic and political actors. All governments have some sort of power-sharing arrangement, regardless of their regime type (Bueno de Mesquita and others 2003). Even in regimes that seem to be dominated by one person, the ethnic composition of the ministerial cabinet is inclusive and proportional to the population, reflecting political bargaining rather than

Box 7.1 Expert survey to identify elites

All social science disciplines and development practitioners recognize the importance of elite actors in determining development outcomes—from Aristotle and his "oligarchy" to early 20th-century "elite theorists" such as Mosca (1939), Pareto ([1927] 1971), and Michels ([1911] 1966), to recent grand theorists of economic and institutional coevolution such as North, Wallis, and Weingast (2009) and Acemoglu and Robinson (2012). The international donor community is looking increasingly at the consequences of different "political settlements," which can be understood as the elite bargaining equilibria that emerge at critical junctures in a country's development (Di John and Putzel 2009; Khan 2010; Parks and Cole 2010). And yet the set of conceptual research tools available to scholars of elite bargaining and to development practitioners remains limited, as does agreement on exactly who are elites.

To help fill this gap, the World Bank, in collaboration with V-Dem (Varieties of Democracy), conducted an expert survey, Measuring Elite Power and Interactions, to generate cross-national indicators that enable comparison of who holds power and how they wield this power (World Bank 2016b). The survey covers over 100 years of data in 12 countries across six regions. The data produced help to identify how the distribution of elites maps onto national power

and the formulation and implementation of laws governing the exercise of power.

The survey reveals that the identity of the powerful elite actors who bargain over national policy decisions differs greatly over space, time, and issue area. For example, although national chief executives were part of the elite ruling coalition in all 12 survey countries in 2015, the other actors varied greatly in both number and representativeness (figures B7.1.1, panel a). With the exception of those in the Russian Federation, Rwanda, and Turkey, where the national chief executives monopolize decision making, the ruling coalition was quite varied. For example, in Bolivia the ruling coalition consisted of legislators, party elites, local governments, labor unions, and civil society organizations.

Ruling elites also differ within countries over time. In the Republic of Korea during the regime of Gen. Park Chung-hee (1963–1979), the bargaining strength of military actors, bureaucratic actors, and economic actors was relatively high (panel b). The post-1987 transition to democracy resulted in greater strength for new actors, particularly political parties, legislators, and the judiciary, but economic and bureaucratic actors remained highly empowered. By contrast, Brazil has experienced much more volatility in empowered elites, particularly before the 1990s (panel c).

Figure B7.1.1 Elite actors within national ruling coalitions vary greatly across countries and over time

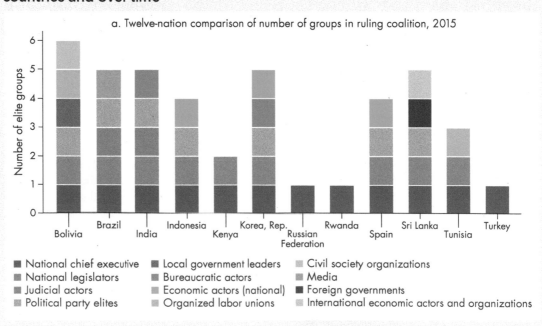

a. Twelve-nation comparison of number of groups in ruling coalition, 2015

Legend:
- National chief executive
- National legislators
- Judicial actors
- Political party elites
- Local government leaders
- Bureaucratic actors
- Economic actors (national)
- Organized labor unions
- Civil society organizations
- Media
- Foreign governments
- International economic actors and organizations

(Box continues next page)

Box 7.1 **Expert survey to identify elites** *(continued)*

Figure B7.1.1 Elite actors within national ruling coalitions vary greatly across countries and over time *(continued)*

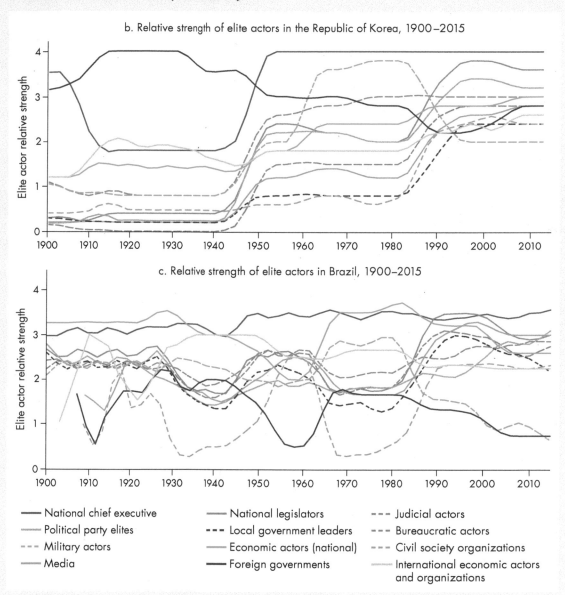

b. Relative strength of elite actors in the Republic of Korea, 1900–2015

c. Relative strength of elite actors in Brazil, 1900–2015

- ——— National chief executive
- ——— Political party elites
- - - - Military actors
- ——— Media
- ——— National legislators
- - - - Local government leaders
- ——— Economic actors (national)
- ——— Foreign governments
- - - - Judicial actors
- - - - Bureaucratic actors
- - - - Civil society organizations
- ——— International economic actors and organizations

Source: WDR 2017 team, using data from World Bank and V-Dem 2016b.

Note: In this figure, relative strength is measured on a 0–4 scale, ranging from 0 (no power to influence decision making) to 4 (group has a lot of power to influence decision making on many issues). Panel a shows the number of elite groups that have a relative strength of greater than 3. For more information on specific variables and survey methodology, see World Bank and V-Dem (2016a) and Coppedge and others (2015).

Source: WDR 2017 team.

Figure 7.1 Preferences of economic elites predict policy adoption more than citizen preferences in the United States

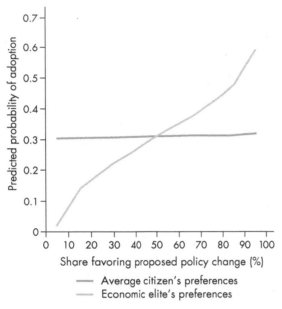

Source: Gilens and Page 2014.

Note: The analysis is based on 1,779 policies in the United States between 1981 and 2002 in which public opinion polls were carried out.

"Big Man" rule (Francois, Rainer, and Trebbi 2012). As they engage in elite bargains, actors have not only different degrees of relative power, but also different incentives and preferences.

For the broad sweep of human history, elites have bargained using deals-based mechanisms. The transition toward more rules-based governance is often thwarted by the incentives that elites face to maintain or maximize *utility*—be it wealth, influence, or reputation. Preserving or maximizing utility depends on preventing expropriation and exploitation by other powerful actors. But the ability of elites to credibly commit to not expropriating from one another is limited because of coordination and common agency challenges. This difficulty in establishing credible internal commitment tends to lead to unstable and nonadaptable short-term bargains. When elite bargains are deals-based, there is a natural tendency to keep coalitions small (Riker 1962). It is easier to coordinate preferences among a small group because bargains become less efficient with many actors (Mailath and Postlewaite 1990), and closer relationships make commitments more credible.

Commitment within the elite bargain may be credible because of the low threshold for small group

coordination, but this credibility depends on maintaining the exclusivity of the bargain.[2] Borrowing from the economic literature on oligopolies, when incumbent elites seek to prevent currently excluded (opposition) elites from entering the ruling coalition, they have three potential strategies: block (to prevent entry); deter (modify incumbent behavior to deter entry); and accommodate (allow other elites to enter and modify the behavior of incumbents and new elites). Despite a tendency for limited deals-based bargains, under certain circumstances elite bargains may expand and generate formal rules to help overcome collective action and commitment challenges, often to bring about effective deterrence or accommodation.

How do bargains adapt to changes in the relative power, incentives, and preferences of elites?

Most elite bargains are deals-based and "exclusive," and they tend to resist adaptation. Bargains with few actors that are less open to external influences have less accountability, which can undermine future adaptability as new actors become powerful. The lack of adaptability of deals-based bargains helps explain why regimes in low- and middle-income countries are tenuous; they experience violent transitions every eight years on average (Cox, North, and Weingast 2015).

In states with deals-based bargains, the distribution of rents tends to be the glue that provides political stability and enables development (North, Wallis, and Weingast 2009). Commitment to distributing rents to those within the coalition may suffice to generate security and tie the state together, but such a state faces difficulties incorporating the new elites perhaps needed to generate growth and equity (see discussion on security in chapter 4). Indeed, these stable bargains can quickly deteriorate when the source of rents breaks down. For example, in South Sudan from the period of the Comprehensive Peace Agreement (CPA) in 2005 through the formation of the state in 2011, the distribution of rents held together heterogeneous factions and structured power relations that were reflected in patronage networks, including well-connected (but unproductive) "tenderpreneurs," who survived on government contracts. However, these rents were unreliable, and undoing them proved difficult: a period of austerity in 2012–13 undermined South Sudan's patronage-based elite bargain, making the country one of the world's most fragile (Twijnstra 2015).

Under certain circumstances, however, elite bargains adapt to changing circumstances by improving state capacity and moving from deals-based agreements to formal rules-based mechanisms for contestability and accountability. In these bargains, elites institutionalize increasingly broad commitments to one another; they move from narrow deals to broad rules.

Elites adopt rules-based mechanisms for two general reasons: to sustain power or to provide insurance against a future loss of power. When actors who have been excluded become stronger, bringing these new actors into credible institutions and granting concessions may be less costly than repressing them. Similarly, expanding the formal accountability space may help provide internal commitments that facilitate agreement. As Tancredi says in *The Leopard*, "If we want things to stay as they are, things will have to change" (Tomasi di Lampedusa [1958] 2007, 40). When ruling elites are no longer confident of their hold on power, the introduction of rules may lower the future costs of losing power by providing "insurance."

The introduction of rules-based mechanisms will coincide with elite self-interest only under certain circumstances. When the cost to ruling elites of losing power is high, they will be less inclined to increase the space for contestability and accountability and to cede power. If ruling elites believe expropriation or violent punishment will result from ceding power, they will reject electoral results that support the opposition (figure 7.2). The most important determinant of the cost of losing is the level of polarization between the preferences of elite groups; starkly opposed preferences raise the likelihood of violence and instability (Vu 2007). Similar or overlapping elite preferences—low levels of polarization—tend to facilitate coordination across different elite groups. When polarization is high, accommodating new groups becomes more challenging because the concessions may be too costly for the ruling elites. When elite polarization decreases, countries are more likely to institutionalize elite interactions and generate rules for contestation and accountability.

The context in which bargains take place also differs according to how much competition or political uncertainty the ruling coalition faces. This relates to both the contestability of access to decision making as well as the degree of internal cohesion in the ruling coalition. When ruling coalitions face competition or when they have only a weak hold on power, political uncertainty about who will be in power in a future period is high. Thus threats to losing power

Figure 7.2 When the cost of losing power is high, elites are more likely to reject electoral results that support the opposition and are less likely to move toward rules-based contestability and accountability

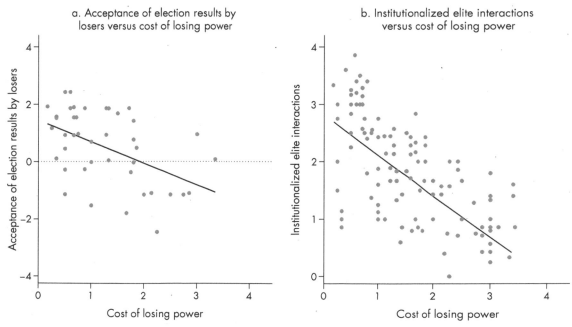

a. Acceptance of election results by losers versus cost of losing power

b. Institutionalized elite interactions versus cost of losing power

Sources: WDR 2017 team, based on V-Dem 2015 and World Bank and V-Dem 2016b.

Note: The cost of losing power, the acceptance of election results by the losers, and institutionalized elite interactions are all measured on an ordinal 0–4 scale, as determined by an expert survey.

are credible.[3] Uncertainty does not necessarily imply instability, but rather simply the unpredictability of who will hold power in the future. When uncertainty is high, ruling coalitions are more likely to implement reforms that will serve as insurance to protect them in the event of losing power. Alternatively, when uncertainty is low and ruling coalition elites are confident of their power, they may take a longer-term perspective and accommodate the demands of other elites through the introduction of new rules that can increase or sustain power.

The cost of losing power and the degree of political uncertainty interact to help determine the likelihood that elites will generate rules for contestability and accountability (box 7.2). Historical contingencies and specific country circumstances ultimately help determine outcomes, but a low cost of losing, and thus low polarization, may be a necessary condition for the emergence of bargains that adapt through the adoption of rules. The discussion that follows provides examples of institutions and rules that ruling coalition elites introduced to enhance power

---

Box 7.2 When do elites have incentives to introduce rules for contestability and accountability?

The cost of losing power—largely determined by the polarization of elite preferences—and the degree of political uncertainty act together to shape elite incentives for introducing rules for contestability and accountability. There are four broad possibilities, considering the high and low values of these two dimensions:

- When uncertainty is high, elites may implement "insurance" reforms to protect themselves in the event of losing power (upper-left quadrant of figure B7.2.1).
- "Insurance" reforms are unlikely to happen, however, if the cost of losing is too high because in this case the commitments of one group of elites to another through either deals or rules are not credible. The result is frequently state collapse or a cycle of violence (upper-right quadrant).
- When uncertainty is low and ruling coalition elites are confident in their power, they may take a longer-term perspective and accommodate the demands of other elites through the introduction of new rules that can increase or sustain power (lower-left quadrant).
- When uncertainty is low but the cost of losing is high, repressive states may arise in which the preferences of the opposition elites are in stark contrast to those of the ruling elites. Repression sustains a large power imbalance between the ruling coalition and the opposition (lower-right quadrant). In this context, it is unlikely that credible rules to regulate contestation and accountability will be introduced.

Results from the Measuring Elite Power and Interactions Survey conducted for WDR 2017 offer empirical evidence to help demonstrate how the cost of losing and political

Figure B7.2.1 The interaction between political uncertainty and the cost of losing power

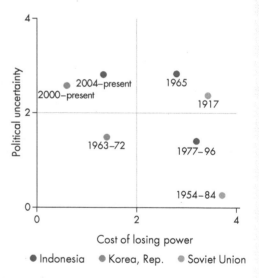

Sources: WDR 2017 team, based on V-Dem 2015 and World Bank and V-Dem 2016b.

Note: "Political uncertainty" is calculated as the average of four variables, each ranging from 0 to 4: (1) elite cohesion in the ruling coalition, (2) elite ideological unity, (3) the relative strength of opposition elites, and (4) the de facto competitiveness of multiparty elections. The "cost of losing power" variable ranges from 0 to 4.

uncertainty can change elite incentives to institute rules-based contestability and accountability. Figure B7.2.1 shows selected historical data points for three countries in the survey: Indonesia, the Republic of Korea, and the Russian

(Box continues next page)

or insure against loss. In some cases, elites generate more capable states; in others, they expand the formal space for contestability and accountability. The concluding section of this chapter discusses when and why these rules persist through continual adaptation.

Elite bargains and uneven state capacity

Over time, state capacity is largely a function of power; ruling elites invest in the capacity of governing structures when it is in their interest to do so—and they neglect those investments when it is not (see chapter 2). Such investments tend to improve institutional functions and development outcomes, but undertaking them is largely a problem of redistributing political power. Increasing the strength of bureaucratic actors is risky, creating the possibility of institutional champions that can contradict ruling elite preferences. And bureaucracies often serve purposes of patronage and rent distribution; undermining these arrangements is politically challenging and can destabilize elite bargains. Despite these challenges, elites

may strengthen the state through bureaucratic and civil service reforms and party institutionalization in search of what this Report calls *outcome legitimacy—* that is, enhancing cooperation and coordination by delivering effectively on commitments.

Under certain conditions, broad administrative reforms that move from patronage to meritocracy may be possible. Although high levels of education and historically strong states may make meritocratic reforms easier, there are no foregone conclusions. Throughout postindependence Africa, individual capacity (education levels) increased while institutional capacity declined as civil service recruitment policies were placed under presidential authority, leading to politicization and deprofessionalization (van de Walle 2001). The Republic of Korea, often assumed to have a "Confucian tradition" of meritocratic civil service, actually undertook massive improvements in bureaucratic quality during the 1960s and 1970s. During the era of the country's first president, Syngman Rhee, the bureaucracy was legally meritocratic, and yet between 1949 and 1961 only 336 bureaucrats passed the High Civil Service

Examination, while 8,263 received "special appointments" (Cheng, Haggard, and Kang 1998).

Reforms to limit patronage frequently arise from top-down initiatives or elite accommodation (Grindle 2012). At times, broad meritocratic reforms may be initiated as part of an effort to strengthen the ruling coalition. In China during the late 1970s, the "Four General Principles" calling for more revolutionary, younger, more professional, and more educated cadres were both technically and politically effective: the reform improved bureaucratic capacity by increasing standards for education and professionalism. Including a "revolutionary" (*geminghua*) requirement made the reform difficult to oppose on ideological grounds, and introducing strict retirement ages at all government levels resulted in the mass retirement of uneducated older cadres, who often opposed economic reforms (Li 1998). With the rapid retirement of 3.4 million revolutionary veterans, it was found that 90 percent of the county-level and above government officials in office in 1988 had been appointed after 1982, and 60 percent of them had college degrees.

Although at times broad administrative reforms are possible, elites are more likely to direct scarce resources and political capital only toward those agencies that help achieve specific goals, resulting in uneven development capabilities. An elite bargaining framework can help explain the emergence of these bureaucratic *pockets of effectiveness*—public agencies that carry out agency objectives effectively despite existing in an environment in which most other agencies are ineffective and subject to predation (Leonard 2008). In these cases, influential elite actors have incentives to ensure the effectiveness of such agencies and use their own political capital to shield the organizations from external interference (box 7.3).

Extending the state's presence to new areas or gaining legitimacy through economic growth may be particularly compelling reasons for developing a noncoercive state capacity. For example, as states have realized they need to know the extent and makeup of their own population (increase "legibility"), they have increased investment in their statistical and census capacity (Scott 1998). In particular, economic

Box 7.3 Pockets of effectiveness in Nigeria

The emergence of "pockets of effectiveness" depends on political support from powerful elite actors. Taking steps to ensure the professionalization and autonomy of an individual government agency often precedes wholesale reform of the bureaucracy because political elites may seek effective management of a particular sector. High-level political interest in and commitment to an agency's success and political insulation from other elites whose interests the autonomous agency may harm are essential for effectiveness. Agency autonomy is most likely to be supported when the agency provides benefits that are immediate, identifiable, and beneficial to an important group of elite actors who "have a conception of the state as a public good, rather than simply as a target of predation or a tool for gaining advantage over others" (Leonard 2008, 25). But autonomy and political support are not enough; bureaucratic pockets of effectiveness require adequate resources as well as managerial factors that support rational decision making, including meritocratic recruitment, internal discipline, and performance-based management.

Consider the National Agency for Food and Drug Administration and Control (NAFDAC) in Nigeria as an illustration of one such pocket of effectiveness (Pogoson and Roll 2014). The agency was created in 1993. In 2001 President Olusegun Obasanjo had a personal interest in combating counterfeit and dangerous drugs as a way to improve Nigeria's international image. He wanted in part to seek debt relief, but also to boost his personal reputation and international prestige. He selected Dora Akunyili to head NAFDAC because of her reputation for incorruptibility. NAFDAC was then granted autonomy from the Ministry of Health to recruit staff and was given an independent budget. It was also allowed to operate free of political control. Under Akunyili's leadership and Obasanjo's direct support and clearance, NAFDAC returned to Nigerian ports, from which it had been banned in 1996, and NAFDAC clearance of imported goods again became compulsory, which broke the clearance monopoly of the Customs Service and plugged a major leak for imported counterfeit products. Challenging the interests of these powerful elite interests (the Customs Service) would not have been possible without agency autonomy and direct support of the president. In 2007 NAFDAC ranked first in a national poll of agency effectiveness (at 70 percent, it was 12 percentage points higher than the second-place agency).

Sources: Leonard (2008); Pogoson and Roll (2014).

Figure 7.3 Horizontal and vertical accountability become more common as party institutionalization increases

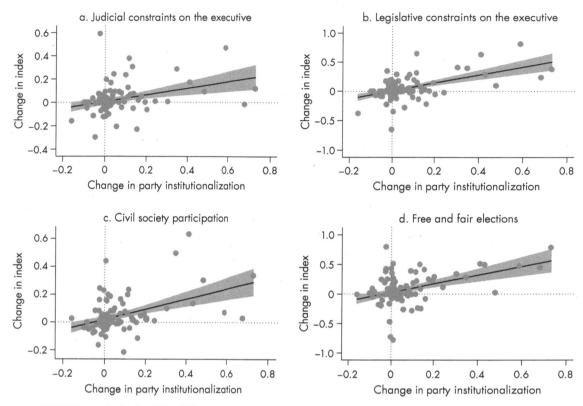

Source: WDR 2017 team, using data from V-Dem 2015.

Note: The data are for 2000 and 2010 and cover 166 countries. All variables range from 0 to 1. Changes are calculated as the difference between 2010 and 2000 values.

goals may be essential for regime legitimacy. In Brazil under its military dictatorship, industrial promotion agencies were turned into islands of excellence to ensure growth (Schneider 1991). In Korea, General Park installed technocrats in ministries related to economic development, but filled nondevelopment ministries (such as home affairs, construction, and transportation) with military cronies (Kang 2002).

Often, the institution in which elite groups choose to invest resources is a political party. Chapter 8 looks at political parties as mechanisms for *citizen* collective action, but parties are also key channels to resolve coordination and commitment challenges among elites. Institutionalization constrains party elites from arbitrary decision making by increasing their accountability to party subordinates and constituents, thereby solving the internal commitment problem and making parties more effective (Panebianco 1988). Party institutionalization may facilitate collective action by supporters of the regime, helping to produce credible commitments and greater private

investment by tying leaders' hands (Gehlbach and Keefer 2012). In doing so, parties contribute to regime durability (Brownlee 2008). When parties become more institutionalized, other formal accountability mechanisms also tend to emerge (figure 7.3).

Broadening the policy arena to enhance elite power

In 16th-century France, jurist and political philosopher Jean Bodin advised absolutist French monarchs to voluntarily relinquish power, arguing that "limitations placed upon [a monarch's] caprice markedly increase his capacity to govern and to achieve his steady aims" (Gandhi 2009, 186). Many elites have followed this advice, institutionalizing bargains among elites through greater contestability and accountability in order to increase and sustain power. Elites in these cases make concessions in order to enhance their own position. This can be done by co-opting newly powerful actors into formal institutional mechanisms for contestation (institutionalizing horizontal contestability) or by increasing horizontal and vertical accountability.

Institutionalizing horizontal contestability (broadening coalitions)

To maintain their own power, ruling coalitions may provide rising elites with payoffs or co-opt potential opposition by creating formal mechanisms to channel their preferences. To sustain coalitions, elites must provide their coalition partners with benefits. Despite a preference for keeping coalitions small, politicians may broaden coalitions when the potential for conflict arises (Riker 1962). Indeed, broadened coalitions help improve regime stability, although there are difficulties in quantifying this effect. In Africa, the addition of one cabinet member lowers the risk of a coup by 23–25 percent, all else being equal (Arriola 2009).

Broadening the bargaining arena by including new actors in the formal decision-making bodies of the state—*institutional co-optation*—may be cheaper and more sustainable than increasing payoffs. When rising elites are paid off instead of being included in decision making, systems may become overly dependent on the source of rents, making them unable to withstand shocks that undermine this rent source, as illustrated by the case of South Sudan described earlier in this chapter.

Ruling coalitions may be strengthened by bringing local or communal elites into the ruling coalition, often by co-opting existing informal institutions into more formal structures. Co-opting local elites rather than replacing them can increase the power of the ruling coalition. In Somaliland, the 1993 clan conference (*shir beeleed*) in the capital city of Borama brought together 500 elites from the modern and traditional sectors and institutionalized these clans and elders into formal governing bodies, a clan (*beel*) system that has led to 20 years of stability in a fragile region (Kaplan 2008). In Sub-Saharan Africa more broadly, when ruling authoritarian coalitions incorporated local authorities rather than replace them, these authoritarian incumbents had more support and were stronger during the democratic transition (Riedl 2014).

However, the participation of new actors is a two-way street: it mitigates conflict and creates "insiders" with incentives to support the ruling coalition, but in providing new actors with commitments, it also tends to empower these actors and the sectors they represent at the expense of the current elite, giving them the ability to influence policy formulation and implementation. Decision-making elites likely see co-optation solely as a means of staving off opposition demands rather than as a means of changing the balance of power within the arena. But both processes inevitably occur. Rising elites can in this sense be considered Trojan horses for expressing new demands internally.

Often, the co-opted parties are new economic interests that have grown more powerful over the course of development. The inclusion of business interests in formal institutions can lead to improved economic outcomes through more successful state-business coordination (see chapter 5 on growth). Formal rules for inclusion provide a credible commitment that noninstitutionalized efforts at coordination would not achieve. In Chile, President Augusto Pinochet's co-optation of business elites to lead ministries and agencies during the 1980s arose out of fear that these elites would turn to the opposition. Their entry in the state led to systematic consultations with peak industries, benefiting business elites themselves while also improving coordination and strengthening the state beyond Pinochet's rule (Silva 1996). In China, the Communist Party's decision to add entrepreneurs to its ranks in the early 2000s signaled an increased commitment to the private sector, helping spur growth and also leading to further changes in regime policy and legal development, including constitutional change in 2004 that strengthened legal protection for private property.

Ruling coalitions may also introduce formal institutional "checks" on their behavior to maintain power and sustain rents. Consider the case of authoritarian legislatures. They are not mere window dressing; they provide a safety valve to vent political pressures, co-opt the opposition, signal regime strength, help regimes withstand leadership transitions, and distribute rents.[4] However, authoritarian legislatures do not just serve the political purposes that spawn their creation; they can also lead to positive feedback loops. For example, the existence of legislatures in authoritarian regimes increases investment by raising the cost of expropriation (Wright 2008; Gandhi 2009), helping foster negotiations among private actors (Jensen, Malesky, and Weymouth 2014), and providing useful policy information that improves resource allocation (Boix and Svolik 2013).

Institutionalizing vertical accountability

The introduction of elections or electoral reforms may be a rational elite strategy to maintain power or privilege, particularly in the face of rising demands from opposition elites. When there are splits among elite actors, the introduction of vertical account-ability mechanisms and responsiveness to citizens may enhance the power of one faction. For example, countries without elections at the national level may introduce local elections to appease local interests, gain information, and solve the principal-agent con-trol problems of local elites by recruiting citizens to monitor local elites on behalf of the central elites. These local elections may strengthen the regime, but they also may lead to better social outcomes, as in the introduction of village elections in China (Martinez-Bravo and others 2011).

When bottom-up citizen movements (discussed in chapter 8) threaten elite interests, elites may intro-duce mechanisms to respond to societal demands before such pressures reach a tipping point. When asked "Why liberalize?" for example, the former pres-ident of Tanzania Julius Nyerere responded, "When you see your neighbor being shaved, you should wet your beard. Otherwise you could get a rough shave" (Levitsky and Way 2010, 16). In 19th- and 20th-century Europe, the extension of suffrage was predicted by the threat of revolution, proxied by revolutionary activity in neighboring countries (Aidt and Jensen 2014) and by strikes or riots in the home country (Kim 2007; Przeworski 2009).

Even without a direct threat from below, many democratic transitions are initiated from a position of strength to ensure maximum benefits for empowered elites. In a "conceding-to-thrive" scenario, the ruling coalition recognizes a future threat to the regime, but it maintains enough strength relative to the opposi-tion to not fear losing an election (Slater and Wong 2013). It may be rational for elites to engage in democ-ratization *now* in order to maintain power because the stronger ruling elites are during democratic transitions, the less the economic redistribution after transition (Albertus and Menaldo 2014). For exam-ple, in Spain after the autocratic Franco era, because the left had been undermined, conservative elites did not think that the advent of democracy would threaten property rights (Alexander 2002). In Latin America, economic elites allowed democratization when conservative parties were in charge and could protect their interests (Rueschemeyer, Stephens, and Stephens 1992).

Where elections are introduced to strengthen an elite bargain, electoral rules may serve to favor the continued dominance of those in power. Following democratization in post–World War II Japan, rural voters had twice the voting power of urban voters (Hata 1990). In Korea, Japan, and Taiwan, China, the combination of single nontransferable votes and multimember districts undermined the power of emerging parties by creating nationwide coordina-tion challenges for smaller parties, which allowed the dominant parties to maximize legislative seats.[5]

When binding rules for accountability serve as political insurance

Sometimes, ruling coalition elites, acknowledging threats to their continued dominance, introduce power-constraining rules that they hope will bind not only themselves, but also their successors. In particular circumstances, the adoption of cohesive and constraining institutions increases with the like-lihood that the incumbents will be replaced (Besley and Persson 2011).

Although greater political competition may increase the likelihood that elites introduce binding rules, the credibility of these new rules depends critically on continued competition. When power imbalances grow between the ruling elites and oppo-sition forces, rules may fail to bind. For example, in Bangladesh in the 1990s equal power between the ruling and opposition parties led to a constitutional amendment in 1996 that called for establishment of a neutral caretaker government at the end of each term, headed by the last Supreme Court chief justice, to facilitate rules-based transitions. This constitu-tional arrangement collapsed in 2007 when the ruling Balochistan National Party (BNP) interfered with Supreme Court retirement dates, resulting in a violent standoff (Khan 2013).

Horizontal accountability as political insurance

Competition among elites helps explain the emer-gence of horizontal checks and autonomous insti-tutions in new or weak democracies. Competitive systems facing political uncertainty are more likely to adopt independent judiciaries because the current ruling elites know they will be better off subject to independent actors than to the machinations and retaliations of political rivals. For example, although Argentina's ruling Peronist party agreed as early as 1994 to strengthen an independent judiciary, such reforms were not implemented until the Peronists thought they would lose power, at which point judi-cial independence was granted in order to control the opposition after ceding power (Finkel 2004).

Other judicial reforms, including judicial review, also become more common when greater competition increases the likelihood that the ruling coalition elites will lose power. In new democracies, the constraint on arbitrary power imposed by judicial review can serve as insurance to potential electoral losers, providing support for democracy, as was the case during democratic transitions in some East Asian democracies such as Korea and Mongolia (Ginsburg 2003). The adoption of constitutional review in 204 countries from 1781 to 2011 was driven largely by electoral politics, which served as political insurance when the ruling party was in jeopardy (Ginsburg and Versteeg 2014).

The same logic applies to accountability, oversight, and transparency laws. In eastern European economies in transition in the 1990s, governments were less likely to extract resources from the state when political competition was high, and they were more likely to introduce institutions of accountability and oversight, particularly those related to civil service, accounting, and anticorruption (Grzymala-Busse 2006). In Brazil, audit courts are more effective in localities with a greater turnover of elites (governors) because these localities have delegated authority to independent auditors as an insurance mechanism (Melo, Pereira, and Figueiredo 2009). Fiscal transparency ties not only the hands of current elites, but also those of successors (Alt, Lassen, and Rose 2006). This is consistent with the actions of certain states in Mexico. Although access to information and transparency laws were strengthened at the federal level after the political change in 2000, and more recently in 2016, such laws were more likely to be passed at the state level when opposition parties were stronger and when there was greater executive office turnover (Berliner and Erlich 2015).

Vertical accountability as political insurance

Elites sometimes introduce elections from a position of strength; at other times, they may do so to insure themselves against exploitation by other elites. Movements toward democracy may result as new economic elites seek to safeguard (ensure a commitment to) their new position and wealth. Under authoritarian regimes, the commitment to protect resources and property is often weak.[6] Broken commitments can lead empowered economic elites to part ways with the ruling coalition and support the democratic transition because they view it as more likely to prevent further exploitation.

When elites introduce elections as a way to insure themselves against exploitation by other elites, the electoral rules are also likely to reflect the interests of these declining powers. When power is weakened,

manipulation of the terms of democratization can serve as a source of political insurance. During República Bolivariana de Venezuela's democratic transition in 1958, the three main political parties signed the Punto Fijo Pact, which not only established respect for constitutions and elections, but also determined that electoral winners should put members of all three parties into positions of power to create national unity governments (excluding the Communists). The pact helped ensure the survival of democracy, but also made outcomes less likely to reflect the will of the people (Myers 2004).

When elites adapt through rules-based mechanisms

In the examples just discussed, elites enhanced state capacity or introduced rules to manage contestation and increase accountability to adapt to changes spurred by the development process that affected the relative power, preferences, and incentives of actors (see part I of this Report). Such adaptation is essential for long-term development.

Adaptation is not a one-off trait. Rather, it is a continual process as the needs and demands of society change over the course of development. At low-income levels, deals may be sufficient to overcome elite coordination and commitment challenges; patronage can effectively provide credible commitment and give the elite ruling coalitions cohesion. At middle-income levels, however, rising societal demands make the transaction costs of coordinating interests greater, potentially undermining deals-based bargains. This situation helps explain why low-income countries that are successful in terms of medium-term economic growth tend to not have governments that are appreciably cleaner than those of comparator countries, whereas upper-middle-income countries that grow to high-income levels experience a sharp decline in perceived corruption relative to those countries that remain at the middle-income level. They also experience greater increases in horizontal and vertical accountability (see spotlight 6 on the middle-income trap).

Bargains that can adapt to accommodate evolving elite interests may nevertheless struggle to adapt to growing citizen demands. Many countries experiencing spells of rapid growth have engaged in rights violations, particularly of student and labor organizations, as a way to support the interests of the state, bureaucratic, and business elites in the ruling coalition (Leftwich 1995). In these cases, the tensions between growth outcomes and equity outcomes and between legitimizing outcomes and legitimizing processes have increased. Regimes may be delegitimized when decision-making processes are insufficiently inclusive, even when other development outcomes appear successful—that is, process legitimacy may become more important than outcome legitimacy. As discussed in part I of this Report, cooperation and coordination—collective action—are weakened as a result of a "legitimacy deficit."

Overcoming delegitimization requires greater inclusion in the political process. As elite ruling coalitions grow in size, coordination difficulties increase, elite splits become more likely, and the space widens for citizen groups to enter. Here, the interaction between citizens and elites becomes key, particularly in the development of social movements. When bureaucratic interests diverge from political interests, for example, they may attempt to organize citizens in their support. But this co-optation of citizens follows the same logic as the institutionalized co-optation of other elites: once citizens gain a seat at the table, vertical accountability increases and citizen interests are articulated and reflected in elite bargains. The interaction between elites and citizens is thus a two-way dynamic with both sides playing decisive roles— elites in seeking citizen support and opening up new spaces for contestation and citizens in organizing to overcome collective action problems and apply pressure on elites, as discussed in chapter 8.

Adaptation is necessary for long-term development, but most elite bargains cannot be adapted. Adaptability in elite bargains requires feedback mechanisms, as well as an ability to accommodate rising and falling powers. The free flow of information and greater freedom of association make such accommodation more likely. Many of the reforms described earlier are complementary and make further reform more likely, leading to a virtuous circle. For example, many reforms that tie the hands of elites are embodied in new organizations, including independent bureaucracies, anticorruption agencies, and legislatures. The actors in these organizations can then directly contest in the policy bargaining arena. Stronger organizations want institutional improvements that support themselves, leading to a self-reinforcing virtuous circle (North, Wallis, and Weingast 2009).

Many of the reforms described earlier also tend to lead to further adaptation because the degree of institutionalization of the policy bargaining arena itself influences the level of uncertainty and the cost of losing. The rules that govern formal bargaining by elites help them overcome common agency problems and also provide the structure for repeated interactions

that can lead to credible commitments. Credible institutions can lower the costs of losing by tying the hands of competing elites, thereby lessening polarization and making change more likely. Conversely, informal patrimonialism pushes regimes to resist democratic reforms because the costs of transition are higher (Bratton and van de Walle 1997).

Although the conditions that determine whether elites will adapt through rules are historically contingent and highly context-specific, there are a few circumstances in which such adaptability becomes more likely: when elites have exogenous reasons to find common ground; when national institutions produce leaders who effectively shape the incentives and preferences of other elites; and when countries have more balanced, diversified, and organized business interests. These circumstances are discussed in the sections that follow.

Common ground: Reducing polarization by maximizing shared elite interests

When elite preferences converge and polarization decreases, coordination and cooperation become less challenging. Often, there are exogenous reasons for such reductions in polarization. External threats or internal threats from nonelites increase the fusion between ruling and opposition elites. When citizens are united against elite interests, the opposition and ruling coalition can more easily find common ground—the cost of losing to the opposition becomes smaller. In Southeast Asian countries that feared class revolution, elite groups with opposing class and ethnic backgrounds made "protection pacts" with one another to resist mass mobilization (Slater 2010). For example, in Malaysia the threat of urban communists enabled ethnic Chinese businesses to unite across ethnic and ideological lines with traditional Malaysian elites.

Polarization can also decline through shared ideologies and shared experience. When elites share an ideology, they can more readily solve internal collective action challenges, enhancing cohesion and making rules-based bargains more viable (figure 7.4). Shared military and revolutionary backgrounds help to explain the cohesion and long-term stability of Mexico's Institutional Revolutionary Party (Partido Revolucionario Institucional, PRI) and China's CPC (Knight 1992). Shared schooling can achieve similar outcomes. Public schooling with nationally determined curricula can generate a national identity that may help overcome underlying schisms. However, education can also increase polarization; ideologically diverse societies may prefer school choice, which can

Adaptation is necessary for long-term development, but most elite bargains cannot be adapted. Adaptability in elite bargains requires feedback mechanisms, as well as an ability to accommodate rising and falling powers.

Figure 7.4 Greater ideological unity among elites is associated with greater cohesion of the ruling coalition, as well as more institutionalized elite interactions

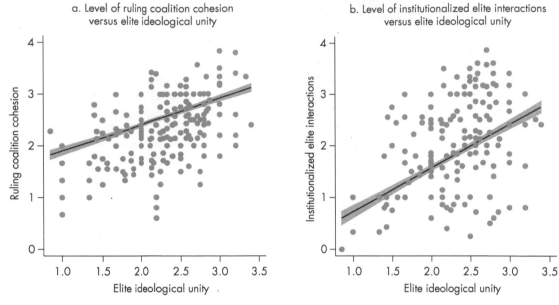

a. Level of ruling coalition cohesion versus elite ideological unity

b. Level of institutionalized elite interactions versus elite ideological unity

Sources: WDR 2017 team, based on V-Dem 2015 and World Bank and V-Dem 2016b.

Note: All variables are ordinal and range from 0 to 4, based on expert survey responses. The charts plot nonoverlapping decadal observations for 12 countries.

result in greater ideological and cultural segmentation over time (Kremer and Sarychev 2000).

Specialized "elite" schools may be able to reduce the polarization of elite preferences and facilitate bargains. In Somaliland, elite secondary schools played a crucial role in generating a unified leadership; the highly selective Sheekh Secondary School, which enrolls only 50 students a year, includes students from all clans and has produced three out of four presidents and numerous vice presidents and cabinet members. According to one graduate, "The graduates of Sheekh School have had a huge influence on Somaliland, on its development, its politics. . . . Elite leadership was trained in us there" (Phillips 2013, 70).

Effective leadership: Shaping elite preferences and incentives

Effective leadership can change the parameters of elite bargains. In an elite bargaining framework, the importance of leaders is not in selecting the "right" policy, but in spurring new ways in which organizations can interact (Andrews 2013). Leaders are instrumental in determining outcomes by solving coordination challenges or by transforming the beliefs and preferences of followers (Ahlquist and Levi 2011). The ability to solve coordination challenges corresponds with a "transactional" role for leaders.[7] Using an array of bargaining tactics and strategies, these leaders

coordinate among elite actors to overcome common agency problems and reach positive sum (win-win) outcomes. They also may change the incentives of other elites, taking into consideration who wins and who loses over time (the intertemporal dimensions).

Transactional leaders, by means of "good politics," can reduce the polarization of elite preferences without shifting norms. In the United States, Lyndon Johnson, as Senate majority leader before becoming president, pushed through the Civil Rights Act of 1957 despite resistance from the opposition as well as the anti–civil rights southern bloc of his own party. By taking personal risks to force a resolution, he overcame a natural tendency of Congress to avoid risk (Schofield 2006). And he did this less by changing beliefs than through good politics, including deals, trades, threats, and ego stroking (Caro 2002).

By contrast, "transformational" leaders can change elite preferences or gain followings by shaping preferences. They are entrepreneurial in coordinating norms and can effect large changes in society by changing the environment in which politics is played out, often by reducing the polarization of elites. Lyndon Johnson would not have been able to push through the more far-reaching Civil Rights Act of 1964 had not the Reverend Martin Luther King Jr. and his fellow civil rights activists successfully shifted the contours of the conversation on race, nonviolence, and human rights in the United States through self-sacrifice, nonviolent struggle, moral courage, and oratorical brilliance.

Transformational national leaders can indelibly alter the nature of the policy arena and the state itself. Perhaps most notably, ideological nation-building efforts can create political and social stability and identity that can lead to greater trust, cooperation, and commitment to ethnically neutral policies (Gellner 1983). In Tanzania, Julius Nyerere's "extended family" (*ujamaa*) socialism served as the ethnically unifying basis for national development. Although economic development did not improve initially, mass compulsory education and the widespread use of Swahili helped overcome tribal cleavages and produce a more unified and stable state. In Indonesia, President Sukarno introduced the Five Pillars (*Pancasila*) to unite disparate elements of society during the process of state formation. The concept survived a military coup as well as the transition to democracy,

helping to maintain a coherent national state during destabilizing times (Fukuyama 2014).

National institutions help determine leader quality both through selection (ex ante accountability) and punishment (ex post accountability)—see Maskin and Tirole (2004). When subsets of the population—such as women (see box 7.4)—are excluded from leadership positions, competitive selection is less likely to produce effective leaders. In democracies, political leaders must be elected, and local competition can prove a fertile ground for demonstrating capacity for higher office (see spotlight 9 on decentralization). Regardless of whether citizens or a small elite elect or select leaders, transparency and information provision are critical for screening good candidates (see chapter 8).

For leaders to be effective, they must be not only well-meaning, but also constrained by strong norms or formal institutions, including parties and legislatures (Ezrow and Frantz 2011). Term limits can encourage party-based decisions rather than

Box 7.4 Female elites and female leaders

When half the population is excluded from leadership competition, the political processes are half as likely to generate good candidates. Although gender gaps are narrowing around the world in several domains, female elites remain underrepresented. The proportion of seats held by women in national parliaments is 22.5 percent worldwide; in the world's largest 200 companies in 2014, women accounted for only 17.8 percent of members of boards of directors; and the average share of female justices in constitutional courts worldwide is 22.4 percent.[a] Even when women do gain positions of power, they are often constrained. For example, when women are appointed ministers (in a sample of 117 countries worldwide), they are largely assigned to less strategic and more "feminine" policy areas (Krook and O'Brien 2012).

The lack of female elite representation has negative effects on the introduction of inclusive policies (see chapter 6) because the preferences of female leaders may be systematically different from male preferences. In the context of elite bargaining, female leaders are also more likely to engage in inclusive decision-making processes. In the United States, female city managers are more likely to

take citizens' inputs into account in decision making (Fox and Schuhmann 1999); female mayors tend to favor cooperation rather than a hierarchical approach to governing (Tolleson-Rinehart 1991); and female chairs of state legislature committees act more as facilitators in committee hearings than do male chairs, who instead use their power to control the direction of the hearings (Lyn 1994).

There is also evidence that female leaders are less prone to patronage politics and corruption. In Africa, women are less likely to become ministers in settings in which incumbents use patronage to support ethnic constituencies (Arriola and Johnson 2014). In India, the 1993 constitutional amendment that mandated the reservation of one-third of local government council positions for women also reduced the incidence of corruption (Beaman and others 2011). In Brazil, random audits of government administrations showed that female municipal mayors were less likely than male mayors to be corrupt and were also less engaged in patronage (Brollo and Troiano 2016). More broadly, countries with a higher representation of women in parliament have lower levels of corruption (Dollar, Fisman, and Gatti 2001).

Source: WDR 2017 team.

a. Data are from the World Bank, World Development Indicators (database); Globe Women, Corporate Women Directors International; and World Bank, Women, Business and the Law (database).

personalistic decisions, as well as the cultivation of successors (Ginsburg, Melton, and Elkins 2011). Term limits also help with informal coordination by signaling to rivals. Even in autocratic settings, higher leadership turnover is associated with more successful economic and human development (Besley and Kudamatsu 2007).

Balanced, diversified, and organized business interests

Economic conditions help determine the adaptability of elite bargaining. Where productive business interests dominate, ruling coalitions are likely to be more dynamic and adaptive; where monopoly interests dominate, policies are more likely to prevent the emergence of new economic elites. Concentrated economic power makes adaptability to external shocks and internal change less likely, with important political consequences. More concentrated economic power tends to lead to concentrated political power that reflects this economic distribution. And when economic power translates into political power, institutions of accountability are less likely to develop (figure 7.5). For this reason, reforms that concentrate economic power without institutions in place to deal with new powerful interests may be ineffective, as in many postcommunist countries, where the initial beneficiaries of market reforms became economically and politically powerful enough to block further reform (Hellman 1998).

When diverse productive interests gain in strength because of external shocks and internal change, they can improve elite bargains. For example, in the conflict between the English Parliament and the monarchy during the 17th-century civil war, traders provided parliamentary moderates who lacked mercantile interests with financial assets and company shares, creating a broad parliamentary majority that overcame monarchic rule and changed the mechanisms by which Parliament operated (Jha 2015).

Business associations can help diverse business interests overcome collective action problems and gain influence in elite bargains. They can push for institutionalized consultations that can enhance coordination and decrease elite polarization. Chile's movement from particularistic state-business relations in the 1970s to peak business association consultations in the 1980s improved economic efficiency, and by aligning the interests of political insiders and business elites it helped pave the way for a smoother democratic transition (Silva 1996). Business associations can also act to balance the power of entrenched political elites. In Korea, the nature of empowered businesses led to a form of business-state collusion that was pro-development, in contrast to business-state relations in the Philippines that tended to be much less conducive to broad-based development (Kang 2002). In these cases, the key to effective business associations is the representation of diverse interests: when business associations represent a diversity of interests, they are more inclined to push for universalistic rules and institutional reforms (Maxfield and Schneider 1997).

Entry points for change through elite adaptation

How can a deeper understanding of elite bargains point to entry points for change? First, changes in the rules of the game in the policy arena are driven by the relative power of self-interested actors. Trying to impose reforms for contestability or accountability is not likely to gain traction. This chapter focuses on national elites, but the same analysis could also consider the subnational level and agency-specific reforms. In all of these cases, reform of the rules by which actors interact can succeed only when the rules reflect the actual distribution of power and interests. Rules that do not reflect this power distribution or change this power distribution will not stick.

Second, under certain circumstances elites do choose to tie their own hands, so there is room for optimism. Trying to create these circumstances by

Figure 7.5 When economic power maps onto political power, there are fewer institutional checks on power

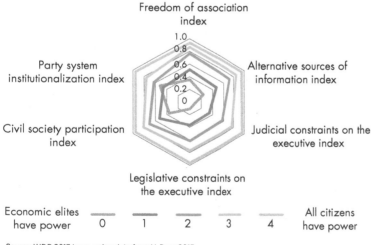

Source: WDR 2017 team, using data from V-Dem 2015.

Note: The figure maps the association between economic and political power. The analysis is based on data for 170 countries in 2012. The variable indicating how economic power maps onto political power is from V-Dem, based on expert surveys. A score of 0 means that economic elites have a monopoly on political power; a score of 4 means that all citizens have equal power, regardless of economic position.

altering incentives, preferences, and contestability at the margins may be an effective way to help change rules. Although there are few entry points, there are ways to facilitate this process and support development of homegrown rules:

- *Effectively change the incentives of elite actors.* Even when the relative power of actors remains the same, the nature of elite bargains can change when the elites in power face changed incentives, often as a result of shocks or gradual processes of economic development. Economic diversification can undermine rent-based elite bargains, changing the incentives of ruling elites to support more broad-based policies. Effective transactional leaders can engage in "good politics" to change the incentives facing other elites in the policy arena. When citizens overcome their collective action challenges to pressure elites, they change the incentives of elites to respond to their demands (see chapter 8). External actors can help change elite incentives when they present inducements or threats, such as conditional development assistance or the possibility for membership in the European Union or World Trade Organization (see chapter 9).
- *Reshape preferences in the policy arena.* The nature of elite bargains can also change when actor preferences evolve. Often, changes in preferences occur slowly over extended periods, such as global trends over centuries to view the practices of slavery and torture as immoral. In the shorter term, transformational leaders can coordinate norms and change beliefs. Increasing the frequency and depth of interactions between elite actors can help them find common ground. And more cross-border flows of ideas and information can change the preferences of domestic actors through the diffusion of norms and interactions between communities of experts (see chapter 9).
- *Make the policy arena more contestable.* When more actors are allowed to contest in the policy arena, elites are more likely to move from limited deals-based bargains to broader rules-based bargains. When newly powerful elites are allowed to contest in formal institutions, bargains can adapt to the changing balance of power. Empowering agencies by increasing their resources or the technical skills, information, and data available to them can enable them to bargain more effectively. And helping groups of elites or citizens overcome collective action challenges can also lead to newly powerful actors who can directly influence the policy arena. Chapters 8 and 9 discuss the potential influence of

other actors (citizens and international actors) to change the nature of elite bargains.

Notes

1. The same analysis could also consider the subnational level and agency-specific reforms.
2. This leads to the "limited access orders" described in North, Wallis, and Weingast (2009) and the "extractive" political institutions described in Acemoglu and Robinson (2012).
3. This can happen in both autocratic and democratic settings. In autocracies, elites face a "dictator's dilemma": their hold on power is tenuous, and they usually are overthrown from within (Svolik 2012). In democracies with significant oppositions, voting regularizes (institutionalizes) uncertainty because a change of administration entails a loss of power for incumbents.
4. For safety valves, see Malesky and Schuler (2010); for co-optation, Gandhi and Przeworski (2006), Langston (2006), and Gandhi (2009); for signaling, Geddes (2005); for leadership transitions, Ezrow and Frantz (2011); and for rent distribution, Lust-Okar (2006).
5. Brady and Mo (1992); Cox and Niou (1994); Cox (1996).
6. From 1950 to 2002, the majority of Latin American countries under an autocracy engaged in at least one large-scale expropriation of private finance, land, or natural resources (Albertus and Menaldo 2012).
7. For the distinction between transactional and transformational leaders, see Burns (1978).

References[a]

Acemoglu, Daron, and James A. Robinson. 2012. *Why Nations Fail: The Origins of Power, Prosperity, and Poverty.* New York: Crown Business.

Ahlquist, John S., and Margaret Levi. 2011. "Leadership: What It Means, What It Does, and What We Want to Know about It." *Annual Review of Political Science* 14 (1): 1–24.

Aidt, Toke S., and Peter S. Jensen. 2014. "Workers of the World, Unite! Franchise Extensions and the Threat of Revolution in Europe, 1820–1938." *European Economic Review* 72 (C): 52–75.

Albertus, Michael, and Victor Menaldo. 2012. "If You're against Them, You're with Us: The Effect of Expropriation on Autocratic Survival." *Comparative Political Studies* 45 (8): 973–1003.

———. 2014. "Gaming Democracy: Elite Dominance during Transition and the Prospects for Redistribution." *British Journal of Political Science* 44 (3): 575–603.

Alexander, Gerard. 2002. *The Sources of Democratic Consolidation.* Ithaca, NY: Cornell University Press.

a. References to titles of publications that include Taiwan, Hong Kong, and Macau refer to the regions currently named Taiwan, China; Hong Kong SAR, China; and Macau SAR, China, respectively.

Alt, James E., David Dreyer Lassen, and Shannan Rose. 2006. "The Causes of Transparency: Evidence from the American States." *IMF Staff Papers* 30 (special issue): 30–57.

Andrews, Matt. 2013. "Who Really Leads Development?" CID Working Paper 258, Center for International Development, Harvard University, Cambridge, MA.

Arriola, Leonardo R. 2009. "Patronage and Political Stability in Africa." *Comparative Political Studies* 42 (10): 1339–62.

Arriola, Leonardo R., and Martha C. Johnson. 2014. "Ethnic Politics and Women's Empowerment in Africa: Ministerial Appointments to Executive Cabinets." *American Journal of Political Science* 58 (2): 495–510.

Beaman, Lori, Esther Duflo, Rohini Pande, and Petia Topalova. 2011. "Political Reservation and Substantive Representation: Evidence from Indian Village Councils." In *India Policy Forum 2010-2011*, Vol. 7, edited by Suman Bery, Barry Bosworth, and Arvind Panagariya. New Delhi: National Council of Applied Economic Research and the Brookings Institution.

Berliner, Daniel, and Aaron Erlich. 2015. "Competing for Transparency: Political Competition and Institutional Reform in Mexican States." *American Political Science Review* 109 (1): 110–28.

Besley, Timothy, and Masayuki Kudamatsu. 2007. "Making Autocracy Work." Economic Organisation and Public Policy Discussion Paper 48, London School of Economics and Political Science, London.

Besley, Timothy, and Torsten Persson. 2011. *Pillars of Prosperity: The Political Economics of Development Clusters.* Princeton, NJ: Princeton University Press.

Boix, Carles, and Milan Svolik. 2013. "The Foundations of Limited Authoritarian Government: Institutions and Power-Sharing in Dictatorships." *Journal of Politics* 75 (2): 300–16.

Brady, David, and Jongryn Mo. 1992. "Electoral Systems and Institutional Choice: A Case Study of the 1988 Korean Elections." *Comparative Political Studies* 24 (4): 405–29.

Bratton, Michael, and Nicolas van de Walle. 1997. *Democratic Experiments in Africa: Regime Transitions in Comparative Perspective.* Cambridge Studies in Comparative Politics Series. New York: Cambridge University Press.

Brollo, Fernanda, and Ugo Troiano. 2016. "What Happens When a Woman Wins an Election? Evidence from Close Races in Brazil." *Journal of Development Economics* 122 (September): 28–45.

Brownlee, Jason. 2008. "Bound to Rule: Party Institutions and Regime Trajectories in Malaysia and the Philippines." *Journal of East Asian Studies* 8 (1): 89–118.

Bueno de Mesquita, Bruce, Alastair Smith, Randolph M. Siverson, and James D. Morrow. 2003. *The Logic of Political Survival.* Cambridge, MA: MIT Press.

Burns, James MacGregor. 1978. *Leadership.* New York: Harper and Row.

Campos, Jose Edgardo, and Hilton L. Root. 1996. *The Key to the Asian Miracle: Making Shared Growth Credible.* Washington, DC: Brookings Institution Press.

Caro, Robert A. 2002. *Master of the Senate: The Years of Lyndon Johnson.* New York: Knopf.

Cheng, Tun-jen, Stephan Haggard, and David Kang. 1998. "Institutions and Growth in Korea and Taiwan: The Bureaucracy." *Journal of Development Studies* 34 (6): 87–111.

Coppedge, Michael, John Gerring, Staffan I. Lindberg, Jan Teorell, David Altman, Michael Bernhard, M. Steven Fish, and others. 2015. *Varieties of Democracy: Codebook v4.* Gothenburg, Sweden: Varieties of Democracy (V-Dem) Project, V-Dem Institute, University of Gothenburg; Notre Dame, IN: Helen Kellogg Institute for International Studies, University of Notre Dame.

Cox, Gary W. 1996. "Is the Single Nontransferable Vote Superproportional? Evidence from Japan and Taiwan." *American Journal of Political Science* 40 (3): 740–55.

Cox, Gary W., and Emerson Niou. 1994. "Seat Bonuses under the Single Nontransferable Vote System: Evidence from Japan and Taiwan." *Comparative Politics* 26 (2): 221–36.

Cox, Gary W., Douglass C. North, and Barry R. Weingast. 2015. "The Violence Trap: A Political-Economic Approach to the Problems of Development." Working Paper, Hoover Institution, Stanford University, Stanford, CA.

Di John, Jonathan, and James Putzel. 2009. "Political Settlements." Issues paper, Governance and Social Development Resource Centre, University of Birmingham, Birmingham, U.K.

Dollar, David, Sandra Fisman, and Roberta Gatti. 2001. "Are Women Really the Fairer Sex? Corruption and Women in Government." *Journal of Economic Behavior and Organization* 46 (4): 423–29.

Ezrow, Natasha M., and Erica Frantz. 2011. "State Institutions and the Survival of Dictatorships." *Journal of International Affairs* 65 (1): 1–13.

Finkel, Jodi. 2004. "Judicial Reform in Argentina in the 1990s: How Electoral Incentives Shape Institutional Change." *Latin American Research Review* 39 (3): 56–80.

Fox, Richard L., and Robert A. Schuhmann. 1999. "Gender and Local Government: A Comparison of Women and Men City Managers." *Public Administration Review* 59 (3): 231–42.

Francois, Patrick, Ilia Rainer, and Francesco Trebbi. 2012. "How Is Power Shared in Africa?" NBER Working Paper 18425, National Bureau of Economic Research, Cambridge, MA.

Fukuyama, Francis. 2014. *Political Order and Political Decay: From the Industrial Revolution to the Globalization of Democracy.* New York: Farrar, Straus, and Giroux.

Gandhi, Jennifer. 2009. *Political Institutions under Dictatorship.* New York: Cambridge University Press.

Gandhi, Jennifer, and Adam Przeworski. 2006. "Cooperation, Cooptation, and Rebellion under Dictatorships." *Economics and Politics* 18 (1): 1–26.

Geddes, Barbara. 2005. "Why Parties and Elections in Authoritarian Regimes?" Paper presented at the American Political Science Association's Annual Meeting, APSA 2005, Washington, DC, August 31–September 3.

Gehlbach, Scott, and Philip Keefer. 2012. "Investment without Democracy: Ruling-Party Institutionalization and Credible Commitment in Autocracies." *Journal of Comparative Economics* 39 (2): 123–39.

Gellner, Ernest. 1983. *Nations and Nationalism.* Ithaca, NY: Cornell University Press.

Gilens, Martin, and Benjamin I. Page. 2014. "Testing Theories of American Politics: Elites, Interest Groups, and Average Citizens." *Perspectives on Politics* 12 (3): 564–81.

Ginsburg, Tom. 2003. *Judicial Review in New Democracies: Constitutional Courts in Asian Cases.* Cambridge, U.K.: Cambridge University Press.

Ginsburg, Tom, James Melton, and Zachary Elkins. 2011. "On the Evasion of Executive Term Limits." *William and Mary Law Review* 52 (6): 1807–72.

Ginsburg, Tom, and Mila Versteeg. 2014. "Why Do Countries Adopt Constitutional Review?" *Journal of Law, Economics, and Organization* 30 (3): 587–622.

Globe Women. 2015. Corporate Women Directors International (CWDI). Washington, DC, https://www.globewomen.org/cwdi/2015FG200KeyFindings.html.

Grindle, Merilee. 2012. *Jobs for the Boys: Patronage and the State in Comparative Perspective.* Cambridge, MA: Harvard University Press.

Grzymala-Busse, Anna. 2006. "The Discreet Charm of Formal Institutions: Post-Communist Party Competition and State Oversight." *Comparative Political Studies* 39 (10): 1–30.

Hata, Hiroyuki. 1990. "Malapportionment of Representation in the National Diet." *Law and Contemporary Problems* 53 (2): 157–70.

Hellman, Joel S. 1998. "Winners Take All: The Politics of Partial Reform in Postcommunist Transitions." *World Politics* 50 (2): 203–34.

Jensen, Nathan, Edmund Malesky, and Stephen Weymouth. 2014. "Unbundling the Relationship between Authoritarian Legislatures and Political Risk." *British Journal of Political Science* 44 (3): 655–84.

Jha, Saumitra. 2015. "Financial Asset Holdings and Political Attitudes: Evidence from Revolutionary England." *Quarterly Journal of Economics* 103 (3): 1485–1545.

Kang, David. 2002. *Crony Capitalism: Corruption and Development in South Korea and the Philippines.* New York: Cambridge University Press.

Kaplan, Seth. 2008. "The Remarkable Story of Somaliland." *Journal of Democracy* 19 (3): 143–57.

Khan, Mushtaq H. 2010. "Political Settlements and the Governance of Growth-Enhancing Institutions." Draft paper, Growth-Enhancing Governance Series, School of Oriental and African Studies, University of London.

———. 2013. "Bangladesh: Economic Growth in a Vulnerable LAO." In *In the Shadow of Violence: Politics, Economics, and the Problems of Development,* edited by Douglass C. North, John Joseph Wallis, Steven B. Webb, and Barry R. Weingast, 24–69. New York: Cambridge University Press.

Kim, Wonik. 2007. "Social Insurance Expansion and Political Regime Dynamics in Europe, 1880–1945." *Social Science Quarterly* 88 (2): 494–514.

Knight, Jack. 1992. *Institutions and Social Conflict.* Cambridge, U.K.: Cambridge University Press.

Kremer, Michael, and Andrei Sarychev. 2000. "Why Do Governments Operate Schools?" Unpublished working paper, Harvard University, Cambridge, MA.

Krook, Mona Lena, and Diana Z. O'Brien. 2012. "All the President's Men? The Appointment of Female Cabinet Ministers Worldwide." *Journal of Politics* 74 (3): 840–55.

Lampton, David M. 1987. "Chinese Politics: The Bargaining Treadmill." *Issues and Studies* 23 (3): 11–41.

Langston, Joy. 2006. "The Birth and Transformation of the Dedazo in Mexico." In *Informal Institutions and Democracy: Lessons from Latin America,* edited by Gretchen Helmke and Steven Levitsky, 143–59. Baltimore: Johns Hopkins University Press.

Leftwich, Adrian. 1995. "Bringing Politics Back In: Towards a Model of the Developmental State." *Journal of Development Studies* 31 (3).

Leonard, David K. 2008. "Where Are 'Pockets' of Effective Agencies Likely in Weak Governance States and Why? A Propositional Inventory." IDS Working Paper 306 (July), Institute of Development Studies, University of Sussex, Brighton, U.K.

Levitsky, Steven, and Lucan Way. 2010. *Competitive Authoritarianism: Hybrid Regimes after the Cold War.* Cambridge, U.K.: Cambridge University Press.

Li, David D. 1998. "Changing Incentives of the Chinese Bureaucracy." *American Economic Review* 88 (2): 393–97.

Lust-Okar, Ellen. 2006. "Elections under Authoritarianism: Preliminary Lessons from Jordan." *Democratization* 13 (3): 456–71.

Lyn, Kathlene. 1994. "Power and Influence in State Legislative Policy-Making: The Interaction of Gender and Position in Committee Hearing Debates." *American Political Science Review* 88 (3): 560–76.

Mailath, George J., and Andrew Postlewaite. 1990. "Asymmetric Information Bargaining Problems with Many Agents." *Review of Economic Studies* 57 (3): 351–67.

Malesky, Edmund, and Paul Schuler. 2010. "Nodding or Needling: Analyzing Delegate Responsiveness in an Authoritarian Parliament." *American Political Science Review* 104 (3): 1–21.

Martinez-Bravo, Monica, Gerard Padró i Miquel, Nancy Qian, and Yang Yao. 2011. "Do Local Elections in Non-democracies Increase Accountability? Evidence from Rural China." NBER Working Paper 16948, National Bureau of Economic Research, Cambridge, MA.

Maskin, Eric S., and Jean Tirole. 2004. "The Politician and the Judge: Accountability in Government." *American Economic Review* 94 (4): 1034–54.

Maxfield, Sylvia, and Ben Ross Schneider. 1997. *Business and the State in Developing Countries*. Ithaca, NY: Cornell University Press.

Melo, Marcus André, Carlos Pereira, and Carlos Mauricio Figueiredo. 2009. "Political and Institutional Checks on Corruption: Explaining the Performance of Brazilian Audit Institutions." *Comparative Political Studies* 42 (9): 1217–44.

Michels, Robert. [1911] 1966. *Political Parties: A Sociological Study of the Oligarchical Tendencies of Modern Democracy*. New York: Free Press.

Mills, C. Wright. 1956. *The Power Elite*. New York: Oxford University Press.

Mosca, Gaetano. 1939. *The Ruling Class (Elementi di Scienza Politica)*. New York: McGraw-Hill.

Myers, David. 2004. "The Normalization of Punto Fijo Democracy." In *The Unraveling of Representative Democracy in Venezuela*, edited by Jennifer L. McCoy and David J. Myers, 11–32. Baltimore: Johns Hopkins University Press.

North, Douglass C., John Joseph Wallis, and Barry R. Weingast. 2009. *Violence and Social Orders: A Conceptual Framework for Interpreting Recorded Human History*. New York: Cambridge University Press.

Panebianco, Angelo. 1988. *Political Parties: Organization and Power*. Cambridge, U.K.: Cambridge University Press.

Pareto, Vilfredo. [1927] 1971. *Manual of Political Economy*. New York: August M. Kelley.

Parks, Thomas, and William Cole. 2010. "Political Settlements: Implications for International Development Policy and Practice." Occasional Paper No. 2, Asia Foundation, San Francisco.

Phillips, Sarah. 2013. "Political Settlements and State Formation: The Case of Somaliland." Research Paper 23, Development Leadership Program, University of Birmingham, Birmingham, U.K.

Pogoson, A. Irene, and Michael Roll. 2014. "Turning Nigeria's Drug Sector Around: The National Agency for Food and Drug Administration and Control (NAFDAC)." In *The Politics of Public Sector Performance: Pockets of Effectiveness in Developing Countries*, edited by Michael Roll, 97–127. Abingdon, U.K.: Routledge.

Przeworski, Adam. 2009. "Conquered or Granted? A History of Suffrage Extensions." *British Journal of Political Science* 39 (2): 291–321.

Riedl, Rachel Beatty. 2014. *Authoritarian Origins of Democratic Party Systems in Africa*. New York: Cambridge University Press.

Riker, William H. 1962. *The Theory of Political Coalitions*. New Haven, CT: Yale University Press.

Rueschemeyer, Dietrich, Evelyne Huber Stephens, and John D. Stephens. 1992. *Capitalist Development and Democracy*. Chicago: University of Chicago Press.

Schneider, Ben Ross. 1991. *Politics within the State: Elite Bureaucrats and Industrial Policy in Authoritarian Brazil*. Pittsburgh: University of Pittsburgh Press.

Schofield, Norman. 2006. *Architects of Political Change: Constitutional Quandaries and Social Choice Theory*. Political Economy of Institutions and Decisions Series. New York: Cambridge University Press.

Scott, James C. 1998. *Seeing Like a State: How Certain Schemes to Improve the Human Condition Have Failed*. New Haven, CT: Yale University Press.

Silva, Eduardo. 1996. "From Dictatorship to Democracy: The Business-State Nexus in Chile's Economic Transformation, 1975–1994." *Comparative Politics* 28 (3): 299–320.

Slater, Dan. 2010. *Ordering Power: Contentious Politics and Authoritarian Leviathans in Southeast Asia*. New York: Cambridge University Press.

Slater, Dan, and Joseph Wong. 2013. "The Strength to Concede: Ruling Parties and Democratization in Developmental Asia." *Perspectives on Politics* 11 (3): 717–33.

Svolik, Milan. 2012. *The Politics of Authoritarian Rule*. New York: Cambridge University Press.

Tolleson-Rinehart, Sue. 1991. "Do Women Leaders Make a Difference? Substance, Style, and Perceptions." In *Gender and Policymaking: Studies of Women in Office*, edited by Debra L. Dodson, 93–102. The Impact of Women in Public Office Series. New Brunswick, NJ: Center for American Women and Politics, Rutgers University.

Tomasi di Lampedusa, Guiseppe. [1958] 2007. *The Leopard*. Translated by Archibald Colquohoun. New York: Pantheon Books.

Twijnstra, Rens. 2015. "'Recycling Oil Money': Procurement Politics and (Un)productive Entrepreneurship in South Sudan." *Journal of Eastern African Studies* 9 (4): 685–703.

van de Walle, Nicolas. 2001. *African Economies and the Politics of Permanent Crisis, 1979–1999*. New York: Cambridge University Press.

V-Dem (Varieties of Democracy). 2015. Database hosted by Gothenburg Institute (Europe) and Kellogg Institute (United States), https://www.v-dem.net/en/.

Vu, Tuong. 2007. "State Formation and the Origins of Developmental States in South Korea and Indonesia." *Studies in Comparative International Development* 41 (4): 27–56.

Winters, Jeffrey. 2011. *Oligarchy*. New York: Cambridge University Press.

World Bank. Various years. Women, Business and the Law (database). Washington, DC, http://wbl.worldbank.org/.

World Bank and V-Dem (Varieties of Democracy). 2016a. "Codebook: Measuring Elite Power and Interactions." Background paper, WDR 2017, World Bank, Washington, DC.

———. 2016b. Measuring Elite Power and Interactions Survey (database).

Wright, Joseph. 2008. "Do Authoritarian Institutions Constrain? How Legislatures Affect Economic Growth and Investment." *American Journal of Political Science* 52 (2): 322–43.

Decentralization

At their most effective, decentralized systems can spur experimentation that helps localities adapt proactively to changing circumstances. In the United States, Supreme Court justice Louis Brandeis famously referred in 1932 to the 50 states as "laboratories for democracy" that could "try novel social and economic experiments without risk to the rest of the country."[1]

By multiplying the number of more or less autonomous arenas within which public authority is exercised, decentralization increases the opportunities for policy innovations and the emergence of effective leaders (Tendler 1997; Campbell 2003). Often these innovations are spurred by political outsiders, who may not have access to the national policy arena but are more likely to acquire citizen support locally and spur local institutional reforms. For example, after direct mayoral elections were introduced in Colombia in the 1990s, municipalities led by political outsiders invested heavily in upgrading their administrative capacities (Fiszbein 1997).

Although decentralization increases *opportunities* for innovation and the entry of political outsiders, only certain arrangements provide the correct *incentives* for experimentation. To generate adaptive and innovative local governance, it is essential to have a well-defined assignment of responsibilities across levels of government and a clear expectation that subnational governments will be held responsible for their performance. To prevent clientelism or capture at the local level, citizens or central elites must have both the ability to hold local elites accountable and the incentives to do so.

Decentralized governance can create incentives for competent individuals to pursue political leadership, societal groups to invest in building political parties, or existing subnational governments to adopt innovative policy solutions. Competitive local elections can enable the entry of political outsiders and provide incentives for incumbent administrations to strive to show competence in governance. In India, which has a decentralized system, several regionally based parties have grown to form national coalitions, whereas two dynastic parties have dominated the politics of Bangladesh, a more centralized state. As a result, India has introduced a far greater range of policy innovations than has Bangladesh in spheres such as language and management of internal conflict (Norris 2008).

If the career prospects of subnational officials depend on their performance in running subnational governments, they have a strong incentive to seek policy innovations to address local governance challenges. In China, local policy autonomy has served as an incentive for local institutional innovations; leadership personnel decisions are determined by upper-level party and government institutions in an arrangement dubbed "experimentation under hierarchy" (Heilmann 2008).

The nature of decentralization and central-local relations shape local incentives for innovation. For example, different incentives and pressures arise when local parties are in opposition to central parties. In Lagos, Nigeria, the opposition leadership could not rely on intergovernmental transfers from the center, and thus it put in place innovative approaches to secure greater internally generated revenues. Because new actors needed to be persuaded to cooperate in

WDR 2017 team, based on inputs from Yasuhiko Matsuda.

order to secure these revenues, more contestability emerged in the local policy bargains (Watts 2016).

National diffusion of local innovations

Even when successful, idiosyncratic local innovations in isolated local governments may not translate into systemic adaptation; these innovations must be diffused across jurisdictions. Decentralization can increase policy experimentation, but it also can increase the number of veto players. In some cases, a nimble unitary state may be more agile in policy adaptation, compensating for the reduced number of opportunities for experimentation and outsider entry.

Certain governance environments and power relationships encourage efficient diffusion of local innovations. Diffusion through "demonstration effects" requires both competition among local governments in different jurisdictions and relatively free flows of information, so that elites and citizens can identify innovations in other jurisdictions. In Brazil, participatory budgeting began in a handful of municipalities in southern parts of the country and eventually spread to hundreds of local governments. In this case, diffusion followed more or less partisan lines, demonstrating the effectiveness of political parties as institutional mechanisms to transmit information (see chapter 8).

Diffusion may also be facilitated by strong central control. In China, where subnational governments have acquired significant levels of autonomy over fiscal and economic affairs but where local leaders face accountability to upper-level governments, individual jurisdictions have emulated successes from other jurisdictions. When provinces faced a challenge of controlling local inflation soon after market-oriented reforms were introduced in the late 1980s, more effective approaches—such as a market-oriented measure adopted by one of the reform front-runners, the province of Guangdong—drove out less effective ones—such as a price-control policy introduced by the more conservative province of Heilongjiang, bordering Siberia (Montinola, Qian, and Weingast 1995).

Local innovations can translate into nationwide reforms through processes of political renewal when local leadership—whether through parties or as individuals—wins national power and leads their country in a new direction. Subnational political leaders are more likely to step up to the national level in a political system in which decentralization is institutionalized and political leaders have opportunities to demonstrate their competence and deliver performance in numerous subnational governments (Myerson 2011). In recent years, Mauricio Macri of Argentina, Narendra Modi of India, and Joko Widodo of Indonesia all demonstrated their effectiveness as local governors before winning national office. Decentralized democracies allow opposition political parties to gain support in specific localities or regions and eventually to challenge the dominant national party. In India, the Bharatiya Janata Party (BJP), which carried Modi into the national government, gained strength over time by winning several elections at the state level (Rudolph and Rudolph 2001).

The politics of decentralization

The decision to decentralize can be spurred by many different combinations of incentives and arrangements of relative power among various actors. A split may arise among central actors, and to gain strength they may turn to supportive local actors. Sometimes, ruling elites have attempted to diffuse popular discontent with the performance of the national government by decentralizing roles and responsibilities to subnational governments. The military regime that governed Brazil from 1964 to 1985, for example, formed tacit alliances with subnational political elites to maintain both a modicum of political legitimacy and coalitional support (Hagopian 1996). In other instances, elites have tried to preempt rising demands for regional autonomy through greater decentralization, such as Bolivia in the 1990s and Indonesia in the early 2000s, or have introduced more decentralization to signify a move away from the authoritarian centralization of power and resources, such as the Philippines after the fall of Ferdinand Marcos. Formalization of a decentralized governance structure can also be a form of "settlement" after a prolonged internal conflict (see chapter 4).

Even after a political system decides to decentralize, the central-local relationship constantly develops; it is not linear. Changing power dynamics can generate pushes for recentralization if national and subnational elites are in competition. For example, in the Philippines, during legislative consideration of the Local Government Code in 1991, members of the House of Representatives, who were elected from congressional districts (typically smaller than a province), opted to weaken the fiscal resource base of provincial governments whose governors were viewed as potential rivals as dispensers of local patronage.

Senators, who were elected nationally, were more willing to devolve more power to the provinces (Eaton 2001; Matsuda 2011).

As these cases demonstrate, political incentives shape important aspects of the design of intergovernmental relations, with lasting consequences for the ability of the decentralized governance arrangement to adapt to emerging challenges. Decisions to decentralize (or recentralize) are primarily politically motivated and involve bargains among multiple stakeholders in which technocratic criteria often take a back seat. Outcomes reflect the relative bargaining powers of competing interests, mediated by the existing political institutions. Understanding how these bargains take place can help produce more effective, adaptive, and context-specific decentralization designs.

Note

1. *New State Ice Co. v. Liebmann*, 285 U.S. 262 (1932).

References

Campbell, Tim. 2003. *The Quiet Revolution: Decentralization and the Rise of Political Participation in Latin American Cities*. Pittsburgh: University of Pittsburgh Press.

Eaton, Kent. 2001. "Political Obstacles to Decentralization: Evidence from Argentina and the Philippines." *Development and Change* 32 (1): 101–27.

Fiszbein, Ariel. 1997. "The Emergence of Local Capacity: Lessons from Colombia." *World Development* 25 (7): 1029–43.

Hagopian, Frances. 1996. *Traditional Politics and Regime Change in Brazil*. New York: Cambridge University Press.

Heilmann, Sebastian. 2008. "Policy Experimentation in China's Economic Rise." *Studies in Comparative International Development* 43 (1): 1–26.

Matsuda, Yasuhiko. 2011. "Ripe for a Big Bang? Assessing the Political Feasibility of Legislative Reforms in the Philippines' Local Government Code." Policy Research Working Paper 5792, World Bank, Washington, DC.

Montinola, Gabriella, Yingyi Qian, and Barry R. Weingast. 1995. "Federalism, Chinese Style: The Political Basis for Economic Success in China." *World Politics* 48 (1): 50–81.

Myerson, Roger B. 2011. "Toward a Theory of Leadership and State Building." *Proceedings of the National Academy of Sciences* 108 (Supplement 4): 21297–301.

Norris, Pippa. 2008. *Driving Democracy: Do Power-Sharing Institutions Work?* New York: Cambridge University Press.

Rudolph, Lloyd I., and Susanne Hoeber Rudolph. 2001. "Redoing the Constitutional Design: From an Interventionist to a Regulatory State." In *The Success of India's Democracy*, edited by Atul Kohli, 127–62. Contemporary South Asia Series. New York: Cambridge University Press.

Tendler, Judith. 1997. *Good Government in the Tropics*. Baltimore: Johns Hopkins University Press.

Watts, Michael. 2016. "The Lagos Model: Political Reform and Asymmetrical State Capabilities in an Oil State." Background paper, WDR 2017, World Bank, Washington, DC.

Public service reform

In the United States, the Pendleton Civil Service Reform Act of 1883 sought to abolish the spoils system then at work in the federal government. To this end, it established a meritocratic public service, governed by rules that restricted politicians' power over their administrative agents (Horn 1995). Implementation of these rules took a long time; a half-century later, about 75 percent of public servants were subject to them (Grindle 2012, 1). Fast-forward to April 2003 when Mexico's president, Vincente Fox, signed into law the Professional Career Service (Servicio Profesional de Carrera, SPC), which set up meritocratic rules for middle- and high-level positions in the federal public administration. As of early 2015, only a tiny fraction (1.8 percent) of all federal public servants were part of the SPC (World Bank 2016).

Public services have yielded to reformers, but only slowly and incrementally. Change has been messy and nonlinear—new color added to an old painting, not a fresh canvas. This pattern holds regardless of the direction or objectives of change—whether reformers were fighting against patronage[1] and for a merito-cratic, (politically) neutral, and stable Weberian-style career public service[2] (Weber 1956), or hoping to make rule-bound bureaucracies more responsive and performance-oriented, such as during the New Public Management (NPM) movement in the 1980s. Why has it been so difficult to change institutional logics within the public service? What does this imply for reformers' strategies?

A case in point: Mexico's Professional Career Service

Mexico's SPC law of 2003 was a historical milestone, passed at a moment of opportunity after the National Action Party (Partido Acción Nacional, PAN) won the presidency.[3] It aimed to put an end to the spoils system of the Institutional Revolutionary Party (Partido Revolucionario Institucional, PRI), in place for over 70 years, by establishing meritocratic rules for middle- and senior-level management positions. Patronage had served the PRI well: the prospect of landing a public job mobilized citizens for its electoral campaigns, and the system permitted it to deliver on presidential agendas, recruiting both expertise and loyalty while co-opting dissenters.

A context of growing electoral competition, and thus a growing risk of losing power, enabled cross-party support for adoption of the SPC by Mexico's Congress. The law had been conceived by an elite coalition of presidential advisers, academics, and leg-islators. Legislators from all major parties supported the SPC law.

Implementation of the SPC encountered resis-tance, however, and was rapidly subverted. The initial challenges did not assuage the critics: it often took months to fill vacant positions under the new recruit-ment processes. Managers, accustomed to the flex-ibility afforded by patronage, felt overly constrained and unable to build their own teams. Ministries, departments, and agencies (MDAs) bypassed the SPC law by appointing large numbers of staff to temporary positions and advisory roles. In 2007 new regulations gave the MDAs autonomy to run the SPC recruitment process themselves, which the Ministry of Public

Prepared for WDR 2017 by Jürgen René Blum.

Service (MoPS) had originally conducted centrally. Today, the SPC remains alive. In early 2015 it covered about 79 percent of the positions that it should cover under the law (World Bank 2016). But challenges persist. For example, the MDAs continue to exploit a loophole in the SPC legislation (Article 34[4]) to bypass its competitive process. In 2014 about 45 percent of all SPC appointees entered through this loophole.

Adverse politics

As in Mexico, reformers have frequently capitalized on moments of crisis or political change to advocate for enacting new public service legislation (Grindle 2012, 256). In Mexico, the opportunity was presented by the increasing party competition. In the United States, the Pendleton Act was passed only after President James Garfield was assassinated by an infuriated benefactor of the spoils system,[5] although voters' discontent with politicians buying and selling offices had been growing beforehand (Wilson 1989, 239). Advocates of meritocratic reform have depended on such rare windows of opportunity because the balance of power has often been skewed against it, facing opposition from powerful veto players.

Patronage—or deals-based—systems have served political elites and their constituents well in many ways. Patronage, employed rightly, can drive government performance. It can enable political principals to pick the most able and loyal candidate for the job. But it can also serve to reward constituents with public jobs, helping politicians survive in office (as in Mexico before 2000), especially when a politician's base is narrow (see chapter 6). As Robinson and Verdier (2013) argue, the promise of revocable public jobs is a politically attractive form of clientelistic transfer because it ensures mutual commitment. Politicians can easily fire disloyal constituents, and constituents can easily observe whether they receive the promised jobs in return for votes. Short electoral cycles also favor clientelism. A public job is an immediate and secure reward for constituents, whereas political investments in meritocratic principles may translate into better services only in the distant—and uncertain—future.

Meritocratic reforms have had to be politically constructed because they require collective action (Schneider 1999; Grindle 2012). They have rarely figured prominently in electoral platforms because they benefit a dispersed and disorganized broad electorate (Schneider 1999). Meanwhile, reform opponents—political and public service elites and civil servants themselves—tend to be powerful veto players, concentrated

and well organized. Within elite circles, legislators must commit to tying their own hands and giving up patronage. This is more credible when electoral competition makes future changes in power likely, such as after Mexico's 2000 election (Geddes 1994). In this case, meritocracy can serve as insurance that partisans will retain their jobs (see chapter 7). Meritocracy can also help politicians credibly commit to policies beyond their own time in office. President Franklin Roosevelt, for example, expanded merit protection to his liberal appointees out of fear that his New Deal policies might not outlast his administration (Horn 1995, 103).

Programmatic political parties can help overcome these collective action problems by disciplining legislators to act collectively in their party's interest (chapter 8), as, for example, in Mexico. Statistical analysis of over 160 World Bank civil service reform projects around the world supports these findings. Cruz and Keefer (2015) find that these projects on average performed better where programmatic political parties were present.[6] Concentrated decision-making power can also help.[7] Several states with centralized power, ranging from Prussia to Rwanda, have employed concentrated power to enforce meritocratic reforms.

Reinterpreting ambiguous rules

Even when new public service rules are adopted, notoriously vast gaps between paper and practice tend to persist. In Mexico, much of the battle over the SPC was fought over the (re)interpretation of the new rules after they had been signed into law. Public service rules are vulnerable to such "political skirmishing" (Mahoney and Thelen 2009, 12) because they are ambiguous (compared with, for example, a change in tax rates) and because of principal-agent problems (Schneider 1999).

Public servants—the very agents asked to implement the new rules—may be reluctant to follow them because they do not reflect the social norms (and beliefs) that shape their identities—that is, the prevailing informal institutions. Identities can be slow to adapt, despite changes in formal rules. In Austria, for example, about a decade after the adoption of NPM-style reforms, 58 percent of surveyed officials continued to identify themselves as "servants of the state," consistent with long-standing bureaucratic-legalistic (*Rechtsstaat*) virtues rather than managerial ones (Meyer and Hammerschmid 2006).

Not least, political principals themselves may seek to only partially implement reforms in a hunt for legitimacy rather than performance (DiMaggio and Powell 1983). Moynihan (2006), for example, documents that U.S. states only partially adopted performance management reforms in the 1990s. Managers were held to account more tightly for results, which were politically attractive to announce. But in the face of union resistance, among other factors, many states failed, in return, to give managers more discretion over their staff.

Implications for public service reform strategies

In summary, public service reform paths have been nonlinear and messy because reform initiatives often face adversity and because new rules risk being subverted in practice. What does this imply for reform strategies?

Above all, realistic public service paths and strategies depend on context. Paths vary because of distinct points of departure. Historical legacies—beyond political institutions—have limited the room in which reformers can maneuver. Pollitt and Bouckaert (2011, 94), for example, highlight how administrative traditions persist. Countries in the *Rechtsstaat* or Napoleonic tradition,[8] such as Austria, Germany, and France, have been much more cautious in dismantling a unified public service and assimilating it with private sector employment than their Anglo-Saxon "public interest" peers. China's unique cadre management system has successfully married long-standing norms of loyalty to the Communist Party of China (CPC) with meritocratic recruitment and cadres' accountability for achieving performance targets far from the apolitical Weberian model (Rothstein 2015).

Realistic reform strategies also need to balance competing and evolving objectives. In member countries of the Organisation for Economic Co-operation and Development (OECD), problem definitions have shifted from containing patronage through meritocratic reforms in the 19th century, to ensuring equal access and treatment in the 1950s, to increasing responsiveness in the 1970s (and performance in the 1990s), as reflected in the NPM movement (Blum and Manning 2009). Postconflict settings perhaps most starkly illustrate competing ends: discretion over public jobs may be the price for peace, trumping all concerns over merit. South Sudan's Comprehensive Peace Agreement (CPA) of 2005, for example, provided its 10 states with vast discretion over recruiting public servants to hold a fragile coalition of formerly warring tribes together and prevent them from reverting to violence (Blum, Ferreiro-Rodriguez, and Srivastava 2016).

Skillfully bundling public service reforms with other policies can help mobilize a broader electorate beyond a small elite of reformers (Schneider and Heredia 2003, 18). Reformers in Argentina and Brazil, for example, framed administrative reforms as essential to making popular stabilization programs viable (Schneider 1999). Such bundling may, however, come at the price of tying the longer-term prospects of public service reform to the "fortunes of the larger agenda" (Schneider 1999).

Especially where political cohesion is weak, selective and asymmetric reform strategies can reduce resistance, seeking to build "islands of effectiveness" in selected agencies. Indonesia's Bureaucracy Reform, for example, successfully increased pay and accountability for performance in a few priority agencies, and it was later gradually rolled out to others (World Bank 2014). In Afghanistan in 2003, reformers adopted an asymmetric reform approach to rebuilding the administration, recognizing that political divisions made comprehensive administrative reforms impossible (Hakimi and others 2004, 11). Yet, selective strategies are risky and no panacea. They can entail generalization pressures, as in Afghanistan (Blum, Ferreiro-Rodriguez, and Srivastava 2016); interagency competition for skills, as in Brazil (Shepherd 2003); or well-paid jobs becoming the target of political patronage, as in Uganda's Revenue Authority (Robinson 2007).

Not least, the process of formulating ideas for reform matters. Where leaders frequently engage with stakeholders—especially public servants—in defining problems and solutions, public servants may be more prepared to accept and identify with new rules (Andrews 2013). New research corroborates the promise of influencing employees' beliefs and organizations' cultures, short of changing formal practices. In a quasi-experimental study, Blader and others (2015) show that merely introducing drivers of a U.S. trucking company to "lean management ideas" that emphasize continual improvement through teamwork and collective responsibility is associated with higher employee engagement and, in turn, better driving performance. Understanding how public servants' identities matter and change remains a promising field for future empirical research.

Notes

1. Following Reid and Kurth (1988), *patronage* is defined here as the power to hire and fire an employee at will.
2. The key feature of a meritocratic civil service is that it restricts politicians' power over their administrative

agents. Meritocracy is understood here as broadly comprising a variety of forms. In the narrow Weberian sense, it refers to a career-based public service, with entry through competitive exams, and government by principles of political neutrality.

3. The argument in this spotlight and the opening example draw strongly on Grindle (2012).

4. Article 34 of the Law of the Professional Career Service establishes that in exceptional cases and in cases of public emergencies the ministers or the chief administrative officers may authorize the appointment of a public servant to a career position without the need for an open competition and on a temporary basis (OECD 2011, 195). These exceptions are only vaguely defined.

5. Reform required a political crisis triggered by the assassination of Garfield by Charles Guiteau, who killed the president in an act of revenge when Garfield refused to appoint him as the U.S. ambassador to France.

6. Project performance is measured based on the Independent Evaluation Group's project outcome ratings. These ratings are meant to assess the extent to which "there were . . . shortcomings in the operation's achievement of its objectives, in its efficiency or in its relevance" on a six-point ordinal scale, ranging from "highly satisfactory" to "highly unsatisfactory" (World Bank 2005, 1). It is important to note that these ratings have very large caveats. Among others, they are corporate measures of project performance, not of government performance; they suffer from endogeneity bias (as objectives are project-specific); and they inevitably contain elements of subjectivity.

7. Besides concentration of power and programmatic political parties, the literature highlights many contextual factors that can influence public service reforms, including the degree of fusion between bureaucrats and politicians (Schneider and Heredia 2003) and the prior influence of class elites in the public service (Grindle 2012). See Pollitt and Bouckaert (2011) for a comprehensive discussion of NPM reforms.

8. From the *Rechtsstaat* perspective, the state is a central integrating force within society, and its central concern is with the preparation and enforcement of laws. By contrast, the public interest model "accords the state a less extensive or dominant role within society" and government is regarded as "something of a necessary evil" (Pollitt and Bouckaert 2011, 62).

References

Andrews, Matt. 2013. *The Limits of Institutional Reform in Development: Changing Rules for Realistic Solutions*. New York: Cambridge University Press.

Blader, Steven, Claudine Gartenberg, Rebecca Henderson, and Andrea Prat. 2015. "The Real Effects of Relational Contracts." *American Economic Review* 105 (5): 452–56.

Blum, J., and N. Manning. 2009. "Public Management Reforms across OECD Countries." In *Public Management and Governance*. 2nd ed., edited by T. Bovaird and E. Loffler. London: Routledge.

Blum, Jürgen René, Marcos Ferreiro-Rodriguez, and Vivek Srivastava. 2016. *Building Public Services in Post-conflict Countries: A Comparative Analysis of Reform Trajectories*. Washington, DC: World Bank.

Cruz, Cesi, and Philip Keefer. 2015. "Political Parties, Clientelism, and Bureaucratic Reform." *Comparative Political Studies* 48 (14): 1942–73.

DiMaggio, Paul J., and Walter W. Powell. 1983. "The Iron Cage Revisited: Institutional Isomorphism and Collective Rationality in Organizational Fields." *American Sociological Review* 48 (2): 147–60.

Geddes, Barbara. 1994. *Politician's Dilemma: Building State Capacity in Latin America*. Berkeley: University of California Press.

Grindle, Merilee S. 2012. *Jobs for the Boys*. Cambridge, MA: Harvard University Press.

Hakimi, Eklil, Nick Manning, Satyendra Prasad, and Keire Prince. 2004. *Asymmetric Reforms: Agency-Level Reforms in the Afghan Civil Service*. Washington, DC: World Bank.

Horn, Murray J. 1995. *The Political Economy of Public Administration: Institutional Choice in the Public Sector*. Political Economy of Institutions and Decisions Series. Cambridge, U.K.: Cambridge University Press.

Mahoney, James, and Kathleen Thelen. 2009. *Explaining Institutional Change: Ambiguity, Agency, and Power*. New York: Cambridge University Press.

Meyer, Renate E., and Gerhard Hammerschmid. 2006. "Changing Institutional Logics and Executive Identities: A Managerial Challenge to Public Administration in Austria." *American Behavioral Scientist* 49 (7): 1000–14.

Moynihan, Donald P. 2006. "Managing for Results in State Government: Evaluating a Decade of Reform." *Public Administration Review* 66 (1): 77–89.

OECD (Organisation for Economic Co-operation and Development). 2011. *Towards More Effective and Dynamic Public Management in Mexico*. OECD Public Governance Reviews Series. Paris: OECD.

Pollitt, Christopher, and Geert Bouckaert. 2011. *Public Management Reform, a Comparative Analysis: New Public Management, Governance, and the Neo-Weberian State*. Oxford, U.K.: Oxford University Press.

Reid, Joseph D., and Michael M. Kurth. 1988. "Public Employees in Political Firms, Part A: The Patronage Era." *Public Choice* 59 (3): 253–62.

Robinson, James A., and Thierry Verdier. 2013. "The Political Economy of Clientelism." *Scandinavian Journal of Economics* 115 (2): 260–91.

Robinson, Mark. 2007. "The Political Economy of Governance Reforms in Uganda." *Commonwealth and Comparative Politics* 45 (4): 452–74.

Rothstein, Bo. 2015. "The Chinese Paradox of High Growth and Low Quality of Government: The Cadre

Organization Meets Max Weber." *Governance* 28 (4): 533–48.

Schneider, Ben Ross. 1999. "The Politics of Administrative Reform: Intractable Dilemmas and Improbable Solutions." Paper presented at the Federal Reserve Bank of Atlanta's 1999 Fiscal Conference: Sustainable Public Sector Finance in Latin America, Atlanta, November 1–2.

Schneider, Ben Ross, and Blanca Heredia. 2003. *Reinventing Leviathan: The Politics of Administrative Reform in Developing Countries*. Miami: North-South Center Press.

Shepherd, Geoffrey. 2003. "Civil Service Reform in Developing Countries: Why Is It Going Badly?" Paper presented at the World Bank's 11th International Anti-corruption Conference, Seoul, Republic of Korea, May 25–28.

Weber, Max. 1956. *Economy and Society*. 2 vols. Berkeley: University of California Press.

Wilson, James Q. 1989. *Bureaucracy: What Government Agencies Do and Why They Do It*. New York: Basic Books.

World Bank. 2005. "Harmonized Evaluation Criteria for ICR and OED Evaluations." World Bank, Washington, DC.

World Bank. 2014. "Pay Flexibility and Government Performance: A Multicountry Study." Working Paper 88486 (June 1), World Bank, Washington, DC.

———. 2016. *Mexico Public Expenditure Review*. Report AUS10694 (March 30). Washington, DC: World Bank.

CHAPTER 8

Citizens as agents of change

For most of the 19th and 20th centuries in Uruguay, the overall quality of public services was low, and political connections were the main vehicle for accessing the goods and services provided by the state. In fact, clientelist (patron-client) practices were the norm. Yet, in recent decades, government performance in Uruguay has steadily improved, making the country a rare contemporary overachiever—a society that has succeeded in curbing corruption and promoting a virtuous cycle of institutional change toward better governance (Mungiu-Pippidi 2015; Buquet and Piñeiro 2016). Today, Uruguay is ranked the world's 21st least-corrupt country, according to Transparency International's 2015 Corruption Perceptions Index (Transparency International 2015).

What accounts for Uruguay's successful transformation? Although a complex set of circumstances and contingencies was ultimately responsible, evolving action on the part of Uruguay's citizens and their interaction with elites in the policy arena were essential ingredients. The creation of programmatic parties after civilian rule was reestablished in 1985 played an important role. Social groups made efforts to build coalitions with interest groups that shared the same preferences—such as the urban sector hit by the economic crisis—and to channel popular demands through a new coalition of political actors (Frente Amplio) that would become a political option to the traditional groups in power. The new coalition increased contestability and managed to bring into the policy arena new demands for equitable access to public resources, accountability, and better-quality services. Eventually, elections rewarded the politicians who delivered on— and credibly committed to—their announced reforms, changing the incentives of elites and increasing the opportunity costs of old clientelist practices. Over

time, political, administrative, and economic reforms increasingly reduced politicians' opportunities to capture state resources for private purposes.

The experience of Uruguay illustrates how multiple mechanisms of engagement can help citizens influence the policy arena by changing incentives, preferences, and contestability to generate more equitable development. Modes of citizen engagement include elections, political organizations, social organizations, and direct participation and deliberation. Because all these expressions of collective action are imperfect, they complement rather than substitute for one another. As the example of Uruguay shows, it is their strategic combination that makes governments more responsive to citizens' needs and opens up opportunities for sustainable change.

Chapter 7 points out that elites are not monolithic; rather, they engage in bargains that reflect diverse preferences and incentives and ultimately shape policy formulation and implementation. Such differences in objectives among elites can open up opportunities for citizens to support change. Indeed, important changes in history have been driven by coalitions between reforming elites and organized citizens that support reform initiatives and overcome the opposition of other elites (Fukuyama 2014; Fox 2015).

The ways in which elites and citizens interact to create coalitions for change are often shaped by existing institutions of vertical and horizontal accountability that define the rules of the game in the policy arena. As discussed in chapter 7, these rules are often the result of elite-elite bargains that are designed primarily to serve elite interests. As this chapter shows, however, certain accountability institutions can perform new functions and create an enabling environment for citizen agency, opening up opportunities

Important changes in history have been driven by coalitions between reforming elites and organized citizens that support reform initiatives.

for enhanced contestability and elite-citizen interaction in ways often not anticipated by the actors who originally designed them. Yet, the outcomes of such institutional reforms are not predetermined. Citizen agency can help translate favorable conditions into effective reforms that drive positive change.

This chapter focuses primarily on the conditions under which citizen engagement can be a driver of positive change, while recognizing that each mechanism of engagement—elections, political organizations, social organizations, and public deliberation—has inherent limitations. Indeed, none of these mechanisms is a panacea: at times, elections may legitimize socially undesirable policies; political and social organizations can lead to violence and rent-seeking; and deliberation can be captured by private interests and opportunistic elites. These mechanisms, however, play a fundamental role in the process of interaction among state and nonstate actors to design and implement policies and to bring about changes in formal rules, particularly in areas that affect minority groups and those generally excluded from the policy arena. When effective, the interaction of these mechanisms of citizen engagement can bring about significant changes in governance through nonviolent means.

Bringing change through the ballot box

Elections are among the most well-established mechanisms available to citizens to strengthen accountability and responsiveness to their demands.[1] When effective, elections can help improve the level and quality of services provided by the state by selecting and sanctioning leaders based on their performance in providing *public goods*. They can help citizens overcome collective action problems so they can give leaders incentives to support the public goods favored by the majority of citizens. However, elections can be an unhealthy form of citizen engagement when they instead serve to select and sanction leaders based on their provision of *private goods* (Khemani and others 2016). Elections can be subject to manipulation, fraud, violence, vote buying, and patronage, which undermine their effectiveness in holding leaders to account, resulting in perverse incentives.

How elections strengthen vertical accountability and responsiveness to citizen demands

Elections can be particularly effective at the local level, where voters might be better able to coordinate and shape the incentives of local politicians to deliver—including by curbing corrupt behavior. In China, for example, the introduction of village-level elections increased total local expenditures on public goods by about 50 percent and helped curb the rent-seeking behavior of local officials and reduce inequality by promoting land redistribution to local villagers (Shen and Yao 2008; Martinez-Bravo and others 2011). Likewise, during the phasing in of decentralization and the shift to direct elections across districts in Indonesia in the late 1900s, districts in which governors were directly elected experienced more efficient revenue collection and spending than districts ruled by centrally appointed governors (Skoufias and others 2011; Martinez-Bravo 2014).

Elections can also curb ethnic favoritism in the allocation of public resources by placing constraints on executive power. In Kenya, for example, during the authoritarian period districts that shared the ethnicity of the president received three times as much public investment in roads (figure 8.1). However, under multiparty electoral democracy this effect has disappeared, suggesting that elections successfully constrained the ability of leaders to divert public resources for partisan goals (Burgess and others 2015). Likewise, a comparison of fertility rates across 28 countries in Sub-Saharan Africa reveals that multiparty elections and leadership changes associated with electoral mechanisms significantly reduced infant mortality rates through improved health care (Kudamatsu 2012).

Encouragingly, opportunities for citizens to engage in the public decision-making process through voting have increased substantially over the last half-century. At the beginning of the so-called Third Wave of democratization in 1974, there were only about 40 electoral democracies in the world, mostly confined to the industrialized Western world (Huntington 1991). Today, the number has more than doubled (to about 100), with more than half of the world's countries choosing their leaders through elections in which a change in government is a real possibility. Elections have become a fast-spreading norm to legitimize state authority and organize human societies (Diamond 2008). Even in places where open contestation at the national level is absent or restricted, elections have been introduced at the local level to improve oversight of local officials, opening opportunities for participation and contestation of public policies (Gandhi and Lust-Okar 2009).

Despite the global spread of elections, the space for effective citizen engagement is compromised by the perception that, on average, the quality of the electoral process is declining worldwide (figure 8.2). Although regular elections can improve the overall level of economic policies by disciplining leaders, this structural effect is conditional on the quality of those elections (Chauvet and Collier 2009). Newly established democracies in low-income countries are especially vulnerable to electoral manipulation. Indeed, the experience of many developing countries suggests that the principle of one person, one vote is often undermined in practice by incumbent leaders who seek to minimize the risk of losing power. Elites can resort to multiple strategies of manipulation that undermine the integrity of the electoral process, including the use of legal instruments that ban certain political parties or individual candidates from joining the electoral contest, the adoption of complex voting registration regulations that effectively disenfranchise certain groups of voters, the resort to electoral fraud, and, in extreme cases, voter intimidation and physical repression of political opponents (Schedler 2002).

Challenges to free and fair elections are reflected in the widespread dissatisfaction and disillusionment among citizens. While on average almost 90 percent of respondents worldwide view free and fair elections as an important instrument for improving economic conditions in their country, they often do not trust their quality. Less than half of respondents to the latest world Gallup survey, on average, have confidence in the integrity of the electoral process; mistrust is especially high in Europe and Central Asia and in Latin America and the Caribbean (figure 8.3). These perceptions matter because they shape citizen engagement and citizens' propensity to vote (Birch 2010). Figure 8.4 is consistent with this claim, showing that voter turnout is declining worldwide. Moreover, the lack of electoral integrity and a persistent climate of mistrust over time undermine the legitimacy of the political system, fueling protests, mass demonstrations, and, in extreme cases, outbreaks of electoral violence and civil war.[2] The 2007 Kenyan election, with an estimated 1,200 deaths and the displacement of more than 300,000 people, dramatically illustrates this point.

Changing incentives: Transparency, information, and the media

Transparency and the provision of timely and relevant information can help improve the quality and effectiveness of elections (Khemani and others 2016). The average voter may not have the information

Figure 8.1 In Kenya, elections changed the incentives of the ruling elites, reducing the scope of ethnic favoritism

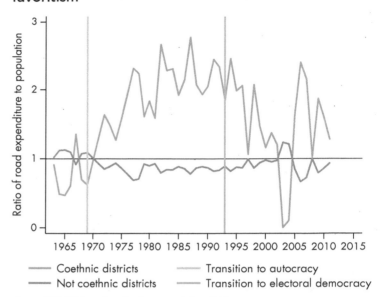

Source: WDR 2017 team, based on Burgess and others 2015.

Note: The figure covers the years 1963–2011. The share of road development expenditure and the share of population are relative to district populations in 1963. A district is defined as coethnic if more than 50 percent of its residents are from the same ethnic group as that of the president in the given year. A ratio above 1 indicates the presence of ethnic favoritism.

Figure 8.2 Electoral democracies are spreading, but the integrity of elections is declining

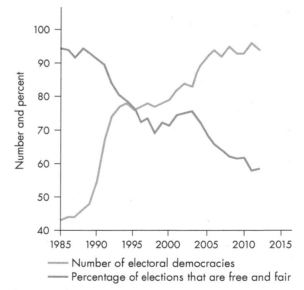

Sources: WDR 2017 team, using data from the Center for Systemic Peace, Polity IV (database), various years (number of electoral democracies) and Bishop and Hoeffler 2014 (free and fair elections).

Note: Over time, there is a larger number of countries where elections are the main instrument to select leaders; the decline in the share of "free and fair" elections could be partially driven by the incorporation of new, less developed electoral systems, but that is unlikely to explain the total decline.

Figure 8.3 Although citizens value elections as an important route to economic development, less than half of respondents worldwide have confidence in the integrity of elections

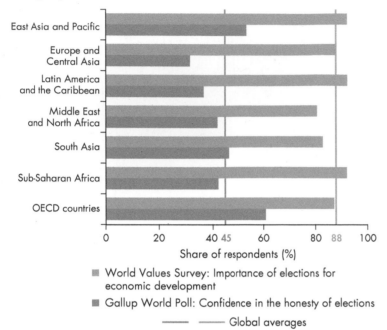

Share of respondents (%)

■ World Values Survey: Importance of elections for economic development

■ Gallup World Poll: Confidence in the honesty of elections

—— —— Global averages

Sources: WDR 2017 team, using data from World Values Survey, Wave 6, 2010–14, and Gallup Organization, Gallup World Poll, 2010–15.

Note: The World Values Survey covers a sample of 41 countries, and the Gallup World Poll covers a sample of 142 countries. OECD = Organisation of Economic Co-operation and Development.

Figure 8.4 Voter turnout worldwide from 1945 to 2015 indicates unequal citizen participation and the risk of biased representation of policy preferences

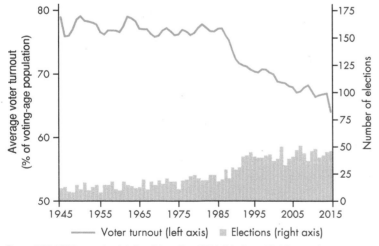

—— Voter turnout (left axis) ■ Elections (right axis)

Source: WDR 2017 team, using data from International IDEA, Voter Turnout Database, various years.

Note: The line refers to average voter turnout using locally weighted smoothing, while the bars indicate absolute number of elections in a given year.

required to properly assess government performance and clearly assign responsibilities. Giving voters accurate and credible information from trustworthy sources such as independent media or oversight institutions can change the prevailing social norms, thereby reducing information asymmetries and increasing voters' willingness to punish incumbents for poor performance and bad practices such as corruption. For example, in 2003 the federal government of Brazil launched a national anticorruption program that targeted municipal governments with random audits by the national audit agency. The results were publicly disseminated through the media (radio, television, and newspapers). When the audit reports disclosed information about corrupt practices, corrupt mayors were punished at the polls, while mayors with no irregularities were rewarded with reelection. These effects were stronger in municipalities with local radio stations, pointing to the important role played by the media in amplifying and disseminating campaign messages (Ferraz and Finan 2008). Similar results have been reported in Mexico and Puerto Rico, using information disclosed in audit reports (Larreguy, Marshall, and Snyder 2015; Bobonis, Cámara Fuertes, and Schwabe 2016), and in India, using report cards on the performance of incumbent politicians (Banerjee and others 2011).

Information can strengthen the quality of citizen engagement even in countries in which partisan loyalties are strong and a dominant party has been entrenched for some time. In Sierra Leone, increased access to information about local politicians through radio campaigns had a significant effect in shaping behavior and increasing voters' willingness to cast their ballot for a politician of a different party and outside their own coethnic group (Casey 2015).

However, as discussed in the *World Development Report 2016: Digital Dividends* (WDR 2016), when the information disclosed is not salient to voters or when attributing individual responsibility is difficult, the incentives of politicians to respond with better service provision remain low, and transparency can have no effect on vertical accountability (see spotlight 11 on transparency and accountability initiatives). In Uganda, the provision of scorecards on the performance of members of the parliament did not have any impact on politicians' selection or performance (Humphreys and Weinstein 2012). Likewise, radio-based information campaigns on public health and primary education in rural Benin had no effect on shaping politicians' incentives to improve health and education services, despite reducing voters' support for patronage practices (Keefer and Khemani 2014). Sometimes, politicians can respond to the disclosure of information by increasing their vote-buying efforts, thereby preempting its potential effect on voting behavior. In the Philippines, an initiative to share information about a large public spending program ahead of municipal elections prompted incumbent politicians to increase vote buying. In the end, the campaign had no discernible effect on voting behavior (Cruz, Keefer, and Labonne 2015).

In the presence of preexisting preferences and entrenched social norms, transparency alone is unlikely to trigger change—and might even lead to more polarized preferences (see spotlight 12 on the media). In these circumstances, citizen engagement through sustained processes of policy deliberation might increase the likelihood of better results (as discussed later in this chapter).

Overcoming the challenge of persistent preferences

Citizens' expectations of what politicians can and should deliver can also be shaped by social norms and so-called mental models, as discussed in the *World Development Report 2015: Mind, Society, and Behavior* (World Bank 2015).[3] These norms and mental models can lead to inefficient demands. To cite a notable example, many societies are organized around patron-client (or clientelist) exchanges, in which voters expect politicians to deliver private benefits in return for political support, and they reward or punish politicians based on these expectations (see chapter 6).[4] An attempt by either party involved to break the terms of the exchange is costly and likely to fail. In the terminology of this Report, these relationships often constitute self-reinforcing equilibria. A field experiment during the 2001 presidential elections in Benin illustrates this point. National candidates who adopted clientelistic messages were more effective in mobilizing electoral support than competitors who used broad-based policy messages (Wantchekon 2003).

Recent empirical studies on voting behavior in the United States illustrate the perverse effects that citizens' beliefs can have in shaping public policies, thereby challenging the conventional logic of democratic theory. Achen and Bartels (2016b) argue that the average citizen has little incentive to study complex political issues, engaging in what public choice theorists call "rational ignorance." As a result, voting behavior is based not on policy preferences but on citizens' social identities and partisan loyalties. Caplan (2008) goes a step further and argues that citizens demand policies based on ideological positions without considering the trade-offs and costs they might entail: voters not only lack information, but they also have systematic biases in favor of economic policies that have been proven wrong empirically. The persistence of popular demands for energy and fuel subsidies despite their proven fiscal and environmental costs illustrates how these behavioral dynamics are also relevant for many developing countries, undermining the opportunity to bring change through elections alone (Clements and others 2013).

Enhancing contestability: De facto enfranchisement of voters

Even where de jure voting rights exist and direct electoral manipulation is limited, elections may fail to effectively sanction and select leaders when citizens opt out. Voter turnout is not uniform and is often biased toward certain income groups, which leads to unequal influence in the policy arena. In this sense, the extent to which citizens engage in the electoral process is an important determinant of the effect of elections. In high-income countries, wealth and literacy rates predict turnout, suggesting that poor voters face constraints that reduce their propensity to vote.[5] The lack of engagement of disadvantaged groups in turn shapes politicians' incentives to adopt pro-poor, redistributive policies, thereby reducing social spending and reinforcing existing inequalities (see chapter 6 of this Report).

This logic implies that the de facto enfranchisement of disadvantaged voters can improve accountability by better capturing their policy preferences. In Brazil, for example, the introduction of electronic voting technology has simplified the process of casting ballots and substantially reduced the number of error-ridden and undercounted votes among the poor. The intervention effectively enfranchised 11 percent of the electorate, mainly the poorest and less educated, and contributed to higher spending on public health care, which in turn increased the access of poor pregnant women to prenatal care and reduced the incidence of underweight births (Fujiwara 2015).

Enfranchising poor voters, however, is not sufficient to change public policies. In fact, in developing countries poor people are *more* likely to vote than wealthy citizens. This finding implies that higher levels of turnout may not necessarily reflect greater political mobilization by the poor but rather their tendency to be more receptive to the clientelist practices used by elites to mobilize them (Pande

2011; Beramendiz and Amat 2014). Consistent with this logic, Kasara and Suryanarayan (2015) find that in poor societies rich voters are less likely to vote because the state's extractive capacity is low, and the threat of wealth redistribution through taxation is not credible. However, as the bureaucratic capacity of the state improves and political competition becomes primarily programmatic in nature, the better-off are more likely to engage and influence fiscal policies through voting. In other words, the effect of poor voters' enfranchisement on public policy is contingent on the nature of political competition, the specific mobilization strategies adopted by political parties, and the presence of "credible political alternatives for marginalized citizens" (Kasara and Suryanarayan 2015, 624). Programmatic political parties and social movements play an important mediating role in this respect, as discussed later in this chapter.

Why elections alone are not enough to bring change

These analyses suggest that the common belief that elections are a sufficient mechanism to produce responsive and accountable government is based on questionable assumptions. Even when elections are more effective in changing voters' preferences and the incentives of politicians, they are a limited instrument of control. Voting is an individual action, and citizens face significant coordination challenges when considering whether to remove poorly performing governments, thereby limiting the credibility of the threat to punish elected officials (Manin, Przeworski, and Stokes 1999). Moreover, even when citizens manage to remove politicians whose performance is poor or diverges from their preferences, elections alone offer no credible guarantee that, once elected, new leaders will not shirk their electoral promises and credibly commit to citizens' demands.

Overcoming the limits of collective action and electoral representation requires organizations that represent citizens' collective interests, including political parties, interest groups, and civic associations. These organizations have the potential to strengthen the ability of citizens to monitor government performance, thereby increasing the costs for politicians shirking their electoral promises and making political commitments more credible (Ashworth 2012; Keefer 2013). As Achen and Bartels (2016a, 275) point out, "Ordinary citizens' interests are likely to matter only insofar as the organised groups representing those interests . . . are themselves politically engaged, well-resourced, and internally accountable." It is to these organized groups that this chapter now turns.

> Citizens face significant coordination challenges when considering whether to remove poorly performing governments, thereby limiting the credibility of the threat to punish elected officials.

Bringing change through political organization: The role of political parties

Through voting, individual actions can shape collective outcomes. Citizen collective action—for example, through political organizations—can also shape outcomes. Political parties are a mechanism that can solve collective action problems and can represent and articulate citizens' collective interests, aggregate their preferences, and channel their demands in the policy-making process (Sartori 1976; Kitschelt and Wilkinson 2007).[6]

Enhancing contestability: Why political parties matter

By solving citizens' coordination problems and providing them with the information cues needed to evaluate the performance of incumbents, political parties play a critical role in strengthening vertical accountability (Aldrich 1995). By recruiting and socializing political leadership, political parties also play an important social function in integrating citizens into the political process and allowing different social groups to have a stake in supporting the system, thereby promoting a culture of compromise and reducing societal tensions through enhanced contestability (Diamond and Gunther 2001, 7–8; Randall and Svåsand 2002). In Tanzania, for example, the power-sharing agreements within the Chama Cha Mapinduzi party were instrumental (before the demise of Julius Nyerere) in accommodating the demands of various ethnic and religious groups, allowing power to alternate between Christian and Muslim leaders (Ezrow and Frantz 2011). This arrangement helps explain why the country was not plagued by the ethnic conflicts that prevailed in many countries in the region, despite the presence of more than 140 distinct ethnic groups.

Over the last 40 years, the global landscape of political party systems has changed. Across all income groups, unelected legislatures and single-party systems have become rare, and multiple political organizations are increasingly allowed to enter the policy arena, articulating societal interests and citizens' demands. However, a closer look reveals important differences: in many developing countries, competition is constrained de facto by the dominant nature of the party system (figure 8.5). Where one party dominates the legislative and executive offices, the ability of citizens to influence the policy-making process through representation is reduced (Sartori 1976; Manin, Przeworski, and Stokes 1999, 48). Although, as discussed in chapter 7, dominant party systems may continue to facilitate cooperation and commitment among elites, they undermine citizen collective action by reducing the attractiveness of electoral politics as a mechanism to alter power asymmetries. Over time, the exclusionary nature of this bargaining could undermine the legitimacy of the political system.

The strategies adopted by political parties to mobilize voters have important implications for development because they directly shape the nature of elite-citizen bargaining. On one end of the spectrum—as discussed in chapter 6—*clientelistic political parties* mobilize support through targeted transfers, cash payments, pork barrel public investment projects, patronage jobs, and other private goods (Kitschelt and Wilkinson 2007). On the opposite end of the spectrum, *programmatic political parties* maintain a coherent position on key policy issues, stick to these policy commitments over repeated electoral rounds as their main appeal to attract votes, and deliver on them once in office.[7]

Because the electoral success of programmatic parties—and their own political survival—depends heavily on the credibility of their policy commitments, these parties are more likely to develop organizational arrangements that prevent free-riding and shirking by party members, and so they are more likely to deliver on their electoral promises. Consequently, the quality of public services is significantly higher in countries in which the main parties (government and opposition alike) exhibit programmatic characteristics, and the effect is larger under conditions of electoral competition (figure 8.6). Likewise, programmatic parties increase the possibility that public sector reforms will be adopted and successfully implemented (Keefer 2011, 2013; Cruz and Keefer 2013).

Shaping preferences and incentives: How programmatic parties emerge

Unfortunately, entrenched clientelistic political parties can be difficult to remove. They can become a self-reinforcing equilibrium as they deliver on their commitment to provide private benefits to constituents. Under these circumstances, increased party competition can lead to more—not less—clientelism because poorer voters are more vulnerable to vote buying and therefore less likely to demand programs or policies. The experience of many low-income countries in Sub-Saharan Africa is consistent with this argument and illustrates how multiparty competition has fueled, rather than reduced, clientelism.[8]

Voters selecting between a programmatic party and a clientelistic party must weigh the credibility of each party's commitments and also compare the

Figure 8.5 Although the spread of multiparty systems has increased opportunities for citizen engagement, dominant parties place de facto limits on electoral competition

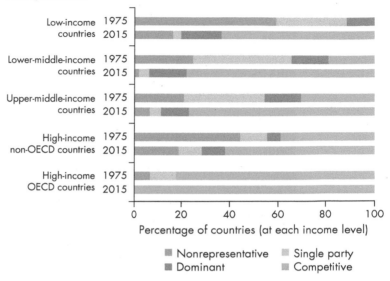

Source: WDR 2017 team, based on Database of Political Institutions (Cruz, Keefer, and Scartascini 2016).

Note: Income groups of countries reflect the latest categorization by the World Bank. A party system is classified as dominant when incumbents control 75 percent or more of seats in the legislature. OECD = Organisation for Economic Co-operation and Development.

Figure 8.6 Programmatic parties perform better than clientelist parties in improving the quality of public services, especially in competitive party systems

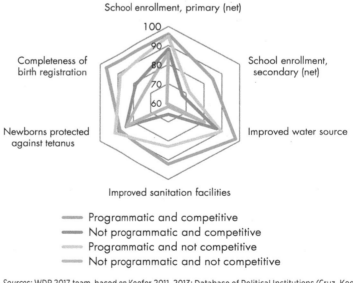

Sources: WDR 2017 team, based on Keefer 2011, 2013; Database of Political Institutions (Cruz, Keefer, and Scartascini 2015); and World Bank, World Development Indicators (database), various years.

benefits promised by each party. To be viable, programmatic parties must successfully deliver on their promises. However, even well-intended politicians often cannot credibly commit to deliver because of weak state capacity and the absence of favorable institutional arrangements—such as strong checks and balances, a well-functioning parliament, and independent judiciaries—that can sanction leaders who renege on their promises. Historical evidence suggests that where meritocratic civil service recruitment predated the development of mass-based political parties, politicians were prevented from capturing the bureaucracy for patronage purposes, and programmatic parties were more likely to develop (Shefter 1977). However, where clientelistic parties already exist, making the commitments of programmatic parties more credible in the short term is difficult because it depends on building state capacity that itself may require the elimination of clientelism.

At times, however, a clientelistic equilibrium can be broken by a change in the relative benefits of clientelistic versus programmatic parties. Indeed, reducing the benefits of clientelism helps explain why developed countries are more likely to have programmatic parties (figure 8.7). At low levels of economic development, the average voters tend to reward clientelist practices rather than support uncertain programmatic platforms because they lack alternative means to secure basic services and are most vulnerable to adverse economic shocks. However, as societies develop, the marginal impact of targeted benefits on the welfare of the average voter is negligible relative to the potential benefits they can derive from public policies. Consequently, citizens' expectations change; they demand higher-quality services and public goods and become less credible in their commitment to "sell" their vote to politicians (Kitschelt and Wilkinson 2007; Stokes and others 2013).

A similar logic explains why political parties tend to diversify their "portfolio" across the national territory and adopt a combination of clientelist and programmatic strategies to mobilize voters, depending on their expected electoral benefits (Kitschelt and Wilkinson 2007, 30–31). In Argentina and Mexico, for example, municipalities that exhibited higher levels of electoral competition and had a larger middle class received the largest influx of public goods, changing politicians' incentives to opt out of clientelism as a strategy to maintain political support (Magaloni, Diaz-Cayeros, and Estévez 2006; Weitz-Shapiro 2014).

At other times, economic crises or stagnation can undermine systems of patronage, triggering the emergence of programmatic parties. In the Republic of Korea, for example, the financial crisis of 1997 reduced the resource base for clientelist practices and triggered policy reforms—such as regulations aimed at improving transparency in political party

finances—that reconfigured partisan competition around programmatic lines (Hellmann 2011; Wang 2012). The outcome of these shocks, however, is not predetermined; worsening economic conditions can also trigger populist appeals that result in political outsiders gaining power on the basis of vague policy proposals. By subordinating the execution of these proposals to the will of a charismatic leader, populism undermines the emergence of programmatic parties and can lead to a shrinking bargaining space, reducing opportunities for citizens to hold elites accountable.[9]

Finally, the commitments of programmatic parties may be more credible at the local level. Decentralization reforms can lower the barriers to the entry of grassroots movements and local civic associations that may be able to compete in elections on a programmatic platform. In Bolivia in the 1990s,

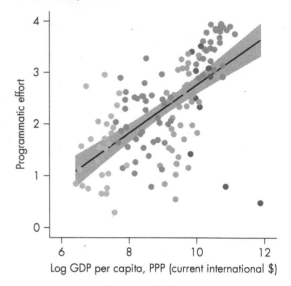

Figure 8.7 Programmatic parties tend to emerge at higher levels of development, but significant variation exists among countries at similar stages of development

- High-income OECD countries
- High-income non-OECD countries
- Upper-middle-income countries
- Lower-middle-income countries
- Low-income countries

Sources: WDR 2017 team, using data from World Bank, World Development Indicators (database), 2016, and V-Dem 2016.

Note: Income is represented by the natural log of the average per capita income in purchasing power parity (PPP) terms in 2008–09. A given party's "programmatic effort" refers to the set of "goods" that the party offers in exchange for political support. The ranks range from 0 (= clientelistic efforts) to 4 (= policy/programmatic efforts). Intermediate values reflect combinations of both strategies (Coppedge and others 2016, 102). OECD = Organisation for Economic Co-operation and Development.

indigenous peoples' movements took advantage of decentralization reforms and newly institutionalized spaces for citizen participation to overcome their divisions, organize collectively through autonomous political parties, and effectively bargain for collective and territorial rights in various municipalities.[10] These experiences created demonstration effects in other municipalities, strengthening the electoral base of indigenous parties and paving the way for their access to the presidency (Van Cott 2005, 2006).

Why political parties alone are not enough to bring about change

When political parties become tools in elite bargains to help solve coordination and commitment challenges among elites, they may fail to represent and articulate the demands and preferences of ordinary citizens. Political parties can act as gatekeepers, adopting laws and regulations that grant ruling elites special advantages and increase the barriers to entry for potential challengers. This behavior can undermine vertical accountability because certain groups of citizens (and the interests they represent) may find themselves systematically excluded from the policy arena or unable to bargain within a level playing field. In South Africa, for example, the National Party enforced the apartheid regime through formal legislation from 1948 to 1994, denying basic political, social, and civil rights to the black majority on the basis of ethnic prejudice.

Political parties can also deliberately try to reduce contestability in the policy arena by adopting political financing laws and regulations that work in their favor. Because of the rising costs of politics and often in reaction to major political corruption scandals, many countries across the world have introduced public funding regulations. These aim to create a level playing field, helping new interest groups and small opposition parties compete on a more equitable basis with incumbent parties, while also reducing the influence of big corporations and private interests in shaping party agendas. However, countries with dominant party systems are less likely to introduce public funding regulations (figure 8.8), reducing the level of contestability. In Africa, for example, only a minority of countries have adopted and effectively enforced public funding laws, contrary to global trends. This regional trend is often coupled with limited transparency on party financing and a heavy reliance on funding from private—often illicit—sources.[11]

Well-established political parties can also become risk averse and opportunistic in the way they articulate citizens' demands. They may "sponsor" societal preferences only when the expected returns in terms

Figure 8.8 Dominant party systems are less likely than competitive systems to introduce legal provisions for public funding, suggesting efforts to reduce contestability

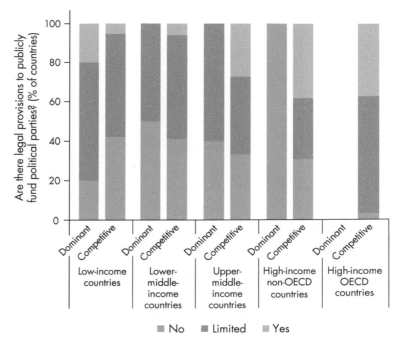

Sources: WDR 2017 team, using data from International IDEA, Political Finance Database, 2016, and Database of Political Institutions (Cruz, Keefer, and Scartascini 2016). Countries are classified based on the presence or absence of legal provisions for direct public funding of political parties. Income groups reflect the latest categorization by the World Bank.

Note: OECD = Organisation for Economic Co-operation and Development.

of electoral gains are positive and large, ignoring demands that are salient to only a small segment of the electorate or that appear too risky because they deviate from established social norms. As a result, the policy arena can shrink considerably and become biased against disadvantaged citizens such as women, indigenous people, and ethnic and sexual minorities.

Taken together, these tendencies often make political parties part of the problem rather than the solution. Public opinion surveys suggest that political parties are now the least-trusted political institution worldwide (figure 8.9). Although significant variation exists across income groups as well as between and within regions, these perceptions highlight an important crisis of representation for traditional representative institutions, forcing citizens to look for alternative mechanisms to organize collectively and bring their demands into the policy arena. The decline of party activism and membership in the Organisation for Economic Co-operation and Development (OECD) is consistent with this argument (Whiteley 2011). However, through social movements,

Figure 8.9 Political parties are on average the least-trusted political institution worldwide

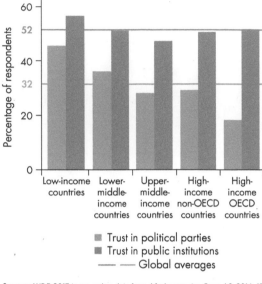

Trust in political parties
Trust in public institutions
— — — Global averages

Sources: WDR 2017 team, using data from Afrobarometer, Round 6, 2014–15; Arab Barometer, Wave 2, 2010–11; Center for East Asia Democratic Studies, National Taiwan University (located in Taiwan, China), Asian Barometer, Wave 3, 2012–14; European Commission, Eurobarometer, 2015; Vanderbilt University, Latin American Public Opinion Project, 2014.

Note: "Average trust in public institutions" is the average of trust in the government, legislature, judiciary, police, and army. Trust is calculated as the sum of all positive answers. Trust in parties also decreases as societies develop, suggesting growing demands and expectations from citizens.

civic associations, and spaces of deliberation, citizens can enhance contestability and change the incentives of the existing political parties, making them more likely to adapt and respond to new societal demands, as discussed in the following sections.

Bringing change through social organization

By coordinating action among citizens around specific issues, social organizations can bring to prominence new demands and interests (Heller 2013). In doing so, social organizations can potentially affect the three levers of change—incentives, preferences and beliefs, and contestability. First, they can *change the incentives of elites* by increasing the political cost of opposing specific policies. Second, they can *reshape the preferences and beliefs of actors* through the creation of new collective identities and the integration of new interests in the policy arena. And, third, they can *enhance contestability* by aligning with actors that can effectively challenge the existing elites and limit their bargaining power.[12] In these ways, social

movements can broaden policy debates and push for new laws and policies that rebalance access to (and distribution of) power among groups within societies, including gender equality laws, indigenous territorial rights, and transparency and right to information laws. However, social organization can also lead to undesirable social outcomes such as opposing reform, creating violence, and reinforcing rent-seeking for specific clientelistic groups. The discussion that follows emphasizes ways in which social organization creates positive change.[13]

Understanding the operating environment of social organizations: Recent trends

Across the world in recent years, thousands of citizens have taken to the streets to question the legitimacy of fiscal austerity policies, condemn corruption scandals, and protest the failure of governments to address the growing inequalities within societies, among other issues (Ortiz and others 2013; Carothers and Youngs 2016).[14]

These trends suggest that ordinary citizens are increasingly willing and able to mobilize peacefully to hold government accountable and voice their discontent when their confidence in public institutions is undermined and when they perceive that the formal mechanisms of representation—such as elections and political parties—have weakened their capacity to articulate their interests and channel their demands.[15]

This process is not accidental. Social movements—as an example of a specific type of social organization—are embedded in broader institutional and socioeconomic environments that shape the strategies and choices available to political actors (Tarrow 1998).[16] Over the last 40 years, the institutional environment for civic activism and social movements has become increasingly more permissive: the spread of democratic norms and practices has widened the civic space, with a growing number of countries enacting laws and regulations to enable and support the formation and functioning of autonomous civic society organizations. Likewise, government interventions to control or censor the media have declined globally (figure 8.10), allowing independent media actors to bring new issues into the national debate, publicizing the claims of social movements, and magnifying their demands (see spotlight 12 on the media). The diffusion of new information and communication technologies (ICTs) has further enabled citizen collective action by facilitating access to information, lowering transaction costs for the creation and development of associational networks, and providing effective coordination tools for disadvantaged groups across

Figure 8.10 After decades of progress, civic space is shrinking globally, driven by higher government restrictions on media and CSO entry

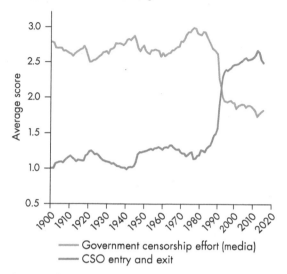

Source: WDR 2017 team, using data from V-Dem (database), 2016.

Note: The average is based on a sample of 78 countries for which there is consistent data for all years presented. The "CSO entry and exit" variable is measured on a 0–4 scale, ranging from 0 (more constrained) to 4 (less constrained). The "government censorship effort (media)" variable is reversed and measured on a 0–4 scale, ranging from 0 (less censorship) to 4 (more censorship). More information on specific variables and survey methodology can be found in World Bank and V-Dem (2016) and Coppedge and others (2015). CSO = civil society organization.

Figure 8.11 Taking advantage of the digital revolution, social movements are increasingly organized across national boundaries

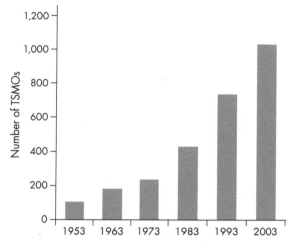

Source: WDR 2017 team, based on Smith 2008.

Note: The bars measure the number of Transnational Social Movement Organizations (TSMOs), defined as organizations that combine activists from multiple countries around common social change goals.

the globe (Bennett and Segerberg 2012). As a result of these processes, social movements are now increasingly organized across national boundaries (figure 8.11)—see Goodwin and Jasper (2015, 157).

Evidence from the last decade, however, suggests that the global trend may be a shrinking civic space (figure 8.10). Many governments are changing the institutional environment in which citizens engage, establishing legal barriers to restrict the functioning of media and civic society organizations, and reducing their autonomy from the state. For example, in the case of media, governments may award broadcast frequencies on the basis of political motivations, withdraw financial support of media organizations and activities, or enforce complex registration requirements that raise barriers to entry into a government-controlled media market. In the case of nongovernmental organizations (NGOs), governments might resort to legal measures to restrict public and private financing or pass stricter laws that restrain associational rights (Carothers and Brechenmacher 2014). Although these initiatives are sometimes motivated by legitimate concerns for public order and national security, they can be used by elites as a strategy to narrow

the policy space and limit the channels available to citizens to engage and influence the policy arena.

Changing incentives: How social organizations can effectively build coalitions for change

Differing incentives and preferences among elite actors open opportunities for social organizations to support change by forming coalitions with reforming elites (Fukuyama 2014; Fox 2015). When economic crises or other external shocks shift the incentives and relative power of elite actors, they may be more likely to defect from the ruling coalition and build alliances with excluded citizen groups. In the Philippines, for example, business elites that originally supported Ferdinand Marcos's coup in 1972 began to defect under the pressures of economic decline. When a major event—the assassination of the main opposition leader in 1983—triggered a wave of protests, grassroots associations forged an anti-Marcos reform coalition, the People Power movement, comprising members of the private sector, representatives of the opposition, religious leaders, and civic organizations. The mobilization culminated in peaceful demonstrations that brought millions of citizens to the streets, forcing Marcos to resign in 1986 and paving the way for the restoration of democratic institutions (Blitz 2000).

In the absence of an identifiable shock, social organizations may be able to shift elite incentives

Box 8.1 Social movements and bottom-up pressures for reform: Right to information legislation in India

Since independence, the Indian government has operated under the colonial Official Secrets Act (OSA) of 1923. Officially conceived as a legal instrument to prevent the disclosure of information that can affect security and national sovereignty, in practice the OSA has empowered authorities to withhold information from citizens at the government's discretion. This situation has created a culture of secrecy that characterizes administrative and political practices, undermining the accountability of state institutions. Despite several attempts at reform by technical working groups and parliamentary commissions, the OSA has never been repealed (Mander and Joshi 1999).

In the 1990s, a rural-based social movement emerged in the state of Rajasthan, demanding access to information on behalf of wage workers and small farmers. The rural poor were often cheated and not paid their full wages, and they could not challenge the paymasters because they were denied access to attendance registers. The movement eventually spread nationwide, leading to the formation of the National Campaign for Peoples' Right to Information (NCPRI) in 1996. Members of NCPRI built strategic alliances with other societal groups, including journalists, lawyers, and human rights activists, thereby creating a strong constituency for reform that moved demands for transparency to the forefront of the political agenda and eventually succeeded in pushing adoption of the Right to Information Act in 2005 (Bari, Chand, and Singh 2015).

Source: WDR 2017 team.

to form a coalition through sustained efforts over a longer period of time. In India, for example, the Right to Information Act (RTIA) was passed in 2005 after a 10-year struggle (box 8.1). Factors such as ideology, religion, leadership, and provision of selective incentives can help sustain commitment to social movements despite lack of short-term success. Labor unions, for example, may provide members with services to sustain participation in the aftermath of failed bargains.

Changing preferences: How social organizations can bring new interests into the policy arena

Elite bargains can have unintended consequences, as discussed in chapter 7. Sometimes, they can create the conditions for social movements to emerge and bring new interests into the policy arena. In Tunisia, for example, progress on gender equality following independence was largely a by-product of an elite bargain—between political and business elites to recruit skilled labor for the growing manufacturing sector—rather than the outcome of feminist mobilization. The top-down policy choices associated with this bargain then created an enabling environment in which women's organizations emerged and were strengthened over time. In 2011 the Jasmine Revolution provided women's organizations with a window of opportunity to leverage their organizational strength and lobby successfully for a mandatory gender quota for elections to the National Constituent Assembly, boosting women's representation in the Assembly to 26 percent. This initial success in turn allowed women's organizations to change elite preferences—shaping the agenda of political parties—which led to the integration of gender provisions in the new constitution (O'Neil and Domingo 2016).

Major political events such as wars and post-conflict constitutional design processes can also alter the balance of power within societies, playing the role of coordination devices to enable collective action among marginalized groups to mobilize and influence the policy arena (box 8.2). In Afghanistan, for example, sustained efforts over the last decade by domestic women's organizations, in collaboration with international donors and NGOs, played a key role in changing the preferences of members of parliament and state officials within the bureaucracy. That change influenced the drafting of a controversial law on the Elimination of Violence Against Women, which introduced criminalization of gender violence for the first time in Afghan history (Larson 2016).[17]

Changing contestability: How social organizations use the law to claim rights

Law plays different roles in society (see chapter 3). It orders behavior, legitimating social hierarchies and power relationships. It can also be used by citizens to contest power and make legal claims to challenge the status quo and push the boundaries of citizenship

Box 8.2 The mobilization of women and promotion of gender-based policies in postconflict settings: The case of Sub-Saharan Africa

Across the world, women's political representation is on average higher in postconflict countries than in countries that have not experienced conflict (figure B8.2.1).[a] This trend is particularly evident in the Middle East and North Africa and Sub-Saharan Africa, where women's presence in parliaments is almost double the level in countries with no conflict. Tripp (2015) provides a possible explanation for these patterns, focusing on Sub-Saharan Africa where postconflict countries have been more successful in promoting gender equality laws across multiple policy

Figure B8.2.1 The rate of political participation of women is higher in countries emerging from conflict

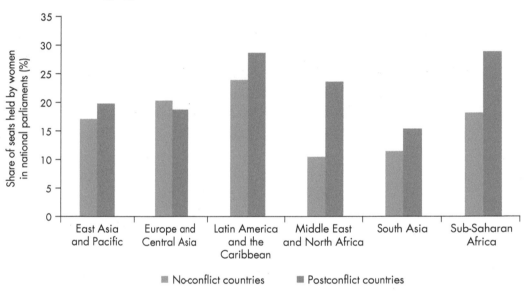

Sources: WDR 2017 team, using data from UCDP/PRIO, Armed Conflict Dataset, 2015; World Bank, World Development Indicators (database), 2016.

Note: The figure indicates the proportion of seats held by women in national parliaments. Postconflict countries are those that had at least one year of conflict after 1985 with more than 1,000 deaths. Countries with ongoing conflict as of 2014, and high-income members of the Organisation for Economic Co-operation and Development (OECD), were excluded.

areas—including integrating women's rights in their constitutions (figure B8.2.2). Rather than looking at a single driver, Tripp highlights the interaction among three drivers. The first is the disruption in gender relations that is specific to conflict-prone countries; women take over many of the traditional tasks of men, leading to shifts in gender norms (see chapter 4). The second is the rise of domestic women's movements, facilitated by the inclusive and competitive nature of the postconflict environment. The third is the influence of international processes and actors involved in the promotion of gender laws and international norms on gender inclusion (further discussed in chapter 9).

The experience in Rwanda reflects the interplay and relative strength of these three factors. In Rwanda, women played a critical role in the Rwandan Patriotic Front (RPF), holding executive positions within the movement while in exile. In the postconflict period, women activists have been powerful agents of transformation, advocating for greater responsibilities in light of the leadership roles played by women in the armed struggle. Even before the establishment of quotas, women held nearly 50 percent of the seats that the RPF controlled in the parliament (Powley 2005). Moreover, women's involvement in the constitution-making processes and later in the parliament provided them with the organizational strength and legitimacy to advocate for the passage of many gender equality and antidiscrimination laws, including the 1999 inheritance law, the 2004 National Land Policy, the 2005 Organic Land Law (Powley 2005),

(Box continues next page)

Figure B8.2.2 **In Africa, postconflict countries have been more likely to integrate women's rights in their constitutions**

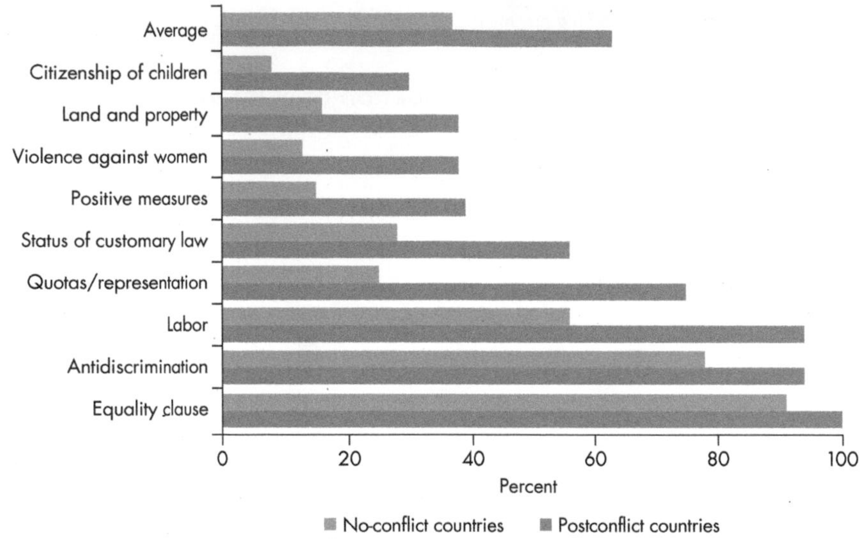

Percent

- No-conflict countries ■ Postconflict countries

Source: Tripp 2015, 1275.

Note: The figure shows the percentage of African countries with constitutional provisions related to women's rights.

and the 2009 legislation against gender-based violence. This influence also explains why—once the new 2003 constitution introduced a quota of 30 percent women in all decision-making bodies—Rwanda far exceeded the target, becoming a front-runner of gender equality and women's political participation in the world, with 64 percent of total seats in the parliament occupied by women, followed by Bolivia (53 percent) and Cuba (49 percent).[b]

Source: WDR 2017 team.

a. This box largely relies and builds on Tripp (2015).
b. Hunt (2014). For the world classification, see http://www.ipu.org/wmn-e/classif.htm.

rights (McCann 2004). It is not a coincidence that the most transformative cases of social movements of the 20th century—including labor, women's rights, and civil rights, and, more recently, indigenous and environmental movements—have all explicitly adopted the language of law and the discourse of rights as *legal* entitlements, creating a "shared normative base" that has facilitated collective action (Heller 2013, 4).

Legal institutions of horizontal accountability such as national courts and ombudsmen offices can also be a strategic asset for organized groups of citizens. By activating these institutions, social movements can raise awareness of collective entitlements and citizenship rights, forging the collective identities of disadvantaged citizens and raising the salience of individual grievances (Peruzzotti and Smulovitz 2006; Fox 2015). Moreover, the ability to achieve legal victories in court can boost confidence among social actors, strengthening the commitment to organize by effectively using legal instruments in their favor. Mass media campaigns are often used as a complementary strategy to publicize court victories and put the news at the forefront of the national agenda (see spotlight 12 on the media). As the history of U.S. civil rights movements suggests, legal mobilizations have often generated a "contagion effect," transforming local victories into nationwide struggles for rights (McCann 1994). Similar dynamics are also spreading in developing countries. In Botswana, for example, women's groups successfully challenged discriminatory customary laws and pushed for the implementation of gender equality principles enshrined in the constitution by adopting litigation strategies that culminated in a series of victories in far-reaching cases before national courts (Hasan and Tanzer 2013).

The effectiveness of legal strategies, however, often depends on the presence of a well-functioning and independent judiciary and a strong network of legal aid experts who can support the claims of social organizations and resist pressures to deny them. Unfortunately, judicial independence is often undermined in many countries, leading some scholars to criticize the faith placed in courts as mechanisms of social change as nothing more than "hollow hope" (Rosenberg 1991). Other studies, however, contend that the spread of international courts and legal bodies associated with international human rights laws provide social movements with additional toolkits to overcome the limitations of state courts and change the incentives of elites, pushing for compliance with laws and regulations ratified by national governments (Keck and Sikkink 1998). The role of these international bodies is explored in chapter 9.

Why social organizations alone are not enough to bring change

Social movements can give voice to powerless groups and put pressure on public authorities, but they often fail to consider the trade-offs associated with the proliferation of competing interests in the policy arena. In many developing countries, state capacity is weak and political parties are unable to perform their function to filter these demands and subordinate them to higher public priorities. In these circumstances, public institutions could become overloaded with multiple pressures, undermining the coherence and effectiveness of public policies. This overloading could generate frustrations and discontent among citizens that, if not properly addressed, can eventually lead to violence, conflict, and political decay (Huntington 1968)—chapter 4 explores violence as a manifestation of governance failure.

Moreover, citizen engagement through social organizations is not necessarily motivated by a vision of a more equal and just society. On the contrary, these organizations can also reinforce social hierarchies, be captured by narrow interests, or be used by reactionary and extremist groups for exclusionary purposes (Gaventa and Barrett 2012, 2399–2401). As

discussed later in this chapter, "civil society failure" is also possible—the risk that social groups "may also face significant problems of coordination, asymmetric information, and inequality, which may limit their ability to respond to and resolve market and government failures" (Mansuri and Rao 2013, 285). When social movements are captured by narrow interests, they may reinforce existing inequalities rather than overcome them. Even when not captured, social organizations may be decidedly "uncivil" and specifically designed to deny equal rights to other groups (Heller 2013).

The role of induced participation and public deliberation

Social movements drive "organic participation" in which citizens contest state policy from outside the state. "Induced participation," in which citizens deliberate policies through formal state interventions, is also important for articulating citizens' interests and overcoming collective action challenges. In the area of development assistance, induced participation takes the form of decentralization and community-driven development, but in a broader context it includes various forms of direct democracy and public deliberation. Public deliberation—spaces and processes that allow group-based discussion and weighting of alternative preferences—can help level the playing field in the policy arena. In certain contexts, deliberation can leverage marginalized groups' efforts to rebalance power relationships in their favor. And citizen participation can be instrumental in improving the quality of deliberation and the legitimacy of decisions by clarifying the needs and demands of local constituencies (Heller and Rao 2015).

Induced participation and public deliberation not only increase the contestability of the policy arena, but also have the potential to aggregate preferences and reshape them through dialogue and argumentation. In *Of the Social Contract*, Jean-Jacques Rousseau ([1762] 2004) argues that participation is not merely a way of reaching a decision, but also a process through which citizens develop a civic consciousness, develop empathy for other views, and learn to take the public interest into account. In other words, participatory processes can help achieve cooperation by shifting preferences.

Public deliberation is most feasible, and thus most successful, at the local level, and it is often seen as a complement to decentralization reforms. In Brazil, following decentralization in 1988, the city of Porto

> Public deliberation—spaces and processes that allow group-based discussion and weighting of alternative preferences—can help level the playing field in the policy arena.

Alegre introduced participatory budgeting in 1990. A decade later, participatory budgeting assemblies drew over 14,000 participants, many of them poor. They led to improved outcomes, with more money dedicated to pro-poor investments, resulting in improved sewerage and water coverage, higher school enrollment, and more affordable housing (Baiocchi 2005). In India, the 73rd amendment to the constitution, approved in 1993, mandated village elections at three levels—village councils (*panchayats*), block councils (block *panchayats*), and district councils (*zila panchayats*)—as well as regular village meetings (*gram sabhas*) open to the entire village. In the state of Kerala, authorities subsequently devolved 40 percent of the development budget to village councils, increasing the demand for local participation (Mansuri and Rao 2013).

However, participatory approaches to development sometimes fail to consider the possibility of civil society failures, where, in weakly institutionalized environments, the poor are less likely to participate and participatory mechanisms can be captured by local elites (Devarajan and Kanbur 2012; Mansuri and Rao 2013). Contestability depends on de facto participation, but demand-driven participation can exclude the weakest individuals, groups, and communities, especially because the poor may face higher opportunity costs for participation. Evidence suggests that participants in public deliberations are wealthier, more educated, male, and more politically connected. Moreover, deliberations often attract similar types of people and fail to promote cross-group cohesion.

When only homogeneous groups of the relatively powerful are included, participation neither enhances contestation nor serves to shift preferences. Moreover, efforts at induced deliberation may be captured by narrow interest groups, whose preferences may be overrepresented, reinforcing existing inequalities rather than overcoming them. For that reason, efforts to "export" participatory budget initiatives sometimes do not work (Baiocchi, Heller, and Silva 2011). Local-level deliberation may be especially subject to capture because of the entrenched influence of local elites (Abraham and Platteau 2004). Consequently, evidence reveals that the poor often benefit less than the nonpoor from participatory processes, especially in communities with high levels of inequality and with particularly salient and significant caste, race, or gender disparities (Mansuri and Rao 2013).

Such failures are not necessarily ameliorated by the availability of new digital technologies (Gaventa and Barrett 2012). On the contrary, as discussed in the 2016 WDR, ICT instruments may actually reinforce socioeconomic inequalities in citizen engagement (World Bank 2016). In Brazil, for example, the use of internet voting on municipal budget proposals reveals stark demographic differences between online and offline voters: online voters are more likely to be male, university-educated, and richer (figure 8.12).

The design of deliberative mechanisms can help overcome problems of exclusion and capture, particularly when such mechanisms are designed in conjunction with other reforms to improve accountability and transparency. For example, there is evidence that participatory community programs are more likely to be successful when they occur in favorable political environments—that is, when local governments have discretion and are already downwardly accountable (Mansuri and Rao 2013).

Providing information on specific policy issues and creating conditions favorable to making informed decisions can also change citizens' preferences and act as an important mechanism to improve the terms of a policy debate and open the way for future changes in public policies. Recent experiences in deliberative polling illustrate this point, providing an innovative approach to ascertain informed, thoughtful, and representative public views on complex policy issues (Fishkin 2011).[18] The media can play an important role in providing information and promoting political participation. For example, recent evidence from Kenya reveals that exposure to a weekly panel discussion program aimed at building a national conversation on governance in Kenya increased both knowledge

Figure 8.12 In Brazil, online voting in participatory budgeting can reinforce existing inequalities

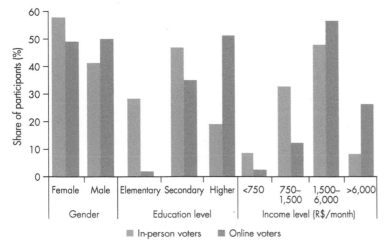

Source: WDR 2017 team, based on Spada and others 2015.

Note: R$ = Brazilian real.

of governance issues and participation in politics (Githitho Muriithi and Page 2014).

Entry points for change: Understanding citizen agency as a collective action problem

This chapter has analyzed the role that ordinary citizens play in driving processes of societal transformation and institutional change. Surveying historical and contemporary experiences, it argues that citizens face collective action problems that prevent them from bargaining effectively and holding government accountable. To strengthen their influence in the policy arena, citizens need to engage through multiple mechanisms designed to solve collective action problems, including voting, political parties, social movements, civic associations, and other less conventional spaces for policy deliberation. Because all these expressions of collective action are imperfect, it is their strategic combination that maximizes the chances to promote change and make governments more responsive to citizens' needs.

As this chapter shows, citizen-led change is possible, but it is often a difficult and long-term process fraught with uncertainties. In India, grassroots organizations spent 10 years scaling up local mobilization efforts, translating rural activism into a multistakeholder coalition for reform, and finally shifting the incentives of state authorities toward the adoption and implementation of right to information legislation.

The analysis in this chapter highlights multiple drivers whose interaction can contribute to lower barriers to collective action and facilitate citizen mobilization through the mechanisms just identified. First, institutions that enhance contestability in the policy arena—such as media regulations, political finance regulations, and constitutional provisions that establish mechanisms to protect citizens' rights—can create an enabling environment for citizen agency by facilitating cooperation and promoting more inclusive and equitable bargaining spaces. While often the outcome of elite bargains, these institutions can nevertheless open up opportunities for previously marginalized groups to mobilize and bargain for their collective interests.

Second, external shocks—corruption scandals, economic crises—can act as important triggers that help citizens overcome otherwise unfavorable circumstances and create opportunities for change.

Third, coalition-building strategies matter for results: chances to promote institutional change and policy reforms are maximized when the incentives of reformers from above (elites) and mobilization from below (citizens) converge and mutually reinforce each other against defenders of the status quo (Fox 2015). This points to the important role that agency and leadership play in seizing windows of opportunities for action.

Notes

1. This section builds on Khemani and others (2016).
2. Collier and Vicente (2011); Bekoe (2012); Norris, Frank, and Martinez (2015).
3. Mental models include categories, concepts, identities, prototypes, stereotypes, causal narratives, and worldviews (World Bank 2015, 62).
4. Stokes (2005); Kitschelt and Wilkinson (2007); Schaffer (2007); Stokes and others (2013).
5. Gallego (2010); Fumagalli and Narciso (2012); Mahler, Jesuit, and Paradowski (2013).
6. As discussed in chapter 7, political parties can also be an instrument to solve coordination and commitment problems among elites.
7. In the real world, political parties do not fall into neat divisions of programmatic or clientelistic. Rather, they are located along a spectrum, and they may display different strategies simultaneously. The focus is on the extent to which a specific strategy prevails over competing alternatives (Kitschelt and Wang 2014).
8. Kitschelt (2000); Keefer and Vlaicu (2008); Bates (2010); Kitschelt and Kselman (2013).
9. Although programmatic parties can have charismatic leaders, the organizational strength and autonomy of the party constrain the power of individual leaders, subordinating them to the party program. Under populism, the relationship is reversed, and the party has no internal mechanisms to sanction leaders if they fail to deliver on their programmatic agenda. This also explains why populist leaders tend to resist efforts to strengthen the party as an autonomous organization, and why such parties are often nothing more than electoral machines that disappear soon after the charismatic leader leaves office (Mainwaring and Torcal 2005).
10. The 1995 Law of Local Participation provided legal recognition of the territorial rights of peasant and indigenous communities, allowing over 15,000 grassroots territorial organizations to participate in local planning (Kohl and Farthing 2006, 125–36). Decentralization, however, was a necessary but not sufficient condition to enable programmatic parties to emerge because its effects were mediated by the geographic distribution of indigenous groups.

Indigenous mobilization was less successful in Peru because the indigenous population accounted for at least one-fourth of the population in only 28 percent of subnational districts in Peru, compared with 79 percent of subnational districts in Bolivia (Van Cott 2005, 218–19).

11. Pinto-Duschinsky (2002); Van Biezen and Kopecky (2007); Norris, Abel van Es, and Fennis (2015).

12. Defining the impact or success of social organizations continues to be a subject of debate among scholars. On the one hand, social organizations are not homogeneous groups, and not all members might perceive a given change as an indicator of success. On the other hand, social organizations often generate impacts in different areas of human affairs (political, cultural, and social), as well as consequences for individuals and societies at large. These impacts and consequences are difficult to disentangle and capture empirically, making causal inferences problematic (Giugni, McAdam, and Tilly 1999; Giugni 2007; Amenta and others 2010; Gaventa and Barrett 2012).

13. Khemani and others (2016) label this positive change "healthy citizen engagement."

14. The spread of civil society groups and citizen activism does not, however, necessarily imply their effectiveness in bringing about change. Only about 37 percent of the reported protests that occurred from 2006 to 2013 were successful in producing demonstrable achievements and prompting authorities to respond with policy changes and reforms (Ortiz and others 2013).

15. In other words, rather than simply exiting the political process—for example, by abstaining from voting or even migrating (Hirschman 1970; Clausen, Kraay, and Nyiri 2009)—citizens seek to voice their opinions and directly influence the policy bargaining arena.

16. Social movements are defined by scholars in different ways. This Report uses a definition commonly embraced by political scientists and sociologists: "*Social movements* [are] a sustained series of interactions between powerholders and persons successfully claiming to speak on behalf of a constituency lacking formal representation, in the course of which those persons make publicly visible demands for changes in the distribution or exercise of power and back those demands with public demonstrations of support" (Tilly 1984, 306).

17. Despite ongoing implementation challenges, the law has become a critical reference point for women's activists, who increasingly use it for litigation purposes, helping to strengthen gender equality (Larson 2016, 23).

18. For short summaries of recent applications of deliberative polling, see http://cdd.stanford.edu.

References[a]

Abraham, Anita, and Jean-Philippe Platteau. 2004. "Participatory Development: When Culture Creeps." In *Culture and Public Action*, edited by Vijayendra Rao and Michael Walton, 210–33. Stanford Social Sciences Series. Stanford, CA: Stanford University Press.

Achen, Christopher H., and Larry M. Bartels. 2016a. "Democracy for Realists: Holding Up a Mirror to the Electorate." *Juncture* 22 (4): 269–75.

————. 2016b. *Democracy for Realists: Why Elections Do Not Produce Responsive Government.* Princeton, NJ: Princeton University Press.

Afrobarometer. Various years. http://www.afrobarometer .org/about.

Aldrich, John H. 1995. *Why Parties? The Origin and Transformation of Political Parties in America.* Chicago: University of Chicago Press.

Amenta, Edwin, Neal Caren, Elizabeth Chiarello, and Yang Su. 2010. "The Political Consequences of Social Movements." *Annual Review of Sociology* 36 (1): 287–307.

Arab Barometer. Various years. http://www.arabbaro meter.org/.

Ashworth, Scott. 2012. "Electoral Accountability: Recent Theoretical and Empirical Work." *Annual Review of Political Science* 15 (1): 183–201.

Baiocchi, Gianpaolo. 2005. *Militants and Citizens: The Politics of Participatory Democracy in Porto Alegre.* Stanford, CA: Stanford University Press.

Baiocchi, Gianpaolo, Patrick Heller, and Marcelo Kunrath Silva. 2011. *Bootstrapping Democracy: Transforming Local Governance and Civil Society in Brazil.* Stanford, CA: Stanford University Press.

Banerjee, Abhijit V., Selvan Kumar, Rohini Pande, and Felix Su. 2011. "Do Informed Voters Make Better Choices? Experimental Evidence from Urban India." Working Paper, Abdul Latif Jameel Poverty Action Lab, Massachusetts Institute of Technology, Cambridge, MA.

Bari, Shamsul, Vikram K. Chand, and Shekhar Singh. 2015. *Empowerment through Information: The Evolution of Transparency Regimes in South Asia.* New Delhi: Transparency Advisory Group.

Bates, Robert H. 2010. "Democracy in Africa: A Very Short History." *Social Research* 77 (4): 1133–48.

Bekoe, Dorina. 2012. *Voting in Fear: Electoral Violence in Sub-Saharan Africa.* Washington, DC: United States Institute of Peace.

Bennett, W. Lance, and Alexandra Segerberg. 2012. "The Logic of Connective Action: Digital Media and the

---

a. References to titles of publications that include Taiwan, Hong Kong, and Macau refer to the regions currently named Taiwan, China; Hong Kong SAR, China; and Macau SAR, China, respectively.

Personalization of Contentious Politics." *Information, Communication and Society* 15 (5): 739–68.

Beramendi, Pablo, and Francesca Amat. 2014. "Inequality and Electoral Participation in Developed and Developing Democracies." Unpublished working paper, Duke University, Durham, NC.

Birch, Sarah. 2010. "Perceptions of Electoral Fairness and Voter Turnout." *Comparative Political Studies* 43 (12): 1601–22.

Bishop, Sylvia, and Anke Hoeffler. 2014. "Free and Fair Elections: A New Database." CSAE Working Paper 2014–14, Center for the Study of African Economics, Department of Economics, Oxford University, Oxford, U.K.

Blitz, Amy. 2000. *The Contested State: American Foreign Policy and Regime Change in the Philippines*. Lanham, MD: Rowman and Littlefield.

Bobonis, Gustavo J., Luis R. Cámara Fuertes, and Rainer Schwabe. 2016. "Monitoring Corruptible Politicians." *American Economic Review* 106 (8): 2371–2405.

Buquet, Daniel, and Rafael Piñeiro. 2016. "Uruguay's Shift from Clientelism." *Journal of Democracy* 27 (1): 139–51.

Burgess, Robin, Remi Jedwab, Edward Miguel, Ameet Morjaria, and Gerard Padró i Miquel. 2015. "The Value of Democracy: Evidence from Road Building in Kenya." *American Economic Review* 105 (6): 1817–51.

Caplan, Bryan. 2008. *The Myth of the Rational Voter: Why Democracies Choose Bad Policies*. Princeton, NJ: Princeton University Press.

Carothers, Thomas, and Saskia Brechenmacher. 2014. *Closing Space: Democracy and Human Rights Support under Fire*. Washington, DC: Carnegie Endowment for International Peace.

Carothers, Thomas, and Richard Youngs. 2016. *The Complexities of Global Protests*. Washington, DC: Carnegie Endowment for International Peace.

Casey, Katherine. 2015. "Crossing Party Lines: The Effects of Information on Redistributive Politics." *American Economic Review* 105 (8): 2410–48.

Center for East Asia Democratic Studies, National Taiwan University. Various years. Asian Barometer. Taipei, http://www.asianbarometer.org/.

Center for Systemic Peace. Various years. Polity IV (database). Vienna, VA, http://www.systemicpeace.org /polityproject.html.

Chauvet, Lisa, and Paul Collier. 2009. "Elections and Economic Policy in Developing Countries." *Economic Policy* 24 (59): 509–50.

Clausen, Bianca, Aart Kraay, and Zsolt Nyiri. 2009. "Corruption and Confidence in Public Institutions: Evidence from a Global Survey." Policy Research Working Paper 5157, World Bank, Washington, DC.

Clements, Benedict J., David Coady, Stefania Fabrizio, Sanjeev Gupta, Trevor Alleyne, and Carlo Sdralevich. 2013. *Energy Subsidy Reform: Lessons and Implications*. Washington, DC: International Monetary Fund.

Collier, Paul, and Pedro Vicente. 2011. "Violence, Bribery, and Fraud: The Political Economy of Elections in Sub-Saharan Africa." *Public Choice* 153 (1): 1–31.

Coppedge, Michael, John Gerring, Staffan I. Lindberg, Svend-Erik Skaaning, Jan Teorell, David Altman, Frida Andersson, and others. 2016. *V-Dem Codebook v6*. Gothenburg, Sweden: Varieties of Democracy (V-Dem) Project, V-Dem Institute, University of Gothenburg; Notre Dame, IN: Helen Kellogg Institute for International Studies, University of Notre Dame.

Cruz, Cesi, and Philip Keefer. 2013. "The Organization of Political Parties and the Politics of Bureaucratic Reform." Policy Research Working Paper 6686, World Bank, Washington, DC.

Cruz, Cesi, Philip Keefer, and Julien Labonne. 2015. "Incumbent Advantage, Voter Information, and Vote Buying." IDB Working Paper 711, Inter-American Development Bank, Washington, DC.

Cruz, Cesi, Philip Keefer, and Carlos Scartascini. 2016. "Database of Political Institutions Codebook, 2015 Update (DPI2015)." Inter-American Development Bank, Washington, DC. Updated version of Thorsten Beck, George Clarke, Alberto Groff, Philip Keefer, and Patrick Walsh. 2001. "New Tools in Comparative Political Economy: The Database of Political Institutions." *World Bank Economic Review* 15 (1): 165–76.

Devarajan, Shantayanan, and Ravi Kanbur. 2012. "The Evolution of Development Strategy as Balancing Market and Government Failure." Working Paper 9, Charles H. Dyson School of Applied Economics and Management, Cornell University, Ithaca, NY.

Diamond, Larry. 2008. *The Spirit of Democracy: The Struggle to Build Free Societies throughout the World*. New York: Times Books.

Diamond, Larry, and Richard Gunther. 2001. *Political Parties and Democracy*. Baltimore: Johns Hopkins University Press.

European Commission. Various years. Eurobarometer. Brussels, http://ec.europa.eu/COMMFrontOffice /publicopinion/index.cfm.

Ezrow, Natasha M., and Erica Frantz. 2011. "State Institutions and the Survival of Dictatorships." *Journal of International Affairs* 65 (1): 1–13.

Ferraz, Claudio, and Frederico Finan. 2008. "Exposing Corrupt Politicians: The Effect of Brazil's Publicly Released Audits on Electoral Outcomes." *Quarterly Journal of Economics* 123 (2): 703–45.

Fishkin, James. 2011. *When the People Speak: Deliberative Democracy and Public Consultation*. Oxford, U.K.: Oxford University Press.

Fox, Jonathan A. 2015. "Social Accountability: What Does the Evidence Really Say?" *World Development* 72 (C): 346–61.

Fujiwara, Thomas. 2015. "Voting Technology, Political Responsiveness, and Infant Health: Evidence from Brazil." *Econometrica* 83 (2): 423–64.

Fukuyama, Francis. 2014. *Political Order and Political Decay: From the Industrial Revolution to the Globalization of Democracy.* New York: Farrar, Straus, and Giroux.

Fumagalli, Eileen, and Gaia Narciso. 2012. "Political Institutions, Voter Turnout, and Policy Outcomes." *European Journal of Political Economy* 28 (2): 162–73.

Gallego, Aina. 2010. "Understanding Unequal Turnout: Education and Voting in Comparative Perspective." *Electoral Studies* 29 (2): 239–47.

Gallup Organization. Various years. Gallup World Poll. Washington, DC, http://www.gallup.com/services/170945/world-poll.aspx.

Gandhi, Jennifer, and Ellen Lust-Okar. 2009. "Elections under Authoritarianism." *Annual Review of Political Science* 12 (1): 403–22.

Gaventa, John, and Gregory Barrett. 2012. "Mapping the Outcomes of Citizen Engagement." *World Development* 40 (12): 2399–2410.

Githitho Muriithi, Angela, and Georgina Page. 2014. "What Was the Role of the Debate Programme Sema Kenya (Kenya Speaks) in the Kenyan Election 2013?" Research Report 5, BBC Media Action, London.

Giugni, Marco. 2007. "Useless Protest? A Time-Series Analysis of the Policy Outcomes of Ecology, Antinuclear, and Peace Movements in the United States, 1977–1995." *Mobilization: An International Quarterly* 12 (1): 53–77.

Giugni, Mario, Doug McAdam, and Charles Tilly. 1999. *How Movements Matter: Theoretical and Comparative Studies on the Consequences of Social Movements.* Minneapolis: University of Minnesota Press.

Goodwin, Jeff, and James M. Jasper, eds. 2015. *The Social Movement Reader: Cases and Concepts.* 3rd ed. Chichester, U.K.: John Wiley.

Hasan, Tazeen, and Ziona Tanzer. 2013. "Botswana Women's Movements, Plural Legal Systems, and the Botswana Constitution: How Reform Happens." Policy Research Working Paper 6690, World Bank, Washington, DC.

Heller, Patrick. 2013. "Challenges and Opportunities: Civil Society in a Globalizing World." UNDP-HDRO Occasional Paper 2013/06, Human Development Report Office, United Nations Development Programme, New York.

Heller, Patrick, and Vijayendra Rao, eds. 2015. *Deliberation and Development: Rethinking the Role of Voice and Collective Action in Unequal Societies.* Equity and Development Series. Washington, DC: World Bank.

Hellmann, Olli. 2011. "A Historical Institutionalist Approach to Political Party Organization: The Case of South Korea." *Government and Opposition* 46 (4): 464–84.

Hirschman, Albert O. 1970. *Exit, Voice, and Loyalty: Responses to Decline in Firms, Organizations, and States.* Cambridge, MA: Harvard University Press.

Humphreys, Macartan, and Jeremy Weinstein. 2012. "Policing Politicians: Citizen Empowerment and Political Accountability in Uganda, Preliminary Analysis." Working paper, International Growth Centre, London School of Economics and Political Science, London.

Hunt, Swanee. 2014. "The Rise of Rwanda Women: Rebuilding and Reuniting a Nation." *Foreign Affairs* 93 (3): 150–57.

Huntington, Samuel P. 1968. *Political Order in Changing Societies.* New Haven, CT: Yale University Press.

———. 1991. *The Third Wave: Democratization in the Late Twentieth Century.* Norman: University of Oklahoma Press.

International IDEA (Institute for Democracy and Electoral Assistance). Various years. Voter Turnout Database. Stockholm, http://www.idea.int/data-tools/data/voter-turnout.

———. 2016. Political Finance Database. Stockholm, http://www.idea.int/data-tools/data/political-finance-database.

Kasara, Kimuli, and Pavithra Suryanarayan. 2015. "When Do the Rich Vote Less than the Poor and Why? Explaining Turnout Inequality across the World." *American Journal of Political Science* 59 (3): 613–27.

Keck, Margaret, and Kathryn Sikkink. 1998. *Activists beyond Borders: Advocacy Networks in International Politics.* Ithaca, NY: Cornell University Press.

Keefer, Philip. 2011. "Collective Action, Political Parties and Pro-development Public Policy." *Asian Development Review* 28 (1): 94–118.

———. 2013. "Organizing for Prosperity: Collective Action, Political Parties, and the Political Economy of Development." In *Oxford Handbook of the Politics of Development*, edited by Carol Lancaster and Nicolas van de Walle. New York: Oxford University Press.

Keefer, Philip, and Stuti Khemani. 2014. "Mass Media and Public Education: The Effects of Access to Community Radio in Benin." *Journal of Development Economics* 109 (C): 57–72.

Keefer, Philip, and Razvan Vlaicu. 2008. "Democracy, Credibility, and Clientelism." *Journal of Law, Economics and Organization* 24 (2): 371–406.

Khemani, Stuti, Ernesto Dal Bó, Claudio Ferraz, Frederico Finan, Corinne Stephenson, Adesinaola Odugbemi, Dikshya Thapa, and Scott Abrahams. 2016. *Making Politics Work for Development: Harnessing Transparency and Citizen Engagement.* Policy Research Report. Washington, DC: World Bank.

Kitschelt, Herbert. 2000. "Linkages between Citizens and Politicians in Democratic Politics." *Comparative Political Studies* 33 (6–7): 845–79.

Kitschelt, Herbert, and Daniel M. Kselman. 2013. "Economic Development, Democratic Experience, and Political Parties' Linkage Strategies." *Comparative Political Studies* 46 (11): 1453–84.

Kitschelt, Herbert, and Yi-Ting Wang. 2014. "Programmatic Parties and Party Systems: Opportunities and Constraints." In *Politics Meets Policies: The Emergence of Programmatic Political Parties*, edited by Nic Cheeseman, Juan Pablo Luna, Herbert Kitschelt, Dan Paget,

Fernando Rosenblatt, Kristen Sample, Sergio Toro, and others, 43–73. Stockholm: International Institute for Democracy and Electoral Assistance.

Kitschelt, Herbert, and Steven I. Wilkinson. 2007. "Citizen-Politician Linkages: An Introduction." In *Patrons, Clients, and Policies: Patterns of Democratic Accountability and Political Competition*, edited by Herbert Kitschelt and Steven I. Wilkinson, 1–49. Cambridge, U.K.: Cambridge University Press.

Kohl, Benjamin, and Linda C. Farthing. 2006. *Impasse in Bolivia: Neoliberal Hegemony and Popular Resistance*. London: Zed Books.

Kudamatsu, Masayuki. 2012. "Has Democratization Reduced Infant Mortality in Sub-Saharan Africa? Evidence from Micro Data." *Journal of the European Economic Association* 10 (6): 1294–317.

Larreguy, Horacio A., John Marshall, and James M. Snyder. 2015. "Revealing Malfeasance: How Local Media Facilitates Electoral Sanctioning of Mayors in Mexico." NBER Working Paper 20697, National Bureau of Economic Research, Cambridge, MA.

Larson, Anna. 2016. *Women and Power: Mobilising around Afghanistan's Elimination of Violence against Women Law*. London: Overseas Development Institute.

Magaloni, Beatriz, Alberto Diaz-Cayeros, and Federico Estévez. 2006. "Clientelism and Portfolio Diversification: A Model of Electoral Investment with Applications to Mexico." In *Patrons, Clients, and Policies: Patterns of Democratic Accountability and Political Competition*, edited by Herbert Kitschelt and Steven I. Wilkinson, 182–205. Cambridge, U.K.: Cambridge University Press.

Mahler, Vincent, David Jesuit, and Piotr Paradowski. 2013. "Electoral Turnout and State Redistribution: A Cross-National Study of Fourteen Developed Countries." *Political Research Quarterly* 67 (2): 361–73.

Mainwaring, Scott, and Mariano Torcal. 2005. "Party System Institutionalization and Party System Theory after the Third Wave of Democratization." Working Paper 319, Kellogg Institute for International Studies, University of Notre Dame, Notre Dame, IN.

Mander, Harsh, and Abha Joshi. 1999. "The Movement for Right to Information in India: People's Power for the Control of Corruption." Paper presented at the Conference on Pan Commonwealth Advocacy, Harare, Zimbabwe, January 21–24.

Manin, Bernard, Adam Przeworski, and Susan C. Stokes. 1999. "Elections and Representation." In *Democracy, Accountability, and Representation*, edited by Adam Przeworski, Susan C. Stokes, and Bernard Manin, 29–54. Cambridge, U.K.: Cambridge University Press.

Mansuri, Ghazala, and Vijayendra Rao. 2013. *Localizing Development: Does Participation Work?* Policy Research Report. Washington, DC: World Bank.

Martinez-Bravo, Monica. 2014. "The Role of Local Officials in New Democracies: Evidence from Indonesia." *American Economic Review* 104 (4): 1244–87.

Martinez-Bravo, Monica, Gerard Padró-i-Miquel, Nancy Qian, and Yang Yao. 2011. "Do Local Elections Increase Accountability in Non-democracies? Evidence from Rural China." Working Paper 16948, National Bureau of Economic Research, Cambridge, MA.

McCann, Michael W. 1994. *Rights at Work: Pay Equity Reform and the Politics of Legal Mobilization*. Chicago: University of Chicago Press.

———. 2004. *Law and Social Movements*. Oxford, U.K.: Blackwell Publishing.

Mungiu-Pippidi, Alina. 2015. *The Quest for Good Governance*. Cambridge, U.K.: Cambridge University Press.

Norris, Pippa, Andrea Abel van Es, and Lisa Fennis. 2015. *Checkbook Elections: Political Finance in Comparative Perspective*. Oxford, U.K.: Oxford University Press.

Norris, Pippa, Richard W. Frank, and Ferran Martinez. 2015. *Contentious Elections: From Ballots to Barricades*. London: Routledge.

O'Neil, Tam, and Pilar Domingo. 2016. "Women and Power: Overcoming Barriers to Leadership and Influence." Research Reports and Studies, Overseas Development Institute, London.

Ortiz, Isabel, Sara Burke, Mohamed Berrada, and Hernan Cortes. 2013. "World Protests 2006–2013." Working Paper 2013, Initiative for Policy Dialogue and Friedrich-Ebert-Stiftung, New York.

Pande, Rohini. 2011. "Can Informed Voters Enforce Better Governance? Experiments in Low-Income Democracies." *Annual Review of Economics* 3 (1): 215–37.

Peruzzotti, Enrique, and Catalina Smulovitz. 2006. *Enforcing the Rule of Law: Social Accountability in New Latin American Democracies*. Pittsburgh: University of Pittsburgh Press.

Pinto-Duschinsky, Michael. 2002. "Financing Politics: A Global View." *Journal of Democracy* 13 (4): 69–86.

Powley, Elizabeth. 2005. "Rwanda: Women Hold Up Half the Parliament." In *Women in Parliament: Beyond Numbers*, edited by Julie Ballington and Azza Karam, 154–63. Stockholm: International Institute for Democracy and Electoral Assistance.

Randall, Vicky, and Lars Svåsand. 2002. "Party Institutionalization in New Democracies." *Party Politics* 8 (1): 5–29.

Rosenberg, Gerald. 1991. *The Hollow Hope: Can Courts Bring about Social Change?* Chicago: University of Chicago Press.

Rousseau, Jean-Jacques. [1762] 2004. *Of the Social Contract, or Principles of Political Right*. Translated by G. D. H. Cole. Whitefish, MT: Kessinger Publishing.

Sartori, Giovanni. 1976. *Parties and Party Systems: A Framework for Analysis*. Cambridge, U.K.: Cambridge University Press.

Schaffer, Frederic Charles. 2007. *Elections for Sale: The Causes and Consequences of Vote Buying*. Boulder, CO: Lynne Rienner Publishers.

Schedler, Andreas. 2002. "The Menu of Manipulation." *Journal of Democracy* 13 (2): 36–50.

Shefter, Martin. 1977. "Party and Patronage: Germany, England, and Italy." *Politics and Society* 7 (4): 403–51.

Shen, Yan, and Yang Yao. 2008. "Does Grassroots Democracy Reduce Income Inequality in China?" *Journal of Public Economics* 92 (10–11): 2182–98.

Skoufias, Emmanuel, Ambar Narayan, Basab Dasgupta, and Kai Kaiser. 2011. "Electoral Accountability, Fiscal Decentralization and Service Delivery in Indonesia." Policy Research Working Paper 5641, World Bank, Washington, DC.

Smith, Jackie. 2008. *Social Movements for Global Democracy.* Baltimore: Johns Hopkins University Press.

Spada, Paolo, Jonathan Mellon, Tiago Peixoto, and Fredrik Sjoberg. 2015. "Effects of the Internet on Participation: Study of a Policy Referendum in Brazil." Policy Research Working Paper 7204, World Bank, Washington, DC.

Stokes, Susan C. 2005. "Perverse Accountability." *American Political Science Review* 99 (3): 315–25.

Stokes, Susan C., Thad Dunning, Marcelo Nazareno, and Valeria Brusco. 2013. *Brokers, Voters, and Clientelism: The Puzzle of Distributive Politics.* Cambridge, U.K.: Cambridge University Press.

Tarrow, Sidney. 1998. *Power in Movement: Social Movements, Collective Action, and Politics.* Cambridge, U.K.: Cambridge University Press.

Tilly, Charles. 1984. *Big Structures, Large Processes, Huge Comparisons.* New York: Russell Sage Foundation.

Transparency International. 2015. Corruption Perceptions Index. Berlin, http://www.transparency.org/cpi2015.

Tripp, Ali Mari. 2015. *Women and Power in Post-conflict Africa.* Cambridge, U.K.: Cambridge University Press.

UCDP/PRIO (Uppsala Conflict Data Program/Peace Research Institute Oslo). 2015. Armed Conflict Dataset Version 4-2015 (1946–2014). Uppsala University, Sweden, http://www.pcr.uu.se/research/ucdp/datasets/ucdp_prio_armed_conflict_dataset/.

Van Biezen, Ingrid, and Petr Kopecky. 2007. "The State and the Parties: Public Funding, Public Regulation, and Rent-Seeking in Contemporary Democracies." *Party Politics* 13 (2): 235–54.

Van Cott, Donna Lee. 2005. *From Movements to Parties in Latin America.* Cambridge, U.K.: Cambridge University Press.

———. 2006. "Radical Democracy in the Andes: Indigenous Parties and the Quality of Democracy in Latin America." Working Paper 333, Kellogg Institute for International Studies, University of Notre Dame, Notre Dame, IN.

Vanderbilt University. Various years. Latin American Public Opinion Project (LAPOP). Nashville, http://www.vanderbilt.edu/lapop/.

V-Dem (Varieties of Democracy). 2016. Database hosted by Gothenburg Institute (Europe) and Kellogg Institute (United States), https://www.v-dem.net/en/.

Wang, Yi-ting. 2012. "A Case Study of Parties' Programmatic and Clientelistic Electoral Appeals in South Korea." In *Research and Dialogue on Programmatic Parties and Party Systems: Case Study Reports,* edited by Herbert Kitschelt and Yi-ting Wang, 138–60. Stockholm: International Institute for Democracy and Electoral Assistance.

Wantchekon, Leonard. 2003. "Clientelism and Voting Behavior: Evidence from a Field Experiment in Benin." *World Politics* 55 (3): 399–422.

Weitz-Shapiro, Rebecca. 2014. *Curbing Clientelism in Argentina: Politics, Poverty, and Social Policy.* New York: Cambridge University Press.

Whiteley, Paul F. 2011. "Is the Party Over? The Decline of Party Activism and Membership across the Democratic World." *Party Politics* 17 (1): 21–44.

World Bank. Various years. World Development Indicators (database). Washington, DC, http://data.worldbank.org/data-catalog/world-development-indicators.

———. 2015. *World Development Report 2015: Mind, Society, and Behavior.* Washington, DC: World Bank.

———. 2016. *World Development Report 2016: Digital Dividends.* Washington, DC: World Bank.

World Values Survey. Various years. Stockholm, http://www.worldvaluessurvey.org/wvs.jsp.

From transparency to accountability through citizen engagement

The increased visibility of social movements and citizens' demands for well-functioning governance over the last decade has been accompanied by an increase in transparency and accountability initiatives (TAIs) in many countries. Driven by combinations of grassroots organizations, transnational advocacy networks, and international donors, these initiatives seek to harness information and citizen participation to strengthen accountability from public officials. They include citizen monitoring and oversight of public sector performance, access to and dissemination of information, public complaint and grievance redress mechanisms, and citizen participation in public decision making. TAIs are supported by the growing number, influence, and range of "social intermediaries" (such as nongovernmental organizations, community-based organizations, and the media), and they are backed by the availability of new modes of communication (mobile phones, internet, and social media).

A growing body of empirical evidence and analysis points to the mixed results of TAIs in terms of improved outcomes.[1] For all of the widely touted success stories, similar interventions have had poor results or even negative consequences in other contexts. For example, participatory budgeting in Porto Alegre, Brazil, has resulted in increased investment in services for the poor (Ackerman 2004), but it has not been successfully replicated elsewhere (Baiocchi, Heller, and Silva 2011).[2] Social audits in the Indian state of Andhra Pradesh have contributed to combating corruption; however, they have been largely unsuccessful in the state of Bihar (Srinivasan and Park 2013; Dutta and others 2014). In Uganda, community

scorecards for health services helped reduce under-5 mortality by one-third (Bjorkman and Svensson 2009), but community monitoring of health providers in Sierra Leone had limited results in light of accountability gaps up the chain of command (Grandvoinnet, Aslam, and Raha 2015). Interpreted from the perspective of this Report, TAIs seek to reshape the policy arena by enhancing contestability and, when successful, effectively changing the incentives of decision makers in favor of certain outcomes.

How power asymmetries shape TAI effectiveness: Transparency, publicity, and accountability

Typical approaches to TAIs tend to focus on reducing information asymmetries. However, as this Report acknowledges, providing information alone will not be effective in changing outcomes unless the underlying power asymmetries are addressed as well. Information asymmetries, while arising from problems of whether actions or outcomes are unobservable, are in the end rarely an accident of history. Rather, the lack of disclosure of information is often the result of powerful actors intentionally withholding information or resisting attempts to make it accessible—in other words, information asymmetries are also embedded in existing power asymmetries.

This Report highlights the three key conditions needed for effective information initiatives: transparency, publicity, and accountability (Naurin 2006). However, making information available, making it accessible, and ensuring that it leads to consequences

WDR 2017 team, based on inputs from Helene Grandvoinnet.

Figure S11.1 Transparency is not enough: Three conditions for the effectiveness of information initiatives

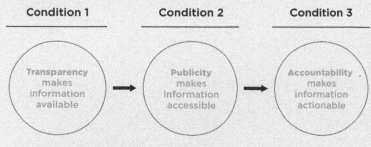

Condition 1	Condition 2	Condition 3

Transparency makes information available → Publicity makes information accessible → Accountability makes information actionable

Source: WDR 2017 team, based on Naurin 2006.

all involve challenging dynamics related to the nature of the policy arena (figure S11.1).

Transparency

Making information available through transparency initiatives is an important first step toward increasing accountability. However, to effectively change the incentives—political costs—of those in power to adopt such initiatives, citizens need to organize collectively to amplify their bargaining power. Successful reform coalitions often involve various civil society groups collaborating with interested elites, including sympathetic government agencies such as law courts or an ombudsman's office. This type of coalition was a key factor in the successful passage of the Right to Information Act in India (see chapter 8) because a coalition of government officials and eminent citizens helped give voice to initially isolated rural activists.

However, the demand for greater transparency per se may not produce incentives powerful enough to stimulate collective action. Reducing the extent of information asymmetries is not enough. Citizens frequently possess in-depth knowledge of state weaknesses and failures, and yet in most cases, without a process to support their demands, they would rather exit the system than challenge it (Hirschman 1970). Supporting the coordination of citizens' preferences is therefore essential to catalyzing change. Indeed, citizens are not a homogeneous group with common preferences, and in coordinating these preferences there is risk of capture by subgroups (see chapters 6 and 8). Civil society is not immune to power relations, and different civil society actors may have different incentives to maintain or to challenge existing rules. It is not uncommon for representatives to emerge voicing demands reflecting special interests rather than the public good, thereby strengthening rather

than confronting the existing power structures (Mansuri and Rao 2013).

Publicity

Although transparency laws are a necessary first condition, they are far from sufficient for effectively promoting accountability. Publicity, the second condition for effectiveness, requires that the available information be made public and reach the intended actors, particularly those for whom the information matters. Publicity thus activates the potential power of transparency. However, whether information reaches the intended audiences depends on who has the incentives, the means, and the power to publicize it. Even when laws on paper support transparency, citizens may lack the incentives to pursue publication of information if doing so increases the risk of reprisal or the perception that there will be no consequences once the information is publicly available.

The media are a key actor in this regard because their de facto power originates from the decisions they make on what information is made public (see spotlight 12). However, civil society can also play an important role. Information can be made more salient through issue framing and perceived as reliable through dissemination by respected individuals or groups within society (such as local leaders, grassroots organizations, parent-teacher associations, or health committees). The availability of new digital technologies and social media platforms has amplified the possibilities for citizens to play a role in both generating content and publicizing it, especially when the traditional media channels may have limited freedom to do so. Although the social media have been powerful in publicizing more egregious government scandals such as corrupt high-level politicians or the excessive use of force by police, they have been less powerful in mobilizing citizens around everyday issues such as failures in service delivery (World Bank 2016). A growing number of civil society organizations have emerged around the world precisely to solve these types of failures by aggregating and publicizing information from citizens on issues such as bribery or teacher absenteeism. However, an analysis of 17 such initiatives found that only three of them had a high impact in terms of government responsiveness (World Bank 2016).

Accountability

Once information is made public, the effectiveness of TAIs to promote government responsiveness ultimately depends on their ability to reshape the policy arena by rebalancing the power asymmetries.

Responsiveness is a function of the incentives public officials face in terms of the chances of being held accountable. Citizen engagement may succeed in shifting those incentives by applying pressure on authorities and increasing the cost of inaction (especially where there is a direct possibility of being sanctioned or being voted out of office).

The road from transparency to accountability, however, is not free of hurdles. Depending on its nature, citizen engagement can lead to positive or negative outcomes. Although assessment of these experiences faces the challenge of defining clearly the dimension over which results are expected, Gaventa and Barrett (2012) propose four dimensions across which to measure these outcomes (table S11.1).[3] According to their analysis of over 800 examples of citizen engagement strategies, the highest percentage of positive outcomes for the indicator *enhanced state responsiveness and accountability* is the result of multiple engagement strategies (as opposed to a single engagement strategy).[4]

In addition to multiple engagement strategies, the effectiveness of citizen engagement to promote accountability also depends on the effectiveness of a broader set of institutional incentives, mechanisms to enforce sanctions, and coalitions with a broad set of actors (including political elites). For example, the need among elite actors to maintain relationships both horizontally (with other elite groups) and vertically (with organized social groups) in order to preserve their influence can create strong incentives to respond (or not) to particular demands, which may vary by sector or over time (Bukenya, Hickey, and King 2012). Some agencies or levels of government are more amenable than others to partnering with civil society to ensure the accountability of other state actors— such as oversight institutions, a central government eager to monitor local governments or agencies, or a regulatory agency partnering with citizens to check the policy of an energy ministry. The judiciary can be an important actor as well to the extent that it has the space and incentives to challenge public authorities (see spotlight 3 on effective and equitable legal institutions). During Hosni Mubarak's rule in the Arab Republic of Egypt, for example, human rights groups took advantage of an important window of judicial independence to systematically challenge repressive legislation through the Supreme Constitutional Court (Moustafa 2007; Staton 2010).

Creating coalitions across different levels of the policy arena can also be critical for scaling up the success of localized interventions. For example, when local obstacles stem from weaknesses at a higher level, improving local accountability alone will not be sufficient (the different policy arenas in which players interact are not independent of each other). In Sierra Leone, a process of community scorecards reached a ceiling when nurses and community members proved unable to resolve issues that involved greater power imbalances or larger institutional breakdowns. Strategies of *vertical integration,* or the coordination of civil society oversight at different levels of public decision making, are important not only for identifying possible (interconnected) entry points

Table S11.1 Positive and negative outcomes of citizen engagement

Positive	Negative
Construction of citizenship	
Increased civic and political knowledge	Reliance on knowledge intermediaries
Greater sense of empowerment and agency	Disempowerment and reduced sense of agency
Practices of citizen participation	
Increased capacities for collective action	New capacities used for "negative" purposes
New forms of participation	Tokenistic or "captured" forms of participation
Deepening of networks and solidarities	Lack of accountability and representation in networks
Responsive and accountable states	
Greater access to state services and resources	Denial of state services and resources
Greater realization of rights	Social, economic, and political reprisals
Enhanced state responsiveness and accountability	Violent or coercive state response
Inclusive and cohesive societies	
Inclusion of new actors and issues in public spaces	Reinforcement of social hierarchies and exclusion
Greater social cohesion across groups	Increased horizontal conflict and violence

Source: Gaventa and Barrett 2012, table 1.

for reform, but also for strengthening the bargaining power of actors to actually pressure for reform. The initiative Textbook Count in the Philippines reveals how this type of strategy was successful in reducing textbook funds lost to corruption as well as improving the quality, cost, and delivery time of textbooks. However, the initiative also reveals how the challenge of sustaining such gains relies on the ability to overcome power asymmetries that prevent commitment to longer-term reform objectives (Fox and Aceron 2016).

Transparency and accountability: Complements for policy effectiveness

The road from transparency to accountability via citizen engagement and coalition building requires an effective reshaping of the policy arena. This can be done through two entry points: enhancing contestability and effectively changing the incentives of decision makers. In other words, transparency and access to information are not effective if the preexisting relative bargaining power of actors remains unchanged.

Accountability is effective when citizens, acting individually in response to new information, vote out those who are politically responsible for bad policies (Khemani and others 2016). Accountability is also strengthened by collective mobilization that increases the cost of inaction for those with the authority to hold others responsible (Grandvoinnet, Aslam, and Raha 2015). As experience shows, coalitions between different groups (citizens and elites) at different levels (local, national, and international) tend to be the most effective ones to bring about change.

Notes

1. For overviews of the evidence, see Gaventa and McGee (2013); Joshi (2013); Fox (2015); Grandvoinnet, Aslam, and Raha (2015); Fox and Aceron (2016); and Khemani and others (2016).
2. See chapter 8 for a more in-depth discussion of the case of Brazil.
3. Grandvoinnet, Aslam, and Raha (2015) propose an alternative set of categories based on within-state, state-society, and within-society outcomes, as well as on whether outcomes are more "instrumental" or "institutional."

4. The single engagement strategies analyzed include local associations, social movements and campaigns, and formal participatory governance spaces.

References

Ackerman, John. 2004. "Co-governance for Accountability: Beyond 'Exit' and 'Voice.'" *World Development* 32 (3): 447–63.

Baiocchi, Gianpaolo, Patrick Heller, and Marcelo Kunrath Silva. 2011. *Bootstrapping Democracy: Transforming Local Governance and Civil Society in Brazil.* Stanford, CA: Stanford University Press.

Bjorkman, Martina, and Jakob Svensson. 2009. "Power to the People: Evidence from a Randomized Field Experiment on Community-Based Monitoring in Uganda." *Quarterly Journal of Economics* 124 (2): 735–69.

Bukenya, Badru, Sam Hickey, and Sophie King. 2012. "Understanding the Role of Context in Shaping Social Accountability Interventions: Toward an Evidence-Based Approach." Social Accountability and Demand for Good Governance Team Report, World Bank, Washington, DC.

Dutta, Puja, Rinku Murgai, Martin Ravallion, and Dominique van de Walle. 2014. *Right to Work? Assessing India's Employment Guarantee Scheme in Bihar.* Equity and Development Series. Washington, DC: World Bank.

Fox, Jonathan A. 2015. "Social Accountability: What Does the Evidence Really Say?" *World Development* 72 (August): 346–61.

Fox, Jonathan A., and Joy Aceron. 2016. "Doing Accountability Differently: A Proposal for the Vertical Integration of Civil Society Monitoring and Advocacy." U4 Issue 4 (August), U4 Anti-corruption Resource Center, Chr. Michelsen Institute, Bergen, Norway.

Gaventa, John, and Gregory Barrett. 2012. "Mapping the Outcomes of Citizen Engagement." *World Development* 40 (12): 2399–410.

Gaventa, John, and Rosemary McGee. 2013. "The Impact and Effectiveness of Transparency and Accountability Initiatives." *Development Policy Review* 31 (7): 3–28.

Grandvoinnet, Helene, Ghazia Aslam, and Shomikho Raha. 2015. *Opening the Black Box: The Contextual Drivers of Social Accountability.* New Frontiers of Social Policy Series. Washington, DC: World Bank.

Hirschman, Albert O. 1970. *Exit, Voice, and Loyalty: Responses to Decline in Firms, Organizations, and States.* Cambridge, MA: Harvard University Press.

Joshi, Anuradha. 2013. "Do They Work? Assessing the Impact of Transparency and Accountability Initiatives in Service Delivery." *Development Policy Review* 31 (7): 29–48.

Khemani, Stuti, Ernesto Dal Bó, Claudio Ferraz, Frederico Finan, Corinne Stephenson, Adesinaola Odugbemi,

Dikshya Thapa, and Scott Abrahams. 2016. *Making Politics Work for Development: Harnessing Transparency and Citizen Engagement.* Policy Research Report. Washington, DC: World Bank.

Mansuri, Ghazala, and Vijayendra Rao. 2013. *Localizing Development: Does Participation Work?* Policy Research Report. Washington, DC: World Bank.

Moustafa, Tamir. 2007. *The Struggle for Constitutional Power: Law, Politics, and Economic Development in Egypt.* New York: Cambridge University Press.

Naurin, Daniel. 2006. "Transparency, Publicity, Accountability: The Missing Links." *Swiss Political Science Review* 12 (3): 90–98.

Srinivasan, S., and S. Park. 2013. "Conducting Social Audits to Monitor Social Service Delivery: A Guidance Note." Draft paper (October), World Bank, Washington, DC.

Staton, Jeffrey K. 2010. *Judicial Power and Strategic Communication in Mexico.* New York: Cambridge University Press.

World Bank. 2016. *World Development Report 2016: Digital Dividends.* Washington, DC: World Bank.

SPOTLIGHT 12

The media

Under the presidency of Alberto Fujimori (1990–2000) in Peru, the bribing of politicians, judges, and news media companies was a well-established practice to weaken accountability and co-opt the opposition. The architect of the system, Fujimori's security chief, Vladimiro Montesinos, kept a detailed record—both on paper and on video—of all payments made. However, Montesinos failed to secure the support of one TV channel (Channel N), which continued to publicize independent analysis and investigations of the regime's performance (McMillan and Zoido 2004).[1] This channel then made public the first "Vladivideos" in 2000, thereby revealing the magnitude of the corruption and the rent-seeking behavior of elites. The popular outrage generated by disclosure of the videos helped opposition forces mobilize, leading to the disintegration of the regime and the ousting of Fujimori a few months later.

This case highlights the central role that the media can play as an agent of accountability. By publicizing information that is reliable and salient for citizens, the media can change the incentives of elites by increasing the costs of certain behavior or policy decisions, reshape preferences and beliefs, and make the policy arena more contestable (Khemani and others 2016). But precisely because of their role, the media can be captured by powerful interests and undermine—rather than support—possible entry points for change.

Changing incentives: The watchdog role of media

The media can play a role as "public sentinels" (Norris 2010), generating and publicizing information about

government performance, shaping the incentives of politicians to deliver, and making governments more responsive to voters, thereby improving the quality of public policies. By making information public, media companies can strengthen the bargaining power of citizens, increasing the costs for public officials to engage in rent-seeking behavior (see chapter 8). Indeed, the media can facilitate the efforts of civic associations to mobilize citizens around an anticorruption agenda and help citizens monitor the quality of government services, acting as important agents of "social accountability" (Peruzzotti and Smulovitz 2006). In Uganda, for example, elite capture undermined public service provision, with local schools receiving on average only 24 percent of the central government grants to which they were entitled. After a media campaign publicized the amount the schools were supposed to receive, the average funding increased to 80 percent, improving school enrollment and learning outcomes. The effects were larger in schools that were closer to a newspaper outlet (Reinikka and Svensson 2005).

Access to media makes government more responsive to citizens' needs. For example, a comparison of Indian states from 1958 to 1992 found that government spending was more responsive to local needs in areas in which newspaper circulation was higher (Besley and Burgess 2002). However, this type of relationship can also generate biases against citizens who do not have access to media, especially the poor living in rural areas (Strömberg 2015). For information to reach the intended audiences (the publicity condition described in spotlight 11), the media need to make information accessible to all. According to data from the Gallup World Poll, the media sources that citizens rely on vary dramatically across regions, although television

WDR 2017 team.

and radio are consistently more popular than news-papers. Moreover, the means by which citizens can access media are also starkly different; despite huge gains in internet penetration rates in recent decades, cell phone ownership far outstrips rates of access to computers or internet at home (Khemani and others 2016; World Bank 2016).

Reshaping preferences: The agenda-setting role of the media

As discussed in the *World Development Report 2015: Mind, Society, and Behavior* (World Bank 2015), the media can play an important role in reshaping prefer-ences and social norms within societies.[2] Media "both entertain and educate, in order to increase audience members' knowledge about an educational issue, create favorable attitudes, shift social norms, and change overt behavior" (Singhal and Rogers 2004, 5). A growing body of studies based on randomized con-trolled trials and quasi-experimental design provides empirical support for this claim, pointing at the trans-formative potential of "educational entertainment" (or "edutainment"). For example, in Brazil, watching a soap opera that shows female characters who have few or no children has been associated with significant drops in fertility rates, changing preferences for family size (La Ferrara, Chong, and Duryea 2012). In India, access to television has improved gender norms, altered son pref-erence, and decreased fertility (Jensen and Oster 2009). In Tanzania, exposure to a particular radio program was associated with a significant increase in condom use and reduction in the number of sexual partners (Vaughan and others 2000). In Rwanda, exposure to radio programs changed citizens' attitudes toward authorities, promoting more pro-social behavior and more active participation in conflict resolution (Paluck and Green 2009). Ultimately, the role of the media, rang-ing from local radio stations to international broadcast-ing networks, in reaching broad audiences and reshap-ing the demands of what they expect from both their government and their media is essential for ensuring the sustainability of progress in promoting more con-testable and participatory spaces of policy dialogue.

Changing contestability: The political economy of media capture and competition

Control of the media is one instrument through which elites bargain. They can capture the media to shape coverage and content, reducing contestability. Although it is difficult to quantify the relative impor-tance of controlling the media compared with other institutions aimed at ensuring checks and balances, in Peru it was estimated that bribing the media was in fact 10 times more expensive than bribing legislators and judges during the Fujimori regime. The television channel with the largest viewership received US$1.5 million a month (McMillan and Zoido 2004). Another strategy governments can use is to adopt regulations that favor a specific media outlet or buy advertising space in exchange for political support. For example, in Argentina the amount of coverage of corruption scandals significantly declined for newspapers that received government-related advertising from 1998 to 2007 (Di Tella and Franceschelli 2011). Private inter-ests can also capture media markets: as of 2016 about 6 percent of all the world's billionaires were involved in some media business, reaching peaks of more than 20 percent in countries such as Mexico, Poland, and República Bolivariana de Venezuela.[3] Other research shows that media capture by narrow interest groups is more likely when media ownership is more con-centrated and income inequalities are higher (Corneo 2006; Petrova 2008).

These findings suggest that more competition and entry in the media market are fundamental to increasing contestability in the policy-making arena (Khemani and others 2016). Ensuring the media's independence from government ownership works toward the same effect. However, ownership of the media and press freedom are also the by-products of elite bargains and power relations, creating an equilibrium that is difficult to change. One important factor driving the growth of independent media is the advertising market. A study of U.S. newspapers in the 19th century revealed that independent media are more likely to emerge in places with higher adver-tising revenues (Petrova 2011). When advertising revenues increase, media outlets have alternative rev-enue sources and therefore are less willing to distort news coverage to protect the interests of subsidizing groups, especially if such distortion undermines their ability to secure advertising revenues.

The international donor community can also provide an alternative revenue stream to media as a means of fostering more independent markets and reducing dependency on government funding. For example, aid flows to support the independence of the media in Tanzania led to important gains in media freedom and the growth of newspapers and tele-vision stations (Tripp 2012). However, international funding of the media tends to be limited. In 2014 only

0.3 percent of total official development assistance was allocated to media support.[4] That said, monetary support of the media is often insufficient to overcome the existing political challenges, and it may in fact lead to unintended consequences.

In some cases, elite bargains can open up opportunities for more competitive media markets and lead to unexpected changes in contestability. In Malaysia, for example, ruling elites invested in internet infrastructure as a way to attract foreign investment. This led to a "democratizing" effect in the media market, with independent bloggers publicizing news on government performance. This development has had an important effect on voting behavior: in districts with higher internet access, the loss of political support for the ruling party has been more pronounced (Miner 2015). Similar effects have been found in the Russian Federation, where the access to a privately owned and independent television channel (NTS) was associated with a higher propensity to vote for the opposition (Enikolopov, Petrova, and Zhuravskaya 2011).

Media content is often decided by elites. The effect of media bias as an instrument to reduce contestability, reinforce prior beliefs, and increase polarization among social groups is well documented in the literature (Strömberg 2015, 2016). Elites can also use the media as a coordinating device for propaganda purposes and—in extreme cases—for repression. For example, 10 percent of the reported killings during the genocide in Rwanda have been attributed to radio broadcasting, which facilitated militia targeting of the Tutsi population (Yanagizawa-Drott 2014).

Under certain circumstances, new social media can counteract elite control of the media market. The anti-G-20 movements following the global financial crisis in 2008–09 (Bennett and Segerberg 2012), the Occupy Wall Street movement in 2011, the Arab Spring that began to spread in early 2011, and the massive protests that erupted in Brazil surrounding the 2014 World Cup (Lemieux 2015)—all demonstrate the instrumental role played by the internet and new social media in facilitating citizens' collective action. The same events, however, also highlight the limitations of social media. Social media can be effective in generating sudden spikes of protests and in coordinating uprising, but they alone cannot yield sustained representation of interests and promote social change (Ackland and Tanaka 2015). According to the *World Development Report 2016: Digital Dividends* (World Bank 2016), "analog" complements are needed to maximize the potential of social media as drivers of change. Political and social organizations can act as such complements (see chapter 8).

Notes

1. It is unclear whether Montesinos failed to secure the support of Channel N because the owners of the channel rejected the bribe or because Montesinos made a strategic mistake by undervaluing the importance of a cable channel with only a few thousand subscribers (McMillan and Zoido 2004).
2. This section largely relies and builds on the *World Development Report 2015: Mind, Society, and Behavior* (World Bank 2015). A background paper for that Report, "The Impact of Entertainment Education," provides a recent review of the literature, analysis of selected cases, and evidence on results.
3. WDR 2017 team, based on *Forbes*, "The World's Billionaires," http://www.forbes.com/billionaires/.
4. WDR 2017 team estimates, based on data supplied by the Organisation for Economic Co-operation and Development.

References

Ackland, Robert, and Kyosuke Tanaka. 2015. "Development Impact of Social Media." Background paper, *World Development Report 2016: Mind, Society, and Behavior*, World Bank, Washington, DC.

Bennett, W. Lance, and Alexandra Segerberg. 2012. "The Logic of Connective Action." *Information, Communication, and Society* 15 (5): 739–68.

Besley, Timothy, and Robin S. L. Burgess. 2002. "The Political Economy of Government Responsiveness: Theory and Evidence from India." *Quarterly Journal of Economics* 117 (4): 1415–51.

Corneo, Giacomo. 2006. "Media Capture in a Democracy: The Role of Wealth Concentration." *Journal of Public Economics* 90 (1–2): 37–58.

Di Tella, Rafael, and Ignacio Franceschelli. 2011. "Government Advertising and Media Coverage of Corruption Scandals." *American Economic Journal: Applied Economics* 3 (4): 119–51.

Enikolopov, Ruben, Maria Petrova, and Ekaterina Zhuravskaya. 2011. "Media and Political Persuasion: Evidence from Russia." *American Economic Review* 101 (7): 3253–85.

Gallup Organization. Various years. Gallup World Poll. Washington, DC, http://www.gallup.com/services /170945/world-poll.aspx.

Jensen, Robert, and Emily Oster. 2009. "The Power of TV: Cable Television and Women's Status in India." *Quarterly Journal of Economics* 124 (3): 1057–94.

Khemani, Stuti, Ernesto Dal Bó, Claudio Ferraz, Frederico Finan, Corinne Stephenson, Adesinaola Odugbemi, Dikshya Thapa, and Scott Abrahams. 2016. *Making Politics Work for Development: Harnessing Transparency and Citizen Engagement*. Policy Research Report. Washington, DC: World Bank.

La Ferrara, Eliana, Alberto Chong, and Suzanne Duryea. 2012. "Soap Operas and Fertility: Evidence from Brazil." *American Economic Journal: Applied Economics* 4 (4): 1–31.

Lemieux, Victoria Louise. 2015. "'We Feel Fine': Big Data Observations of Citizen Sentiment about State Institutions and Social Inclusion." Working Paper 99486, World Bank, Washington, DC.

McMillan, John, and Pablo Zoido. 2004. "How to Subvert Democracy: Montesinos in Peru." *Journal of Economic Perspectives* 18 (4): 69–92.

Miner, Luke. 2015. "The Unintended Consequences of Internet Diffusion: Evidence from Malaysia." *Journal of Public Economics* 132 (C): 66–78.

Norris, Pippa, ed. 2010. *Public Sentinel: The News Media and Governance Reform*. Washington, DC: World Bank.

Paluck, Elizabeth Levy, and Donald P. Green. 2009. "Deference, Dissent, and Dispute Resolution: An Experimental Intervention Using Mass Media to Change Norms and Behavior in Rwanda." *American Political Science Review* 103 (4): 622–44.

Peruzzotti, Enrique, and Catalina Smulovitz, eds. 2006. *Enforcing the Rule of Law: Social Accountability in the New Latin American Democracies*. Pitt Latin American Studies Series. Pittsburgh: University of Pittsburgh Press.

Petrova, Maria. 2008. "Inequality and Media Capture." *Journal of Public Economics* 92 (1–2): 183–212.

———. 2011. "Newspapers and Parties: How Advertising Revenue Created an Independent Press." *American Political Science Review* 105 (4): 790–808.

Reinikka, Ritva, and Jakob Svensson. 2005. "Fighting Corruption to Improve Schooling: Evidence from a Newspaper Campaign in Uganda." *Journal of the European Economic Association* 3 (2–3): 259–67.

Singhal, Arvind, and Everett M. Rogers. 2004. "The Status of Entertainment Education Worldwide." In *Entertainment-Education and Social Change: History, Research, and Practice*, edited by Arvind Singhal, Michael J. Cody, Everett M. Rogers, and Miguel Sabido, 3–20. Routledge Communication Series. Mahwah, NJ: Lawrence Erlbaum Associates.

Strömberg, David. 2015. "Media and Politics." *Annual Review of Economics* 7 (1): 173–205.

———. 2016. "Media Coverage and Political Accountability: Theory and Evidence." In *Handbook of Media Economics*, Vol. 1A, edited by Simon P. Anderson, David Strömberg, and Joel Waldfogel, 595–622. Handbooks in Economics Series. Amsterdam: Elsevier.

Tripp, Aili Mari. 2012. "Donor Assistance and Political Reform in Tanzania." UNU-WIDER Working Paper 2012/37, United Nations University-World Institute for Development Economics Research, Helsinki.

Vaughan, Peter W., Everett M. Rogers, Arvind Singhal, and Ramadhan M. Swalehe. 2000. "Entertainment-Education and HIV/AIDS Prevention: A Field Experiment in Tanzania." *Journal of Health Communication* 5 (8): 81–100.

World Bank. 2015. *World Development Report 2015: Mind, Society, and Behavior*. Washington, DC: World Bank.

———. 2016. *World Development Report 2016: Digital Dividends*. Washington, DC: World Bank.

Yanagizawa-Drott, David. 2014. "Propaganda and Conflict: Evidence from the Rwandan Genocide." *Quarterly Journal of Economics* 1.

CHAPTER 9

Governance in an interconnected world

The dynamics of governance do not play out solely within the boundaries of nation-states. Countries today face an interconnected, globalized world characterized by a high velocity and magnitude of flows of capital, trade, ideas, technology, and people. From 1960 to 2011, global trade's share of the global gross domestic product (GDP) more than doubled, from 25 percent to over 60 percent.[1] The share of foreign direct investment (FDI) increased from less than 10 percent to over 40 percent from 1992 to 2010.[2] Meanwhile, foreign debt's share of the global GDP grew from only 11 percent in 1970 to 90 percent in 2010.[3] Today, the world is very different from the one in which the current developed countries emerged: cross-border flows were low; they received no aid; and they were not subject to a proliferation of transnational treaties, norms, and regulatory mechanisms. For developing countries, the era of globalization and "global governance" presents both opportunities and challenges.

Globalization can greatly benefit countries in search of sustained and inclusive development. The rapid diffusion of technology and greater access to capital and world markets have enabled annual growth rates of over 7 percent for a subset of developing countries—a previously unfathomable rate of growth that helped lift over 1 billion people out of poverty from 1981 to 2012 (Spence 2011).

Globalization can, however, also present great challenges. By making it possible for domestic actors to send money and resources abroad, transnational flows increase the capacity for them to opt out of local bargains. These flows have also been associated with a marked rise in inequality within countries and with a greater vulnerability of countries to global economic crises, such as the 1997 Asian financial crisis and the 2008–09 global financial crisis.[4] Global interactions can undermine domestic social and economic development by exerting power in ways that prevent the adoption of policies fit for the domestic or local context or by reinforcing preexisting conditions that sustain socially undesirable outcomes. The resurgence today of populist politics and its rejection of trade and migration in several Western countries can be seen as a reaction to these negative effects.

Transnationalism and the domestic policy arena

The policy bargaining framework discussed in this Report provides a lens for discerning how to maximize the positive impacts of transnational flows and international actors to achieve security, growth, and equity. These flows can be critical instruments for enhancing the ability of domestic actors to commit, coordinate, and cooperate to advance development outcomes. But they also can disrupt these functions by confusing expectations, competing with social norms, and undermining citizen-state accountability. Understanding these effects requires in turn understanding how transnational factors shape the incentives of domestic actors, influence their preferences to change outcomes, and affect contestability in the policy arena.

At times, international actors enter directly into the policy arena (figure 9.1, panel a). Foreign states, multinational corporations, development agencies, or transnational nongovernmental organizations (NGOs) can gain a seat at the domestic bargaining table as they pursue specific goals or support domestic efforts that are aligned with their interests.

For developing countries, the era of globalization and "global governance" presents both opportunities and challenges.

Figure 9.1 International actors can affect the domestic policy arena by changing the dynamics of contestation, shifting actor incentives, or shaping actor norms

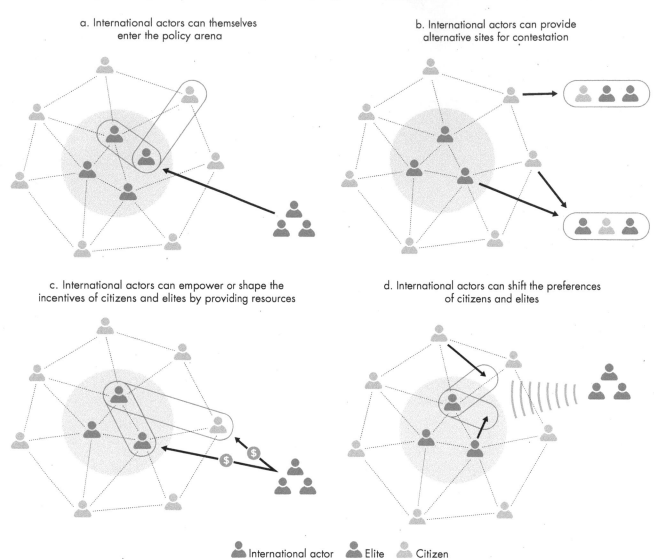

a. International actors can themselves enter the policy arena

b. International actors can provide alternative sites for contestation

c. International actors can empower or shape the incentives of citizens and elites by providing resources

d. International actors can shift the preferences of citizens and elites

International actor   Elite   Citizen

Source: WDR 2017 team.

However, international actors and mechanisms largely affect the policy arena indirectly. In doing so, they may change incentives and preferences toward enabling or constraining institutional functions for development and open or foreclose the possibilities for contestation.

International actors can shape the arena in which policy making and contestation occur by creating alternative spaces in which actors can bargain (figure 9.1, panel b). For example, foreign investors can bring states to the International Centre for Settlement of Investment Disputes (ICSID) for independent arbitration rather than rely on the legal mechanisms of the host state. Citizens of countries party to the European

Court of Human Rights can bring claims against their home state. Several international human rights treaties require states to report and answer to an international expert body. And a vast number of international and transnational forums exist for the development of industry-specific rules, monitoring their application and sanctioning violations to various degrees. The proliferation of these forums raises unresolved questions about their functional design, political legitimacy, and accountability. For example, as states increasingly subcontract government functions such as public infrastructure and service delivery, the tools of commercial arbitration may undercut the role of citizens in accountability. This challenge is reflected in contemporary public concerns about the role of investor-state dispute settlement in bilateral and multilateral investment treaties such as the Trans-Pacific Partnership.

Transnational flows and mechanisms can change the payoff structure and incentives of domestic actors by providing inducements or threats (figure 9.1, panel c). For example, conditions attached to foreign aid (conditionality) can make assistance dependent on specific behavior by domestic actors. Similarly, the desire to attract foreign investment can act as an incentive for positive changes in domestic governance. For example, the pursuit of foreign investment in China and Vietnam spurred institutional improvements in economic management at the provincial level, with greater flows leading to even more institutional reforms (Dang 2013; Long, Yang, and Zhang 2015). International trade agreements, by changing the incentives of domestic actors, can serve as a commitment device. At the same time, the incentives and payoffs may be structured in favor of private goods rather than global or national public goods. A government may sign a trade agreement to tie its hands in the face of domestic vested interests that might induce it to implement suboptimal policies such as high tariffs, or it may use transnational flows as a reason to avoid regulating a costly and challenging issue, such as the environmental damage caused by mines (Maggi and Rodríguez-Clare 1998, 2007; Shemberg 2009).

International actors and transnational interactions also shape preferences by influencing the ideas and beliefs of actors in the domestic policy arena (figure 9.1, panel d). Improvements in technology, by facilitating greater global connectivity, have helped spread international ideas and norms. Transnational networks of technical experts can play an important role in changing preferences and internalizing new norms through the diffusion of evidence and authoritative expertise.[5] In China, the interaction of the National Environmental Protection Agency (NEPA) with experts resulted in new perspectives, peer standards, data, and research findings that NEPA drew on to shape the debate over accession to the Montreal Protocol to protect the ozone layer, shifting the views of other political actors and allowing successful bargaining with more domestically grounded agencies, including the State Meteorological Administration (Economy 2001). Beyond finance and other forms of leverage, development actors can be most influential through the dissemination of knowledge and evidence. But, as Michel Foucault has argued, knowledge and evidence can also reflect particular agendas and

reduce the space of public discourse (Lukes 1986). Development indicators, for example, provide certainty and an impression that a clear trajectory exists to changing phenomena that are inherently complex and contested, such as peace or well-being (Davis, Kingsbury, and Merry 2012).

This chapter looks at how international actors can influence domestic governance dynamics through two primary instruments: (1) the introduction and diffusion of transnational rules, norms, and regulations and (2) the distribution of official development assistance or foreign aid. In discussing both instruments, this chapter focuses on the mechanisms through which these instruments act on the incentives and preferences of actors in the policy arena and the contestability of that arena.

Transnational rules and regulations: Enhanced cooperation and focal points for change

As the flows across borders expand, the instruments and mechanisms used to manage them expand as well (figure 9.2). Since the late 20th century, an ever-increasing number of international and transnational efforts have been made to govern the activities, relationships, and behavior that transcend national frontiers. These efforts stem in part from the nature of today's global challenges—such as climate, finance, and cross-border crime—which require solutions that go beyond the traditional state model of regulation. Unlike traditional international relations, these transnational efforts involve a broad array of actors—nation-states, multilateral organizations, private actors, and advocacy groups—and cover a wide range of issues—business transactions, labor, crime, information management, intellectual property, procurement, utility regulation, human rights, food and safety standards, and environmental sustainability (Hale and Held 2011).

Much of this proliferation of regulation has been in pursuit of further deregulation, as exemplified by the increasing de jure openness of capital accounts (figure 9.2, panel a). Other regulations and treaties are intended to enhance coordination on issues of global importance. For example, more than 1,000 multilateral and 1,300 bilateral environmental agreements are now in place (Green 2014).

The formation and diffusion of this overlapping web of transnational rules mirror this Report's framework on a transnational level. The nature and content

As the flows across borders expand, the instruments and mechanisms used to manage them expand as well.

Figure 9.2 Regulations and legal agreements have proliferated across borders

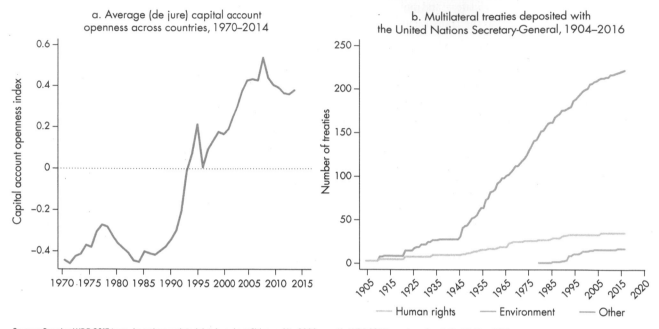

a. Average (de jure) capital account openness across countries, 1970–2014

b. Multilateral treaties deposited with the United Nations Secretary-General, 1904–2016

Human rights   Environment   Other

Sources: Panel a: WDR 2017 team, based on updated database from Chinn and Ito 2006; panel b: WDR 2017 team, based on United Nations 2016.

Note: The category "human rights" in panel b refers to treaties related to human rights, human trafficking, refugees and displaced persons, and the status of women.

of each regime are a product of contestation among multiple actors with varying incentives, preferences, and relative power. Transnational rules are institutionalized in some form of instrument, from authoritative/binding legal instruments to nonbinding declarations of norms and voluntary standards and regulatory regimes.[6] These instruments perform the functions of commitment, coordination, or cooperation through various mechanisms, from coercion to socialization (table 9.1). They may directly target state governments, as do the European Union's (EU's) fiscal and monetary rules or labor and tax standards aimed at avoiding a race to the bottom. They may bypass state governments to directly regulate private actors, as do voluntary industry regimes such as the Roundtable on Sustainable Palm Oil. Or they may reach out directly to citizens by legitimating local grievances through international rights and norms (Braithwaite and Drahos 2000; Shaffer 2013).

What follows is a closer look at how transnational rules interact with the policy arena—specifically, (1) the rules that seek to achieve international cooperation on global goods by changing incentives; (2) the rules that help induce a credible commitment to domestic reform through trade and regional integration incentives; and (3) the rules that serve as focal points for domestic actors to shift preferences and

improve coordination to overcome collective action challenges.

International cooperation: Changing incentives to prevent races to the bottom

In the same way that firms in competitive markets lower prices to attract consumers, when goods, services, and capital are freely exchanged and move internationally countries have an incentive to adopt competitive strategies to gain market share or attract investment. To attract productive investments, countries may lower taxes on corporate income for foreign companies. Competition among countries on these forms of taxation has the effect of depleting the domestic tax base and considerably decreasing revenue. It also tends to shift taxation onto less mobile factors such as labor. In turn, lower revenue means that countries have to shrink spending, with detrimental effects on the well-being of the poorest and least powerful in society. Moreover, competition to boost exports may result in lax labor and environmental standards (Chau and Kanbur 2005). These are examples of *races to the bottom.*

Once competition pushes countries to a low equilibrium, they have no incentive to change policy. An attempt by one country to raise taxes on goods and services, capital, or corporate income would result in

Table 9.1 Transnational actors, instruments, and mechanisms for influencing domestic governance through incentives, preferences, and contestability

Actors	Instruments	Mechanisms
International governmental organizations • United Nations (multiple agencies) • International financial institutions • World Trade Organization • International courts and tribunals **Regional organizations** • European Union • African Union • ASEAN • OECD **International nongovernmental organizations** • Multinational corporations • Professional associations • Advocacy organizations • Epistemic communities **Domestic actors** • Government officials • Political actors • Private sector actors • Local civil society groups • Grassroots organizations	**Legal and rule-based instruments** • International and regional treaties and conventions • International and regional standards, principles, and guidelines • Bilateral treaties • Voluntary standards and norm regimes • Contracts • International courts and arbitration mechanisms **Expert knowledge and evidence** **Public and private capital flows** **Migration and professional exchanges** **Security operations**	**Incentives** • Coercion (economic, military, political) • Rewards • Reciprocity **Preferences** • Knowledge and capacity transfer • Persuasion • Socialization • Demonstration **Contestability** • Coalition building • Substitution for domestic arena • Empowerment

Sources: WDR 2017 team, drawing on Braithwaite and Drahos 2000; Hale and Held 2011; and Shaffer 2013.

Note: ASEAN = Association of Southeast Asian Nations; OECD = Organisation for Economic Co-operation and Development.

a loss of sales or investments. Any intervention that could enhance employees' welfare or the sustainability of production would also raise costs and thus reduce exports and output. Because of the sensitivity of global capital to domestic adjustments and perceptions of investment risk, policy makers seeking global investment may become largely accountable to external actors rather than to domestic constituents. For example, policy makers seeking to increase domestic debt levels to finance an expanded education budget may be prevented from doing so by the fear that international ratings agencies will downgrade their country's sovereign bond rating, leading to capital flight.

Global coordination is needed to prevent races to the bottom, underprovision of global public goods, and negative cross-border externalities. International actors can strengthen the commitment capacity of states through agreements on specific issues such as investment or environmental standards, labor standards, or tax coordination. If all countries coordinate and adopt the same policy, such as international labor standards (Basu and others 2003), they will all be better off. For example, in parallel with the creation of a common market, the EU set up a Code of Conduct to prevent countries from engaging in harmful tax competition and to harmonize value added taxes on goods and services and, less successfully, corporate taxes and capital income taxes.

Such agreements can strengthen the commitment of countries to specific minimum standards that prevent the occurrence or perpetuation of an undesirable equilibrium. However, in the absence of credible sanctions, incentives to defect are very high. Preventing defection requires recognition that achieving a sustainable agreement is a *two-level game*, involving both an international bargaining process and a domestic bargaining process (box 9.1). Ultimately, the

Box 9.1 Legitimizing the second-best: Governance options for global public goods and the Paris Agreement on climate change

Climate change is a global public goods problem. Solving it requires universal participation (all countries need to reduce emissions), but there is an incentive to free-ride in any agreement. An obvious solution is a global governance body that ensures the participation of all countries and a fair distribution of efforts. From the United Nations Framework Convention on Climate Change (UNFCCC) in 1992 through the Kyoto Protocol in 1997 and the Copenhagen negotiations in 2009, international negotiations have tried to create such a framework to decide on a global target for temperature change, country-specific emission targets, and a set of processes to ensure flexibility and compliance.

The Kyoto Protocol failed to achieve universal participation. Developing countries were reluctant to take on commitments that could slow their economic growth, and many countries were reluctant to expose themselves to possible sanctions from a supranational body (Stewart and Wiener 2003). As predicted by economic theory, in the absence of a supranational governance body a credible commitment was impossible to achieve (Carraro and Siniscalco 1992; Barrett 1994). The 2015 Copenhagen conference, however, was a paradigm shift, moving away from the first-best option of sanctions to a system of "pledge-and-review," by which countries make unilateral commitments that are reviewed and monitored by the international community (Barrett, Carraro, and de Melo 2015).

These developments led to universal participation in the Paris Agreement, underpinned by 162 unilateral commitments to contribute to reductions in global emissions. The agreement, which went into effect in November 2016, also includes provisions to facilitate the adaptation to climate change, support to cope with unavoidable loss and damage, financial flows and financing instruments, and processes for the monitoring and revision of commitments.

The pledge-and-review scheme has two obvious limitations. First, there is no reason to expect that the sum of the unilateral commitments will meet the global target of maximum temperature change, and indeed they currently do not meet the goal of the Paris Agreement (limit warming to 2 degrees and try to achieve 1.5 degrees). The hope is that commitment revisions will lead to a gradual increase in ambition (van Asselt 2016). By providing a "ratcheting mechanism" that encourages countries to follow the lead of others in increasing commitments, the Paris Agreement is an important coordination mechanism (Keohane and Victor 2016). But if the problem is one of cooperation—that is, some countries care more about climate change than others—then such a cycle of revisions could lead to a stagnation of ambition, or even to a race to the bottom (Nordhaus 2015).

The second limitation is the lack of a compliance mechanism beyond monitoring that enables "naming and shaming" of countries that do not deliver on their commitment (Aldy 2014). However, climate negotiations are part of a broader network of agreements. Thus failing to deliver on climate commitments may not lead to direct sanctions, but it could have a cost in other areas such as trade or technological cooperation. Nordhaus (2015) suggests that even a minimum trade-related cost for noncompliance would lead to much greater participation and ambition.

Even though the Paris Agreement is far from an optimal mechanism to govern global public goods (Stiglitz 2015), it is an attractive second-best option, building on countries' self-interest in implementing climate policy actions at the country level (Busby 2016; Keohane and Victor 2016).

Source: Prepared for WDR 2017 by Stéphane Hallegatte.

preferences and relative power of the relevant domestic actors determine the credibility of commitment and the effectiveness of international sanctions.

Transnational rules that provide incentives for a credible commitment to domestic reform: Trade agreements

The desire to attract investment and expand trade can also provide incentives for improvements in domestic governance. Indeed, international agreements on economic integration can mean that domestic actors will make credible commitments to follow through on economic reforms. The success of the EU integration process, for example, demonstrates the power of inducements. Prospective member countries have to change their domestic rules to abide by the 80,000 pages of regulations in the acquis communautaire. For those countries that have joined the EU, the potential economic benefits of joining outweighed any loss of domestic autonomy in specific areas, and the benefits of accession were used by elites to overcome domestic resistance to the required reforms.

EU membership contributed to the consolidation of democratic institutions in former dictatorships in the European periphery, such as Greece, Portugal, and Spain in the 1980s, and in central and eastern European countries in the former communist bloc in the 1990s and 2000s.

The possibility of accession to the General Agreement on Tariffs and Trade (GATT) and then its successor, the World Trade Organization (WTO), has induced considerable domestic reforms in nations that seek to develop through global trade. WTO accession has had the strongest growth-promoting effects in countries that undertook deeper commitments as part of their accession negotiations, including China and Vietnam. Moreover, this pro-growth effect of accession has been strongest in countries with the weakest domestic governance (Tang and Wei 2009).

In China, the process of WTO accession at the turn of the millennium led to a major restructuring of the economy toward more market- and rules-based mechanisms, with accession acting as a "wrecking ball" for the closed command economy (Woo 2001; Jin 2002). China's leadership leveraged foreign competition and external commitment to accelerate domestic reforms, including reductions in tariff and nontariff barriers, market access for foreign firms, and protection of intellectual property. China's commitments to liberalizing its trade in services have been the most radical of any country acceding to the WTO (Mattoo 2004). The accession helped China's leadership overcome domestic opposition to reforms, and it also signaled to the emerging private sector that reforms were credible. The reforms enhanced the commercial legal environment and forced state-owned enterprises and state-owned banks to restructure and compete on a market basis, facilitating a more modern financial system and rapid private sector growth (Lardy 2002).

Another example of a trade agreement that led to domestic reforms is the Multi Fibre Arrangement (MFA), which went into force in 1974 under GATT. In response to pressure by the United States to protect the U.S. domestic clothing industry, the MFA set quotas for textile exports from developing countries, but it excluded some of the world's least-developed countries from the quota system. As a result, countries such as Bangladesh, Cambodia, and Tunisia, which could produce more and set prices higher than their competitors, received "quota rents." In Bangladesh, this positive shock prompted the government to facilitate institutional innovations, including back-to-back letters of credit and the bonded warehouse, which enabled a transformation of the Bangladeshi economy and an evolution of the elite bargain that determined governance dynamics and political reform (Khan 2013).

Trade agreements can help achieve commitment to domestic reforms by empowering new domestic actors. For example, workers at a Nike factory in Mexico succeeded in unionizing by leveraging the corporate codes of conduct and transnational advocacy networks that developed after implementation of the North American Free Trade Agreement (NAFTA)—see Rodríguez Garavito (2005). In Cambodia, a surge in garment exports to the United States following implementation of the MFA led to a bilateral trade agreement in 1999 that used export quotas as a mechanism for improving domestic labor standards, thereby giving greater bargaining power to Cambodian workers. Specifically, the United States agreed to increase garment quotas by 14 percent a year if working conditions complied with international standards, and an International Labour Organization (ILO) project was established to independently monitor workers' conditions in Cambodian garment factories. This enhanced commitment led to significant improvements in freedom of association following the agreement, with the share of unionized garment workers rising from only 12 percent in 2000 to nearly 50 percent by 2005 (Adler and Woolcock 2009).

And yet the substance and institutional design of trade agreements can harm poor constituencies. At times, they may prompt a regulatory race to the bottom for low-wage or casual workers, such as those in Mexican *maquiladoras* or the Bangladeshi garment industry (Carr and Chen 2002; Santos 2012). Policy makers and publics are well aware of this problem, and a body of transnational law and regulations has emerged to complement the domestic efforts just described. These efforts, though, face ongoing institutional design challenges—in particular, how to build participatory legitimacy along with effective enforcement. Meanwhile, as these efforts to foster transnational coordination proliferate, evidence suggests that the coordination effects of regulatory instruments should not be overstated. In WTO jurisprudence, whether a restriction on imports counts as a legitimate regulation or a nontariff barrier is indeterminate—a phenomenon recognized by WTO lawyers and staff themselves. The indeterminacy is part of the strength of the regulatory regime: the concept of the nontariff barrier is flexible and potentially context-specific (Lang 2011). And yet those players who know how to navigate the WTO rulemaking and appeals system will do better than those who do not. Among developing nations, this is often those who have the capacity and staff to be repeat players at the WTO (Santos 2012).

> Trade agreements can help achieve commitment to domestic reforms by empowering new domestic actors.

Transnational rules as focal points to shift preferences and induce coordination

The last century has witnessed a "Rights Revolution" in which global treaties and norms have facilitated the spread of the notion of rights (figure 9.3)—see Pinker (2011). International human rights and gender quotas illustrate the ways in which transnational ideas diffuse and the mechanisms through which those ideas affect domestic governance arrangements. Although a range of incentives can lead to the formal adoption of such norms, the norms eventually become effective and internalized according to the extent to which they reshape societal preferences.

Since passage of the Universal Declaration of Human Rights in 1948, human rights have been increasingly specified and embedded in international treaties, institutions, and organizations. Country adoption and participation have been widespread. However, international treaties are not always effective in changing state behavior and practices. Indeed, a persistent implementation gap exists between the de jure pledge to protect human rights—as measured by states' ratification of major international human rights treaties and conventions—and actual compliance (figure 9.4). Some scholars argue that human rights are nothing more than window dressing or empty promises that are unable to constrain power or change the behavior of domestic actors (Posner 2014).

Explaining why state compliance with human rights treaties and conventions varies requires taking a closer look at the interaction between international norms and the domestic bargaining process. Once signed, international treaties "empower individuals, groups, or parts of the state with different rights preferences that were not empowered to the same extent in the absence of the treaties" (Simmons 2009, 125). By referring to international norms, ordinary citizens and disadvantaged groups can strengthen the legitimacy of their claims and successfully challenge the prevailing norms, pressuring governments to transform state institutions and reform public policies. Elite resistance frequently increases the incentives for domestic actors to build transnational alliances to support their claims. Often referred to as the "boomerang effect," this dynamic process increases the costs incurred by state actors when resisting change and eventually leads to compliance (Keck and Sikkink 1999). The human rights struggles in Latin American countries during military dictatorships illustrate this point, as well as the mobilization against the apartheid government in South Africa. Indeed, the most transformative social movements of the 20th century—including

Figure 9.3 The "Rights Revolution" has led to a global spread of rights-related norms, facilitated and supported by global treaties and agreements

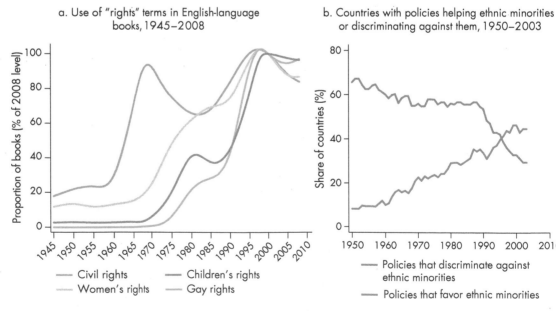

a. Use of "rights" terms in English-language books, 1945–2008

b. Countries with policies helping ethnic minorities or discriminating against them, 1950–2003

— Civil rights — Children's rights
— Women's rights — Gay rights

— Policies that discriminate against ethnic minorities

— Policies that favor ethnic minorities

Source: WDR 2017 team, using data from Google Books Ngram Viewer, based on Pinker 2011.

Source: WDR 2017 team, using data from Asal and Pate (2005).

Note: Policies include economic and political policies that discriminate or favor any ethnic group in a given country-year.

Figure 9.4 Human rights treaties are spreading, but de facto changes in state performance are lagging behind

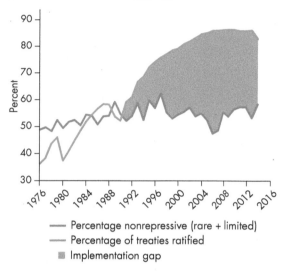

Percentage nonrepressive (rare + limited)
Percentage of treaties ratified
■ Implementation gap

Source: WDR 2017 team, based on Hafner-Burton and Tsutsui 2005.

Note: "Percentage of treaties ratified" measures the share of six core human rights treaties that the average state has ratified in a given year. "Percentage nonrepressive" measures the percentage of states that reported very rare or limited violations of personal integrity rights in a given year, based on data from the Political Terror Scale (Gibney and others 2016).

Figure 9.5 Gender quota laws have spread worldwide since 1990

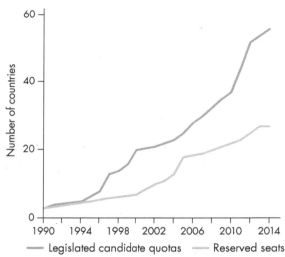

Legislated candidate quotas   Reserved seats

Sources: WDR 2017 team, based on Center for Systemic Peace, Polity IV (database), various years; Norris and Dahlerup 2015; and International IDEA, Inter-Parliamentary Union, and Stockholm University, Global Database of Quotas for Women, various years.

Note: The figure includes only quotas introduced at the national level. Moreover, it does not include voluntary party quotas (adopted in 32 countries) because the adoption year varies across parties in a given country.

labor rights, women's rights, and civil rights, and, more recently, indigenous and environmental movements—have all explicitly adopted the language and instruments of international rights (Heller 2013).

Over the last 25 years, different forms of gender quotas for representation in national legislatures—including legislated quotas, reserved seats, and voluntary party quotas—have spread to more than 100 countries (figure 9.5).[7] These new provisions have helped double the percentage of women in the lower house of national legislatures from approximately 10 percent in 1995 to 22 percent in 2015 (Norris and Dahlerup 2015). Quotas for women in local government positions, as in India, are also increasingly common.[8] In early adopters—mainly European countries that introduced voluntary party quotas in the 1980s—domestic social movements and left-leaning political parties were especially influential (Ramirez, Soysal, and Shanahan 1997). By contrast, international nongovernmental organizations and multilateral organizations have become increasingly influential for late adopters among developing countries, especially postconflict countries largely dependent on international assistance (Krook 2006; Celis, Krook, and Meier 2011).

These processes of international norm diffusion interact with domestic factors to strengthen the bargaining power of women's organizations and improve their capacity to influence constitutional reforms and lobby for the adoption of gender-sensitive policies. Many countries, however, still face important challenges in closing their implementation gap and achieving the level of political participation for women defined in the quota laws. The gap is larger for legislative quotas. Although these gaps may reflect in part overly ambitious targets, the short time since adoption of the quota, and the weakness of mechanisms to sanction noncompliance, evidence suggests that social norms also play a role. In Spain, for example, a recent study found that political parties nominate female candidates for seats in areas where they have little chance of being elected in order to reduce the risk of losing decision-making power within the party (Esteve-Volart and Bagues 2012). It is yet to be seen how more recent reform efforts by some parties, such as the adoption of "zipper systems" in which male and female candidates are alternated on ballot lists, will influence these dynamics within Spain. Major shocks—such as conflict—can speed up the process of changing norms and create new windows of opportunity for disadvantaged groups. A process of "policy learning" can also occur; initially ineffective quota laws have been revised to improve their effect on the de facto political representation of women (Norris and Dahlerup 2015).

Foreign aid and governance

Since the end of World War II, foreign aid has been one of the most prominent policy tools used by high-income countries to promote security, growth, and equity in low-income countries.[9] Primarily intended to fill capital shortfalls, official development assistance (ODA) has become a means of meeting a range of development, humanitarian, strategic, and commercial goals. In addition to finance, aid includes the transfer of knowledge, expertise, and ideas intended to influence norms, capacity, and power (box 9.2).

Between 1960 and 2013, member countries of the Organisation for Economic Co-operation and

---

Box 9.2 Aid as a delivery mechanism for transnational rules and ideas

Development actors, especially the international financial institutions, have been among the most influential generators of transnational rules, norms, and ideas, using aid as a diffusion mechanism. Just as economic orthodoxy has evolved over time—from an emphasis on the role of the state in planning and investment in the 1960s and 1970s, to the macroeconomic discipline and market liberalization of the Washington Consensus in the 1980s, to poverty alleviation and market institutions in the 1990s, to achievement of the Millennium Development Goals (MDGs) and improvement of governance institutions in the 2000s—so, too, have aid modalities evolved in search of more effective means of translating these norms into development outcomes.

Ex ante conditionality. Structural adjustment lending policies in the 1980s marked the high point of ex ante conditionality—that is, aid transfers depended on the recipient's adoption of preset conditions. Today, however, this approach has been largely regarded as a failure because conditional loans proved ineffective as a commitment device. In theory, the threat of nondisbursement, or reward of disbursement, was an incentive to government actors to overcome obstacles to reform because of either opposing objectives or domestic political economy factors. Although ex ante conditionality could sometimes strengthen the hand of reformist governments that needed to swing domestic opinion behind these changes, it proved ineffective in changing incentives and the preferences of opposing elites (Collier and others 1997). This outcome was due in large part to the lack of a credible threat and the time consistency problem: more often than not, donors submitted to pressures to disburse despite the failure of recipients to meet the prescribed conditions (Killick 1997; Kanbur 2000). More fundamentally, the prescribed conditions were often politically infeasible because they sought to disable the systems of patronage needed to hold coalitions together (Mbembe 2001). In short, the diffusion of norms through coercion was incapable of changing the much stronger dynamics of the domestic bargaining arena (Temple 2010).

Ex post conditionality. In the 1990s, ex ante conditionality was largely replaced by aid modalities based on principles of partnership and ownership, assuming that aid would be more effective in good policy environments (World Bank 1998; Dollar and Burnside 2000). Many donors adopted a form of ex post conditionality under which aid in the form of budget support (mostly unconditional funds) would be directed to countries that themselves adopted good economic and governance policies. Although aid still served as an incentive, its primary role was to amplify reform efforts and maximize poverty reduction in those places most likely to achieve results. Yet another feature was an emphasis on social participation in the development of policies, as introduced in the Poverty Reduction Strategy Paper (PRSP) process adopted by the International Monetary Fund (IMF) and the World Bank as a means of enhancing the contestability of the policy arena. These developments were also subject to criticism, most notably around the imperfect science of measuring institutional performance for purposes of aid allocation and the questionable concept of "ownership" in view of the power imbalance both between donors and recipients and between government elites and other domestic constituencies (Wilhelm and Krause 2008). At worst, such an approach can give rise to enhanced legitimacy for governments that go through the motions of "ownership," while in fact reducing the space for local contestation and innovation. Some observers questioned the extent to which this method was an answer to the flaws of ex ante conditionality.[a]

Outcome-based conditionality. The most recent generation of aid instruments seeks to overcome the difficulty of influencing the bargaining arena to yield "good" policies by focusing instead on outcomes. Donors have introduced a range of results-based approaches, such as the World Bank's Performance for Results (PforR) instrument, which disburses upon achievement of results according to agreed-on performance indicators. This outcome-based conditionality is particularly suited to social sector outcomes such as those set out

(Box continues next page)

Development (OECD) that are also members of the Development Assistance Committee (DAC) provided some US$3.5 trillion (constant 2009 dollars) in aid. Non-OECD economies are an increasingly important source of aid: in 2014 the flow of aid to developing countries from both DAC and non-DAC contributors amounted to over US$161 billion (map 9.1). Although aid has ebbed and flowed over time, its significant increase over the last two decades coincides with the establishment of the Millennium Development Goals, as well as with the surge in flows toward conflict-affected countries in the aftermath of the cold war.[10]

Map 9.1 Aid flows amounted to over US$161 billion from donor countries (purple) to recipient countries (orange and green) in 2014

Aid flows (US$)

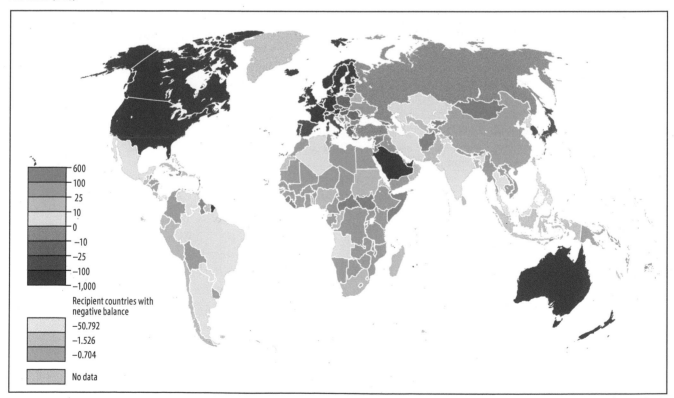

IBRD 42496 | SEPTEMBER 2016

Source: WDR 2017 team, using data from the Organisation for Economic Co-operation and Development.

Note: Data are on a per capita basis as of 2014. Shades of orange denote recipient countries. Shades of purple denote donor countries. The darker the country, the higher is the amount of aid received or transferred. Green countries (China, Indonesia, and Panama) are recipient countries in which the flow of aid received is smaller than the repayment of debts.

Figure 9.6 Aid makes up a large share of GDP and revenue in many developing countries

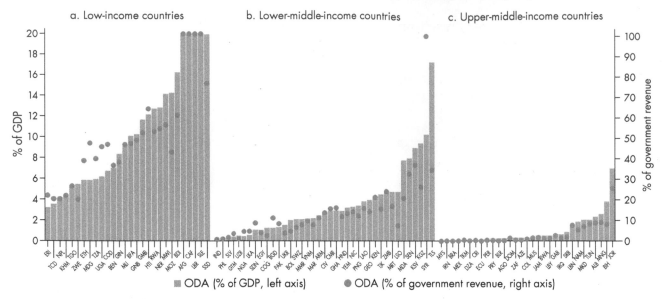

a. Low-income countries b. Lower-middle-income countries c. Upper-middle-income countries

■ ODA (% of GDP, left axis) ● ODA (% of government revenue, right axis)

Sources: WDR 2017 team. Official development assistance (ODA) data: Organisation for Economic Co-operation and Development; government revenue data: IMF, *World Economic Outlook*, various years.

Note: The graphs show ODA from all donors to all recipients in low- and middle-income countries with a population of at least 1 million. Figures for ODA (percent of GDP) are capped at 20 percent of GDP for the sake of visualization. The underlying uncapped data are Afghanistan, 24.1 percent; Central African Republic, 35.4 percent; Liberia, 37.0 percent; and Malawi, 21.8 percent. Figures for ODA (percent of government revenue) are capped at 100 percent for the sake of visualization. The underlying uncapped data are Afghanistan, 105.2 percent; Central African Republic, 260.6 percent; Liberia, 126.0 percent; and Sierra Leone, 143.2 percent.

Still, few donors have met the ODA target of 0.7 percent of gross national income (GNI), which they first agreed to in 1970.

Although the volume of aid is increasing, its share relative to flows of private capital and other sources of finance is decreasing. In middle-income countries, aid makes up only 1.9 percent of GDP (median), compared with 9.6 percent in low-income countries. Foreign direct investment—largely reflecting new and increased exploitation of natural resources—and remittances have overtaken aid as a percentage of GDP in 21 out of 43 African countries based on the available data.[11] Nevertheless, aid makes up more than 10 percent of GDP for half of all low-income countries and over 30 percent of total revenues for 26 developing countries (figure 9.6).

A look at the impact of more than five decades of development aid on security, growth, and equity reveals the great variation across regions and countries (figure 9.7). As this Report explores, aid has to be understood in terms of how it interacts with the existing domestic power imbalances and how it affects the decision-making processes and the allocation of resources. Some groups and actors are better positioned to channel foreign aid flows to their benefit or to that of their constituencies, whether in or outside government, and thus strengthen their position of

Figure 9.7 Low- and lower-middle-income countries vary greatly in the amount of aid received and improvement in GDP per capita

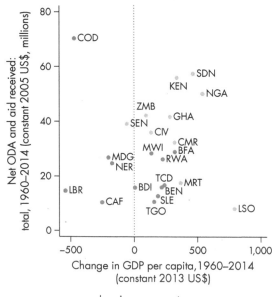

Source: WDR 2017 team, using data from the World Bank, World Development Indicators (database).

Note: GDP = gross domestic product; ODA = official development assistance.

influence. In this way, aid, like other resources, can reinforce or offset existing power imbalances, resulting in heterogeneous outcomes when it comes to growth and equity, depending on the specific context.

Understanding the impact of aggregate aid flows on governance

Two decades ago, an influential study concluded that the link between aid and growth is much stronger in countries with sound policy and institutions, leading to calls for donors to direct assistance to those states that could demonstrate good governance (Burnside and Dollar 2000).[12] But what effect can aid have on governance? This question has been the subject of considerable debate among leading scholars, spawning an array of attempts to measure empirically whether aid in the aggregate promotes or undermines the quality of institutions in recipient countries. Some of the pessimists, including Deaton (2013) and Easterly (2006), claim that large amounts of aid can deepen pathologies in countries with poor governance.[13] Conversely, the optimists argue that aid can help overcome resistance to good policies and support the development of political institutions, including democracy.[14] Unfortunately, the evidence belies clear answers, in large part because of the inherent methodological flaws, including the fact that aid aggregations lump together different sources (bilateral and multilateral); different modalities (budget support, project finance, technical assistance); different desired outcomes (development, democracy, humanitarian relief); and different local contexts. Ultimately, aid is neither inherently good nor bad for governance. What matters is how aid interacts with the prevailing domestic context and which groups or actors see their influence enhanced.

Although empirically inconclusive, the literature converges on a set of analytical arguments that sheds light on the conditions under which aid can have a positive or a negative impact on governance. Studies of aid in the aggregate include large amounts of bilateral aid, which historically has been used to project a dynamic mix of the donor's strategic, commercial, and programmatic priorities. Significant correlations have been documented between the allocation of aid and a range of donor interests, including former colonial ties, voting record in the United Nations, business opportunities, and supply-side factors such as a food surplus (Alesina and Dollar 2000; Qian 2015). According to one argument, in inherently unstable or institutionally fragile environments, the multiple purposes often projected through ODA—stability, security, humanitarian assistance, state building—frequently

have contradictory and—most often—unintended effects (Paris and Sisk 2007). When aid is granted without making the development objective of the recipient country the priority, it is more likely to have negative effects on governance.

Another argument focuses on the great potential for aid funds to be misused by those in power, whether through outright embezzlement (perhaps best illustrated by the case of Mobutu Sese Seko, former dictator of the Democratic Republic of Congo, who reportedly appropriated $12 billion in aid money) or through the diversion of aid money—or government funds freed up by the injection of aid money—to nondevelopment aims that reinforce extractive, patrimonial, and exclusionary power structures (Ahmed 2012; Deaton 2013). Several econometric studies have found a negative correlation between high levels of aid and the accountability of political institutions.[15] This risk is even greater where aid is unconditional and where political elites do not face organized opposition (Acemoglu, Robinson, and Verdier 2004).[16] Some investigators have argued that large amounts of aid may encourage political instability and coup attempts as individuals and groups vie for the opportunity to control aid-financed assets (Grossman 1992).

Underlying these arguments is the claim that aid can undermine the relationship between the state and its citizens by making the state less responsive to their demands. The more a state relies on revenues from the international community, the fewer incentives it has to build the public institutions necessary to mobilize domestic revenues through taxation. And the less a state relies on its domestic tax base, the more its state-citizen accountability erodes (Moore 2004). Aid has thus been likened to the natural resource curse: a windfall of unearned income that enables irresponsible government spending and behavior, unconstrained by the kind of state-citizen social contract thought to lie at the heart of modern democracies.[17] However, the empirical evidence linking aid flows to domestic taxation is mixed (box 9.3).

Aid and the policy arena: Incentives, preferences, and contestability

A growing theoretical and empirical literature is examining how development projects interact with the policy arena to produce three possible outcomes for governance: no effects, negative effects, or positive (generative) effects.

The first category includes projects that, intentionally or not, miss opportunities to reshape elite incentives and preferences. Projects that deliver goods directly, and thus circumvent government

Ultimately, aid is neither inherently good nor bad for governance. What matters is how aid interacts with the prevailing domestic context and which groups or actors see their influence enhanced.

Box 9.3 The impact of aid on domestic resource mobilization: What does the evidence say?

There is a growing consensus that increasing the mobilization of domestic resources can enhance accountability, particularly if such efforts are explicitly linked to the provision of public goods. If policy makers need to depend on broad-based taxation—or indebtedness, which implies more taxation in the future—they are more likely to include citizens and elites in policy discussions. The need for revenue to finance wars led European states to bargain with subject populations for greater taxation (Tilly 1990). Once taxed, citizens demand a greater say in state affairs. As 18th-century American colonists claimed, "Taxation without representation is tyranny." More recently, in Sub-Saharan Africa paying taxes has been shown to increase political interest (Broms 2015).

Does foreign aid undermine domestic resource mobilization and thus accountability to citizens? Studies testing that hypothesis initially showed a negative correlation between the two (most notably, Gupta and others 2004). More recently, these studies have been refuted by the adoption of different data sets (Morrissey and Torrance 2015) or econometric techniques.[a] Although the behavioral effect of aid flows in undermining accountability has been

tested and isolated in experimental settings (Martin 2014; Paler 2014), in reality the relationship is more complex and seems to depend on three factors: (1) the type of aid (for example, grant or debt, budget support, or project-specific); (2) the contemporaneous effects of policies associated with the aid; and (3) more important, the governance setting specific to each country.

The effects of domestic resource mobilization also depend on the nature of taxation. Some taxes do not enhance accountability (resource taxation) or have distortionary effects (trade taxes). International corporate tax competition has diminished states' capacity for domestic resource mobilization (see earlier discussion on races to the bottom). In environments with low savings rates or the potential for capital flight and tax evasion, consumption taxes are most likely to be effective, but also likely to be regressive. In 9 out of 25 countries with household survey data available for circa 2010, the net effect of all government taxing and spending was to leave the poor worse off in terms of actual consumption of private goods and services (Lustig 2016).

Source: WDR 2017 team.

a. Clist and Morrissey (2011) invalidate the contemporaneous negative correlation found in Gupta and others (2004) by introducing a lagged effect of aid on taxation, concluding that the relationship is negligible.

---

systems, may succeed in the immediate effort (and, indeed, this can be a worthy result), but they may have little to no effect on the quality of governance. Some community-driven development initiatives fall into this category.[18]

Projects that aim to directly improve governance arrangements, such as public sector reform or demand-side initiatives, may end up creating negative dynamics by providing incentives that reinforce the preexisting power imbalances. The tendency of donors to introduce reforms based on best-practice solutions that worked elsewhere (with the expectation that tight monitoring of top-down implementation will yield similar results) has been called an example of *isomorphic mimicry*, a term drawn from organizational sociology (DiMaggio and Powell 1983). These reforms focus on forms—such as laws, systems, and procedures—without paying attention to how they change the nature of the policy arena. This practice can create "capability traps" when recipient governments adopt these forms to ensure flows of donor financing and to reap

legitimacy gains, while evading more fundamental reforms to make the functioning of institutions more effective. Not only does this approach leave recipients with unsustainable and dysfunctional institutions, but it also may reduce the space for local innovation and collective action (Pritchett, Woolcock, and Andrews 2010; Andrews, Pritchett, and Woolcock 2013).

Positive effects are also possible when donor engagement supports the emergence of more accountable and equitable governing arrangements embedded in the domestic context. Certainly, many projects do succeed in doing so, but when and how generative effects take place are difficult to predict in advance because of the web of intersecting and evolving factors that determine how donor initiatives engage with local spaces, including the vagaries of internal politics, shocks of various sizes and effects, and a range of contextual factors. Indeed, many people have been trying to think "politically" about aid in order to overcome challenges to its effectiveness (box 9.4). A burgeoning literature on ways to increase the chances of generative

Box 9.4 Beyond technocratic approaches: Opening the door to considerations of politics and power in development policy

The last 10 years have seen a striking rise in discussions of politics and power in development policy circles. This new focus reflects a reaction against technocratic approaches that rely on the provision of capital and injections of technical know-how to overcome development challenges. It grows out of the evolution of governance programming, which, after emerging in the 1990s, encountered serious limits when well-intended efforts to strengthen governance institutions in poor countries faced entrenched resistance to reform and other structural obstacles.

One result has been the progressive incorporation of political economy analysis by many development organizations and practitioners as a basic tool of program design. Debates over how much the growing use of political economy analysis is actually resulting in more effective development programs remain heated, but most organizations are now willing to concede that attempting to operate in complex, challenging, and diverse national contexts does require at least some concerted efforts to understand the local political economy of reform—that is, who are the winners and the losers and who holds the balance of power in such processes.

Potentially, much deeper change involves establishing new types of development programming that embody recognition of development as an inherently political process—one that consists, in the words of the late Adrian Leftwich (2004, 115), of "conflict, cooperation and negotiation in the way we use, produce, and distribute resources." Adherents of the "Doing Development Differently" manifesto emphasize the importance of focusing on local solutions advanced by local conveners in processes legitimized at all levels, while proceeding through rapid cycles of planning, action, and reflection, and managing risks by making small bets. The Developmental Leadership Program stresses the importance of leadership in development, defining leadership as a political process involving authority and a capacity to mobilize people and resources and to forge coalitions.

The recently launched Global Partnership on Collaborative Leadership for Development seeks to put leadership and coalitions at the center of development, and the Global Delivery Initiative is developing an evidence base for using principles of the science of delivery. At the U.K. Department for International Development, serious attention to how political settlements are established and sustained in fragile states is a central element of politically smart development work. An informal coalition of practitioners organized under the rubric of "Thinking and Working Politically" aims to advance innovative efforts to move politics and power from the margins to the core of development thinking and action. This approach entails ensuring that attention to these issues extends well beyond their original home in governance work to all major areas of development practice, from health and education to transportation and food, among other things.

A strong sense of "At last!" accompanies this push to take politics in development seriously—relief that outdated, artificial walls created in the early days of development assistance are finally being dismantled. Yet, changing development practices is hard. Many of the operational imperatives that arise from greater attention to politics and power—such as the need to increase the flexibility of implementation, to tolerate greater risk and ambiguity, to devolve power from aid providers to aid partners, and to avoid simplistic linear schemes for measuring results—run up against long-established bureaucratic structures, practices, and habits. In addition, taking politics seriously in development points directly to the need to challenge the interests of the power holders that control institutions—something that many development organizations have not yet decided they are willing to do, especially in the current environment of heightened sensitivity in many countries about national sovereignty. The development community is talking the talk of politics. How much it will walk the walk is not yet clear.

Source: Prepared for WDR 2017 by Thomas Carothers, Vice President for Studies, Carnegie Endowment for International Peace.

outcomes points to a common set of principles, which are discussed in the next section.

Using aid to foster positive governance dynamics for development

Recognition that development is an inherently contentious process that implicates power imbalances and social norms is not new. Hirschman documented this observation most eloquently using World Bank projects in his 1967 classic, *Development Projects Observed*. Building on the literature and knowledge base that have emerged over the last few decades, the framework explored in this Report points to the following four principles to guide efforts to use aid in ways that foster positive governance dynamics for development outcomes.

Diagnose the underlying functional problem. As discussed in chapter 2, diagnoses of development problems—and proposed prescriptions—often focus on proximate causes. The *World Development Report 2015: Mind, Society, and Behavior* (World Bank 2015) called for expanding diagnostic methods to identify the individual psychological, behavioral, and social obstacles underlying development problems. This Report has emphasized the need to understand the underlying governance challenges that hinder the adoption and implementation of policies that can improve security, growth, and equity outcomes. Diagnostic approaches should home in on the specific commitment and collective action problems that stand in the way of achieving outcomes and on the ways in which power asymmetries in the policy arena constrain these functions.

Target development cooperation in ways that overcome obstacles in the policy arena. At times, it is most appropriate for aid to steer clear of the policy arena in order to deliver direct benefits to populations in need. Emergency and disaster responses, humanitarian aid, and, in some cases, direct service delivery may warrant aid approaches that work in parallel with domestic governance.[19] However, where aid is intended to support sustained improvements in development outcomes, the most important role it can play is to facilitate changes in the policy arena that will alleviate existing constraints to the adoption and implementation of development-oriented policies. As emphasized in this Report, this means focusing on three key levers of change: incentives, preferences and beliefs, and contestability.

The use of financial forms of aid as an incentive to influence the policy arena is discussed in box 9.2. Beyond providing monetary support, aid in the form of technical assistance, analytical expertise, and knowledge sharing can be a powerful means of changing preferences, especially where it enables internal debate and adaptation. Supporting the generation of evidence about the effectiveness of policies and making such evidence publicly available in transparent ways will enhance an informed public debate about policy (Banerjee 2007; Devarajan and Khemani 2016).

Understanding of the role of aid in promoting contestability is at an earlier stage. The last decade has seen the proliferation of demand-side, participatory, and multistakeholder donor–funded aid initiatives under the rubrics of social accountability, legal empowerment, open governance and transparency, and citizen engagement. Evaluations of such programs have pointed to the need to strengthen the dissemination of information and bottom-up approaches, but also to focus on creating enabling environments that activate collective action and promote a commitment to respond (Fox 2015; Khemani and others 2016).

Time frames are critical. Ultimately, aid can only nudge or accelerate a development trajectory that is determined by a complex set of intricately connected, self-reinforcing factors. Indeed, it may be ill-advised for those pursuing development aims that confront deep-vested interests or threaten a delicate stability to use aid in ways that disrupt the existing agreements in the policy arena. Although interventions may have little impact within the life span of a project, they can aim to set in motion a collective dynamic that, over time, will reduce power asymmetries, effectively change incentives, and reshape preferences. Attention to the dynamics of elite bargains, as discussed in chapter 7, can help identify strategic opportunities to invest in ways that align with the interest of influential groups and also bring other actors into the policy arena, enhancing the adaptive capacity of societies in more inclusive ways.

Anticipate opposition, shifting interests, and unintended consequences. Over the last few years, development practitioners have seized on a principle long established in the organizational change literature: complex problems require solutions based on incremental and adaptive efforts supported by strong learning feedback loops (see box 9.4). This principle is particularly important because efforts to change the policy arena will often trigger opposition and backsliding, and they may yield unanticipated consequences—both positive and negative. It should be assumed that the progress of reform will not be linear, that adaptations will be necessary, and that domestic coalitions for reform must be supported to reduce the risk of reversal.

Applying such measures will require not only particular skill sets and methodologies, but, most important, an enabling environment within development institutions. Several multilateral and bilateral organizations are exploring ways in which the development community can implement internal reforms as they seek more agile, more flexible, and more adaptive projects. Partnerships such as the Global Delivery Initiative also look at the methodologies and approaches available for development practitioners to work more adaptively through citizen engagement tools and feedback mechanisms, information and communication technologies, and real-time practitioner exchanges in order to overcome complex problems, such as those faced during governance projects.

Several multilateral and bilateral organizations are exploring ways in which the development community can implement internal reforms as they seek more agile, more flexible, and more adaptive projects.

Look beyond the traditional aid modalities. The declining role of official development assistance relative to other forms of capital and the inherent limitations of the traditional foreign aid model in dealing with many of today's challenges call for a broader approach to achieving the United Nations' Sustainable Development Goals. As discussed in this chapter, the increasingly complex and interconnected realm of transnational rules, agreements, and regulations driven by the public and private actors has a significant influence on domestic governance and the achievement of development outcomes. In many cases, the domestic policy space for tackling development challenges is significantly constrained by actions and decisions made elsewhere. Control of corruption, crime, and security at the country level, for example, may depend on how the flows of goods, capital, and migrants are regulated at the transnational level or in the domestic policy arenas of other states (see spotlight 13 on illicit financial flows). The impact of foreign direct investment on local outcomes may be largely determined by how multinational corporations are regulated by their home states as well as through transnational rules that encourage races to the top rather than the bottom. The growing role of private actors and finance in a wide range of development activities—from utilities to education to infrastructure—also highlights the importance of upstream policy arenas that aim to ensure accountability for the public good.

International actors should enhance efforts to engage in the two-level game, using transnational coordination and commitment devices backed by the promotion of incentives, preferences, and contestability in the domestic policy arena to help achieve security, growth, and equity goals. They also might look inward to the ways in which their own policy arenas have increasingly significant impacts on development outcomes across the globe.

Notes

1. World Bank, World Development Indicators (database), various years, sum of exports and imports of goods and services worldwide.
2. Updated and extended version of data set constructed by Lane and Milesi-Ferretti (2007).
3. Updated and extended version of data set constructed by Lane and Milesi-Ferretti (2007).
4. Bourguignon (2015) and Milanović (2016) have shown that inequality *among* nations has decreased substantially, whereas inequality *within* countries has soared, with the exception of Latin American countries, where income inequality has decreased slightly over the last 15 years.

5. Haas (1992, 3) describes an epistemic community as "a network of professionals with recognized expertise and competence in a particular domain and an authoritative claim to policy-relevant knowledge within that domain or issue-area."
6. Transnational rules are similar to the so-called international regimes in the international relations and international political economy literature. See, for example, Ruggie (1975) and Krasner (1983).
7. Legislated gender quotas and reserved seats are typically introduced through changes in electoral laws or constitutions, whereas voluntary party quotas are adopted by individual parties that commit to a specific share of female candidates.
8. About 40 percent of the world's countries have some form of gender quota, according to the World Bank's 2016 Women, Business, and the Law database: 73 countries have quotas at the national level, and 65 countries have quotas at the local government level. Some countries have quotas at both the national and local levels; others have one but not both. For example, India adopted a quota at the local level but not at the national level.
9. Foreign aid refers to official development assistance as defined by the Organisation for Economic Co-operation and Development.
10. This increase in foreign aid accompanied the steep rise in peacekeeping operations in the 1990s and the post–9/11 interventions in Iraq and Afghanistan.
11. WDR 2017 team, based on data from OECD (ODA); World Bank, Africa Development Indicators, various years (FDI/GDP); and World Bank, World Development Indicators (database, GDP and remittances/GDP). FDI and remittances refer to the latest available data point.
12. See also World Bank (1998). The findings of Burnside and Dollar (2000) have been called into question by Easterly, Levine, and Roodman (2003).
13. This leads to the unsettling view that "when the 'conditions for development' are present, aid is not required. When local conditions are hostile to development, aid is not useful, and it will do harm if it perpetuates those conditions" (Deaton 2013, 273). See also Easterly (2006).
14. See, for example, Goldsmith (2001); Dunning (2004); Wright (2009); and Dietrich and Wright (2013).
15. Among the cross-country studies that find a negative correlation between aid and governance quality are Braütigam and Knack (2004); Moss, Pettersson, and van de Walle (2006); Djankov, Montalvo, and Reynal-Querol (2008); Bueno de Mesquita and Smith (2009); Busse and Gröning (2009); and Rajan and Subramanian (2011).
16. But also see Tavares (2003).
17. The "aid curse" argument is made by Moss, Pettersson, and van de Walle (2006); Collier (2007); and Djankov, Montalvo, and Reynal-Querol (2008).

18. See Casey, Glennerster, and Miguel (2012); Wong (2012); King (2013); Mansuri and Rao (2013); and Humphreys, Sanchez de la Sierra, and Van der Windt (2015).

19. But even these interventions can have significant indirect impacts on governance in both negative and positive ways.

References

Acemoglu, Daron, James A. Robinson, and Thierry Verdier. 2004. "Kleptocracy and Divide-and-Rule: A Model of Personal Rule." *Journal of the European Economic Association* 2 (2–3): 132–92.

Adler, Daniel, and Michael Woolcock. 2009. "Justice without the Rule of Law? The Challenge of Rights-Based Industrial Relations in Contemporary Cambodia." Justice and Development Working Paper 2 (2), World Bank, Washington, DC.

Ahmed, Faisal Z. 2012. "The Perils of Unearned Foreign Income: Aid, Remittances, and Government Survival." *American Political Science Review* 106 (1): 146–65.

Aldy, Joseph E. 2014. "The Crucial Role of Policy Surveillance in International Climate Policy." *Climatic Change* 126 (3): 279–92.

Alesina, Alberto, and David Dollar. 2000. "Who Gives Foreign Aid to Whom and Why?" *Journal of Economic Growth* 5 (1): 33–63.

Andrews, Matt, Lant Pritchett, and Michael Woolcock. 2013. "Escaping Capability Traps through Problem-Driven Iterative Adaptation (PDIA)." *World Development* 51 (C): 234–44.

Asal, Victor, and Amy Pate. 2005. "The Decline of Ethnic Political Discrimination, 1990–2003." In *Peace and Conflict 2005: A Global Survey of Armed Conflicts, Self-Determination Movements, and Democracy*, edited by T. R. Gurr and M. G. Marshall. College Park, MD: Center for International Development and Conflict Management.

Banerjee, Abhijit Vinayak. 2007. *Making Aid Work*. Cambridge, MA: MIT Press.

Barrett, Scott. 1994. "Self-Enforcing International Environmental Agreements." *Oxford Economic Papers* 46 (Supplement 1): 878–94.

Barrett, Scott, Carlo Carraro, and Jaime de Melo, eds. 2015. *Towards a Workable and Effective Climate Regime*. London: CEPR Press; Clermont-Ferrand, France: Ferdi.

Basu, Kaushik, Henrik Horn, Lisa Román, and Judith Shapiro, eds. 2003. *International Labor Standards: History, Theory, and Policy Options*. Malden, MA: Blackwell.

Bourguignon, François. 2015. *The Globalization of Inequality*. Translated by Thomas Scott-Railton. Princeton, NJ: Princeton University Press.

Braithwaite, John, and Peter Drahos. 2000. *Global Business Regulation*. Cambridge, U.K.: Cambridge University Press.

Braütigam, Deborah A., and Stephen Knack. 2004. "Foreign Aid, Institutions, and Governance in Sub-Saharan Africa." *Economic Development and Cultural Change* 52 (2): 255–85.

Broms, Rasmus. 2015. "Putting Up or Shutting Up: On the Individual-Level Relationship between Taxpaying and Political Interest in a Developmental Context." *Journal of Development Studies* 51 (1): 93–109.

Bueno de Mesquita, Bruce, and Alastair Smith. 2009. "A Political Economy of Aid." *International Organization* 63 (2): 309–40.

Burnside, Craig, and David Dollar. 2000. "Aid, Policies, and Growth." *American Economic Review* 90 (4): 847–68.

Busby, Joshua. 2016. "After Paris: Good Enough Climate Governance." *Current History* 115 (777): 3–9.

Busse, Matthias, and Steffen Gröning. 2009. "Does Foreign Aid Improve Governance?" *Economics Letters* 104 (2): 76–78.

Carr, Marilyn, and Martha Chen. 2002. "Globalization and the Informal Economy: How Global Trade and Investment Impact on the Working Poor." Working Paper on the Informal Economy, International Labour Office, Geneva.

Carraro, Carlo, and Domenico Siniscalco. 1992. "The International Dimension of Environmental Policy." *European Economic Review* 36 (2–3): 379–87.

Casey, Katherine, Rachel Glennerster, and Edward Miguel. 2012. "Reshaping Institutions: Evidence on Aid Impacts Using a Preanalysis Plan." *Quarterly Journal of Economics* 127 (4): 1755–1812.

Celis, Karen, Mona Lena Krook, and Petra Meier. 2011. "The Rise of Gender Quota Laws: Expanding the Spectrum of Determinants for Electoral Reform." *West European Politics* 34 (3): 514–30.

Center for Systemic Peace. Various years. Polity IV (database). Vienna, VA, http://www.systemicpeace.org /polityproject.html.

Chau, Nancy H., and Ravi Kanbur. 2005. "The Race to the Bottom, from the Bottom." *Economica* 73 (290): 193–228.

Chinn, Menzie D., and Hiro Ito. 2006. "What Matters for Financial Development? Capital Controls, Institutions, and Interactions." *Journal of Development Economics* 81 (1): 163–92.

Clist, Paul, and Oliver Morrissey. 2011. "Aid and Tax Revenue: Signs of a Positive Effect since the 1980s." *Journal of International Development* 23 (2): 165–80.

Collier, Paul. 2007. *The Bottom Billion: Why the Poorest Countries Are Failing and What Can Be Done about It*. Oxford, U.K.: Oxford University Press.

Collier, Paul, Patrick Guillaumont, Sylviane Guillaumont, and Jan Willem Gunning. 1997. "Redesigning Conditionality." *World Development* 25 (9): 1399–1407.

Craig, David, and Douglas Porter. 2003. "Poverty Reduction Strategy Papers: A New Convergence." *World Development* 30 (1): 53–69.

Dang, Duc Anh. 2013. "How Foreign Direct Investment Promotes Institutional Quality: Evidence from Vietnam." *Journal of Comparative Economics* 41 (4): 1054–72.

Davis, Kevin, Benedict Kingsbury, and Sally Engle Merry. 2012. "Indicators as a Technology of Global Governance." *Law and Society Review* 46 (1): 71–104.

Deaton, Angus. 2013. *The Great Escape: Health, Wealth, and the Origins of Inequality.* Princeton, NJ: Princeton University Press.

Devarajan, Shantayanan, and Stuti Khemani. 2016. "If Politics Is the Problem, How Can External Actors Be Part of the Solution?" Policy Research Working Paper 7761, World Bank, Washington, DC.

Dietrich, Simone, and Joseph Wright. 2013. "Foreign Aid and Democratic Development in Africa." In *Democratic Trajectories in Africa: Unravelling the Impact of Foreign Aid*, edited by Danielle Resnick and Nicolas van de Walle, 56–86. WIDER Studies in Development Economics. Helsinki: United Nations University-World Institute for Development Economics Research; New York: Oxford University Press.

DiMaggio, Paul J., and Walter W. Powell. 1983. "The Iron Cage Revisited: Institutional Isomorphism and Collective Rationality in Organizational Fields." *American Sociological Review* 48 (2): 147–60.

Djankov, Simeon, José García Montalvo, and Marta Reynal-Querol. 2008. "The Curse of Aid." *Journal of Economic Growth* 13 (3): 169–94.

Dollar, David, and Craig Burnside. 2000. "Aid, Policies, and Growth." *American Economics Review* 90 (4): 847–68.

Dunning, Thad. 2004. "Conditioning the Effects of Aid: Cold War Politics, Donor Credibility, and Democracy in Africa." *International Organization* 58 (2): 409–23.

Easterly, William Russell. 2006. *The White Man's Burden: Why the West's Efforts to Aid the Rest Have Done So Much Ill and So Little Good.* New York: Penguin Press.

Easterly, William Russell, Ross Levine, and David Roodman. 2003. "New Data, New Doubts: A Comment on Burnside and Dollar's 'Aid, Policies, and Growth' (2000)." *American Economic Review* 94 (3): 774–80.

Economy, Elizabeth. 2001. "The Impact of International Regimes on Chinese Foreign Policy-Making: Broadening Perspectives and Policies . . . But Only to a Point." In *The Making of Chinese Foreign and Security Policy in the Era of Reform, 1978-2000*, edited by David M. Lampton, 230–56. Stanford, CA: Stanford University Press.

Esteve-Volart, Berta, and Manuel Bagues. 2012. "Are Women Pawns in the Political Game? Evidence from Elections to the Spanish Senate." *Journal of Public Economics* 96 (3): 387–99.

Fox, Jonathan A. 2015. "Social Accountability: What Does the Evidence Really Say?" *World Development* 72 (C): 346–61.

Gibney, Mark, Linda Cornett, Reed Wood, Peter Haschke, and Daniel Arnon. 2016. The Political Terror Scale 1976-2015. http://www.politicalterrorscale.org.

Goldsmith, Arthur A. 2001. "Foreign Aid and Statehood in Africa." *International Organization* 55 (1): 123–48.

Green, Jessica F. 2014. *Rethinking Private Authority: Agents and Entrepreneurs in Global Environmental Governance.* Princeton, NJ: Princeton University Press.

Grossman, Herschel I. 1992. "Foreign Aid and Insurrection." *Defense Economics* 3 (4): 275–88.

Gupta, Sanjeev, Benedict J. Clemens, Alexander Pivovarsky, and Erwin R. Tiongson. 2004. "Foreign Aid and Revenue Response: Does the Composition of Aid Matter?" In *Helping Countries Develop: The Role of Fiscal Policy*, edited by Sanjeev Gupta, Benedict J. Clements, and Gabriela Inchauste, 385–406. Washington, DC: International Monetary Fund.

Haas, Peter M. 1992. "Epistemic Communities and International Policy Coordination." *International Organization* 46 (1): 1–35.

Hafner-Burton, Emilie, and Kiyoteru Tsutsui. 2005. "Human Rights in a Globalizing World: The Paradox of Empty Promises." *American Journal of Sociology* 110 (5): 1373–1411.

Hale, Thomas, and David Held, eds. 2011. *Handbook on Transnational Governance.* New York: Polity.

Heller, Kevin Jon. 2013. "'One Hell of a Killing Machine': Signature Strikes and International Law." *Journal of International Criminal Justice* 11 (1): 89–119.

Hirschman, Albert. 1967. *Development Projects Observed.* Washington, DC: Brookings Institution Press.

Humphreys, Macartan, Raul Sanchez de la Sierra, and Peter Van der Windt. 2015. "Social Engineering in the Tropics: A Grassroots Democratization Experiment in the Congo." Working paper, Columbia University, New York.

IMF (International Monetary Fund). Various issues. *World Economic Outlook.* Washington, DC: IMF.

International IDEA, Inter-Parliamentary Union, and Stockholm University. Various years. Global Database of Quotas for Women. http://www.quotaproject.org.

Jin, Liqun. 2002. "China: One Year into the WTO Process." Address to the International Monetary Fund and the World Bank, Washington, DC, October 22.

Kanbur, Ravi. 2000. "Aid, Conditionality, and Debt in Africa." In *Foreign Aid and Development: Lessons Learnt and Directions for the Future*, edited by Finn Tarp, 318–28. Routledge Studies in Development Economics Series. London: Routledge.

Keck, Margaret E., and Kathryn Sikkink. 1999. "Transnational Advocacy Networks in International and Regional Politics." *International Social Science Journal* 51 (159): 89–101.

Keohane, Robert O., and David G. Victor. 2016. "Cooperation and Discord in Global Climate Policy." *Nature Climate Change* 6 (6): 570–75.

Khan, Mushtaq H. 2013. "Bangladesh: Economic Growth in a Vulnerable LAO." In *In the Shadow of Violence: Politics, Economics, and the Problems of Development*, edited by Douglass C. North, John Joseph Wallis, Steven B.

Webb, and Barry R. Weingast, 24–69. New York: Cambridge University Press.

Khemani, Stuti, Ernesto Dal Bó, Claudio Ferraz, Frederico Finan, Corinne Stephenson, Adesinaola Odugbemi, Dikshya Thapa, and Scott Abrahams. 2016. *Making Politics Work for Development: Harnessing Transparency and Citizen Engagement.* Policy Research Report. Washington, DC: World Bank.

Killick, Tony. 1997. "Principals, Agents, and the Failings of Conditionality." *Journal of International Development* 9 (4): 483–95.

King, Elisabeth. 2013. "A Critical Review of Community-Driven Development Programmes in Conflict-Affected Contexts." Technical report, U.K. Department for International Development and International Rescue Committee, London.

Krasner, Stephen D. 1983. *International Regimes.* Ithaca, NY: Cornell University Press.

Krook, Mona Lena. 2006. "Reforming Representation: The Diffusion of Candidate Gender Quotas Worldwide." *Politics and Gender* 2 (3): 303–27.

Lane, Philip R., and Gian Maria Milesi-Ferretti. 2007. "The External Wealth of Nations Mark II: Revised and Extended Estimates of Foreign Assets and Liabilities, 1970–2004." *Journal of International Economics* 73 (2): 223–50.

Lang, Andrew. 2011. *World Trade Law after Neoliberalism: Reimagining the Global Economic Order.* Oxford, U.K.: Oxford University Press.

Lardy, Nicholas R. 2002. *Integrating China into the Global Economy.* Washington, DC: Brookings Institution Press.

Leftwich, Adrian. 2004. *What Is Politics? The Activity and Its Study.* Cambridge, U.K.: Polity Press.

Long, Cheryl, Jin Yang, and Jin Zhang. 2015. "Institutional Impact of Foreign Direct Investment in China." *World Development* 66 (C): 31–48.

Lukes, Steven. 1986. *Power (Readings in Social and Political Theory, No. 4).* New York: NYU Press.

Lustig, Nora. 2016. "Domestic Resource Mobilization and the Poor." Background paper, WDR 2017, World Bank, Washington, DC.

Maggi, Giovanni, and Andrés Rodríguez-Clare. 1998. "The Value of Trade Agreements in the Presence of Political Pressures." *Journal of Political Economy* 106 (3): 574–601.

———. 2007. "A Political-Economy Theory of Trade Agreements." *American Economic Review* 97 (4): 1374–1406.

Mansuri, Ghazala, and Vijayendra Rao. 2013. *Localizing Development: Does Participation Work?* Washington, DC: World Bank.

Martin, Lucy. 2014. "Taxation, Loss Aversion, and Accountability: Theory and Experimental Evidence for Taxation's Effect on Citizen Behavior." Working paper, Yale University, New Haven, CT.

Mattoo, Aaditya. 2004. "The Services Dimension of China's Accession to the WTO." In *China and the WTO: Accession, Policy Reform, and Poverty Reduction Strategies,* edited by Deepak Bhattasali, Shantong Li, and Will Martin, 117–41. Washington, DC: World Bank.

Mbembe, Achille. 2001. *On the Postcolony.* Berkeley: University of California Press.

Milanović, Branko. 2016. *Global Inequality: A New Approach for the Age of Globalization.* Cambridge, MA: Harvard University Press.

Moore, Mick. 2004. "Revenues, State Formation, and the Quality of Governance in Developing Countries." *International Political Science Review* 25 (3): 297–319.

Morrissey, O., and S. Torrance. 2015. "Aid and Taxation." In *Handbook on the Economics of Foreign Aid,* edited by B. Mak Arvin and Byron Lew, 555–76. Cheltenham, U.K.: Edward Elgar.

Moss, Todd, Gunilla Pettersson, and Nicolas van de Walle. 2006. "An Aid-Institutions Paradox? A Review Essay on Aid Dependency and State Building in Sub-Saharan Africa." Working Paper 74, Center for Global Development, Washington, DC.

Nordhaus, William. 2015. "Climate Clubs: Overcoming Free-Riding in International Climate Policy." *American Economic Review* 105 (4): 1339–70.

Norris, Pippa, and Drude Dahlerup. 2015. "On the Fast Track: The Spread of Gender Quota Policies for Elected Office." HKS Working Paper 15-041, Harvard Kennedy School, Cambridge, MA.

Paler, Laura. 2014. "Keeping the Public Purse: An Experiment in Windfalls, Taxes, and the Incentives to Restrain Government." *American Political Science Review* 107 (4): 706–25.

Paris, Ronald, and Timothy D. Sisk. 2007. *Managing Contradictions: The Inherent Dilemmas of Postwar Statebuilding.* New York: International Peace Academy.

Pinker, Steven. 2011. *The Better Angels of Our Nature: Why Violence Has Declined.* New York: Penguin.

Posner, Eric A. 2014. *The Twilight of Human Rights Law.* Inalienable Rights Series. New York: Oxford University Press.

Pritchett, Lant, Michael Woolcock, and Matt Andrews. 2010. "Capability Traps? The Mechanisms of Persistent Implementation Failure." Working Paper 234, Center for Global Development, Washington, DC.

Qian, Nancy. 2015. "Making Progress on Foreign Aid." *Annual Review of Economics* 7 (1): 277–308.

Rajan, Raghuram G., and Arvind Subramanian. 2011. "Aid, Dutch Disease, and Manufacturing Growth." *Journal of Development Economics* 94 (1): 106–18.

Ramirez, Francisco O., Yasemin Soysal, and Suzanne Shanahan. 1997. "The Changing Logic of Political Citizenship: Cross-National Acquisition of Women's Suffrage Rights, 1890 to 1990." *American Sociological Review* 62 (5): 735–45.

Rodríguez Garavito, César A. 2005. "Global Governance and Labor Rights: Codes of Conduct and Anti-sweatshop Struggles in Global Apparel Factories in Mexico and Guatemala." *Politics and Society* 33 (2): 203–33.

Ruggie, John Gerard. 1975. "International Responses to Technology." *International Organization* 29 (3): 557–84.

Santos, Alvaro. 2012. "Carving Out Policy Autonomy for Developing Countries in the World Trade Organization: The Experience of Brazil and Mexico." *Virginia Journal of International Law* 52 (3): 551–632.

Shaffer, Gregory. 2013. *Transnational Legal Ordering and State Change.* New York: Cambridge University Press.

Shemberg, Andrea. 2009. "Stabilization Clauses and Human Rights." Research Report, United Nations Special Representative on Human Rights, Transnational Corporations, and Other Business Enterprises, New York.

Simmons, Beth A. 2009. *Mobilizing for Human Rights: International Law in Domestic Politics.* New York: Cambridge University Press.

Spence, Michael. 2011. *The Next Convergence: The Future of Economic Growth in a Multispeed World.* New York: Farrar, Straus, and Giroux.

Stewart, Richard B., and Jonathan Baert Wiener. 2003. *Reconstructing Climate Policy: Beyond Kyoto.* Washington, DC: American Enterprise Institute Press.

Stiglitz, Joseph E. 2015. "Overcoming the Copenhagen Failure with Flexible Commitments." *Economics of Energy and Environmental Policy* 4 (2): 29–36.

Tang, Man-Keung, and Shang-Jin Wei. 2009. "The Value of Making Commitments Externally: Evidence from WTO Accessions." *Journal of International Economics* 78 (2): 216–29.

Tavares, José. 2003. "Does Foreign Aid Corrupt?" *Economics Letters* 79 (1): 99–106.

Temple, Jonathan. 2010. "Aid and Conditionality." In *The Handbook of Development Economics,* edited by Dani Rodrik and Mark R. Rosenzweig, 4415–23, Vol. 5 of *Handbooks in Economics.* Amsterdam: Elsevier North Holland.

Tilly, Charles. 1990. *Coercion, Capital, and European States, A.D. 990–1990.* Cambridge, MA: Basil Blackwell.

United Nations. 2016. United Nations Treaty Collection. New York, https://treaties.un.org/.

van Asselt, Harro. 2016. "International Climate Change Law in a Bottom-Up World." *Questions of International Law* 26: 5–15.

van de Walle, Nicolas. 2005. *Overcoming Stagnation in Aid-Dependent Countries.* Washington, DC: Center for Global Development.

Wilhelm, Vera, and Philipp Krause, eds. 2008. *Minding the Gaps: Integrating Poverty Reduction Strategies and Budgets for Domestic Accountability.* Washington, DC: World Bank.

Wong, Susan. 2012. *What Have Been the Impacts of World Bank Community-Driven Development Programs? CDD Impact Evaluation Review and Operational and Research Implications.* Washington, DC: World Bank.

Woo, Wing Thye. 2001. "Recent Claims of China's Economic Exceptionalism: Reflections Inspired by WTO Accession." *China Economic Review* 12 (2–3): 107–36.

World Bank. Various years. Africa Development Indicators. Washington, DC, http://data.worldbank.org/data-catalog/africa-development-indicators.

———. Various years. Women, Business, and the Law (database). Washington, DC, http://wbl.worldbank.org/.

———. Various years. World Development Indicators (database). Washington, DC, http://data.worldbank.org/data-catalog/world-development-indicators.

———. 1998. *Assessing Aid: What Works, What Doesn't, and Why?* Policy Research Report. Washington, DC: World Bank; New York: Oxford University Press.

———. 2015. *World Development Report 2015: Mind, Society, and Behavior.* Washington, DC: World Bank.

Wright, Joseph. 2009. "How Foreign Aid Can Foster Democratization in Authoritarian Regimes." *American Journal of Political Sciences* 53 (3): 552–71.

Illicit financial flows

In spring 2016, 11.5 million confidential documents were leaked from a private legal firm based in Panama. News of the leak quickly spread worldwide. The documents contained information on assets held in offshore companies in more than 40 countries by wealthy individuals, including public officials.[1] Although holding assets in a tax haven is not illegal per se, the prevailing sentiment expressed in newspaper articles and the reaction from the public mainly took the form of condemnation and criticism of a practice interpreted as powerful economic and political elites concealing taxable income from domestic fiscal authorities, with the assistance of the financial systems of many developed countries.

What are IFFs?

These undisclosed accounts are one manifestation of what has become known as illicit financial flows (IFFs). The definitions of IFFs vary, but there are two main interpretations of what makes these financial flows illicit (see Epstein 2005, 7).[2] The normative interpretation suggests that financial flows become illicit not only because they hinder development, but also because they are deemed "illegitimate from the perspective of an existing consensus about the social (developmental) good" (Blankenburg and Khan 2012, 32).

The legal interpretation, on which the empirical literature on IFFs is predominantly built, suggests that IFFs refer to money that is earned, transferred, or used in contravention to existing law. In some cases, this could mean money that is earned legally

WDR 2017 team, based on inputs from Peter Reuter.

but transferred out of the country illegally to evade taxes or currency controls. There are many different sources of illegally earned IFFs, ranging from drug trafficking to embezzlement. IFFs can be classified based on whether the actors involved are criminal organizations, individuals, or corporations (Janský 2013). Table S13.1 presents a few examples.

Although estimates of the size of IFFs are controversial, the consensus among development scholars and practitioners is that IFF outflows on average actually exceed official development assistance in developing countries (Herkenrath 2014).

Rethinking the approach to IFFs

IFFs deprive developing countries of resources that could be used at least partially for redistribution, for financing public goods, and for fostering private investments in local businesses. In doing so, IFFs support existing inequalities and are particularly detrimental to the poor. IFFs are also deeply connected to the governance process. Corruption and embezzlement thrive in environments in which accountability to citizens is low, which in turn weakens trust in state institutions. Tax evasion—a manifestation of a lack of cooperation in society—is fueled by a state's lack of commitment to using resources for the delivery of public goods. That lack of commitment in turn undermines the outcome legitimacy of the state, which is based on the delivery of public services. Criminality also flourishes in environments in which trust is low and the state fails to provide the means for large population groups to effectively participate in the

Table S13.1 Actions generating illicit financial flows

		Source of earnings	
		Money legally earned	Money illegally earned
Actors involved	Criminal organizations		• Drug trafficking • Human smuggling
	Individuals	• Tax evasion • Evasion of currency controls	• Corruption • Embezzlement
	Corporations	• Tax evasion • Profit shifting	• Violation of intellectual property rights • Illegal exploitation of natural resources

Source: WDR 2017 team.

legitimate economy. The WDR 2017 framework sheds light on how to think about approaching reforms to combat IFFs.

Think not only about the form of institutions, but also about their functions

As discussed in chapter 1, importing forms of institutions is not enough to change the facts. Kenya is often cited as a major destination for the proceeds from piracy in the Indian Ocean and a key transit point for terrorist funds to neighboring Somalia. Seeking to fight illicit financial activities, especially money laundering and terrorism financing, Kenya established the Financial Reporting Centre (FRC) in 2012. Although creating the FRC enabled Kenya to be removed from the list of countries that could be sanctioned for noncompliance by the Financial Action Task Force (FATF), little else seems to have changed.[3] There was substantial evidence of high-level corruption in the Kenyan government at that time, and yet no cases were brought against senior officials for violating money laundering regulations. To make the FRC meaningful, the administration would have had to pursue many of its own senior members.

Think not only about capacity building, but also about power asymmetries

The lack of capacity of developing countries to manage complex laws and regulations is often cited as the source of their difficulties in curbing IFFs. Some developing countries do not have any transfer pricing rules, thereby ensuring that a multinational corporation operating in their jurisdiction can transfer as much of its profits elsewhere as it wishes.[4] However, the low capacity of developing countries is often based on power: it is in the interest of someone to keep capacity low because it allows them to extract rents (Leite 2012). Lack of political incentives has

indeed been recognized as more difficult to overcome than any legal, institutional, or operational issues in this context (Stephenson and others 2011).

Think not only about the rule of law, but also about the role of law

Incumbents may appear to be complying with international laws and regulations to gain legitimacy, while continuing to do business as usual. One important requirement of the FATF Anti-Money Laundering (AML) regime is to facilitate requests for information and cooperation from nations that are pursuing money laundering cases involving another country's nationals (Recommendations 35–40). Most nations have adopted statutes and regulations that conform to the FATF rules. However, authorities in many countries have a history of dragging out the process of cooperation for so long that, in fact, the laws are effectively nullified. For example, countries may delay responding to requests by other countries made under the aegis of Mutual Legal Assistance (MLA) about where illicit funds are hidden (Chêne 2008). On the other hand, using delays to deny politically motivated requests from developing countries through the MLA may be fair in systems that are essentially corrupt (Terracol 2015).

A way forward

Fighting the illicit flow of capital abroad is an important development concern. In 2009 Switzerland returned US$93 million to Peru from the accounts of Vladimiro Montesinos, the de facto chief of intelligence and main adviser to former Peruvian president Alberto Fujimori (1990–2000). In 2004 the Philippines recovered US$683 million from the Swiss accounts of Ferdinand and Imelda Marcos, the former president and first lady of the Philippines (1965–86). In both cases, the money recovered would have been enough to fill at least 25 percent of the nation's poverty gaps in the same year.[5]

In the aftermath of the 2016 legal document leak described earlier, the top five European economies (France, Germany, Italy, Spain, and the United Kingdom) announced actions to improve information sharing in order to fight tax evasion and money laundering. Of these economies, the United Kingdom plays a particularly important role in this respect because a number of its Overseas Territories and Crown Dependencies, such as the British Virgin Islands and Jersey, derive a substantial share of their gross domestic product (GDP) from providing financial nonresident depositor services. Recently, all such offshore jurisdictions have joined this initiative and started to implement rising transparency standards. Panama has also recently taken steps to strengthen its tax transparency and financial integrity frameworks. Fundamental reforms that seemed imaginary just 10 years ago are now being discussed as active proposals by powerful bodies such as the G-7, G-20, and Organisation for Economic Co-operation and Development (OECD). These proposals include country-by-country reporting of corporate profits, which facilitates detection of transfer pricing abuses and other instruments to shift profits to low-tax jurisdictions, and the creation of public lists of beneficial ownership to prevent concealment through shell corporations.[6]

That said, each type of IFF featured in table S13.1 involves a different and complex network of actors, including domestic and foreign state institutions, domestic and foreign public officials, and foreign financial institutions, all influenced by different factors for moving money abroad and using different channels (such as bulk cash smuggling, shell corporations, informal value transfer systems, or trade-based money laundering). Failure to take into account the mutually sustainable relations of incentives among all the actors involved in IFFs—and to disaggregate the different types of IFFs—risks generating ineffective reforms (Reuter 2016). In particular, attempts to solve the issue should concentrate not only on the countries of origin, but also on the countries receiving IFFs.

Notes

1. Although the legal firm in question was based in Panama, more than 75 percent of the offshore companies were in jurisdictions outside the country.
2. For a recent review of the various definitions found in the literature, see Tropina (2016).

3. The FATF is an intergovernmental body established in 1989 by the ministers of its member jurisdictions to set standards and promote effective implementation of legal, regulatory, and operational measures for combating money laundering, terrorist financing, and other threats related to the integrity of the international financial system. Currently, it comprises 35 member jurisdictions and two regional organizations (the European Commission and the Gulf Cooperation Council). As for the situation in Kenya, Findley, Nielson, and Sharman (2014) find that in that country it is easier than elsewhere to open an anonymous shell company, one of criminals' preferred devices for transferring money internationally.
4. Multinational corporations are often the initiating actors in these matters. See, for example, Global Witness (2006).
5. WDR 2017 team estimates, based on the World Bank and United Nations Office on Drugs and Crime's StAR (Stolen Asset Recovery Initiative) database and the World Bank's World Development Indicators (database). According to the StAR, recovered assets amounted to US$5 billion in the 15 years up to 2011 (Brun and others 2011). Although "currently no single tool or process can effectively establish a comprehensive measure of IFFs at the global or country level" (United Nations 2016, 37), such recovered assets would be only a tiny share of the total flow according to different estimates—for example, taking the lower bound estimates of US$20 billion per year from Brun and others (2011), the recovery rate would be just 0.5 percent.
6. For a summary of the measures currently adopted and being discussed within OECD and the G-20, see OECD (2016).

References

Blankenburg, Stephanie, and Mushtaq Khan. 2012. "Governance and Illicit Flows." In *Draining Development? Controlling Flows of Illicit Funds from Developing Countries*, edited by Peter Reuter, 21–68. Washington, DC: World Bank.

Brun, Jean-Pierre, Clive Scott, Kevin M. Stephenson, and Larissa Gray. 2011. *Asset Recovery Handbook: A Guide for Practitioners*. Washington, DC: World Bank-United Nations Office on Drugs and Crime (UNODC).

Chêne, Marie. 2008. "Mutual Legal Assistance Treaties and Money Laundering." U4 Expert Answer (July 29), U4 Anti-Corruption Resource Center, Chr. Michelsen Institute, Bergen, Norway.

Epstein, Gerald A., ed. 2005. *Capital Flight and Capital Controls in Developing Countries*. Cheltenham, U.K.: Edward Elgar.

Findley, Michael G., Daniel L. Nielson, and J. C. Sharman. 2014. *Global Shell Games: Experiments in Transnational Relations, Crime, and Terrorism*. Cambridge Studies in International Relations Series. Cambridge, U.K.: Cambridge University Press.

Global Witness. 2006. "Heavy Mittal? A State within a State: The Inequitable Mineral Development Agreement between the Government of Liberia and Mittal Steel Holdings NV." Global Witness, Washington, DC, October.

Herkenrath, Marc. 2014. "Illicit Financial Flows and Their Developmental Impacts: An Overview." *International Development Policy*, Articles and Debates 5.3, Graduate Institute, Geneva.

Janský, Petr. 2013. "Illicit Financial Flows and the 2013 Commitment to Development Index." CGD Policy Paper 034 (December), Center for Global Development, Washington, DC.

Leite, Carlos A. 2012. "The Role of Transfer Pricing in Illicit Financial Flows." In *Draining Development? Controlling Flows of Illicit Funds from Developing Countries*, edited by Peter Reuter, 235–64. Washington, DC: World Bank.

OECD (Organisation for Economic Co-operation and Development). 2016. "OECD Secretary-General Report to G20 Leaders, Hangzhou, China, September 2016." OECD, Paris.

Reuter, Peter. 2016. "Illicit Financial Flows and Governance: The Importance of Disaggregation." Background paper, WDR 2017, World Bank, Washington, DC.

Stephenson, Kevin, Larissa Gray, Ric Power, Jean-Pierre Brun, Gabriele Dunker, and Melissa Panjer. 2011. *Barriers to Asset Recovery: An Analysis of the Key Barriers and Recommendations for Action*. StAR Initiative Series. Washington, DC: World Bank.

Terracol, Marie. 2015. "Mutual Legal Assistance and Corruption." U4 Expert Answer 17 (September 24), U4 Anti-Corruption Resource Center, Chr. Michelsen Institute, Bergen, Norway.

Tropina, Tatiana. 2016. "Do Digital Technologies Facilitate Illicit Financial Flows?" Background paper, *World Development Report 2016: Digital Dividends*, World Bank, Washington, DC.

United Nations. 2015. "Resolution Adopted by the General Assembly on 27 July 2015, 69/313: Addis Ababa Action Agenda of the Third International Conference on Financing for Development (Addis Ababa Action Agenda)." Document A/RES/69/313 (August 17), United Nations, New York.

———. 2016. *Addis Ababa Action Agenda: Monitoring Commitments and Actions*. New York: Inter-Agency Task Force on Financing for Development, United Nations.

World Bank. Various years. World Development Indicators (database). Washington, DC, http://data.world bank.org/datacatalog/world-development-indicators.

World Bank and United Nations Office on Drugs and Crime. Various years. The Stolen Asset Recovery Initiative (StAR). Washington, DC, http://star.worldbank.org/star/.